Managing Hospitality Organizations

Achieving Excellence in the Guest Experience

Second Edition

Robert C. Ford
University of Central Florida

Michael C. Sturman
Rutgers University

Los Angeles | London | New Delhi
Singapore | Washington DC | Melbourne

FOR INFORMATION:

SAGE Publications, Inc.
2455 Teller Road
Thousand Oaks, California 91320
E-mail: order@sagepub.com
SAGE Publications Ltd.

1 Oliver's Yard
55 City Road
London, EC1Y 1SP
United Kingdom

SAGE Publications India Pvt. Ltd.
B 1/I 1 Mohan Cooperative Industrial Area
Mathura Road, New Delhi 110 044
India

SAGE Publications Asia-Pacific Pte. Ltd.
18 Cross Street #10-10/11/12
China Square Central
Singapore 048423

Acquisitions Editor: Maggie Stanley
Senior Content Development Editor: Darcy Scelsi
Editorial Assistant: Alissa Nance
Marketing Manager: Sarah Panella
Production Editor: Veronica Stapleton Hooper
Copy Editor: Lynne Curry
Typesetter: Hurix Digital
Proofreader: Sally Jaskold
Indexer: Robie Grant
Cover Designer: Janet Kiesel

Printed in the United States of America

Library of Congress Cataloging-in-Publication Data

Names: Ford, Robert C. (Robert Clayton), author. | Sturman, Michael C. (Michael Craig), author.

Title: Managing hospitality organizations : achieving excellence in the guest experience / Robert C. Ford and Michael C. Sturman.

Other titles: Managing quality service in hospitality

Description: Second edition. | Thousand Oaks, CA : Sage, [2020] | Previous edition: Managing quality service in hospitality : how organizations achieve excellence in the guest experience. | Includes bibliographical references and index.

Identifiers: LCCN 2018043450 | ISBN 9781544321509 (pbk. : alk. paper)

Subjects: LCSH: Hospitality industry–Management. | Hospitality industry–Customer services. | Hospitality industry–Personnel management.

Classification: LCC TX911.3.M27 F68 2020 | DDC 647.94068–dc23 LC record available at https://lccn.loc.gov/2018043450

This book is printed on acid-free paper.

SFI label applies to text stock

18 19 20 21 22 10 9 8 7 6 5 4 3 2 1

BRIEF CONTENTS

DETAILED CONTENTS

CHAPTER 3 SETTING THE SCENE FOR THE GUEST EXPERIENCE 80

CHAPTER 4 DEVELOPING THE HOSPITALITY CULTURE: EVERYONE SERVES! 110

SECTION 2: THE HOSPITALITY SERVICE STAFF 141

CHAPTER 5 STAFFING FOR SERVICE 142

CHAPTER 6 TRAINING AND DEVELOPING EMPLOYEES TO SERVE 186

CHAPTER 7 SERVING WITH A SMILE: MOTIVATING EXCEPTIONAL SERVICE 222

FOREWORD

Whenever I am in the Orlando area, I try to meet with Bob Ford. He is one of the best scholars of hospitality management. I find that spending an afternoon with Bob fills me with both energy and curiosity. He has an uncanny ability to identify areas of opportunity and to discuss common practices in the hospitality industry and how we can investigate ways to improve them. I value his insights and his ability to recognize the real issues that we need to resolve with service delivery systems, so much so that I have had him come to Houston to spend a day with our faculty.

Through this book, everyone can spend a day with Professor Robert Ford. Bob loves to spend time with hospitality executives, discussing what keeps them up at night. This discussion provides him with not only a real understanding of the industry but also anecdotes he uses to illustrate his text. The examples of best practices presented in this book make it an interesting read. This book is structured as a textbook, but any manager of a hospitality organization will find the time spent reading this book a good investment.

The research suggests that there truly are important differences between managing a service organization and managing a tangible goods producing organization. Yet, there are very few books on the management of services. This book is the only one I know of on the management of hospitality services. When I taught services management, my choice for a text was Bob's [first edition] *Managing the Guest Experience in Hospitality.* I come from a marketing background. Bob often reminds me that marketers make promises and operators have to deliver those promises. This book explains how to deliver those promises.

This book has been completely updated with new examples and the latest thought on service management. Although Disney provides great examples of how to deliver great service, the book has been expanded to include examples from a diverse set of hospitality organizations, including international organizations. This inclusion will make it interesting and relevant to students going into any area of the hospitality industry and to students from across the globe.

Michael Sturman, now a professor at Rutgers University's School of Management and Labor Relations, was previously the Kenneth and Marjorie Blanchard Professor of Human Resources at Cornell University, having researched and taught at the Hotel School for 18 years. One of Michael's additions is his knowledge of compensation and staffing in the hospitality industry. Michael's research articles have been featured in the top management journals. He is known for his ability to communicate the implications of this research to practitioners and is former editor of and a frequent contributor to the *Cornell Hospitality Quarterly.*

I am delighted that Bob and Mike have created the second edition, newly titled *Managing Hospitality Organizations: Achieving Excellence in the Guest Experience.* I am delighted not only for myself, but also for my guests, the students of hospitality management. I strongly recommend *Managing Hospitality Organizations: Achieving Excellence in the Guest Experience* as a must read for hospitality managers and a text for hospitality management programs.

John Bowen
Dean and Barron Hilton Distinguished Chair
Conrad N. Hilton College
University of Houston

PREFACE

Welcome to *Managing Hospitality Organizations: Achieving Excellence in the Guest Experience*, **SECOND EDITION**. This second edition, like the first edition, continues to be based on the principles of *guestology,* and that means we practice in writing this book what we teach in class. So, we kept the positive features of the earlier book while changing those that our readers said needed to be changed.

The book is based on much of what the first author learned when he came to Orlando to head the hospitality program at the University of Central Florida. There, he learned about many different aspects of the hospitality industry from The Walt Disney Company, and specifically about the principles of guestology from its "father," Bruce Laval. Disney was then and still is today a benchmark hospitality organization. People come from all over the world to learn how to use Disney's guestological techniques and apply those principles to their own guest-focused organizations. If there seems to be an abundance of examples in this book from Walt Disney World, there is a reason. This is a visible and familiar service exemplar that most students can relate to easily and which many have visited. Disney also provides an exceptionally wide representation of the hospitality industry. It has successful examples of restaurants from quick-serve to fine dining; lodging from campgrounds to upscale hotels; a transportation system that includes trains, boats, buses, and monorails; catering services, convention and meeting planning services, entertainment and night clubs, retail stores, golf courses, and cruise ships. These organizations include almost every specific job category in the hospitality field. The range of jobs for study on the Disney property—in terms of staffing, training, motivating, and job performance—is very wide. Disney hires and trains thousands of people annually to fill 1,100 different positions.

But there are many other exemplars: companies that use best practices to successfully deliver great service. Aside from Disney, there are many examples from hotels, casinos, restaurants, amusement parks, airlines, and even others that may, at first glance, not appear to be in the service industry. In today's business environment, all companies need to know how to provide exceptional service, or their customers will go to their competitors that can. We hope that you will be able to learn from these examples, from firms both familiar and new to you, and see the application of the principles and ideas in the book to whatever hospitality organizations are near you.

We also hope that you will find this book as clearly written and rich in content and real-world examples as its predecessor book. We worked hard to improve the aspects of the book that our student readers and faculty teachers liked while changing what needed to be changed. A lot has happened in the past decade, especially in technology, and this book contains new content to reflect those changes. We hope you like our work and invite you to tell us how well we did or where we could have done better. As practicing guestologists, we sought the input of many former guests and those who were seeking more coverage of managerial topics than is currently available in hospitality texts. We did what we tell you to do as practicing guestologists—ask, ask, ask your guests what they want, need, and expect from an experience. After all, it doesn't matter what we think is a great book if our guests don't see it that way.

We have made two big changes while writing this edition. The first involves the changes that have occurred with people. Guests of the late twentieth century are different from today's guests. The current generation of employees now entering the labor force have different expectations, capabilities, and behaviors than previous generations. The second big change is in the forces impacting the organization. Competitors and the nature of competition have changed. Suppliers are different, technology is very different, the ecological environment is different, and hospitality organizations have discovered that the global nature that all businesses operate in today affects them too. We are all interconnected, and the result of these global connections is a change in how we manage the guest experience in hospitality.

We have made other changes as well to make the book more relevant in an era where social responsibility, ethics, and environmental concerns are increasingly part of the hospitality manager's world. In each chapter, we again provided an ethical dilemma to discuss. Our references have been updated to give the student and instructor further information on each chapter's topics for expanding lectures, opening knowledge doors for papers, more in-depth study of related topics, and starting places for further research. We have also included classic references to allow the student to trace the evolution of ideas back to their roots.

Finally, we want to point out that customer service by itself will not remedy a bad strategy, ineffective staffing, or poorly designed and operated business systems. On the other hand, the research shows that once a business is efficiently run, customer service can give it a sustainable competitive advantage. A big friendly smile won't make up for a ruined meal, but a "wow" service encounter with a well-trained and motivated server can make a routine experience into an unmatchable "wow" that guests will remember and come back to have again. The exciting thing to us is how great an opportunity this is for gaining a competitive advantage over others in whatever hospitality business in which you compete. A quick look at the most recent American Customer Satisfaction Index (online) will show that most businesses are at the "C" level in providing customer satisfaction. Where else in the world can you be only a little above average to be seen as "outstanding"? We hope that the lessons learned and the concepts presented here will help you become accomplished guestologists and receive an "outstanding" from your guests.

PURPOSE OF THE BOOK

This book is an attempt to organize, integrate, and present information about managing hospitality organizations, some of which comes from academic studies and some from the school of experience. We wrote the book to meet the needs of college classes devoted to or including exploration of this exciting, undeveloped area. It should also be of help to executives and managers who seek to implement a guest-focused service strategy in any hospitality or service organization that wants to compete successfully in today's customer-driven market.

This book fills a void. Up until now, instructors and students in hospitality management classes have had to use a text that combined services marketing with some services management, with specific applications to restaurants, lodging, and other hospitality areas made by the instructor or by means of handouts and articles on serving guests in hospitality settings. *Managing Hospitality Organizations: Achieving Excellence in the Guest Experience* fills that void. It combines the findings of the most significant research on services and hospitality services in particular with the best practices of leading hospitality organizations such as The Walt Disney Company, Four Seasons, Hilton Hotels, Marriott, Darden Restaurants, Southwest Airlines, and many others.

In addition to reviews by numerous college and university instructors of hospitality, the material has been reviewed by practicing executives from many successful hospitality organizations, such as The Walt Disney Company, Four Seasons, Gaylord Hotels, Hyatt Hotels, Sodexo, Darden Restaurants, Sheraton Hotels, and many others. These academic and practitioner reviews have assured that the text content is supported by sound theoretical underpinnings and real-world findings.

THE HOSPITALITY PRINCIPLES

Managing Hospitality Organizations: Achieving Excellence in the Guest Experience represents theory that has passed the test of relevance. A proven principle of hospitality management keys each chapter of this book. Leading hospitality organizations have found these principles to be important, workable, and useful. They represent the key points to keep in mind when putting the book's material into practice. They can guide hospitality organizations and their managers as they seek to reach the levels of excellence achieved by the benchmark organizations.

SYSTEMATIC SEQUENCE

To communicate the content of *Managing Hospitality Organizations: Achieving Excellence in the Guest Experience* as clearly as possible, we have used a simple structure for the book so that its organization could be one of this book's major features. One section is devoted to each of hospitality management's three major concerns: *strategy, staffing,* and *systems.* Each of the fourteen chapters is keyed to a principle of successful hospitality management.

Section 1, *The Hospitality Service Strategy,* begins by Chapter 1 explaining some of the book's major concepts: some differences between products and services; what is meant by guestology; meeting customer expectations; the three parts of the guest experience; and the definitions of quality, value, and cost in a guest service context. This section then moves to Chapter 2's thorough coverage of the planning processes used to assess and meet guest expectations. Also explained are essential planning topics such as quantitative and qualitative forecasting tools; the importance of demographic trends; and the organization's service strategy origins in its vision, purpose, and mission, which themselves are based on the organization's careful assessment of guest expectations. Chapter 3 describes why the service setting or environment is crucial to service success. We have employed numerous examples to illustrate the principles and best practices of creating an appropriate setting. Section 1 concludes with Chapter 4's discussion of the importance to the hospitality organization of a total service culture and how to achieve it.

Section 2, *The Hospitality Service Staff,* covers how to recruit and hire "persons who love to serve" in Chapter 5, how to train them in Chapter 6, and then how to motivate and empower them to provide outstanding guest service in Chapter 7. A topic that many students and practitioners find particularly important is covered in Chapter 8, how the hospitality organization can, when the conditions are right, encourage and help guests co-produce, or participate in co-creating, their own experiences!

Section 3, *The Hospitality Service Delivery System,* shows how to glue the different parts of the guest experience together by communicating information to the right person at the right time, described in Chapter 9. Chapter 10 then describes the critically important tasks involved in planning and creating the service delivery system. This includes projecting to meet demand, monitoring the system, and engaging in continuous improvement. Because no organization's server/system combinations can match demand perfectly, Chapter 11 describes techniques for managing the inevitable waits for service. Chapter 12 presents some ways of measuring results in terms of service quality and guest satisfaction so organizations and servers know how well they are meeting guests' expectations. All organizations try to provide perfect experiences, but the leading ones plan for the inevitable failures. Chapter 13 therefore focuses on how to avoid service failures and problems. But because no servers and systems have yet been devised that can provide so complex a service as the guest experience perfectly every time, we have also discussed planning for, finding, and fixing service failures when they occur. Section 3 and the book concludes with Chapter 14, which explains how the organization's people, units, and their efforts must be tied together to provide remarkable guest service that delights guests. That alignment—of strategy, staffing, and systems—is accomplished by outstanding organizational leadership.

LEARNING OBJECTIVES, KEY TERMS, AND DISCUSSION QUESTIONS

Every chapter opens with a comprehensive set of learning objectives addressing the chapter's main points. The learning objectives are reiterated in the chapter, and we end each chapter with a summary of the key lessons learned associated with each learning objective. The list of key terms and concepts provides a review of the subjects and ideas in the chapter. These terms and concepts are boldfaced and defined when they are first discussed in the chapter. The discussion questions at each chapter's end are designed to provoke thought and classroom interaction about chapter content and to enable students to make self-assessments of how well they have understood the material.

ACTIVITIES AND CASE STUDIES

Each chapter includes at least one hospitality activity to encourage students to visit local hospitality organizations and study them from the perspective of the book's ideas. Some activities suggest that students talk with guests, employees, and managers to obtain a variety of perspectives on the guest experience. Other activities suggest exploration of the internet to visit sites established by hospitality organizations and to acquire further information on the book's concepts and ideas. Case studies provide an opportunity to discuss hospitality concepts and principles in terms of real or (if disguised) hypothetical hotels, restaurants, and other business types found in the hospitality industry.

ETHICAL SCENARIOS

Unethical practices in business are a growing concern. Newspapers commonly report on scandals where someone has embezzled, stolen, forged, misappropriated funds, etc. But even when not dealing with blatantly illegal activities, employees and managers will likely be faced with tough decisions that require uncomfortable choices. The purpose of the "Ethics in Business" section, at the end of each chapter, is to raise such issues that students may need to wrestle with in the services industry. Each chapter presents an issue that students can think about and discuss regarding what is the "right" way to respond. Students are encouraged to consider different perspectives for each scenario, weighing how different individuals may consider the same situation in different ways.

ADDITIONAL READINGS

We did not create this book on our own; rather, we stood on the shoulders of many giants who have come before us. Each chapter is based on substantial research that has been conducted in service businesses, on hospitality companies, and from insights from academics and practitioners. For those interested in better understanding the foundations of our thinking, or if you are interested in learning more about a particular topic, we have provided a list of additional readings for each chapter. These readings include classic articles on the particular topic, as well as recent research on timely and relevant topics. We hope to give additional breadth and depth to teachers' classroom and executive education presentations. We also hope to give students a rich resource they can use to dig deeper into topics of interest that they discover in the book. We fully appreciate that we have only scratched the surface of this amazing array of knowledge and hope we can offer some suggested readings for those who are inspired to explore further.

TO THE STUDENT

Managing Hospitality Organizations: Achieving Excellence in the Guest Experience is designed for you. The material has been taught in many classes during the past decade to students with backgrounds similar to yours. The information presented is based on the best available research on services and hospitality services in particular, and on the best practices of leading hospitality organizations. The book should give you a thorough understanding of the principles of managing a hospitality organization. We hope you will want to keep the book if you enter the hospitality field or work in any of the many service organizations that dominate the economy. What we can learn from hospitality leaders is valuable in managing any customer-focused for-profit or nonprofit organization.

NEW TO THIS EDITION

- All learning objectives have been revised and are stated using terminology that is measurable and actionable.
- Key terms can now be found at the end of each chapter.
- A running glossary has been added. Key terms with definitions appear in the margin of the reading.
- Learning objectives have been correlated to each primary heading in the reading.
- Updates focusing on technology and innovations in technology have been expanded in the reading. An icon will appear to highlight and draw attention to this emerging trend in hospitality management.
- Content on sustainability has also been incorporated into the reading. An icon will appear to highlight and draw attention to this emerging trend in hospitality management.

Technology

Sustainability

CHAPTER 1

- Content has been reorganized to improve flow and comprehension
- Expanded discussion of the trending experience economy
- Expanded focus on competitive advantage
- Incorporated new examples from more businesses such as Carnival Cruises, Bahama Breeze, Melting Pot, and Country Walker
- Incorporation of new studies and literature

CHAPTER 2

- Chapter is significantly revised for flow and clarity
- Expanded discussion on environmental assessment
- Expanded discussion on generational groups/categories, particularly Millennials and Generation Z
- Added discussion of changing social and political expectations
- Expanded discussion of the green movement and environmental sustainability
- Expanded discussion of operating environments
- Expanded discussion of action plans including management performance plans, employee hiring, training, and retention plans, financial plans, and marketing plans
- Expanded discussion of competitive environments
- Incorporated new examples from more businesses such as Ruth Chris's Steak House, Alaska Airlines, Mind's Eye Travel, Panera, Applebee's, and Aloft
- Updated review questions
- Incorporation of new studies and literature

CHAPTER 3

- Incorporated international examples such as Kavevala and Shanghai Disney
- Incorporated new examples from more businesses such as Fred Harvey Company, Amplatz Children's Hospital, Medieval Times, Kavevala, and Seasons 52
- Incorporation of new studies and literature

CHAPTER 4

- Expanded discussion of corporate culture, defining, creating, and communicating to support and enhance the service experience
- Examples from the Gaylord Hotel STARS program
- Incorporated new examples from more businesses such as Hyatt Hotels and Google
- Incorporation of new studies and literature

CHAPTER 5

- Added discussion of human resource management, including planning, online recruitment, professional networks, and career fairs
- Added discussion of emotional labor
- Added discussion of new technologies in recruitment and screening
- Incorporated new examples from more businesses such as Southwest Airlines, Eleven Madison Park, Hilton Hotels, and Kimpton Hotels

- Revised review questions
- Incorporation of new studies and literature

CHAPTER 6

- Significantly revised and revamped chapter providing new examples and expanded discussions. Revised and reorganized for better flow and clarity.
- Fully revamped and revised discussion on training, types of training and training methods, including simulations and e-learning
- New introductory example from The Inn from Pittsburgh
- Added discussion on use of big data
- Added discussion of costs of training and return on investment
- Incorporated new examples from more businesses such as Cheesecake Factory, Four Seasons, JetBlue, LaQuinta, and Scandinavian Airline Service
- Incorporation of new studies and literature

CHAPTER 7

- Very heavily revised chapter adding discussions on many emerging topical areas such as sexual harassment, ethical leadership, equity, teamwork, and generational and cultural differences
- Added discussion of the service-profit chain
- Expanded discussion of motivation
- Introduced concept of hedonic treadmill
- Added discussion of growth needs
- Removed content on roles and satisfaction
- Incorporation of new studies and literature

CHAPTER 8

- Places increased emphasis on assisting the guest with co-production of the experience and co-creation of its value
- Incorporated new examples from more businesses such as Uber, Lyft, Living Social, and Marriott
- Incorporation of new studies and literature

CHAPTER 9

- Added discussion of new and emerging technologies such as virtual reality, data analytics, self-service kiosks, artificial intelligence, web mapping and geocoding, and social media
- Added example of overbooking of flights
- Incorporated new examples from more businesses such as Amazon, Whole Foods, Ocean House and Harrah's
- Incorporation of new studies and literature

CHAPTER 10

- Expanded discussion of service standards using Gaylord Hotels STARS program as an example
- Added example of Wendy's ambassador programs in training
- Incorporatied new studies and literature

CHAPTER 11

- Added discussion of use of technology to allow guests to plan according to statistics made available and through use of mobile apps
- Incorporated new examples from more businesses such as Pandora–World of Avatar
- Incorporation of new studies and literature

CHAPTER 12

- Added discussion of Leading Hotels of the World Standards
- Added discussion of use of new technologies such as apps, tablets, and the web, as well as social media
- Incorporated new examples from more businesses such as Carrabba's, Hampton Inn, Eleven Madison Park, Planet Hollywood Orlando, and Continental Airlines
- Incorporation of new studies and literature

CHAPTER 13

- New examples of handling service failures, such as Ocean House and Caesars Entertainment
- Incorporation of new studies and literature

CHAPTER 14

- Reorganized for improvement of flow and clarity
- Added discussion of training
- Added discussion on innovation, including examples of William Cameron Coup, restaurant incubators, and eco-innovations
- Added a section on leading and managing
- Incorporated new examples from more businesses such as Emirates Air and WestJet
- Incorporation of new studies and literature

DIGITAL RESOURCES

SAGE edge offers a robust online environment featuring an impressive array of tools and resources for review, study, and further exploration, keeping both instructors and students on the cutting edge of teaching and learning. SAGE edge content is open access and available on demand. Learning and teaching has never been easier! You can access your SAGE Edge content at edge.sagepub.com/ford2e.

SAGE edge for Students provides a personalized approach to help students accomplish their coursework goals in an easy-to-use learning environment.

- Mobile-friendly flashcards strengthen understanding of key terms and concepts.
- Mobile-friendly practice quizzes allow for independent assessment by students of their mastery of course material.
- Learning objectives reinforce the most important material.
- Video and multimedia links appeal to different learning styles.
- Additional Readings for further study.

SAGE edge for Instructors supports teaching by making it easy to integrate quality content and create a rich learning environment for students.

- Test banks provide a diverse range of pre-written options as well as the opportunity to edit any question and/or insert personalized questions to assess students' progress and understanding. Questions are correlated to Bloom's taxonomy and the current AACSB standards.
- Sample course syllabi for semester and quarter courses provide suggested models for structuring one's course.
- Editable, chapter-specific PowerPoint® slides offer complete flexibility for creating a multimedia presentation for the course.
- Video and multimedia links appeal to students with different learning styles.
- Instructor's Manual containing lecture outlines, answers to review questions, suggested activities, suggested discussion topics for Ethics in Business Feature, and case notes.
- Additional Readings are assignable for further study.

This book is dedicated to Bruce Laval—the father of guestology.

ACKNOWLEDGMENTS

Once again and always, we thank our wives, Barbara Ford and Kelly Sturman, for unfailing support and for continuing to exceed our expectations; they put the wow! in our lives. We also want to thank the great people at Sage for their patience and support. A special thanks to Cherrill Heaton, whose writing and organizational skills made this book possible.

Robert C. Ford
Michael C. Sturman

INDUSTRY AND PRACTITIONER REVIEWERS

Rick Allen, The Walt Disney Company (retired)
Wendy Anderson, Earle Enterprises
Anthony Bernazar, FreshPoinit
Christopher Brumbaugh, Gaylord Hotels
Carol Cooley, Gaylord Hotels
Richard J. Corcoran, R. J. Corcoran & Associates
Ed Evans, Four Seasons Hotels and Resorts
Vanessa George, Hyatt Hotel Corporation
Pallava Goenka, Specialty Restaurant Corporation
Will Guidara, Eleven Madison Park
Laurie Hobbs, Ocean House
Mark Jacob, The Dolder Grand
Stacey Jacobs, Hilton
Rich Jeffers, Darden Restaurants
Melanie Jones, Southwest
Carol Kanfoush, Maxie's Supper Club and Oyster Bar
Janna Kiuru, Klaus K Hotel
Johann Krieger, Gaylord Hotels
Bruce Laval, The Walt Disney Company (retired)
Meagen Mills, Red Lobster
Katie Reed, Hilton
Don Riddel, Don Riddle Images
Maureen Silver, Gaylord Palms
Blaine Sweatt, Darden Restuarants (retired)
Rich Ungaro, formerly of Starbucks
Britni Webster, Freshpoint
Megan Zamiska, J. Wade Public Relations

ACADEMIC REVIEWERS

Sherry Andre, Johnson & Wales University, Miami
Paul Bagdan, Johnson & Wales University, Providence
Bill Bennett, Southwest Minnesota State University
Marisa B. Boff, Bradford School
Denise A. Braley, Mitchell College
Kathleen Pearl Brewer, University of Nevada, Las Vegas
Steven A. Carvell, Cornell University
John C. Crotts, College of Charleston
Jonathan Deutsch, Drexel University
Duncan Dickson, University of Central Florida
Rick Florsheim, University of Central Florida
Babu P. George, University of Southern Mississippi
Susan Gregory, Eastern Michigan University
Demian Hodari, Ecole hôtelière de Lausanne
Nan Hua, University of Central Florida
Leonard A. Jackson, University of Central Florida
Miyoung Jeong, University of South Carolina
Richard R. Perdue, Virginia Polytechnic Institute and State University
Peter Ricci, Florida Atlantic University
Heejung Ro, University of Central Florida
Theda L. Rudd, The School of Hospitality Business, Michigan State University
Wei Wang, University of Southern Mississippi
Alistair Williams, Johnson & Wales University
Katherine Wilson, University of Central Florida
Chih-Lun Yen, Ball State University

ABOUT THE AUTHORS

Robert C. Ford (Ph.D., Arizona State University) is professor emeritus of management in the College of Business Administration (COBA) of the University of Central Florida (UCF) where he has taught management of service organizations. He joined UCF as the chair of its hospitality department. He was also the COBA Associate Dean for Graduate and External Programs.

Bob has authored or coauthored numerous publications in both top research and practitioner journals. He has served on several editorial boards including *Cornell Hospitality Quarterly, British Journal of Management, Journal of Leadership and Organizational Studies, Journal of Convention and Event Tourism, and Journal of Service Management.* He has also published several books including *Managing the Guest Experience in Hospitality, Achieving Service Excellence: Strategies for Health Care, Managing Destination Marketing Organizations,* and *The Fun Minute Manager.*

Bob has been an active participant in many professional organizations. He has served the Academy of Management (AOM) as editor of *The Academy of Management Executive,* Director of Placement, board member of the HRM and Careers divisions, Division Chair for both its Management History and its Management Education and Development divisions, a member and chair of its Ethics Adjudication Committee, and a co-founder of the Community of Academy Senior Scholars. Bob has served the Southern Management Association (SMA) in every elective office including president. He was a founding member and Chair of the Accreditation Commission for Programs in Hospitality Administration and served on the Destination Marketing Accreditation Program.

Bob has been recognized for his service by many organizations. He received the Distinguished Service Award from AOM's MED, the Richard Hodgett's Distinguished Career Award from Management History, and SMA's Distinguished Service Award and was elected to SMA Fellows. In recognition of his service to hospitality education, he was given the Paul Brown Award by the Florida Hotel and Lodging Association. He was also twice awarded a W. James Whyte Research Fellow by the University of Queensland.

Michael C. Sturman (Ph.D., Cornell University) is a Professor of Human Resource Management in the Rutgers' School of Management and Labor Relations. His research focuses on the prediction of individual job performance over time and the influence of compensation systems. He also examines the use of HR Analytics and Metrics to improve HR decision-making and the return on HR investments. Michael has published research articles in journals such as the *Academy of Management Journal, Journal of Applied Psychology, Journal of Management, Organizational Research Methods,* and *Personnel Psychology.* He has also published practitioner-oriented papers in *Compensation and Benefits Review,* the *American Compensation Association Journal, Cornell Hospitality Quarterly, International Journal of Hospitality Management, Lodging Magazine,* and *Lodging HR,* and is a presenter in Salary.com's CompX Compensation Education series. Before coming to Rutgers, Michael was the Kenneth and Marjorie Blanchard Professor of Human Resources at Cornell University's College of Business, where he held appointments in the Management Area and the School of Hotel Administration, as well as a courtesy appointment with the School of Industrial and Labor Relations. Michael holds a Ph.D., M.S., and B.S. from Cornell University's School of Industrial and Labor Relations, and is a Senior Professional of Human Resources as certified by the Society for Human Resource Management. He teaches undergraduate, graduate, and executive courses on human resource management, HR Analytics, compensation, and analytical methods. He is an Associate Editor for the *Journal of Applied Psychology* and serves on the editorial boards of *Journal of Management* and *Organizational Research Methods.*

INTRODUCTION

SERVICE RULES!

The modern economy is dominated by service organizations. The service sector constitutes 75% to 80% of the U.S. economy and is growing. Even businesses dealing primarily in physical goods now often view themselves primarily as service providers, with the offered good being an important part of the service. These firms have adopted traditional service terms such as customer satisfaction, customer retention, and customer relationships. Some, like IBM, have realized that their future flow of revenues and profits will come from their service businesses.

Yet, surprisingly few articles and books focus on how to manage service organizations, even fewer on how to manage hospitality organizations. The purpose of this book is to provide a comprehensive review of the best that is known about managing hospitality organizations. From the neighborhood restaurant to the resort hotel, from the small convention center to the huge theme park, the principles of managing hospitality organizations are the same. Even more important, they are different from the principles of managing manufacturing organizations taught in most business schools.

HOSPITALITY IS DIFFERENT

Traditional bureaucratic structures and manufacturing management principles get turned on their heads in the hospitality sector. It's one thing to design, organize, and control a work process and motivate a workforce when the product is tangible and the production process takes place in a big closed brick factory with an "Employees Only" sign on the door. A totally different challenge arises when the customer is consuming your "product" while you're producing it. The challenge is often intensified by the product's intangibility: "Hospitality" is intangible, and the hospitality experience may not even physically exist! Designing and producing such an experience is quite different from the design and production of goods.

These "production" problems in the hospitality industry are matched or exceeded by the challenge of managing employees who must be carefully trained to provide a service whose quality and value are defined by each guest. To top it off, employees must be taught to provide this service not behind closed doors but while customers, guests, or clients are watching, asking questions, and changing their minds about what they want. Most even participate jointly with the employees in co-producing the guest experience itself! Manufacturing managers sometimes moan about how hard it is to teach their employees to perform the necessary manufacturing steps accurately. They should talk to their colleagues in the hospitality industry, who have to teach their employees not only how to "manufacture" the product but also how to do so with the guest watching and co-producing. These managers know that the principles taught in smokestack management courses in traditional business schools don't seem too relevant. Managing in the hospitality industry is a very different world.

STUDY THE BEST

Only recently have researchers and management scholars begun to study this different world as a separate field, and much of what is known is still based on anecdotal information and case-study examples. This makes perfect sense. In the early stages of inquiry into any field of business, the logical approach is to find the best organizations and study them to discover the principles that drive what they do. A review of the service management literature quickly reveals several benchmark organizations. The list includes Darden Restaurants, Four Seasons Hotels and Resorts, Hilton, JetBlue Airways, Marriott International, Nordstrom's Department Store, Southwest Airlines, and The Walt Disney Company. And there are, of course, many others large and small. These organizations learned long ago the importance of understanding what their customers expect from all parts of their service experience, and they manage their businesses around satisfying those expectations. Because they have studied their guests long and hard, they know what their guests want, what they are willing to pay for it, and how to give it to them. The magic of Disney and the other outstanding hospitality organizations is that they meet guest expectations, of course, and then exceed them in a thousand ways that get guests not only to say "wow!" on the first visit but to return repeatedly and say "wow!" every time. Customers, clients, patrons, and guests return to the great organizations—manufacturing or service—because they get it right and then some.

FOCUS ON YOUR GUEST

Two fundamental concepts, based on the practices of successful hospitality organizations, will appear in one form or another throughout the book. First, everything the organization does should focus on the guest. Most managers think first about their organization, their production requirements, and their employee needs. They are used to starting with themselves or their employees when they design their product, create the setting or environment in which the customer interacts with the organization, and set up the system for delivering the goods or services that their customers buy. They manage from the inside out. This first fundamental that we stress is that you must manage from the outside in! Start with the guests. Study them endlessly; know what they want, need, value, expect, and actually do. Then focus everyone in the organization on figuring out how to do a better job of meeting and exceeding guest expectations in a way that allows the organization to make a profit.

YOUR CUSTOMER IS YOUR GUEST

The second fundamental concept that must be part of the hospitality organization's culture is that you must treat each customer like a guest. If appropriate to the organization (and it probably is appropriate in all hospitality organizations), always use the term *guest* and not *customer*. Create a guest-focused culture. Most important of all, train employees to think of the people in front of them as their guests, whom they are hosting for the organization. This is not a simple change in terminology; it is a big deal. In fact, outstanding companies like Disney think it's such a big deal that they use the term *guest* instead of *customer* for their millions of visitors. They know the importance of constantly reminding their thousands of employees to think of their customers as guests in everything they do. Disney even coined the term *guestology* to refer to the scientific study of guest behavior to learn more about meeting—and exceeding—the expectations of its guests.

Looking at a customer as a guest changes everything an organization and its employees do. A customer comes to the organization seeking to buy something that the organization sells, and the only obligation of the organization and its employees is to execute a commercial transaction in an effective, businesslike manner. The person comes in the door expecting to be treated like a customer, at best. But if the organization can provide a hospitable experience of which the actual commercial transaction is only a part, the customer will think "wow!" Creating an experience instead of merely selling a product or service is important to turn customers into patrons or guests. Rather than thinking of selling admission tickets or hotel rooms, the truly guest-focused organizations such as The Four Seasons Hotels try to create a memorable event for their customers. They provide the commercial transaction within a warm, friendly experience that makes an emotional connection so memorable that it brings the customer back time after time. The Four Seasons and all other excellent hospitality organizations know that it is cheaper to keep loyal customers than it is to attract new ones, and that repeat business is the key to long-term profitability.

To become a believer in this fundamental concept, think about the business organizations you deal with. To some, you are merely a component in a commercial transaction; others treat you like a guest. The difference is so clear it is unforgettable. Anyone who has been to a Disney theme park or a Hyatt Regency hotel knows the special way they treat their guests. The idea of treating customers like guests is a lesson that any hospitality organization—in fact, any organization that seeks to compete successfully in the modern service-dominated economy—must learn. Customers are increasingly aware of who treats them right and who does not. They know more about what does and does not have value for them, and they expect more from the organizations they deal with. Even more important, the organizations that have discovered and use the principles explained in this book are taking business away from those organizations that still don't understand them. While the best keep raising the bar for each other, they are also making it increasingly difficult for the rest to understand why their customers are never satisfied with their service or product. This book organizes what the best hospitality organizations know and what the rest must learn to compete successfully in an increasingly customer-driven marketplace.

Although focusing on customers and treating them like guests sound simple enough, these tasks are actually huge managerial challenges that the exemplars in hospitality services spend enormous amounts of time, money, and energy to meet. They spend countless hours and dollars investing in a service culture that continually reinforces their customer service values.

SOME THEORETICAL UNDERPINNINGS

In addition to studying the best practices of exemplars in the hospitality industry, we have reviewed the services management, marketing, hospitality, and human resource literatures. The concepts and principles contained in this book represent a unique combination of what the academic literature says should work and what the long experience of some of the most successful hospitality organizations in the world have found does work.

STRATEGY, STAFF, AND SYSTEMS

We have organized the best that is known about hospitality management according to the three critical *S*s of the successful hospitality organization: strategy, staff, and systems. Each *S* organizes the material in one of the book's three major sections. Each *S* is equally important in providing superior service. First comes strategy and the definition of what plans hospitality organizations must make to be effective in achieving their service mission. Next is the staff. Although every organization wants an effective staff, the hospitality organization depends almost completely upon its personnel to deliver the high-quality guest experience that distinguishes the excellent hospitality organization from the merely good. Finally, the third *S* represents the systems. The best hospitality staff in the world cannot succeed without an effective array of systems to back them up in delivering the service that the customer comes for. An impressive mission statement and a big server smile can't make up for a burned lasagna, a dirty room, a late flight, unpredictable room service, or a broken air conditioner.

Although the hospitality organization's strategy, staff, and systems are obviously related to one another, they all have one focus—the guest—and exist for one overriding purpose: to provide guest satisfaction.

PROVIDE THE BETTER CHOICE

Service in the hospitality industry is too often unsatisfactory. Dissatisfied guests can easily switch to competing organizations or even choose alternatives to this industry. Hospitality owners and managers are increasingly aware that if they want guests to keep coming back to their hotel, restaurant, destination, cruise line, or airline instead of going elsewhere, they'd better learn to give good service. If guests feel that they are receiving unsatisfactory service from one organization, they can probably find a similar organization just down the street, and they will go there. Indeed, with the increasing availability of virtual experiences, they can find many alternative ways to spend their money.

Everybody sees the problems with guest service, and many people looking for answers ask: who does it right, and how? This book, which combines the key principles of good hospitality service management research with examples drawn from some of the world's most successful hospitality organizations, should help any hospitality organization or manager who aspires to be a guestologist and provide better service to guests.

STRUCTURE AND THE FOURTEEN PRINCIPLES OF HOSPITALITY MANAGEMENT

Within this overall three-section structure, we have framed the information under fourteen principles in fourteen chapters. Here is an overview of how all this fits together.

THE HOSPITALITY SERVICE STRATEGY

1. Provide the service quality and value that guests expect.
2. Focus strategy on the key drivers of guest satisfaction.
3. Provide the service setting that guests expect.
4. Define and sustain a total service culture.

THE HOSPITALITY SERVICE STAFF

5. Find and hire people who love to serve.
6. Train your employees, then train them some more.
7. Motivate and empower your employees.
8. Empower guests to co-create their experiences.

THE HOSPITALITY SERVICE SYSTEMS

9. Glue the guest experience elements together with information.
10. Provide seamless service delivery.
11. Manage the guest's wait.
12. Pursue perfection relentlessly.
13. Don't fail the guest twice.
14. Lead others to excel.

Within this structure, we think we have captured the important aspects of managing in hospitality organizations. We hope it will be fun for readers to learn more about this fascinating industry and how the best manage to be the best.

Courtesy of Hilton Hotels

SECTION 1

The Hospitality Service Strategy

If you don't have a road map, or know where you are, you may be there already.

—Norman Brinker, Former CEO, Chili's Restaurants

Running a business without a plan is like going into the forest, shooting off your rifle and hoping that dinner runs into the bullet.

—Herman Cain, Former Chairman and CEO, Godfather's Pizza

Johner Images

1 The Basics of Wow! The Guest Knows Best

Hospitality Principle: Provide the Service Quality and Value that Guests Expect

Of course he is a crank, but we must please him. It is our business to please cranks. Anyone can please a gentleman.

—Fred Harvey

Learning Objectives

After reading this chapter, you should be able to

1.1 Describe the key differences between making products and creating experiences for guests.

1.2 Recognize the importance of the guest experience.

1.3 Identify the components of the guest experience.

1.4 State the importance of meeting the hospitality guest's expectations.

1.5 Define *service quality* and *service value* in hospitality.

1.6 Explain the reasons why "it all starts with the guest."

INTRODUCTION

Serving guests and making products are such different activities they require different management principles and concepts. Catching a defective tire or a paint blemish on a car's finish at the final inspection stage of an assembly line production process is one thing. Quite another is listening to irate guests telling you in no uncertain terms that your hotel, restaurant, or airline has failed to deliver the service experience they expected. In the first instance, the quality inspector—one of many people between the maker of the product and the final customer—can send the defective product back for rework without the customer ever knowing. In the second situation, there is usually no one to buffer the relationship between the person delivering the unsatisfactory service and the guest dissatisfied with it.

At its most basic level, the **hospitality** industry is made up of organizations that offer guests courteous, professional food, drink, and lodging services, alone or in combination. But the hospitality industry is more than just hotels and restaurants. Beyond these, the industry is defined in many ways. An expanded definition includes theme parks, airlines, gaming centers, cruise ships, trade shows, fairs, meeting planning, and convention organizations. Indeed, everyone involved in the vast travel and tourism industry may be considered part of the hospitality industry. We believe the principles and practices presented in this book have wide application, therefore we are going to use this more expanded concept of the industry. The challenge for all organizations in this industry is to ensure their personnel always provide at least the level of service their guests want and expect—every time, perfectly. This book is designed to show all those working in this industry and those who manage them how to do that.

hospitality An industry consisting basically of organizations that offer guests courteous, professional food, drink, and lodging services, alone or in combination, but in an expanded definition also includes theme parks, gaming facilities, cruise ships, trade shows, fairs, meetings and events, and convention organizations.

Even more challenging for those in hospitality organizations is the simple reality that service quality and service value are defined not by managers, auditors, or rating organizations: They are defined entirely in the mind of the guest. Although there are a few organizations, such as J. D. Power and AAA, and many websites, such as Trip Advisor and Yelp, that rate the service quality of the local Holiday Inn, Carnival Cruises, or Olive Garden, individual guests still make their own decisions on whether the quality and value of the service they experienced met their expectations. *BusinessWeek* annually rates the best service companies and the American Customer Satisfaction Index (ACSI) and *Consumer Reports* from time to time offer evaluations of the major airline, hotel, and restaurant companies. In the final analysis, however, the decision about the quality and value of a hospitality experience is made anew by each individual guest in every transaction with a specific unit of a hospitality organization on a particular date with a certain service staff. If the guest comes on a date or at a time when the organization for whatever reasons fails to meet expectations, for that guest the restaurant is no good, the airline inept, and the hotel a major disappointment. One unfortunate incident can negatively influence the opinion of the guest and anyone the guest talks to both in person and virtually, through a website posting or social media site.

You will find this text is very different from traditional management texts, because hospitality organizations are very different businesses to run from those discussed in traditional management texts. Most texts emphasize different principles and guidelines for managers seeking to run these organizations well; however, the success or failure of the guest experience may depend on how a single moment of truth between a hospitality employee and the guest is handled. Management's responsibility is to ensure that each moment of truth has been prepared for—has been managed—as well as humanly possible to yield a satisfying, even outstanding, outcome for the guest.

How to achieve such outcomes is the focus of this book. Once dominated by the manufacturing sector, the economy is now overwhelmingly dominated by the service sector. This shift to a service economy, and then beyond ultimately to what is now known as the experience economy, requires traditional management models and methods be reorganized and redirected if they are to meet the unique challenges and opportunities of hospitality organizations.

GUESTOLOGY: WHAT IS IT?

guestology The study of guests—their wants, needs, expectations, and behaviors—with the aim of aligning the organization's strategy, staff, and systems so as to provide outstanding service to guests.

In this book, we organize the available knowledge about meeting these challenges and opportunities around **guestology**, a term originated by Bruce Laval of The Walt Disney Company.[1] Customer-guests are, to the extent possible, studied scientifically (the *-ology* in *guestology*). Guests' behaviors within the hospitality organization are carefully observed. Their wants, needs, capabilities, and expectations regarding the hospitality guest experience are determined. The result of all this study is that the service product is tailored to meet their demands and those of future guests.

The use of "guest" in guestology also has meaning as it implies that all the organization's employees must treat customers as if they were guests in their own homes. Guestology then simply means that the organization should study the guests to manage everything it does from the guest's point of view. All the while, this is a business, and an eye must be kept on the bottom line to ensure that services can continue to be provided in the future. The good news is that guestology makes good business sense. The practice of guestology makes it possible to increase guest satisfaction, which leads to more repeat visits, which in turn drives revenues up. The findings of guestology turn into the organizational practices that provide sustained outstanding services. The organization's strategy, staff, and systems are aligned to meet or exceed the customer's expectations regarding the three aspects of the guest experience: service product, service setting (also called service environment or servicescape), and service delivery. These aspects or elements are carefully woven together to give guests what they want and expect, plus a little bit more. "It all starts with the guest" is not just an inspirational slogan; in the service-centered hospitality organization it is the truth and everybody accepts and lives by it.

Guestology turns traditional management thinking on its head. Instead of focusing on elaborate organizational design, strict adherence to managerial hierarchy, and lean production systems to maximize organizational efficiency, guestology forces the organization to start everything it does by looking systematically at the guest experience from the customer's or guest's point of view. What customers do and want are first systematically studied, modeled, and predicted. Only then can the rest of the organizational

[1] Robert C. Ford and Duncan D. Dickson, "The Father of Guestology: An Interview with Bruce Laval," *Journal of Applied Management and Entrepreneurship* 13, no.3 (2008): 80–90.

issues be addressed. The goal is to create and sustain an organization that can effectively meet the customer's expectations and still be efficient enough to make a profit.

Meeting Customer Expectations

Customers come to a service provider with certain **expectations** for themselves, their businesses, and/or their families. First-time guests may have general expectations. For example, a first-time guest of a major hotel may simply expect a nice room, a comfortable mattress, clean surroundings, satisfactory meals, and a reasonable price. A repeat guest may have more specific expectations based on past experiences. Olive Garden knows that all guests, new and repeat, have certain expectations that drive their evaluation of the quality and value of the Olive Garden experience. From extensive research of their customers, Olive Garden leaders know their guests' key drivers are food of good quality, fast and attentive service, cleanliness, and a pleasant atmosphere. Olive Garden not only asks and studies its guests to find their key drivers, it also solicits comments about how well it delivered on those characteristics by gathering customer feedback.

expectations
Characteristics that a guest hopes and assumes will be associated with a service experience.

A **guestologist** seeks to understand and plan for the expectations of an organization's targeted customers before they ever enter the service setting, so that everything is ready for each guest to have a successful and enjoyable experience. The road from the Magic Kingdom's Main Street, U.S.A. hub off to the right to Tomorrowland in Orlando's Walt Disney World Resort is wider than the road to Adventureland which is off to the left. This is because Disney carefully studied guest behavior and discovered that when people were otherwise indifferent as to which direction to go, they tended to go in the direction of their handedness. Since there are more right-handed than left-handed guests, Disney made the road to the right wider than the other roads off the main hub anticipating that more people would go in that direction. That is guestology in practice. Here is a second illustration of the concept. Disney knows one of its greatest assets is its reputation for cleanliness. Keeping a theme park clean is a big job, so the Disney organization encourages its guests to help out by disposing of their own trash. After all, whatever people throw away themselves does not have to be cleaned up by a paid employee. In studying guest behavior, Disney learned two things. First, if cast members (the Disney term for its employees) are visible constantly picking up even the smallest bits of trash, park guests tend to dispose of their own trash. The cast members model the desired behavior of keeping the parks clean to show respect for cleanliness, and guests copy them. Second, people tend to throw their trash away if trash cans are convenient, easily seen, and not far apart. Disney locates the trash cans to match these criteria. If you visit the Magic Kingdom on a quiet day when the crowds are not distracting, you will notice that Main Street, U.S.A. looks like a forest of trash cans, located 25 to 27 paces apart. Understanding how guests respond to environmental cues and using that knowledge to help maintain a high standard of cleanliness is guestology in practice.

guestologist
A specialist in identifying how hospitality organizations can best respond to the needs, wants, expectations, and behaviors of their targeted guest markets.

Managers of all hospitality organizations can extend the lessons learned by Disney guestologists and other leading hospitality firms to their own companies. If the organizational goal is to provide an outstanding guest experience, then the organization must understand why its guests come to the hospitality organization, what those guests expect, and what the company can and will actually do in order to meet the guests' expectations. Many people think running a restaurant is simple: Offer good food at a fair price, and everything else takes care of itself. Profitable restaurants know that guests patronize them—or get angry and leave—for a variety of reasons other than food quality and value. Managing the total dining experience is a much bigger job than merely executing a good recipe. Guestology involves systematically determining what those factors are, modeling them for study, measuring their impact on the guest experience, testing various strategies that might improve the quality of the experience, and then providing the combination of factors or elements that attracts guests and keeps them coming back.

Understanding the Guest

To well-managed hospitality organizations, guests are not statistical entities, vague concepts, or abstractions. Even with the availability of massive amounts of information on customers "big data" analytics can provide, the best service providers never forget that within the heterogeneous mass of people they serve or want to serve, each is an individual, each is unique. Some companies use the term VIP to remind their employees they are serving "Very Individual People." Each guest brings to the guest experience a different bundle of needs, wants, capabilities, and expectations. Most Melting Pot guests know how to use the fondue pots. Others need to be taught so they don't burn themselves. Most Dave & Buster's guests will arrive happy and excited about whatever is going to happen to them. Others will arrive unhappy, bored, or even angry. Even more challenging is the possibility that the happy, excited guest who came yesterday is the unhappy angry guest coming in the door today. The hospitality organization must not only strive to satisfy each of the guests it seeks to serve in its target market but also adapt what it does to account for the changes in expectations, wants, needs, capabilities, and even behaviors those guests may have from visit to visit.

The first step in understanding how to manage the guest experience then is to understand the guests in a target market, to whatever extent possible. Ideally, this understanding would include (1) the traditional demographic breakdowns of age, race, gender, and guests' home locations; (2) the psychographic breakdowns of how they feel, what their attitudes, beliefs, and values are, and what kind of experience they need, want, and expect the hospitality organization to deliver; and (3) the capabilities (their knowledge, skills, and abilities known as **KSAs**) to co-produce the experience.

KSAs An abbreviation for knowledge, skills, and abilities necessary to do a job.

Meeting the expectations of a customer who arrives needing but not really wanting the service or who may even be angry at the service provider, and perhaps even at the world itself, is difficult. In such situations, ensuring the quality of the service experience is even more crucial because of the circumstances leading to the need for the services. For example, those employing the services of a funeral home rarely do so under happy circumstances. Most dental patients coming in for a root canal will neither enter nor leave the dentist's office filled with joy. In hospitality, sometimes people must travel but don't particularly want to, like the overtired business traveler, the reluctant wedding guest, or the child forced to go on the family vacation or out to a family dinner. Fortunately, most guests of hospitality organizations are not only capable of performing whatever tasks they must perform to co-produce the experience but are also eagerly anticipating the service and have no problems with needing it or wanting it. They are easier to keep happy than the person waiting for the dentist's drill, surgeon's knife, divorce lawyer's advice, or otherwise forced into circumstances not by their choosing.

Understanding and appreciating that guests, their expectations, and their capabilities are varied motivates the guest-focused organization to design each guest experience from each guest's point of view. This allows it to deliver a personalized experience to the extent possible and ensures the hospitality organization has systems and procedures in place to accommodate variations in guests' capabilities. Not everyone is able to do the walking required in a visit to Six Flags, so each Six Flags park has motorized scooters available for those guests needing help.

Serving Internal Customers

In addition to public consumers, the hospitality organization has within itself many **internal customers**, persons and units that depend on each other and "serve" each other. The principles for providing an outstanding service experience for external customers also apply to these many internal customers. For example, a computer help desk that serves internal customers should understand and fulfill the expectations of these customers just as any organization tries to meet and exceed the expectations of its external customers.

internal customers Persons or units within the organization that depend on and serve each other.

This logic can easily and rightfully be extended to the level of the individual employee. The organization must meet or exceed the expectations of employees about how they will be treated. Smart hospitality organizations know their employees must get the same care and consideration they want their employees to extend to their guests. They understand they can't mistreat their own employees and expect them to then treat the customers well. They know the way in which the organization treats its own employees will inevitably spill over onto the way their employees treat guests and each other. In these organizations, everyone works hard to avoid employee mistreatment and unfairness. As expressed in the Southwest Airlines mission statement, "Employees will be provided the same concern, respect, and caring attitude within the organization that they are expected to share externally with every Southwest customer." Extending guest treatment to employees is so important to organizational success that much of Chapter 7, on employee motivation and empowerment, will be devoted to it.

Technology

Service

We have frequently spoken of **service**, a word with numerous meanings. A common way to think of service is as the intangible part of a transaction relationship that creates value between a provider organization and its customer, client, or guest.[2] More simply, a service is something that is done for us. Services can be provided directly to the customer (e.g., a spa treatment, a haircut, and medical procedures) or for the customer (e.g., finding and purchasing tickets to a show, lawn care, and car repair). The services can be provided by a person (e.g., by a service associate in a restaurant or by a concierge) or via technology (e.g., by booking a ticket online, getting a restaurant reservation on a smartphone app, or using an ATM). Some of these relationships are depicted graphically in Exhibit 1.1, later in the chapter. And, of course, services can be provided as a combination of these characteristics.

service An action or performed task that takes place through contact between the customer or guest and representatives of the service organization.

Most services include a tangible physical product or tangible materials and equipment in the transaction as well. At McDonald's guests get a hamburger they can see, touch, eat, or take home in a box; they also get service along with the hamburger. A cruise line will include a ship, a dining experience will provide food, and a teacher's lesson may require a PowerPoint slide deck, texts, and notes. Other service transactions—for example, a session with a psychiatrist, or a massage therapist, or a job counselor—offer only the customer-provider interaction.

Service Product

Another, perhaps even more common, meaning of service refers to the entire bundle of tangibles and intangibles in a transaction with a significant service component. If you leave town for a month and pay for pet-sitting service, the organization or individual may buy and serve pet food, brush and comb your pets, interact with them, bring them toys, clean their litter box, and so forth. Some of what you pay for when you purchase the pet-sitting service is tangible (e.g., the dog food); some is intangible (e.g., petting the dog). For such tangible-intangible mixtures or bundles, the term **service package** or **service product** is often used. The terms are used to describe pure services as well, since the pure service provided is the product the organization offers for sale. Although these overlapping meanings can be confusing (*service* sometimes referring to a tangible-intangible mixture, *service product* sometimes referring to a pure service with no tangible product), the way the term is used in context should make clear what we are talking about in this book. In different contexts, sometimes one term will feel appropriate, sometimes the other.

service package, service product The entire bundle of tangibles and intangibles provided by a hospitality organization to guests during a service experience.

[2] John Bowen and Robert C. Ford, "Managing Service Organizations: Does Having a 'Thing' Make a Difference?" *Journal of Management* 28, no. 3 (2002): 447–469.

Courtesy of Darden Restaurant

Bahama Breeze uses its architecture, landscaping, and design to help communicate to the customer the Caribbean theme of the restaurant.

One necessary distinction to realize is that the service product does not refer specifically to the tangible items that may accompany the transaction, though it can include them. That is, if you go to Bahama Breeze for dinner, the actual meal is not the service product; it is just a tangible part of the service product that Bahama Breeze delivers to diners within a building themed to resemble a Caribbean restaurant and a feeling that "Your island getaway begins here." Likewise, Starbucks knows it's not just selling coffee but everything that goes along with a full and enjoyable coffee-house experience. A final point about the service product: Both the organization and the guest define it, and the definitions may not be the same. The organization may think its service product is the well-made, tasty hamburger, reliably consistent from location to location. But the guest may be "buying" a more extended service product: a well-made, tasty, consistent hamburger delivered quickly in clean surroundings by a cheerful server. Cleanliness and cheerfulness may be as important as burger taste for many guests. Since it all starts with the guest, a hospitality organization always needs to define its service product not in terms of its own interests but in terms of what its guests want and expect. Charles Revson, founder of Revlon, Inc., long ago drew this important distinction between what his organization makes and what the clientele buys: "In the factory we make cosmetics; in the store we sell hope."[3]

Service Industries

Just as the service product is a mixture of tangible and intangible elements, so are the entire industries that provide these products. Although some industries have traditionally been referred to as service industries, marketing writer Theodore Levitt made an important point about service as early as 1972: "There are no such things as service industries. There are only industries whose service components are greater or less than those of other industries. Everybody is in service."[4]

Goods to Services to Experiences

A characteristic of the contemporary economy that hospitality organizations were the first to understand is that, for many consumers, receiving well-made goods or well-rendered services may no longer be sufficient. If you build a better mousetrap today, the world may or may not beat a path to your door. More and more, today's consumers want their goods and services packaged as part of a memorable experience that has an emotional impact. Of course, today's airlines must fly passengers safely from point to point on schedule; restaurants must serve tasty, safe-to-eat food; hotels must provide clean rooms—all at a price customers are willing to pay. But the most successful hospitality organizations, and an ever-increasing number of organizations of all types, are recognizing the **competitive advantage** they can gain by providing carefully designed experiences that are so engaging they remain in the memories of their customers, clients, and guests. B. Joseph Pine and James H. Gilmore were among the

competitive advantage Something an organization does or has that makes it somehow better than its competitors in the eyes of its targeted customers.

[3] Theodore Levitt, "Production-Line Approach to Service," *Harvard Business Review* 50, no. 5 (1972): 41–52.
[4] Levitt, 41.

first to note that just as we had moved from an industrial to a service economy, we have now transitioned to an experience economy.[5] If this is true, thinking in terms of providing customer experiences is important for many organizations in varied industries; in the hospitality industry, such thinking is already considered essential to a successful strategy for gaining a competitive advantage.

A firm can gain a competitive advantage a number of ways. For example, it can have a unique (and legally protected) feature like Disney's Mickey Mouse, or a McDonald's franchise, or use of a respected brand name. It can also be gained by controlling non-substitutable resources like a secret sauce no one else has for its barbecue, a service culture that attracts the best employees, or a plot of Napa Valley land famous for producing exceptional wine. The point is that controlling a valuable and rare resource or having a capability that others can't use, imitate, or substitute for gives a hospitality organization a competitive advantage. Having and keeping a competitive advantage can lead to long-term success.

The competition for guest loyalty and dollars (or euros, pesos, rupees, won, yen, yuan, or even a cryptocurrency like Bitcoin) is intense and will only grow more so in the future. New hospitality organizations spring up every day, and for new organizations to survive, they need to develop and sustain a competitive advantage. Although opening a hospitality organization such as a hotel, convention center, cruise line, or airline costs a lot of money, for thousands of restaurants, hospitality suppliers, tour operators, web designers, and convention services organizations, the amount of start-up capital needed is comparatively small. This book is not just for large corporations. These smaller organizations, like the larger ones, hope to survive and prosper in this competitive environment and therefore need to master and practice the principles of guestology. If they don't provide the experience their guests expect, someone else will.

THE GUEST EXPERIENCE

A term we have already repeatedly mentioned and will recur many times in the following pages is **guest experience**. The guest experience, often referred to as **service experience** in other service industries, is the sum total of the experiences the guest has with the service provider on a given occasion or set of occasions. If a guest tells a friend that last night she had a "wonderful evening at the concert," she is referring to the evening as a whole and is thinking of it that way; the evening of music was the guest experience. Providing her with the different phases and aspects that made up her wonderful evening, however, involved many employees, some of whom she saw and many of whom she was not even aware, who produced those different activities and projects flawlessly. For purposes of planning and execution, most hospitality organizations divide the total experience they offer into convenient units or components. For purposes of explaining the total guest experience, we shall do the same, even though such a division is to an extent artificial.

guest experience The sum total of the experiences (consisting of the service product, setting, and delivery system) that the guest has with the service provider on a given occasion or set of occasions; often referred to as service experience in other service industries.

service experience Same as guest experience, but sometimes used in service industries that do not typically refer to their customers as guests.

Valerie Zeithhaml and her coauthors suggest even traditional manufacturing organizations should be aware of the importance of the service component of their manufactured product as they have recognized the value of the total product offering to include the services associated with it.[6] In the experience economy, customers should be considered as guests whether they are having the experience of participating in the purchase of a physical product or of an intangible service.

[5] B. Joseph Pine and James H. Gilmore, "Welcome to the Experience Economy," *Harvard Business Review* 76, No. 4 (1998): 97–105.

[6] Valarie A. Zeithaml and Stephen W. Brown, *Profiting from Services and Solutions: What Product-Centric Firms Need to Know* (New York, NY: Business Expert Press, 2014).

Product, Setting, and Delivery

In a way, this entire book can be oversimplified into one (fairly long!) sentence: We are going to show how the best hospitality organizations use their strategy, staff, and systems to provide each guest with a seamless three-part guest experience—service product, service setting, and service delivery—each part of which will at least meet the guest's expectations and the sum total of which ideally will make the guest say, or at least think, "wow!" In a simple service situation, the entire guest experience might be delivered by a single person in a single moment, but for the typical guest experience, speaking of a service delivery system seems more accurate. That system consists of an inanimate technology part (including organization and information systems and process techniques) and the people part—most importantly, the frontline server who delivers, or presents the service, or co-produces it with the guest.

Here is the basic equation that captures all the components of the customer experience that must be effectively managed by the guestologist:

Guest experience = service product + service setting + service delivery system

All the moments spent at the concert add up to the guest experience later described as a "a great concert." But the guest probably had many smaller service experiences during the evening. If, for example, at intermission she went to a designated area and received beverage service, that short experience would have its own service, setting, and delivery system. Any time a consumer goes to a vacation resort, takes a cruise, flies, or visits a theme park, she will have numerous separate service experiences, and will ultimately make a judgment about the quality and value of the *overall* guest experience. If a guest spends three days or a week at a resort—as many people do—each day's individual guest experiences will add up to the overall day's experience, and the one-day experiences will add up to the overall resort experience.

Unique, Yet Similar

Incidents and occurrences are never exactly the same for two people—whether at a concert, hotel, vacation resort, restaurant, or on a cruise ship—therefore no two guest experiences are exactly alike. Even if the incidents and occurrences were exactly the same, each guest's experience of them will be unique because the wants, needs, tastes, preferences, capabilities, and expectations each guest brings to the experience are uniquely theirs and may even change from day to day. Add in the intangibility of service itself, and the uniqueness of each guest experience cannot be questioned. That uniqueness is what provides the primary challenge to the hospitality service provider. The old saying has it that "you can't please every guest," but the hospitality organization has to try, even though everybody is different.

On the other hand, guests do respond to many experiences in similar if not identical ways. These categories of responses can be sampled, studied, and modeled to produce extremely accurate predictive models of guests' behaviors. Probabilistic statistics is a major tool in the guestologist's toolkit for identifying how hospitality organizations can best respond to the needs, wants, capabilities, and expectations of their targeted guest markets. Successful hospitality organizations spend considerable time, effort, and money studying their guests to ensure each part of the entire guest experience adds something positive to it. They also expend significant resources finding and fixing the inevitable mistakes as best they can.

Components of the Guest Experience

Though the three elements the hospitality organization has to work with should blend seamlessly into one experience, for the purpose of discussion we break them out into the service product, service setting, and service delivery system. Here is a fuller description of each.

The Service Product

The service product, sometimes called the service package or service/product mix, is why the customer, client, or guest comes to the organization in the first place. An organization's reason for being is often embodied in the name of the business: Pacific Playground Amusement Park, the Continental Hotel, the Casino Royale, Cheers Bar and Grill. Recall that the basic product can be relatively tangible, like a hotel room, or relatively intangible, like a rock concert. Most service products have both tangible and intangible elements and can range from mostly product with little service to mostly service with little if any product.

The Service Setting

The second component of the guest experience is the **service setting** or **service environment** in which the experience takes place. The term **servicescape**, the landscape within which service is experienced, has been used to describe the aspects of the setting that contribute to the guest's overall feel of the experience. Las Vegas casinos are famous for using their hotels' designs to make the focus of the service setting on the gambling. Hotel lobbies are lavishly decorated, making the customer feel he or she is in a resort. Everything the customer needs—the rooms, bars, fancy restaurants, fast food, shopping, and shows—is conveniently inside the casino. And to get to any service the guest needs—for example, the front desk to check in or out, or to get to any restaurant—the guest must always pass through the casino. The design of the service setting keeps the customer focused on where the hotel makes its money: the casino. The servicescape is also extremely important to themed eatertainment restaurants

service setting, service environment, servicescape The physical location and its characteristics within which the organization provides service to guests.

©iStock.com/ DavorLovincic

Casinos use the servicescape as part of the overall experience to keep the guest's focus on the many opportunities for gambling.

like Bahama Breeze, Hard Rock Cafe, and Rainforest Cafe. They use the distinctive theme of the food-service setting—from the building exterior, to decorations inside the restaurant, to background music choice, to table and menu design—as an important means of making themselves memorable and distinguishing themselves from other restaurants.

The Service Delivery System

service delivery system The human components and the physical production processes, plus the organizational and information systems, involved in delivering the service to the customer.

The third part of the guest experience is the **service delivery system**, including the human components (the restaurant server who places the meal on the table or the sound engineer at the rock concert) and the physical production processes (the kitchen facilities in the restaurant or the rock concert's sophisticated amplification system) plus the organizational and information systems and techniques that help deliver the service to the customer. Unlike a factory's assembly line system, which is generally distant from and unobservable to consumers, many parts of service delivery systems must necessarily be open to consumers who can avail themselves of the services directly and co-produce the experience. Also, the output products of an assembly line system can be touched, physically owned, and seen; the services produced by the service delivery system are intangible memories of experiences that exist only in guests' minds.

While all aspects of the service delivery system are important, the people interacting with customers or guests are by far the most able to make a difference in how customers feel about the value and quality of the experience. Even if there is little they can do when the food is ruined or the concert amps fail, customer contact employees can make the difference in both how angry the customers are with a failure in the service experience and how happy they are when everything went right. For hospitality organizations, they can be the most important component of the service delivery system and the most challenging to manage. It is the wait staff, the cabin crew, the front desk agents, the valet parkers—their genuine attitude, authentic friendliness, sincere concern, and helpfulness in ensuring the success of the guest's co-production—who largely determine both the value and the quality of the experience for the guest. At the moment or over the series of moments when the service is experienced, that single employee is the service department, the entire organization, and even perhaps the entire hospitality industry to the guest. The feeling the guest takes away from the experience is largely derived from what happens during the encounters or interactions between the guest and the employees, and the less tangible the service product, the more important the servers become in defining the quality and value of the guest experience. The single service employee makes the "wow." No wonder the leading hotels, restaurants, and other hospitality organizations invest substantial time and money into finding, training, and supporting their frontline employees. If these folks fail to do it right, the guest and everyone the guest ever tells about the experience may be lost.

Service Encounters and Moments of Truth

service encounter The person-to-person interactions or series of interactions between the customer and the persons delivering the service.

The term **service encounter** is often used to refer to the person-to-person interaction or series of interactions between the customer and the person delivering the service. Although both parties are usually people, the many situations or interactions between organization and guest that are now automated—the automatic teller machine, check-in kiosks, and mobile app transactions being familiar examples—may also be considered service encounters. The heart of a service is the encounter between the server and the customer. It is here where emotions meet economics in real time and where most customers judge the quality of service.[7]

[7] Alex M. Susskind, K. Michele Kacmar, and Carl P. Borchgrevink, "Guest-Server Exchange Model and Performance: The Connection Between Service Climate and Unit-Level Sales in Multiunit Restaurants," *Journal of Hospitality & Tourism Research* 42, No. 1 (2016): 122–141.

ImagesBazaar via Getty Images

The check-in is often the first moment of truth for the hotel guest.

An encounter is the period of time during which the organization and the guest interact. The length of a typical service encounter will vary from one service experience to another. The purchase of a ticket is a brief service encounter; the interaction between guest and agent at a hotel front desk is usually somewhat longer; and the series of interactions between guest and server comprising a restaurant meal is an even longer encounter. A day in a theme park may involve fifty to a hundred different service encounters.

Other service encounters can last for an extended time. For example, at Club Med, where vacationers may spend more than a week at a resort, the guests—called GMs *(Gentil Members)*—regularly interact with Club Med staff—called GOs *(Gentils Organisateurs)*—who play, dance, dine, and drink with the guests every day and night. On cruises, guests may develop a personal relationship with their cabin steward over a multiday voyage. Lindblad Expeditions offers week-long trips to exotic locations, which make for extended interactions between service providers and guests on a ship with at most 148 or as few as 12 guests.

Service encounters or interactions, and especially certain critical moments within them, are obviously of crucial importance to the guest's evaluation of service quality; they can make or break the entire guest experience. Jan Carlzon, the former president of Scandinavian Airline Services (SAS), coined a term to refer to the key moments during these interactions, and to some brief encounters or interactions themselves, as a **moment of truth**.[8] Another term often used in the services literature is **critical incident.** Dwayne Gremmler, in his review of the technique for collecting data on critical customer experiences, describes its uses, advantages, and disadvantages. His extensive review of the technique offers a helpful checklist of how to use it and interpret its findings.[9]

moment of truth Any key or crucial moment or period during a service encounter, a make-or-break moment; subsequently expanded by others to include any significant or memorable interaction point between organization and guest.

critical incident A memorable event that deviates significantly, either positively or negatively, from what the guest expects or considers normal in a service encounter.

Regardless of whether it is termed a moment of truth or critical incident, if the airplane wouldn't fly, the meal was bad, or the air conditioning in the hotel room didn't work, the guests won't care how pleasant the server was or how good that person made them feel. While a server can often make any bad situation better, when a failure occurs, there is a problem with the service experience that needs the full attention of the hospitality manager. On the other hand, since most plane rides are like other rides, most meals are similar to other meals, and most hotel rooms are like other hotel rooms, the distinguishing characteristic of most guest experiences is how the people providing the service did it! Even if the plane ride, meal, or hotel room is the best of one's life, a rude or careless service person can wreck the guest experience in a moment. If that happens, all of the organization's other efforts and expenditures are wasted. It is little wonder the most effective hospitality organizations spend serious time and money managing these moments.

For example, a potential passenger's first interaction with airline personnel is an obvious moment of truth; it can determine whether the potential passenger leaves your airline and goes to another, or whether a potentially lifetime relationship with the passenger is begun. Carlzon managed the entire airline so as to provide good service at the moment of truth, "the fifteen golden seconds" during which an entire airline is

[8] Jan Carlzon and Tom Peters, *Moments of Truth* (New York, NY: Harper Business, 1989).

[9] Dwayne D. Gremler, "The Critical Incident Technique in Service Research," *Journal of Service Research* 7, No. 1 (2004): 65–89.

represented to one guest by one server, because the success of the entire organization depends on those first fifteen seconds. The original definition of moment of truth was Carlzon's, but other writers have expanded the term to include any significant or memorable interaction point between server and guest or, if no server is present as at an ATM or on a smartphone app, or a website, between organization and guest. In most hospitality organizations, the first fifteen seconds are make-or-break moments as the hospitality organization, like everyone else, gets only one chance to make a first impression.

At the moment of truth, a server or other organizational representative is typically present and attempting to provide service. Some writers include interactions with inanimate objects as potential moments of truth. Opening the door of a hotel room might be such a moment. If the guest's first impression of a room's appearance is negative, or if the organization has slipped up and forgotten to clean the room, for example, a crucial moment has not been properly managed and a guest, possibly an excellent long-term customer, may be lost for good.

Each moment of truth also offers the possibility of making the experience memorable in a way that differentiates this organization's service from all others—to create a competitive advantage. Disney, for example, asks its employees to create magical moments for its guests by seeking opportunities to make a routine guest experience special. From simple examples such as replacing for free and with a smile a dropped ice cream cone to more complex examples such as making sure a guest gets to greet a loved character, Disney encourages its cast members to find opportunities to "wow" its guests. While many of these wow moments are created by a cast member who sees an opportunity to turn a service failure or an "ow" into a "wow," there are many stories told to remind all cast members they should look for ways to make a moment of truth a wow moment.

The moment-of-truth concept is very important: Each guest may have only a few moments of truth during a single guest experience or many moments in a lifetime relationship with a company, but each one needs to be positive. The best organizations identify when and where these moments of truth occur and ensure they are managed well. Since many involve a customer co-producing an experience with an employee, these organizations make a special commitment to ensuring their servers know how to deliver on the many make-or-break moments of truth every day by not only delivering a flawless service but by doing so in a way that is memorable to the guest.

Many hospitality organizations ask their employees to identify such moments of truth or critical incidents and record them in a database. Gaylord Hotels, Hyatt, and Disney, for example, ask their staff members to share stories about critical incidents they have observed so they can use these stories to help teach employees about their service culture.

The Nature of Services

Services and manufactured products have traditionally been seen as having different characteristics. Manufactured products tend to be tangible—produced, shipped, and purchased now for consumption later. Although there is a growing trend by some manufacturers to also consider the service aspects of their manufactured product, most production organizations don't spend much time on assessing the customer service issues that are created by interaction between the manufacturer and the consumer. Services, on the other hand, tend to be intangible, purchased (if not always paid for) first, then simultaneously produced and consumed, and accompanied by considerable provider-customer interaction.[10] Let's look at these characteristics more closely.

[10] Robert C. Ford and David E. Bowen, "A Service-Dominant Logic for Management Education: It's Time," *Academy of Management Learning & Education* 7, No. 2 (2008): 224–243.

Services Are Partly or Wholly Intangible

Even when the service rendered includes a tangible item (e.g., the Mickey Mouse hat, Mardi Gras beads, a good meal), the total guest experience is the sum of the tangibles plus the intangibles included in the service-product mix, the environment within which it is delivered, and the service product's delivery. Because all or part of the service product is intangible, it is impossible to assess the product's quality or value accurately or objectively, to inventory it, or to repair it (although we will talk later about correcting service failures). Since the customer decides whether or not the quality is acceptable or value equals expectations, the only way to measure either quality or value is through subjective assessment techniques, the most basic of which is to ask the customer.

A second implication of this intangibility characteristic is that every guest experience is unique. Even though a given room at the Ritz-Carlton looks the same to everyone, the overall experience at the Ritz will be different for each guest each time. The less tangible the service provided, the more likely each guest will define the experience differently. The point is simple: since every guest is unique, every guest experience will also be unique.

Another implication of intangibility is that hospitality organizations cannot keep an inventory of guest experiences. Service products are perishable. The stockpile of airline seats on today's 10 a.m. flight to New York is gone after the plane leaves. Tonight's unsold hotel rooms cannot be held over until tomorrow night, nor can seats at tonight's rock concert. Once a convention ends, the opportunity to participate in an exciting meeting session is gone. The inability to inventory experiences has important implications for hospitality organizations. One of the more important is the management of capacity. Because capacity is limited and demand for guest experiences varies over periods of time, capacity must be carefully managed to meet demand. If demand exceeds capacity, then guests have to wait or don't get served at all. If capacity exceeds demand, then the hospitality organization's human and physical resources sit idle.

Finally, because services are intangible and therefore difficult to fully anticipate before they are delivered and actually experienced, organizations wanting guests to try their services rather than those of competitors must find ways to make the intangible tangible—through photographs in advertising, a virtual tour of a hotel interior on the internet, using cloth versus plastic tablecloths at a restaurant, hanging awards on the hotel lobby wall, getting endorsements by famous people, and so forth. Such efforts to give tangible evidence of service quality help the employees as well. After all, the service is as intangible for the organization's employees as it is for guests. A tangible picture can be worth a thousand words in helping organization members form a mental image of what their service should be like and what their organization's quality level should be.

Services Are Consumed at the Moment or During the Period of Production or Delivery

Even if the guest takes home the Mickey Mouse hat, or the Mardi Gras beads, or the full stomach, or even if the luncheon was prepared an hour before the customer had it, the service as a whole and from the customer's perspective was consumed as it was delivered. The customer can take home the hat, beads, and the memory of the experience but not the service itself. What are the important implications of this characteristic for hospitality managers? Organizational systems must be carefully designed to ensure the service is consistently produced so each guest has a high-quality experience that both meets expectations and is nearly equal to that experienced by every other guest (except for differences supplied by servers in response to each guest's unique needs and co-production capabilities). In addition, the experience must at least equal that which the same guest had in previous visits. The hospitality organization must think through the service delivery process by *working from the guest backward.*

This working backward to meet customer desires and expectations is a major difference between hospitality organizations and typical bureaucratic functional organizations, which are often designed for the convenience and efficiency of organizational members. In a well-designed hospitality organization, the focus is on the guest experience and those who co-produce it. All the traditional organizational and managerial concepts that have been classically taught as the best way to manage are turned upside down. Instead of concentrating on top-down managerial control systems to ensure consistency and employee predictability, hospitality organizations must concentrate on *employee empowerment.* They know managers cannot watch every guest-employee interaction. The guest experience cannot be held back until the boss checks it for errors, as would be true of a new book, tractor, or suit. The frontline service provider who cares about the service, the organization, and the guest must be selected in the employment process and then trained and trusted to deliver the guest experience as well as that person knows how. Instead of managers following the traditional model of reviewing employee performance after the fact, in the hospitality organization they must use goal setting skills and create service standards that help the employee know how and why the consistent delivery of a high-quality guest experience is critical to guest satisfaction and organizational success. Instead of tracing information and authority from the top down, the guest-focused organization must trace it from the bottom up.

Services Require Interaction Between the Service Provider and the Customer, Client, or Guest

This interaction can be as short as the brief encounter between the customer and the order taker at a McDonald's drive thru, or as long as the lifetime relationship between the patient and the family physician. These interactions can be face to face, over the phone, on the web, or by mail, e-mail, or texting.

When the interaction is face to face, customers and employees must be taught how to co-produce the experience in some systematic way. The Melting Pot Restaurant trains its servers how to train guests on the proper way to cook in a fondue pot, a hotel's convention services group stations people at key places to give directions to attendees, and an airline has staff at its check-in counter to help passengers navigate any problems with the technology. When the experience happens at the moment of its consumption, then the organization needs to plan on how to ensure new, untrained, inexperienced, and unknowledgeable customers get the same service experience quality and value that the returning, trained, experienced, and knowledgeable ones get. Since each customer is different, the organization cannot expect each customer to consume the same amount of time or resources in the experience. Accommodating the variability in customer differences is how a guestologist can make an important contribution by careful research and thoughtful planning to adjust the service experience provided for each customer. As Ford and McColl-Kennedy write, the organization must "mind the gap."[11]

Technology

Exhibit 1.1 displays four types of relationships between provider and customer, with examples of each type noted inside the respective boxes. Different service situations call for different strategies in systems, personnel, and service environment by the service provider to "mind the gap." If the provider is not going to be present in the encounter, the service system must be foolproof for all types of customers who are in the targeted market to use it. In many places throughout the United States, ATMs and self-service kiosks, for example, ask customers whether they want to read

[11] Robert C. Ford and Janet R. McColl-Kennedy, "Organizational Strategies for Filling the Customer Can-Do/Must-Do Gap," *Business Horizons* 58, No. 4 (2015): 459–468.

EXHIBIT 1.1

The Different Relationships Between Customer/Guest/Client and Service Provider

	Customer present	Customer not present
Service provider present	Hospitality, medical, professional	Lawn service, jewelry repair
Service provider not present	Electric/gas/phone/internet utilities, ATMs, vending machines	Online stores and travel services, technical help, answering services

the instructions on the screen in English, Spanish, or even some other language. Some ATMs at hotels that target global travelers give people the choice of many languages with which to complete their transactions. Web designers spend considerable time testing how people access their web pages to ensure they are logical, easily used, and quick to load so impatient users don't click off. On the other hand, if the provider is present, the organization must focus on the customer's interactions with the provider as a major means for adding value to the service product. A full-service hotel or restaurant, for example, relies extensively on its employees to deliver value in the guest experience; the owner of a website does not.

Many services are delivered with customers present at some stages but not all. At car dealerships, most car repairs take place out of the customer's sight. Two points of contact occur: at the customer service desk and the payment window. The appearance of both the physical setting and the people at those contact points is quite different from those back in the repair area, beyond the sight of customers. Each type of customer contact may call for a different managerial strategy, environment, and delivery system.

GUEST EXPECTATIONS

Guests arrive with a set of expectations as to what that chosen hotel or restaurant can and should do, how it should do it, how the people providing the service should behave, how the physical setting should appear, what capabilities guests should have to perform their roles or responsibilities in co-producing the experience, how the guest should dress and act, and what the cost and value of the successfully delivered service should be. First-time guests arrive with a mindset of expectations based on advertising, familiar brand names, promotional devices, their previous experiences with other hospitality organizations, their own imaginations, and stories and experiences of people they know who have already been guests. The organizational responsibility for bringing first-time or infrequent guests to the organization usually lies with the marketing department's ability to make promises about what expectations will be met.

Repeat guests' past experiences with an organization provide the primary basis for their expectations regarding future experiences. In many instances, this sets a high standard to meet: what may create a "wow" experience for guests upon a first visit may be only "as expected" the next time. The organizational responsibility for getting the repeat business of both new and previous customers rests on the service providers' ability to meet and maybe even exceed both the promises that marketing has made and prior experiences of repeat guests. Depending on what sort of business you are in, you may or may not want to under-promise; but the key to "wowing" customers is to consistently over-deliver.

Most hospitality organizations try to provide their guests with accurate information ahead of time, so these customers come to the experience with expectations the organization can meet or exceed. If the hospitality organization does not provide that information, guests will obtain or infer it, accurately or inaccurately, from other sources: perhaps the organization's general reputation, ads, experiences their friends have had with the organization, those they themselves have had with similar organizations, online reviews, or from social media. People going to Wendy's, for example, have well-defined expectations about the quick-serve experience and quickly notice if the food is not up to par, service is slow, the rest rooms are dirty, or something else is different from what they expected. Likewise, diners at a Michelin three-star restaurant bring their well-defined expectations about the fine dining experience and will quickly notice when something is not up to their expectations. Both Wendy's and the three-star restaurant will have customers bringing their dining expectations, but the expectations will be very different. To be successful both restaurants must know what these expectations are and at least meet them.

Meeting Expectations

The major responsibility for meeting or exceeding the expectations created by the marketing department and by the past experiences of repeat guests lies with the operations side of the organization. If what guests experience falls short of what they have been led to expect or have learned to expect, they will be unhappy. They will not remember later a delightful, carefully planned guest experience; they will remember their unmet expectations as poor service and a bad experience. To preserve its reputation and customer base, the hospitality organization must meet or exceed the expectations of its guests. If it cannot or does not, it must either change its marketing strategy and create different guest expectations or change its service product, service setting, and/or service delivery system so it can meet present guests' expectations. If enough people tell their friends what a terrible experience your restaurant or hotel provided or write negative online reviews, your reputation will be gone. With easy access to the web through smartphones and handheld devices, happy and unhappy guests are no longer restricted to talking with friends and neighbors over the backyard fence or on the phone. Angry customers can instantly tweet their friends and followers or post their complaints on reputable websites or blogs dedicated to providing a means for customers to convey their experiences with different organizations or products. With such sites easily accessed—and indeed frequently used by individuals when planning trips—customers can convey their opinions about any hospitality organization almost instantly to thousands of strangers all over the world! A visit to TripAdvisor or Yelp will provide good examples of the power of individuals to influence others across the world.

Technology

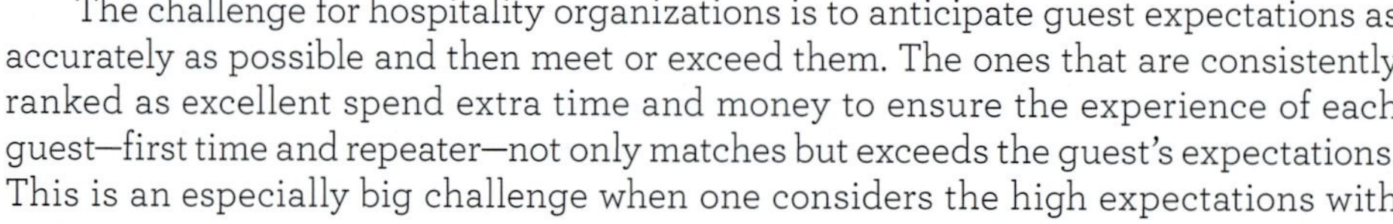

The challenge for hospitality organizations is to anticipate guest expectations as accurately as possible and then meet or exceed them. The ones that are consistently ranked as excellent spend extra time and money to ensure the experience of each guest—first time and repeater—not only matches but exceeds the guest's expectations. This is an especially big challenge when one considers the high expectations with which guests arrive at, say, a luxury cruise ship. First-time customers have probably received travel agency brochures, seen cruise ships in movies and on television for years, and viewed YouTube videos of other's cruises. They probably know of the cruise line's outstanding reputation and what the brand promises. Repeat passengers arrive with high expectations based on prior cruises. The cruise line wants both new and repeat customers to leave the trip wowed and makes a concerted effort to exceed each passenger's expectations.

The same is true throughout the hospitality industry. The Rocky Mountaineer claims that it proudly offers "The Most Spectacular Train Trips in the World" and Country Walkers claims on its web page, "With over 36 years of experience, we know exactly how to create an unforgettable itinerary. From walks off the beaten path to a world of inclusions—encompassing everything from meals and park fees to beer and wine with dinner—we offer unparalleled tours."[12]

If the organization cannot meet certain types of expectations, it should not say it can; it should not promise more than it can deliver. During difficult times for airlines, no-frills Southwest Airlines has continued to do well. One reason is superb service. But another key reason for its real success is that it does not promise more than it can deliver. As one person noted on Yelp, "I really like Southwest Airlines. While not fancy, they do exactly what they are supposed to do—get you where you are going safely and efficiently—with your luggage!"[13] The hospitality organization must assess guest expectations in its target market, assess its own competencies in meeting them, and try to meet or exceed them wholeheartedly.

Do Not Provide More Hospitality Than Guests Want

Organizations must be careful not to over-deliver to the point of making guests feel uncomfortable or unpleasantly surprised. If customers enter Eat 'n' Run, which looks and sounds like a fast-food restaurant, and see white linen tablecloths, they may feel they are about to experience expensive, leisurely, "fine" dining and incur a bigger cost than they expected. Most restaurant-goers enjoy fine dining, but they want to pick the occasion, not be surprised when it occurs.

Waiters are supposed to be attentive and polite. But consider a dining experience during which the waiter constantly hovers and speaks to the diners. If Mary Jones has taken her boss out for an important business discussion, or Bob Smith has come to the restaurant with his love interest in hopes of finding a quiet moment to propose marriage, the constant presence of an overly attentive wait staff will be a major annoyance and too much service. When does enough service become too much? The excellent hospitality organization will do two things to find out. First, it will spend the time and money to train its employees to be alert to customer cues, signals, and body language so they can fine-tune their interaction with their customers. Second, it will constantly survey or ask its guests what they thought about the experience, to ensure guests receive more service value than they expect but not so much more as to detract from the experience. As former Chili's Restaurants CEO Norman Brinker said, "Listen to your customers. They'll tell you what to do."[14]

Just What Does the Guest Expect?

Most guests have the same general expectations when they go to a hospitality organization for service. Surveys and interviews are not required to determine that most guests expect to have the service experience they came for including cleanliness,

[12] https://www.countrywalkers.com/about-us/. Accessed February 2, 2018.

[13] Yelp, "Southwest Airlines," Yelp (blog), accessed February 2, 2018, http://www.yelp.com/biz/southwest-airlines-phoenix-3.

[14] Norman Brinker and Donald T. Phillips, *On the Brink: The Life and Leadership of Norman Brinker* (Arlington, TX: Summit Publishing Group, 1996), p. 192.

courtesy, responsiveness, reliability, friendliness, and the desired service product delivered in the appropriate service setting.

Customers complain when they do not get what they expect or when they have an unpleasant experience. Another way to understand what customers expect is to examine their complaints. Marketing expert Leonard Berry has listed the ten most common customer complaints. Considering what customers do not want can provide insight into what they do want. A common thread running through the complaints suggests that what bothers customers most is disrespect. Here are Berry's ten complaints[15]; they can help us arrive at a still general but slightly more specific set of guest expectations:

1. *Guest Complaint:* Lying, dishonesty, unfairness.
   Guest Expectation: To be told the truth and treated fairly.
2. *Guest Complaint:* Harsh, disrespectful treatment by employees.
   Guest Expectation: To be treated with respect.
3. *Guest Complaint:* Carelessness, mistakes, broken promises.
   Guest Expectation: To receive mistake free, careful, reliable service.
4. *Guest Complaint:* Employees without the desire or authority to solve problems.
   Guest Expectation: To receive prompt solutions to problems from empowered employees who care.
5. *Guest Complaint:* Waiting in line because some service lanes or counters are closed.
   Guest Expectation: To wait as short a time as possible.
6. *Guest Complaint:* Impersonal service.
   Guest Expectation: To receive personal attention and genuine interest from service employees.
7. *Guest Complaint:* Inadequate communication after problems arise.
   Guest Expectation: To be kept informed about recovery efforts after having or reporting problems or service failures.
8. *Guest Complaint:* Employees unwilling to make extra effort or who seem annoyed by requests for assistance.
   Guest Expectation: To receive assistance rendered willingly by helpful and trained service employees.
9. *Guest Complaint:* Employees who don't know what's happening.
   Guest Expectation: To receive accurate answers from service employees knowledgeable about both service product and organizational procedures.
10. *Guest Complaint:* Employees who put their own interests first, conduct personal business, are texting instead of paying attention to the customer or chatting with each other while the customers wait.
    Guest Expectation: To have customers' interests come first.

[15] Leonard L. Berry, *Discovering the Soul of Service: The Nine Drivers of Sustainable Business Success* (New York, NY: The Free Press, 1999), 31.

Being aware of these common guest concerns and expectations should be part of any hospitality organization's knowledge base and training program. As we shall see later, however, the best organizations others use as benchmarks dig deeper to discover the more specific guest expectations, which allow them to personalize each guest's experience as much as possible. Some organizations keep a record of these specific expectations in their database to be sure of meeting them on the guest's next visit.

QUALITY, VALUE, AND COST DEFINED

In the hospitality industry, the terms *quality, value,* and *cost* have specialized meanings to fit the guest-focused orientation of the benchmark firms.

Quality

Two "equations" can help make clear what quality, value, and cost mean to the guestologist and why we say quality and value are determined not in any absolute sense, as they might be in other situations, but entirely by the guest.[16] The **service quality** of the entire guest experience or of any part of it is defined as the difference between the quality the guest expects and the quality the guest gets. If the two are the same, then quality in this special sense is as expected; the guest got what was expected and was satisfied. If the guest got more than was expected, quality was positive; if the guest got less than was expected, quality was negative. For example, a guest stays on successive nights at a Hyatt resort hotel and at a Knight's Inn hotel. If the Hyatt hotel did not live up to the guest's high-quality expectations and the Knight's Inn exceeded the guest's somewhat lower-quality expectations, according to the preceding definition, the Knight's Inn guest experience was of higher quality.

service quality The difference between the service that the customer expects to get and the service that the customer actually receives.

The first equation that follows describes these relationships for the quality of the guest experience, Q_e. It is equal to the quality of the experience as delivered, Q_{ed}, minus the quality expected, Q_{ee}. If the delivered and expected quality are about the same, quality is not zero as it would be if these were true mathematical equations but average or as expected. If quality is average or above average, the guest can be described as satisfied. If quality is below average, the guest is dissatisfied.

$$Q_e = Q_{ed} - Q_{ee}$$

As reflected on the right side of the equation, quality as perceived by the guest will be affected by changes in either guest expectations or organizational performance. If Q_e is high enough, the guest had an exceptional, memorable, or wow service experience. The quality of any aspect of the service experience could be described in the same way.

Quality is independent of cost or value. Quality can be high and cost also high; quality can be high and cost low, and so forth.

Value

The **service value** of the guest experience (V_e) is equal to the quality of the experience (Q_e) as "calculated" using the first equation divided by all the costs incurred by the guest to obtain the experience:

service value The relationship of the quality of the service to its cost, or service quality divided by all costs incurred by the guest for service.

$$V_e = \frac{Q_e}{\text{All costs incurred by guest}}$$

[16] James L. Heskett and W. Earl Sasser, *Service Breakthroughs: Changing the Rules of the Game* (New York, NY: Free Press, 1990), 2.

If the quality and cost of the experience are about the same, the value of the experience to the guest would be normal or as expected; the guest would be satisfied by this fair value but not wowed. Low quality and low cost, and high quality and high cost, satisfy the guest about the same, because they match the guest's expectations. Organizations add value to their guests' experiences by providing additional features and amenities without increasing the cost to guests.

Cost

cost The financial and non-financial burden incurred by a guest to obtain a service, including tangible quantifiable costs (like price) and intangible non-quantifiable costs like opportunity costs of foregoing alternative opportunities, annoyance at receiving unsatisfactory service, and so forth.

One source of **cost** difference to a guest having lunch today at your restaurant rather than someone else's is, of course, the price of the meal. In addition, experienced restaurant and other hospitality managers appreciate that the guest has also incurred other, less quantifiable costs, including the so-called opportunity costs of missing out on alternative meals at competing restaurants and foregoing experiences or opportunities other than eating a restaurant meal. The cost of the guest's time and the cost of any risks associated with entering into this service transaction must also enter the equation. The guest's time may not be worth an exact dollar figure per minute or hour, but it is certainly worth *something* to the guest, so time expenditures (time spent getting to your restaurant, waiting for a table, waiting for service) are also costly. Finally, the customer at your restaurant runs some risks, slim but real and potentially costly. The customer runs the risk that your restaurant cannot meet expectations or the risk that your service staff will embarrass the customer in front of the customer's own special guest today, as in our previous examples, Mary Jones with her boss or Bob Smith with his love interest.

All these tangible and intangible, financial and nonfinancial costs comprise the "all costs incurred by guest" denominator of the second equation. They make up the total burden on the guest who chooses a given guest experience.

Cost of Quality

An important concept in service organizations is the cost of quality. Interestingly enough, *cost of quality* is often used as a reminder not of how much it costs the organization to provide service quality at a high level but of how little it costs compared to the cost of not providing quality. If the organization thinks about the costs of fixing errors, compensating guests for failures, lost customers, low employee morale, and negative word of mouth that can result from poor service, the cost of quality is low indeed and the cost of not providing quality enormous. That is why the best hospitality organizations expend whatever resources are necessary to accomplish two complementary goals: exceed expectations to deliver "wow" to the level of guest delight and prevent failures. Because preventing and recovering from failure are so important, we devote Chapter 13 to these topics.

Who Defines Quality and Value?

Because service is intangible and guest expectations are variable, no objective determination of quality level (and therefore of value) can be made. In some areas of business, a quality inspector might be able to define and determine the quality of a product before a customer ever sees it. In the hospitality field, however, only the guest can define quality and value. No matter how brilliantly the organization designs the service, the environment, and the delivery system or develops measurable service standards, if the guest is dissatisfied with any of these elements, the organization has failed to meet the guest's expectations; it has not provided a guest experience of acceptable quality and value.

Of course, the hospitality organization may help the guest to perceive quality and value by offering a guarantee or a pledge of satisfaction that can be exercised by the guest when the guest feels the experience did not meet expectations. Premier Inn in the UK likewise has used a "Good Night Guarantee" that provides its guests with some customer-defined tangibility to its promise of service quality. Its guarantee states, "In fact, we're so confident you'll have a great night's sleep that, if you don't, we'll give you your money back. Just speak to one of our friendly reception team. This is our Good Night Guarantee."[17]

To meet or exceed the expectations of all types of guests with their different needs, wants, experiences, capabilities, and moods is the fundamental and most exciting challenge of a hospitality organization. If the hospitality manager does not believe the guest is always right (at least in the guest's mind), then the manager had better find a new career. Even when guests are wrong by any reasonable standard, the hospitality manager must find ways to let them be wrong with dignity so their self-esteem and satisfaction with the guest experience and the organization are not negatively affected.

THE IMPORTANCE OF GUESTOLOGY

While guestology is obviously most helpful in organizing knowledge about the management of hospitality businesses—like hotels and restaurants, which have traditionally spoken of their clientele as guests—it can be used to study and understand any organization in which people are served in some way. Even manufacturing firms have "guests" or people they should treat like guests: their customers, their own employees, and their strategic partners. Nevertheless, the traditional management model found in typical texts tends to be oriented toward the manufacturing sector, the making of physical products. Using the manufacturing model to describe how to provide hospitality services and experiences is a questionable approach.

Is hospitality management different from traditional management? Do hospitality organizations face challenges different from those faced by other business organizations? Should they therefore design themselves differently and set different types of goals? Do managers of hospitality organizations face different types of problems and require different training than managers of traditional manufacturing organizations? Do hospitality employees respond best to managerial strategies different from those to which manufacturing employees respond? The growing literature on hospitality management and the experience of successful hospitality organizations indicate the answer to all these questions is yes.[18] A purpose of this book is to show why.

Why bother to consider the guest part of this guestology material seriously? Why should I think of my subordinate as a guest, the person walking into my hotel lobby as my guest, or the family coming off I-81 to my tourist attraction as guests? Let's look at the service situation from your perspective for a moment. What hospitality organizations do you personally patronize, and what kind of restaurant or hotel would you yourself want to work for? Those that treat you like a special guest, or those that make you feel like an interruption to their organizational procedures and policies?

The answers to all these questions are plain. The hotels you return to, the restaurant you dine at again and again, and the theme park you enjoy and recommend to friends and family are the ones that take the time to figure out what you seek in the guest experience, offer it to you, and then make clear in all they say and do that it was their pleasure that you sought it out from them. If they understand you and give you what you seek in that experience, you will like them, ascribe high value to the guest experience they provide, return when you need that service, and tell your friends and neighbors what a terrific place that hospitality organization is.

[17] Whitbead PLC, "Good Night Guarantee," Premier Inn, Whitbread PLC, accessed February 2, 2018, https://www.premierinn.com/gb/en/why/sleep/good-night-guarantee.html.

[18] Duncan Dickson, Robert C. Ford, and Bruce Laval, "The Top Ten Excuses for Bad Service (and How to Avoid Needing Them)," *Organizational Dynamics* 34, no. 2 (2005): 168–184.

LESSONS LEARNED

LO 1.1 Describe the key differences between making products and creating experiences for guests.

- The less tangible the guest experience is, the more important the frontline people are in delivering the service to the guest's perception of quality and value.

LO 1.2 Recognize the importance of the guest experience.

- Experiences that evoke a guest's emotions are more memorable.

LO 1.3 Identify the components of the guest experience.

- Manage all three parts of the guest experience: the service product, the service environment, and the service delivery system (both the processes and the people).
- Service product + service environment + service delivery system = guest experience.

LO 1.4 State the importance of meeting the hospitality guest's expectations.

- Provide memorable experiences that exceed guest expectations when possible, but know when enough is enough; deliver more than the guest expects, but not more than the guest wants.

LO 1.5 Define *service quality* and service value in hospitality.

- Your guest defines the value and the quality of your service, so you had better know what your guest wants.
- Ask, ask, ask your guests.
- The cost of providing quality is low compared to the potential cost of not providing quality.
- You may under-promise, but always try to over-deliver.

LO 1.6 Explain the reasons why "it all starts with the guest."

- Treat each customer like a guest, and always start with the guest.

KEY TERMS AND CONCEPTS

competitive advantage 8
cost 22
critical incident 13
expectations 5
guest experience 9
guestologist 5
guestology 4
hospitality 3
internal customers 6
KSAs 6
moment of truth 13
service 7
service delivery system 12
service encounter 12
service environment 11
service experience 9
service package 7
service product 7
service quality 21
service setting 11
service value 21
servicescape 11

REVIEW QUESTIONS

1. Consider the formula presented in the chapter: service product + service environment + service delivery system = guest experience
   A. Although all parts are important, do you think these three types of organizations—a hotel, a restaurant, and an airline—would tend to place a different emphasis on the three parts in providing the total guest experience?
   B. If product + environment + delivery system = 100%, how would the hotel, restaurant, and airline divide up their emphasis? Or, how would these organization types rank the three parts of the guest experience in order of emphasis?
2. Imagine that a Rolex watch, a Casio watch from Walmart, an Eagle Mirado #2 pencil, and a Cross fountain pen are sitting on a table in front of you. Explain which item is highest in quality, and which is lowest in quality?

3. These standard rooms are available in your locality: the Ritz-Carlton Hotel ($956 per night), a Holiday Inn ($170), a No-Tell Motel ($70), and an Airbnb ($50). Which room would you expect to be highest in quality, and which would be lowest in quality? Explain why.
4. Consider the examples in questions 2 and 3 in terms of value. Under what circumstances can quality be high and value low? Value high and quality low?
5. A guest experience is a service, and this chapter explained that services are largely intangible. Think of a somewhat expensive guest experience you have had. What tangibles did the organization use to make you feel your intangible experience was worth the money you paid?
6. Reflect on a recent, enjoyable guest experience and on a disappointing guest experience.
   A. What were the significant events, the moments of truth, during each experience?
   B. How did they contribute to your enjoyment or disappointment?
   C. How do they relate to managing the guest experience in hospitality organizations?
7. This chapter makes some general statements about how people form their expectations for guest experiences.
   A. How do those statements match up with the way you personally form your expectations for a new upcoming experience?
   B. If you are going for a repeat experience, would your expectations be based totally on previous experiences?
   C. If you were a hospitality manager, what level and type of expectations would you want to create in your guests, and how would you try to create them?
   D. How would you take into account the fact that some guests are new, some are repeaters, and you may not know which are which?
8. You are probably familiar with the expression "too much of a good thing." In the hospitality setting, that would describe over-delivering the service guests have come to receive.
   A. How much service is too much service? Have you ever experienced excessive service?
   B. How does a hospitality manager ensure guest expectations are met or exceeded without going overboard?
9. From an article in a guest services magazine: "What brings hotel guests back? A fluffy robe hanging on a padded hanger? Creamy chocolate reposing on the pillow? The jungle safari bedroom decor? Or plain vanilla, old-fashioned service?" What do you say?
10. How is service quality related to guest satisfaction?
11. Why is it important to start with the guest in everything the hospitality organization does? How does the practice of guestology enable hospitality organizations to be successful in starting everything with the guest?

ACTIVITIES

Many of the chapters in this book will include suggested hospitality field exercises or activities that might involve speaking to customers, employees, and managers of hospitality organizations. Your instructor will guide you on whether to do these assignments and how to go about them. You will also have assignments that ask you to report on a service failure or write a letter of complaint. You are doing these assignments to learn, not to make trouble for hospitality employees, so don't use real names in your reports unless your instructor gives permission. Don't send a fake complaint to an organization to see how they respond; this could get you in real trouble.

Excellent sources for study are your own organization, if you are presently working, and the organizations in which your friends may be working. Ideally, your information will come from hospitality organizations but if your personal situation does not permit that, study some other type of service organization. If you are really at a loss, consider the "service" provided by the instructors of your classes. For some of the requested firsthand information, however, you may have to visit the organization and talk with its people. If so, be a good guest!

For the following three exercises, and all the others in this book, you will write your responses or prepare to discuss them in class, as your instructor directs.

1. Pick two service organizations, in the same service field, you have patronized recently or can visit conveniently. Compare them in terms of the service quality and value you received.
2. Think about the last business establishment of any kind you visited. What were the tangibles of its service product? What were the intangibles?
3. Divide up into groups. On the basis of the group's collective experience, discuss what good service is. Mention some organizations that deliver good service. Compare notes with other groups.

ETHICS IN BUSINESS

This chapter has emphasized the idea of serving the customer's needs, and the general notion that "the guest is always right." Of course, there are times when the guest goes too far, or wants too much. As mentioned earlier in the chapter, in such circumstances, "the hospitality manager must find ways to let the guest be wrong with dignity so their self-esteem and satisfaction with the guest experience and the organization are not negatively affected." So, how would you suggest handling the following situations?

- A guest leaves a message that he will be interviewing job candidates in his suite at noon, and so needs the room made up immediately, while he is out for breakfast. The housekeeper sent to the room reports that some illegal drugs were left in the bathroom, and she refuses to make up the room.
- A long-time customer has drunk a bit too much in your hotel bar. He is staying at the hotel that evening, he is not driving, and he insists on one more drink. He says that if the hotel refuses to serve him, he will take his business elsewhere.
- You are working at a fancy restaurant and serving a family. The family orders a 1990 Chateau Margaux (a bottle of wine that will run you roughly $3,700 at Eleven Madison Park in New York City). They want you to pour "just a taste" for their child, so that he may share in the experience of trying this exceptional wine. You are unsure what the local laws are, and you simply do not know if you are allowed to serve alcohol to a minor, even with the parents' consent. They, however, insist it is just a taste, and there is no harm.

CASE STUDY

Eastern States Air Environment

Gloria Rooney assumed the presidency of Eastern States Air in the early 2010s, after proving her ability as executive vice president with two other major airlines. Like most other surviving airlines, Eastern States Air weathered rough times during the mid-2000s. But as the year 2018 neared, Rooney was running an airline that was doing well. Naturally, Rooney couldn't be satisfied with simply staying the course; she wanted to do better. And she thought she knew how.

Rooney saw that service in the airline industry had been in a state of steady decline for several years. More and more passengers were flying than ever before, but their level of satisfaction had gone down. Crowded airports, flight delays, overbooking, cramped seating, add-on costs for luggage, the occasional disastrous customer-service incident, and other factors had combined to raise industry complaints to all-time-high levels just when passenger flight miles were also at an all-time high.

In that atmosphere, Rooney finally had an opportunity to put into practice one of her most deeply held beliefs about running an airline: "It's not what you do; it's how you do it." She told her staff time after time: "The 'what' is the easy part. What we do is take passengers from here to there at a competitive price. The way we can distinguish ourselves favorably from our competitors is in the 'how.'"

Eastern States Air became known as "the airline that put the Frills back into Flying." A small lounge was added to all planes that could accommodate one. For people not wanting to leave their seats, two complimentary drinks per passenger per flight, delivered to the seat, became the standard. An internationally known chef was hired to supervise a food-service system that produced meals as close to the gourmet level as was possible given the state of technology. Just before passengers exited each Eastern States flight, they were surveyed to see how satisfied they had been with the basics of the flight and with the frills that Eastern States had put back into flying. Early results of Rooney's campaign showed passenger satisfaction levels were off the chart at the top. In one astonishing month, the airline received no complaints about anything. Rooney was overjoyed. "They said zero defects was an impossible standard in airline service. We proved them wrong." The passengers who raved about Eastern States Air and flew the airline as often as they could, sometimes simply for sheer pleasure, understood there is no free lunch. Eastern States had to raise its fares considerably to provide outstanding service, but some people paid the higher prices happily.

Unfortunately, the number of passengers flying Eastern States Air took a disastrous drop. The ones who stayed loved the airline. They became unpaid spokespeople for Eastern States Air, but there were not enough of them. Rooney realized she had been somewhat deceived by the excellent survey results. The results were biased because she had only surveyed those who stayed, not those who left.

Surveying a broader cross-section of passengers, former passengers, and passengers of other airlines led Rooney to change her strategy. "When you get right down to it," she said, "this is really a very simple business. Steamships used to be a mode of transportation; now they provide luxury cruises that end up where they started. But in our business, what people want is to get from here to there as inexpensively as possible. In the current market, cheap airfares are what people expect, and that's what we need to give them. But we won't forget the loyal customers who have stayed with us. If we do this right, we can appeal to both groups."

To implement the new strategy, Eastern States Air cut back on the number of seats in first class but increased their size, along with first-class appointments and level of service, to retain the airline guests who had been satisfied to have the frills put back into flying and were willing to pay for them. Throughout the rest of the plane, however, economy became the watchword. More seats were stuffed into each plane, the number of flight attendants was reduced, and "meals" could be purchased for an extra fee. They not only added a fee for luggage, they even charged for carry-ons.

Eastern States began to make a financial comeback, but the number of complaints skyrocketed to record levels. The following comments were typical:

> "You are putting all your service into the front of the plane. What about those of us stuck in the back?"
>
> "I've seen the animals in cattle cars treated better than this."
>
> "I used to be able to get by a window or on the aisle; now I always seem to get stuck in the middle seat. Why is that?"
>
> "I see that your industry is enjoying record profits. How about using some of that dough to give us a better ride?"
>
> "I'm a little over six feet tall, and I have to twist my legs to fit in that cramped space you give me."
>
> "Seats too narrow, too close together. Flight attendant didn't even ask me if I wanted a drink or a meal."
>
> "I've had better seats and better service on the cross-town bus."
>
> "How can you charge me to stick my own bag under my own feet?"

Some of these disappointed and angry passengers took out their resentment on the flight crews. Morale among the pilots and flight attendants began to drop. Rooney was baffled and disappointed. "You can't win in this business. You give people what they want, and the complaints go through the roof." She was quite concerned about the next board of directors meeting and what the board would have to say about her management of the airline.

1. What is the service product of the airline industry?
2. What were Rooney's mistakes?
3. How could they have been avoided?
4. What now?

Further readings on the topics in this chapter are listed in "Additional Readings" on pages 493–495.

Get the tools you need to sharpen your study skills. SAGE edge offers a robust online environment featuring an impressive array of free tools and resources.

Access practice quizzes, eFlashcards, video, and multimedia at **edge.sagepub.com/Ford2e**.

Visit **edge.sagepub.com/Ford2e** to help you accomplish your coursework goals in an easy-to-use learning environment.

©iStock.com/ PeopleImages

2 Meeting Guest Expectations Through Planning

Hospitality Principle: Focus Strategy on the Key Drivers of Guest Satisfaction

High performing organizations design work processes from the customer backward to ensure a flow that makes sense from a customer's perspective.

—Ken Blanchard, Jesse Stoner, and Scott Blanchard, *Serving Customers at a Higher Level*, in Ken Blanchard's *Leading at a Higher Level*

Learning Objectives

After reading this chapter, you should be able to

2.1 Distinguish between the three generic strategies for positioning products and services.

2.2 Explain how the elements of the organizational planning cycle result in the establishment of the hospitality organization's overall strategic plan and service strategy.

2.3 Recognize the quantitative and qualitative tools used for forecasting in the hospitality environment—external and internal.

2.4 Identify the key external and internal factors that must be examined for successful planning.

2.5 Describe the process to determine core competencies.

2.6 Describe the importance of a mission and vision statement in focusing the strategic plan on the best way to fit core competencies with strategic premises.

2.7 State the importance of including the key drivers of guest satisfaction in the planning process.

2.8 Describe a planning model, showing how components are tied together and action plans are developed.

2.9 Recognize the value added to the planning process by including those affected by the plans.

2.10 Recall that while plans are necessary, organizations must be ready and capable of change.

INTRODUCTION

When guests show up at a hotel, restaurant, or any other hospitality service provider, they have certain expectations of both what will and will not happen. To give guests what they expect requires research to determine exactly what those expectations are. Translating those expectations into a service product that aligns or fits the organization's mission and values takes detailed planning, forecasting, and sound intuitive judgment. Managers of the best hospitality organizations try to mix all three together into a strategy that allows them to give guests exactly what they expect and even a bit more. Guests will return only if their experiences meet, if not exceed, their expectations. The **service strategy** is the organization's plan for providing the experience guests expect.

service strategy The organization's plan for providing the experience guests expect.

Planning and strategy making are simple to talk about but difficult to do. In theory, all one has to do is to assess the environment within which the organization operates, assess the organization's capabilities, decide where the organization wants to go within that environment, and in light of those capabilities, make a plan to get there. Unfortunately, the needs, wants, capabilities, and expectations of real customers change; competitors find ways to duplicate the firm's strategic advantage of the moment; governments pass new laws; and advances in technology require the firm to scrap its old delivery system and create a new one. In other words, people change, their needs and expectations change, the competition changes, the environment changes, and so must the hospitality organization. Finding ways to deliver what customers expect in light of the many uncertainties created by such changes is a major challenge.

THREE GENERIC STRATEGIES

A saying in business is, "Price, quality, speed—pick any two." The implication is that no organization can do it all, so no customer should expect it all; the organization must determine the basis on which it hopes to compete. Wendy's provides speed and price; the Ruth Chris's Steak Houses provides quality. In addition to price, quality, and speed, the organization could compete on variety, convenience, friendliness, no-frills, uniqueness, helpfulness, or some other basis.

According to strategy scholar Michael Porter, an organization usually employs one or more of three different generic strategies.[1] First, it can aim to be the low-cost producer and low-price provider in its industry, area, or market segment. Second, it can find ways to differentiate its product or service from those of its competitors. Third, it can identify and fill a particular market niche or need. Successful hospitality organizations establish a strategy that includes one or more of these generic strategies and stick with it

A Lower Price

low-price provider An organization that tries to compete within its market primarily by maximizing operational or production efficiencies and minimizing organizational costs so as to offer the same service as competitors at a lower price.

"We will not be undersold!" The **low-price provider** tries to design and provide pretty much the same service the competition sells, but at a lower price. Management's focus is on maximizing operational or production efficiencies to minimize the organization's costs. Southwest Airlines focuses on reducing the costs of running the airline (turnaround times, loading and unloading, food service, and so forth) to achieve the lowest production cost per mile in the industry. Walmart focuses on selling for less by controlling inventory and cutting merchandise costs through mass buying. The low-price provider tries to offer the service at a price so low competitors cannot offer the same service and value at that lower price without losing money. Red Roof Inn and Motel 6 are competing with Budgetel and Sleep Inn, not with Ritz-Carlton and Four Seasons. Of course, all hospitality organizations are cost conscious, but some focus on offering bargain prices to reach a wider market rather than focusing on differentiating their service in a wide market or meeting the special needs of a narrow market.

Companies employing the low-price strategy must recognize that if they reduce prices to customers by reducing their own costs, the deterioration in the guest experience that results may decrease the value of the experience to guests and drive them to competitors. Although some are still able to offer excellent customer service, such as Alaska Airlines and Southwest, it is through the delivery system (e.g., employees, scheduling, and standardization of aircraft) that they add value and not through offering a more expensive service product or employing more staff.

A Differentiated Product

differentiation A strategy designed to create in the guest's mind desirable differences, either real or driven by marketing and advertising, between the service or product offered by the organization and other competing services and products.

All hospitality organizations practice product **differentiation** to an extent; all want to be perceived as offering a service product—the guest experience itself—that is different in ways their customers find important. Many try to attract guests by emphasizing these differences rather than by offering low prices.

Differentiating one's product in the marketplace results from creating in the customer's mind desirable differences, either real or driven by marketing and advertising, between that product and others available at about the same price. In an era when so many hotel rooms of different brands look so similar, the Ice Hotel in Jukkasjärvi, Sweden—located 200 km north of the Arctic Circle—is constructed each year out of snow and ice, featuring reindeer skin beds, an ice bar, and magnificent ice sculptures in the lobby; it certainly provides a unique experience that differentiates it from every other hotel in the world.

[1] Michael E. Porter, *Competitive Strategy: Techniques for Analyzing Industries and Competition* (New York, NY: The Free Press, 1980), 40–41.

While not all hotels strive to be as unique as the Ice Hotel, hotel companies do try to differentiate themselves in the marketplace by advertising, creating a brand identity that is valued by the targeted customers, or offering special amenities ("Free continental breakfast!" "Gourmet room service!" "Kids eat free!" "Heavenly Bed") that are attractive to that market segment. They hope a potential guest looking for a place to spend the night will remember what the brand stands for, want the amenities offered, and therefore book a room, for example, at a Westin Hotel instead of a Hilton, or vice versa, for what is essentially the same service product: a clean room in which to sleep.

For example, the Nickelodeon Hotels & Resorts at Punta Cana, Dominican Republic, differentiates itself from most other hotels by focusing on families with children offering suites themed after Nickelodeon's popular children's characters. Besides its unique reproduction of SpongeBob's Bikini Bottom home, The Pineapple, it also offers "Slime O Clock Somewhere" activities, which include an interactive kids-only dinner show with a chance to meet Nickelodeon's characters like SpongeBob SquarePants. The hotel offers a special play area with supervised activities for younger kids, "Just Kiddin," for parents' peace of mind. This hotel's strategy is to position itself as a unique, family friendly location themed with a readily recognized SpongeBob theme.

Courtesy of Nickelodeon Hotel & Resorts

The Nickelodeon Hotels & Resorts—located at Punta Cana, Dominican Republic—allows guests to stay in SpongeBob SquarePants' pineapple house.

The Brand Image

A major way to differentiate one's service from those of competitors is through the creation of a strong **brand image**.[2] A brand represents a promise to guests of what the quality and value of experiences associated with the brand will offer them, every time and every place they see the brand. A strong brand promise reduces customer uncertainty about the hospitality experience the organization offers and, consequently, creates a brand preference and increases customer loyalty. Once a strong brand preference is established, it can provide some protection against cost cutting or other competitive strategies that can get guests to switch to other competing products. A strong **brand name** can also extend the company's reach into new markets. Because services are mostly intangible—with no dress, guitar, or SUV to touch and try out before buying—brands are particularly important in both adding value to the guest experience and differentiating it from competing services. Even producers of mostly tangible products, like detergents and autos, know the value of a brand and work hard to protect its integrity and image. The Golden Arches is a brand worth a great deal as a symbol of quality and value, and it provides McDonald's with a tremendous competitive advantage. The McDonald's brand communicates a certain consistency in quality, price, and type of food served. Although specific menu items may vary worldwide—a guest can't get beef, but can get the beef-less McCurry Pan in India; beer in Germany; a McRice Burger in Taiwan; and Gallo Pinto (rice and beans) in Costa Rica—the mission of each restaurant is the same: to "be our customers' favorite place and way to eat." A McDonald's restaurant is instantly recognizable, and thus any of its restaurants anywhere in the world is immediately

brand image The image or icon associated with a specific product, service, or organization, meant to help customers differentiate the organization's offerings from those of competitors.

brand name The name of a specific product, service, or organization, used to differentiate the organization's offerings from those of competitors.

[2] Kevin L. Keller, *Strategic Brand Management: Building, Measuring, and Managing Brand Equity*, 4th ed. (Boston, MA: Pearson, 2013).

differentiated from any other fast-food operation. McDonald's works hard to protect the valuable symbol of its brand logo and maintain the reputation for which it stands.

A high-quality brand name and brand image is a source of competitive advantage. They enable companies like McDonald's, Disney, or Marriott to gain acceptance for anything new they bring to the marketplace. Customers will usually be willing to give the new product or service a try simply because of the brand's reputation. For example, thousands of people, many of them families that had never before felt comfortable going on a cruise, booked trips on the Disney Magic even before the ship was launched. They knew Disney would not risk hurting its brand by putting it on something inconsistent with the quality of products and services customers have come to expect from Disney. A brand represents a powerful marketing tool to communicate a promise of quality and value for any experience with that brand. Therefore, companies spend a lot of money to create and protect their brands.

Having a strong brand may sometimes be a disadvantage. When Disney entered the European market by opening Disneyland Paris, it discovered the Disney brand was not seen favorably by some, who associated the brand with promoting American values. Furthermore, fear of hurting the brand image may unnecessarily inhibit a company from exploring new market opportunities or putting its name on a potentially profitable product or service just because doing so may seem inconsistent with the brand image. Compared to the advantages of instant and favorable product differentiation, this disadvantage is small, and most companies with strong brands are happy to pay this price.

A Special Niche

market niche A gap in a market that an organization seeks out, focuses on, and attempts to fill to attract customers and compete successfully.

Finally, an organization can try to find and fill a particular **market niche** or gap. It can focus on a specific part of the total market by offering a special appeal—like quality, value, location, or exceptional service—to attract customers in that market segment.

The airline industry is one that is constantly seeking to create and fill niches. For example, JetBlue, WestJet, and Southwest Airlines all elected to pursue a short-haul, low-fare, high-frequency, point-to-point strategy to carve out a specific niche in the airline market. This has been a successful strategy, allowing them to achieve success in comparison to the legacy carriers using a hub-and-spoke, business-class traveler-focused strategy. This strategy has been replicated in Europe as well, with the creation of EasyJet, WOW, and Norwegian Air.

Warren Buffet, the legendary chairman of Berkshire Hathaway, has taken the airline niche strategy further by investing in what may become a new type of airline travel: The company, NetJets, uses a concept called fractional ownership. NetJets owns its aircraft, flies anywhere in the world, adheres to rigorous safety and maintenance standards, and uses a high-tech operations center to keep an eye on every plane in its fleet. But the resemblances to traditional carriers end there. By purchasing a NetJets' Share, customers can travel on their own schedules, avoid check-in and security lines, stretch out in comfort in spacious cabins, and fly with only the passengers they choose.[3]

Joe Raedle/Getty Images

Panera Bread is an American chain of fast causal restaurants, seeking to position itself in the market niche between casual-dining and fast food.

[3] NetJets, "More Than 50 Years of Leadership: And Still Going Strong," NetJets, Berkshire Hathaway, accessed February 3, 2018, https://www.netjets.com/AboutNetJets/.

There are many other examples across the hospitality industry where companies have sought niches that will appeal to specific groups of potential customers. For example, the niche tour industry now includes specialty tours focused on people who want to combine a tour experience with such activities as bicycling; walking; volunteering; golfing; sampling wines, cuisines, or pub beers; associating only with a specific group of people, like a university's alumni, families, or members of the LGBTQ community; or exploring a specific culture, ecology, or heritage. The Society for Accessible Travel & Hospitality reports organizations have designed special tours for the disabled, such as the cruises designed for people with visual impairments offered by Mind's-Eye Travel.[4] Theme parks also have increasingly found niches. Customers can choose among Christian (Holy Land), kiddie (Wannado City), heritage (Wild West City, Dollywood), water (Aquatica), animal experience (Marineland, Discovery Cove), human bodies (Corpus), and other niche theme parks.

In the fast-food market and budget-hotel market, the competitive positioning of a McDonald's or Day's Inn is to be the low-cost producer in the budget segment of the market. Casual-dining restaurants like Olive Garden and Chili's have tried to position themselves in the dining-out market by offering price and food values at a point above fast-food and below fine-dining restaurants. Others, like Panera, Chipotle, and Zaxby's, have found a new niche by positioning themselves between casual-dining and fast food. Still others, like fast-fine, food trucks, grocery chains' prepared food, and home delivered meal-kits, continue seeking and serving new niches. A Norwegian architectural firm has even designed a restaurant, Under, that will be 16 feet underwater to fill a niche of customers wishing to dine under the sea. By focusing on one particular part of the total market, each of these concepts hopes to distinguish itself from other types of eating options. Other market niches that have been identified and used as a focus for organizational strategies are the healthy-eating niche in restaurants, convention hotels in lodging, medical needs in tourism, and water parks in parks and attractions. In all these instances, the market niche is carefully defined demographically, psychographically, or geographically. The organization seeks to build a top-of-mind awareness with customers in its targeted market as to how unique the experience provided is, and how it uniquely meets their particular needs by focusing on that particular market segment.

The distinction between a *differentiation strategy* and *finding a niche strategy* is not clear cut. One way to think of it is that the organization determines the market in which it wants to compete, the niche it hopes to fill, and then uses strategies to differentiate itself from other organizations in that same market or niche. The most common strategy is to try to differentiate its product or service from similar products or services.

The organization that concentrates on filling niches is often a market innovator seeking to be the first to move into a market segment to meet an unfulfilled customer need, perhaps a need customers don't recognize until they see the product the innovator offers to fulfill it: a high-priced luxury airline for rich people, a sandwich wrap for drivers eating dashboard cuisine, an Airbnb for more adventurous travelers, or any other of the thousands of innovative products and services brought to the marketplace each year. This unfulfilled need might be identified by careful market research, serious study of population and demographic trends, a lucky guess, or an intuitive combination of these approaches. Some researchers argue this combination is the most likely way for managers to develop a **strategic plan**, especially those that make a real difference in an organization's success.[5]

strategic plan The specific steps that detail how the organization intends to get from where it is to where it wishes to be in order to achieve its mission and vision.

The differences between these three competitive strategies—lower cost, product differentiation, and defined market scope (niche vs. broad market reach)—are illustrated in these three restaurant examples. The fast-food, limited-menu restaurants like McDonald's compete on price, Red Lobster differentiates itself from other full-service restaurants

[4] Society for Accessible Travel and Hospitality, "Home Page," Society for Accessible Travel and Hospitality (SATH), accessed February 3, 2018, http://www.sath.org/.

[5] Julia Sloan, *Learning to Think Strategically*, 3rd ed. (New York, NY: Taylor & Francis, 2016).

by specializing in seafood, and Dave and Buster's fits into a niche, the "eatertainment" restaurant. The differences between the three strategies, however, are not always clear and many authors classify strategies in various ways.[6] Consider the Hyatt hotel company. Does it seek to compete on a niche (high-end business and convention traveler) or on price (the best price in its market segment)? Marriott has developed 30 brands to fit the various market niches it seeks to reach as well as the price points within those segments. It differentiates its brands on the basis of both price and targeted market niche. The point is that a number of strategic opportunities exist for hospitality organizations to consider when choosing its competitive strategy. Each of these opportunities has advantages and disadvantages that an in-depth review of strategic planning will reveal.[7]

Combining Strategies

The strategies just discussed are not mutually exclusive. An organization can seek to differentiate its product from all others in the market by positioning the product in people's minds as the best value for the lowest cost. This combination of strategies requires the organization to use both effective marketing techniques that reach this best-value, lowest-cost market segment and operating efficiencies that allow it to make money at the low price. Successful theme parks seek to apply this combination by advertising a park visit as a high-value, low-cost, family-entertainment experience while keeping their costs, especially labor costs, low. JetBlue and Southwest Airlines follow the strategy of offering both low prices and excellent service to provide a high-value, low-cost experience in the airline industry to the broadest array of customers possible.

Reinventing the Industry

Picking and following a strategy is an important decision for any hospitality manager seeking to find the best match of the company's mission with its current and emerging uncertainties. If drastic change is forecast, the organization might even have to reinvent itself and develop new ways to compete more effectively. A strategy might be to become cheaper, or better, or faster. These are all reactive strategies most organizations could adopt as circumstances change.

Most companies listen to their customers and then respond to their articulated needs. But some rare, highly creative organizations can actually create the future for themselves and their industries. Organizational strategists Gary Hamel and C. K. Prahalad note in their now classic book, *Competing for the Future,* the organization might even need to "lead customers where they want to go but don't know it yet."[8] They "do more than satisfy customers, they constantly amaze them."[9] In other words, they will need to be capable of reinventing their industry through constant innovation.

The creation of Disneyland Park is a great example of a visionary leader reinventing an industry by leading customers to a place they didn't know they wanted to go. Disneyland was an attempt to move beyond the Coney Island amusement park concept to something new, cleaner, more organized, and safer. Instead of a disjointed array of amusement rides, barkers, and arcades, Walt Disney created within a single setting the feel of being actual participants in a motion picture. The traditional amusement park was embellished in creative ways with new technology and the introduction of theming to become an experience: The theme park didn't exist until Disney and his creative team imagined it and built it.

---

[6] Porter, *Competitive Strategy,* 40–41.

[7] Michael A. Hitt, R. Duane Ireland, and Robert E. Hoskisson, *Strategic Management Cases: Competitiveness and Globalization,* 12th ed. (Boston, MA: Cengage Learning, 2017); Arthur A. Thompson Jr. and Margaret A. Peteraf, *Crafting & Executing Strategy: The Quest for Competitive Advantage, 21st ed.* (New York, NY: McGraw-Hill Education, 2017); Nigel Evans, *Strategic Management for Tourism, Hospitality and Events,* 2nd ed. (Abingdon, Oxon: Routledge, 2015); Fevzi Okumus, Levent Altinay, and Prakash Chathoth, *Strategic Management for Hospitality and Tourism* (Abington, Oxon: Routledge, 2010).

[8] Gary Hamel and C. K. Prahalad, *Competing for the Future* (Boston, MA: Harvard Business School Press, 1994).

[9] Hamel and Prahalad, *Competing for the Future,* 109.

No Matter the Strategy, Provide Better Service

In this section, we've discussed three generic strategies—competing on price, differentiating, and finding a niche. Each of these strategies may work for a while, but they also have potential shortcomings. If you compete on price, somebody is eventually going to undercut your price. Also, the costs associated with establishing a close and lasting relationship with guests are difficult to cover if you stress your low price. If you find a niche and succeed there, an imitator eventually will join you in the niche, and soon it will be just another market segment. If you differentiate successfully, somebody will copy your differentiation feature. Many successful service organizations have found that the best way to succeed in the long term is to differentiate on the basis of superlative service quality and value. Provide better service and value than the competition does, and they can't beat you. As author Dr. Tony Alessandra says, "Being on par with price and quality only gets you into the game, service wins the game."[10] The well-known management writer Tom Peters echoes this idea. He writes, "You can knock off everything . . . except awesome service."[11]

THE HOSPITALITY PLANNING CYCLE

Leading guests to where they want to go but don't know it yet is how the truly outstanding hospitality organizations become and stay outstanding. The focus of this chapter is to help readers appreciate how service organizations find a way to give guests what they want, when they want it, even if they don't know yet exactly what they want. The organization gathers as much information as it can on what its present customers want, need, and do, tries to imagine what kinds of experiences their future guests will find satisfying, and then plans ways to deliver them. For example, Walt Disney planned out a theme park he knew would wow park visitors long before they knew what a theme park was. As a more recent example, bank customers didn't know they needed debit cards (on which expenditures are deducted directly from the customer's checking account) until banks offered them. Similarly, phone customers didn't recognize their need for a single telephone number that can be used anywhere and includes texting, picture taking, e-mail, GPS, and internet capabilities until wireless companies made them aware of how convenient such services could be. Hospitality organizations did not know they needed a website and smartphone apps until the ideas were introduced.

The way to reach these outcomes is through the strategic planning process. The process has two basic steps: assessment (external and internal) and figuring out what to do on the basis of that assessment. The external assessment of environmental opportunities and threats leads to the generation of strategic premises about the future environment. The internal assessment of organizational strengths and weaknesses leads to a redefinition or reaffirmation of the organization's capabilities.

As seen in Exhibit 2.1, hospitality planning follows a continuous ongoing cycle that begins at the big-picture level and ends in specific action plans with departmental or project budgets, and individual yearly objectives that can be tested against performance metrics. Typically, such planning is done annually and begins with management's simultaneous consideration of three elements: the external environment with its opportunities and threats, the internal organization with its strengths and weaknesses, and the relationship of these elements to the statements of organizational vision and mission. The cycle renews itself as the performance metrics tell the planners what went right and what didn't. This periodic review is the beginning point of the new planning cycle as one cycle's performance becomes the starting point for the next cycle.

[10] AZQuotes, "Tony Alessandra Quotes," AZQuotes, accessed February 3, 2018. http://www.azquotes.com/author/40353-Tony_Alessandra.
[11] Tom Peters, *The Circle of Innovation: You Can't Shrink Your Way to Greatness* (New York, NY: Vintage Books 1997), 457.

EXHIBIT 2.1

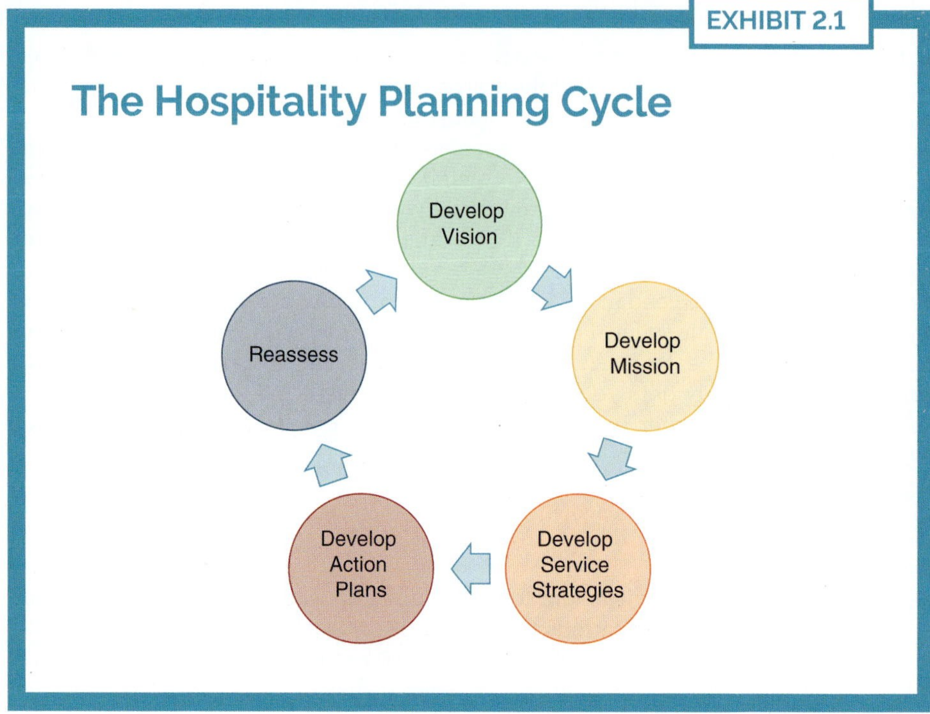

Applebee's, for example, found in reviewing its performance metrics in 2017 that it was producing unhappy customers and losing money. Its strategy of branding itself as a modern millennium hangout was frustrating its longtime regulars who were confused by the new menu items and modern décor. The review led to it adopting a new strategy of returning to its roots, eliminating menu items like the turkey sandwich with sriracha chile lime sauce and bringing back old favorites.[12] Whether this strategy works will be determined when the next review at the end of the planning cycle takes place. The point is that a strategic planning cycle is ongoing and not a one-time process.

environmental assessment A careful examination of the present opportunities and threats in the external business environment, and forecast of the future environment, within which the organization operates to determine the impact of external factors on the organization and to discover the key drivers that will satisfy present and future guests; carried out as part of long-term strategic planning and sometimes called the long look around.

key drivers Primary factors within a guest experience valued highly by the guest and leading to guest satisfaction, determined by surveying and studying guests.

Looking Around

The **environmental assessment**, or the long look around for opportunities and threats, in turn defines the strategic premises. These premises are the beliefs of the managers assessing all long-term aspects of the external environment and trying to use them to discover what forces will impact their business in the future and especially what customers will want in that future environment. They seek to identify what the **key drivers** or value drivers of guest satisfaction will be in the intermediate-term and longer-term future. Although guests will not always know what the key drivers of their future satisfaction will be, the guestologist will try to find the critical aspects of experiences guests think will satisfy them in the future.

For example, in response to its recognition of growing concerns over the public health issues with obesity and public interest in calories found in restaurant meals that led to a number of local laws, Darden Restaurants led a restaurant industry proposal for legislation requiring nutrition information to be posted. It sensed its customers were increasingly interested in having access to that information and, as one of the largest restaurant chains in the United States, it knew the importance of listening to

[12] Abha Bhattari, "Applebee's Halts Millennial Chase," *Orlando Sentinel*, August 15, 2017, A8.

what its customers were asking it to do. Although the entire industry initially opposed any federal regulation, it proposed the Labeling Education and Nutrition (LEAN) Act in 2009. Darden chose to show its support for this act by immediately posting online the nutritional values and calories for each of its menu items. A visit to its Olive Garden website shows this information along with a commitment to reduce sodium and enhance the nutritional content of its children's menus.[13]

Looking Within

The **internal assessment**, or the searching look within for strengths and weaknesses, defines the organization's capabilities, and considers the organization's strong and weak points in terms of its ability to compete in the future. It is here that the organization determines what it does well, what it does not do well, and how its strengths and weaknesses pair with what it wants to accomplish.

internal assessment A careful examination of the organization's present internal condition, its strengths (see core competencies), and weaknesses; carried out as part of long-term strategic planning and sometimes called the searching look within.

On the basis of its own internal assessment, for example, Gaylord Hotels realized it needed to develop a stronger guest focus among its employees. Gaylord Hotels wanted to compete by providing exceptional service; yet, it did not feel it had a corporate culture that helped to direct all employee efforts to fulfill this goal. Using a strategic approach to create a guest-focused culture, it was able to overcome this internal weakness, develop a strong service culture among its employees, and transform it into an area of strength.

The Necessity for Planning

The process described in Exhibit 2.1 seems to many like an attempt to apply rationality to an irrational world and to predict an unpredictable future. It will, therefore, lead to errors, wasted time, and frustration. Nevertheless, the planning process is worthwhile. There is an old saying that those who fail to plan, plan to fail. Every hospitality organization needs a road map to unite and focus the efforts of the organization's members and get them prepared for the future the organizational planners predict. Everyone makes decisions today that they must live with in the future, and most managers want to make those decisions as rationally as possible. Even though no one, including planners, knows what the future will bring, only by creating and implementing plans can we communicate to those both inside and outside the organization where we want to go, what criteria we should use to allocate our scarce resources, and which activities we should pursue or avoid. To successful hospitality organizations, doing nothing to prepare for an uncertain future is not an option.

Adriana Zebrauskas/Bloomberg via Getty Images

Food trucks are becoming increasingly popular around the world and part of the recent pop-up restaurant phenomenon. Food trucks offer a relatively inexpensive way for restaurateurs to quickly enter into the restaurant industry, offering gourmet cuisines in various locations. This food truck offers Japanese food in a market in Mexico City.

This is the kind of thinking that encouraged Warren Buffet to invest in NetJets, the cruise industry to build new very large ships, and China to invest in theme parks. No organization can instantly create such magnificent facilities and equipment. The only way it can get to the future it envisions is to invest today. Although no one's foresight as to what customers of tomorrow will want can be perfect, everyone must

[13] Olive Garden Italian Kitchen, "Home," Olive Garden, Darden Concepts, accessed February 3, 2018. www.olivegarden.com/home.

make decisions today that anticipate the future they expect to see. Creating and following a careful strategic plan is the best known way to do so.

Once the hospitality planning process is complete, the cycle should begin again in some predefined time frame. The planning process should never stop because the world in which any organization operates never stops changing. Moreover, the assessment of the performance metrics associated with each action plan will offer valuable feedback to the organization's leadership as it reviews its strengths, weaknesses, opportunities, and threats in the next cycle of the planning process.

Forecasting

forecasting Process of making predictions of future trends, or the impact of current trends on future business.

quantitative forecasting tools Forecasting tools that use quantitative, objective information or data to make projections.

qualitative forecasting tools Forecasting tools that use non-quantitative, subjective information to make projections.

Assessing the future depends on a chosen **forecasting** process. Forecasting techniques range from the heavily quantitative tools, which are fairly objective, to the highly qualitative tools, which are heavily subjective. The **quantitative forecasting tools** include the powerful tools of statistical forecasting. The **qualitative forecasting tools** include scenario building, the Delphi technique, and pure creative guesswork. Most forecasting techniques are based on the idea that the future is somehow related to the past, that what has already happened has some predictable relationship to what will happen.[14] If a restaurant's customer growth rate has been about 10% per year for five years, then forecasting that this growth rate will continue next year seems reasonable. If records show that by 10 A.M. on an average day 20% of all visitors who will come into a zoo for that day are already on the grounds, then the day's total attendance can be reliably forecasted by 10:15 A.M. On a grander scale, if the growth rate of tourists coming to a Caribbean island paradise has been 10% per year for the past decade, then predicting this growth rate will continue for at least a few more years seems reasonable for planning purposes even if history also tells us that hurricanes may occur to disrupt that trend.

The problem with assuming the past can be used to predict the future is that all too frequently the assumption does not hold true. In the early days of the telephone, the ratio of phones to operators was very small. If only population trends and that ratio had been used to predict the number of telephone operators needed in the distant future, the prediction might well have been that half the people in the United States would now be working as telephone operators. Major improvements in technology and work productivity have greatly increased the ratio of telephones to operators. As the bursting of the housing bubble and the subsequent financial meltdown of 2008 showed to the dismay of many investors and retirees, any forecast based only on the past can be thrown off by unexpected technological, economic, societal, environmental, or political changes.

Forecasting techniques are useful to capture the impact of current trends on future business. However, they are only one source of input into the creative process by which thoughtful hospitality managers develop strategic plans. The appendix at the end of this chapter offers a review of the more popular quantitative and qualitative tools such as econometric models, regression analysis, time-series and trend analyses, brain-storming, and focus groups; the reader is encouraged to review them.

ASSESSING THE ENVIRONMENT

Exhibit 2.2 provides details of each of the steps in the planning cycle. The exhibit shows the hospitality planning process begins with a long look around the environment. Here, the organization carefully studies the opportunities and

[14] Bo Peng, Haiyan Song, and Geoffrey I. Crouch, "A Meta-analysis of International Tourism Demand Forecasting and Implications for Practice," *Tourism Management* 45, (2014): 181–193. Doris Chenguang Wu, Haiyan Song, and Shujie Shen, "New Developments in Tourism and Hotel Demand Modeling and Forecasting," *International Journal of Contemporary Hospitality Management* 29, no. 1 (2017): 507–529.

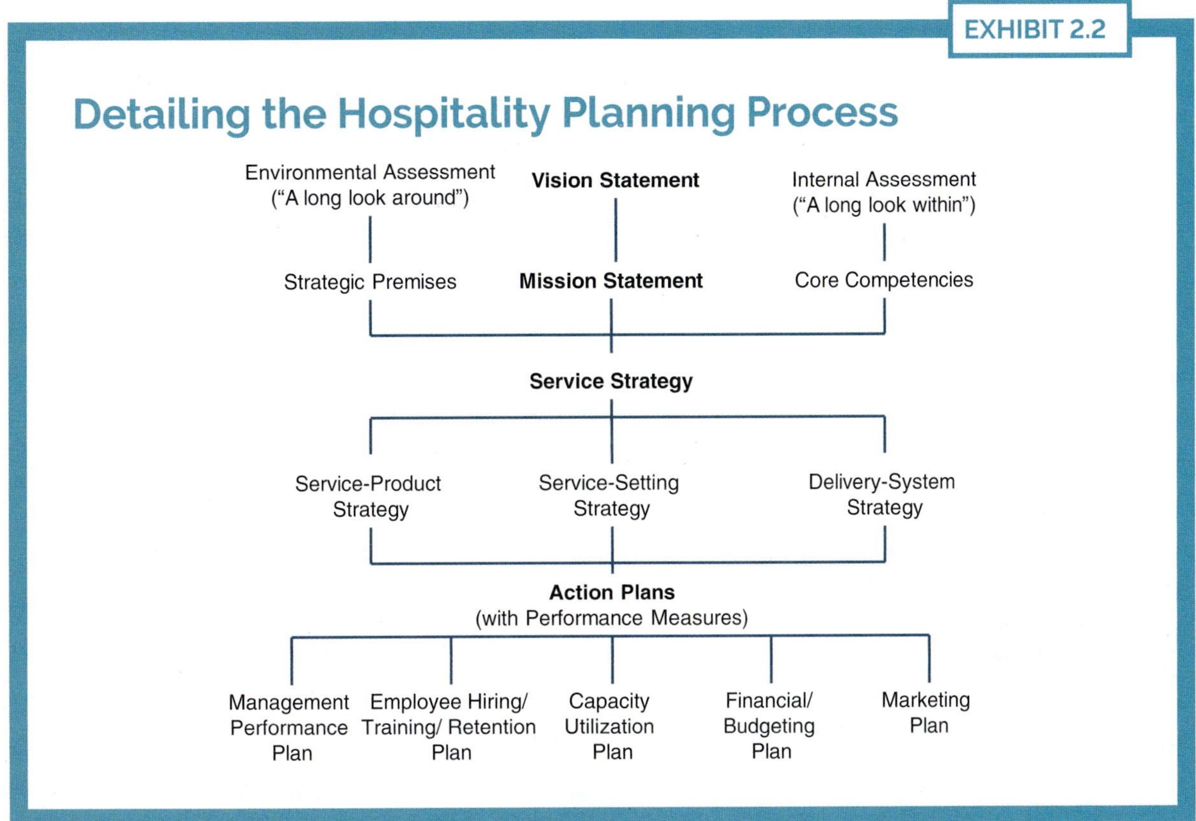

threats the future holds for both it and its industry. Exhibit 2.3 presents the three categories of factors that should be included in an environmental assessment: those in the overall environment, the industry environment, and the company's operating environment.

The Overall Environment

Among the many factors the hospitality organization must forecast for the uncertain future, it must try to predict potential changes in the economy, societal and demographic trends, political leadership, technology, and even the natural environment. All of these environmental factors impact the way a hospitality organization operates, as well as affecting the guests who seek its services.

The Economy

The organization must consider the effects of governmental economic policies on its suppliers of capital, the ability of its customers to buy the service, its own cost structure, and direct and indirect competitors' ability to compete. The economic meltdown of 2008 continues to have a major impact on the hospitality industry. Not only did it lead to a virtual halt on new construction but also directly influenced consumer confidence and willingness to spend on vacations, time shares, second homes, and other hospitality and tourism services. Likewise, the resulting governmental intervention and financial subsidies given to the financial and industrial sectors led to public outrage over any business spending viewed as excessive or wasteful, such as resort hotel golfing retreats, meetings in Las Vegas, first class travel, luxury boxes, and premium entertaining. Hospitality organizations serving these governmentally subsidized

EXHIBIT 2.3

Factors to Include in Environmental Assessment

The Overall Environment

The Economy. What do we project for economic growth, inflation, interest rates, capital and credit availability, consumer confidence, consumer purchasing power? How will changes in the global market affect our business?

Society and Demographics. How will shifts in social attitudes/values regarding childbearing, marriage, family-work balance, lifestyle, racial equality, retirement, pollution, etc. affect us? How will shifts in population characteristics, language, age distribution, educational backgrounds, health, ethnic mix, cultural values, etc., affect us?

Politics and Changing Social Expectations. What sort of government policy changes regarding antitrust activities, regulation, foreign trade, health care, taxation, depreciation, environmental protection, and foreign trade barriers can we expect? What political factors or legal constraints will affect international business?

Technology. Where is it going? What new products, services, or breakthroughs might we anticipate?

Ecology. Are there foreseeable natural or man-made caused disasters ahead? Environmental legislation? Customer expectations?

The Industry Environment

Changing Competitors. Who will our new competitors be? Will technological advances enable them to offset our present competitive advantages (economies of scale, brand-name differentiation, market niche, availability of capital)?

Changes in Other Relevant Groups

Resource Suppliers. How stable, big, and reliable are our current suppliers? Might any become potential competitors? Are substitute suppliers available? Can we supply ourselves?

Capital Suppliers. Will we have enough credit to finance growth? Will we stay worthy of credit? Do we have enough cash if we need it?

Labor market. Will we have enough employees, with the right skills, when and where we need them? What are the skill sets of new entrants to the labor market? When are people retiring? What changes are ahead for unions?

The Operating Environment

Strategic Premises. What are the fundamental assumptions about the industry, market, and environment that the organization is making to determine how it will compete in the future? Is the organization offering a service product that customers want? Will the organization's service product be something customers will continue to demand in the future?

Predicting the Competitive Environment. Which customer needs are not being met by our or competitors' existing products? Are R&D efforts underway to fill these needs? What marketing and distribution channels should we use? How will demographic and population changes affect our markets? Any new market segments? What technologies are customers using to experience hospitality products in our competitive market domain?

Surprises. Not all changes in the overall environment, industry, or operating environment can be predicted. Nonetheless, major disruptions seem inevitable. Is the organization capable of weathering a major incident, like an environmental disaster or a terrorist attack? Even if not directly affected by major changes to the operating environment, the indirect effect on the market can be substantial. Organizations need to at least consider how unpredictable future events can impact what customers want and the services the organization offers.

businesses increasingly found themselves on the defensive justifying to a skeptical public why these expenditures made good business sense.

The 2008 financial crunch reminded everyone of the implications of business cycles. In other words, the lack of clear forecasting of the downside of the business cycle and overreliance on a continuing upside caused then and may cause again many financial challenges and employee hardships for all parts of the hospitality industry across the world.

In addition to the financial environment, organizations in the hospitality industry must also consider, besides the influences from the financial environment, numerous other economic factors in their strategic planning process. For example, one important consideration is the future directions of the local, regional, national, and even international economies and how these directions will influence the demand for hospitality services. Consider foreign currency exchange rates. If the euro is less valuable in foreign exchange than the U.S. dollar, foreign tourists will consider going to visit a country in the European Union rather than coming to the United States. In the labor intensive service sector, the influence of inflation on competitiveness is especially important. If inflation rates move up or down, the organization's cost of capital—its ability to expand the business, buy new equipment, and keep up with rising wage expectations—will be affected. Other economic factors would include productivity growth, income distribution, tax laws, and stage in the business cycle. Most hospitality organizations are more sensitive to variations in general economic health than organizations making and selling necessities. When the economy is in a downward cycle, so too is the travel and tourism industry. People must buy groceries and clothing; they don't have to take vacations, go to meetings and conferences, or go out to eat.

Society and Demographics

Assessing demographic trends and their effects may require both qualitative and quantitative forecasts. Hospitality organizations already know a lot about their future guests since so many of them are already here. As of 2017, there are more than 323 million people in the United States.[15] Of these, 49 million (approximately 15.2% of the population) are older than age sixty-five. Another 18.8% were 0–14 (61 million), 13.5% were 15–24 (approx. 44 million), 39.6% were 25–54 (128 million), and 12.8% (41 million) were 55–64. This breakdown includes the Baby Boomers (those born between 1945 and 1964) who represent about 77 million and 24% of the total population.

Baby Boomers. This large group of aging people has had and will continue to have a major impact on the hospitality industry as customers, investors, and employees. Baby Boomers and older Americans outnumbered teenagers in 2017, and most will continue to be active twenty to thirty years more than prior generations. The aging Baby Boomers are retiring at the rate of about 10,000 each day with a substantial sum of money available for discretionary use. This relatively affluent demographic group will continue to be a prime target of the hospitality industry. Although many have at least some child care responsibility for their single-parent children's children, they have the time, money, and physical ability to travel and participate in many guest experiences unimaginable to their parents at comparable times in their lives.

This group of seniors now either in retirement or nearing it will continue to change the workforce and the marketplace for hospitality organizations. They are healthier, financially better off, more willing to travel, are more used to having things "their way," and generally have higher expectations than their parents had. They have the money, time, energy, and inclination to do what they want to do. The hospitality industry will benefit from this large group of potential customers. Moreover, if they follow the trends set by the generation before them, many will work longer in order to enjoy the social benefits of working, delay the consequences of their unwillingness to set aside enough wealth to live as they wish in retirement, and fill jobs that require their expertise and experience. Others will use their retirement to seek new and higher-involvement experiences (e.g., voluntourism, adventure tourism, ecotourism).

[15] United States Census Bureau, "Population," Census.gov, U.S. Department of Commerce, accessed September 15, 2017, https://www.census.gov/topics/population.html.

In other words, many of these seniors not only will stay in the workforce longer compared to their predecessors but also may change jobs to pursue an encore career in an entirely different profession, set up entrepreneurial ventures to do something they always wanted to do, or take jobs like teaching and in not-for-profits that their family financial commitments would not have allowed them to take earlier in their lives. There are stories told of people who retired and moved to Orlando to work for Disney because they had always wanted to work in a "magical" place. Likewise, there are people who have always wanted to run a restaurant, open a bed and breakfast, become a full-time meeting or event planner, or cruise line lecturer. Hospitality organizations may find it desirable to look closely at this labor pool.

Generation X, Generation Y (Millennials), and Generation Z (Next-Gens). In contrast, the generations succeeding the boomers (Generations X, Y, and Z) have or expect to have few defined benefit retirement plans. Instead, they must worry about the future of Social Security and must depend on their own investment successes (or luck) to fund their retirement years. At the same time, they are also in the middle of public health crises with both obesity and opioids and are increasingly responsible for their own health care expenses and retirement savings in a world that has fewer domestic industrial jobs. They must also face the prospect of funding one of the largest government debts in American history, incurred as a result of the 2008 financial meltdown, spending on the Iraq, Afghanistan, and Syrian conflicts, the 2017 Tax Reform, investments in infrastructure, health care costs, and many other financial issues. These generations face the possibility of having a lower standard of living than their parents, working more years before retiring, and paying more for the large number of retirees in Social Security and Medicare, the national debt, and the health care fallout of obesity and drug abuse.

Many future market opportunities can be identified by reviewing information already known about Baby Boomers and the Generation X, Generation Y, and Generation Z segments of the population. The 65.7 million Americans born in the years 1965–1980 make up Generation X. Generation Y (Millennials) Americans are those born in the years 1981–1997, and Generation Z (Next-Gens, iGens,) are those born after 1997 to at least 2017. In 2017, these segments represented 20%, 24%, and 23%, respectively, of the population of the United States. The roughly 74 million Americans of Generation Z, also called the iGen Generation, currently between the ages of 0 and 19, represent a significant demographic category and constitute the future and present new entries into the workforce. What education and training these people will have completed will determine the entry-level employee competence and the emerging customer expectations for hospitality experiences. Looking at the demographics, the relatively large bulges in the Generation X and Generation Y numbers will continue to translate into important trends in both employment and marketing strategies for the hospitality industry. While the Generation Y Millennials have become an important and unique force of their own, Generation Z will be even more interesting and unpredictable as it evolves. This generation will be different because the world it has to deal with is quite different from the one its parents faced. Moreover, the Z generation will face this new world with their smartphones. Because of the time they spend on their phones, they are working less, driving less, dating less, hanging out in person with others less, and are less happy than their preceding generation.[16] While Millennials have been known as job hoppers with large college debt, they tend not to be as much interested in taking risks as the more entrepreneurial, self-directed Generation Z. Organizations seeking to employ these iGens will need to offer personal flexibility, educational opportunities, remote or virtual job options, and advanced technology.[17]

---

[16] Jean M. Twenge, "Have Smartphones Destroyed a Generation?" *The Atlantic*, September 2017; Jean M. Twenge, *iGen: Why Today's Super-Connected Kids Are Growing Up Less Rebellious, More Tolerant, Less Happy—and Completely Unprepared for Adulthood—and What That Means for the Rest of Us* (New York, NY: Atria Books, 2017).

[17] Gabriel Hitt, "Gen Z Makes Its Labor Force Debut—Is Your Company Ready?," Universum Global Top 100, Universum Global, last revised 2017, http://universumglobaltop100.com/articles/gen-z-makes-its-labor-force-debut-is-your-company-ready.

Technology

Hospitality organizations are making attempts to attract these groups of people. For example, hotels seeking to appeal to a Generation Y group of Millennials will offer different amenities and features than those targeting boomers. Their research shows that Millennials rarely unpack their suitcases and are as likely to work on beds instead of desks. Moreover, over two thirds of them use availability of in-room wi-fi in selecting a hotel.[18] Choice Hotels created a new chain, Cambria Suites, to appeal to this demographic. Its theme is, "Where everybody is somebody." It offers all suite rooms, high-speed internet, barista coffee service, posh gyms, and retail shops that emphasize health foods. The in-room amenities include MediaHub plug and play technology for laptops and game consoles. To make sure their emphasis is missed by no one, they call their exercise rooms "Refresh," their restaurants "Reflect," and their shops "Renew."[19] Similarly, Aloft, one of Starwood Hotels' brands, also targets the Millennial market. "We see millennial travelers more as explorers than tourists," said Brian McGuinness, global brand leader, Starwood's Specialty Select Brands. "Our Aloft hotels are specifically designed with them in mind." Aloft features free wi-fi, areas for working poolside or in the bar, and even a robotic bellhop that appeals to this tech-savvy generation. Guests who are too busy to talk to a human can order from an emoji room-service menu by texting a string of emojis with their last name and room number to Aloft TiGi (Text it. Get it.).[20] Hotel companies realize that not all generations of guests want the same experience, and so they market different products to appeal to different groups.

Demographic Implications. Changing demographics have several implications for all organizations serving the public, but some of them will have special impact on the labor-intensive hospitality industry. As aging Baby Boomers press for allocation of more government dollars to their growing health care and retirement needs, funding for education has come under pressure. In this scenario, agile hospitality companies can define themselves as white knights to schools and their students by finding innovative ways to promote their products and services while helping schools achieve their educational mission. The production of support lesson plans, videos, edutainment, and electronic media will represent prime opportunities for companies to do good things for school systems and for themselves. Organizations that have a fundamental appeal to children, like those running theme parks or makers of children's products, can seize these opportunities in education as a cost-efficient and focused marketing strategy for reaching this market estimated to be worth $100 billion per year and for creating good will to attract future employees.

Managerial Implications of Generation Y in the Workforce. Generation Ys have been called the "most praised generation," as their entire young lives have been filled with positive feedback from parents, teachers, coaches, and others. They won soccer trophies as children just for showing up, ribbons for participating in school events, and were routinely told they were special. Now as members of the labor force, they require different strategies to manage; as customers, they require different strategies to satisfy.[21]

Technology

The characteristics of these Millennials have other important implications for managing the workforce of hospitality organizations. As the presence of tech-savvy Millennials grows in the work force, businesses can expect to see greater use of communication tools

[18] Andrea Peterson, "Secrets of a Hotel Test Lab," *Wall Street Journal*, October 1, 2015, http://online.wsj.com/public/resources/documents/print/WSJ_-D001-20151001.pdf.

[19] Choice Hotels International, "HOME," Choice Hotels International Inc., accessed February 3, 2018, https://www.choicehotels.com.

[20] Dinah Eng, "What Do Millennials Want? Hotels Have Some Ideas," *New York Times*, April 4, 2016, https://www.nytimes.com/2016/04/10/travel/millennials-hotels.html.

[21] Jeanine S. Stewart, Elizabeth Goad Oliver, Karen S. Cravens, and Shigehiro Oishi, "Managing Millennials: Embracing Generational Differences," *Business Horizons* 60, no. 1 (2017): 45–54; Malinvisa Sakdiyakorn and Walanchalee Wattanacharoensil, "Generational Diversity in the Workplace: A Systematic Review in the Hospitality Context," *Cornell Hospitality Quarterly* 59, no. 2 (2017): 1–25.

like live chat, project management platforms, and collaboration technology, replacing traditional e-mails. Business leaders are also finding Millennials work better by eliminating cubicles and divided departments, allowing for open meeting spaces and seating areas. Finally, because Millennials are comfortable with technology, they seek jobs with more scheduling flexibility by using technology to work when and where it works best for them. The divergence between the haves and the have-nots is already wide among today's school children and tomorrow's workers, and it will likely grow wider. As technology morphs from being a luxury to a necessity, the chasm between the performance of low-income students and their more affluent peers is a growing concern. Some note the tech movement is further exacerbating the already-large achievement gap; in education circles, this phenomenon is dubbed the "connectivity gap" or the "digital divide." Discrepancies exist among schools and across districts, but they also spread to individual students, many of whom live in homes without sufficient connectivity.[22]

Today's children will be the eighteen- to twenty-one-year-old workers of 2025 and 2030. Those who enter the workforce without the requisite basic skills will represent a major training and development challenge for the many hospitality organizations that depend upon young, eager, tech savvy, and educated employees to provide and ensure guest satisfaction. The challenge for managers will be to keep this new group of employees, especially the have-nots, competitive with the rapidly emerging, highly educated workforce of the Asian rim countries, who are now investing heavily in technology, education, and training. The labor pool companies can hire from is rapidly becoming global, and workers from many nations are competing for the same jobs. Advances in technology and communication that allow many jobs to be done by remotely located employees, a crowdsourced grouping, or even by robots make where a person is located less important than what the person can do. When a pizza can be delivered by a robot or room service provided by Aloft's Botlr, the need to find new hires with improved capabilities becomes obvious. Indeed, the more sophisticated the requirements are for entry employees, the more challenging it will be to sustain the traditional paths of opportunity for the underprepared and disadvantaged in the hospitality industry. Some estimate that between 75 million and 375 million people will need to switch jobs because of artificial intelligence and automation.[23] As lower skilled jobs like taxi, delivery truck, and pizza driver get taken over by self-driving vehicles, the ability of hospitality organizations to offer a hand up to new entrants trying to climb the economic ladder declines.

Technology

New entrants into the workforce will be different in other ways as well. As the first generation to have easy access to instant and almost constant worldwide communication through their hand-held devices, Generation Ys and now Zs define their friends and their interests globally instead of restricting themselves to the neighborhood. This trend has both positive and negative aspects: The power of neighborhood and community over individual beliefs, values, and behavior (its social capital) will decline while a global perspective and the diversity of thinking that such a perspective brings will increase. Finally, and more importantly, Generation Ys have grown up expecting to find anything they need—products, knowledge, entertainment, and services—on the web. Google and Wikipedia provide a means to access information instantly. Websites like Amazon, eBay, and Craigslist sell everything imaginable and may even offer same day delivery. Other sites provide instant hotel, restaurant, or conference reservations. They learn online from educational institutions, news sources, and (sometimes fake) blogs; they entertain themselves online through music and video access; they create online content through YouTube and Instagram; and they connect online through various social media like Facebook and Snapchat. The Millennial generation is truly a digital generation

[22] Stuart M. Brotman, "The Real Digital Divide in Educational Technology," Brookings Foundation, January 28, 2016, https://www.brookings.edu/blog/techtank/2016/01/28/the-real-digital-divide-in-educational-technology/; Alexander JAM Van Deursen and Jan AGM Van Dijk, "The Digital Divide Shifts to Differences in Usage," *New Media & Society* 16, no. 3 (2014): 507–526.

[23] Daniela Hernandez, "Seven Jobs Robots Will Create-or Expand," *Wall Street Journal*, April 30, 2018, accessed 8/31/18, https://www.wsj.com/articles/seven-jobs-robots-will-createor-expand-1525054021.

and the Z Generation will be even more so. Recognizing this trend, and in particular the extent to which individuals spend time on their smartphones, Disney has added an app that provides interactive entertainment for guests while waiting in line or just walking.

A Different Way of Thinking. In school and preparing to enter the workforce are the Generation Z, or iGens. Here, a child's waking moments are carefully scheduled and planned by "helicopter parents," who hope that by packing their kids' days with soccer practice, tennis lessons, foreign language lessons, extra math tutoring, and judo, they can ensure their children's future success.

Grandparents remember how family and friends would regularly visit, and parents remember how they spent their youth playing with neighborhood friends in pick-up games and spontaneous play. Today's children pick up their smartphones, Xbox or PlayStation for play, participate in massive multiuser online role-playing games, compete with online friends in first-person shooter games, or just check Snapchat to see what their friends are doing in the little time left to them after their working parents pick them up from after-school care or structured activities. The impact of such trends on both the future customer and on employee creativity and ability to develop new ideas may be profound. The real question is, how do these generational differences in the amount of free time children have—and in how they use what free time they have—affect what kinds of knowledge, skills, and abilities they will bring into the workplace?

Conventional wisdom would have us believe that when a child has a handheld game console or a smartphone, with virtual or mixed reality games and graphics, plus instant access to social media, the motivation to stretch and grow one's own imagination and creativity is limited. However, numerous studies conducted by cognitive scientists, psychologists, and neurologists point to just the opposite conclusion: Time spent watching TV and playing mixed reality Pokémon Go or other computer games actually enhances creativity, patience, social competence, cognitive abilities, including pattern recognition, strategic thinking, priority setting, interpretive analysis, plan formulation and execution, and the ability to adapt rapidly to change.[24]

While many may assume this generation will have difficulty moving from a virtual entertainment world to the real world of work, there are reasons to predict this generation of workers will actually be quite well prepared. For example, cognitive scientists have found that video games exploit the "regime of competence" principle, carefully balancing reward and frustration, demanding that players work at the very limit of their levels of competence. One study showed gamers consistently outperformed non-gamers on standard tests that measure attention span and information-processing time. Other research has revealed gamers to be significantly more confident, more socially capable, and more creative in problem solving than non-gamers.[25]

What kind of cognitive skills should we expect to find in Next-Gens? They're going to think well about systems; they're going to be good at exploring; they're going to be good at reconceptualizing their goals based on their experience; they're not going to judge people's intelligence just by how fast and efficient they are; and they're going to think nonliterally.[26]

Changing Social and Political Expectations

Another factor in an organization's long look around is society's changing expectations for all its institutions, including those in the hospitality industry, as well as emerging social trends and institutional changes. "Dashboard cuisine" with its use of wraps did

[24] Russell Hamm, Lauren Pinkus, Amanda Wilkins, and Maria Town, "The Impact of Web-Based Game Play on Soft Skills Education," Department of Labor, accessed February 3, 2018, https://www.dol.gov/odep/documents/Soft%20Skills%20Fact%20Sheet%20Fina17%2015_508%20compliant.pdf.

[25] Isabela Granic, Adam Lobel, and Rutger CME Engels, "The Benefits of Playing Video Games," *American Psychologist* 69: 1 (2014): 66–78; Sacip Toker and Meltem Huri Baturay, "Antecedents and Consequences of Game Addiction," *Computers in Human Behavior* 55 (Part B) (2016): 668–679.

[26] Dina H. Bassiouni and Chris Hackley, "Generation Z Children's Adaptation to Digital Consumer Culture: A Critical Literature Review," *Journal of Customer Behaviour* 13, no. 2 (2014): 113–133.

not exist as a food-service category until a decade ago. Changing social trends led to this new category as very busy families sought a way to find food they could eat in their cars without making a mess. Similarly, a recent concept is the weekly family meal preparation and delivery service like Blue Apron, Plated, and HelloFresh. These services ship to people's homes a week's worth of meals with the fresh ingredients pre-portioned and ready for assembly and cooking. They claim close partnerships with farmers to get high-quality ingredients and special menus developed by their skilled chefs. Their target market is busy families who want to prepare meals at home but without the time-consuming inconvenience of gathering the ingredients, prepping, or menu planning. Other families not interested in making their own meals can use home delivery of restaurant meals though such services as UberEats, Doordash, and Grubhub.

Some changing expectations are expressed through trade associations that monitor social trends and their impacts on the industry. Others wind up in the political process and result in new laws, rules, or regulations. An example is the emergence of Uber and Lyft as alternatives to taxis. The local people transportation business was primarily the domain of taxi companies until the arrival of ride sharing companies like Uber. This innovation in ride sharing disrupted the local laws and legislation governing the taxi industry and caused significant concerns by these regulated companies in the face of this new and largely unregulated competition.[27] While the final resolution of these concerns remains unclear as local governments continue to sort out the implications of this innovation on laws and regulations, the reality is that people desiring temporary transportation have new options that were unavailable before the invention of ride sharing technology. A second example is Airbnb, which is being challenged by the traditional hotel associations as short term housing requiring application of the same rules and regulations as they face.

Legislation impacts the way in which hospitality organizations operate, and so do nongovernmental organizations (NGOs) and interest groups. Because they are so dependent on maintaining a good relationship with the public, hospitality organizations are especially vulnerable to protests or demonstrations by interest groups that object to management policies or business decisions. If a hospitality organization has any thoughts of building a major facility in a historically significant area, it can expect that groups wanting to preserve the area in its present state will generate negative publicity. Even if constructing the facility is a good business decision, public opposition may make it a bad customer-relations decision. Any hospitality organization dependent on a broad customer base has a real challenge when every action it takes is so visible to its guests.

Technology

Technology

Several developments other than the population trends that are changing the workforce and customer base will affect the strategies of hospitality organizations. Dramatic changes in technology will continue to have a major influence on both organizations and the industry. While many demographic trends shift slowly, changes in technology, especially information technology, occur rapidly, and so they and their impact are difficult to forecast.

The communications and computing power now found in a handheld device were unthinkable only ten years ago. Today, anyone with a smartphone can search (or ask their personal artificial intelligence (AI) assistant to search) for the lowest airfare to a destination, make a plane reservation, book a hotel room, reserve a rental car, get recommendations on a destination from other travelers, or even take a virtual tour of a hotel, theme park, or destination, all at the same time they are talking. Yesterday's comic-strip fantasy was Dick Tracy's two-way wrist radio. Today, anyone with an Apple Watch can answer calls, search with Siri, stream music, track fitness, or

[27] Scott S. McCartney, "The Uber Airport Rules," *Wall Street Journal*, July 7, 2016, https://www.wsj.com/articles/you-cant-take-an-uber-home-from-these-airports-1467829592.

check in for a flight. The implications of fifth-generation technology and the Internet of Things capabilities for travel agents, hotels controlling their room inventory, and other existing—and yet to be created—parts of the travel, tourism, and other hospitality markets are enormous.[28] The rapid growth of cloud computing, which relies entirely on the internet to access both programs and data files, allows unforeseen opportunities for information sharing, collaboration, and networking by people across the globe.

On the other hand, the ever-present smartphones have been found to be a distraction that disrupts task concentration, problem solving, and the application of thoughtful brainpower.[29] Moreover, the constant availability of many online "friends" sharing their life's details tends to make our face to face conversations shallower and less satisfying and impact our personal relationships in other ways as well. Research shows smartphones inhibit the development of interpersonal closeness and trust and diminishes the extent to which the user feels empathy and understanding from their partners. Finally, there is evidence that smartphones may make us dumber as we tend to not bother to learn things when we know they can be instantly Googled. Researchers have called this the "Google effect." The problem this creates for hospitality organizations seeking to hire them as employees or entice them as customers is that the more Generation Ys and Millennials are willing to offload their store of knowledge to the web, the less likely it is that they are able to make the associations between things they know to things they don't to handle new situations, ideas, and tasks.

Other aspects of technological change will be equally important to managing the hospitality organization. The need to blend innovative high-tech solutions into high-touch service situations will be increasingly recognized as a competitive strategy and, when done successfully, rewarded in the marketplace. Hotels, restaurants, and other guest service organizations will find new ways to substitute technology for people, to reduce their dependence on this expensive and increasingly scarce resource. At the same time, these same organizations will need to find ways to maintain the high level of personal contact that defines a memorable guest experience. The challenge is to substitute technology for labor in ways the guest perceives as either a positive increase in service quality and value or does not perceive at all. One restaurant in the Netherlands has a robot that scales a 26-foot-high bar to tap bottles of homemade gin, whiskey, and limoncello so that bartenders don't have to climb ladders. In Japan these collaborative robots, known as cobots, place takeout dumplings in boxes. Because cobots use AI to complement the work of the employees, they offer new ways to complement employees' task performance that save labor costs while adding time to employees to provide more of the valued human touch.[30] The potential of robots is one way to deliver quality service with a person-like machine while the potential of virtual reality will change how conferences, trade shows, and conventions are produced in yet unforeseen ways.[31]

Self check-in at hotels or airports is an example of technology with which guests have become

VCG/VCG via Getty Images

This restaurant with robot servers shows just one way that changing technology can affect the hospitality industry.

[28] Ulrike Gretzel, Marianna Sigala, Zheng Xiang, and Chulmo Koo, "Smart Tourism: Foundations and Developments," *Electronic Markets* 25, no. 3 (2015): 179–188.

[29] Nicholas Carr, "How Smartphones Hijack Our Minds," *Wall Street Journal*, October 7–8, (2017): C1–2.

[30] Natasha Khan, "Robots Shift from Factories to New Jobs," *Wall Street Journal*, June 11, (2018): B4.

[31] Carole B. Sox, Sheryl F. Kline, and Tena B. Crews, "Identifying Best Practices, Opportunities and Barriers in Meeting Planning for Generation Y," *International Journal of Hospitality Management* 36 (2014): 244–254.

comfortable. While most luxury hotels still check in guests wanting this personal service, they also offer the technology for those who prefer the convenience of checking in themselves. Self check-in is more convenient for those comfortable with the technology, usually takes less time, and is considerably cheaper for the hotel than staffing up to check in guests manually. For some people, the substitution with technology can increase their perception of service quality and value. In contrast, others may want to have a person to talk to and check them in. For these guests, technology decreases their perception of service quality and value rendered by the organization. The point is that some guests like technology and some do not. It is the task of the guestologist to find ways to use technology when it meets guests' needs and not use it when it does not.

Sustainability

Ecology

green movement
A diverse set of political, scientific, and social movements advocating for sustainable management of resources and addressing issues of climate change.

Perhaps no movement has received more attention recently than the **green movement**. Not only has it become a national priority, but it has been the subject of industry initiatives across hospitality. Some states, for example, Florida, offer green certification for hotels that implement environmentally friendly practices. Other organizations across the globe have developed green certification programs, such as GreenGlobe, Europe's Green Tourism, and the USA's Green Seal. There is even a Green Hotel Association, which includes many members of the leading hotel chains.[32] Healthy Stays has a website (environmentallyfriendlyhotels.com) where customers can find lodging that matches their commitment to environmental actions.[33] Being green can involve a wide range of practices (see Exhibit 2.4). Some hotels only employ basic environmental practices (e.g., a linen reuse program, greater recycling, lower energy consuming light fixtures and appliances), but others employ much more intensive and sophisticated practices. One hotel, for example, offers a bar of "Waste Reducing Exfoliating Body Cleanser" that has a hole in the middle as its green replacement for the traditional soap bar. Its box proclaims, "This innovative ergo-nomically shaped 'waste reducing' soap has been designed to eliminate the unused center of traditional soap bars. This soap is cruelty free and contains no animal fat or byproducts. The carton is made from recycled packaging and printed with soy-based inks." Whether this is motivated by a cost savings or a sincere commitment to the environment is immaterial as this represents a way to provide a win-win solution to an environmental issue. The hotel saves money by spending less on soap while the environment is spared the effects of producing a bar of soap that is only partially used before disposal.

Most "green" programs seek to do both to encourage hotels to engage in environmentally beneficial activities. Their requirements are attempts to have hotels do well while doing good. Thus, when a Hyatt or Marriott saves one shift of laundry workers plus the soap, water, and electricity by not cleaning sheets and towels for those guests in stay-over rooms, it is doing both. Likewise, when resorts offer carbon-neutral vacations, they are trying to appeal to customers who are increasingly demanding this increased level of environmental sensitivity while still making a profit. The Playa Nicuesa Rainforest Lodge in Costa Rica, for example, states on its website that it lives in "harmony with nature" through its eco-friendly policies. Playa Nicuesa is located on a 165-acre preserve within the lush rainforest of the Piedras Blancas National Park.[34] It also fronts the pristine Pacific coastline of the Golfo Dulce in the undeveloped Osa Peninsula/Golfo Dulce region of Southern Costa Rica. Besides claiming a carbon neutral operation, they advertise, "We provide intimate experiences to connect with the natural world of the rainforest and

---

[32] Mark Scott Rosenbaum and Ipkin Anthony Wong, "Green Marketing Programs as Strategic Initiatives in Hospitality," *Journal of Services Marketing* 29, no. 2 (2015): 81–92.

[33] Brigitte Prud'homme and Louis Raymon, "Implementation of Sustainable Development Practices in the Hospitality Industry: A Case Study of Five Canadian Hotels," *International Journal of Contemporary Hospitality Management* 28, no. 3 (2016): 609–639.

[34] Playa Nicuesa Rainforest Lodge, "Sustainability: Eco-friendly Lodge Near Puerto Jimenez, Costa Rica," Nicuesa Lodge, accessed February 3, 2018, https://www.nicuesalodge.com/sustainability.aspx.

EXHIBIT 2.4

Examples of Environmental Best Practices for a Hotel

Fundamentals

- Install insulated windows to reduce heating and cooling costs.
- Monitor electric, gas, water, and waste usage on a monthly and annual basis.
- Use ENERGY STAR certified appliances, equipment, and light fixtures
- Install low-flow toilets, urinals, sinks, and showers.
- Implement a towel and linen reuse program.
- Implement a recycling program for guest waste, electronics, and light bulbs.
- Order in bulk, where feasible, to reduce packaging waste.
- Donate overproduced food, compost food waste, and recycle used vegetable oil.
- Change menu seasonally in accordance with regionally fresh foods.
- Develop and implement an environmentally conscious purchasing plan from sustainable sources.
- Recycle and donate unused guest room amenities.
- Utilize environmentally friendly cleaning products.
- Develop, document, and implement a preventative maintenance program.

Next Steps

- Form an Environmental Committee responsible for developing policies to improve sustainability and reduce environmental impact.
- Use renewable energy where possible.
- Use smart thermostats to adjust rooms' temperatures according to season, time, and occupancy.
- Landscape with native or drought-tolerant plants.
- Ensure that all disposable cups, plates, and utensils are biodegradable.

Innovations

- Reclaim greywater (outflow from sources other than toilets, such as washing machines) for non-drinking use, such as flushing toilets and watering landscapes
- Conduct environmental benchmarking: compare hotel energy and resource consumption to one's competitive set; tie compensation to environmental performance
- Consider a rooftop garden to regulate temperature and provide local (and marketable!) produce for an in-house kitchen.

ocean through educational and adventure activities while adhering to the highest level of sustainable hospitality. . . . We strive to offer luxury service in an authentic, sustainable and pristine location. Designed in balance with the land, Playa Nicuesa Rainforest Lodge is truly sustainable from its architectural design to every aspect of your experience. Our Sustainability Coordinator ensures that we honor the environment while staying dedicated to the guest experience."[35]

Hotels and luxury lodges are not the only segments of the hospitality industry interested in the environment. The National Restaurant Association has developed an environment program called Conserve/EPA Energy Star Challenge, and the Destination Marketing Association International has included it in their accreditation process. Greening of hospitality is a big issue today and will only become more so in the future as more stakeholders and customers show their concern for the devastation of the rain forest, the melting of the glaciers, and the changes in the earth's environment. Even tourism destinations like Iceland and Venice, Italy, are having discussions among their stakeholders as to the extent to which these places can sustain the volume of tourists now visiting. The issue of **sustainability** is a politically sensitive conversation in many destinations from the Great Barrier Reef, Australia, to Machu Picchu, Peru, where local environmental groups are confronting the tourism interests over how much the natural attraction can be visited without damage to

sustainability The use of resources in a way that protects the future environment and the ability of future generations to meet their own needs.

[35] Playa Nicuesa Rainforest Lodge.

the ecosystem, native culture, infrastructure, or the attraction itself. Even the Great Wall in China can only survive a finite number of feet wearing on it.

At a minimum, those engaged in strategic planning should try to stay aware of shifting social expectations. Including input from social groups can sometimes enhance the strategic planning process greatly. When planning began for Disney's Animal Kingdom theme park, the organization invited representatives of environmental and animal-rights groups to help in the development process. By working with them, Disney was able to develop a park consistent with the environmentalists' ideals. Similarly, as noted earlier, because of increased attention to health issues and particular concerns about obesity, Darden Restaurants posts nutrition information for its restaurants (e.g., Olive Garden, Yard House, Long Horn Steakhouse) online. Although some states are passing laws to require this action, Darden took the lead in making this information available to its consumers and even helped lobby for the passage of such legislation. Restaurants need to keep pace with more than just changing customers' preferences for food; they must also monitor broader trends that influence consumer behaviors. When guests can use a smartphone app to locate which restaurants offer the healthiest meals, those restaurants seeking to attract this market segment might be proactive and offer that information to all guests to signal they care about nutritional concerns.

The Industry Environment

Besides the changes in the overall environment that impact everyone, there are industry specific factors that must be anticipated and forecast as well. This includes changing competitors, both for the specific service product and for substitutes for that product. Convention centers must spend time not only forecasting the impact that other convention providers' capacity and marketing plans will have on their own demand patterns but also the impact online virtual meetings will have on demand for all convention space. Changes in other resource providers—such as for products, labor, and capital—should also be included in the planning cycle. From fish to workers to money, the market will allocate resources to their best and most profitable use. Hospitality organizations must forecast their ability to obtain these resources in the marketplace and have a plan to assure their continuing availability.

Changing Competitors

An organization has existing competitors, potential competitors, and indirect competitors that offer customers a substitute or alternative service either next door or online. These competitors can be local, national, international, or even virtual.

Existing competitors have an established position in your market niche. If you are a small corner restaurant, your competitors are all those other restaurants in the same market area. Since most people go to restaurants within a short drive from their home, these competitors are easy to identify. Potential competitors are those who are likely to enter your market area. The sign may be up, the building begun, and the "buy one, get one free" coupons distributed, to mark the existence of a potential competitor to your restaurant. The alternative or indirect competitors include anyone who sells food. They can range from Weight Watchers, which provides its own branded food products to dieters, to the local grocery store, to a food-delivery service. Anyone who can fill the same basic need with an alternative product may be an indirect industry competitor but is still a direct competitor for your customers' business.

In the theme park industry, a competitor is not only anyone that can offer a more attractive use for a guest's funds in the destination but is also anyone who can encourage customers to spend their leisure dollars at some destination besides yours. Because Orlando visitors and locals can spend money in a wide variety of alternative ways, Orlando theme parks are especially sensitive to this competitive market reality.

And, of course, people can choose not to come to or stay in Orlando at all; the over 8 million annual visitors the parks depend on can go to competitive attractions at other destinations, like Las Vegas, Spain, or London. The Orlando competition includes other theme parks, dinner theaters, civic museums, art galleries, factory-outlet stores, or even a trip to the beach. It even includes noncustomers who stay away from parks entirely and watch videos at home or in a motel room. The guestologist tries to find out how guests in the organization's target market—those who come, those who don't come, and those who don't come back—want to spend their time and money and, ideally, provides desired options rather than letting customers go to competitors.

Changes in Other Relevant Groups

In addition to the various factors and groups we have already discussed, several other groups in the organization's external environment must be included in any environmental forecast: the suppliers of resources and raw material, capital, and labor.

Resource Suppliers. When Red Lobster adds a new seafood item to its menu, it must first check to be sure the demand for it doesn't exhaust the world's supply of that item. Because Red Lobster has so many restaurants, adding or removing a menu item can have a major impact on the supply of that product. If a certain type of shrimp now retails for $9.99 per pound, how much will the price change if Red Lobster buys up half of the world's supply next year? Obviously, the planning process needs to take such supply-related issues into consideration.

Luke Sharrett/Bloomberg via Getty Images

When a restaurant like Red Lobster adds a new seafood item to its menu, it must first make sure that its demand for the product can be satisfied by the current world supply.

Capital Suppliers. A second major interested group is the suppliers of capital. As the capital market has become more global and electronic transfers make movement of capital easier and quicker, the organization may need to spend more time forecasting the availability and cost of capital for its business and industry. If capital availability is driven by the next quarter's financial report, the impact on the organization's decision-making and planning horizon will be considerable. If Wall Street investors demand a certain short-run return on investment, finding the extra resources to develop a new service or to take a chance on a new concept or location may be difficult. The airline industry undergoes a periodic devaluation of its stock prices as the capital market expresses its opinion about the industry's overcapacity problems and how much it will cost to fix them. No matter how good a strategy an organization has, if it can't convince the capital market or if the capital market is unwilling to take the risk, the strategy may be worthless.

The Labor Market. A third supplier of a crucial resource is the labor market. An organization needs the right number of employees, with the right skills, hired at the right cost, in order to deliver its service product successfully. The availability of labor depends on many factors, including the demographics of the relevant labor market, the extent to which the company can recruit enough qualified applicants, the wages paid by the company and its competitors, the KSAs needed to perform the required work, and the extent to which the company is willing and able to train employees in necessary roles. As an organization considers how it will implement its service strategy, it must consider very carefully how it will staff, develop, and motivate employees to fulfill the organization's goals. These issues—staffing, developing, and motivating employees—are so critical that we devote Chapter 5 (Staffing for Service), Chapter 6 (Training and Developing Employees to Serve) and Chapter 7 (Serving with a Smile: Motivating Exceptional Service) to these topics.

The Operating Environment

Changes in the overall environment and the industry impact how the company will compete in the future. These changes affect the fundamental assumptions the organization will make about the future, how it will anticipate changes to its competitive environment, and the potential for surprises that may be major disruptors to the organization and industry.

Hospitality organizations must consider carefully the major aspects of its operating environment in order to be as prepared as possible for its future.

Strategic Premises

strategic premises
Assumptions about the future, based on the results of forecasting, on which the organization's strategic plan is based or premised.

The hospitality organization draws conclusions about the future of its industry and market from its environmental assessment, and then uses this information to make the assumptions, called **strategic premises**, on which its service strategy is based. Strategic premises are educated guesses. The organization's planners may guess wrong; even if they guess right, they may devise the wrong strategy or implement it in an ineffective way. But choosing to do nothing is also a strategy and not to guess at all means reacting day to day to whatever seems to be going on, without a plan or a focus for organizational activities.

Dave Thomas, founder of Wendy's, told how his environmental assessment led to certain premises on which Wendy's corporate strategy was based. When creating his new restaurant in 1969, he identified five trends he thought offered him a market opportunity he had the competence to meet:[36]

1. *People wanted choices.* They were tired of living in a prepackaged world; they wanted some influence over the products they were buying in the marketplace, and they wanted something new.
2. *People were fed up with poor quality.* He saw a big interest in things that were fresh and natural.
3. *People were trying to adjust to a newer, more complicated way of life.* Older people were looking for relief from the many social and political changes occurring during the 1960s, and young people were looking for changes they could handle. Thomas notes, "In a funny way, the old-fashioned decor and the Tiffany lamps provided a novelty for the young adults and nostalgia for the older generation at the same time."
4. *People were on the move.* Any business had to accommodate this restless mobility.
5. *People were ready for an upscale hamburger place.* He felt many people had grown up loving hamburgers, but were not satisfied with the product generally available at fast-food outlets.

Thomas wrote, "Knowing these five trends allowed Wendy's to focus on the right market. My bet is that if you looked at any successful business, you would find factors very much like these behind the business's success. If you're going to bet your bankroll on a business concept, you had better be able to understand those forces.

[36] R. David Thomas, *Dave's Way* (New York, NY: Berkley, 1992), 94.

If you can't describe them, you had better feel them so clearly in your gut that you know you're right."[37]

The recent development of fine-casual or fast-fine dining restaurants shows a successful application of Thomas's trends. Two New York–based award-winning chefs, Will Guidara and Daniel Humm, decided there was a market for fine dining quality food that was served quickly and competitively priced with fast-casual restaurants like Panera and Chipotle, and invented Made Nice to fill that niche. It offers mobile people on the move quality choices. At fast-fine restaurants, you get a made to order, proper meal that allows you to sit down to eat it and then get back to work.[38]

Predicting the Competitive Environment

Changes in the overall environment, the industry, as well as in assumptions made about the operating environment will have varying effects on how the organization competes in the future. But not all factors are equal in either their impact on the organization or in terms of our ability to forecast them fully. Some are predictable and simple, such as the estimated number of teenagers available for work in ten years. Since they have all been born already, predicting the number available in ten years is a straightforward calculation. Some other factors are simple but unpredictable. Using demographics again, estimating the number of skilled and trained employees who will be available in Pocatello, Idaho, in twenty years is a simple number to calculate, but the calculations rest on unpredictable information such as unknown changes in family formation, net migration into southwestern Idaho, local economic changes, and other factors.

As was true of simple future elements, complex future elements are either predictable or unpredictable. Once a certain number of people are in a destination market, a relatively predictable percentage will come to any given tourist attraction on any given day. Calculating the number of people who will be in the market, however, is a complex process; it depends on airline routes and fares, propensity to travel by people all over the world, the price of gasoline, foreign exchange rates, the threat of terrorism, the level of economic activity, consumer confidence, availability of and cost involved in other more attractive destinations, and a variety of other factors.

Technology

The complex and unpredictable outcomes are, of course, the hardest to forecast. An example would be changes in technology. If technology develops to the point that the experience of going to a major attraction or a conference can be duplicated through virtual reality, then people won't have to go through the trouble and expense of coming to the site of the attraction or conference to rent cars, stay in hotels, and buy admissions. As this technology becomes reality, the entire area surrounding the attraction or destination will suffer a severe economic decline. Predicting what economic impact a new technology can have is a major challenge for both hospitality and civic forecasters. The web enabled sharing economy innovations like Airbnb and Uber are only the beginning examples of capacity sharing services. Likewise, major political policy changes can have major impacts on hospitality organizations such as a reduction of guest worker visas making it hard to get summer help on Cape Cod or increases in minimum wages that influence the hiring decisions of a local restaurant.

Some forecasts are easy, because the elements comprising them (which are themselves forecasts) are predictable and the calculations simple, and others are difficult. Guestologists must try to make the forecasts relevant to their organization's future, regardless of ease or difficulty, and include them in their strategic planning processes. Since things that can be counted are often more comfortable to deal with than those that can't, managers are sometimes tempted to emphasize those factors that are numerical while ignoring those that cannot be easily measured.

[37] R. David Thomas, p. 94.

[38] Jane Black, "A Grown-Up Guide to Fast-Fine," *Wall Street Journal*, June 11, 2017. https://www.wsj.com/articles/a-grown-ups-guide-to-fast-fine-Dining-1496923201.

Unfortunately for those managers, in real life the crucial factors are usually those to which we can't apply numbers.

Surprises

The final external issue to address in this long look around at the environment is the potential for surprises. While one cannot often predict real estate or financial market crashes, terrorist attacks, political movements, wars, or natural disasters, thoughtful planners consider these possibilities. Preparing for such events means having a plan in place to deal with the immediate consequences (such as on the day of the disaster) and the longer-term implications.

Many "unique" disasters have certain commonalities: loss of power, inability of guests to leave while new guests are arriving, failure of communication networks, fear on the part of both guests and staff, and so forth. Although specific events cannot be predicted, the better companies are well prepared when some sort of disaster occurs.[39] This involves having a plan for where guests will go or stay, what to do with food in the refrigerators without power or knowing how long the generators will last, what circuits are connected to them, and so forth. A well-thought-out disaster preparedness plan can help make sure employees know how to respond should some unforeseen event occur. Two 2017 hurricanes, Irma and Maria, caused incredible devastation on the Caribbean islands of Puerto Rico and the Virgin Islands, and other destinations that depend heavily on tourism for sustaining their economies, jobs for their residents, and their way of life. While devastation of this magnitude is beyond most individual organizations' planning model, a disaster plan developed by a specific hotel or resort could alleviate some of the storm-related issues faced by its guests, employees, and physical plant. Prepositioning supplies, generators, and communication devices, for example, enabled those organizations that planned for disasters to provide for guests and employees until local power and distribution channels could be restored.

As for longer-term implications, hospitality organizations should consider how surprises can affect overall demand for their service product. If most customers have to drive long distances to get to your service setting, your planners should keep in mind the gas supply problems that intensifying instability in the chief oil-producing nations might create. If your airline serves or your hotel chain is located in an area that seems liable to be a target for terrorist attacks, you need to have a contingency plan. While the terrorist attack of 9/11 may seem like a distant historical event now, continuing terrorist attacks on places where tourists tend to cluster still impact the hospitality industry. Conventions still struggle with attendees' reluctance to fly in the face of the time-consuming ordeal the Transportation Security Administration (TSA) has introduced to flying as a response to terror threats. Cruise lines face the additional inconvenience of enforcing new passport requirements, and destinations dependent upon international travelers suffer from the latter's unwillingness to endure the new security procedures and travel bans for those seeking to enter the United States. While hoping and planning for the best, strategic planners must realize that any number of unpredictable future events can have a severe impact on how many customers want or need the service the organization offers and plan for them.

ASSESSING THE ORGANIZATION ITSELF: THE INTERNAL ASSESSMENT

On the right side of our planning model shown in Exhibit 2.2, opposite the long look around, external assessment, is internal assessment, the searching look

[39] Judith Mair, Brent W. Ritchie, and Gabby Walters, "Towards a Research Agenda for Post-Disaster and Post-Crisis Recovery Strategies for Tourist Destinations: A Narrative Review," *Current Issues in Tourism* 19, no. 1 (2016): 1-26; Yawei Jiang, and Brent W. Ritchie, "Disaster Collaboration in Tourism: Motives, Impediments and Success Factors," *Journal of Hospitality and Tourism Management* 31, (2017): 70-82.

within. The hospitality organization cannot plan with any confidence until it admits its weaknesses and identifies its central strengths, frequently termed its core competencies.

Core Competencies

The definition given by management strategists Hamel and Prahalad is helpful: An organization's **core competence** is the bundle of skills and technologies that gives the organization an important difference in providing customer benefits and perceived value.[40] Ford's core competence is the ability to make cars. The core competence of Marriott is the ability to manage excellent lodging facilities. Southwest's core competence is to have efficient operations while maintaining superior customer service. Knowing its areas of competence will enable an organization to make a key strategic decision: What should we not do because we don't have the competence?

core competence A specific factor or characteristic that a business sees as being a key strength for how it provides its service product.

If a company has proven it has the ability and technology to combine the merchandising of consumer goods, entertainment, and an eating experience in a striking setting, then it can do what Rainforest Cafe and most other theme restaurants have done: Seek to expand the variety of consumer goods it sells alongside its restaurant operations. In contrast, while Darden's core competencies include its ability to effectively manage its supply chain and restaurant operations, it does not have a core competency in the area of information technology. As a result, Darden outsources its IT system because it decided that IT was not part of its core competence and it did not believe that allocating resources to acquire that competence should be part of its strategy. The point is that every successful organization has developed a core competence, an ability to do something very well. As long as it sticks to activities appropriate to that core competence, it will probably continue to succeed. When it strays from its core competence, it may find itself pitting its weaknesses against the strengths of other organizations.

This is why many organizations seek to outsource activities and functions they believe are not their core competence to another organization that has a core competence in those activities and functions. Forming strategic alliances with these organizations allows that outsourcing organization to gain the competence of another organization instead of trying to do everything itself. An airline, for example, will outsource its fueling function to another organization so it can retain its focus on those things that are core to its business and let others handle those things that are not core. Schools and universities outsource their food service to Aramark or Sodexo so they can focus on the academic issues that are core to their mission.

The internal assessment tells the hospitality organization where it stands now, what new strengths it must develop, and what weaknesses it must eliminate to build the core competence it will need to succeed in the future industry it foresees. If an organization accurately perceives itself to be the dominant force in entertainment and foresees the future of entertainment in electronic media, then that company should probably set its sights on dominating any electronic medium that develops and delivers entertainment. Such reasoning is, of course, what made Wall Street applaud Disney when it bought Pixar. For Disney, the fit with its core competence and industry vision was perfect. Pixar had successfully used computers to replace hand-drawn animation, which most, including Disney, had not thought possible. The purchase of Pixar represented a capitulation of Disney's commitment to hand-drawn animation as the future of entertainment in this electronic medium. The success of *Toy Story, Finding Nemo,* and *Coco* proved the value of digital animation. Rarely do the internal and external audits lead to such dramatic changes in strategy.

Technology

[40] Hamel and Prahalad, *Competing for the Future*, 221–222.

Internal Assets

An internal assessment includes an assessment of all the organization's internal assets. Each organization has a reputation, a pool of human capital (its employees), managerial capabilities, material resources, culture, and competitive advantages based on its technology. It also possesses patents, brand names, copyrights, and customer loyalty, all of which help define its core competencies.

The Ritz-Carlton, for example, is generally considered to be one of the world's most able lodging organizations. It knows what it should do to sustain its core competence of providing service excellence in the lodging field. It has a unique, well-established, loyal customer base, a committed pool of employees, strong culture, well-trained management, a strong brand image, and a well-maintained capital base. In an assessment of its own internal strengths and weaknesses, The Ritz-Carlton builds upon its core abilities—by not only acknowledging them as an organizational strength but also incorporating its gold standard into its business plan as a marketable product, to be shared with others through seminars offered at the Ritz-Carlton Leadership Center on how to manage for service excellence.[41]

Likewise, Darden Restaurants understands that one role of planning based on a knowledge of core competencies is to seek business areas the organization should be in and avoid or exit those it should not. When a company perceives it has reached a critical point in penetrating a market segment, it seeks new segments to satisfy customers or new ways to expand its reach or penetration of its current market segment. If a company achieves great success and finds itself with a lot of available cash, as Darden did with the success of Olive Garden and Red Lobster, it is tempted to try new lines of business because it can afford to, and its shareholders expect it to grow. What Darden did was to open Bahama Breeze, Smokey Bones, and Seasons 52, as well as later buy Longhorn Steakhouse and The Capital Grille to expand its penetration of its existing markets. On the other hand, it exited Smokey Bones when its planners determined a sports bar did not fit its core competence of running casual-dining restaurants. As other aspects of the environment and its competitive situation changed, Darden continued to make strategic choices, such as selling Red Lobster and being able to use the cash that such a sale generated to focus on other business needs.

Alternatively, Hilton Worldwide decided to capitalize on its name and core abilities by providing a comprehensive array of service products for the lodging market. This includes timeshares (Hilton Grand Vacations), midscale/select service (Hampton by Hilton, Home2 Suites by Hilton, and Tru by Hilton), upscale (Canopy by Hilton, DoubleTree by Hilton, Hilton Garden Inn, and Homewood Suites by Hilton), upper upscale (Hilton Hotels & Resorts, Curio Collection by Hilton, Embassy Suites by Hilton, Tapestry Collection by Hilton) and luxury (Waldorf Astoria Hotels & Resorts, Conrad Hotel & Resorts). Being a successful multi-brand company requires having the right mix of brands that meet customer demands but also complement each other by facilitating the recollection of the overall organization and affiliated products. Hilton Worldwide wants customers to be comfortable at any of their brands because the name "Hilton" conveys a level of quality and service no matter what the specific hotel. But the various brands also capture different market segments, so that Hilton Worldwide can capture a broad array of the hospitality marketplace.

An unsatisfactory bottom line will motivate a company to take a searching look within. For years, McDonald's focused on selling hamburgers. Falling

Courtesy of Hilton Worldwide

Hilton Worldwide has created 14 brands to appeal to a variety of market niches at a range of price points.

[41] Joseph Michelli, *The New Gold Standard: 5 Leadership Principles for Creating a Legendary Customer Experience Courtesy of the Ritz-Carlton Hotel* Company (New York, NY: McGraw Hill Professional, 2008).

sales and the public's obvious desire for healthier foods convinced the company it had to change the way it executed its core competence: making and selling hamburgers quickly. The company tried to expand its target market to include those customers choosing Starbucks and Panera by offering new menu items and premium coffee. Its falling sales and market research discovered this strategy wasn't working and the customers it lost were not those going to Starbucks or quick-casual competitors but to other fast food restaurants seeking lower priced meals. It changed its strategy in 2017 to lower prices and offering freshly prepared meals. In an experiment in Dallas it offered freshly made quarter pounders to discover whether customers will trade fresh for fast as the made to order quarter pounder takes a minute longer to prepare. With McDonald's drive through times generally slower than many of its competitors already, the further delay of cook to order burgers created additional concerns over customer service time. In the fast food market that extra time can seem like an eternity. Early results have been encouraging with the Dallas test market reporting an increase in sales by 20% to 50%.[42]

VISION AND MISSION STATEMENTS

Exhibit 2.2 shows that a vision statement and mission statement are key parts of the hospitality planning process. Most organizations spend a great deal of time trying to articulate these concepts, and the reason is clear: If you (and your employees) don't know what you want to do, how can you (and they) decide how to do it? Most companies wind up writing mission and vision statements—and other statements such as credos, beliefs, and values—but not all need to. Often, smaller organizations have leaders who know what they are doing and where they are heading without writing it down. Vision and mission statements vary from the simple to the complex, but in general, the simpler the better.

The Vision Statement

A **vision statement** articulates what the organization hopes to look like and be like in the future. Rather than presenting specific principles, goals, and objectives, the vision presents hopes and dreams; it creates a picture toward which the organization aspires; it provides inspiration for the journey ahead. It depicts what the organization hopes to become, not what the organization needs to do to get there. The vision statement is used to unite and inspire employees to achieve the common ideal and to define for external stakeholders what the organization seeks to accomplish. As examples, Hilton Hotels' vision is "To fill the earth with the light and warmth of hospitality—by delivering exceptional experiences—every hotel, every guest, every time," and Visit Orlando's vision is "To be the most visited travel destination in the world."

vision statement An articulation of what the organization hopes to look like and be like in the future.

Though mission and vision are to an extent overlapping terms, the vision is the really big picture of hopes for the future. Hamel and Prahalad call this vision definition the "quest for industry foresight," as the organization defines what its future could be and works backward to what it must do today to make that future happen. The creative imagination of management and the entire organization needs to be focused on articulating the vision and how to achieve it. Hamel and Prahalad describe the difficulties involved in getting from here to there, from today to tomorrow:

> Although potentially useful, technology forecasting, market research, scenario planning, and competitor analysis won't necessarily yield industry foresight.

[42] Julie Jargon, "McDonald's Sales Show Improvement," *Wall Street Journal*, July 26, 2017, https://www.wsj.com/articles/mcdonalds-profit-rises-refranchising-drive-dents-revenue-1508851452.

> None of these tools compels senior management to preconceive the corporation and the industries in which it competes. Only by changing the lens through which the corporation is viewed (looking at core competencies versus focusing on only strategic business units), only by changing the lens through which markets are viewed (functionalities versus products), only by broadening the angle of the lens (becoming more inquisitive), only by cleaning off the accumulated grime on the lens (seeing with a child's eyes), and only by occasionally disbelieving what one sees (challenging price-performance conventions, thinking like a contrarian) can the future be anticipated. The quest for industry foresight is the quest to visceralize what doesn't yet exist.... Having imagined the future, a company must find a path that leads from today to tomorrow.[43]

This ability to imagine a future market opportunity that is currently unpopulated with competitors is the focus of a term called blue ocean strategy.[44] This is the idea that the truly innovative organizations seek new market spaces that allow them to operate in a wide-open ocean of opportunity because there is no existing competition or there is nothing like it in the marketplace. An example should make this strategy clear. Cirque du Soleil is neither a circus nor a theatrical show but is instead a combination of the two that is unlike anything that has ever been seen before. By eliminating the costs of a circus and embracing the entertainment focus of a themed theatrical show, Cirque du Soleil made something entirely new. It found a blue ocean opportunity that has been very successful.

Sometimes an organization is created to fulfill a personal vision. Walt Disney wanted to build his theme park, Disneyland, so badly he was willing to borrow against his insurance policy to begin it. He had a vision to fulfill. Selling others on the same vision was a difficult challenge. After all, who else could imagine a theme park built on 182 acres of citrus grove in the middle of then-undeveloped Anaheim, California? The park would wind up costing $17 million to build, far exceeding the original estimates. While Disneyland was a visionary project, it pales in comparison with the vision required to conceive a Walt Disney World Resort and bring the park into being. Disney bought nearly 28,000 acres, mostly citrus groves, near the quiet town of Orlando, Florida, on which to build his dream. It included not only an expanded version of his Disneyland theme park but also hotels, restaurants, and even Epcot, the city of the future. Epcot was originally envisioned as a complete, self-contained city with its own schools, apartments, and shopping facilities. The development of the Celebration community brought to fruition this final part of Walt Disney's grand vision.[45]

The Mission Statement

mission statement
An articulation of the organization's purpose, the reason for which it was founded and for which it continues to exist.

An organization's **mission statement** articulates the organization's purpose, the reason for which it was founded and for which it continues to exist. The mission statement defines the path to the vision, given the strategic premises and the organization's core competencies. The mission statement is a guide to defining the how, what, who, and where for the organization's overall service strategy that in turn drives the design of the service product, service environment, and service delivery system. These definitions form the basis for all of the other steps and decisions that put resources in place to fulfill those plans.

The mission statement should guide managers as they allocate resources, focus organizational marketing efforts, and define for all employees how they should deal

[43] Hamel and Prahalad, *Competing for the Future*, 114–115.

[44] W. Chan Kim and Renée Mauborgne, *Blue Ocean Shift: Beyond Competing—Proven Steps To Inspire Confidence and Seize New Growth* (Boston, MA: Hachette Books 2017).

[45] Brian J. Robb, *A Brief History of Disney* (London: Little, Brown Book Company, 2014).

with guests and customers. A typical mission statement will include, at a minimum, the following three elements:

1. What you do (What is the product or service you are providing to the customer?),
2. Who you do it for (Who is the targeted customer?),
3. How or where you do it (Where is the product or service going to be provided to the targeted customers? Place, niche, or market segment?).

Four Seasons Hotels and Resorts

Four Seasons Hotels and Resorts displays its' Pillars of Service in all of their properties.

An example would be the simple but elegant "Pillars of Service" that are posted in every Four Seasons property. The pillars explain "Who We Are," "What We Believe," "How We Behave," and "How We Succeed." These pillars demonstrate, for all employees and guests to see, the core values, beliefs, principles, and goals behind the award-winning service that Four Seasons seeks to deliver.[46]

Darden Restaurants states its mission as "To be financially successful through great people consistently delivering outstanding food, drinks, and service in an inviting atmosphere, making every guest loyal."[47] Starbucks defines its mission as "To inspire and nurture the human spirit–one person, one cup, and one neighborhood at a time."[48] The organization's statement of mission often includes its core values. Walmart founder Sam Walton combined mission and values when he said, "We put the customer ahead of everything else. . . . If you're not serving the customer, or supporting the folks who do, we don't need you."[49] All these organizations recognize the importance of providing straightforward guidance to all employees as to how the organization expects them to act in their jobs.

Southwest Airlines started out in 1971 with this mission: "Get your passengers to their destinations when they want to get there, on time, at the lowest possible fares, and make darn sure they have a good time doing it." Here is the Southwest mission statement of today:[50]

> The mission of Southwest Airlines is dedication to the highest quality of Customer Service delivered with a sense of warmth, friendliness, individual pride, and Company Spirit.
>
> **To Our Employees**
>
> We are committed to provide our Employees a stable work environment with equal opportunity for learning and personal growth. Creativity and innovation are encouraged for improving the effectiveness of Southwest Airlines. Above all, Employees will be provided the same concern, respect, and caring

[46] Four Seasons Press Room. "Awards and Accolades for Four Seasons Hotels and Resorts," accessed June 11, 2018, https://press.fourseasons.com/news-releases/awards-and-accolades-for-four-seasons-hotels-and-resorts/.

[47] Darden Concepts Inc., "Frequently Asked Questions," Darden Corporation, accessed February 3, 2018. https://www.darden.com/legal-notices.

[48] Starbucks, Inc. "Starbucks Mission Statement," Starbucks, accessed February 3, 2018, https://www.thebalance.com/starbucks-mission-statement-2891826.

[49] James Charles Collins and Jerry I. Porras, *Built to Last: Successful Habits of Visionary Companies* (New York, NY: Random House, 2005), 74.

[50] Southwest Airlines Co, "About Southwest," southwest, Southwest Airlines Co, accessed February 3, 2018, https://www.southwest.com/html/about-southwest/.

attitude within the organization that they are expected to share externally with every Southwest Customer.

DEVELOPING THE SERVICE STRATEGY

Once the external and internal assessment factors have been examined in light of the corporate vision and mission, the hospitality organization is ready to define its service strategy. This strategy is critical to any service organization's success because it provides guidance in how to make every organizational decision, from capital budgeting to handling a customer complaint. Defining and creating the service strategy are as much art as science and should involve the voice, ideas, and enthusiasm of its many stakeholders. According to service expert Leonard Berry, an excellent service strategy has four characteristics: quality, value, service, and achievement.[51]

First, the excellent strategy emphasizes quality. Without a commitment to *quality,* nothing else matters. Any hospitality organization can write a mission statement, but those truly committed to excellence start by committing the organization to providing the customer with a guest experience of high quality.

Second, an excellent service strategy emphasizes *value.* It commits the organization to providing customers with more benefits from the guest experience than their costs. Recall that value and cost cannot be defined solely in monetary terms. If "time is money," organizations can provide value by saving time for customers. Organizations doing so fill a significant market niche. The many people who pay extra for personal shoppers in retail stores believe they receive good value in time saved for the money they spend on having someone shop for them. Home-delivered pizza is even a better value; time is saved, and the cost is no more than going to the restaurant. Organizations must budget funds for measuring the perceived value of their services to customers. No matter what the service costs, customers must believe they are getting significant value for their money.

The third characteristic of an excellent service strategy is that it focuses the entire organizational effort on *service.* This strategy commits the organization to hiring people who believe in service, employee training programs emphasize the commitment to service quality, resources are allocated to serving the customer, the performance and reward systems carefully reinforce the entire workforce's commitment to service, and all organizational efforts seek to support the service mission. The service strategy should ensure everyone in the organization walks the service-quality walk by constantly reflecting total commitment to service excellence.

Finally, the service strategy should foster among employees a sense of genuine achievement. It should stretch and push every employee to grow and develop so the employee group stretches and develops the entire organization to do things no one thought were possible. Taco Bell found a way to stretch its employees so it could operate 90% of its company-owned restaurants without a full-time manager. According to Berry, "These locations are team managed by their mostly younger person crews who order inventory, schedule work hours, and recruit and train, among other functions."[52]

The organization must now define its market's key drivers, craft its service product to meet that market's needs, create the appropriate service environment, and design the service systems to reach the target market. In Chapter 1 we discussed these key components of the hospitality organization, and this is when the strategy must be

[51] Leonard Berry, "The Employee as a Customer," in *Services Marketing: Text, Cases & Readings*, Ed. Christopher H. Lovelock (Englewood Cliffs, NJ: Prentice Hall), 65–68.

[52] Berry, 67.

translated into specific actions. If the company mission is to deliver a service product to an upscale, educated, retired socioeconomic group, then the service delivery system should be high touch, and the service environment should be elegant and congruent with what an upscale market wants. Knowing what any market wants takes us back to an important point from the first chapter: Ask the customer.

Determining the Service-Product Strategy

Developing a service-product strategy requires an organization to determine what service product it should provide for its customers. And usually, the best way to know what your customers want or expect is to ask them. The organization should not only look inside to evaluate its core competencies but must also ask its customers to determine the key drivers of customer satisfaction. Customers can tell the organization what they really value, and these values should drive the decision process on resource allocations. The customers will tell the organization if its core competencies are properly aligned with providing customer value and satisfaction, and excellent hospitality organizations measure these key drivers carefully and frequently.

As a true believer in identifying key drivers, Disney surveys its guests constantly. On one such survey, Walt Disney World Resort guests were asked a variety of questions about their experiences and how those experiences related to both their intention to return to the parks and their overall satisfaction with Walt Disney World Resort. Fast food in the parks received relatively low ratings. However, analysis of the data revealed only a weak statistical relationship between these low ratings and both intention to return and overall satisfaction with Walt Disney World Resort. The quality of the fast food did not seem to matter all that much. On the other hand, ratings of attractions, entertainment, and fireworks were strongly related to both the return intention and the satisfaction measure.

Guided by the survey results, Disney invested its available funds in new attractions, entertainment, and expanded fireworks displays. Although the organization felt competent to improve fast food, it allocated scarce resources to improving areas of key importance to guests. The strategic planning process did not just involve managers introspectively looking at organizational core competencies. It incorporated the wishes and expectations of guests into these decisions. Guest-focused organizations do the same. They find out what key factors drive the experiences of guests, and they work hard to ensure the organization has or develops the core competencies to provide and enhance those key drivers.

Determining the Service-Setting Strategy

Developing a service-setting strategy requires the organization to determine how it is going to provide exceptional service environment for its customers. This strategy is realized by the way the organization designs and builds the setting in which the experience takes place. The guest must not only feel comfortable in the setting, but the setting should contain clues and cues to help the guest realize the quality and value of the experience. Since the quality and value of the hospitality experience is entirely defined by how the guest sees it, every visual and environment cue should be carefully aligned to reinforce it. Thus, the environmental cues that impact the senses should be assessed to ensure they add value to the guest. Too hot or cold, too much light or too little, too many things to see or not enough, are only a few of the design elements that need to be considered in creating an environment strategy. Because the hospitality experience is largely intangible, the strategy must include as many cues as possible to communicate with the tangible environment the quality and value of the experience. This topic is so important that we devote Chapter 3 to it.

Determining the Delivery-System Strategy

Once the service-product and service-setting strategies have been defined, the organization possesses the basis for ensuring the customers' key drivers are addressed, by determining what the organization's service product should be and what the service environment in which the service product is provided or delivered should look and feel like. The final step is to determine how the service delivery system makes the service product available to the guest.

If the organizational mission, for example, is to create and sustain a low-cost airline to serve the budget market in western Canada, the service product must be designed to meet that market's expectations, the service environment must be designed to fit the product and match or exceed the guest's expectation of how this type of airline experience should look and feel, and the service delivery system must be designed to ensure the service product is provided to the guest in a way that is congruent with how the guest expects to experience that service. The joint consideration of these three guest-experience components leads to the short-run action plans that can support and implement the components and thereby achieve the organization's mission.

ACTION PLANS

action plans The specific plans that lay out the specifics of how the organization will operate, what everyone needs to do in the next time period, usually a year, what resources are available to implement them, and, through the assessment metrics, how valuable feedback will be elicited on progress in achieving the plan.

Once the organization has a clear idea of the characteristics of its targeted guests, where, what, and how it wants to serve them, what its strengths and weaknesses are in providing that service to those guests, what its overall mission and goals are, and how it delivers its services through service-product, service-setting, and service-delivery strategies, it can proceed to developing **action plans**. The action plans along with appropriate measurement metrics and budget allocations represent the leadership's decisions on how to best implement the service strategy in specific terms that will motivate and guide the rest of the organization's members toward accomplishing the overall service strategy and organizational mission. These plans lay out the specifics of how the organization will operate, what everyone needs to do in the next time period, usually a year, what resources are available to implement them, and, through the assessment metrics, how valuable feedback will be elicited on progress in achieving the plan.

The bottom tier of Exhibit 2.2 indicates the five key areas in which action plans, performance metrics, and budget allocations should be established: management, staffing, capacity utilization, finance, and marketing. Benchmark organizations not only develop plans in each of these areas but also make sure each area has a means that is as objective as possible for measuring the degree to which those plans were achieved. They know what gets measured gets managed, so they spend the time and effort to communicate to all that their performance metrics are fair and tightly aligned with the plans. Not only must employees understand the direction in which everyone is supposed to go but also everyone must know what getting there looks like. The measures ensure the right actions are taken, the right goals are achieved, and the employees can see how well they're doing as they work toward achieving the goals of the action plans. Good plans are accompanied by appropriate resource allocations and objective measures of achievement so everyone knows how the plans are working.

Management Performance Plans

Action plans need to be translated into management tasks, roles, and responsibilities. Once a strategic plan has been established, managers should be assigned goals and objectives that focus their actions and activities to those that must be done to implement the plan and then hold them accountable for their effectiveness in doing the right things. As has been noted earlier, what gets measured gets managed and what gets managed gets done. The management performance plans, consequently, must be connected with appropriate measures to the strategy so managers stay focused on and rewarded for executing that strategy.

Employee Hiring, Training, and Retention Plans

A strategic plan will inevitably require employees at all levels to do new things, add new skills, and acquire new knowledge. The action plans for employee hiring, training, and retention should consider several issues before they are established and performance metrics set. If the strategic plan requires new KSAs from existing employees then a plan is required to develop these. If the strategic plan requires new types or additional numbers of employees at present or future locations, then a plan for recruiting and hiring needs to be created. Finally, if turnover is seen as a critical issue in implementing the strategy, then the plan to retain productive employees is needed as well. The hospitality industry is so dependent upon its employees and their ability to successfully deliver the guest experience that we devote a chapter (Chapter 5: Staffing for Service) to this important topic.

Capacity Utilization Plans

There are many tools that can be used to plan the best ways to build and manage capacity. Three in particular that are frequently used in hospitality are design day, yield management, and the related concept of revenue management. Each offers hospitality managers a planning tool to match capacity with guest demand.

The Design Day

A basic problem for many hospitality organizations is that demand is uncertain and capacity is fixed. An important concept in capacity planning for hospitality organizations is the **design day**.[53] Whenever a new restaurant, hotel, theme park, cruise ship, or other service facility is created, management must determine how big to build it. How many people should the new physical facility be able to handle at one time? It should not be designed to accommodate demand on the busiest day of the year, because for the other 364 days, at least some of its capacity will exceed demand and be unused. On the other hand, if the facility is designed to meet demand on the slowest day, capacity will not be sufficient to meet demand for the rest of the year and customers will be denied service. The idea of a design day is to decide which day of the year to build for when determining the design capacity of an attraction or any hospitality facility.

design day The day of the year the organization uses to calculate designed capacity. Capacity is built to meet or exceed demand at a percentage of the year where management believes the costs of turning guests away is less than the costs of building more capacity.

As an example, a theme park could use past and predicted attendance figures to set the design day at the 50th percentile, so overall park demand (and demand for particular rides and attractions) would exceed capacity on about half the days, and about half the time capacity would exceed demand. But a successful park does not want guests to experience excessive wait times for half the days of the year. The park designers must decide what percentile level they want to establish for their design day. The higher the percentile level chosen, the lower the number of days the organization will exceed its design-day standards for guest wait times. However, higher demand days cost more—greater capacity must be built—but yield greater guest satisfaction. For example, if they choose a 75th percentile design day, the park will exceed wait-time standards on about 90 days of the year; if they choose a 90th percentile design day, they will exceed their wait-time standards on only about 36 days per year.

[53] Duncan Dickson, Robert C. Ford, and Bruce Laval, "Managing Real and Virtual Waits in Hospitality and Service Organizations," *Cornell Hotel and Restaurant Administration Quarterly* 46, no. 1 (2005): 52–68.

The design-day percentile is a critical management decision for any hospitality organization. A higher percentile day means increasing capital investment to increase park, restaurant, cruise ship, convention center, or hotel capacity. Building physical capacity based on selecting a lower percentile day will cost less to build and sustain during the nonpeak times, but guest dissatisfaction will likely be higher during peak times. Once the design-day capacity is exceeded, the quality of the experience will be diluted for guests. They will be forced to wait a greater length of time or abandon the idea of experiencing what the organization offers. In either case, customers may be dissatisfied. This dissatisfaction will have a negative impact on repeat visitation, long-term attendance growth, and revenue. Management must balance carefully the trade-off between the increased costs of investment in capacity and dissatisfied guests.

Every hospitality organization uses some method to plan its capacity and decide how big to build its physical facility. The design-day concept is one way to find the best balance between investing in and carrying the costs of excess capacity and ensuring the quality and value of each guest's experience. Costs are associated with buildings, grounds, staff, and inventory. But customers expect the service to be available to them when they want it; otherwise they are dissatisfied with the quality and value of their experience. Finding the best balance between economic realities and the guest satisfaction strategy and mission is what guestologists do.

Consider a theme park with numerous rides and other attractions. Once the design-day decision has been made that is consistent with its mission, the park management can calculate how many demand units (people per time period per attraction) will be in the park to consume or enjoy the capacity available. Thus, if the park attendance on a design day is 18,000 people and a new ride or attraction that takes thirty minutes is expected to capture 3% of this capacity per hour, the hourly capacity of the ride has to equal 270. With this capacity and assuming a continuous flow of people coming to enjoy an attraction, no one will have to wait more than thirty minutes. As the ride or attraction begins, the first of the next 270 people wanting to enjoy it will start forming a new waiting line. As soon as the ride gets back to its starting point or the show ends, the 270 people who have been waiting for varying lengths of time will enter the ride or show, and a new waiting line will start to form. If the design-day decision includes allowing guests to wait for a fixed amount of time (e.g., an average of 15 minutes across all park attractions), the actual capacity of the new attraction can be less than 270 because the capacity will assume a certain acceptable number of people waiting in line. The point is this important capital-allocation decision—how big to build a new ride or other attraction—can be based on straightforward calculations that are themselves based on design-day decisions made long ago, which are in turn based on the organization's estimates of what quality and value customers expect.

For any hospitality organization, the original design-day decision is based on forecasts of guest demand, information derived from organizational past experience, and perhaps from knowledge of similar facilities. Once real information can be gathered through real experience with real people or some other change occurs, the design-day decision can be refined. Because most hospitality organizations would rather add capacity than tear down existing capacity or let it stand idle, the original design-day decision for a new facility should probably use conservative estimates.

yield management
A technique for managing the pricing of an organization's units of capacity, using forecasts based on past results, to maximize the profitability of that capacity; in other words, selling the right capacity to the right customer at the right time, for the right price.

Yield Management and Revenue Management

A capacity-management concept that has gained substantial favor in the airline, lodging, restaurant, spa, cruise line, and convention industries is **yield management**—managing the sale of units of capacity to maximize the profitability of that capacity. Yield management involves selling the right capacity to the right customer at the most advantageous price, to maximize both capacity use and revenue. This concept is based on the idea that guest demand patterns can be predicted to some extent and those predictions can be used to allow the hospitality organization to charge different rates to different people (or groups) based on (1) when reservations are made and (2) the capacity projected to be available at any given time.[54]

A related concept is **revenue management**, which is concerned with maximizing revenue in much the same way as yield management, but also considers the cost of selling the service product and money made from other services. Whereas yield management is specific to setting price for a specific service or product, revenue management considers more of the several factors that comprise the "big picture." So, for example, yield management may be focused on setting the price of a hotel room to maximize room revenue; whereas revenue management takes into account not just revenues from the hotel rooms, but also from other services such as parking, food and beverage revenue, and other services the hotel offers.

revenue management
A technique for selling the right capacity to the right customer at the most advantageous price, to maximize both capacity use and revenue from all components of the service product.

Early reservations with restrictions (e.g., no refund fares or paying a high financial penalty for any schedule changes) will yield the lowest prices. Guests who wait until later to make reservations, with fewer restrictions and more flexibility, can expect and are usually willing to pay more. Balancing capacity, demand, and price is primarily the task of job revenue managers, often with the aid of (and sometimes substituted by) a computerized yield-management system.

For example, a sophisticated yield management system will predict the demand pattern for reservations on a specific flight from Los Angeles to New York four months from now, and then price each seat in a way that exactly meets the forecasted demand for travel on that flight. That is, the airline will know how many seats it should set aside on that flight for full-fare guests (who will book their reservations late and will expect to pay more) and how many it must sell at lower prices. Using historical data, the yield management program may estimate that 20% of the flight's capacity should be reserved for full-fare guests who book late. It may also forecast or calculate a pick-up rate indicating how additional passengers will book reservations from now until the plane flies four months from now. This rate, also based on historical experience, can be a smooth curve or any other distribution that describes how guests make reservations.

The airline's goal is to sell as many seats as possible at the highest rate possible. It will start by setting aside the expected full-fare capacity and then calculate the capacities to be set aside at each successively lower rate. As most travelers know, the farther out from the flight date the reservation is made, generally the lower the ticket price. The closer to the actual date of the flight, generally the higher the ticket price. The yield-management process is designed to set aside seats at each price level in such a way as to sell each seat at the highest possible price. The airline might set aside the 20% mentioned earlier at full fare, 30% at a 10% discount, 40% at a 20% discount, and 10% at half price. If the airline's predictions are accurate, the bargain hunters will make their reservations early and fill up the half-price seats, followed by the later bargain hunters who were not willing or able to commit to the flight soon enough to fly at half price. They will be disappointed they can't get the 50% off fares but are happy with a 20% discount anyway. The guests who commit even later can't get the 20% discount but are still relieved not to pay full price. People paying full price are those who have no choice but to travel on that particular day or business travelers who must book their flights close to the actual departure date.

The reservation process is dynamic, and an effective yield-management system will continuously compare the actual reservation rate to the forecasted rate. The number of seats set aside in each price category or the price of seats in each category can be modified based on the actual, evolving relationships between the supply of that flight's seats and the demand for those seats. If the pick-up rate prediction is incorrect, the airline can always advertise the empty remaining seats on its web page at a substantial discount that still covers its direct costs and contributes to the flight's total revenue, or it can sell the seats to a consolidator.

[54] Sheryl E. Kimes and Jochen Wirtz, "Revenue Management: Advanced Strategies and Tools to Enhance Firm Profitability," *Foundations and Trends in Marketing* 8, 1 (2015): 1–68.

A good yield-management model can maximize the revenue on every flight by filling up every seat at a price that perfectly balances seat supply with passenger demand. Yield management is an important capacity-planning device not only for airlines but also for other organizations that have both capacity limitations and a perishable commodity, like a room for the night, a cruise date, convention centers, or even athletic events. Because the organization's salespeople must have accurate and timely information about guest demand and available capacity, yield management can hardly be accomplished without the power of computer analysis but still relies in many instances on a person's judgment. In the hotel industry, for example, it is usually one person at a resort hotel who makes the decision as to how many rooms to assign to Hotels.com or to Priceline.com for a given night. While the statistics from data mining the historical demand patterns are a critical starting point, that person will have the responsibility of assessing the usefulness of the predictions based on real-time judgment.

Financial Budget Plans

The actions and activities identified in the strategic planning process will require resources, and the financial budget plan is where the organization puts its money to make these actions and activities happen. The financial plan that is reflected in the budget represents the way the organization plans to pay for the actions it needs to take, the managers it needs to hire, the employees it needs to train, the capacity it must create, and the marketing it will do to create and fulfill its targeted customers' expectations in the hospitality experience. While some actions can be taken that don't require new funding, such as adding employee recognition to the company newsletter or encouraging guests to choose times when lines are less likely, most activities cost money. These will require creating a budget item that allocates the available funds to those things identified by the strategic plan as important to its guests. Since few organizations have unlimited funds to spend, this allocation process is usually a difficult one. Everyone involved in planning typically has some preference as to how the budget should be allocated. The best planners will start with studying guest preferences and use those data to allocate money to those actions and activities that will yield the most likely improvement in the guest experience.

Marketing Plans

Every strategic plan should result in a marketing plan to ensure the targeted customers (and the employees) know the promised quality and value of the experience the hospitality organization offers. This plan should reflect the planning done to identify the targeted market's key drivers in the service product, service environment, and service delivery system.While a detailed discussion of how this plan should be created and measured is extensively covered in services marketing, it is important for hospitality managers to participate in the promises marketing makes. When a guest enters a hotel, restaurant, theme park or cruise ship, the guest will come with expectations that are largely created by advertising and marketing. If the expectations are unmet and the guest disappointed, it is the organization's management that receives the complaints and its employees who deal with the disappointment. While the marketing plan defines the promises that bring the guests in, it will be how well operations delivers on those promises that brings guests back.

Action Plans as an Integrated Whole

All action plans need to be considered as a whole and individually. No marketing plan or capacity utilization plan, for example, should be set without also taking into account the financial budgeting plan. Similarly, no managerial performance plan can be set without carefully planning for the necessary resources that will allow managers to reach their targeted goals. Just as it makes no sense to put a lot of resources into a marketing plan that will draw many customers without considering the capacity decisions, it also makes little sense to develop performance targets for managers without also considering what physical, financial, marketing, and human resources they will need to reach their targets. This process defines hospitality service planning. The plan lays out the necessary steps and identifies the mileposts along the path the organization must follow to fulfill its mission, to achieve its vision. If the organization foresees its future inaccurately, misdiagnoses its core competencies, defines its mission poorly, or chooses the wrong service strategy, it will soon lose its competitive stature.

INVOLVING EMPLOYEES IN PLANNING

In February 2007, JetBlue created a major customer service failure when it was forced to cancel 250 flights in the wake of a major ice storm that closed down New York City. The next day was even worse, as the disruptions of the storm were compounded when the airline was unable to fully recover in the days that followed. JetBlue, which books 80% of its tickets online, did not have enough reservations agents on its toll-free line to handle all the rescheduling. At Kennedy Airport, there was not enough trained staff to work on rebooking. In addition, the unit in charge of locating pilots and flight attendants and assigning them to their next flight was overwhelmed. In effect, the airline had to shut down and restart. One plane that sat for 10 hours on the New York tarmac became a symbol of the whole mess. Across the system, there were numerous customer complaints, national news (and late-night comedian) coverage, and the recognition that its then president and CEO, David Neeleman, should issue a public apology. The carefully built reputation for excellence in customer service that was the pride of the employees and a competitive advantage was severely damaged in a few hours. The customer relations fallout as well as the employee morale impact of this mistake led the company to undertake a top-to-bottom review of how it ran the airline. One of JetBlue University's leaders was tasked with organizing and interviewing groups of employees at several of the major destinations JetBlue served. The question he asked was, "What are we doing wrong and how do we fix it?"

Over the course of four months, the employees generated about 25 action items that were then presented to management for implementation. These included relatively simple things such as reorganizing the crew scheduling organization, creating a new division to manage transportation and accommodations for flight crews away from home base, redesigning training programs for crew scheduling and operations, and more complex things like whether to upgrade or replace the information systems used to track airplanes and crews. JetBlue's leadership reviewed these items, recognized their worth, and put most of them in place. Things immediately improved, as seen in both employee morale and customer satisfaction scores.

The JetBlue example reinforces the need to plan for the probable and to be nimble enough to react quickly and appropriately if the improbable occurs. Increasingly, hospitality organizations are including their employees in the planning processes. They have learned that good things come from widespread employee participation. First, the frontline employees know more about guests than anyone else does, because they are the ones who guests share their compliments and complaints with and who see guests smile or frown in the hospitality experience. They know what makes guests happy and what doesn't. They also have ideas about what products or services the organization could add, redesign, or delete to add value to the guest's experience or to reduce costs. Second, to implement any strategic plan requires that everyone understands it and commits to its logic. What better way to gain understanding and obtain employee buy-in than to have the employees help develop the plan? There is an old saying that those who plan the battle seldom battle the plan. If employees are involved in understanding the need to plan and how the plan will help the organization solve problems and reach the future, why wouldn't they support it and try to implement it? Most managers have learned the hard way that the best plan in the world is worthless unless those who have to make it work want to make it work.

A Walmart store in Louisiana had a shoplifting problem, so the manager stationed an elderly man at the door to "greet" customers as they entered and left. Potential shoplifters learned someone would be observing them directly as they left, but even more significantly, honest customers were impressed by this friendly touch. The idea spread to other stores, and Walmart became known for its friendly greeters.

Was this company success the product of strategic planning, or any planning? A Walmart executive of that time said, "We live by the motto, 'Do it. Fix it. Try it.' If you try something and it works, you keep it. If it doesn't work, you fix it or try something else."[55] The Louisiana manager tried it, and it worked far better than the manager thought it would, so the whole company kept it.

That's one way to run an organization, and Sam Walton built a hugely successful company. Hospitality organizations can learn from Walmart's use of employee ideas. When everyone is responsible for thinking strategically about how to fulfill the organization's mission, the power of individual creativity can be unleashed in very positive ways. A planning process should include the people who must make the plans become reality, or the effort will be at least partly wasted. The best plan in the world is worthless without implementation, and the benchmark organizations have learned the power of employee participation in planning to achieve implementation more smoothly and efficiently.

THE UNCERTAIN FUTURE

Of course, unforeseen developments may disrupt or overturn even the best laid plans. Good plans attempt to bring rationality and stability to the organization's operations and efforts, but organizations seldom operate in purely rational or stable situations. Indeed, the very plans that made a firm competitive under one set of circumstances may make it uncompetitive if managers get so wedded to the plans they ignore or don't see changes in the marketplace.

Courtesy of Airbnb

In 2008, Brian Chesky, Joe Gebbia, and Nate Blecharczyk founded Airbnb. You never know where the next big change to the hospitality industry will come from and what it will look like.

The strategic planning model in Exhibits 2.1 and 2.2 are neat and orderly. Unfortunately, the world is not a neat and orderly place. The cycle of planning may be deftly tied to a yearly calendar and duly placed on everyone's time management screen. But the plans laid out in August may be turned totally upside down in September by such external events as competitors' innovations, terrorist attacks, a financial meltdown, technological developments, or an organizational disaster such as the illness or death of a CEO, a labor dispute, or an unfavorable judgment in a lawsuit. If such events occur, the organization cannot wait until next August to revise its plan.

[55] Collins and Porras, *Built to Last*, 98.

Plans are designed to be flexible guides along the path between today and tomorrow, not the final word on everything. Effective hospitality organizations stay nimble in responding to the many uncertainties that can affect their operations and the services they provide. Many create contingency plans, which offer alternative strategies to meet changed circumstances. But since no one can anticipate everything that may happen to an organization, contingency planning can go only so far.

LESSONS LEARNED

LO 2.1 Distinguish between the three generic strategies for positioning products and services.

- The three generic strategies are lower price, a differentiated product, or a special niche. Select the generic strategy that best fits your internal and external assessments and your mission.

LO 2.2 Explain how the elements of the organizational planning cycle result in the establishment of the hospitality organization's overall strategic plan and service strategy.

- Use the organization's vision to define your mission and communicate the mission to everyone inside and outside your organization so they know what you seek to do, who you seek to serve, and where and when you will do it.

LO 2.3 Recognize the quantitative and qualitative tools used for forecasting in the hospitality environment—external and internal.

- Try to understand the future environment and what it might do to you and your future guests.
- Use appropriate, powerful forecasting tools, but use them to inform, not replace, managerial judgment to determine strategic premises.

LO 2.4 Identify the key external and internal factors that must be examined for successful planning.

- The key internal and external factors that must be examined for strategic planning are your core competencies and strategic premises.

LO 2.5 Describe the process to determine core competencies.

- Know your core competencies, why they are your core, and why you are competent in them.
- Know which core competencies you need to build or acquire for the future.

LO 2.6 Describe the importance of a mission and vision statement in focusing the strategic plan on the best way to fit core competencies with strategic premises.

- Pick the best strategy—low-cost provider, differentiated service, or occupying a market niche—to fulfill your organization's mission.

LO 2.7 State the importance of including the key drivers of guest satisfaction in the planning process.

- Strategy starts with the guest. Know what key factors drive the guest's determination of quality and value.

LO 2.8 Describe a planning model, showing how components are tied together and action plans are developed.

- Begin developing your action plan by examining your external environment, knowing your organization's strengths and weaknesses, and understanding the relationship of these elements to your mission.
- Action plans are the result of strategic planning.

LO 2.9 Recognize the value added to the planning process by including those affected by the plans

- Involve employees in planning. Those who plan the battle are unlikely to battle the plan.
- Your employees represent the one competitive advantage that your competitors can't easily duplicate.

LO 2.10 Recall that while plans are necessary, organizations must be ready and capable of change.

- While plans are necessary, companies must recognize that not all contingencies can be anticipated.

KEY TERMS AND CONCEPTS

action plan 64
brainstorming 77
brand image 33
brand name 33
core competence 57
Delphi technique 77
design day 65
differentiation 32
econometric models 75
environmental assessment 38
focus group 78
forecasting 40
green movement 50
internal assessment 39
key drivers 38
low-price provider 32
market niche 34
mission statement 60
qualitative forecasting tools 40
quantitative forecasting tools 40
regression analysis 76
revenue management 67
scenario building 78
service strategy 31
strategic plan 35
strategic premises 54
sustainability 51
time-series and trend analyses 76
vision statement 59
yield management 66

REVIEW QUESTIONS

1. You are about to start your own restaurant and need to articulate a strategic plan. Think of five key decisions you need to make and tell how you will make them.
2. How does knowing key drivers help a manager meet guest expectations in a guest experience?
3. Think about kids in junior high school today; they will be part of tomorrow's workforce and customer base. What management and guest-service changes will hospitality organizations have to make if they want to succeed with these future employees and customers?
4. Think of a hospitality organization that you are familiar with.
   A. What seem to be the key drivers of the guests in its target market?
   B. How do these key drivers influence how the organization operates?
   C. How should they influence how that organization operates?
5. Think of a product, service, or brand to which you are loyal. Why are you loyal to that product, service, or brand? What did the organization do to acquire your loyalty, and what has it done to maintain it? Based on the reasons for your loyalty, what one piece of advice would you give to future hospitality managers?
6. List a few necessary core competencies for successfully operating a fast-food restaurant versus a fine-dining restaurant versus a casual-dining restaurant.
   A. Why are these competencies core?
   B. Why do they differ from one type of restaurant to another?
7. How do you define *service?* What are the components of good and bad service? Which components of bad service are due to not getting something that you expected or wanted? Getting something that you don't expect or want?
8. Find the mission and vision statements of a hospitality company. What do these statements do to help the organization focus its efforts?

9. If an organization like an airline uses yield-management techniques, guests end up paying different prices for what is essentially the same service. What are the implications of that difference, if any, for guest expectations, service quality, value, and guest satisfaction?
10. Consider the expression "Price, quality, speed—pick any two." Do you think a company strategic planner said it, or a customer? Is the expression fair and accurate in today's business world?
11. Why do you think getting employee input is important in the planning process? What do line employees know that management may not know?

ACTIVITIES

1. In the chapter appendix, there are four qualitative techniques that can be used for forecasting: brainstorming, the Delphi technique, focus groups, and scenario building. Divide up into groups and, as your instructor directs, come up with a forecasting problem that a local hospitality organization might face and try to arrive at a conclusion about it by using one or more of the techniques. Different groups might use different techniques for the same problem to see if they come up with the same conclusion or problem solution.
2. Find a hospitality organization that uses forecasting techniques. How does the organization use them to predict its staffing and product supply needs, or for other purposes? How does the organization gather data? Does it use prediction models and statistical techniques, or is forecasting done mainly by the seat of someone's pants?
3. This chapter suggests an organization should focus on its core competencies, not spread itself into areas in which it may not be competent. Some competency pairings are generally accepted, like bar and grill. Others might reflect an organizational intention to operate in unrelated areas, like college and fish camp or blacksmith and nail care. Look for unusual competency pairings in business names you come across and report them back to the class.
4. Go on the web or across your community and see what the companies you find claim as their mission. What is your estimation of how well this mission helps define strategic decisions they make?

ETHICS IN BUSINESS

The Kelilah Hotel, an independent four-star property, like most of its competitors, advertises on the web. It knows from asking its guests that most customers compare prices on travel sites like Orbitz, Travelocity, and Hotels.com to find the best rates for a hotel at their desired destination. While customers do check out online ratings of prospective hotels, they largely select the cheapest listing in the desired hotel category. The Kelilah Hotel has taken a page out of the airlines' pricing strategy in the face of their customers' changing behavior with the new technology and now lists the lowest price they can. What they do when the customer checks in is to add fees to make up the difference in their revenue stream from lowering prices. Thus, they now charge a wireless fee, a parking fee, a health club fee, a fee for a view room, and a few other fees they have added to increase revenue on the low-priced rooms. When asked why they use all these fees, they respond that it is a competitive necessity. Websites advertising room rates do not specify when additional fees are charged, so customers are making their purchase decisions without knowing these additional fees are present. It is unclear what fees, if any, The Kelilah Hotel's competitors are charging. What are the ethics of charging all these additional fees?

CASE STUDY

Case 1: Profit? Growth? Survival? Service? Customers? Environment?

Six hospitality management students are having a discussion at the Student Center about the primary goal of hospitality organizations.

Jim said emphatically, "Large hospitality corporations are in business to make as much money as they can. No matter if it's food, lodging, or gaming, profit maximization is their primary goal, and everything else is secondary. Businesses exist to make a profit."

Will agreed, up to a point: "If the hospitality organization is a public corporation, profits are a necessity, but the primary goal of any business is to grow. No business wants to stay small and unimportant. Company officials and stockholders want growth, for the feeling of progress and accomplishment it brings and for the profits that will eventually accompany growth."

Jane said, "There's something to what you both say. Any company needs profits, and any company would like to grow. But survival is the primary goal, because without it you can't have profit or growth."

Sally said, "Any hospitality organization's goal had better be to give good guest service. If the organization achieves that goal, all the rest will fall into place. If they don't, they have no chance anyway."

Spiro said, "My dad owns a restaurant, and he agrees with my professor who said the main goal of any business is to get and keep customers. No customers, no nothing. I agree with my dad."

Betty said, "No matter what you learned in class, you are all kidding yourselves. Primary goals are just for looks anyway. No matter how specific an organization's goals, no matter how carefully it plans, no matter how hard it works to meet those goals, the environment within which the organization markets its product or service will determine the organization's destiny. Organizations react to environmental forces, regardless of goals. To succeed, a business organization doesn't need to establish goals; it needs to be lucky enough to be in the right place at the right time and take advantage of the opportunities presented to it."

1. With whose position would the company's stockholders most likely agree?
2. What do you think the CEO would say? The employees? The guests?
3. Where do you stand on the issue? (Or do you have an even different view?)

Case 2: Economy Airlines

Minor Hamblin had a humanistic dream: to found a company in which every employee would be an owner/manager, a company in which people really would work together. Hamblin started the revolutionary low-fare, no-frills Economy Airlines. Within a few years, Economy was the fifth-largest U.S. passenger carrier. The company had no unions. New employees had to buy and hold 100 shares of Economy common stock, offered at a 70% discount. Profit sharing regularly added substantial amounts to their paychecks. Hamblin believed that participatory management was the style that best suited contemporary employees. One university professor wrote that Economy Airlines was "the most comprehensive and self-conscious effort to fit a business to the capabilities and attitudes of today's workforce. Economy Airlines is doing everything right."

Economy had a flat structure with only three management levels. In terms of the organization chart, pilots and flight attendants were on the same level and had the same clout. The company had no secretaries; managers did their own typing and answered their own phones.

The company rapidly expanded its routes and schedules. Unfortunately, traffic growth failed to keep up with expansion. Other airlines adopted the low-fare, no-frills approach and even attacked Economy directly in their advertising campaigns. Economy's stock plunged from over 100 to 8. One employee observed, "When stock prices were high, profit sharing and stock ownership were great. Now they aren't so great." The Air Line Pilots Association began a drive to unionize Economy's pilots. New government regulations made Minor Hamblin wonder if he could even keep Economy's flying certificate.

Hamblin had a renewed realization that a company can't always control its own destiny. "That professor said I was doing everything right. Now I'm in danger of going belly-up." He wondered if he should convert Economy over to a more traditional structure, with more management layers, a clearly defined chain of command, and specialized employee tasks. Or perhaps he should sell out.

1. What caused Economy's problems?
2. Do you see any way that Economy could have avoided those problems?
3. What steps should Economy Airlines take now?

Case 3: The Diamondback Plaza Hotel

Dwight Robinson owns The Diamondback Plaza, a large hotel in a popular vacation area. Robinson tries to maintain a reputation of casual elegance for his hotel and is known among local hoteliers for his dignified advertising and for sticking to the "rack rate." He feels that to do otherwise is not fair to guests paying full price. Robinson is happy about all aspects of his hotel operation except his average nightly occupancy rate of 68%. The average for his geographic area is 78%.

In an attempt to improve his results, Robinson has hired a consultant who, after studying the situation, has presented the following recommendation:

Mr. Robinson, your rooms are not yielding the income they might because you establish one price for your rooms and then sit back hoping people will stay with you. In today's market that strategy won't work; you have to manage your situation to improve your yield per room.

You need to use all available means to lure travelers into your hotel. When you see at a certain time in the evening that your hotel is not going to be full, you have to cut prices until you sell out. You may not be able to sell every room every night, but don't be satisfied until your occupancy rate is over 95%. Follow this principle: Don't go to sleep yourself until you get people to sleep in all your rooms.

Your debt relative to your property value is low; you don't have high interest charges to cover. So, you can offer lower room prices than your competitors and still make a profit.

Put a big flashing sign outside your hotel. If people aren't checking in and you foresee vacancies, start that sign flashing at $79.99. If you can't fill up at that figure, drop it to $59.99 or even $49.99. Anything is better than nothing.

First thing every morning, check the previous night's records. If the Diamondback wasn't sold out, ask your night manager why! She'll soon get the message.

Sure, your average daily room rate will drop, but so what? That's just a prestige number to brag about when you get together with other local hotel owners. By managing the yield on each unit, you'll maximize your profits, and isn't that why you're in business?

Should Dwight Robinson take the consultant's advice?

APPENDIX

QUANTITATIVE AND QUALITATIVE TOOLS TO PLAN FOR THE FUTURE

Exhibit A2.1 presents and briefly describes some popular quantitative and qualitative forecasting techniques and indicates their cost/complexity. We shall discuss some of the more important techniques.

Quantitative Forecasting Tools

Statistical techniques used for forecasting are of several types: econometric, regression, time-series analysis, and trend analysis. Each is based on the idea that definable and reliable relationships exist between what the organization wishes to forecast and some other variable.

Econometric Models

Econometric models are elaborate mathematical descriptions of multiple and complex relationships that are statistically assembled as systems of multiple regression equations. If a chain of movie theaters in New England wishes to predict the relationship between theater attendance and the level of economic activity in New England, the chain would use a complex econometric model built to describe how New England's level of economic activity and the amount of personal discretionary income allocated to entertainment purchases relate to movie theater admissions.

econometric models
Elaborate mathematical descriptions of multiple and complex relationships, statistically assembled as systems of multiple regression equations; used in forecasting.

EXHIBIT A2.1

Popular Approaches to Forecasting the Future

TECHNIQUE	SHORT DESCRIPTION	COST/COMPLEXITY
Quantitative-Causal Models		
Econometric models	Simultaneous systems of multiple regression equations	High
Regression analysis: Single and Multiple	Variations in dependent variables are explained by variations in one or more independent variables	Medium/high
Time-series models	Linear, exponential, S-curve, or other types of projections	Medium
Trend analysis	Forecasts obtained by linear or exponential smoothing or averaging of past actual values	Medium
Qualitative or Judgmental Models		
Brainstorming	Idea generation in a noncritical group situation	Medium
Delphi technique	Experts guided toward consensus	Medium
Focus groups, customer surveys, market research	Learning about intentions of potential customers or plans of businesses	Medium/high
Scenario building	Impacts of anticipated conditions imagined by forecasters	Medium

Source: Pearce, J. A. II & Robinson, R. B. Jr. 2009. *Strategic Management: Formulation, Implementation, and Control*. New York: McGraw-Hill, pp. 121–122. With permission of The McGraw-Hill Companies.

Regression Analysis

regression analysis A statistical technique used to examine the relationship or degree of association between one or more variables to predict a dependent variable of interest; used in forecasting.

In **regression analysis**, the relationship between variables of interest is studied so they can be statistically associated. If statistical studies of a theme park's visitors show that in July and August visitors consumed an average of 1.5 Cokes per visit, determining how many Cokes, cups, servers, and how much ice will be needed on a particular day in those two months is a straightforward calculation. Using regression analysis, we can further predict sales on the basis of other known numbers (probable park visitors) and the known relationships between these numbers and the variable of interest (in this case, Coke sales). If we know that a convention is bringing 15,000 visitors to a city in a certain month, we can predict through regression analysis the number of rooms a hotel is likely to sell, the number of meals that will be consumed at a restaurant, and the number of taxi rides that will be taken in that time period.

Time-Series and Trend Analyses

time-series and trend analyses Statistical methods for projecting past information or trends into the future; used in forecasting.

Time-series and trend analyses are other ways to extrapolate the past into the future. If we know how much our market has grown every year for the last ten years, a time-series forecast will project that rate of growth into the future to tell us what our park attendance, hotel occupancy rate, or covers (the number of meals served at a restaurant) will be in a given future year. These numbers can be adjusted for changes in the economy, seasonal fluctuations, revised assumptions about tourism and population growth rates, or what the competition is doing.

The opening of Walt Disney World Resort's fourth park, Animal Kingdom, changed the historical visitor's patterns in the Orlando area in a major way, so the historical time-series and trend-analysis statistical formulae also had to change. If, for example, visitors to Orlando spend their average five-day visit on Disney property (or connect to Disney Cruise Lines), the number who have extra days to go to Universal Studios, Sea World, or Gatorland drops significantly, unless the number of tourists or average length of stay rises. These other attractions have had to create new strategies to market themselves and all of Orlando as a destination separate from Walt Disney World Resort. If they can convince travelers that there are good ways to enjoy a wonderful family vacation in Orlando besides visiting Walt Disney World, they can attract a new market of visitors who are not planning to visit Walt Disney World Resort or who have been there and done that and are looking for something new to do. The creation of the Universal Studios/Islands of Adventure/Sea World/Aquatica/Wet'n Wild combination ticket (Orlando Flex Ticket) that offers both Universal Orlando Resort's second theme park, Islands of Adventure, and Sea World's water park, Aquatica, is a strategic response to the important changes in visitor patterns created by the opening of Disney's Animal Kingdom. These other theme parks had to define and attract a new market segment by opening up new facilities that would redefine how visitors saw Orlando as a destination that was more than just Disney World.

Qualitative Forecasting Tools

While objective forecasting tools offer many advantages, they require a sufficient quantity of relevant data. Sometimes, particularly when trying to forecast demand for new products and services, relevant data simply do not exist. Here, other forecasting tools can be used to make more qualitative or subjective forecasts. Among them are brainstorming, the Delphi technique, focus groups, and scenario building or war gaming.

Brainstorming

Brainstorming is a well-known strategy of asking a group of people to ponder the future and what it may mean, based on what they already know. Brainstorming can be formal and structured, requiring participation from everyone, or very informal and unstructured. As a forecasting tool, it assumes everyone has some degree of creativity, that people will voluntarily contribute their ideas in an open group discussion, that the sharing of those ideas will spark others to generate even more new ideas, and that the sum total of those ideas will be a more comprehensive forecast than that of any one person. Although these sessions often yield good new ideas, these assumptions do not always hold up. Many participants forced to brainstorm often view the time spent as wasted in aimless discussions dominated by a few who loudly express their ideas and convince others to keep their ideas to themselves.

brainstorming As a qualitative forecasting tool, a method in which a group of people generate and share ideas in open discussion, often in a free-association way, about what the future may bring.

The Delphi Technique

The **Delphi technique** is a more structured process for tapping into the knowledge of experts to create a forecast of future events that are unknown or unknowable. For example, if one wanted to know the market potential of tourism in Botswana, one could empanel a group of experts on the most probable scenario for the future of the tourism and hospitality industry in that country. Likewise, if a convention center wants to know what percent of its center capacity will be filled at this time five years from now, the Delphi technique offers a good tool to use. A group of industry experts would be asked to make individual estimates for five years from now, and the estimates would be combined or averaged. That average estimate would then be communicated back to the experts, along with the thinking that went into the estimates above and below that average. The experts would then be asked to consider this new information and invited to offer a second round of estimates. After several iterations of this procedure, the typical Delphi process tends to yield a fairly tight estimate of the future—in this example, the capacity utilization of the convention center five years from now.

Even though this process cannot guarantee a forecast of such future unknowables as precisely how many Kiwanis Club members will attend a national convention or exactly how many meals will be eaten away from home next year, combining expert estimates can yield the best estimate possible.

Delphi technique As a qualitative forecasting tool, a rather formal process involving surveying experts to get their individual forecasts, then combining or averaging those forecasts, often followed by another round of estimates based on a sharing of the individual and combined forecasts, the goal being to arrive at a final combined forecast.

Focus Groups

focus group As a qualitative forecasting tool, a group of people—frequently guests—discuss with a trained group discussion leader their future hopes and expectations of the organization; often used to sound out guests about planned organizational innovations.

Focus groups are asked to concentrate on an issue and discuss their thoughts about it with a trained group-discussion leader. Focus groups, which will be discussed in more detail in a later chapter, are perhaps most frequently used in assessing the quality of service already rendered and identifying customer key drivers. They can also be helpful in forecasting what innovations people are apt to like and not like about a service experience. If an organization has an innovation in mind, it can form a focus group that is demographically and psychographically representative of its target market and see how the group reacts to the innovation. For example, groups of young teens living in trend-setting areas are frequently used to predict clothing fashion trends that retailers use to order clothing inventories.

Scenarios

scenario building As a qualitative forecasting tool, a group of people—frequently organizational employees—assume a certain future situation or set of circumstances, then try to assess its implications for the organization; sometimes called war gaming.

Scenario building, or war gaming, has become a fairly popular subjective forecasting technique. We assume a certain future situation or scenario, and then try to assess its implications for our organization. If a hospitality organization has a major investment in Florida and California theme parks, a future scenario of concern might be the rapid developments that are occurring in virtual-reality technology. If this scenario occurs, making quick and easy access to virtual theme parks possible for millions of people, what will its impact be on the willingness of people to travel to distant, fixed-site locations for actual theme park experiences?

Scenario builders often need to act quickly. All one has to do is to look at Wii, PlayStation, Xbox and the other computer games and virtual worlds (e.g., Second Life) that are increasingly available on the web, inexpensive, and extensively used by the iGens Generation to see the potential threat and opportunity they represent for the hospitality industry. Scenario builders are in danger of looking up from their industry scenarios or service simulations to find that the scenario is already here, online, and free.

Further readings on the topics in this chapter are listed in "Additional Readings" on pages 495–499.

Get the tools you need to sharpen your study skills. SAGE edge offers a robust online environment featuring an impressive array of free tools and resources.

Access practice quizzes, eFlashcards, video, and multimedia at **edge.sagepub.com/Ford2e**.

Visit **edge.sagepub.com/Ford2e** to help you accomplish your coursework goals in an easy-to-use learning environment.

Gustavo Caballero/Getty Images

3 Setting the Scene for the Guest Experience

Hospitality Principle: Provide the Service Setting that Guests Expect

I don't want the public to see the world they live in while they're in the Park. I want them to feel they're in another world.

—Walt Disney

Learning Objectives

After reading this chapter, you should be able to

3.1 Explain how theming the service setting pays off in guest satisfaction.

3.2 Discuss why the service setting or service environment is important.

3.3 Explain how the service environment affects guests and employees.

3.4 Discuss why providing a service environment in which guests feel safe and secure is critical.

3.5 Identify which elements of the service environment need to be managed.

3.6 Describe how individual factors moderate or affect the responses of guests to the service environment, according to Bitner's servicescape model.

INTRODUCTION

In Chapter 1, we defined the guest experience as consisting of three component elements: the service itself, the service environment, and the service delivery system (the people and the processes that provide the service to the guest). This chapter focuses on the service environment or setting in which the guest experience takes place. For a restaurant, the environment can be a Rainforest Café or Margaritaville, where the physical structure is an integral part of the guest experience, or it can be a Denny's with simple booths. The difference between these two types of restaurants is something more than just the food. An eatertainment restaurant, such as House of Blues, ESPN Club, and Hard Rock Café, creates an environment that enhances the eating experience well beyond the meals it serves. They deliver a high-quality meal, but they also offer an elaborately themed décor to add a show-like experience for their guests and uniquely differentiate their restaurants from competitors. Although all service organizations give some thought to the service setting, its importance to the customer experience has been most thoroughly understood by those who view and treat their customers as guests—the hospitality industry.

Some in the hospitality industry have embraced the idea of guestology and have developed service environments to meet or exceed the customers' expectations. Truly amazing examples can be found in amusement parks, hotels, and restaurants, where the entire service setting is crafted to create a specific look and feel for the guest. This service setting is an important part of the service experience being delivered. This chapter will focus on why managing the setting for the hospitality experience is so important, and what major components the guestologist needs to consider doing it well.

CREATING "THE SHOW"

A term coined by Walt Disney, **"the show"** refers to everyone and everything that interfaces with guests. It reflects his belief that a theme park should make guests feel like they are immersed in a living motion picture, where everything the guest sees, feels, and senses is part of the story being told. Although employees and other customers are also part of any guest service organization's "show" or service environment, the physical aspects of the service setting are equally important.

"the show" A Disney term for everyone and everything that interfaces or interacts with guests on a Disney property.

Without question, the physical aspects of the service setting can have a major influence on the guest's determination of the quality and value of a guest experience.

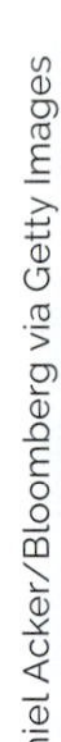

The Bright Angel Lodge, designed by Mary Colter, provides a unifying architectural theme for guests staying at the Grand Canyon.

For some experiences offered to guests, the environment is in effect the setting for a dramatic production or play in which the guest is a participant.[1] Occasionally, the environment is so significant to the enjoyment of the fantasy that it should perhaps be considered a part of the service itself.

Perhaps more than any other organization, Disney understands that its guests have extraordinary experiences largely because of the attention Disney pays to creating the show. Some claim Walt Disney's extensive use of theming was an extension of the ideas originated by architect Mary Colter (1869–1958) of the Fred Harvey Company, seen in her pioneering designs for the Hopi House, Bright Angel Lodge, and other structures at the Grand Canyon, as well as in other buildings The Fred Harvey Company built in the early 1900s.[2] Her idea was that a guest experience can be unified and enhanced if it is based on a theme. Today, The Walt Disney Company shows its belief in that idea by spending endless time and effort ensuring the environment and the cast members/employees within each of its parks—the show—are organized around a central theme, as consistently and accurately as possible.

Many companies use a theme to create a feeling that guests are somehow immersed in another place and time to provide them with extraordinary experiences. The lesson Disney has taught is that by paying attention to the details of creating a themed show, they can add quality and value to the guest experience. Successful hospitality organizations have learned a great show is well worth spending considerable time and effort.

Much of Walt Disney's early success with Disneyland resulted from his insight that many guests would enjoy feeling like active participants in a drama or movie rather than simply being passive observers. In making movies, Walt learned to present stories that offered viewers the opportunity to experience fantasy vicariously. Why not set up parks and rides including characters and fantastic settings within which guests could move and participate as if they were immersed in a movie? For an organization offering such an intangible feeling as its "product," the service setting is critical to success.

Themes Create Fantasy

When a company uses the physical environment and other visual cues to create a show as part of its service experience, it is trying to transport its guests into a fantasy world. This strategy can be used for an amusement park, a restaurant, a hotel, a cruise ship, or any place where the hospitality experience would be enhanced by adding some fantasy. Many hospitality organizations have used the environment to create a sense of fantasy through **theming**, as they have learned the value of creating a unique and memorable setting that enhances and contributes to the total guest experience. For example, when the environment serves as an important part of the dining experience,

theming The organization and presentation of the guest experience around a unifying idea or theme, often a fantasy theme, to give guests the illusion of being in a place and time other than "the here and now"; most often used in connection with theme parks and theme restaurants

[1] B. Joseph Pine and James H. Gilmore, *The Experience Economy: Work Is Theatre and Every Business a Stage* (Boston, MA: Harvard Business School Press); Kirk L. Wakefield and Jeffrey Blodgett, "Retrospective: The importance of servicescapes in leisure service settings," *Journal of Services Marketing* 30, no.7 (2016): 686–69.

[2] Molly H. Mullin, "The Great Southwest of the Fred Harvey Company and the Santa Fe Railway," *Museum Anthropology* 20, 1 (1996): 79–80.

the theme of the setting within which the meal is presented needs to be consistent with the food served.

Walt Disney's genius was to take guests out of the real world and transport them into a world of make-believe, which he accomplished by carefully integrating all the components of the guest experience in his themed parks. Seeing the success of Disney, others adopted this idea. The Medieval Times restaurant created a theme that transports guests to an eleventh-century feast and tournament, where knights joust on horseback and dinner is eaten without any utensils. The listings in the "Experiences" section on the Unusual Hotels of the World website show an amazing variety of themed hotels available for customers.[3] The variety of themed hotels listed include: an igloo, cave dwellings, 200 meters underground, a train car, prisons, and even one where each room is themed after an automobile (Would you like to stay in the Mercedes Benz room, the Morris Minor room, or might the Volkswagen room be more your style?). Regardless of the type of hospitality experience or the specific theme, to visit one of these business establishments is to experience a fantasy. That's what guests want and expect. The details of the environment and employees are carefully themed—organized and presented around a unifying idea, often a fantasy idea—to create the feeling within the guest that every part of the environment is an accurate representation of what the guest might reasonably expect to see if the fantasy were true.

Roberto Machado Noa/LightRocket via Getty Images

The Medieval Times restaurant creates a theme that transports guests to an eleventh-century feast and tournament.

In historic Colonial Williamsburg, for example, not only are employees dressed in authentic eighteenth-century attire, each of the working craftsmen uses methods appropriate to that time period to create tools, parts, or other items needed by other parts of the historic community. You can watch the blacksmith make nails, which will be used to restore a barn, which will eventually house sheep, whose wool will be used to create new period clothing to be worn by future employees.

To Theme or Not to Theme?

Theming can effectively tie all the elements of the service experience together. Yet, by its very nature, a themed service may limit the appeal of the service offering to some people, and theming also limits the sort of new ventures of service products such a company can provide, because any new elements must remain consistent with the theme. Therefore, the decision whether to theme or not must be considered very carefully.

On the positive side, theming is a way to add value to the guest experience, if used effectively by enhancing it. For a Rainforest Cafe, many Las Vegas hotels, a Medieval Times castle, or a Disney theme park, the theming contributes to maintenance of the fantasy, enhances visual stimulation, and helps to find one's way around with the visual cues it provides. It gives guests something to talk about after they've gone home; it reinforces their remembrance of what they've done; it can create an emotional connection with the experience; and it provides additional confirmation of the experience's value. Theming is an opportunity for the organization to add "wow" to the experience, by providing more than guests expect.

[3] The Unusual Company Ltd., "Go Unusual Travel Ideas," *Unusual Hotels of the World*, The Unusual Company Ltd., access date February 6, 2018. http://www.unusualhotelsoftheworld.com/.

Consider a five-star restaurant. It is a kind of fantasyland. It takes guests out of the real world and serves them a memorable meal in a memorable environment. The setting is designed to send signals or cues to its guests that this is a place of consistently high quality, as the setting enhances and contributes to the total guest experience. While the memorable part is intended to be the world-class meal and the way it is served, it is the first impression created by the physical environment that sets up the guest's expectations for the great meal that follows.

Contrast the fantasy created by the five-star restaurant with the fantasy created by a Rainforest Café, Margaritaville, Bahama Breeze restaurant, or any good ethnic restaurant you can name. These restaurants and many other organizations within and outside the hospitality industry have created a service setting through theming. They realize that blending the sights, sounds, and even the tastes and smells of the service setting to fit in with an overall theme can enhance the guest's experience and make it more memorable by appealing to all the guests' senses. Restaurants have been themed for many years, but at such totally themed restaurants as Medieval Times, Murder Mystery Dinner Theatre, and House of Blues, the food may become a secondary aspect of the overall guest experience. A walk down the Las Vegas strip offers several illustrations of how hotels have added theming to enhance the guest experience. There, one can find structures that remind guests of New York, Venice, Paris, and a circus. Likewise, the cruise industry has added theming to its cruises and ships to make them immediately recognizable and different for guests. Theming makes a trip on a ship like the *Disney Magic* or the *Disney Wonder* memorable. The theming begins with the ship's outward appearance, and continues with the hallways, food, and activities, all of which carefully and consistently reinforce the fantasy. Today's guests have become accustomed to enriched environments in their homes, offices, entertainment sites, and automobiles. Organizing the experience around a theme is one way for hospitality organizations to meet guest expectations of an enriched service setting, especially when the setting tells a story.

The health care industry has also recognized the value of theming. For example, Minneapolis, Minnesota's Amplatz Children's Hospital adopted a "Passport to Discovery" theme.[4] It designated each floor of the hospital as a unique habitat and assigned each clinical area a "storyteller" that is an animal from that habitat. The storyteller for each floor is incorporated in all signage. Each patient is issued a "passport" at check-in. As they go through the hospital, they receive stamps on their passport. Amplatz's goal was to use a theme they could easily incorporate into its many architectural spaces. It would be imbedded in walls, ceilings, floor patterns, lighting fixtures, signage, and furniture. The theme would inform the color scheme: yellow for the grassland floor, orange for the desert floor, and so on. The theming "clues" embedded in the various architectural and graphic elements would create a "treasure hunt" that encouraged ambulatory patients to move about their floor, helping to relieve the boredom of a long hospital stay while providing information about natural habitats and the diverse cultures that reside in them. Even in the parking

Mark Andrews/Disney via Getty Images

The Disney Wonder is one of Disney's four themed cruise ships.

[4] Rulon F. Stacey and Carolyn Wilson, "Benefits of a Codesign Model in Healthcare Don't End with the New Building," *Frontiers of Health Services Management* 31," no. 1 (2014): 31–38.

garage accent colors were used to identify parking levels. The result is a space that is integrated down to the last detail. The theme would add value to the hospital by educating, entertaining, and engaging patients. Children often find hospitals scary and boring, but the theming strategy helps make it less scary and more interesting.[5]

On the negative side, a themed environment can be more expensive to construct and take more time to get all the elements right to make it memorable for the guest. Further, theming is not always appropriate, and theming has its risks. By definition, theming places limits on what the organization can offer in terms of service, setting, and delivery system. Compared to an all-purpose non-themed restaurant, a themed restaurant will generally have a narrower range of menu offerings. Medieval Times has a fixed choice menu with the only options being a chicken or vegetarian dinner and a limited variety of drinks. Patrons of Lone Star Steakhouse and Saloon want and expect to find steak, ribs, chicken, barbecue, and chili on the menu, and a hot sauce on the table. Only if the market for those offerings continues to be strong will Lone Star or Medieval Times succeed.

Few organizations are fortunate or insightful enough to develop themes with universal appeal. Hooters, a Florida-based limited-menu restaurant chain, whose waitresses dress in tight orange shorts and skimpy, figure-hugging t-shirts, attracts primarily young white males and not older customers or other ethnic groups. The more specialized the theme, the more it will appeal to customers who already liked the theme anyway, but the narrower the market will be. This appeal to a relatively narrow market niche, however, can succeed. No hospitality organization can be all things to all guests. Hard Rock Cafe does not try to appeal to small children, and rock fans are not the key customers whose expectations Chuck E. Cheese is trying to meet. Even organizations whose themes appeal to a broad audience—like Hard Rock and its music stars—must find ways to sustain their novelty by changing their exhibits and improving menu items to keep the experience fresh for returning guests.[6] Otherwise, guests will come once, or perhaps a few times for the novelty, and then seek other experiences. People even become tired of superstars and music memorabilia.

The organization must provide a service setting consistent with the guest's expectations for the overall guest experience. Theming is one approach toward achieving that goal. All aspects of the physical setting—building design, layout of physical objects, lighting, colors, equipment, signs, employee uniforms, smells, sounds, materials—must complement and support each other and give a feeling of integrated design.

Control and Focus

To maintain the illusion of fantasy in a themed service setting, the experience, as is true of any good story, must be controlled and focused. The guests should see what the storyteller wants them to see. This can be accomplished in a variety of ways. In a theme park, most attractions are designed to control the experience. Rides are designed to give guests the feeling of moving through a story. Guests are positioned to see the right visual cues and not the wrong ones. In a Pirates of the Caribbean or a Haunted Mansion, the positioning of the vehicles on the ride, the use of light and dark, smells, the pace of the ride, as well as other elements of the environment create the experience the storyteller envisioned.[7] Hospitality organizations can also limit where the guests can actually go or what they can see. Bushes are planted to block guest movement to where they are not supposed to go, and pathways are paved to promote movement to where they should go. Likewise, buildings and foliage are placed to block sightlines,

---

[5] Jennifer Silvis, "What's in A Theme?" *Health Care Design Magazine*, December 21, 2011, https://www.healthcaredesignmagazine.com/architecture/whats-theme/.

[6] Jooyeon Ha and SooCheong Jang, "Boredom and Moderating Variables for Customers' Novelty Seeking," *Journal of Foodservice Business Research* 18, no. 4 (2015): 404–422.

[7] Stephen M. Fjellman, *Vinyl Leaves: Walt Disney World and America* (Boulder, CO: Westview Press, 1992), 257.

ensuring what is supposed to be seen is seen and what should be out of sight is unseen. Support functions are carefully hidden from the guest. You never see an un-costumed cast member at Disney, you never see the modern kitchen at Medieval Times, and the lawn is mowed with power lawnmowers at Colonial Williamsburg early in the morning before any guests arrive. Guest flow through a themed setting is carefully planned so the guests experience only what the company intends them to experience.

The Architecture

The same idea, of having the attention of guests engaged in specific things that will reinforce the experience or a story, is carried forward in the architectural theming of the hospitality organization. For example, the Klaus K hotel in Finland was created with a theme based on the Finnish national epic *Kalevala*. The designers studied the story and Finnish history to realize that the country and *Kalevala* are about strong contrasts: life and death, light and dark, pride and humility. Their task was to weave these contrasts, creating a theme in such a way to evoke the story. As scholar Lena Mossberg describes it, "We created an interior design that partly reflects the Finnish nature, temperament, and the country's modern history. The hotel rooms were sectioned into categories like 'passion,' 'jealousy,' 'desire,' and 'mysticism.'"[8]

As an example of another architectural detail used to be consistent with this story of *Kalevala,* which explains how the world and universe were created from seven eggs, the front desk of the hotel is shaped like an egg and depicts a bird's nest theme. These sorts of details are pervasive through the structural design of the hotel, as well as in all of its artwork. There are many such architectural details throughout the hotel, but the appeal of this theming is of course in the eye of the customer. As Mossberg also felt, "The Americans didn't get it, but the Finns loved it."[9]

Courtesy of Klaus K Hotels

The Klaus K hotel in Helsinki, Finland, was designed so that the architecture reflected Finnish nature, temperament, and the country's modern history.

Former New Business Development President and Executive Vice President of Darden Restaurants Blaine Sweatt described his development team's design approach when creating the innovative Seasons 52 facilities: "Tremendous attention was given to every detail of the design to be sure it both reinforced the conceptual positioning of the brand and enhanced the comfort of the guests. This encompassed designing the look and feel of the restaurant to create a relaxing, yet sophisticated atmosphere that actually feels as though it embraces guests from the moment they arrive until the time they leave." This philosophy guided the design team as it analyzed each phase of the restaurant visit to ensure that each would add to the guest experience. For example, the "approach" phase transitions guests from the outside world to a relaxing experience. From the time arriving guests step out of their cars through the moment when they're enjoying their first sip of wine, the design elements were carefully combined to slowly draw the guests into the sights, sounds, and smells of a rich, earthy culinary adventure.

Early in the design phase the team decided to incorporate many of the design principles that Frank Lloyd Wright first articulated. Notably these included designing

[8] Lena Mossberg, "Extraordinary Experiences through Storytelling," *Scandinavian Journal of Hospitality and Tourism* 8, no. 3 (2008): 204.

[9] Lena Mossberg, p. 204.

structures to harmonize with nature and creating visually interesting structures that emphasized long linear lines, wide roof overhangs, and flowing water. The Seasons 52 design evolved to include significant amounts of stonework, natural woods, open beam-work and earthy colors as were often found in Wright's classic architecture. The restaurant building itself incorporated carefully prescribed mature landscaping to create a woodsy feeling and a cascading water feature to produce the relaxing sounds of falling waters.

Courtesy of Darden

Seasons 52 gave careful consideration to every design detail to ensure that each aspect reinforced the conceptual positioning of the brand and enhanced the comfort of the guests.

Equal attention was given to the subsequent phases of the dining experience. The "Entry to the Host and Lobby Areas" phase was designed to communicate, through lighting, space use, and wood tones, a sense of arrival at a destination that guests would experience as exciting and stylish. An open flame oven was purposely located near the entrance to reinforce the raw essence of cooking right at the front of the restaurant, subtly reminding arriving guests of the primal importance of fire to life. Darden's new concept development team believed the purposely blended tapestry of colors, lighting, sight line angles, textures, design accents, aromas, and music were so important to creating the guest experience that nearly one-third of a 100-page document describing lessons learned from Seasons 52 was dedicated to these design issues.

Similarly, extensive uses of architecture to reinforce a theme can be found throughout the world of hospitality, such as The Forum Shops connected to Caesars Palace in Las Vegas, Nevada. The use of simulated ancient Roman architecture, streets, fountains, statues, and facades help complete an image the hotel is trying to portray.

Some settings can be experienced from a single location. Most architectural structures—environments that often cost millions of dollars to create—can best be experienced by moving through them to perceive the intersecting planes, spaces, and shapes of which architecture is made. Colonial Williamsburg allows guests to experience life in an eighteenth-century town, around the time of the American Revolutionary War. You can explore the town, tour the governor's mansion and numerous other buildings, observe (and sometimes assist) craftsmen using authentic eighteenth-century methods in their shops, watch historical reenactments outside the courthouse or capitol building, dine in period restaurants, and otherwise fully immerse yourself in this time period. The mission of the Colonial Williamsburg Foundation is to operate the world's largest living history museum, and in doing so, seeks to replicate with as much authenticity as possible the original architecture of this historic location. The architecture is just one part of the overall theme that situates the guests and develops the narrative story as the guest moves through it and becomes immersed in the illusion.

Michael S. Williamson/The Washington Post via Getty Images

Colonial Williamsburg seeks to immerse guests into the world's largest living history museum.

Robert C. Ford

Walt Disney World's Casting Center Doorknobs: "One Good Turn Deserves Another."

The creation of a movie-type of experience in Disney's Orlando Resort is most evident in the rides, but it is also an important element in the overall architecture of the park. A walk down Main Street, U.S.A., in the Magic Kingdom, for instance, opens up carefully planned and themed vistas, with Cinderella Castle always looming in the distance. The Cinderella Castle appears at first to be far away, as if this symbol of childhood fantasy is only a distant memory, a part of a small middle-American town's collective memory.[10] As guests move toward the castle, they see it more distinctly, and they can eventually reexperience the fantasy by entering the castle.

The Casting Center building used for interviewing and hiring staff is themed in a way that introduces potential employees into the Disney culture. Applicants walk up a long incline to a reception desk. The art and architecture along the way portray important Disney images and symbols. The design communicates to prospective cast members some of the Disney culture and a feeling of an open invitation to join the Disney family. In the reception lobby are statues of fifteen famous Disney characters. Even the knobs on the building's front door are designed to replicate the doorknobs from the classic animated feature *Alice in Wonderland* to send the subtle message to potential hires that they are entering a place unlike any other.

Sights and Sounds

Sound is often an important service-setting element. Music is a particularly potent environmental factor.[11] A convenience store that was plagued by some teenagers hanging out at the store and bothering patrons began playing elevator music through its sound system. Unable to fit the classic music to their rebellious self-image, the troublemakers moved on.

The basic principle, of course, is that environmental sounds should serve a purpose. In general, the sounds (most often music) should complement the experience the organization is trying to provide to its target guests. Again, in general, but with many exceptions, louder, faster music in the service setting appeals to younger guests; softer, slower music appeals to older guests. The sounds of music can also affect guest behavior. Studies have shown that bar patrons finish their drinks faster or slower depending on the tempo and subject matter of the music being played. People tend to eat faster and drink more (and leave sooner, meaning that more tables are typically turned) if the music is fast and loud. Slow music encourages people to dine in a leisurely fashion. A study of diners at an Italian restaurant in Scotland found that both music tempo and preference were related to time spent by guests in the restaurant. A more detailed analysis indicated the target guests' music preference was the best explanation of the relationship between music and guest behavior.[12] Similarly, a study in a wine store showed that French wine sold more when French music was playing,

[10] Shelton S. Waldrep, "Monuments to Walt," in *Inside the Mouse: Work and Play at Disney World*, ed. Jane Kuenz, Shelton Waldrep, Susan Willis, and Karen Klugman (Durham, NC: Duke University Press, 1995), 212–213.

[11] Rajnish Jain and Shilpa Bagdare, "Music and Consumption Experience: A Review," *International Journal of Retail & Distribution Management* 39, no. 4 (2011): 289–302.

[12] Clare Caldwell and Sally A. Hibbert, "The Influence of Music Tempo and Musical Preference on Restaurant Patrons' Behavior," *Psychology & Marketing* 19, no. 11 (2002): 895–917.

while German wine sold more when German music was playing.[13] Clearly, the sights and sounds in the background affect the way consumers behave—and spend their money.

Lighting is an important feature of most service settings. Some guest experiences are best delivered in bright lights, some in dim. Glare and lights at eye level are unpleasant in any setting. If you enter a service setting and don't notice the lighting, it is probably well done. Lighting can focus the eye toward visual cues that emphasize the theme of the experience and away from things that detract from the theme. In a Rainforest Cafe, you see not the lighting but what is lit. Lights should be selected, turned on, and directed not just to avoid darkness. Like every other aspect of the setting, the lighting should be an element of a greater design with the purpose of enhancing the guest experience.

Courtesy of the Klaus K Hotel

Lighting can be used to affect an establishment's moods, as shown here in the Klaus K's bar and lounge.

In prescribing the design features for the Seasons 52 restaurants, the Darden design team specified five specific guidelines in their use of lighting. These are:

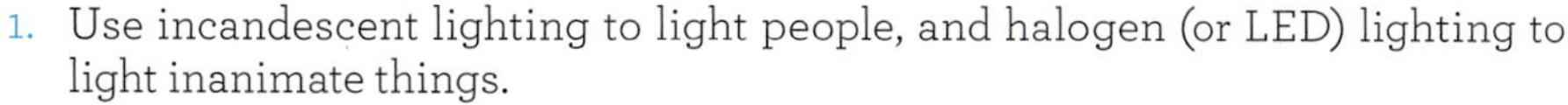

1. Use incandescent lighting to light people, and halogen (or LED) lighting to light inanimate things.
2. Never allow guests to see where a light comes from, only where it hits.
3. If you're spending money on a decoration (a painting, vase, shelving), spend the money to illuminate it so it can be seen.
4. When illuminating particular design features, have beams directed at different angles to avoid glare from straight-on lighting of surfaces.
5. Physically check that no light source is visible from any place a guest may be seated or standing.

At Walt Disney's Magic Kingdom, careful attention is paid to the meshing of visual and auditory effects to enhance the guest's experience. Music and spoken words are carefully integrated into the design of individual rides so the guest has a continuing, seamless experience while moving on the ride or through a park area. As the guest moves away from one room or segment area to another of the Haunted Mansion, Pirates of the Caribbean, or It's A Small World, the sounds and visual effects merge, with no sense of overlap, to provide a smooth transition from one phase of the fantasy to the next.[14]

The Entertainment Control System

Technology

Disney's Entertainment Control System (DECS) at the Magic Kingdom is designed to maximize each guest's experience by managing the visual and auditory aspects of the setting. For parades covering the wide geographic area of the Magic Kingdom, the visual and musical effects could easily clash. Since the floats move and the

[13] Adrian C. North, David J. Hargreaves, and Jennifer McKendrick, "In-store Music Affects Product Choice," *Nature* 390: 6656 (1997): 132; Charles Spence and Maya U. Shankar, "The Influence of Auditory Cues on the Perception of, and Responses to, Food and Drink," *Journal of Sensory Studies* 25, no. 3 (2010): 406–430.

[14] Waldrep, 212–213.

guests stand still, Disney has found a way to accompany each float with appropriate lighting and music as it moves through the 24 zones of the parade route. Disney uses two technological solutions. The first is a series of remote interface cabinets linked together through fiber-optic cable to the DECS. As the parade floats pass by the buried antennae, the DECS reads the code associated with each float and then creates appropriate lights and music, from hidden loudspeakers, near the float. Each float carries an FM wireless receiver, audio amplifier, and speaker system. Each float is designed to carry one channel of the audio signal sent by the DECS and play it through its own sound system. The result is that guests experience the same light-and-sound show, part of which emanates from the float and another part from the hidden light-and-sound sources in each zone, all these media synchronized by the DECS.

WHY IS THE ENVIRONMENT IMPORTANT?

Hospitality managers must pay attention to the environment for several major reasons. It influences guest expectations, creates and maintains the mood, and has positive effects on employees. Finally, the environment serves several functional purposes as part of the service itself. While every hospitality organization has a service environment, the best, such as the memorable ones in theme restaurants, hotels, cruise ships, and parks, know how important they are in creating value and quality for their guests' experiences. They know their environments are key parts of the service experience and carefully plan their service settings to ensure each component adds to the theme that ties the whole experience together.

Guest Expectations

First, the environment influences the guest's expectations, even before the service is delivered. If the outside of the restaurant is dirty, guests will enter with negative expectations, if they enter at all. Objectively, the number of cigarette butts on the ground next to the restaurant's front door has nothing to do with the chef's ability to prepare a high-quality meal and the staff's ability to present it, but guests do not view the environment objectively. If the restaurant does not care enough to clean up outside its building, the guest may conclude it does not clean up its kitchen either and probably does not care about how it prepares the meal. Many guests evaluate a restaurant by using the restroom test, to see how much the restaurant cares about cleanliness. Good restaurant managers make sure that procedures are in place to keep the restrooms clean.

Guest Mood

Second, the environment sets and maintains the mood after the guest begins the guest experience. Once the guest enters the Magic Kingdom, the entire focus is on establishing the fantasy and maintaining the "magic." One way to do so is to maintain the consistency between what the guest expects to see and what the guest actually sees. Guests expect the cast members in Disney costumes to stay in character, and they do. Most are not allowed to speak because if they did, Mickey would probably not sound the way he does in the cartoons. Better to make guests wonder than to disappoint them. Those that do speak are carefully trained in not only the words to use but also how to speak in character. When you go to the Royal Summerhus at WDW's Epcot to meet and get your picture taken with Princess Anna and Queen Elsa, Anna will be very upbeat, talkative, welcoming, and warm. Elsa will still be friendly but more reserved and regal. If the characters were allowed to take off their head masks or any other part of their costumes while in public view or allowed to act in any way they choose, they might destroy the magic of the illusion or ruin a child's feelings about the character she loves. A Disney rule requires that character costumes must be transported in black bags to ensure that no child will accidentally see a lifeless Mickey or other beloved character being hauled in the back of a van.

In a similar effort, to use the environment to set the mood, Disney spends considerable money on ensuring the park grounds are clean, the lawns carefully manicured, and the flowers always in bloom. The company has learned through studies of guests that people associate *clean and orderly* with *safe and high in quality.* They know everyone has been to a typical amusement park and seen the dirt and debris scattered all over the grounds. Walt Disney wanted to differentiate his parks from traditional amusement parks, and cleanliness is one way to do so. The real world is not always a clean place, so providing a sparkling-clean park is yet another way to enable guests to leave the outside world behind and feel safe in the fantasy environment Disney has created.

Main Street, Disney

As the example of Seasons 52 Restaurant suggested, even the architecture should be used to enhance the mood the hospitality organization strives to create and maintain. Every guest at the Disneyland Park or Walt Disney World's Magic Kingdom must pass through their Main Street. The Main Street building and streets are constructed to enhance the feeling of being not in a huge and spectacular park but in a cozy, friendly place. The architectural technique, called forced perspective, led to designing the first floors of the buildings along Main Street, U.S.A. in Disneyland Park at 9/10th scale, the second floors at 7/8, and the third floors at 5/8 scale. According to David Koenig in *Mouse Tales,*

> The decreasing heights make the shops appear taller than they are, yet still cozy. The Sleeping Beauty Castle uses the same effect, its stones large at the base and increasingly smaller up high. On the Matterhorn, trees and shrubs halfway up are smaller than those at the base. The Mark Twain [steamboat], Disneyland Railroad, and Main Street vehicles are all 5/8 scale and other structures were built in various scales based on what looked most effective to the designers.[15]

While this old production technique saves space and costs in building movie sets, it is also an effective means for creating an environment that reinforces the feeling Disneyland Park seeks to create. Disney consciously conceives and creates all aspects of the service environment, from building architecture to doorknobs, in order to set and maintain whatever mood is appropriate to each fantasy in the series of fantasies comprising the overall guest experience of a Disney theme park. This attention to detail also creates a competitive advantage. Other organizations use their physical structures and settings to do the same. A doctor hangs her diplomas on the wall to reassure patients she has the training necessary to provide high-quality medical care. Carrabba's uses an open grille concept to allow its guests to easily see the cleanliness of its food-preparation people and their cooking areas. A checklist of how often the bathrooms have been cleaned is posted on the bathroom door for all McDonald's customers to see. Good hoteliers are constantly stopping to pick up pieces of paper and other debris in their hallways and other hotel spaces, to serve as a role model for others to emulate and to keep the hotel spotless. They know the degree to which guests associate cleanliness with overall quality.

[15] David Koenig, *Mouse Tales: A Behind-the-Ears Look at Disneyland* (Irvine, CA: Bonaventure Press, 1994), 42–43.

Employee Satisfaction

A third contribution of the service setting to the guest experience is its effect on a group of people who do not even use the service: the employees who co-produce it. Although the environment is designed primarily to enhance the guest's experience, insofar as possible it should be supportive of and compatible with the employee's experience as well. Nobody wants to work in a dangerous or dirty environment. Employees spend a lot more time in the service setting than guests do, and a well-designed environment can promote employee satisfaction, which some argue is highly correlated with guest satisfaction.[16] Hyatt Hotels believes in this philosophy so strongly it improved its employee entry-way so that it looks as nice as the one used by its guests. They believe if their employees are happy with the physical environment that impacts their working conditions in the back of the house, that happiness will carry over into the way they serve their guests in the front of the house.

Care and attention to environmental details show employees that the organization is committed to guest satisfaction and service quality. Hyatt employees know any company that spends the amount of time and energy Hyatt does on the details of the hotel, even on those details most guests will never notice, must really care about the quality of the guest experience. The impact of this caring on the employees is immeasurable; in ways large and small, it shows employees the commitment the company expects from itself and from them.

Gaylord Hotels discovered that several of its initiatives to enhance the service environment spill over to its employee satisfaction. At Opryland, there is an employee named Davine. She is a woman, dressed as a tree, and standing on stilts. Her job is to position herself at various points in the atrium. She entertains people by making slight movements that catch people by surprise as they think she is part of the background scenery and not an animate object. Because the employees know she is there surprising guests, they too are entertained. One of the byproducts of the hospitality industry is utilized fully by Gaylord as it knows that by creating a fun setting for its customers it also creates a fun work setting for its employees.

Setting as a Part of Service

The environment may serve merely as a neutral backdrop for some guest experiences. But for many organizations, the environment is so significant to the success of its guest experience it represents a fourth important component to consider for hospitality managers: The setting for such guest experiences should be considered as part of the service itself. The guest co-producing the experience is, in effect, inside the "service production factory." Unlike the typical manufacturing production facility, the service production factory has the guest inside it on the production floor and often in the middle of the production process. When the guest is present and co-producing the experience in the hospitality "service factory," the setting represents a major part of what the guest is paying for and seeking from the guest experience. No one wants to go to a fine-dining restaurant and sit on plastic seats, to eat a gourmet meal served on paper plates by a waiter dressed in blue jeans and t-shirt who is trying to turn the table in forty-five minutes. No matter how good the meal, the quality of the food, or the presentation on the paper plates, the guest will be dissatisfied with the fine-dining experience in such an environment. Not only must the meal be good, the decor, ambience, tablecloth, attire of the servers, number and

[16] Ingrid Y. Lin and Anna S. Mattila, "Restaurant Servicescape, Service Encounter, and Perceived Congruency on Customers' Emotions and Satisfaction," *Journal of Hospitality Marketing & Management* 19, no. 8 (2010): 819–84.

appearance of other guests, and place setting must all be consistent with what the guest expects in a fine-dining experience.

The quality of the environmental context within which the guest's experience occurs affects the quality of the experience itself and also the guest's opinion of the hospitality organization's overall quality. In a fascinating experiment broadcast on Food Network's *Food Detectives,*[17] two groups of individuals were invited to have a meal at what they were told was a possible new restaurant. Both groups received the same food. The first group, however, was served on plastic plates, on tables with plastic tablecloths, and the food was given boring names (like seafood filet and chocolate cake). The second group, however, was served on tables with linen tablecloths, and the food had names like Succulent Italian Seafood Filet and Belgian Black Forest Double Chocolate Cake. Although the food was identically prepared, the group in the fancier environment reported it tasting better and also reported being willing to spend more money for it. Clearly, one's environment affects the way the guest experience is perceived and even valued.

The Functional Value of the Setting

Finally, the environment is important for several pragmatic and functional reasons. The guest relies on the hospitality organization to create an environment that is safe and easy to use and understand. Environmental features must be such that the guest can easily and safely enter, experience, and then leave without getting lost, hurt, or disoriented.

For the modern hospitality organization, the issue of safety and security has become more important than ever before. People worry increasingly about whether they will be safe from harm or injury when they go to a concert, restaurant, hotel, cruise, or convention. Guests must believe the service settings have a high level of safety and security, and hospitality organizations should find ways to communicate to guests that they are safe places to be. Light, open space, smiling employees making eye contact with guests, and cleanliness make guests feel secure. Such environmental elements as well-lit parking lots and pathways, low-cut hedges behind which no one can hide, and the presence of uniformed employees are appropriate and reassuring in just about any service situation. Many hotels post security guards at entry points to give their customers a feeling of security as they enter and leave the property; hotels also train their employees to emphasize their presence by looking at guests, making eye contact, and speaking to them; and theme parks have vehicles cruising the well-lit parking lots to reassure guests they are about to enter a crime-free world. Shanghai Disneyland Resort recognized the crowd control problems it was likely to face in a location that has seen some of the largest crowds in the world. It decided to enhance guest safety by redesigning its park's entrance. Instead of allowing guests to enter along a traditional "Main Street," Shanghai guests will enter into a jumbo-sized oval with a garden maze designed to slow the

John Tlumacki/The Boston Globe via Getty Images

With increased security concerns, travelers are willing to be subjected to increased levels of security.

[17] The Food Network, "Liquid Nitrogen Cocktails," Food Detectives, Season 2, Episode 9, directed by Bob Tuschman, aired July 16, 2009 (New York, NY: Scripps Networks, 2018), Television.

expected hurried scramble of entering guests.[18] Most hospitality organizations want guests to relax and enjoy the guest experience. In a world where terrorists are an ongoing threat, guests will even tolerate inconveniences if those body scans at airports, checking of bags and purses at concerts, and the many other security checks guests encounter make them feel safe. Because guests cannot relax if they fear for their safety, managers must provide a safe and secure environment. It's as simple as that.

A second functional aspect of the setting is making it easy for guests to find their way to do whatever it is they seek in the experience. If what guests seek is a specific location, like a meeting room in a hotel or the Hogwarts Express in Universal Studios, clear, simple signage or strategically located employees can help them find their way. If it is a web page or an app, like for making an online restaurant reservation or a hotel self-check-out, it is important not only to make sure it works properly but also that there are clear, easy-to-follow directions on how to navigate the page or use the technology to avoid guest frustration. The point is guests who feel lost or confused are generally unhappy and dissatisfied with their experience and the hospitality organization. All organizations that want their guests to successfully operate their self-service technology or find their way in a physical or virtual setting must carefully study guest behavior to ensure their directions and wayfinding guides are accurate, clear, and easy to find and use and, most importantly, that they work.

A MODEL: HOW THE SERVICE ENVIRONMENT AFFECTS THE GUEST

As we know, the hospitality manager seeking to provide an excellent and memorable experience should give as much attention to managing the setting as to the service product itself and the service delivery system. The rest of this chapter will be based on Exhibit 3.1. This exhibit is based on a broader model proposed by Mary Jo Bitner for understanding the environment-user relationship in service organizations.[19] Her term for this is "servicescape" and her model seeks to describe how the components of a service environment influence a guest's willingness to stay in the experience or leave. Although other writers[20] have modified this model, our exhibit follows Bitner's model and focuses on the environmental influences that operate on the guest to determine the guest's reaction to the service setting. The combination of elements can cause the guest (and employees as well) to want to approach the setting and remain in it or to leave the setting and avoid it in the future. Even though our model focuses on guests, it should be noted again it is equally important in seeing the relationship between the environment and employee behavior.[21]

As seen in Exhibit 3.1, which is to be read from left to right, five environmental components (first block) comprise the service setting as perceived by guests: ambient conditions; use of space; functional congruence; signs, symbols, and artifacts; and other people, comprising employees and other guests. No guest is likely to be aware (at least consciously) of all environmental elements. Consciously and subconsciously, each guest

---

[18] James T. Areddy, "In China, Disney Aims to Keep Security Behind the Scenes," *Wall Street Journal*, June 10, 2016, https://www.wsj.com/articles/in-china-disney-aims-to-keep-security-behind-the-scenes-1465464602.

[19] Mary J. Bitner, "Servicescapes: The Impact of Physical Surroundings on Customers and Employees," *The Journal of Marketing* (1992): 57–71; Woo G. Kim and Yun J. Moon, "Customers' Cognitive, Emotional, and Actionable Response to the Servicescape: A Test of the Moderating Effect of the Restaurant Type," *International Journal of Hospitality Management* 28, No. 1 (2009): 144–156.

[20] Michela Mari and Sara Poggesi, "Servicescape Cues and Customer Behavior: A Systematic Literature Review and Research Agenda," *The Service Industries Journal* 33, no. 2 (2013): 171–199; David Ballantyne and Elin Nilsson, "All That Is Solid Melts into Air: the Servicescape in Digital Service Space," *Journal of Services Marketing* 31, no. 3 (2017): 226–235; Mark S. Rosenbaum and Carolyn Massiah, "An Expanded Servicescape Perspective," *Journal of Service Management* 22, no. 4 (2011): 471–490.

[21] Chang-Yen Tsai et al., "Work Environment and Atmosphere: The Role of Organizational Support in the Creativity Performance of Tourism and Hospitality Organizations," *International Journal of Hospitality Management* 46 (2015): 26–35.

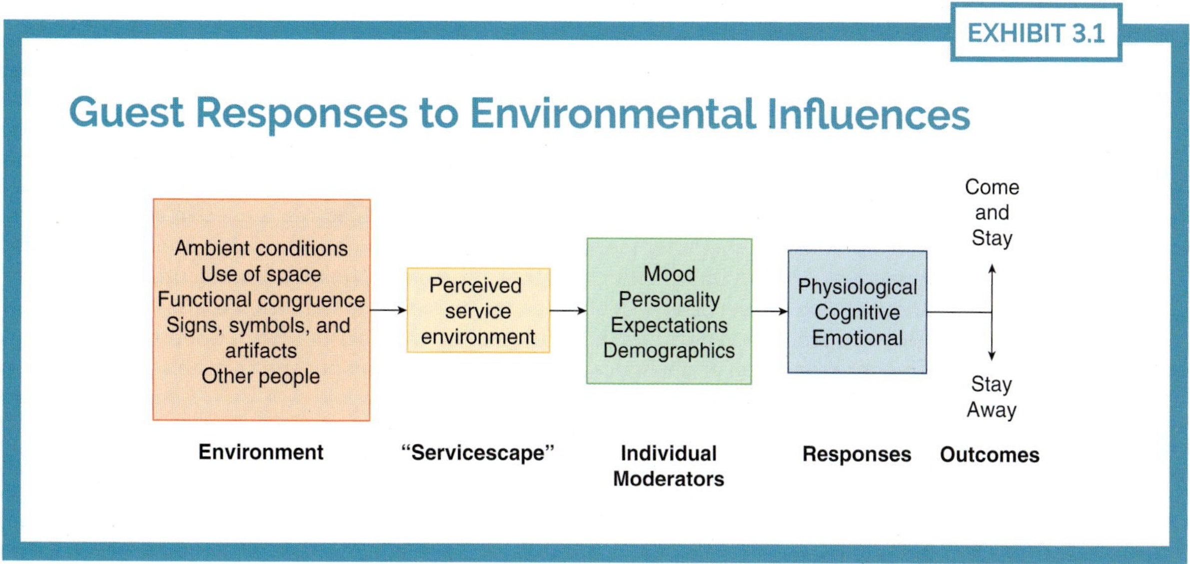

selects the combination of elements that comprises, for that guest, the perceived service landscape, or servicescape, as a whole. Each guest will respond differently to the individual elements of that servicescape, depending on the guest's individual characteristics and prior experiences. The responses will not only be different, but they may be different within any or a combination of three general response types: physiological, cognitive, or emotional. Finally, the guest's overall response to the setting will cause the guest to want to come and stay (or make a purchase, or use the service, etc.) or to avoid it.

Each element in the setting is capable of infinite variation. These variable elements also can be combined in an infinite variety of ways. Thus, each guest's experience of the setting is unique to that guest and more than likely unique to that particular time and place. People change from one service encounter to another and the way they perceive the experience at one time may also change.

Now, let's look at the servicescape model in Exhibit 3.1 in more detail.

Environment

The first group of factors in the servicescape model are those that make up the environment in which the guest experience takes place. These factors include the ambient conditions in the environment, the use of its space, functional congruence of the physical elements, its signs, symbols, and artifacts, plus any other people that are present.

Ambient Conditions

Ambient conditions in the environment—the ergonomic factors such as temperature, humidity, air quality, smells, sounds, physical comfort, and light—affect the nature of the guest experience. The effect on a guest of a dark, humid, quiet tunnel with intermittent noises and cool air blowing is different from the effect of a light, airy, music-filled shopping mall. The first setting feels ominous and scary, the second warm and positive. The whole category of "dark" theme park rides and attractions, like Disney's Haunted Mansion, Pirates of the Caribbean, and The Twilight Zone Tower of Terror, is designed around the concept that darkness has an element of suspense, surprise, and potential terror that light does not have. On the other hand, the romantic feel of dimly lit restaurants with soft music, comfortable chairs, and tempting smells is due to the careful management of ambient conditions.

Use of Space

The second environmental category is the use of space. It refers to how the equipment and furnishings are arranged in the hospitality service setting, the size and shape of those objects, their accessibility to the customers, and the spatial relationships among them.

The organization's use of space affects the nature of the guest experience. Depending on how the waiting space is designed, waiting lines can feel open and friendly or they can make a customer feel closed in and alone. How pathways are laid out to get from one location in a facility, whether it be a zoo, hospital, museum, or a hotel, to another also influences the feeling of openness or closedness the guest experiences. Closed spaces evoke different feelings than areas with a lot of open space or light. The basic decision about space is how to use it to lay out the service setting so as to complement and enhance the guest's experience.

Space, however, is expensive and must be used wisely. A restaurant with too many tables and seats or a hotel with too many rooms within its available space may be both unattractive to guests and a poor investment. An organization that attempts to increase the revenue-producing space within which it provides guest experiences at the expense of essential but non-revenue-producing space (e.g., for public areas, offices, kitchens, supplies, and utilities) may have a memorable service setting, but its delivery system will be unable to reliably provide the service product required for a memorable guest experience.

The space layout should also help guests to know where they are and how to find their way to where they want to go. People do not like being lost or confused as to where they are, and the benchmark hospitality organizations spend considerable time and effort in making guest wayfinding easy by the way they design their space. As Disney said, "Have a single entrance through which all the traffic would flow, then a hub off which the various areas were situated. That gives people a sense of orientation—they know where they are at all times. It also saves a lot of walking."[22] This commitment to orientation can be seen in each park at Walt Disney World Resort. Logical, easy-to-follow pathways lead people in the Magic Kingdom from one attraction to another. The big circular path around the World Showcase in Epcot makes it easy for guests to go from one attraction to another in an orderly way, and the lake in the middle of everything provides a superb orientation for the guest at any point around the circle. Cinderella Castle in the Magic Kingdom, The Twilight Zone Tower of Terror in Disney's Hollywood Studios, the Tree of Life in Disney's Animal Kingdom, and Spaceship Earth or Epcot Lagoon in Epcot are other landmarks that provide constant points of orientation. Guests know by looking where they are in each of the parks and can see how to get to other locations.

©iStock.com/ MichaelWarrenPix

The layout of Walt Disney World Epcot shows the careful attention to guest orientation.

Within specific Walt Disney World Resort areas, many visual and audio aids are provided to help orient the guest. The cast members in each location are costumed consistently within that location.

[22] Walt Disney, "Walt Disney Famous Quotes," Disney's Kingdom Editions (Lake Buena Vista, FL: The Walt Disney Company, 1994), 29.

Key structures help identify where one is in the Magic Kingdom. The Prince Charming Regal Carrousel in Fantasyland, the Liberty Square riverboat in Frontierland, and Space Mountain in Tomorrowland are examples of key attractions that by location, size, and sounds help guests identify where they are. When there are multiple cues, it is even easier to stay oriented. Adventureland, for example, not only has the Jungle Cruise but also clearly displays Walt Disney's Enchanted Tiki Room to help people know where they are. The challenge is to ensure the physical environment consistently reinforces the feeling of being in a particular section of the park by blocking out the sight of other areas, while providing landmarks that let guests know how to get to other park areas. The need to prevent guests from seeing anything that would make them think they are anywhere else but in Frontierland, for example, is carefully balanced against the need to provide clear and easy guidance to other park locations.

Robert C. Ford

The Enchanted Tiki Room serves as an environmental landmark, serving as a cue to help guests know where they are within the park.

Hospitality managers must maintain the environmental feel of the setting while also providing orientation devices to help guests locate rest rooms, information kiosks, meeting rooms, and exits. All service settings face this challenge. Circus legend P. T. Barnum set up his exhibits and signage to guide customers from start to finish. It is said that he used signs guiding guests along, stating, "This way to the egress." Circus patrons (many not knowing *egress* was another word for exit) found themselves passing smoothly, effortlessly, and efficiently through the exhibit through the final door into the alley outside the building.

Hospitality settings should be designed to ensure smooth flow for both guest and employees. Guests must feel they are moving effortlessly through the service setting. Employees must have sufficient space, traffic routes, and sufficiently short distances to travel to provide timely service to guests. In a restaurant, if waiters entering and leaving the kitchen use the same door, collisions and dropped trays—which, of course, do not enhance the diner's experience—are inevitable. If the kitchen is too far from the dining area, food temperatures will suffer. If tables are too close together, servers cannot move smoothly across the room, and the guest experience suffers.

Restaurants offer a classic example of how the placement of facilities within a space is related to the level and character of the guest experience provided. In a casual-dining restaurant, guests accept a distance of only two to three feet between tables (plus their chairs). In an upscale restaurant, tables must be at least four feet apart. If they are closer together, guests may not be able to put a finger on just what is wrong, but the service environment will not suit their expectations. Restaurants also use spatial design principles to give guests a sense of privacy while preserving the ambiance. By careful measurement of table and seat spacing and attention to heights, they can provide each guest with a feeling of safety and security while not making any guest feel isolated or exposed. For example, if the dimension to the top of a booth's back is kept to 46" it is low enough for guests to see over and high enough for privacy.

Functional Congruence

Functional congruence refers to how well something with a functional purpose fits into the environment in which it serves that purpose. The functioning of the equipment, layout of the physical landscape, design of the building, and the design of the service environment must be congruent with what the guest expects to find in that environment. Entrances should be where guests would logically expect them, rooms should be large enough to house the expected meetings, and restrooms should be large enough to accommodate expected demand at a convention break. In a self-service environment, items and equipment necessary to the experience must be easy to use, or someone had better be available to help guests figure out how to "serve themselves." If customers must perform complicated or unfamiliar tasks, like figure out how to operate a self-service kiosk at an airport or hotel or a virtual reality experience on a computer, the instructions must be clear and easily located. Self-service technology, as in pumps at gas stations, airport check-in kiosks, and self-serve restaurants, requires more focus on spatial design clarity and layout than would service experiences accompanied by a gas attendant, airline counter personnel, or server.[23]

In an effort to obtain a competitive advantage based on differentiating a functional component of any hotel, Westin Hotels introduced its Heavenly Bed in 1999. Since a bed is the essential functional part of any hotel room, Westin wanted to focus its guests' attention on the comfort of its bed, turning the bed into a nonverbal cue that would signal how Westin's bed would provide a good night's sleep. Westin essentially began a competition among hotels in terms of whose bed could offer the best night's sleep. The Heavenly Bed was so successful that every major hotel brand eventually followed suit with the development of signature beds. Westin has continued this effort with upscale amenities like its Heavenly Baths, and by partnering with companies like New Balance and Peloton to provide other amenities that both differentiate the brand, but also create products consumers want for their own homes.[24]

The functional congruence of environmental elements is given great consideration in a well-designed service environment, so whatever physical or environmental element the guest requires for maximum enjoyment of the experience is provided when needed. As the Magic Kingdom guest enters Main Street, U.S.A., stores on the right-hand side sell items useful inside the park, like hats, sun screen, and snacks. Disney carefully places theme park eating places where guests can find them, often just after a ride or attraction. Retail shops are located at the exit points of rides for guests wanting a souvenir of the experience they have just enjoyed. As guests leave the park, retail outlets on their right side sell souvenirs. Disney knows most guests will be looking and walking on the right-hand side of the street, so they make sure shops on the right sell those things guests will be looking for at that stage of their park visit.

Signs, Symbols, and Artifacts

The fourth component of the environment is the signs, symbols, and artifacts that communicate information to the guest. Carl Sewell and Paul Brown, authors of the classic *Customers for Life,* state signs serve one or more of only three purposes: to name the business (e.g., Nordstrom's Department Store, Ramada Inn, Shula's Steak House), to describe the product or service (e.g., Rooms for Rent, Hot Dogs, Rest Rooms), and to give direction (e.g., Entrance, Do Not Enter, Pay Here, No Smoking, Employees Only, Wrong Way, You Are Here).[25]

Signs are explicit physical representations of information the organization thinks guests might want, need, or expect to find. Signs must be easy to read, clear, and located in obvious places where they can direct and teach people how to use the

---

[23] Cees J. Gelderman, W. Th Ghijsen, Paul, and Ronnie Van Diemen, "Choosing Self-service Technologies or Interpersonal Services—The Impact of Situational Factors and Technology-related Attitudes," *Journal of Retailing and Consumer Services* 18, 5 (2011): 414–421.

[24] Allison Olmsted, "Travelers: Your Hotel Workout and Fitness Options Just Got Much Better," *Forbes*, April 26, 2017, Accessed 2/7/2018, https://www.forbes.com/sites/allisonolms/2017/04/26/travelers-your-hotel-workout-fitness-options-just-got-much-better/#69301d6d6c69.

[25] Carl Sewell and Paul B. Brown, *Customers for Life: How to Turn That One-Time Buyer into a Lifetime Customer* (New York, NY: Doubleday, 2002).

service easily. Tourist cities wanting international visitors to come back know that, to encourage returns, they must stimulate positive emotional and cognitive responses within visitors from many countries. Taking guests' national origins and cultural backgrounds (demographics is one of the individual moderators [see Exhibit 3.1]) into account, they go to great effort and expense to create not small signs in English (which would cause negative cognitive and emotional responses in non-English-speaking visitors) but large, easy-to-see street and directional signs with universal symbols on them to make it easy for all tourists to find their way.

Even such an apparently small and easy job as making a sign must be done from the guest's point of view, rather than the organization's. For example, hotels, airports, and other tourist locations often use "You Are Here" signs to help orient guests within the service environment. If these signs are not done carefully, and from the perspective of a total stranger to the environment, they can cause more confusion than if there was no sign in the first place. Poorly designed signs leave the customer not only lost or disoriented but also feeling stupid, and customers do not continue to patronize organizations that make them feel stupid.

Signs are so important that Miami's airport hired a person to specifically audit the naming logic and consistency of its signage when it realized its existing signage was confusing its visitors trying to find flights, services, or exits. Wayfinding signage is especially important for airports as they deal with so many hurried, tired, global travelers who may be unfamiliar with an airport or the language.[26] Signs are used to convey messages through the use of symbols, often language itself. Some signs contain not words but other symbols, such as representational icons that can replace any specific language. These signs, of course, are especially important in travel and tourism settings, to which guests come from many nations, cultures, and linguistic backgrounds. If the customer must remember the information on the sign, a symbol often works best. Universal Studios uses its famous movies to represent sections in the parking lot. When parking their cars, the sign is combined with ambient signals such as music from *Jaws,* colors, and sounds to increase the likelihood that people will remember where their cars are. At the end of the day, people should be able to more easily remember that the car is in the Jaws section than in Section 17A or Section 31D. A National Geographic television series, Crowd Control, narrated by psychologist Daniel Pink, provides a visual example of how colors, themed decorations, smells, and sounds can be used in an airport parking garage to help people remember where to find their cars.[27] The goal in both parking examples is to use as many sensory cues as possible to make the car's location memorable.

Artifacts are physical objects that represent something beyond their functional use. As such, they are a type of symbol. Darden's Seasons 52 requires each table to have a candle centered on it. The candle is not needed for lighting, but is there as an artifact to stir guests' vestigial memories of their ancestors sitting around their campfires. From an

Robert C. Ford

The entrance to SeaWorld in Orlando, Florida, helps to both situate the guest and clearly convey the theme of the establishment.

[26] Paul Symonds, "Wayfinding Signage Considerations in International Airports," *Interdisciplinary Journal of Signage and Wayfinding* 1, no. 2 (2017): 60–80.

[27] National Geographic, "Top 5 Parking Jobs: Crowd Control," YouTube video, 1:34, posted November 16, 2014, https://www.youtube.com/watch?v=PcKlsS1Shfl.

anthropological viewpoint, campfires represent a place of safety, security, and social gathering. Thus, the candles' fire subtly evokes a feeling of warmth, fellowship, and being alive. Themed restaurants use artifacts extensively to help convey the theme. What would Margaritaville be without an erupting volcano to support the Jimmy Buffet theme?

Other People

The last component of the environment is the other people in it: employees, other guests, or perhaps even audio-animatronic creations that guests come to think of as real people. Guests often want to see other guests. If they are alone, they wonder why; are they foolish to be where no one else is? Many people do not like to eat in an empty restaurant; you can eat alone at home. A positive eating experience generally requires the presence of other diners enjoying their meals. Guests of many hospitality organizations expect to see other people also enjoying the experience. Happiness and satisfaction are contagious. Many service settings would feel depressing and lonely without other guests.

Employees are environmentally important even before they deliver the anticipated service. A restaurant that employs well-dressed, well-groomed people will have an atmosphere very different from that of a place where everyone wears torn and dirty uniforms. Most guest-service activities have standards of dress and personal appearance codes for employees and guests that can be very structured and specific. Employees must look like what guests expect to see when they enter the organization. If the guests view clean, neat, appropriate attire as a mark of respect for them and congruent with the type of place they want to be, then employees need to meet those expectations. Although there are some hospitality organizations that seek to cater to guests who want and expect unshaven, overly made-up, or haphazardly attired employees with multicolored spiked hair and visible body decorations, this is a specific market segment. Though society's standards of dress and appearance are more casual than they once were, that market niche is still fairly small.

Guests also arrive in some service settings with expectations for each other. Although patrons of a fancy restaurant may not expect other guests to dress up to employee standards (who may be wearing tuxedos), most people would be unhappy about paying fine-dining prices when some guests are sitting around in cut-off shorts and halter tops. On the other hand, patrons at an open-air fish camp restaurant or at the Phantom Ranch at the bottom of the Grand Canyon would expect a more relaxed dress code for both employees and guests. Some restaurants seeking to serve both types of guests have devised ways to divide their restaurant into separated spaces so that similarly attired guests sit together and apart from dissimilarly attired guests.

Although Exhibit 3.1 includes other people as part of the environment, and clearly they often are, they sometimes seem almost like part of the service itself. If you go to a baseball camp, dude ranch, a conference, or on an Outward Bound team-building trip through the wilderness, other people are not just wallflowers or scenery; they are necessary to the experience, and you may even participate in or co-produce it with them. However, although the other customers may be an important or even a necessary part of a guest experience, and can even sometimes make it or break it, their presence is only rarely the reason why you sought out the experience. They are usually best thought of as part of the environment within which the service is delivered, which has to be carefully managed so that these other people are congruent with the guest expectations, rather than as part of the service itself, though the distinction is not always clear.

The Servicescape

Temperature, smells, sounds, lights, signs, physical structures, furnishings, green space, open space, other people—although no guest ever singles out or even notices all the elements within the environment, they do combine to create an overall, unified impression of that environment. In the model seen in Exhibit 3.1, we use the term *perceived service environment* for the general perception or whole picture the guest draws from the countless individual environmental factors. As noted earlier, the *servicescape* is what the individual environmental factors add up to for each guest.

Because each guest perceives different environmental elements, each guest's servicescape is a little bit different.

Individual Moderators

Making even more difficult what might have seemed an easy task—providing a setting within which to deliver the service—the hospitality service provider must realize that each guest's reaction to the perceived servicescape is affected or "moderated" by the guest's mood, personality, expectations, and demographic characteristics. Even if they perceive the servicescape similarly, a shy seventy-year-old female entering a wild night club by mistake is going to have a reaction different from that of a twenty-four-year-old male accustomed to spending most evenings there. Not only that, but both the seventy-year-old and the twenty-four-year-old may be in different moods and have different expectations of the night club experience. Service experience designers and hospitality managers must realize the guest whose perception of the servicescape has been moderated by the guest's individual differences from all other guests is going to respond to the servicescape in one, or perhaps more likely in some combination, of three ways: physiologically, emotionally, and cognitively. We shall discuss each of these below.

Not only do different guests respond differently to the same environment, but even the same guest may respond differently from day to day or even hour to hour. Although the hospitality organization usually provides the same servicescape elements for everyone, it should always remember the uniqueness of guests.

We label as moderators the individual, personal factors that cause guests to respond to the service setting in different ways. Guests bring a particular day's moods, purposes, demographic characteristics, and personality traits to a particular day's guest experience. These factors affect or moderate each guest's response to the servicescape.

Some people like to be alone and object to standing in long, crowded lines. Other people love to be around crowds and view rubbing elbows and sharing harmless gripes with people in line as part of the fun. Some customers arrive in a happy mood while others are angry or upset. Some older people have a hard time walking longer distances while most young adults don't mind and may prefer it. Some parents don't like to get wet on a ride while most teens think it's great. Some people have been there and done that before and have certain expectations of what the environment should be like while others are first timers and find everything fascinating.

Cultural values and beliefs also influence how guests respond to the servicescape. Some cultures find red a happy color, and others find it threatening; some find handshakes a positive gesture, and others are offended. Some cultures believe in waiting in line and others do not. Each culture produces a multitude of cultural nuances, and hospitality managers can only do their best to recognize the individual variations these differences create and design an environment that will offer a guest experience of high quality and value to most people.

Moderators also include the individual moods that people bring to the servicescape. When people are upset or angry, they may not be able to perceive any environment as positive or fun. Every restaurant server dreads the arrival of an unhappy diner. Regardless of how good the service, fine the dinner, or exciting and pleasant the environment, the diner is likely to leave as unhappy (and unlikely to leave a generous tip) as when that person arrived.

People arriving either in a neutral mood or unfamiliar with the experience awaiting them will be most influenced by environmental cues. The wonderful smell of freshly popped popcorn or baking cinnamon buns will influence the neutral guest to consider purchasing the food product. Smart retailers make sure these familiar odors are fanned out into the wandering crowd to encourage product awareness and interest. Cinnabon does its best to ensure that everyone walking by its retail stores smells the tempting aroma of cinnamon. Among other smells it can produce, the Disney Smellitzer machine reproduces and projects the aroma of freshly baking chocolate-chip cookies to tempt the crowds walking by the bakery on Main Street, U.S.A., in the Magic Kingdom.

Responding to the Servicescape

A guest can respond to a service setting in one or more of three ways: physiologically, emotionally, and cognitively. The moderating factors discussed in the previous section will affect the nature of the response.

Physiological Responses

The environment can influence the guest's decision to stay or leave in two ways. The first is the effect of the environment on the guest's senses or the way in which the experience looks, smells, feels to the touch, tastes, or sounds. The second is the guest's ability to absorb and process the quality and quantity of information the environment provides. Each is important in determining the guest's response.

The Senses. A physiological response results primarily from the servicescape's effects on the guest's senses. Most physiological responses to the environment are responses to such ambient conditions as temperature, humidity, air quality, smells, sounds, and light. The effects of the ambient conditions, however, are moderated or influenced by the guest's mood, personality, expectations, and demographic factors. Different age groups, for example, will respond differently to a darkened restaurant and guests from different cultures will respond differently to different colors.

Information Processing. A second type of physiological response to the environment is the information-processing capabilities of the brain. A well-known study of how much unfamiliar information a human brain could process at any one time found the capacity was seven (plus or minus two) random pieces of information, such as random numbers. The study was done for the phone company, which wanted to know how long a telephone number people could remember. The study results led to using combinations of words and numbers (like REpublic-45914) to help people overcome their physiological limitations by combining a familiar word with five unfamiliar numbers. We can see variations on this method today in the word-based phone numbers used by organizations competing for our business with easy-to-remember numbers, such as 1-800-I-FLY-SWA, 1-800-HOLIDAY, 1-800-HILTONS.

The importance of this concept to those managing the service environment is to recognize that what is familiar to those who work there is unfamiliar and random information to most guests. Random information will quickly overtax the capacity of the guest's mind to comprehend the environment and enjoy the service experience. It doesn't take much unconnected information—a lengthy menu in an unfamiliar restaurant, for example, or a vast assortment of machines in a self-serve photocopy center—to confuse a customer, and many service experiences are unfamiliar territory to their customers. Guests become frustrated when confused, lost, or overwhelmed with too much information or too many options for their minds to comprehend. Organizations must respect the information-processing limitations that all people share and devise ways to make random information nonrandom and familiar.

One way to help guests cope with information overload is to provide cues that prime subconscious memory in the service setting.[28] These are typically sensory cues where a smell, sound, sight, taste, or touch calls forth a memory that helps guests respond appropriately in the present setting. If a hotel, for example, wishes to remind guests to take environmentally friendly actions, it can not only provide tent cards on its desks that remind people to "save our environment" by reusing towels, but also infuse the air with a forest smell, display art portraying environmental beauty, and play background music of forest sounds.

Rich and Lean Environments. Environments can be made **information rich** or **information lean**. Obviously, an information-lean environment will help when guests are expected to be unfamiliar with the setting, or when they have to process a lot of information, whereas an information-rich environment can be used when guests are familiar with the setting or have few choices or decisions to make. The directional or instructional parts of the environment must be kept lean enough to make sure guests can figure out what they are supposed to do or where they are supposed to go; the richer or more elaborate environments can be used when guests have no responsibility for figuring anything out. Thus, a themed restaurant can be rich in detail and content because the guest only has to sit, observe, and eat. If customers must make decisions about where they are or what to do next, as in a major convention hotel complex, the setting should be kept relatively simple and familiar. This point ties in well with the cognitive aspects of the environmental experience.

information-rich environment An environment which requires considerable information processing because there are large amounts of data to process.

information-lean environment An environment which does not require extensive information processing because there are few data to process.

Cognitive Responses

Every guest brings a unique background and knowledge based on what that guest has experienced and learned in a lifetime of prior experiences. These many past experiences influence what a guest expects from the experience being offered. The best hospitality organizations recognize the influence their guests' pasts have on their future expectations and design their environment to include familiar reminders to the many different past experiences their many different guests have had.

Expectations and the Servicescape. The cognitive impact of an experience depends on the knowledge the guest brings to the experience. Guests enter every experience with a set of expectations based on what they have seen, heard about, or done before. The human tendency is to seek points of similarity between what we have done, seen, or experienced before and what we encounter in the new situation. These prior experiences build expectations as to what ought to be seen, which obviously influences what is perceived. For example, whn readng sentences, what we expct to read infuenses what we thnk the wrds say. As an example, just consider that last sentence. Likewise, if we enter a cafeteria similar to one we have visited before, we have our behavior scripted to perform the tasks necessary to eat by the familiar cues in the environment (the arrow pointing to the beginning of the line, the arrangement of the trays, the rack for the silverware, and the bars upon which our tray should slide as we review the food items available).

Indeed, one advantage of chain or branded restaurants is that we know what to expect because we have been there before. We know the environment in one Subway is pretty much like the environment in another, and so we know immediately how to get our food selections after a quick scan of the physical facility to confirm that it is set up the same as every other Subway. Imagine, in contrast, the customer who has never seen a Subway before and has had no similar experience. Or worse, what if Subway's managers were authorized to lay out the restaurants however they

[28] Robert C. Ford, "Prime Time: The Strategic Use of Subconscious Priming to Enhance Customer Satisfaction," *Business Horizons* 57, no. 2 (2014): 269–277.

Andreas von Einsiedel via Getty Images

Creative Touch Imaging Ltd./NurPhoto via Getty Images

A restaurant's servicescape helps convey the type of experience the establishment will deliver.

wished, as a cafeteria, a typical restaurant, or otherwise? Without any previously scripted behavior patterns to rely on, customers new to each location would be quite confused and would require employee time and assistance to navigate through this unfamiliar experience.

The point is hospitality organizations should recognize the information-processing limitations of their guests and seek to introduce the environmental cues necessary to ensure the present experience ties into some previously built and familiar guest mental map. As noted earlier, theming is used extensively to simplify the ability of guests to orient themselves to a location. If you are in the Magic Kingdom's Frontierland, all the streets, decorations, cast-member costumes, and even the trash cans are themed to provide the multiple cues that help guests quickly determine where in the park they are. The more familiar the organization can make the experience to the guest, the less confusion, frustration, and unhappiness the guest will have. Of course, sometimes guests are seeking a unique experience, and so will purposely seek out an unfamiliar restaurant, perhaps to have an experience unlike ones they have had anywhere else.

Nonverbal Cues and Communication.

Those aspects of the environmental setting that evoke a cognitive response can be viewed as a form of nonverbal communication whereby the designers of the guest experience communicate what the experience is and teach the guest how to enjoy it. If patrons see an array of cues such as white linen tablecloths in a restaurant, they link that information back to what they have learned previously about the relationship of white linen to restaurant type and price range. In other words, servicescape layout and content tell the guest something about what to expect from the experience. These informational cues tap into previous knowledge and form the expectations about what the experience should be like. If diners find the white-linen-tablecloth restaurant also has inexpensive menu prices and excellent food, they will be wowed about what a great deal the experience represents because they have been cued to expect a big bill. Conversely, if the same diners see disposable china on plastic tables and are then handed menus filled with forty-dollar entrees, they likely will be upset. Guests bring a lifetime of their own experiences and expectations that influences what they expect to find. Whether or not their expectations are met obviously bears on their satisfaction with the experience, so physical cues—like all other aspects of the experience—must be carefully constructed and managed to be consistent with the expected experience.

Emotional Responses

Finally, the customer may react emotionally to the servicescape. Old graduates get choked up when they return for reunions at their college campuses. Children and adults alike are emotionally touched by holiday decorations. The flags flying, the breeze blowing, the dramatic music, and the majesty of the distinguished speakers have strong emotional impact on many American visitors to Epcot's American Adventure. Young children have the same emotional reaction when SpongeBob SquarePants walks by. It not only represents an individual physical act but also builds an emotional tie to the entire park experience that many children never forget.

Emotional responses have two distinct elements of interest to the hospitality organization. The first is the degree of arousal, and the second is the amount or degree of pleasure/displeasure the experience represents. The emotional response the hospitality organization seeks to create should have elements of arousal and pleasure to gain the emotional interest of its guests. People want to spend time and money in pleasurable environments; they avoid unpleasant environments; those that create high levels of arousal are viewed positively unless the arousal is unpleasurable. A sudden explosion that creates loud noise, confusion, and overstimulation would be high on arousal but low on pleasure, except on national holidays like the Fourth of July or during an expected fireworks display. Most people avoid explosive settings.

On the other hand, some people seek out high levels of arousal and pleasure in such activities as sky diving, ultra-light plane flying, playing or watching extreme sports, stock car racing, or rock climbing. A trip on a roller coaster is a scary but not terrifying ride, which yields high levels of pleasant experience combined with high levels of arousal. In such activities, a little fear stimulates a positive experience for the customer. Arousal can also be obtained in other ways, such as the appeal to patriotism in Fourth of July celebrations or Irish music at a St. Patrick's Day parade.

Good hospitality managers have learned to use arousal cues effectively. For example, in the morning when hotel guests are heading to breakfast, the music will be mellow. Lunch music will be upbeat, higher energy for cocktail hour, and slower music for dinner.[29] Morning guests arriving at a theme park will likely hear upbeat, up-tempo music; employees would greet guests in strong, enthusiastic voices to sustain the positive feelings and high level of energy with which guests come into the park. When guests are leaving at the end of the day, both the music and the final comments of employees should probably be sedate and restrained, to be consonant with the lower arousal level of the tired guests.

The Bottom Line: Come and Stay, or Stay Away

These three response factors—physiological, cognitive, and emotional—operating together lead the guests to make one of two choices: to become patrons (i.e., come and stay) or to give their business elsewhere (i.e., stay away) (see far right of Exhibit 3.1). Leaving the service and its delivery out of the equation, the guest can decide that the experience of the service environment was, on the whole, positive or negative. Servicescape perceptions can encourage the guest to stay longer and come again, or go away and stay away. Hospitality organizations must work hard to create environments that encourage the longer stays and repeat visits that result in increased revenues.

The model in Exhibit 3.1 should help hospitality managers to choose and arrange environmental factors so as to provide servicescapes that enhance the service and its delivery and that guests, in their infinite variety, will generally respond to in a positive way.

---

[29] A. Peterson, "It's Checkout Time, Kenny G: The New Hotel Music Strategy," *Wall Street Journal*, July 30, 2015.

LESSONS LEARNED

LO 3.1 Explain how theming the service setting pays off in guest satisfaction.

- Theming can add quality and value to the setting by making it memorable.

LO 3.2 Discuss why the service setting or service environment is important.

- Design the space to fit the guest's needs, wants, and expectations.

LO 3.3 Explain how the service environment affects guests and employees.

- Recognize that guests can differ in mood, expectations, and experience from one experience to the next; what was a wow for a guest today may only be an as-expected tomorrow.
- Do not overload the environment with information; recognize that most people can process only small amounts of unfamiliar information at one time.
- Envision and create the service setting from the guest's point of view, not your own.

LO 3.4 Discuss why providing a service environment in which guests feel safe and secure is critical.

- Manage the environment to maintain the guest's feeling of safety and security.

LO 3.5 Identify which elements of the service environment need to be managed.

- Supply information-rich environments when and where guests have time to appreciate and enjoy them; use information-lean environments when and where guests are trying to figure out what they should do or where they should go.
- Use signs and symbols to make it easy for guests to go where they want to go and to know where they are, whether in your physical space or on your website.
- Make sure the functional parts of the setting work and work the way the guest expects.
- Realize that for each guest both other guests and employees are part of the setting.
- Know and manage the cognitive, physiological, and emotional impact of your environment on guests.

LO 3.6 Describe how individual factors moderate or affect the responses of guests to the service environment, according to Bitner's servicescape model.

- Remember each guest arrives with different moods, personalities, demographics, and past experiences that influence their reaction to the service setting.

KEY TERMS AND CONCEPTS

REVIEW QUESTIONS

1. Consider how theming a guest experience adds value or improves the quality of the guest experience. Compare two similar experiences you have had, such as one restaurant that offered a themed experience and another that did not. What differences did you note between the quality and value of the two experiences?
2. Why should managers pay attention to the environmental setting in which the guest experience occurs?
3. Reflect on the service environments of two different hospitality organizations, one that felt good to you and one that felt uncomfortable. Use the factors in the model in Exhibit 3.1 to determine why they felt different.

4. Imagine yourself as a first-time visitor to your town or your campus.
   A. How hard or how easy would it be to direct yourself to the location where you are right now?
   B. How could you make finding this location easier for an unfamiliar visitor, using the ideas suggested in this chapter?
5. Think about the environmental and "people" factors that make you feel safe and secure in the location where you live.
   A. To what extent are these same factors applicable to hospitality environments?
   B. Have you ever been in a hospitality setting in which you did not feel safe and secure? What more could or should the organization have done to enhance your feelings of safety and security?
6. Consider the places you go as a guest or customer.
   A. Are these environments too rich or too lean with information, and why do you make that judgment?
   B. How would you change those environments to make the amount of information in those environments just right for achieving whatever it is you need to do when you are in that particular situation?
7. Consider the places you have worked (or observed service employees working) to provide guest experiences.
   A. Did any of the environmental factors (identified in the servicescape model) influence how you felt (or the person you've observed appeared to feel) in the safety, comfort, or ability to provide the quality of service experience you (or the server you observed) wanted to provide your guests?
   B. How would you change the environment to improve your ability (or the person you've observed) to provide the quality of service you wanted to provide your guests?

ACTIVITIES

1. The hospitality service product is largely intangible. Observe and report how one or more hospitality organizations with which you are familiar use environmental design cues to give a degree of tangibility to this intangible service product.
2. Using Exhibit 3.1 as your reference, go to a hospitality organization and take note of as many environmental factors as you can. Which ones seem to have been "managed" by someone? Which factors can and cannot be managed by the local manager? Which ones seem managed well and which ones do not?

ETHICS IN BUSINESS

A number of themed establishments try to represent different eras in history. While accurately representing history can be both educational and entertaining, different periods in history have had very different norms, mores, and construction and safety standards. In particular, many of the attitudes and policies toward women, minorities, and non-Christians in the eighteenth and nineteenth centuries would be considered highly offensive today. To some extent, a themed establishment wants to remain "true" to its historical basis. For example, think of a historic area like Colonial Williamsburg that tries to represent and recreate life in the eighteenth century. To what extent should an establishment try to be historically accurate, versus artificially injecting modern construction and interpersonal standards into the experience especially in regard to the way the actors behave when providing their services?

CASE STUDY

Case 1: Safety at the Downtown Hotel

It is 2020. Faramarz has recently purchased the Downtown Hotel, a 125-unit facility in downtown Central City, a large city in the northeast. The Downtown Hotel was originally a

Holiday Inn, built in 1990 and owned by the parent company, InterContinental Hotels Group, rather than a franchisee. The hotel was later rebranded as a Holiday Inn Express. Since its launch in 1991, Holiday Inn Express had grown from 0 to 500 properties by 1996, and had locations throughout the United States, Europe, the Middle East, Africa, and the Asia Pacific. When the Central City Holiday Inn was built, it was located near the bustling central business district, but in a neighborhood that was typical of the older northeast working-class ethnic neighborhoods. Although most Holiday Inn hotels built in or near central business districts at that time were many stories tall, a zoning peculiarity on this site restricted the building to two levels.

Around 2000, as part of restructuring at InterContinental Hotels Group, the property in Central City was sold. By this time, the neighborhood in which the hotel was located had become more dangerous, the inner-city central district was less desirable to businesses, and the hotel building had begun to look dated. Faramarz knew these facts but bought the property anyway; the price was right, and he anticipated he could revitalize it. The building was still structurally sound and located next to an interstate highway. It still had a 50% occupancy rate, although the rate had been gradually falling over the past few years. Faramarz attributed the falling occupancy rate to poor management and facility deterioration; he thought he could do better.

Faramarz spent considerable money refurbishing the property. When he was finished, the rooms were nicely decorated, the amenities appropriate for the intended market segment, and the exterior pleasant to look at.

The design of the hotel was typical of early 1990s construction: two levels of rooms facing the street with exterior entrances to rooms on both levels, the guests on the second level entering their rooms from an open balcony facing the street. Guests parked their cars in front of the rooms in an unfenced lot. The original bushes and trees that were planted years ago were now fully mature and, in combination with the two-level building structure, gave the property a shaded country feel.

Now that he had enhanced the attractiveness of his building and its rooms, Faramarz wanted to develop a strategy to improve the Downtown Hotel's occupancy rate. His basic information source was guest comment cards and mystery shoppers. The common theme of their feedback was that while they appreciated the modernization and the country feel of the place, they felt rather unsafe here. Many guests said that they did not intend to return to the hotel on future visits to Central City. Faramarz could see he had a problem but didn't know quite how to solve it.

Based on the ideas in this chapter and what your own common sense tells you (and any interviews you might obtain with hotel personnel), develop a strategy for making Faramarz's guests feel safer at the Downtown Hotel.

Case 2: Fine Dining at the Silver Slipper

After profitable careers in the stock brokerage industry, Fred and Song Yi attended Chef Elmo's School of Culinary Arts. When they graduated, they fulfilled their dream of many years: They opened their own fine-dining restaurant, The Silver Slipper.

They found a building in what they concluded was an excellent location. It had originally been a Denny's Restaurant. The next owner, Bella Starr, had converted the family restaurant into a steakhouse, the Tombstone Restaurant and Saloon. She left most of the Denny's decor intact but superimposed on the interior the rough timbers and boards that Americans have come to expect in their western steakhouses.

Buying the Tombstone Restaurant and Saloon used up a large chunk of Fred and Song Yi's available capital. They decided since their focus was to be excellent food, they would invest the rest of their funds in an upgrade of the kitchen. They patterned their kitchen after the model fine-dining kitchens at Chef Elmo's School. The couple realized the dining area needed refurbishing and upgrading, but they couldn't do everything at once. They decided to struggle along with the vinyl upholstery, plastic furnishings, and rough-hewn timbers and boards until their superb meals had generated some profits. After all, guests came to a fine-dining restaurant for fine dining, not for the decor. They knew that some of Europe's finest restaurants, with the highest prices, were simple and basic almost to the point of bareness. They had graduated at the top of their culinary class, had served apprenticeships at excellent restaurants, and knew they could provide tastier culinary creations than any other chefs in town.

The big night came; Fred and Song Yi were open for business! Their reputations as trained chefs had preceded them, and many guests arrived in response to the excitement created by the new fine-dining opportunity. Fred and Song Yi received many compliments on the excellence of the food. But more than a few guest comment cards also referred to how expensive the meals were.

Although comments on the food continued to be highly favorable, the crowds of diners began to dwindle as the initial excitement wore off. Within a few weeks, though the small numbers of diners still willing to pay premium prices continued to rave about the food, Fred and Song Yi saw they had to do something, or they weren't going to make it. Song Yi even had to begin selling mutual funds on the side.

Fred wrote a letter to Chef Elmo, asking him for advice. Chef Elmo offered to "help out in the kitchen" for a weekend, after which he would give his frank opinion as to how Fred and Song Yi should proceed.

What do you think Chef Elmo will tell Fred and Song Yi is wrong with their new business endeavor? What advice do you think he will give them?

Further readings on the topics in this chapter are listed in "Additional Readings" on pages 499–502.

Alfred Eisenstaedt/The LIFE Picture Collection/Getty Images

4 Developing the Hospitality Culture: Everyone Serves!

Hospitality Principle: Define and Sustain a Total Service Culture

My role? Well you know I was stumped one day when a little boy asked, "Do you draw Mickey Mouse?" I had to admit I do not draw anymore. "Then you think up all the jokes and ideas?" "No," I said, "I don't do that." Finally, he looked up at me and said, "Mr. Disney, just what do you do?" "Well," I said, "sometimes I think of myself as a little bee. I go from one area of the studio to another and gather pollen and sort of stimulate everyone. I guess that's the job I do."

—Walt Disney

Learning Objectives

After reading this chapter, you should be able to

4.1 State why the organization's leaders are so important to defining, developing, teaching, and maintaining its culture through their words and actions.

4.2 Relate a hospitality organization's culture to service success.

4.3 Discuss the essential roles the organization's beliefs, values, and norms play.

4.4 Describe how the external world influences the internal culture.

4.5 Explain how the organization communicates its culture to its employees—through laws, language, stories, legends, heroes, symbols, and rituals.

4.6 Describe how the organization can accomplish the difficult task of changing its culture, if that becomes necessary.

INTRODUCTION

When guests go to the Walt Disney World Resort, fly on Southwest Airlines, shop at Nordstrom, or stay at a Four Seasons hotel, they can sense something special about the organization and the people who work there. If customers of these organizations are asked about the experience, they invariably describe it as better than they expected. What's even more amazing is the employees will also tell you that the organizations are different. The Disney cast members talk about their commitment to the quality of "the show" they produce for park visitors. The Four Seasons and Nordstrom employees talk about their commitment to guest service, and Southwest Airlines employees talk about their commitment to providing a unique and pleasurable flying experience. Not only do employees talk about these corporate values—they believe in them. And they demonstrate their commitment to the customer in a thousand different ways every day. The hospitality manager seeking excellence can learn a great deal by examining how these organizations create and sustain their culture of service excellence. This chapter presents the concept of corporate culture, why and how excellent managers communicate culture to employees, the value of creating a strong culture versus a weak culture, how to change an existing culture, and how managers can work with their culture to ensure it supports the organizational mission of service excellence.

THE IMPORTANCE OF LEADERS

Getting everyone in the organization committed to high levels of guest service is a daunting challenge. Not only did Walt Disney, Herb Kelleher of Southwest Airlines, and Isadore Sharp of Four Seasons Hotels and Resorts spend their personal time and energy necessary to create and sustain the organizational culture that still today defines the corporate values for which their organizations are famous, they also got their employees and managers to believe in the culture and adopt the organization's values. They knew that, as leaders, they were responsible for defining the culture. They all had a strong commitment to excellent service, and they communicated it—through their words and deeds—clearly and consistently to those inside and outside the organization.

Can managers who are not the presidents or founders of organizations have the same kind of influence on the culture that these famous leaders have had? They certainly can, and they must, although managers and supervisors are more likely to serve more as translators and teachers of a top manager's cultural values and beliefs than as definers of their own unit's culture. The most important influence on any organizational culture is the behavior of the organization's leader. Viewing this influence from the bottom of the organizational chart, employees try to behave as their supervisors do, supervisors are influenced by the behavior of their managers, the role models for managers are their own managers, and so on until top-level managers, and especially the organization's leaders, become the role models for the whole organization and the ultimate definers of each organization's cultural values.

Supervisory personnel at all levels, then, must realize how important they are as cultural keepers, teachers, and translators. If they do not perform this function well in everything they say, do, and write, the customers' service experience will suffer. Managers must not only consistently walk the walk and talk the talk of excellent service; they must constantly remind all employees that they supervise to do the same. Isadore Sharp, founder of Four Seasons, says, "Employees are natural boss watchers. Everything their bosses say and do tells employees their real concerns, their real goals, priorities, and values."[1] If any manager moving through the service environment sees any employee doing something inconsistent with the culture and ignores it, that manager sends a message to all employees that such behavior is a legitimate option and that not everybody has to focus on guest service all the time. It doesn't matter if the employee is officially supervised by that manager or not. When any manager ignores any employee action that impacts the show or the guest experience negatively, the message is sent loud and clear to everyone that it does not matter that much. After a few instances of managers saying one thing but rewarding or not punishing another, everyone learns the real level of service commitment that is expected.

Sustaining the quality of the customer experience is everyone's job. Not only must all the public and private statements and actions support the idea that everyone serves; the organizational reward system, training programs, and measures of achievement must also support and reinforce this message. When managers publicly and loudly celebrate the service achievements of their employees, they send a very strong message to everyone else about what the organization believes in and what its culture values.

Culture and Reputation

A company's culture, like a person's character, drives its reputation. Companies whose culture honors customers, employees, and shareholders usually have excellent reputations with all three groups. These organizations recognize the importance of a strong culture in the competitive marketplace, a strong culture that everyone believes in, understands, and supports. All organizations have a culture, whether or not anyone spends any time worrying about it, shaping it, or teaching it. Managers who do not effectively manage their organizations' cultures encourage weak organizational cultures or, worse yet, cultures that are structured and defined by someone or a group that may not be concerned with or may even seek to subvert the organization's mission. Unmanaged or mismanaged cultures give weak and inconsistent guidance to their members on what the organization needs them to do, why, how, and when.

Managers of effective hospitality organizations, on the other hand, understand the value of a strong culture and do whatever they can to reaffirm and support what the organization values and believes. If the culture values excellent service, the members learn that providing excellent service is what they are supposed to do. The stronger this cultural norm is and the more the members accept and believe in it, the more likely it is they will try to do whatever they can to create and sustain service excellence.

Unfortunately, many managers don't understand their responsibilities in managing the culture to get this level of employee commitment, and both their employees and customers can tell. Successful hospitality managers spend enormous amounts of

[1] Isadore Sharp, *Four Seasons: The Story of a Business Philosophy* (New York, NY: Penguin, 2009), 101.

VISION	VALUES	SERVICE BASICS
STAR employees delivering flawless service to customers seeking meeting, convention and leisure experiences.	**Service** We serve our Guests and each other every day. **Citizenship** We share a loyalty to our company, our communities and each other. **Integrity** We conduct both business and relationships in an honest, sincere and straightforward manner. **Respect** We care about the beliefs and feelings of others. **Excellence** We seek to set the standard. **Creativity** We pursue the extraordinary in all we do. **Passion** We love what we do and we are taking it to the world.	1 Look Everyone In The Eyes And Smile 2 Speak First And Last 3 Look Sharp 4 Know Your Stuff 5 Discover And Delight 6 Make It Right

STARS

SMILES

TEAMWORK

ATTITUDE

RELIABILITY

SERVICE WITH A PASSION

Courtesy of Gaylord Entertainment Company

Gaylord Hotels uses its vision, presented on this card, to emphasize for its employees the key aspects of its hospitality focus.

time and energy on training new employees in the organization's culture, reminding their existing employees of the cultural values, and rewarding and reinforcing these values at every opportunity. Although there are always other things to do, these managers make the time to reinforce culture.

Gaylord Palms in Orlando is a great example of a company that intentionally built on its Grand Tradition heritage to create a culture that would ensure everyone in it was committed to and would deliver excellent customer service. Its goal was to get the top scores, "5"s, on its customer satisfaction measures and it set out to build a culture that would inspire its employees to get them. Upon its opening, Gaylord Palm's general manager strategically defined a path by which this organization would create and sustain a strong customer-centric culture. He started by emphasizing its then parent organization, Gaylord Entertainment Company's, customer-focused vision and a set of values based on the unique history and entertainment traditions of the Grand Ole Opry. He then selected a leadership team that would appreciate and teach these cultural values and beliefs to all employees (or STARS, as they are termed at Gaylord) as they were hired, oriented, and trained. Gaylord used a variety of communication tools to build trust in and affirm management's commitment to the culture. The term *STARS First* was created to send a strong message of its commitment to the staff, and management backed it up by creating a unique *STAR guarantee*. This guarantee permitted direct access to top management for any employee anywhere who felt the promised employment relationship was not being delivered. The guarantee was created to build trust that management really believed in its STARS First cultural value.

So, does building a customer-centered culture really work? The metrics collected by the Gaylord Palms shows it really does. Not only did the Palms achieve a strong showing in the 10s in its early years, but it has consistently gathered every meeting planning award and best-place-to-work award in its market sixteen years after its opening.[2] This strategy was so effective that when the original cultural strategy developed at Gaylord Palms was later implemented in other Gaylord properties, it led to the same results in employee and customer satisfaction and market performance.

Few hospitality organizations have the opportunity to create a culture in a brand-new operation, as Gaylord Palms did. Its employees understood and participated enthusiastically in the organization's beliefs and values from the very beginning. The Gaylord experience, however, offers a model of how to create new

[2] Robert C. Ford, Celeste P. M. Wilderom, and John Caparella, "Strategically Crafting a Customer-focused Culture: An Inductive Case Study," *Journal of Strategy and Management* 1, no. 2 (2008): 143–167.

cultural values and beliefs even in existing organizations by systematically managing the culture. Its own success in transferring its guest-focused culture to other Gaylord Hotels shows how management can use a culture-based strategy to refocus strong employee commitment to a service excellence vision even where this commitment had been weak.

The Manager's Most Important Leadership Responsibility

Everyone has been in an organization that feels warm, friendly, and helpful, perhaps for reasons they can't quite explain. Similarly, everyone has been in an organization that feels cold, aloof, uncaring, and impersonal. While most people can readily give examples of organizations that fit the two types, few can really explain what makes the two types different.

Making culture different in the right ways is the hospitality manager's responsibility. Fred Cerrone is the founder and CEO of Hotel Equities, a hotel management company. Adopting a practice used by many of the exemplar hospitality organizations, Cerrone asks all his associates to carry a card that defines the company's mission and values. Each day, the general manager of each hotel reviews one of the values listed on the card with the staff. Says Cerrone, "That's a way to instill the culture into our hotels and throughout the organization. Now, our more than 700 employees 'get it.'"[3] Indeed, some leading writers go so far as to maintain that defining and sustaining the culture is every manager's most important responsibility.

THE IMPORTANCE OF CULTURE

In Chapter 2, we talked about defining a service strategy. Strategy is no more than a piece of paper without a supporting culture. An old saying affirms this: "Culture eats strategy for breakfast." The organization's strategy must be connected to its culture. No matter how brilliant and well thought out a strategy is, it will fail if it doesn't fit with the organization's cultural values and beliefs.

Strategy and Employee Commitment

The firm's competitive strategy provides the basis for such critical decisions as how the organization will be structured, what type of service it wants to deliver, what market niche it seeks to fill, what production and service delivery system it will use, who it will hire, and how it will train, reward, promote, and evaluate those people. But only employee commitment to implementing all those critical decisions can turn plans into actions. All the plans in the world are useless without employee understanding, commitment, and support.

Hospitality organizations that seek to provide an exceptional service experience require an especially high level of commitment and understanding from their employees. Hyatt Hotels includes its mission statement in its jobs page on its website to tell potential employees what it expects from them and how it will support them in delivering their best to Hyatt's guests.

> Our Purpose: *We care for people so they can be their best.* We continuously listen, learn and evolve to both meet and anticipate the needs of our colleagues. We believe that being your best is about being your true self — engaged, fulfilled and ready to take on the world.[4]

[3] S. Ricca, "Commitment to Culture," *Hotel and Motel Management* 244, no. 5 (2009): 28–29.

[4] http://www.hyatt.jobs/explore-hyatt/mission-statement/, accessed February 7, 2018.

Hyatt reinforces this mission through its orientation, training, and employee recognition programs where it communicates its core values of respect, empathy, integrity, creativity, humility, and fun.

Because the guest experience is intangible to some extent, and because each moment during the experience is so critical to determining guest satisfaction, employees must not only understand the vision, mission, and strategy of the organization but they must also have the skills needed to provide the service experience, knowledge of the guests they serve, and an ability to respond quickly to the many variations in guest expectations. However, knowledge, skills, and abilities are not enough. Employees must also have high levels of motivation to consistently deliver the hospitality experience in the way it should be done. Culture is the organization's software that tells well-trained, motivated employees how and why to do what when a customer is standing in front of them. Consequently, a strong and focused organizational culture becomes an especially important managerial emphasis in hospitality organizations.

Culture Defined

An **organizational culture** is a way of behaving, thinking, and acting that is learned and shared by the organization's members. A more formal definition is one that follows: the shared philosophies, ideologies, values, assumptions, beliefs, attitudes, and norms that knit a community of different people together. All these interrelated qualities reveal a group's agreement, implicit or explicit, on how its members should approach decisions and problems. In other words, culture is the way people in the organization act and think as they go about doing their jobs. "It's the way we do things around here." Any culture is also dynamic and constantly changing as anyone who has followed the changes in teen music and dress for the past decade can readily confirm. A culture both influences its members and in turn is influenced by its members. The interaction between members over time as they deal with changing circumstances and changing membership means that cultures will change.

organizational culture The shared philosophies, ideologies, values, assumptions, beliefs, attitudes, and norms that knit a community of different people together.

CULTURE AS A COMPETITIVE ADVANTAGE

An organization's culture can be a significant competitive advantage if it has value to its members, is unique, and cannot be easily copied by others. If an organization has a strong culture that others cannot readily duplicate, it can use that culture to attract both customers and employees. In fact, a strong organizational culture can be a major determinant in not just satisfying your customers, but actually delighting them.[5] A good strategy is to identify other organizations with successful cultures and try to emulate the processes used to create those cultures in your own company. For example, Southwest Airlines has a thriving culture others can use as a benchmark for their own. A big part of that culture is "Living the Southwest Way," which means "displaying a Warrior Spirit" (work hard, desire to be the best, be courageous, display a sense of urgency, persevere, and innovate), with a "Servant's Heart" (follow the Golden Rule, adhere to the basic principles, treat others with respect, put others first, be egalitarian, demonstrate proactive customer service, and embrace the SWA family), and embracing a "Fun-LUVing Attitude" (have fun, don't take yourself too seriously, maintain perspective [balance], celebrate successes, enjoy your work, and be a passionate team player).[6]

Working in a culture where the employees truly have the *spirit* is very different from working in a culture where the norm is for employees to work only the typical

[5] Chiu-Ying Kao, Sheng-Hshiung Tsaur, and Tsung-Chiung Emily Wu, "Organizational Culture on Customer Delight in the Hospitality Industry," *International Journal of Hospitality Management* 56 (2016): 98–108.

[6] K. Makovsky, "Behind the Southwest Airlines Culture," *Forbes*, November 21, 2013, accessed February, 2018, https://www.forbes.com/sites/kenmakovsky/2013/11/21/behind-the-southwest-airlines-culture/#39871af23798.

nine-to-five job. More importantly, being a customer who encounters this type of culture is unique and fun. The Southwest culture represents a competitive advantage for them over other airlines.

Management by Culture

The stronger the culture, the less necessary it is to rely on the typical bureaucratic management controls—policies, procedures, and managerial directives—found in traditional industrial organizations. If the culture can effectively substitute for such expensive control mechanisms, that in itself is a pretty good reason for the hospitality organization to spend the time and money needed to build a strong culture. JetBlue teaches its employees its five core values and tells them to use them instead of a rule book in making their decisions. The five values are safety, caring, integrity, passion, and fun.[7] JetBlue believes if employees keep these in mind as they do their jobs, they will always make the best possible decision for the customer and the company. Since hospitality organizations must find ways to delegate more decision-making responsibility and empower their employees, especially their guest-contact employees, they must rely on strong cultural values to ensure their people do the right things the right way for their guests.

A strong culture can also help employees guide guests properly even when the manager is not nearby. Guests are not passive; they almost always participate in co-producing their own hospitality experience with the guidance of employees. Unlike a manufacturing organization, where the production process is fairly predictable, the process of providing a hospitality experience is subject to incredible variation. As many different things can happen as there are many different types of people. Since defining and training for all the possibilities is impossible, the hospitality organization must rely on its employees to understand what each guest can and will do in co-producing the experience in order to fulfill each guest's expectation. The more uncertain the task, the more employees must depend on corporate values instead of managerial instructions, formal policies, and established procedures to guide their behavior.[8]

Courtesy of Katherine Wilson

The uniform of the chef helps reinforce the professional norms of providing consistent quality to every guest.

An Example: The Chef

In some cases, professional values can substitute for or complement values of the organization. The cultural values of the professional chef are particularly strong. While much of any culinary program is devoted to teaching the principles of cooking, implicit in all the culinary training is the cultural value of preparing a consistent fine-dining experience. Regardless of program or type of culinary training, one central value stands out: The chef must strive for flawless production of the food delivered in a fine-dining experience for every guest every time. Indeed, some casual dining chains have sent their cooks to culinary courses not so much to learn how to cook, since a chain's recipes are standardized, but to learn how to respect the

---

[7] http://work-here.jetblue.com/category/get-to-know-us/, accessed February 7, 2018.

[8] Robert C. Ford, and Janet R. McColl-Kennedy, "Organizational Strategies for Filling the Customer Can-Do/Must-Do Gap," *Business Horizons* 58, no. 4 (2015): 459–468.

culinary cultural values of product quality and consistency so the diner at a Chili's or Olive Garden, like the diner at a gourmet Parisian restaurant, will have a consistently prepared meal.

Culture as a Competency

If an organization's culture is strong, it becomes another core competency. As would be true for other core competencies, the organization that seeks to do something incompatible with its culture is likely to fail. If, for example, members of an organization's culture believe they should provide a high-value service experience, any manager trying to implement a cost-saving move that somehow jeopardizes their ability to provide that experience will meet resistance. The story is told about the general manager of the early Fred Harvey Company who visited one of his restaurants located along the Atchinson Topeka and Santa Fe railway. When reviewing the meat inventory, the GM noted 156 people were served steaks the previous day. According to Fred Harvey standards, this was thirteen more than should have been cut from the available supply. The general manager told the restaurant manager, "You are cutting your steaks too thin in order to make your showing of profit better. . . . We will stand for your operating a house without any profit—we will even stand for your operating at a loss . . . but under no circumstances will we permit a lowering of the standard of the food or service we give the public in order to make a showing. While encouraging thrift we would prefer extravagance to scrimping on guests in any particular." The likelihood is great this manager or any who heard this story would not fail to remember Harvey's belief that his company would never sacrifice its reputation for quality for profit.

The basic principle is simple. If the organization is committed to a strategy of service excellence, everything its managers say or do must consistently reflect its cultural norms, beliefs, and values to support the culture of service excellence. Otherwise, excellence will not happen.

Culture and the Outside World

Culture helps an organization's members deal with two core issues all organizations must resolve: how they should relate to the world outside of the organization, and how the organization's members should relate to one another. Noted cultural scholar Edgar Schein defines culture as

> the accumulated shared learning of that group as it solves its problems of external adaptation and internal integration; which has worked well enough to be considered valid and, therefore, to be taught to new members as the correct way to perceive, think, feel, and behave in relation to those problems. This accumulated learning is a pattern or system of beliefs, values, and behavioral norms that come to be taken for granted as basic assumptions and eventually drop out of awareness.[9]

Some managers define how their organizations should deal with the outside world by taking a closed or negative view of whatever those outside the organization are doing and encourage an "us-versus-them" cultural mindset. Members of such a culture are unreceptive to new ideas from the outside; they tend to discard or downplay common industry practices or innovations and are generally secretive about what their organization is doing and protective of its "proprietary knowledge." On the other hand, managers trying to create an open-culture organization constantly encourage their people to learn, grow, and develop by interacting with others in the industry, to benchmark

[9] Edgar H. Schein, *Organizational Culture and Leadership*, 5th ed. (Hoboken, NJ: Wiley, 2016), 6.

against best-practice organizations wherever they can be found, and to consider ideas and innovations developed outside the organizational boundaries. Not surprisingly, people in these open, learning organizations adapt more quickly to changes in customer expectations and respond better to customer needs than those in organizations with closed or negative cultures.

Culture and the Internal Organization: X and Y

Relating to the outside world refers to how the members of the organization see the world, what assumptions they make about the organization's relationship to that world, and how members are supposed to respond to external events. Relating to one another inside the culture refers to how the members see their collective mission, the ways they interact or interrelate with each other to accomplish that mission, and the assumptions they should use in making decisions about those things they control—their functional areas, interpersonal relationships, and attitudes toward change and adaptation. With regard to internal interaction, a culture can be democratic, supportive, friendly, informal, and participatory in its decision-making, or it can be formal, rigid, bureaucratic, and autocratic, allowing only those at the top of the organization to make decisions.

These two extremes reflect the distinction made famous by management scholar Douglas McGregor in his classic discussion of Theory X and Theory Y management styles. These two theories represent two very different sets of assumptions managers can make about how people behave. Theory Y managers assume people like to work, derive real satisfaction from their work, and want to do a good job. Theory X managers assume people will work only as hard as they are made to work, are motivated solely by extrinsic rewards, and need careful direct supervision. In life, of course, most managers fall somewhere between these extremes. People entering one culture type from another quickly learn that the behaviors and actions managers rewarded and respected in their former organization may not be respected or rewarded by managers in the new one. Part of the employee hiring process should include an introduction to the new culture to help new hires learn the cultural norms, values, and beliefs. This becomes especially important when employees join organizations that not only have a distinct organizational culture to learn, but which also include cultural values of other nations or ethnic groupings.

Teaching the New Values

Since everyone brings to a new job the cultural assumptions learned in past experiences, managers of excellent hospitality organizations know they must start teaching new cultural values to employees from day one. Orientation is considered essential in hospitality organizations, and companies known for their strong cultures—like Disney, The Ritz-Carlton, Gaylord, and Four Seasons—earned that reputation by spending considerable time and money on teaching their cultures to new employees.

Gaylord Hotels is a good example. Management believes it is important to socialize its new employees to the Gaylord culture as soon as they join the organization. Its New STAR Premier Orientation begins with two days of training that everybody attends, with an emphasis on culture woven into the entire curriculum. Gaylord believes this cultural training is critical to defining what the company is and what its values are to all who join it. Everyone learns the cultural value of Gaylord's STARS First commitment through the STAR guarantee and the many avenues available for employee communications. Orientation is followed by one to four weeks in the individual departments, where new employees get training in both job skills and further training in the Gaylord culture and its values.

STARS learn there is not supposed to be any difference between serving a guest and serving each other. This initial orientation is followed ninety days later by an "Encore" class reunion to ensure the STARS know their benefits, are comfortable in their job roles, and can see how to apply the flawless service philosophy in their specific departments or areas.

Culture Fills the Gaps

The cultural teachings become employee beliefs about how things should be, values of what has worth, and norms of behavior. They provide guidance to the culture's members as they interact with each other and their customers. In Schein's terms, they guide the members in how they should perceive the world around them, feel about the events they face, and think about what they do and don't do within their jobs. Many bureaucratic organizations believe the best way to make sure employees do the right thing in their jobs is to establish extensive rules and regulations to cover every possible contingency. Ideally, in that view, there would be a rule for every possibility. Excellent hospitality organizations, knowing that rules and procedures cannot cover everything, spend their time defining and teaching the culture so that their employees will know how they should act in treating their guests and one another. These organizations teach their employees as much as they can, and then rely on culture to fill in the inevitable gaps between what can be predicted and what actually happens when guests enter the service setting.[10]

BELIEFS, VALUES, AND NORMS

Culture-driven organizations seek to define the beliefs, values, and norms of the organization through what their managers do, say, and write as well as by who they reward, recognize, and promote. Let's take a closer look at what we mean by beliefs, values, and norms.[11]

Beliefs

Beliefs form the ideological core of the culture. Beliefs define the relationships between causes and effects for the organizational members. A belief is how people in organizations make sense of their relationships with the external world and its influence on the internal organization. If culture is a set of assumptions about how things operate, beliefs are formed to help the people inside the organization make sense of how those assumptions influence what they do inside the organization.

beliefs A body of ideas or tenets believed to be or accepted as true.

Let's consider a simple illustration. If the people in an organization assume the marketplace rewards those organizations that provide good service and punishes those that don't, the importance of providing good customer service becomes a cultural belief. It's something everyone believes in. Obviously, most beliefs are more complex than this; a multitude of assumptions about how the environment operates may translate into a whole system of sense-making beliefs. The point here is that every organization's members make a number of assumptions about the world and develop beliefs that reflect how they will respond as part of an organization to those assumptions. The management of an organization that understands the importance of these beliefs will take an active role in defining both the assumptions and the beliefs those assumptions create.

[10] Duncan Dickson and Robert Ford, "'We Only Need One Rule.' Growing a Service Culture: An Interview with John Caparella, President and Chief Operating Officer of the Venetian Las Vegas, the Palazzo Las Vegas, and Sands Expo and Convention Center," *Journal of Applied Management and Entrepreneurship* 17, no. 3 (2012): 98–114.

[11] For the definitions in this section, we are indebted to Harrison M. Trice and Janice M. Beyer, The Cultures of Work Organizations, (Englewood Cliffs, NJ: Prentice-Hall, 1993), 33–34.

Values

values Preferences for certain ideas, behaviors, and outcomes over others, used and promulgated within organizations to define for members (and sometimes guests) what is right and wrong, preferred and not preferred.

Values are preferences for certain behaviors or certain outcomes over others. Values define for the members what is right and wrong, preferred and not preferred, desirable behavior and undesirable behavior. Obviously, values can be a strong influence on employee behavior within an organizational culture. If management sends a clear signal to all employees that providing good customer service is an important value to the organization, then the employees know they should adopt this value. Consequently, they are more likely to behave in ways that ensure the customer has a good service experience.

Norms

norms Standards of behavior—spoken and unspoken, obvious and subtle—that define how members (and sometimes guests) are expected to act while part of the organization.

Norms are standards of behavior that define how people are expected to act while part of the organization. The typical organization has an intricate set of norms. Some are immediately obvious, and some require the advice and counsel of veteran employees who have learned the norms over time by watching what works and what doesn't work, what gets rewarded, and what gets punished.

Most outstanding hospitality organizations have norms of greeting a guest warmly, smiling, and making eye contact to show interest in the guest. Some use the ten/five-foot rule. Once guests are within ten feet of employees—window washers, engineers, and ground crews, as well as guest-contact persons—they are within the "hospitality zone" and the behavior norm is for employees to make eye contact and smile. Once guests are within five feet of employees, the behavior norm is to briefly speak to or engage the guest. Some organizations print the service norms on cards (like the Gaylord Palms does with their "Service Basics" on their employee card), supplied to every employee to serve as the guidelines for service.

Cultural norms are defined and shaped for the hospitality employee not only by fellow employees and supervisors but also by guests who make their expectations plain. Such guests are an advantage that hospitality organizations have over manufacturing organizations because these guests become potent assistants to the managers in monitoring, reinforcing, and shaping employee behavior. At Disney, the guest service guidelines are so well established even the guests often know them. If a ride operator in the Magic Kingdom fails to make eye contact or doesn't smile, a park patron may comment about the deviation from the service norm ("What's the matter? Did Goofy step on your toe?") or offer a reminder. Ride operators learn quickly what is expected of them by the constant hints, looks, glares, and comments guests make. Guest expectations of normal behavior help shape employee behavior. As with many organizations that make sure their guests know their commitment to service excellence, Disney's guests help reinforce the norms of behavior; they demand Disney cast members live up to their reputation for providing a high-quality Disney experience.

Norms in Advertising

Many hospitality organizations use advertising as a means to sell their services, to show the guest visually what the guest experience should look like. Since the employees see the same ads, they also learn the norms of behavior guests will expect, and this advertising serves to train them just as it informs prospective guests. The guest arrives with predefined expectations, and the hospitality employees know what they are and also know they had better meet or exceed those expectations or the guest will be unhappy and dissatisfied.

Norms of Appearance

In addition to the norms of behavior, most hospitality organizations have norms of appearance and standards of personal grooming. For example, employees may not be allowed to have hair that extends below a certain length; only women may have pierced ears and earrings must be smaller than a certain size; fingernails may not be excessively long or colored in unusual ways; and necklaces, bracelets, beards, moustaches, visible tattoos are not allowed, and so forth. Although such norms can lead to criticism about restrictions on personal freedom of expression regarding appearance, hospitality organizations must meet guest expectations in this regard, as in all areas of service. If Ritz-Carlton guests expect to see clean-cut employees greeting them upon check-in, then the Ritz-Carlton had better hire clean-cut employees. Disney wants its employees to have a conventional appearance; anything other than the *"Disney Look"* would detract from the guest's experience of the Disney show. On the other hand, the Disney norms would not be consistent with the culture at a Hard Rock Cafe, the Iron Horse Saloon, or Lockdown Bar and Grill in Chicago. While organizations where employees do not have direct contact with external customers can ignore such personal-appearance concerns, most hospitality organizations cannot. The latter must carefully define and enforce their norms of appearance to ensure employees have the look guests expect.

With changing times comes changing norms. Here are two modern chefs who don't seek to look like the "traditional" chefs of prior decades.

We have seen that advertising can help predefine guest expectations. Here is an example of how an appearance norm at a southern resort hotel affected the appearance and expectations of the hotel's convention clientele. Traditionally, this hotel required the men on its management team dress in blazers and ties, and the women in blazers and skirts. Whenever meeting planners visited the hotel to discuss potential convention business, they could see by the outfits of the hotel managers the culture was clearly somewhat formal. When these meeting planners went back to their organizations, they reported to their members that the attire for the convention, even though it was to be held in the sunny south, would be jackets and ties, and jackets/skirts or dresses. Now that the hotel's management has stopped requiring its team to wear jackets and instead requires short-sleeve Polo shirts with collars, or skirts and blouses, the entire atmosphere of the meetings held in the hotel has changed. Meeting planners, adopting the new appearance norm, now report to their convention attendees the meeting attire will be informal and relaxed.

Folkways and Mores

Folkways are the customary, habitual ways in which organizational members act or think, without reflecting upon them. Shaking hands (or not shaking hands), addressing everyone by first or last name, and wearing or not wearing a tie would all be examples of folkways. In a restaurant, a folkway might be to roll silverware when there is nothing else to do in the quiet times between crowds. An organization's *mores* are folkways that go beyond being polite. These are customary behaviors that must be followed to preserve the organization's efficient operation and survival. Mores require certain acts and forbid others. At Ritz-Carlton, employees are expected to use guests' names when they interact with guests. This more is part of the Gold Standards, which encompass the values and philosophy by which Ritz-Carlton operates. Other companies have mores, such as discouraging employees from dating each other, and forbidding supervisors from dating subordinates. By indicating what is right and wrong, they form the basis of the organization's code of ethics and accepted behaviors.

CULTURE AND THE ENVIRONMENT

The organization's culture, then, represents a shared learning process that continues over time as the people inside the organization change, grow, and develop while responding to a world that does the same. The world external to the organization (consisting of the physical, technological, and cultural environment) defines the activities and patterns of interactions for the organization's members who have to deal with the external world. Edgar Schein says,

> Culture is pervasive and influences all aspects of how an organization deals with its primary purpose, its various environments, and its internal operations. . . . Culture also covers mission, strategy, structure, and basic operational processes. All of these have been the product of shared learning and will limit the kinds of changes the organization can make.[12]

Learning the Culture, Learning From the Culture

As new people join the organization, they learn the culture from both formal company practices, such as training and reward systems, and informal social interaction with fellow employees, supervisors, and subordinates. They learn the right way and the wrong way to do things in that particular culture. The point is culture is an important influence on how people inside organizations behave while performing their jobs, how they make decisions, how they relate to others, and how they handle new situations.

The guidance that culture can give in handling unusual situations becomes especially meaningful in hospitality organizations. Unlike manufacturing organizations, where the jobs in the production process can be clearly defined in advance through engineering methods and bureaucratic control mechanisms, the hospitality industry is full of unusual events. People ask unbelievably odd questions, make the most outrageous requests, and behave in unpredictable ways. Without a cultural value system to guide them, employees in hospitality organizations would frequently fail the guest because they would not know how their organization wants them to respond to these unusual events. While most product manufacturers need to focus on teaching employees only the hows of producing the product, the hospitality organization must also teach its employees the whys. Developing, reinforcing, and communicating clear cultural norms about what is and is not the right way to deal with customers is a very effective way to teach those whys. A sign frequently seen in customer-focused organizations says:

> **Rule 1:** The customer is always right.
>
> **Rule 2:** If you think the customer is wrong, re-read Rule 1.

While no organization believes all customers are always right in all situations, the two principles are a good guide to behavior in those organizations that want to remind their employees of the organization's fundamental value structure. This sign is a strong symbolic reminder of this important cultural value.

Like everybody else, employees need to make sense out of their environment and how to behave within it. Culture helps them do so. When people collectively make assumptions about how the world operates, they form beliefs that help them make sense of those assumptions, collectively decide upon what is valued, and then define norms that enforce and carry forward those values in the day-to-day behavior of the members.

---

[12] Schein, *Organizational Culture and Leadership*, 11.

It sounds more complicated than it is. Essentially, managers who recognize these concepts and their worth to the organization spend considerable time and effort clarifying and articulating the assumptions, shaping the belief system, and making clear the organizational values to all the members. Members of every culture want to make sense of what they are supposed to do when dealing with those inside and outside the organization and will find a way to do so with or without management help. Hospitality managers wanting to ensure that their primary cultural value is service excellence will continually and consistently emphasize and define that critical value for the entire organization through everything they say, do, and write.

Subcultures

Cultures can often split into subcultures. Usually, the more people involved in the culture, the harder it is for them to stay in communication with one another, the more likely it is the organization will see some subcultures form. Subcultures can be good or bad, supportive or destructive, and consistent with or contrary to the larger corporate culture. Since culture relies on interactions to sustain itself, people who work together may well create a subculture of their own, especially if they don't interact much with other organizational units. Organizations that depend greatly on part-time, temporary contract labor or employees from employment firms ("third party employees") are especially susceptible to subculture formation; the part-timers and temporary contract labor may not spend enough hours in the greater organization to absorb its culture or care enough about the organization and its members to substitute its values for their own.

A third party may have a totally different set of cultural values based on their employment firm's culture. For example, many hotels do not hire their own housekeepers but contract with a housekeeping labor supplier to provide the employees that do these jobs. These housekeepers may wear a Marriott uniform one day and a Hilton or Hyatt uniform on another day. While outsourcing labor can have significant cost advantages, getting temporary or third-party employees to adopt the company's cultural values and beliefs and not create their own sub-culture is a difficult challenge. Moreover, many times permanent, full time employees are unwilling to make an effort to include the part-timers in their interactions and conversations, making it more difficult for them to learn or identify with the company's culture. Despite these challenges, the organization will want to do what it can to ensure that any subcultures are consistent with the core cultural values even if some specific behaviors, beliefs, and norms do vary somewhat from the desired culture. Communication is the key to bringing even part timers into the overall culture.

The authors of *Inside the Mouse* show how the large size of the entire Walt Disney World Resort operation has led to the development of subcultures.[13] The categorizing and subdividing of employees by place (Tomorrowland versus Frontierland), type (food and beverage versus attractions operator), shift (weekend versus weekday), and amount of work (full-time versus part-time) have the effect of forming many and clearly distinguishable subcultures. Cast members tend to associate with others like themselves, who are doing things like what they do in areas where they are likely to meet one another frequently. After all, a culture is a shared experience, and the more it is shared, the more definable it becomes for those sharing it. Pirates of the Caribbean people tend to hang out with other Pirates of the Caribbean people, Haunted Mansion people hang out with other Haunted Mansion people, and so forth.

The subcultures forming within the overall culture can be a managerial challenge if they operate in ways that do not support the overall corporate culture. The Jungle Cruise operators have a tendency to see themselves as excellent stand-up comedians

[13] Shelton S. Waldrep, "Monuments to Walt," in *Inside the Mouse: Work and Play at Disney World*, eds. Jane Kuenz et al. (Durham, NC: Duke University Press, 1995), 212–213.

and compete against one another for the best comedy routine during a Jungle Cruise ride. Although some humor can enhance the show for guests, this subcultural competition promotes values that, if carried to an extreme, could directly conflict with the overall Disney culture. Deviations from the accepted scripts might become so outlandish as to violate the overall cultural value of providing a wholesome and nonoffensive family entertainment experience. Although the worst violators eventually get caught, the damage to the overall Disney experience for some guests may by then be irreparable. The overall culture must be strong enough to override the subcultures on issues important to the organization's guest service mission. While some cultural variation may be tolerated, the overall culture has to be defined and reinforced by management in ways sufficiently strong that the central values of the organization come through in the customer experience.

Subcultures of Nations

Just like subcultures in organizations, organizations themselves can be thought of as subcultures of ethnic populations, nations, or even entire geographic regions. When an organization seeks to open a branch or start a business in a cultural setting it is not accustomed to, it can often have unexpected challenges. Disney was unprepared for the challenges that opening EuroDisney (now Disneyland Paris) would have. The French saw this as an attempt to teach American values as superior to French and resisted it. Four Seasons Hotels learned from this and decided to take a very different approach when it opened its Four Seasons Hotel King George V Paris. After doing a service quality audit to identify some of the differences between French and North American business culture, David Richey, the quality auditor, stated, "There were three things we talked to Four Seasons' executives about, mostly related to employee attitude. First, the staff had an inability to apologize or empathize. . . . Second, the team had a very tough time doing anything that could be described as selling. This is also typically European. For example, say your glass is empty at the bar. In Paris, they may not ask you if you want another drink. Third, the staff were rules and policy oriented. If something went wrong, they would refer to the manual instead of focusing on satisfying the guest."[14]

The point is simple. Just as hospitality managers must pay attention to and manage how they relate to the subcultures that may form in their organizations, they must recognize that they must also pay attention to and manage how they relate to the larger culture in which their organization is embedded. People will bring to work their cultural values, and if there is conflict between those cultural values and those of the organization, the managers will need to find ways to bring them together. The Paris Four Seasons, for example, recognized its employee of the month and year recognition programs might be seen as controversial unless presented as congruent with the French, Anglo-Saxon culture and not as an American scheme.

COMMUNICATING THE CULTURE

While the substance of culture is a set of assumptions that lead to beliefs, values, and norms, culture is communicated to those inside and outside the organization in a variety of ways, including laws, language, stories, legends, heroes, symbols, and rituals. In these ways, people can express, affirm, and communicate their shared beliefs, values, and norms to each other and to those outside the organization. Each way is important in helping the members learn, implement, teach, and reinforce the shared culture. They should be used together and become part of an overall message to members of what the culture stands for. The more these communications support each other in

[14] Roger Hallowell, David Bowen, and Carin-Isabel Knoop, "Four Seasons Goes to Paris," *The Academy of Management Executive* 16, no. 4 (2002): 19.

sending a single clear message to the organizational membership, the stronger the impact of that message will be.

The Gaylord Palms' opening manager knew that communicating culture was critical. Much of the effort to communicate the culture took place in the hiring process, so new entrants immediately learned the emphasis placed on being customer centered. The process started with hiring people who fit with the Palms' culture; management knew, however, this culture had to be reinforced on an ongoing basis. As described earlier in this chapter, this included emphasizing the culture in employee orientation, follow-up training, and through the wallet cards that detail the Gaylord values for easy reference.

Leading hospitality organizations know the importance of these elements in defining their organizational culture. They manage their cultural mechanisms in a holistic way to reinforce, clearly and consistently, those organizational values they expect all employees to have in mind when they meet, greet, and serve customers. Learning the culture becomes part of the training for all new employees. Managers and other experienced employees, internal communications media, and organizational reward structures should all be coordinated to teach, reinforce, and celebrate the corporate culture thereafter.

Laws

The laws of an organization are its rules, policies, and regulations—the norms that are so important they need to be written down so everyone knows exactly what they are. They tell the members what behaviors are expected within that culture and also detail the consequences of violating the norm.

Two norms are so important to Disney they are corporate policies—in effect, laws. First, a cast member in costume must not walk in an area where the costume is inappropriate. An employee in the futuristic Tomorrowland cannot go to Frontierland. Nor may an Epcot World Showcase member of the China Pavilion be found in costume in the Moroccan Pavilion. Second, cast members portraying Disney characters must stay completely in character; they must maintain and fulfill the character expectations of Disney guests. They cannot speak, be seen out of costume, take off any part of the costume in public, or do anything else that might destroy the sense of fantasy for the children (of all ages). Indeed, a policy forbids transporting any character costume in a public area unless it is in a black bag that completely covers all its parts so no child (of any age) will see a favorite fantasy character "in pieces." A cast member violating either norm may be fired.

Language

In addition to the common language of the larger social culture, each organization develops a language of its own, which is frequently incomprehensible to outsiders. The special language is an important vehicle both for communicating the common cultural elements to which the language refers and in reaffirming the identity with the culture those who speak this language share. Terms an insider uses to talk with another insider communicate an important concept quickly and also distinguish that person from an outsider.

For example, everyone at Disney uses certain important terms that carry strong cultural messages. All employees recruited by Casting are called *cast members*. This term sends two important messages. First, everyone is equally part of the overall cast of the organization, a concept reinforced by the use of first names alone on all name tags. Second, the term reminds cast members they are playing "roles" that help make up the Disney show. Other terms reinforce this concept, such as *on stage*, to define all situations and areas where cast members are in front of their customers, and *back stage,* to define areas the customers cannot see. Law enforcement staff are called *security hosts,* and everyone's uniforms are costumes that are checked out daily from wardrobe. In other words, the language of the culture is carefully constructed to ensure cast members constantly think of themselves as participants in an ongoing stage production designed to create a magical fantasy experience. So effective is this training in language that Smith and Eisenberg report no Disneyland Park employee they talked to during their thirty-five half-hour interviews used any of the traditional terms for *uniforms, customers,* or *amusement park,* instead using only *costumes, guests,* and *property.*[15]

Stories, Legends, and Heroes

Stories, legends, and heroes are another way of transmitting cultural beliefs, values, and norms. They communicate proper behaviors and the right and wrong way to do things. The best at building culture use stories extensively. Disney, Four Seasons, Gaylord, and the Ritz-Carlton all have their collection of stories that are used by managers to teach the culture. The Ritz-Carlton is especially noted for using teaching stories and its managers tell many. For example, to teach going the extra mile to serve a customer, the *New Gold Standard* reports how managers use the following letter from a guest as a story to teach its values:

> My wife [accidentally] broke a bottle of makeup that she had brought along and left it in pieces on the counter in the bathroom because she wanted to use as much of it as possible. We came back to the room one day to find a note sitting beside the broken makeup bottle from housekeeping offering to replace the broken bottle they didn't even break.[16]

The best service-oriented companies want to obtain only top scores in customer evaluations, and stories provide a means to define and teach employees what customer-guests will find inspiring enough to give such high evaluations. Some companies, like Disney, have a rich history of stories to draw on. Disney managers have used examples from the *Lion King* to teach the value and importance of the guest service commitment or used the song "Be Our Guest" from *Beauty and the Beast* to build similarly inspirational stories about providing excellent guest service. Newer companies, like the Gaylord Palms, didn't have this past to draw upon for stories but could invent them. To take advantage of the power of stories as a training tool, the Palms' management created a letter from a fictitious customer when it opened to illustrate what the intangible mission of flawless service meant through the customer's eyes until it could collect real customers' letters. In short, the best service-oriented companies collect and use stories to teach employees about what the service they want to provide looks like. To accomplish this, they use real examples with real employees whom everyone knows; those that don't have real examples create heroes with stories to teach the culture.

American Express famously called those employees who have provided exceptional service to customers "Great Performers." To help illustrate this point to new employees, American Express told them stories about their Great Performers. New employees heard, for example, about two customer service people in Florida who got money to a woman in a foreign war zone and helped her get passage on a ship out of the country; travel agents in Columbus, Georgia, who paid a French tourist's bail so he

---

[15] Ruth C. Smith and Eric M. Eisenberg, "Conflict at Disneyland: A Root Metaphor Analysis," *Communications Monographs* 54 (no. 4), (1987): 367–380.

[16] Joesph Michelli, *The New Gold Standard: 5 Leadership Principles for Creating a Legendary Customer Experience Courtesy of the Ritz-Carlton Hotel Company* (New York, NY: McGraw Hill Professional, 2008), 181.

could get out of jail after being arrested for speeding; an employee who drove through a blizzard to take food and blankets to stranded travelers at Kennedy Airport; and an employee who got up in the middle of the night to take an Amex card to a customer stranded at Boston's Logan Airport. Any hospitality organization has its heroes—employees who have gone above and beyond the call of duty—and their stories should be preserved and shared. American Express distributes its Great Performers booklets to all employees worldwide.

Four Seasons also has a rich reservoir of stories to draw upon. Stories about the Power of Personal Service are used to illustrate what this term means in real examples anyone in their organization can understand and use. One story, for example, tells of an employee who accidentally overheard a guest telling his wife how embarrassed he felt as he was the only one without a black tie at a black-tie function. The employee pulled him aside and said he thought he might have a solution. After asking the man to take a seat in his office, he went into a back room, took off his own tuxedo, put on his civilian clothes, rushed to the laundry to clean his tuxedo, and then called in the seamstress to fit the cleaned tux to the guest. What makes this story so rich is that it teaches the values management wants shared by all of Four Seasons' employees. It also shows clearly the connection between customer service and two important business outcomes. First, the guest turned out to be the chairman and CEO of a leading consulting organization, who after this experience directed all his company's business, worth millions in food and lodging, to Four Seasons. Second, the man took every opportunity to tell people in his speeches and conversations what Four Seasons did for him. These testimonials from a leading businessman proved to be priceless word-of-mouth advertising. Teaching the culture through stories can leave a lasting impression on employees as they come to see how the abstract idea of customer service translates into specific employee actions that lead to outcomes that benefit both their company and them.

All organizations can and should use stories, heroes, myths, and legends to help teach their culture, to communicate the values and behaviors the organization seeks from its employees while performing their jobs, and to serve as role models for new situations. Most people love stories. It's so much easier to emotionally connect to a story of what a hero did than to listen to someone lecturing about customer responsiveness in a formal training class. Not only are stories more memorable because of this emotional connection than a few arbitrary points listed on a classroom PowerPoint, but the tales can be embellished in the retelling and the culture thereby made more inspiring. Tales of "Old Joe" and what wondrous things he did while serving customers teach employees the desired responses to customer concerns and reaffirm the organization's cultural values. When Gaylord Palms opened, it had no stories to tell, so its opening general manager invented some to show the kind of service he wanted his STARS to deliver and asked his managers to ask employees at weekly meetings for examples that would replace the fictitious ones with real ones as time went on. Stories are felt to be so powerful in teaching culture at the Gaylord Palms they were collected in a database so managers needing a particular type of story to tell can find one even if their own employees have no examples to share. Now Gaylord uses a newspaper, *KYS: Know Your Stuff,* which is distributed to every employee every day that contains the key information about the day's activities. groups in house, employee birthdays and anniversaries, and a tip of the day to emphasize and reinforce one of the Gaylord values.

Every hospitality organization should capture and preserve the stories and tales of its people, who do amazing things, create magical moments, to wow guests. The effort will yield a wonderful array of inspiring stories for all employees and send a strong message about what the organization values and desires in its employees.

Robert C. Ford

The Team Disney Administration Building uses its architecture as a symbolic reminder of Disney's culture.

symbol A physical object that has organizational significance or communicates an unspoken message (for example, Mickey's ears for Disney).

ritual A symbolic act performed to gain and maintain membership or identity within an organization.

Symbols

A **symbol** is a physical object that has significance beyond itself, a sign that communicates an unspoken message. Cultural symbols are everywhere in organizations. A corner office on the top floor, a company achievement award hanging on the wall or a photo of the individual shaking hands with the CEO displayed on a desk communicates information about the status, importance, or organizational power of the person that transcends the mere physical objects involved. At Walt Disney World Resort, Mickey's famous mouse ears are everywhere. The plants are grown in mouse-ear shapes, the anniversary service pins are mouse ears, awards are mouse ears, the souvenir balloons are ear shaped, the entrance to Team Disney is framed by ears, and Disney's Hollywood Studios landmark water tower (The Earful Tower) has mouse ears on it. Mouse ears are subtly hidden everywhere around the property and serve as a constant symbolic reminder of where Disney began. Not even the employees know where all the mouse ears are. There is even a website devoted to Hidden Mickeys. While this may seem overdone, it ties into the cultural values as they serve as a constant reminder of the reason behind why everyone is there—it all started with a mouse.

Rituals

Rituals are symbolic acts that people perform to gain and maintain membership or identity within an organization. At most hospitality organizations, all employees go through a similar training program. Rituals are mainly informational; new employees learn the organizational basics and cultural heritage. But, like military boot camp or initiation into a sorority, it also has ritualistic significance because everyone goes through the experience upon entry into the company to learn and share the common culture. Most hospitality organizations develop elaborate ritual celebrations of service excellence. These can range from a simple event like a departmental pizza party to honor those receiving positive comments on customer comment cards, to elaborate employee of the year award ceremonies that resemble a major gala. The point is that what the organization celebrates ritualistically and how much effort it makes to celebrate tells the members a lot about what the culture believes in and holds valuable.

Gaylord Palms' management gave extra effort to the development of rituals and celebrations that would reinforce its culture and affirm its commitment to its employees.[17] They created rituals and celebrations specifically designed to reinforce the organization's vision and values. One ritual was designed for celebrating promotions. When a STARS got promoted, the person was put on a three-wheeled bicycle and pedaled around the hotel by his or her new supervisor. The bike would be followed by a camera-toting paparazzo waving a sign and making noise. If the idea was to make the newly promoted person feel special and recognized, this simple celebration certainly did that. Today, the recognition and celebration of new promotions is done differently but still with an emphasis on making the newly promoted STARS feel special and recognized.

[17] Terrence E. Deal and M. K. Key, *Corporate Celebration: Play, Purpose, and Profit at Work* (San Francisco, CA: Berrett-Koehler, 1998).

Indeed, the emphasis on doing things that make employees feel special is carried over in a variety of celebrations that are uniquely special to the person being recognized. For example, a somewhat conservative manager was greeted at the airport by a group of twenty fellow managers with noise makers and in costumes to celebrate his success in representing the Palms in a corporate meeting. The cultural value encourages its STARS to find fun ways to create memorable celebrations for each other. A person being recruited was greeted as he slid down an ice slide at the annual Ice Holiday Display by a group of STARS holding signs saying "We want you to join us."

A second formal event that was specifically designed to celebrate and communicate the culture and its values is the All STARS rally that is held annually. These rallies provide a mechanism to publicly celebrate management's commitment to open communications, to reinforce the importance of the company's values, and to highlight the fun STARS have doing their jobs. They celebrate successes of individual contributors, by selecting STARS in the hotel that best represent all six values seen on the pocket card shown earlier. A number of STARS ranging from as few as four to as many as ten are selected by a committee comprised of the prior year's winners. A three-minute video is prepared on each person and shown at the rally along with the awarding of a plaque. These are emotionally charged entertaining events that make the STARS feel valued, recognized, and appreciated while teaching all in attendance what the company values, recognizes, and appreciates. Value award winners are honored by being included in the Value Wall of Fame, which details the history of value award recipients over the years. Because Gaylord is now one of Marriott Corporation's brands, at the end of each year, one of the winners of the Value Award is nominated for the JW Marriott Award of Excellence, which recognizes people from the entire Marriott Corporation who best represent its values.

Leaders Teach the Culture

Managers of effective hospitality organizations constantly teach the culture to their employees, reinforcing the values, mores, and laws. Strong cultures are reinforced by a strong commitment by top management to the cultural values. Schein suggests "the beliefs, values, and actions of the founder are the biggest determinants of how the culture will evolve."[18] Effective leaders don't just talk about the culture; they act on it every day. They personally model their commitment to the service mission, and they do it visibly. They back up slogans with dramatic, sometimes costly, actions. To instill values, they stress two-way communications, opening their doors to all employees and using weekly work-group meetings to not only inform and inspire but also to discuss and solve service problems. They put values into action by treating employees exactly as they want employees to treat their customers.[19] They use rituals to recognize and reward the behaviors the culture values, and they praise the heroes whose actions have reflected worthy cultural values in the stories they tell. Other employees can use these hero stories as models for their own actions.

Schein offers further insights about how leaders can embed the culture, especially at the time the organization is being formed.[20] Initially, the leader defines and articulates a set of beliefs and assumptions about how the organization will operate. According to Schein, "The leader must have certain insights, clear vision, and the skills to articulate, communicate, and implement the vision."[21] Since new members join the organization with mixed assumptions and beliefs, the leader must carefully and comprehensively define the organization's culture. This process creates the definition of the corporate culture, embeds it in the organization's consciousness, and shows what

[18] Schein, *Organizational Culture and Leadership*, 178.
[19] William H. Davidow and Bro Uttal, *Total Customer Service: The Ultimate Weapon* (New York, NY: Harper Collins, 1989), 107.
[20] Schein, 181–206.
[21] Schein, 352.

behaviors are reinforced. Whatever the leader responds to emotionally or with great passion becomes a powerful signal to which subordinates also respond. Thus, during the period of an organization's creation, the leader must spend some thoughtful time defining what is important, how the organization's members should interpret the world they face, and what principles should guide their actions. Once the organization's culture is in place, the leader constantly adjusts and fine-tunes it as markets, operating environments, and personnel change.

Schein suggests that leaders can use five primary mechanisms to define and strengthen the organization's culture: "(1) what leaders pay attention to, measure, and control; (2) leader reactions to critical incidents and organizational crises; (3) deliberate role modeling, teaching, and coaching by leaders; (4) criteria for allocation of rewards and status; (5) criteria for recruitment, selection, promotion, retirement, and excommunication."[22]

Setting the Example

Bill Marriott Jr. provides a good example of how a leader can help to sustain the culture. He is famous for dropping in at a hotel and chatting with everyone he sees. He has been known to get up early in the morning and wander into the Marriott kitchens to make sure the pancakes are being cooked properly. This intense commitment to personal contact with each and every Marriott employee and visible interest in the details of his operations have become so well known among the Marriott organization that his mere presence on any Marriott property serves as a reminder of the Marriott commitment to service quality.[23]

Kimpton Hotels & Restaurants maintains a culture based on Bill Kimpton's vision. Although Bill Kimpton died in 2001, the culture he cultivated lives on through the organization's new leadership. According to Niki Leondakis, chief operating officer, "One of the things we do at employee orientation is talk to every one of our employees. Once a year, I and one of our senior executives travel around the country on the Kimpton National Tour and bring together all the employees at each hotel. We talk about the culture of care. It means caring for your co-workers, caring for our guests, caring for the environment, our community, our investors."[24]

The clear commitment to the customer-service culture, demonstrated through the actions of those on the top of the organizational chart, sends a strong message to all employees that everyone is responsible for maintaining a high-quality customer experience. This same modeling behavior can be seen in the many hotel managers who visibly and consistently stop to pick up small scraps of paper and debris on the floors as they walk through their properties. Employees see and emulate this care and attention to detail.

A leading hotelier in Orlando has earned a reputation among his employees and fellow hoteliers alike as a can-do manager. A story is told about how he took a chance and bought a bankrupt hotel with very little money and a whole lot of courage. When he was seen mowing his own property's lawn, a legend was born that here was a guy who would do what it took to get the work accomplished. He reinforced the message by his attire. His typical working outfit was blue jeans and a polo shirt. He intentionally wore shoes with soles that he could use to rub out black marks on his tiled floors and was frequently seen doing exactly that. His employees learned, by reputation and by deed, that this owner was ready to work at any job that needed doing. Since he also had a big sign on the interstate that advertised different room rates for each night, he earned a reputation as a relentless competitor. His strategy was to fill his rooms at rates that would allow him

---

[22] Schein, 204.

[23] Hal B. Gregersen and J. Stewart Black, "J. W. Marriott, Jr., on Growing the Legacy," *The Academy of Management Executive* 16, no. 2 (2002): 33–39.

[24] C. Wolff, "What Makes Kimpton Cool," *Lodging Hospitality* 11, no. 8 (2008): 42–43.

to capture his variable costs plus whatever else the market could bear. His flexibility in room rates and his nightly phone calls to his front desk manager, asking about the percentage of rooms sold rather than revenues, sent a powerful message to his organization that its goal was to fill the rooms every night. By his own actions, dress, and style, he has been extraordinarily effective in teaching his employees at all organizational levels the cultural values and norms he wants for his organization.

Hospitality managers must stay close to both their employees and their guests. Only by walking around can they see for themselves that the quality of guest experiences is high, that concerns of guests and employees are being met, and that everyone remains focused on the guest. While managers in the manufacturing industry can rely on statistical reports to tell them how things are going on the production line, hospitality managers need more than these financial and operating reports to really find out how things are going. They use the classic managerial technique of "management by walking around" to stay as close as possible to the point where the service experience is produced—the moments of truth. As Norman Brinker put it, "There's no substitute for spending time with people in their own environment. You not only meet everybody personally, you are able to see and hear for yourself what's going on."[25] Many restaurant managers are told to meet every guest and to make at least one table visit to talk to them; hotel managers spend time in their lobbies to observe the reactions of guests; and bed and breakfast operators monitor the looks on guests' faces to make sure the experience is going well. All these guestology techniques are based on the simple idea that the reason for the organization's existence and basis for its success is the customer. For successful organizations, being out with the customer is an important organizational value and not just a company slogan, and managers from the top down must set the example. As most of them know, the pressures of day-to-day administrative responsibilities can easily push aside this fundamental ingredient in service success, so they build customer-contact time into their schedules. Orlando's Grand Cypress Hyatt has each manager assigned to a door-duty time, to send the message to customers and employees alike it is important to Hyatt that everyone be aware of the guest experience: Even managers must spend some time at the door talking to guests and watching their body language as they enter and leave.

Guests Teach the Culture

Hospitality organizations often have the help of guests in teaching and reinforcing the values, beliefs, and norms expected of the employees. As management scholar Van Maanen reports from his observations of Disneyland Park,

> Ride operators learn how different categories of customers respond to them and the parts they are playing on stage. For example, infants and small children are generally timid, if not frightened, in their presence. School age children are somewhat curious, aware that the operator is at work playing a role but sometimes in awe of the role itself. Nonetheless, the children can be quite critical of any flaw in the operator's performance. Teenagers, especially males in groups, present problems because they sometimes go to great lengths to embarrass, challenge, ridicule, or outwit an operator. . . . The point here is that ride operators learn what the public (or at least their idealized version of the public) expects of their role and find it easier to conform to such expectations than not. Moreover, they discover that when they are bright and lively, others respond to them in like ways.[26]

[25] Norman Brinker and Donald Thomas Phillips, *On the Brink: The Life and Leadership of Norman Brinker* (Arlington, TX: Summit Publishing Group, 1999), 191.

[26] Van Maanen, "The Smile Factory," 70–71.

Culture and the Organization Chart

Schein suggests a leader can use other, secondary mechanisms to reinforce or define the organization's culture.[27] A leader can define the value of a functional area by placing the area at the bottom or near the top of the organizational chart. For example, placing the quality assurance function near the top of the chart and requiring its manager to report to a high-level executive tells the organization's employees the leader values quality. The way in which the leader designs the organizational systems and procedures will also tell everyone in the organization a great deal about what is valued. McDonald's sends a strong value message through its quality checklist and by the procedures it uses to maintain its standards of cleanliness to guarantee its customers the freshness of each hamburger it sells. McDonald's spends a great deal of money sending quality control people out to individual restaurants to check on these key items, to let restaurant managers know what is important, and to make sure customers get what they expect. All McDonald's employees know what's on the quality checklist and how seriously the organization takes these inspections, so the checklist helps to define the cultural values of cleanliness and quality. Employees know that what is expected is inspected.

Culture and Physical Space

The layout of physical space is another secondary mechanism that can send a cultural message. For example, office size and location are traditional symbols of status and prestige. By putting the executive chef in the big office out front, the leader tells the rest of the organization the chef plays an important role in the organizational culture and producing food of high quality is an important organizational function. If the employee break room is put in leftover space, not very nice, and generally non-hospitable, this sends a very different message of the value of employees than a well-lit, well-furnished, and appealing employee cafeteria. Finally, the formal, published statements of the company's mission and vision hanging on the walls not only teach employees the philosophy, creeds, and beliefs by which the organization lives but show them the organization believes in them enough to display them where all employees can be reminded of them. Although some organizations may not say what they really mean in these public statements, the excellent hospitality organization will do so clearly, concisely, consistently, and publicly.

Stephen Brashear/Getty Images

The use of physical space can also communicate aspects of culture, such as how much employees are really valued. Google is known for providing elaborate facilities for its employees, including its famous cafeteria shown here.

Culture and Leadership Skills

The success with which leaders use the mechanisms discussed above to convey cultural values is a good measure of their leadership skills. When they concentrate on using them together in a holistic way, they can ensure all mechanisms convey to employees a consistent set of cultural beliefs, values, and norms. Consistency is important as a powerful reinforcer of the culture. The more consistently these mechanisms are used, the more powerfully reinforced the culture will be. Leaders must take care about what they do, say, and write to ensure the messages they send are what is

[27] Schein, *Organizational Cutlure and Leadership*, 181–206.

intended and explicit. What the leader gets angry or excited about tells everyone what is important. A leader who expresses outrage over a service failure caused by a careless employee sends a strong message to all the employees that good service matters. A story is told of how Bill Marriott Sr. fired an employee on the spot for insulting a guest. When this story got around the organization, there was no question in anyone's mind of the guest orientation that Marriott valued.

At Southwest: Maintaining a Strong Culture

Truly outstanding hospitality organizations engage all their members in teaching each other the organization's culture. Good managers create the opportunities for this teaching and learning to happen. For example, Southwest Airlines created a Culture Committee, whose responsibility was perpetuating the Southwest Spirit.

The Culture Committee was created in 1990 "to take the lead in preserving the airline's unique culture."

> The Culture Committee was created to pull together people who exemplify Southwest's culture. Most of the original committee had ten or so years at Southwest and embraced Southwest's maverick, caring, irreverent way of doing things. They were all great in their individual jobs and were hand-picked for their creativity, expertise, energy, enthusiasm, and most importantly, Southwest Spirit. For the two years they serve on the committee, they engage in leadership activities that protect the company's unique and highly valued culture. Committee members have been known to visit stations with equipment and paint in hand to remodel a break room. Others have gone to one of Southwest's maintenance facilities to serve pizza and ice cream to maintenance employees. Still others simply show up periodically at various field locations to lend a helping hand.
>
> Their labor is really a labor of love; their payoffs are the relationships they build with other workers, the knowledge that they have sparked worthwhile and fun endeavors, and most importantly, the satisfaction of having been a vital part of keeping the Southwest Spirit alive.[28]

Courtesy of Southwest Airlines

Southwest employees show off the uniforms that they created. Employees at the company collaborated to design their own uniforms for each department.

Originally, the committee was made up of 38 people. It has since expanded to well over 350 active and alumni members, with representatives from each station and part of the airline.[29] Even after members end their terms on the committee, these alumni members tend to stay active in support of Culture Committee initiatives.

The Culture Committee has helped maintain Southwest's culture throughout its growth. Southwest even employs a Managing Director of Culture to specifically focus on activities and policies that support its unique culture. Because of its culture, Southwest's employees maintain a strong customer-service-oriented company, repeatedly making the company one of the highest-rated airlines in terms of customer satisfaction

[28] Southwest Airlines Co., "Our History," Southwest Airlines Co., accessed September 7, 2009, https://www.swamedia.com/pages/our-history-sort-by.

[29] Ann McGee-Cooper, Duanne Trammell, and Gary Looper, "The Power of LUV: An Inside Peek at the Innovative Culture Committee of Southwest Airlines," *Reflections: The SoL Journal* 9, no. 1 (2008): 49–55.

and one that is currently recognized by Indeed.com as second on the list of the best companies to work for in America.

CHANGING THE CULTURE

The world changes and the people inside the organization change. The culture must also evolve to help members cope with the new realities the organization faces. Even a culture that starts out with a strong customer orientation may change how it displays that customer centricity over time as the managers, customers, and employees change. No matter how good a job the founder did in defining the culture and getting everyone to buy into it, the next generation of managers must work, perhaps even harder, to sustain those cultural values that should endure while changing those that need changing. They have available, of course, all the tools discussed in this chapter to do this. The communication tools of symbols, legends, language, stories, heroes, and rituals need constant attention to sustain the cultural values in the face of changing circumstances.

Denny's Restaurants

The most difficult task of all is changing an entire culture. When a negative culture is pervasive throughout an organization, it can be very challenging to make a change to a positive culture, even when the culture is causing major problems.

In 1997, Denny's restaurants operated 1,652 restaurants and was generally seen as a successful company. But over the next few years, repeated claims of racial discrimination were made that seemed to indicate racism was ingrained in Denny's culture. In one instance, several black teenagers were refused service unless they paid for their meal in advance; in another, six black Secret Service agents were forced to wait an hour for service while their white counterparts were seated and served promptly. Multiple cases emerged of other black customers being forced to pay a cover charge and prepay their meals while white customers seated and served at the same time were not subjected to the same service. Furthermore, of Denny's thousand-plus restaurants, there was only one black franchisee and none of the suppliers for the company were from companies owned by minorities. Denny's CEO at the time, Jerome Richardson, publicly stated Denny's did not discriminate and the negative events were isolated incidents. It did not seem he really thought racism was an issue. Richardson was quoted as saying, "We hire from the population. We get the good with the bad. But yeah, it makes you wonder if this wasn't blown out of proportion" and "If our African-American guests were mistreated, was it because of racism? I can't tell you. It's impossible to know what's in a person's heart."[30] In subsequent lawsuits, it seemed racism was simply ingrained in Denny's culture. For example, one lawyer said a former manager talked of training he had received on how to deal with what was considered too many blacks in a restaurant at one time, a policy the manager said the company referred to as "a blackout."[31] Although the company seemed to make some efforts to change, the lawsuits kept coming. While they never admitted guilt, Denny's agreed to settle a class-action lawsuit for $54 million to 295,000 customers, the largest public accommodation settlement ever at the time.[32] Yet, despite the bad publicity and high costs, the culture did not change.

---

[30] J. Howard, "Service with a Sneer," *New York Times*, November 6, 1994, http://www.nytimes.com/1994/12/04/magazine/1-service-with-a-sneer-990094.html.

[31] Stephan LaBaton, "Denny's Restaurants to Pay $54 Million in Race Bias Suits," *New York Times*, May 25, 1994, http://www.nytimes.com/1994/05/25/us/denny-s-restaurants-to-pay-54-million-in-race-bias-suits.html?pagewanted=all.

[32] Faye Rice and A. Faircloth, "Denny's Changes Its Spots Not So Long Ago, The Restaurant Chain Was One of America's Most Racist Companies. Today it is a Model of Multicultural Sensitivity. Here is the Inside Story of Denny's About-Face," *Fortune*, May 13, 1996, http://archive.fortune.com/magazines/fortune/fortune_archive/1996/05/13/212386/index.htm.

Change did not begin until new leadership came to the company. In 1995, Jim Adamson was brought in as CEO, and the culture began to change from the top down. In his first meeting as CEO, he told employees, "Anyone who doesn't like the direction this train is moving had better jump off now . . . and I will fire you if you discriminate."[33] Management began to deal with its racial problems instead of trying to explain them away.

Through the change in culture, which began at the top, Denny's radically changed the way it treated minorities. Within a few years, half of Denny's employees were minorities, 32% of supervisory positions were held by minorities, there were dozens of black-owned franchises, and millions of dollars of supplies were purchased from minority-owned suppliers. Today its commitment to minorities is still strong as it claims that of its total workforce is minority, and 45% of the franchisees are held by minority or women.[34]

While changing its customer service culture is challenging for properly treating external customers, it is equally challenging for changing the culture about treating internal customers. An example is the importance of the role of the chef as a cultural leader in restaurants. This person can greatly influence how internal customers—employees—are treated. As the restaurant industry has come under fire for allegations of discrimination, sexism, harassment, and a hostile work environment, especially for women, the chef can play a positive role in needed change. The chef is the leader in the kitchen, and often the leader for the entire restaurant. How the chef behaves, and what the chef tolerates, sets the culture for the entire organization. Emphasizing respect as a key cultural value can prevent the kind of behaviors known to plague the restaurant industry. Changing a hostile culture requires leadership by chefs, the programs that train them, and the owners who employ them. Will Guidara, a New York–based restaurateur and co-owner of the hospitality group *Make It Nice,* has emphasized its efforts to overcome in his restaurants the causes of negative cultures seen in the industry. "We emphasize mutual respect, between the restaurant and the dining room, and among all of the employees. We balance intensity and respect."[35]

Changing a company's culture is a difficult task. It often requires new leadership with a true commitment to the new ideas. Simply providing training or mentioning supposed cultural values in orientation will not work if upper management does not truly embrace the behaviors it hopes its line employees will engage in by what it says, does, and writes every day.

What We Know About Culture

Here are some principles about organizational culture that seem to hold generally true.

- Leaders define the culture (or redefine it if necessary), teach it, and sustain it. Doing so may be their biggest responsibility in the organization.
- An organizational culture that emphasizes interpersonal relationships is uniformly more attractive to professionals than a culture that focuses on work tasks.[36]
- Strong cultures are worth building; they provide guidance for employee behavior in uncertain situations when company supervisors, policies, or procedures are unavailable or unwritten.

---

[33] Rice and Faircloth, 133.

[34] Denny's, "2014-2015 'Guest First' Diversity Report," accessed 10/30/2018, https://www.dennys.com/assets/files/diversity/2014-2015-Dennys-Diversity-Report.pdf?v=2.1.1.295.

[35] Michael C. Sturman, Interview with Will Guidara, Personal interview, December 8, 2017.

[36] Mark G. Ehrhart and Maribeth Kuenzi, "The Impact of Organizational Climate and Culture on Employee Turnover," in *The Wiley Blackwell Handbook of the Psychology of Recruitment, Selection and Employee Retention*, eds. Harold W. Goldstein et al. (Malden, MA: Wiley-Blackwell, 2017), 494–512.

- Subcultures will form in larger organizations. A strong culture will increase the likelihood of keeping the subcultures consistent with the overall culture's values in important areas.
- Sustaining the culture requires constant attention to the means of communicating culture so that they all consistently reinforce and teach the organization's beliefs, values, and norms of behavior to all employees.
- Excellent hospitality organizations hire and retain employees who fit their culture and get rid of those who do not. The fit between the individual and the culture is strongly related to employee turnover, commitment, and satisfaction.[37]

LESSONS LEARNED

LO 4.1 State why the organization's leaders are so important to defining, developing, teaching, and maintaining its culture through their words and actions.

- Leaders know that culture exists, whether they define it or not, so they take responsibility for defining it.
- Leaders know one of their most important jobs is to teach culture.

LO 4.2 Relate a hospitality organization's culture to service success.

- Culture fills in the gaps for employees between what they've been taught and what they must do to satisfy the guest.
- Leaders think carefully about how to be consistent in making sure everything they say, do, or write ties into strengthening the cultural values of guest service.

LO 4.3 Discuss the essential roles the organization's beliefs, values, and norms play.

- Leaders find heroes, tell stories, and repeat legends to teach and reinforce important cultural values, beliefs, and norms.

LO 4.4 Describe how the external world influences the internal culture.

- The physical, technological, and cultural environment defines the activities and patterns of interactions for the organization's members who have to deal with the external world.
- Everything from the national culture to the subgroups of employees within whom individuals work can influence the type of culture that develops in an organization.

LO 4.5 Explain how the organization communicates its culture to its employees—through laws, language, stories, legends, heroes, symbols, and rituals.

- Leaders use all the tools of culture building to shape, change, and reinforce it.
- Leaders define and teach organizational culture to everyone by what they say, do, and write every day, as well as by what they reward and punish.

LO 4.6 Describe how the organization can accomplish the difficult task of changing its culture, if that becomes necessary.

- To create a culture of service excellence, celebrate successful examples of service excellence—publicly.

KEY TERMS AND CONCEPTS

beliefs 119
norms 120
organizational culture 115
ritual 128
symbol 128
values 120

[37] Ehrhart and Kuenzi, 494–512.

REVIEW QUESTIONS

1. Recall any organization in which you were heavily involved as an employee or as a student.
   A. How would you describe the culture of that organization?
   B. What did the managers or leaders do or not do to cause the culture to be as you described it?
   C. What ideas in this chapter could the managers or leaders have used to improve the organizational culture?
   D. How does culture relate to managing the guest experience in hospitality organizations?
2. Why is culture such an important concept to guest service organizations? How does culture influence the guest experience?
3. What is the difference between a strong and a weak culture? What can a manager do to create a strong culture?
4. Does a culture exist whether a manager does anything about it or not?
5. How are stories important to building and sustaining a strong culture?
   A. Give examples of stories you have heard that helped teach cultural values.
   B. How does all that relate to managing the guest experience in hospitality organizations?
6. "Walking the walk" is an expression that one hears in hospitality organizations in connection with the leaders. What are some possible meanings of the concept in the hospitality context?
7. Explain the impact of beliefs, values, and norms on the culture of an organization.
8. What are some of the positive and negative results of the formation of subcultures?
9. Describe a technique that may be employed to change the culture in a restaurant.

ACTIVITIES

1. Divide into groups. Come up with a list of what factors or aspects make up an organizational culture. Which characteristics are the most important?
2. Find a hospitality organization that has a strong, clearly defined service culture. You may work for one yourself or have friends who do. How does the organization create and sustain that culture? What training methods, incentives for managers and employees, and communications techniques are used to create and define the culture? If you know of an organization that has a weak, muddled, unfocused culture, talk about that organization, too.

ETHICS IN BUSINESS

In this chapter, we talked about how companies set standards for appearance and personal grooming. This is done to ensure a certain image of the service providers and help reflect the culture of the organization. These standards are also based on customer expectations. That said, when do these standards go too far? Suppose a hotel wants employees without moustaches or beards. Is this reasonable? What if it violates a potential employee's religious beliefs? How much of a role should the government play in regulating what employers can specify as reasonable? At one extreme, you could argue employers should be able to do whatever they want (which could therefore include selecting people based on gender, race, etc.). At the other extreme, the government could prohibit any sort of regulation that is not clearly and directly job related (and so, make any sort of appearance policy illegal). What do you think is ethically appropriate?

CASE STUDY

Doug's Fried Chicken

Within four years of assuming the presidency, Judy Hart brought the market share of Doug's Fried Chicken from 2% to 20%. She was a risk-taking, innovative entrepreneur. She increased the chain from 400 outlets to 1,743 and rapidly expanded into 27 countries. "I've got to be involved in a continual go-go growth cycle. Because of my successful track record, the franchisees and the board go along with any programs I propose," Hart believed. Hart was flamboyant and sensational. She shifted the annual franchisee convention from Des Moines, Iowa, to New York. She moved headquarters from a converted post office into a new $5.8 million building.

Then, one Friday afternoon, Doug's board of directors dismissed Hart from the presidency. "Judy," said Chairman Doug Jones, "for a while we liked your 'full-steam-ahead' attitude. But you can't seem to slow down. You're trying to change too many things too fast."

The board elevated John Davis, vice president for finance, to the position of president. Davis was a conservative, accommodating executive who watched budgets closely and believed in rigorously controlled expansion. He emphasized fiscal responsibility. Davis set up a centralized purchasing system (which Judy Hart had always opposed). Board Chairman Doug Jones was pleased; he considered Davis to be "in tune with the mood of the board and the franchisees at this point in time."

Judy Hart was unemployed over the weekend. Then she was enthusiastically hired by Berger's Burgers, a company that had achieved financial stability only in the last couple of years. Now they were in a strong cash position. "Judy," said Horace Berger, chairman of the board, "we think we're ready to take off. We want to triple the number of Berger's Burgers outlets within three years. Can you do it?"

"Can do, Mr. Berger," said Judy happily. "But first we've got to refurbish this tacky headquarters building and change the site of the annual convention. I envision a truly spectacular party for the franchisees in Las Vegas."

1. How do you explain Judy Hart's unceremonious dumping from Doug's and her warm welcome at Berger's?
2. Did Doug's make the right decision? Did Berger?

Further readings on the topics in this chapter are listed in "Additional Readings" on pages 502–504.

Get the tools you need to sharpen your study skills. SAGE edge offers a robust online environment featuring an impressive array of free tools and resources.

Access practice quizzes, eFlashcards, video, and multimedia at **edge.sagepub.com/Ford2e**.

Visit **edge.sagepub.com/Ford2e** to help you accomplish your coursework goals in an easy-to-use learning environment.

Steve Debenport via Getty Images

SECTION 2

The Hospitality Service Staff

We're not in the coffee business, serving people;
we are in the people business, serving coffee.

—Howard Schultz, CEO, Starbucks Coffee

Robert Nickelsberg/Getty Images

5 Staffing for Service

Hospitality Principle: Find and Hire People Who Love to Serve

If someone isn't smiling during the interview, what in the world would make you think they will be smiling when faced with a line of customers all in a hurry for service, service, service?

—T. Scott Gross, *Positively Outrageous Service*

Learning Objectives

After reading this chapter, you should be able to

5.1 Explain the importance of staffing for an organization to be able to deliver an exceptional service product.

5.2 Understand why it is critical to study the job before efforts are made to fill it.

5.3 Describe the process of recruiting employees who will give excellent guest service.

5.4 Recognize internal and external recruitment strategies that organizations use.

5.5 Express the importance of a diversified workforce to hospitality organizations.

5.6 Explain the standard approaches and techniques for screening and interviewing job candidates.

5.7 Understand how and why organizations need to balance all of the information gathered in the selection process to hire the right person.

5.8 Explain why organizations need to treat job applicants professionally and with respect, even those they end up not hiring.

5.9 Describe the process of on-boarding and why it is important.

5.10 Discuss why managing turnover is just as important as managing who is hired.

INTRODUCTION

When a guest checks into a hotel, most of the time things go . . . as expected. The guest drives up to the hotel, gets the luggage out, goes to the front desk, and gives the agent his name. She interacts pleasantly while she finds the reservation, handles the check-in, and provides a key. The guest heads up to the room and opens the door to the room without incident. The guest may watch TV to relax, and then goes to sleep. If someone were to ask that guest, "How were the employees of the hotel?" he might think back to his front desk experience and say "Fine." But this answer overlooks the large number of people that were hired, trained, and coordinated to make check-in meet his expectations.

So, who are all the people involved? There was the reservationist who took the reservation, the manager who hired and scheduled the reservationist, the valet who parked the car, the bell person who helped with the luggage, the doorman who let the guest in to the hotel, the front desk agent (whom the guest did remember), the front desk manager who scheduled enough people to be on staff to ensure check-in occurred in a reasonable amount of time, the housekeeper who cleaned the room, the maintenance person who made sure the light bulbs and TV remotes were working, and of course, a host of IT staff who provided the technology that helped make the reservation and kept the information secure, and the executive staff who were responsible for the higher level management activities that ensured the profitability and efficiency of the hotel. It took literally dozens of people to get the guest checked into the room . . . as expected. All those people had to be hired, trained, paid, and managed.

An exceptional service experience requires exceptional servers. Consequently, in organizations whose mission is to provide exceptional service and, especially

human resource management The use of organizational systems to ensure that human talent is used efficiently and effectively to achieve organizational goals.

for those in hospitality services, providing this top-notch level of service requires recruiting, training, and inspiring employees to deliver this exceptional service. The process of **human resource management** (HRM) is all about employing people with the right knowledge, skills, and abilities (KSAs) and then motivating them to deliver exceptional service. It includes applying the science behind the processes of recruiting, selecting, developing, and motivating employees to perform their tasks in ways that are consistent with the service mission of the organization.

This chapter begins a discussion of the human resource issues involved in managing the guest experience, by reviewing the first issue: hiring the right people, who can deliver the experience your guests expect. Chapter 6 will look at what is involved in training and developing the employees you have hired, and Chapter 7 will examine the financial and nonfinancial factors that leaders use to motivate exceptional employee service. The final chapter of this section will consider these human resource management issues as they apply to your guests who can be considered as quasi-employees co-producing and co-creating their own hospitality experiences.

THE MANY EMPLOYEES OF THE HOSPITALITY INDUSTRY

Providing either a tangible or an intangible service product requires many different employees doing many different jobs. Most obvious are the front-of-house employees who interact with the guest. They are directly responsible for providing the value and quality of an exceptional experience because they are the interface between the guests and the company. Back-of-house employees, or what is sometimes called the *heart of the house,* help create the service experience. They cook the meals, clean the sheets, fix the rides, and so forth so that the guest's experience meets or exceeds expectations.

Management also plays a critical role. They hire, train, evaluate, reward, discipline, celebrate, promote, and oversee all the tasks that are required in delivering a service experience. In short, their job is to ensure there is someone at the right time and place ready, willing, and able to serve the guest. Beyond these tasks, there are laws and regulations that must be followed; supplies that must be purchased; accounts that must be balanced; financial statements that must be created; strategies that must be developed and implemented; facilities that must be cleaned and maintained; marketing plans that must be developed; and sales that must be made. All these tasks—and the people who perform them—are critical for a successful business.

Serving the Guests

Scott Gross, in his book *Positively Outrageous Service,*[1] provides numerous examples of how exceptional customer service can make the service experience extraordinary. One such service experience occurred at a Hampton Inn at the St. Louis Airport. A guest arrived very late at night, with an important 9 a.m. meeting the next morning. Unfortunately, his luggage didn't make it, but he needed to look fresh and clean for this important meeting. Upon hearing the dilemma, the night auditor suggested the guest get clothes and other essentials at a local Walmart, which stayed open late. Because the guest had flown in and had no way to get there, the night auditor gave the guest directions *and* the keys to his car!

[1] Scott T. Gross, Andrew Szabo, and Michael Hoffman, *Positively Outrageous Service: How to Delight and Astound Your Customers and Win Them for Life*, 3rd ed. (New York: Allworth Press, 2016).

While many people are involved in the delivery of any service experience, it is the frontline or customer-contact employee, with whom the guest interacts, who has the most direct influence on the guest's perception of the service's quality and value. This employee—the front desk agent, the restaurant server, the character at a theme park, the cabin steward, the driver of the bus, the tour leader, the flight attendant—is frequently the one that can turn a guest experience into a memorable "wow." This can be done in a variety of ways, but one way is for that person to creatively add something extra and unexpected to the experience. The story is often told of a Southwest flight attendant who hid in the overhead compartment to surprise boarding guests with an unexpected greeting. Those who were greeted this way still talk about the pleasant and memorable experience this provided them on an otherwise as expected flight. Such an employee can make the service experience something special, worthy of being told to friends or recorded in books about great service experiences, by adding an extra service to an already outstanding service product.

Both the Hampton Inn and Southwest Airlines examples illustrate the role employees can play in adding something extra to the service experience. It is always possible to simply check a guest into your hotel or help passengers be seated for a flight. Service can be as expected—simple, polite, and efficient—but it won't be especially memorable. The employees the best hospitality organizations seek, however, are the ones who provide exceptional and memorable service experiences. Whether it is by turning a routine encounter into a memorable experience as in the Southwest Airlines example, or by helping solve a guest's problem as in the Hampton Inn case, hiring the right service-oriented employees can create memorable guest experiences. For these guests, these employees made these service experiences a "wow!"

Supporting the Service

If employees are to deliver excellent service, there must be something excellent to deliver in the first place. Just as guest-contact employees must have the right abilities and motivation to interact appropriately and engagingly with guests, so employees in non-contact positions must have the right abilities and motivation to do their jobs in creating an excellent service product for the guest-contact employees to deliver.

For example, Eleven Madison Park has been called the best restaurant in the world.[2] One of the key reasons for its success is the effort it takes to ensure the entire customer experience is exceptional. On a given night, the restaurant serves about 115–120 guests in the dining room, and another 25 in the bar. Providing this service are typically 37 staff members in the dining room, four managers, and a complement of one chef, six sous chefs, and another twenty cooks in the kitchen. At any given moment, there may actually be more employees than there are actual customers in the restaurant. Each employee is there for a reason: to ensure that each customer has an exceptional dining experience. While the customers might interact directly with only a few employees (e.g., maître d', server, wine steward), and while those employees provide exceptional service, these employees are only part of the reason this restaurant is so special. People go to such restaurants both for the exceptional experience that they have by sitting for such a meal and also for the magic occurring out of sight in the kitchen. Says Daniel Humm, the chef and co-owner of the restaurant, "It's so important that we push ourselves and strive for excellence all with the sole goal of providing the absolute best for our guests."[3]

---

[2] "No.1 Eleven Madison Park," The World's 50 Best Restaurants, accessed January 2, 2018. http://www.theworlds50best.com/The-List-2017/1-10/Eleven-Madison-Park.html.

[3] "Elite 100 Speaks to Eleven Madison Park's Daniel Humm," Elitetraveler, accessed January 2, 2018. http://www.elitetraveler.com/features/elite-100-speaks-to-eleven-madison-parks-daniel-humm.

Photo by Jake Chessum

A pre-shift meeting of Eleven Madison Park's large cooking team.

Almost any service encounter requires some back-of-the-house people providing excellent support to those interacting with guests. Meals must be cooked, rooms must be cleaned, laundry must be done, beds must be made, buildings and rides must be maintained, and dishes must be washed. The work of some support services is obvious—a skilled chef is clearly involved in the preparation of a meal served at a fine restaurant. Other functions are less obvious—the Walt Disney World Resort in Orlando, Florida, is supported by a full-time fire department, employing roughly 150 firefighters, emergency medical technicians, and paramedics, who are seen only when needed.

The Role of the Manager

As with all labor-intensive industries, hospitality organizations must also employ managers to supervise, coach, and coordinate the many employees doing the different jobs. Supervisors and managers have a number of important roles, from checking employees' work to creating work schedules, providing training, conducting performance evaluations, and supplying necessary equipment and supplies. Yet managers in service firms are faced with very different issues than managers in product-producing firms.[4] While any performance assessment includes some degree of subjectivity, the critical nature of customer satisfaction and loyalty, the transient nature of guests and the variety of expectations they hold, and the simultaneous production and consumption of services make the hospitality managerial role complex and difficult to spell out. In addition to their administrative responsibilities, hospitality managers are held accountable for success on qualitative measures, and often perform a customer-service role as well. Finding and hiring managers with these capabilities is at least as important, critical, and challenging as hiring customer-service employees.

Managing Emotional Labor

Unlike jobs such as watching a computer monitor that is measuring a manufacturing process, or sitting in isolation in an office cubical balancing accounts, most employees in the service industry (and, more generally, in the service economy) regularly interact with other people: internal customers such as co-workers, subordinates, superiors, as well as external customers and guests. Work that includes interactions with other individuals requires employees to regulate their emotions during these interactions. For positions with guest-contact responsibilities in particular, employees must understand which expressions of emotion are expected by the guest, display those emotions and reactions, and, simultaneously, suppress the emotions and reactions they are feeling but would be inappropriate to display to a guest. Whenever emotional regulation is part of the job, the employee role is not just performing a task but also includes the regulation of emotions, which is **emotional labor**.

emotional labor The process of managing feelings and expressions to fulfill the interactional and emotional requirements of a job.

[4] John Bowen and Robert C. Ford, "Managing Service Organizations: Does Having a 'Thing' Make a Difference?," *Journal of Management* 28, no. 3 (2002): 447–469.

Hospitality and most service employees are expected to be upbeat, cheerful, enthusiastic, and genuinely interested in providing an exceptional service experience to the guest, and they must do so even when they themselves don't feel upbeat or positive. Moreover, they are expected to be this way even when their guests are not equally upbeat, cheerful, enthusiastic, or interested. Doing this is emotional labor and it can be just as tiring as physical labor.[5] When hiring people to perform in customer-contact roles, companies must select individuals who are not only able to successfully perform the assigned tasks, but who are also capable of handling the emotional labor these guest-focused tasks sometimes create. Putting on a happy face when you yourself are having a bad day or are dealing with a really rude or unpleasant guest is hard. When employees' true emotions are not consistent with the emotions the customer expects them to display, they can use one of two strategies: **surface acting**, where they modify their facial expressions and body language to display the expected but not truly felt emotion, or **deep acting**, where they are able to actually change their inner feelings to the degree that they are able to display the desired emotion with conviction and authenticity.[6] Surface acting diminishes the energy an employee has, as the effort it takes to fake or display emotions not truly felt is fatiguing. Think of the last social event you attended when you wished you were somewhere else with someone else and recall how exhausting it was. Deep acting, though, when the employee's inner feelings match the required emotions, leads to less exhaustion and enhances the employee's well-being on the job.

surface acting The process of modifying facial expressions and body language to display the expected emotions, but without the emotion being genuinely felt by the actor.

deep acting The process of changing inner feelings so that the expected emotion is also genuinely felt by the actor, thus allowing the emotion to be displayed with conviction and authenticity.

Not everyone, no matter how service oriented, can be upbeat or positive all the time no matter how positive and upbeat their customers and work situation are. If your job is to greet 20,000 guests a day on the *Spaceship Earth* or at *The Wizarding World of Harry Potter,* it is hard to sustain an upbeat or positive emotional state. In addition, all hospitality employees have had guests who push them to their limits and thus challenge their genuine commitment to provide great service. If the job requires employees to engage in extensive surface acting, eventually the employee will burn out.[7] It is thus critical that organizations hire those who are more capable of truly engaging in deep acting when providing customer service. This means finding applicants with a passion for customer satisfaction, a capacity to deal with complaints/problems, an ability to develop good working relationships, and an appetite for work.[8]

Finally, because service employees will be interacting with the guests, they should also be polite, considerate, and willing to make a genuine effort to help other people. For example, during the hiring process, observe how candidates treat the receptionist before the interview. To put these general abilities together would lead to selecting someone who has the ability to handle emotional labor, can put on a consistent show in front of guests, cares about the quality of the performance and the guest's reaction to it, and does it all with gusto.

Find the Service Naturals

While employees in different positions will obviously play different roles and have different levels of customer contact, ultimately, the hospitality industry comes down to providing service. Each employee helps deliver that service, either directly or

[5] Despoina Xanthopoulou et al., "Need for Recovery after Emotional Labor: Differential Effects of Daily Deep and Surface Acting," *Journal of Organizational Behavior* (2017): 1–14.

[6] Huiwen Lian et al., "Self-control at Work," *Academy of Management Annals* (2017): 703–732.

[7] Ziguang Chen et al., "Chinese Hotel Employees in the Smiling Masks: Roles of Job Satisfaction, Burnout, and Supervisory Support in Relationships between Emotional Labor and Performance," *The International Journal of Human Resource Management* 23, no. 4 (2012): 826–845.

[8] Elizabeth M. Ineson et al., "Seeking Excellent Recruits for Hotel Management Training: An Intercultural Comparative Study," *Journal of Hospitality & Tourism Education* 23, no. 2 (2011): 5–13.

service naturals An individual who instinctively provides great service when presented with the opportunity

indirectly. When one comes across employees who deliver exceptional customer service experiences, they really stand out.

Scott Gross calls these people **service naturals**[9] because they instinctively give great service when provided the opportunity. These are the employees who can change a regular interaction with a customer into something special the guest will both appreciate and remember. Through this experience, the server connects with the guest in a way that builds a relationship. Though often very brief, this relationship makes an emotional connection that leaves the guest feeling good about the experience and believing that something was special and memorable about it. The challenge for hospitality organizations seeking excellence is to find and hire these people who can make such connections with guests.

Gross estimates that service naturals represent only one in ten of the available workforce. As he states, "Ten percent can't get enough of their customers. Five percent want to be left alone. The vast majority, when it comes to customers, can take 'em or leave 'em."[10] If Gross's percentages are accurate, he raises two major challenges for hospitality managers. First, they need to work hard at developing a process that will systematically find, recruit, and select those 10% who are truly committed to providing excellent service. Second, they must work even harder to develop an effective process for showing the rest how to provide the same quality of service that the naturals do naturally. Because naturally talented people are so rare in the labor pool, the organization must identify what skills are lacking in the people they do hire and train them in those skills.

Given the challenges of recruiting and hiring good employees in the hospitality industry, some organizations are tempted to place the service naturals in the guest-contact jobs and hire the rest for support jobs, which don't have direct contact with the guest. Since not all jobs in hospitality organizations require extensive guest contact, putting people not naturally good at service in these behind-the-scenes jobs might seem like a way out. The truly excellent organizations, however, recognize the fallacy of this reasoning. They know that *all* employees are somehow involved in serving either external paying guests or internal fellow workers. Knowing that service effectiveness depends on everyone throughout the organization taking service responsibility seriously, these outstanding organizations try not to hire anyone unwilling or unable to provide outstanding service. There are simply very few places to hide employees who may be outstanding technically but have no service skills.

TOSHIFUMI KITAMURA/AFP/Getty Images

Companies like Ritz-Carlton seek to hire service naturals, who instinctively give great service when provided the opportunity.

The Recruitment and Selection Challenge

Many hospitality companies say they hire the "best and the brightest." Others claim to follow the mantra "select the best and train the rest." But in reality, the process of getting employees into service roles can prove to be difficult for all companies. Entry-level jobs in the hospitality industry are often known for long hours, difficult conditions, and low pay. By its very nature, the business of hospitality often means being open twenty-four hours a

[9] Scott T. Gross, Andrew Szabo, and Michael Hoffman, *Positively Outrageous Service: How to Delight and Astound Your Customers and Win Them for Life*, 3rd ed. (New York: Allworth Press, 2016).
[10] Gross, Szabo, and Hoffman, p. 149.

day, including on holidays and weekends. It is an industry known for its high turnover. Ultimately, finding qualified applicants can prove to be quite a challenge. For all the rhetoric about hiring the best and the brightest, it is not uncommon to hear some managers say, "If the candidate has a pulse, he's hired!"[11] The best organizations know this is a recipe for service disaster. They know the **recruitment** and **selection** process must be carefully planned and executed.

recruitment The process of finding candidates with the KSAs necessary to fill organizational positions.

selection The process of selecting employees to fill organizational positions from the candidates with the necessary KSAs.

Although all companies clearly want to have high-ability, skilled, and motivated employees, the best-performing companies are those that have gained a competitive edge by developing recruitment, training, placement, and reward and recognition programs that motivate all employees to provide outstanding service for customers. It all begins with recruitment and selection. If the organization can somehow attract and select the best potential employees, it will gain a significant advantage over those organizations that do not systematically seek out and find these guest-focused people.

The selection process, in theory, is straightforward. *First,* figure out exactly what you are looking for; *second,* recruit a pool of good candidates; *third,* select the best in the pool; *fourth,* bring the best candidates on board; *fifth,* make the new hires feel welcome; and *sixth,* manage any potential future turnover of employees strategically. Each step requires a number of critical decisions. How do you know who your best candidates are and what does a great candidate look like? Do you look for applicants from inside or outside your company? What tools do you use to collect information (e.g., interviews, psychological testing, references)? How do you combine the information you collect to decide who you should hire? How do you make the new hire feel genuinely welcomed and show your appreciation to that person for agreeing to join your organization?

THE FIRST STEP: STUDY THE JOB

Before looking for a new employee, an organization must take the time to fully understand exactly what sort of job you are going to fill. This will require gathering information on what those on the job do, determining what KSAs are needed to perform the job successfully, and ultimately detailing the exact specifications and competencies that need to be examined in the selection process.

Job Analysis: The Foundation of Human Resources

job analysis A systematic process through which information about the content of a job is gathered and analyzed to determine the exact job specifications and required competencies for the job.

The process known as **job analysis** is what allows an organization to identify the exact job specifications and required competencies for each job classification and type (for an example of the result of a thorough job analysis, see Exhibit 5.1). A job analysis reveals if the job requires physically strong people to assist park visitors into a ride, skilled lifeguards to keep people safe in the water park, or multilingual people to speak to an international clientele.

Many organizations spend a considerable amount of effort identifying the KSAs associated with each major job or job category; they then develop measures to test applicants on the degree to which they have these KSAs. A carefully developed measurement process ensures the tests are both valid and reliable to provide an effective and legally defensible means for putting the right candidates in the right jobs. Further, a careful job analysis to develop accurate selection measures has the added benefit of identifying training needs and building reward structures that are directly connected to the critical KSAs closely linked with job performance.

[11] Bruce J. Tracey, Michael C. Sturman, and Michael J. Tews, "Ability versus Personality: Factors That Predict Employee Job Performance," *Cornell Hotel and Restaurant Administration Quarterly* 48, no. 3 (2007): 313–322.

EXHIBIT 5.1

The Knowledge, Skills, and Abilities Required for an Assistant Front Desk Manager in a Sample Major European Hotel

- Ability to work in a fast-paced environment.
- Outstanding flexibility; must be able to work under stress and pressure and reflect at all times, even under difficult conditions, a positive can-do attitude and the best image of the hotel.
- Ability to analyze complex statistical data and make judgments accordingly.
- Ability to deal effectively with internal and external customers, some of whom will require high levels of patience, tact and diplomacy to defuse anger, collect accurate information, and resolve conflicts.
- High school diploma required. Degree with hospitality focus preferred.
- Minimum two years previous front desk experience required.
- Experience with reservation information systems required.
- Experience in a luxury property of comparable size preferred.
- Operational and/or sales experience required.
- Must be able to deal correctly with confidential information and must be discreet.
- Must be fluent in French and English and must be able to address any kind of information in an adequate manner.
- Must be well groomed and maintain impeccable hygiene standards.
- Extensive walking required and ability to stand on feet for a long time.
- Hours may vary based upon organizational needs and operational demands.
- Strong leadership skills.
- Excellent oral and written communication skills in English and French. Dutch is an asset. German and/or Spanish is a plus.

While the KSA approach is the most widely used strategy for selection in industrial organizations, using it in the hospitality organization is more difficult because of service intangibility and variability in guest expectations. Measuring the strength, height, and manual dexterity necessary for a manufacturing job is far easier than determining the sort of personal and conceptual competencies needed to provide excellent customer service.[12] For this reason, hospitality organizations must go beyond KSAs and consider other factors such as the attitudes and behaviors needed to effectively connect and interact with guests, the decision-making competencies needed to understand and fix different guests' problems in complex situations, and the ability to display the emotions guests expect in service experiences. Indeed, many hospitality organizations find attitude so important they use this staffing principle: Hire for attitude, train for skill. From the guest's perspective, another way of expressing this idea is found in a commonly heard hospitality saying, "Guests don't care how much you know until they know how much you care." Of course, you cannot forget that you need to hire people with the right skills to perform the job, or at least the right abilities to be successfully trained for the job, but employee attitudes, problem-solving skills, and emotional self-regulation can also be important factors in whether a company provides service excellence or a service failure.

---

[12] Sonia Bharwani and Parvaiz Talib, "Competencies of Hotel General Managers: A Conceptual Framework," *International Journal of Contemporary Hospitality Management* 29, no. 1 (2017): 393–418.

Study Your Best Performers

The intangibility of the guest experience and the uniqueness of what each guest expects from it have led some hospitality organizations to use a secondary strategy for identifying good candidates: study the organization's best performers and identify their personal traits, tendencies, talents, and personality characteristics. Then, find candidates who match this profile.

Instead of identifying the KSAs that particular jobs seem to require or will require in the future, this approach starts by defining the KSAs of currently successful employees. In essence, this is benchmarking against your own very best practitioners of the job. The idea is that if you hire only employees who have traits, skills, abilities, tendencies, talents, and personality characteristics that are similar to those found in the current strong job performers, they should be more successful than new employees who don't have those same characteristics. If you want to find a successful new job performer, find an existing successful job performer and hire someone as nearly like that person (in terms of KSAs, behaviors, personality, and attitudes) as possible. The trick, of course, is to discern the distinguishing characteristics that enable your strong performers to succeed.

Develop Talent Profiles

Many organizations have followed the strategy of identifying talent profiles based upon work by the Gallup Corporation, S.R.I., J.D. Power, and other similar organizations. The idea here is to look at an organization's strong performers and, based on their talents, develop talent profiles for each major job category. Then, they use these benchmark profiles to screen new applicants. For example, theme park ticket sellers have traditionally been hired and rewarded on their ability to handle large sums of money transactions quickly and accurately; yet careful analysis showed that the best ticket sellers have additional talents. In effect, the ticket seller is the first point of contact between a theme park and its guests. Newly arriving guests are not typically knowledgeable about the many ticket package options. They often need to talk to a person who can quickly and easily identify what guests really want to do and then sell them the most appropriate ticket package. The talents required of the employee who can do this well include having very good empathetic listening, interpersonal, and coaching skills in addition to the ability to handle large sums of money rapidly and carefully. The successful ticket seller is really something of a vacation planner. Once the talent profile of successful ticket sellers was identified, a reassessment of the selection process, the training involved, and the reward structure for this job could be done.

Of course, competency-based approaches to selection have a few drawbacks. Designing them for a single job or single job category can be quite expensive unless the organization has a lot of people doing that job. While Marriott employs so many hotel assistant managers that developing a competency profile becomes worthwhile, an independent hotel may not believe that the considerable expense of having a professional organization come in to do this work can be recaptured in any selection efficiencies gained. Further, as the necessary competencies change, so too must the selection measures. Finally, it is not clear how helpful developing a competency profile is for a specific job in the long run if the company plans to promote employees into other jobs in the future. Because of this, companies like Marriott and Choice Hotels have developed more generic competency measures, which help avoid some limitations of the single-job measures.

Nonetheless, all competency measures are essentially anchored on the successful practitioners in the current organization. If the organization wants diversity in opinion, training, talents, and personalities to promote change and organizational growth, basing hiring decisions on the mix of existing competencies may impede gaining the benefits of a diverse workforce. To avoid these potential problems, competency measures should be considered as only one tool in the selection process.

Other Key Characteristics for Service Personnel

While certain KSAs or competencies can be identified for a specific job, there are some known characteristics that are needed by employees who are actually serving customers, clients, or guests. One is enthusiasm. To provide exceptional service, guest-contact employees must be able to display *an enthusiastic approach to life*. Enthusiasm is contagious, and guests come to most hospitality organizations expecting to be served by employees who are enthusiastic about the service itself, the organization, and the opportunity to provide service. There are very few guests who do not want and expect a feel-good guest experience that only enthusiastic employees can deliver.

Enthusiastic employees show their enthusiasm in many ways, but one important way is to put on a "show" for their guests. Scott Gross devotes a significant part of *Positively Outrageous Service* to the importance of hiring and training people who can perform a show. He believes a touch of spontaneous, unrehearsed showmanship can sometimes provide the margin of difference between a hospitality experience that merely meets the guest's expectations and one that is truly memorable. Enthusiastic hospitality "showpeople" engage guests in their performances and enable guests to remember the experience. Whether it is the server who bursts unexpectedly into a song during a restaurant meal, the bus driver who delivers a comedic monologue during the ride to an off-airport rental car location, or the amusement park employee who spontaneously turns an unexpected delay for an attraction into a "good show," the point is the same.

Employees who are recruited, hired, and trained to not only perform their jobs in exceptional ways but also create a good show for the guests add value to the guest experience in important ways. First, they make the experience memorable and help keep the hospitality organization in the top of the guest's mind, increasing the likelihood of return or repurchase. Who can forget the Southwest attendant who surprises newly boarded passengers by singing the preflight safety instructions to rap music? This entails more than just "doing the job." Sometimes, guests will get extra value from being entertained while dealing with boring, routine activities like boarding a plane.

Employing servers who interact with guests in this way creates a competitive advantage since no competitor can design into its service experience the same feeling of a unique and personalized show for the guest that the well-selected, well-trained, enthusiastic employee can. The opportunity to provide a show for the guest is a terrific opportunity for properly selected employees to show their enthusiasm in a fun way. An organization that encourages its employees to take every opportunity to be creative and individualistic with guests, connect with guests, and use their showmanship tells employees that the company appreciates their skills and trusts them to do the right thing with customers. For servers who sought the job partly for the opportunity to demonstrate their creativity and originality, performing for guests is a fun part of the job.

human resource planning The process of analyzing an organization's current human resource capabilities and the organization's human resources required to meet organizational objectives.

Human Resource Planning

Once you understand the job you are filling, you must then engage in **human resource planning**. Human resource planning is the process of analyzing an organization's current human resources and projecting what human resource needs will be required to meet the organization's service mission. Based on the organizational strategy, human resource planners must determine what KSAs employees must possess to accomplish its goals, what levels of KSAs employees currently possess in the organization, and whether or not the organization has the people potential or organizational training capabilities to fill the gaps in the needed KSAs in its existing employee group.

HR planning is not only for filling today's gaps but also for the longer run. While most recruitment activity is focused on filling jobs that are currently vacant, some effort should be given to forecasting the long-term employment needs of the organization both in terms of number of employees and KSAs. If, for example, you are planning to build a new hotel or expand an existing one, you must consider whether or not a sufficient number of job candidates with the necessary KSAs will be available for hire when the project is done. If not, plans need to be developed to recruit from distant labor markets, retrain people in the current labor market, or hire away qualified employees from their current employers. Each of these strategies has costs and benefits that should be carefully weighed, but each is also a strategy used to find sufficient numbers of qualified employees.

HR planning also helps determine the best way to staff a position. Does the company need to hire a full-time employee or a part-time employee? Full-time employees are more committed and have less turnover, but does the company really require all those hours of work? HR planning may also reveal that the company doesn't actually even want its own employees. Jobs may be outsourced; that is, the task in question may be performed by another company for a fee. This, of course, gives control over the work to another company, but often other companies that specialize in particular services may be able to perform the work for less money. Many hotels, for example, outsource their housekeeping function. That is, they hire other firms who find and train the labor, provide those employees the required uniforms, and assign them to various hotels as needed. Some hotels find outsourcing dramatically saves money and eliminates the need to manage a position that has fairly high turnover; other hotels do not want to relinquish control over such an important position, and thus hire full-time or part-time employees to handle housekeeping duties.

Companies may also hire temporary workers. If HR planning reveals the employment demand is probably only for the short run, a company may pay a staffing agency to temporarily provide an employee for a particular position. Contingent hiring like this gives companies flexibility to accommodate fluctuations in demand that are common in the hospitality industry. Of course, as with outsourcing, hiring contingent workers gives the company less control over the sort of characteristics and preparation of the workers, and such workers are not as committed to the goals and mission of the company as the company's own employees.

The HR planning process could also reveal that you have too many employees (and so layoffs may be necessary), current KSAs are inappropriate, or your organization needs to acquire more people with different skills. HR may also determine that the organization can acquire the new skills by training current employees (a topic covered in Chapter 6) or by motivating and empowering current employees (Chapter 7), but commonly the best way to acquire the needed KSAs is by hiring new employees.

Human resource planning is an essential task for hospitality companies. Because of growth and changes in the industry, and because of the regular high turnover it experiences, the hospitality industry has a continuous huge appetite for labor. The fact that most of this turnover occurs in entry level jobs, which are also typically lower paying, makes the selection process a constant challenge. Knowing the specific demands for selection that your organization will face can make the difference between being able to attract and hire great personnel, or simply settling for a warm body with a pulse.

THE SECOND STEP: RECRUIT A POOL OF QUALIFIED CANDIDATES

Once an organization knows what it is looking for in new employees, and how many of those employees are needed, it needs a diverse pool of qualified applicants from which it can select them. Where does an organization find them? The most basic choice here is, does the organization consider people from inside the company or outside? Whether the company looks inside or outside depends partially on the level of positions to be filled. If they are entry level, recruiting will occur mainly from outside. If above entry level, the company will have to decide whether to promote from within or look outside.

Hiring Internal Candidates

hiring from within The practice of filling positions within an organization from employees already working for the organization.

Many companies prefer internal recruitment for several reasons. In fact, the practice of **hiring from within** is often seen as a best practice of human resource management to help achieve and reinforce consistency in hospitality services.[13] Hiring internal candidates has a number of advantages, as described below. It is no panacea, however, and the decision to hire from within needs to be considered in light of both its advantages and disadvantages.

The Known Quantity

The most important advantage of promoting from within is that you have much more information—and more accurate information—about your current employees than you do about external candidates.[14] The internal candidate is a known quantity. That person's performance has been available for observation and evaluation every day, and the person's strengths and weaknesses are generally known. Because some external candidates will interview well and some poorly, managers doing the hiring can make mistakes. On the other hand, the good and bad qualities of a person observed every day are evident. Perhaps even more importantly, the present employee has shown loyalty to the organization by staying on and seeking higher levels of responsibility and challenge. For these reasons, many organizations prefer a known inside candidate over an outsider. Because customer relationships are so important in hospitality organizations, it makes considerable sense to promote current employees who have proven successful in their jobs, have shown a commitment to customer service, know and like the company culture, may be connected to the company's customers, and are familiar with the organization's mission and commitment to guest service.

Internal Equity

The second reason for internal hiring is internal equity. Many hospitality organizations employ people from varied backgrounds and with different levels of training and education. Many employees, except those in some technical areas and those with unique qualifications and experience, start at the same entry-level point. Each has an equal opportunity to prove a commitment to service excellence if they wish to get promoted. At a hotel front desk, you might find a recent college graduate, an

[13] Judie M. Gannon, Angela Roper, and Liz Doherty, "Strategic Human Resource Management: Insights from the International Hotel Industry," *International Journal of Hospitality Management* 47, (2015): 65–75.

[14] Michael C. Sturman, Robin A. Cheramie, and Luke H. Cashen, "How to Compare Apples to Oranges: Balancing Internal Candidates' Job-performance Data with External Candidates' Selection-test Results," *Cornell Hotel and Restaurant Administration Quarterly* 43, no. 4 (2002): 27–40.

older person who has changed careers, and a person with a high school or technical school degree—all working side by side and trying to impress the front desk manager with their merits for promotion. If an outsider gets the vacancy at a higher level, these hard-working employees will not feel fairly treated. They helped the organization achieve its success; now they should be recognized for their contributions and allowed to share the rewards.

The Four Seasons subscribes to this internal promotion approach. Says Ed Evans, Executive Vice President and Chief Human Resources Officer:

> Four Seasons has a strong belief in and storied history of promotion from within. It has been the philosophy of our company to hire for attitude and train for skill. We view the hotel teams as families and believe that something special happens when people genuinely know, care about, support and help develop one another, especially in terms of emotional intelligence. Promotion from within should not be confused with promotion based upon tenure. Tenure does not trump talent; it is healthy to bring exceptional experienced talent into the family from outside of the company and outside of the industry in numbers that ensure diversity of thought, experience and approach. Yet, it is of critical importance for a high touch luxury service brand such as Four Seasons to attract, retain, develop and promote strong talent from within in order to protect the cultural fabric of our company.

Experience

Most people, as just mentioned, start in the hospitality industry by taking entry-level jobs. Companies want their employees to know the business from the ground up. This hiring strategy is usually uncompetitive and unattractive for college graduates who have not acquired such experience through co-op or intern programs. While most graduates appreciate the need to take the entry-level jobs as an opportunity to prove themselves, many are unwilling to accept the relatively low starting salaries that hospitality organizations typically offer. This is becoming an even greater issue for the industry as students graduating from college increasingly start their careers with tens of thousands of dollars of debt. These students cannot afford low starting salaries even when they have hope of future promotions and pay raises.

The hospitality industry has, consequently, often relied on growing its own from noncollege talent or finding college students who are so committed to the industry that they will give up current rewards to enter it. In a tight labor market, the belief in the need to start everyone at the entry level has caused the industry some difficulty. Bright college graduates interested in the hospitality industry often have better options even in other service industries who have learned to appreciate the hospitality skills these students can bring to provide a level of customer service that can be a competitive advantage in health care, retail, and other services. The entry-level approach makes attracting MBAs and other advanced-degree holders especially difficult. While this is less of an issue in a loose labor market (i.e., when a lot of people are looking for jobs), there is always a shortage of truly excellent workers, even when there is high unemployment.

Hiring from within makes it possible to gain the employee commitment needed while maintaining the entry-level salary structure. The well-managed hospitality organizations have systems in place to recognize potential and have training programs available to develop that potential. Although they miss out on some college-trained applicants, they are able to build a strong workforce based on their own internal processes. Whether the costs of these internal development programs are worth the trade-off—for not paying higher entry-level salaries—is still debated, but college graduates are often not willing to make the heavy financial sacrifice that the industry asks of them.

Another experience-related point in favor of hiring from within the organization—if the job to be filled is at the managerial or supervisory level—is the belief that you cannot manage someone doing something you've never done. Although hospitality experience and real-life examples can be acquired in one company and brought to another, the most relevant experience and examples are obviously those that are acquired internally. The core competence of hospitality organizations is providing service, and unless you have had experience in providing service, felt the emotional pressure of guests in your face, and found ways to resolve guest problems on the spot, you don't really know what it's like. Given the uniqueness of organizations, and the particulars of companies' cultures, promoting employees from within helps preserve the investment you have made in employees, and keeps that company-specific knowledge working for you. You are in the business of providing an outstanding guest experience and, as a manager, of establishing and sustaining a guest-focused culture within the organization. You need to have real examples from your own experience that help you tell your employees how to provide excellent guest service.

Knowing the Culture

Organizations like to promote internal candidates because much of the training in the organizational culture has already been done. Internal candidates already know the company's beliefs and values and have proven themselves to be comfortable in that culture. The cultural learning curve for promoted internal candidates is substantially reduced as they already know the office political structure, the corporate goals, the real way things get done inside the organization, and what the organization really believes in and rewards.

Lower Cost

Internal recruitment also has the general advantage of reducing costs. There is no need to pay for advertisements and travel expenses of candidates to be interviewed, and the decision often requires less time, which saves money. Also, candidates can be considered before a position is even open, and the company can begin developing them to take on the new responsibility when it becomes available. This way, when an opening does occur, it takes less time to fill the position. Additionally, cost savings occur because there are fewer eligible employees and ultimately fewer applicants for a given position than would be the case had external candidates also been considered. A well-prepared company can use internal selection successfully to move good people up through the organization. But if not well-prepared, it may find itself forced to select from a pool of less qualified employees.

Another advantage of internal selection is that it can reduce turnover. Employee turnover is greatest among new hires, so promoting internally helps decrease the chance that the position will need to be filled again in the near future. Recruiting is an expensive process and reducing turnover reduces costs. Promoting good performers from within will reduce turnover by giving the high performers assurance that the company will let them grow and reward them for their loyalty and dedication. As Leonard Berry puts it, excellent companies "hire entry-level people who share the company's values and, based on performance and leadership potential, promote them into positions of greater responsibility."[15]

[15] Leonard L. Berry, *Discovering the Soul of Service: The Nine Drivers of Sustainable Business Success* (New York: The Free Press, 1999), 45.

Internal Search Strategies

A pool of internal candidates can be created in one of two ways: job postings or a review of personnel records. Many organizations announce open positions to employees via a company intranet, bulletin boards, newsletters, or other means of communication. Sometimes, employees are informed of openings before they are publicly announced, thus giving internal candidates the first chance to apply for positions.

Courtesy of Hilton Hotels

Hilton, as well as many other top hospitality organizations, use sophisticated human resource information systems to help find highly qualified internal candidates.

Some companies use their employee records to identify potentially qualified candidates. For example, Hilton Hotels uses a computer application that tracks such factors as employee profiles, past performance ratings, employment history, skill sets, employee interests and career aspirations, willingness to relocate, and languages spoken. Hilton can instantly access the records of qualified candidates from across its entire set of properties and determine who might be a good fit for, say, a new general manager position in San Diego. In short, there is typically better information available on internal applicants, including useful prior performance information.[16] It also helps employees manage their careers by matching their preferences and qualifications with the requirements of open positions. Employees can then see what they need to do to prepare for positions with greater responsibility.

Some companies, like Darden Restaurants, manage internal promotions and transfers even more proactively. They develop **succession plans**, in which employee careers are planned over a long period, including the progression through a number of key positions or key locations. When a position becomes available, the company already has a list of finalists for that job, or even a person already identified to take on a new role. Succession plans allow a company to identify talented personnel and put them through appropriate training and increasingly challenging job positions to prepare them for taking on greater responsibility.

succession plans A long-term plan for the orderly progression of employees through key positions or key locations.

Hiring External Candidates

Not every job can be filled by an internal candidate. For example, the only source of candidates for entry-level jobs is the external labor market. Nor do organizations always want to promote only from within. Internal recruitment is by definition limiting. A company's internal labor pool is almost always smaller than the total labor pool. In some circumstances, looking outside the company for new employees has a number of advantages.

New Ideas and Fresh Perspectives

One problem with hiring internally—which usually involves promotions and transfers—is that it limits the diversity of experiences of the candidate population. When companies hire only from within for everything except entry-level positions, everyone's experience comes from the same organization. Employees may learn very

[16] Matthew Bidwell, "Managing Talent Flows through Internal and External Labor Markets," in *The Oxford Handbook of Talent Management*, eds. David G. Collings, Kamel Mellahi, and Wayne F. Cascio (New York: Oxford University Press, 2017), 281–298.

well how business is done in their company, but they may have no idea of how other companies are doing the same things, and in particular how others might be handling certain problems in a better way. Some companies have come to rely on hiring from their top-performing competitors as a way to reduce their own training costs while obtaining the talent they need to be competitive. This strategy can be expensive as hiring someone away from an existing external job will generally cost more than developing such a person internally, but for some specialized or senior positions, the benefits gained may be worth the cost (and may actually reduce training costs).

Difficulties With Internal Candidates

The company that promotes from within often promotes its best line-level employees into supervisory or managerial roles; however, good line-level employees do not always make good managers, nor do all of them want to become managers. For example, by promoting the best front desk agent to front desk supervisor, the company may be losing a great agent with great customer service skills and acquiring a bad manager with poor leadership abilities. Convincing a bellman or waitress to become a manager may be difficult as employees in tipped positions frequently make more money than their supervisors. Unless organizations are willing to develop employees systematically to take on the greater responsibilities of higher-level positions, promotion from within might do more harm than good. Similarly, if a culture change is desired, or if a particular talent is unavailable in the internal labor pool, adhering to the practice of promoting from within can fail to produce the characteristics required in new leaders.

Specific Skills and Knowledge

While hiring from within can be a means to motivate and retain lower-level staff interested in a promotion, external candidates may be desirable when a needed ability or combination of abilities in a specific job is unavailable among existing employees. Although most hospitality leaders can tell many stories of general managers who worked their way up from entry-level positions, many aspects of running a hospitality business may require particularly specialized knowledge that a firm may not always be able to provide internally.

Technology

For example, the knowledge of accounting, IT, finance, human resources, law, marketing, revenue management, statistics, and strategy that a general manager needs in order to run a profitable hotel cannot necessarily be "picked up" along the way without some sort of external education or experience at the same level at a different company. Many hospitality organizations must look outside for information systems skills that are not generally acquired through the experience-based internal-development career paths. While organizations would like to promote internal candidates, the technological revolution is happening so fast that the traditional in-house training processes are often not able to keep up. The hospitality industry increasingly looks to the more technologically advanced industries for filling positions that require application of up-to-date technologies to emerging hospitality focus areas. Even entry-level jobs are requiring workers to be tech-savvy, have customer service and communications skills, and have skills like the ability to use customer relations software to even be hired.[17]

The same phenomenon has occurred in the finance area, where the increasing need to have employees skilled in asset-management and capital-budgeting techniques has meant that the traditional approach of growing the necessary skills internally doesn't work well enough or fast enough to keep up with the rapid pace of change. Likewise, in customer service roles, the availability of data analytics to provide customer service is challenging the traditional skill sets of those promoted because they were good at

[17] Anne D'Innocenzio, "Getting in the Door Is Harder Now," *Orlando Sentinel*, June 5, 2018: A9.

providing service. In today's technology driven world, the guest service manager of a casino may undertake a sophisticated data analysis of the casino's customers to see which are profitable and merit free meals and shows and which are not.

In short, the hospitality industry is becoming more technology driven and sophisticated. Companies are recognizing that to acquire specific sorts of skills and experiences, they have to look outside the company for people with particular education, experience, or a good combination of the two. Because the pace at which technologies are changing is so rapid, and because the sophistication of the business of hospitality is increasing, the traditional strategy of "start at the bottom and grow your way to the top by watching others doing it as we've always done it" can no longer be viewed as necessarily the best way to fill all positions.

Diversity

Another concern with promotion from within is that it can limit diversity at higher organizational levels. If a company hires only from within, its diversity in higher-level positions is limited by the employee demographics already present. For example, if women are slightly more likely to leave a company than men, it becomes increasingly unlikely that women will achieve the highest levels when the company hires only from within. Hiring from outside the firm allows a company to enhance its diversity by seeking candidates from different applicant pools.

Of course, simply hiring externally does not guarantee diversity. Enhancing diversity takes a concerted effort to seek diverse applicant pools and to have managers willing to hire people who do not necessarily look or sound like themselves. One company that has clearly made such an effort is Hyatt Hotels. While maintaining its presence on *Fortune*'s list of 100 Best Companies to Work For, Hyatt has also been repeatedly recognized for its diversity efforts, such as "100 Best Workplaces for Women" by *Fortune,* "50 Best Workplaces for Diversity" by *Fortune,* "Best Place to Work for LGBT Equality" by Human Rights Campaign, "American's Best Employers for Diversity" by *Forbes,* and "Best Company for Latinas to Work For in the U.S." by *LATINA Style* magazine to name just a few of their awards. Making a clear commitment to diversity begins at the top of the organization, and this commitment has helped to keep Hyatt Hotels one of the most highly regarded lodging companies in the world.

Embracing diversity is not about being politically correct. It is good business. Clearly you have to act within the law. U.S. federal laws prohibit discrimination on the basis of race, color, national origin, sex, religion, age (if 40 and over), disability status, veteran status, and genetic information. Some (but not all) jurisdictions prohibit discrimination on the basis of sexual orientation and gender identity. Beyond the legal and moral need to comply with antidiscrimination laws, contemporary hospitality organizations have three other very good reasons to foster diversity in their staff.

First, thanks to advances in transportation and communication, global travel patterns, and the breaking down of many cultural and racial barriers, increasingly guests are from diverse cultural and demographic populations. In some service settings, these diverse guests expect that service providers will be similar to themselves or will at least understand the expectations of people like themselves. They want servers who speak their language, figuratively and perhaps literally. Many airlines, for example, try to hire multilingual flight attendants and reimburse attendants for taking language lessons or classes. United Airlines specifically advertises that it offers additional compensation for speakers of designated languages, and it is not uncommon for over 80% of newly hired flight attendants to speak multiple languages.[18] Although no workforce will be as diverse as the broad cultural range of guests, staffing strategies

[18] Andrea Rumbaugh, "After 6 Weeks of Training, Freshly Minted Flight Attendants Soar," *Houston Chronicle*, last modified March 4, 2017, accessed January 2, 2018. http://www.houstonchronicle.com/business/article/After-6-weeks-of-training-freshly-minted-flight-10972075.php.

should be designed to hire guest-contact employees sufficiently insightful to read cues indicating the expectations of guests from different cultures and backgrounds and flexible enough to meet those varied expectations.

A second reason for interest in diversity is that employing a diversified workforce, by tapping all available segments of the general labor pool, will result in *a better workforce* than if the organization limits its hiring to select parts of the labor pool. In a competitive environment, all organizations must look at the entire labor pool for the best employees, regardless of background, cultural heritage, or other differences. The best organizations gain a competitive advantage by seeking out and recruiting talent wherever it may be found. Recognizing and appreciating diversity can be a stimulus to develop innovative ways to recruit. Knowing that Orlando, Florida, has a large Moroccan population, one hotelier sought them out. Since few other hospitality organizations recognize this group's size or bother to understand its proud cultural heritage, this hotel has gained a unique and valuable advantage by recruiting from this relatively untapped resource.

A third reason a company should embrace diversity is that its labor pool and its customers are becoming more diverse. Companies should therefore be proactive so they are prepared for the inevitable demographic shifts they will be seeing. According to the U.S. Census Bureau, roughly 38% of the U.S. population is a racial or ethnic minority. The Census Bureau projects that by 2060 only 56.4% of the U.S. population will be comprised of white, non-Hispanics.[19] In short, businesses need to accept and be prepared for diversity, whether they like it or not. There is no longer a typical hospitality employee for whom the organization can design one-size-fits-all selection, training, or reward systems. Dual-career couples, same-sex partners, single mothers and fathers with child care responsibilities, grown children with elder care responsibilities—all these and many other demographics are apt to be represented in the hospitality organization's workforce. The manager of the modern hospitality organization must be sensitive to the needs of employees from these varied backgrounds and lifestyles.

No matter how diverse the hospitality organization's workforce, the fact remains that guest-contact personnel will be different in most ways from the guests they serve. For example, most restaurant servers are younger than the patrons. The organization must hire people who are adept at interacting with the great variety of guests, who can read guest expectations during the first few moments of the service encounter, and who enjoy the challenge of providing personalized service to today's multicultural hospitality clientele.

External Search Strategies

When looking to hire externally, companies can develop an appropriate pool of applicants in many ways. For large hospitality organizations in cities and towns where the tourism and hospitality industries dominate, these sources are especially important to provide the tremendous number of people the hospitality industry needs. The smart hospitality companies go where the growth is; thus, growth plus replacement needs add up to a big recruitment job. Seasonal fluctuations in demand for hospitality services only compound the problem by requiring intensive recruitment and selection drives to prepare for an expected seasonal rush. Even in tighter economic times or in situations with limited seasonal variation, the high turnover in the hospitality industry makes recruitment a constant challenge, and controlling costs becomes even more important. In the end, regardless of the specific economic or business situation, a major challenge for all hospitality organizations is how to create and maintain a qualified external labor pool in a cost-effective way.

[19] Sandra L. Colby and Jennifer M. Ortman, "Projections of the Size and Composition of the U.S. Population: 2014 to 2060," Current Population Reports, P25-1143, U.S. Census Bureau, Washington, DC, 2014.

Print and Public Advertising

Although there is much discussion of how the internet is replacing print media, help-wanted advertisements are still a very common method for advertising job openings. Almost all newspapers still print help-wanted ads in the traditional way in which they have been printed for decades.

In addition to the advertising in newspapers, magazines, and weeklies targeting potential employees, aggressive recruiters use more creative means to reach people who may not read the help-wanted ads, may not be thinking about changing jobs, or may not even be thinking about working. Just as marketers segment their markets to find likely candidates for their products and services, recruitment managers increasingly segment their markets to reach and attract job candidates. For example, when the Encore hotel was opening in Las Vegas, it needed to hire for every position: roughly 6,000 new employees, including room concierges, dealers, room attendants, management staff, security personnel, and valets. To fill these positions, their managers believed they needed approximately 60,000 applicants. As part of their recruitment effort, the company used skywriting to advertise its openings. Planes flew up and down the California coast leaving messages over every major beach and even over a Los Angeles Angels versus Boston Red Sox baseball game. They received over 25,000 applications on the first day, and they would have received more had not the sheer volume of responses crashed their server.

This type of public advertising can also attract interest from employees who are currently working for someone else. These people might not have thought about working for the organization doing the advertising until they happened to see or hear the ad, which might suggest to them an intriguing opportunity. If these people are at all dissatisfied with their current jobs, the possibility of interesting them in your organization becomes even greater. Even though they aren't looking for a job, their interest may be captured by a billboard; an advertisement at the bus terminal, television, or radio ad; or even a skywriting campaign.

Some public advertising can, however, create problems. For example, having a sign on the marquee of a fast-food restaurant may be an efficient way to advertise for new employees, but it potentially sends a negative message to customers: We don't have enough employees, so our fast-food experience may be a lot slower today. Care must be taken so that any recruitment effort sends the right message to employees, potential employees, guests, and potential guests.

Online Recruitment

Technology

The widespread use and accessibility of the internet and social media have turned internet recruiting into a multibillion dollar industry. Top sites for jobs in general include Indeed.com, CareerBuider.com, Dice.com, Glassdoor.com, Google for Jobs, Idealist.com, LinkedIn.com, LinkUp.com, Monster.com, US.jobs,[20] and many niche job sites as well.[21] A survey by Glassdoor.com reported that employees use an average of 7.6 job sites during their search.[22] The same survey revealed that 89% of Glassdoor users were actively looking for a new job or would consider better opportunities.

Online recruitment tools help to fit employees to jobs and companies they want. Unlike some websites that only post job openings—like a modern help-wanted section—some others ask job seekers questions to assess their fitness for positions or about what they are looking for in a new position. For example, you might be asked if

[20] Alison Doyle, "Top 10 Nest Job Websites: Maximizing Your Online Job Search," *The Balance*, last modified December 7, 2017, accessed January 3, 2018. https://www.thebalance.com/top-best-job-websites-2064080.

[21] Alison Doyle, "Top 18 Niche Job Sites," *The Balance*, last modified August 24, 2016, accessed January 3, 2018. https://www.thebalance.com/top-niche-job-sites-2061866.

[22] "50 HR and Recruiting Statistics for 2017," Glassdoor, Inc., accessed January 3, 2018. http://resources.glassdoor.com/rs/899-LOT-464/images/50hr-recruiting-and-statistics-2017.pdf.

you had managerial responsibility in a previous job, or whether you prefer to work for a large or small company. A job site can then use the information it collects to try to create a fit between the qualifications and preferences of applicants and the characteristics of jobs and companies.

Some companies are trying to stay on top of technological trends to reach out to potential applicants. Most companies have developed Facebook, LinkedIn, and career portals from their corporate websites. A survey by the Society for Human Resource Management showed that 84% of companies currently use social media for recruitment, and two-thirds of these organizations have taken steps to facilitate recruitment through smartphones.[23] All major hotels' websites have links for careers from their main page that allow users to search for available jobs with the company, often by location, job characteristics, job title, and so forth. But new innovations continue to be developed. A company called *Spur* recently launched a smartphone app designed to connect hospitality businesses and workers to fill positions or shifts that otherwise would go unfilled. The idea is to help hospitality companies fill sudden and short-term hiring needs, and allow individuals looking to get some extra money to find an extra job or shift.[24] IHG—whose hotel brands include Intercontinental Hotels and Resorts, Kimpton Hotels, and Crown Plaza—uses an artificial intelligence system to filter applicants and check its regular selection methods. Applicants record videos, and the technology uses computer vision to detect when an employee's words are in conflict with their expressions. The goal, at least of yet, is not to replace people in the recruitment process, but to serve as a check to help reduce or eliminate biases that might otherwise influence the selection process.[25]

Technology

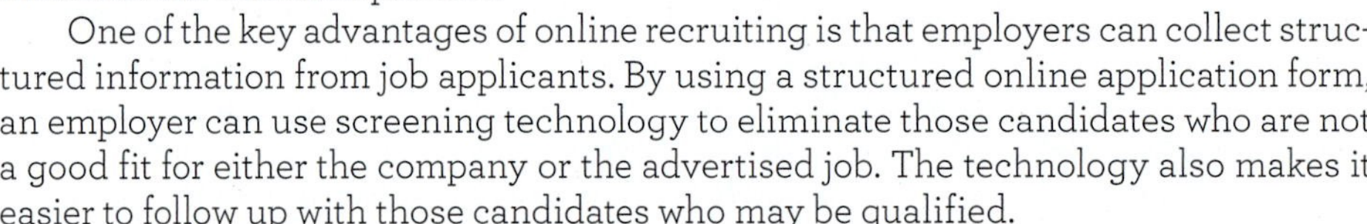

One of the key advantages of online recruiting is that employers can collect structured information from job applicants. By using a structured online application form, an employer can use screening technology to eliminate those candidates who are not a good fit for either the company or the advertised job. The technology also makes it easier to follow up with those candidates who may be qualified.

Of course, this approach is also not without its risks. Companies with blogs and web pages must update their content continuously or they won't look credible. While a well-managed employer brand can help attract employees, a poorly designed web page can discourage potential employees from applying. Also, these pages create opportunities for any company detractors to have more of a voice. Even AI systems, based on sophisticated algorithms, may not be perfect. They may pick up on patterns that can actually perpetuate or amplify prejudices if not carefully designed and implemented. For example, if men are unfairly getting higher performance evaluations than women, the AI system may "learn" that men are higher performers and thus end up providing discriminatory advice in future hiring decisions. While organizations should take advantage of current technology to enhance their recruiting efforts, they need to understand how their use of technology can work against them. Further, they must be prepared to commit the necessary resources to monitor and use the technology well or the entire effort may actually hinder recruitment efforts.

The internet has also changed how employers look for new employees. While previously most employers had to wait for individuals to apply for jobs, sites like LinkedIn, CareerBuilder, and Monster allow individuals to advertise their skills, and employers may actively seek out individuals who have not even applied for given positions. Companies use social media to recruit passive job candidates who might not otherwise apply for a given job. At the same time, companies use social media to screen job

[23] "SHRM Survey Findings: Using Social Media for Talent Acquisition—Recruitment and Screening," Society for Human Resource Management, last modified January 7, 2016, https://www.shrm.org/hr-today/trends-and-forecasting/research-and-surveys/Documents/SHRM-Social-Media-Recruiting-Screening-2015.pdf.

[24] Paul Gattis, "New Huntsville-based App Connects Jobs, Workers in Hospitality Industry," AL.com, last modified October 30, 2017, accessed January 3, 2018.

[25] Alicia Clegg, "Recruiters Turn to AI Algorithms to Spot High-Fliers," *Financial Times*, last modified July 13, 2017, accessed January 3, 2018, https://www.ft.com/content/3045bbaa-6260-11e7-8814-0ac7eb84e5f1.

candidates to help verify information but also to assess if the individual is an appropriate fit with the company.[26] People seeking jobs should therefore think carefully about what information and pictures they post or allow on their sites.

This technology has also changed the way individuals look for a job. Job seekers can use networking opportunities, such as LinkedIn, Plaxo, and others, to look for jobs by networking with their online contacts, finding out about job opportunities, and so forth. The availability of job postings makes it very easy to regularly browse opportunities. Applications like LinkedIn can help people build better resumes, and many job sites allow users to set alerts to let them know if particular types of jobs become available. Employees can check on their cell phones if there are better jobs out there every day on their commute into work. Given the prevalence and ease of technologies related to job searches, many employees are engaged in a continuous job search.

In short, the technology has dramatically changed the way in which people look for, apply for, and find out about jobs. While the internet has not replaced older ways in which companies and job seekers find each other, it certainly has added a host of new communication methods. Although many jobs will still be filled in traditional ways, the information made available through the internet, social media, and smartphone apps has changed the job search and recruitment process dramatically.

Focused Recruitment Efforts

Targeting specific segments of the labor market to identify potential employees is another recruiting strategy. Some organizations target high schools, minorities, associations of differently-abled people, homeless people, or senior citizens. They structure the job opportunities and marketing to appeal to the needs and limitations of that particular segment of the employment pool. For example, many hospitality organizations find that some of their best employees are older, retired people, so they target that group. Retired seniors are often lonely, bored, looking for something to do that will bring them into positive contact with other people, or, realizing that they retired too early, need a job to supplement their Social Security. Many guest-contact jobs can provide this opportunity for them. Organizations that originally recruited older people because of labor shortages have often found to their pleasant surprise that their older employees not only have better attendance records than younger employees, but they bring an enthusiasm for and experience in helping and interacting with guests that makes them great customer-focused employees.

As another example of focused recruitment efforts, Hilton launched "Operation: Opportunity," which was a recruitment effort specifically targeting veterans and military spouses. Hilton saw veterans as a potential pool of applicants that shared their company's values, but also represented a highly trained and available pool of talent. According to Joe Berger, Hilton's Area President for the Americas, they "focused on educating our recruiters and putting one person in charge of military recruiting. We took time with our partners to understand all of the military positions and mapped them out to our hotel positions across the board, from business and finance to accounting, engineering, housekeeping and guest services."[27] The program, which began in August 2013, was a

Courtesy of Hilton Hotels

Hilton Hotel's Operation: Opportunity is the company's recruitment effort that specifically targets veterans and military spouses.

---

[26] "SHRM Survey Findings."

[27] Erika Prafder, "Hilton Hotels Use Special Hiring Program to Recruit Veterans," *New York Post*, last modified March 6, 2017, accessed January 7, 2018. https://nypost.com/2017/03/06/hilton-hotels-use-special-hiring-program-to-recruit-veterans/.

great success, hitting its initial goal of hiring 10,000 veterans by 2018 two years early. Hilton extended the program, committing to adding an additional 20,000 military hires by the end of 2020.

Professional Networks and Placement Services

Successful hospitality managers join professional organizations to find both good employees and good ideas about how to find good employees. The amount of movement back and forth across hospitality organizations causes these professional networks to be strong and informative. Some organizations seek to represent an entire industry (like the American Hotel & Lodging Association), a segment within the industry (like the Asian American Hotel Owners Association), specific professions (like the Society for Human Resource Management), or even particular networks of individuals (like the Cornell Hotel Society). While jobs can be found in many ways, networking is still one of the most effective to find out about potential jobs and potential employees, network, and enable the personal face-to-face connection that can make a potential employee stand out in a large pool of applicants.

Student Recruiting

An important strategy for finding the many people that the hospitality industry needs is student recruiting. A number of programs develop pools of potential employees among young people who are either still in school or have recently graduated. Being young, full of energy, recently educated in state-of-the-art methods, and enthusiastic, students are often ideal hospitality employees. In addition, they come to the job with the anticipation of learning and growing and are, therefore, typically quite comfortable with structured work requirements and extensive training.

One common recruiting strategy is the traditional campus visit by a company recruiter. The institution's placement office schedules eligible students to meet with the recruiter and provides an interview space on campus. The recruiter may interview graduating senior applicants for full-time jobs and undergraduates for summer internships. A variation on this idea is the job fair, where many employers come to the campus on the same day and set up booths where they can meet with potential employees.

Another common approach to hiring young people is to use local career fairs. Local career fairs represent a means for a number of local employers to meet with a large number of prospective employees. They offer an opportunity for companies to find new recruits, and for individuals to find out more about particular companies. Companies can communicate what they are looking for in an employee, such as required skills and experience, and prospective employees can complete applications and conduct brief informal interviews. Such events bring prospective employees from local high schools, colleges, universities, and professional schools. Last year, Hilton hosted more than 100,000 people at 1,260 career events worldwide.[28]

Dania Maxwell/Bloomberg via Getty Images

Job seekers stand on line to register for an interview time slot during a career fair at the Pechanga Resort and Casino in Temecula, California.

[28] Kim Peters and Tabitha Russell Wilhelmsen, "The Skills Challenge: How Four of the World's Best Workplaces Prepare Their Teams for the Future," *Fortune*, last modified October 26, 2017, accessed January 3, 2018, http://fortune.com/2017/10/26/best-companies-to-work-for-global/.

Organizations can sometimes get students to work for them as part of a school experience, such as co-op, internship, or work-experience programs. Nearly all hospitality programs, most schools of business, some other academic majors, and many high schools and junior colleges encourage their students to get some real-world work experience while they are taking academic course work. For example, Cornell University's School of Hotel Administration requires students to work 800 hours in the hospitality field before graduation. The student not only makes some money to help cover education costs but also benefits from seeing the practical application of classroom theory in the real world. This sort of relevant work experience can add value to a college student's résumé or high school student's college application.

The company also benefits from these programs as it gains access to an eager, young, energetic labor pool that does not expect a permanent employment commitment. The smart organizations, however, keep a close eye on these student employees and make sure that impressive student workers know of the company's interest. They offer these students scholarships or put them in special work experiences that prepare them to be fully trained employees upon graduation. Unfortunately, not all organizations use these programs well, and they can work to the student's and the industry's disadvantage. Some short-sighted organizations place young, part-time students only in simple, quickly learned, highly repetitive, and monotonous jobs that provide little learning experience and even less personal growth. The fast-food industry has burned out many students in this way. Putting students in these jobs not only keeps turnover high but, more importantly, has discouraged many bright young people from seeking careers in the food-service industry. These companies have unfortunately taught many young people that the industry is full of jobs suitable only for burger flippers.

Enlightened organizations, taking a longer-term view of the need to get and keep young people interested in the hospitality industry, have designed their work-experience programs to provide some real learning opportunities and growth challenges. McDonald's, for example, proudly advertises that it is "committed to being America's best first job." They advertise benefits like tuition assistance, scholarships, and career development as ways to attract the newest and youngest entrants to the workforce. The point is that student-recruitment programs can be designed and used to get not only employees who learn, earn, and contribute to the business today, but also employees who will be eager to stay in the industry tomorrow upon graduation. The best organizations know how to use these work-experience programs to identify the better students and keep them after they graduate. Since many of these same organizations also place a high premium on people having at least some experience in entry-level positions, these programs give the students the opportunity to pay their dues in these entry-level jobs while they are still in school. This experience puts the students in a better position for promotion to higher-level and better-paying jobs by the time they graduate. Exhibit 5.2 presents descriptions of internship programs at several major hotels.

Helped by the current federal funding emphasis on school-to-work programs and stronger ties between hospitality companies and academic institutions, the hospitality industry has found a variety of ways to effectively create opportunities to attract students. This is an issue because of the large number of new employees required by this industry's growth rate and the high turnover common in the industry. Even while there are a lot of students looking for work, and particularly when economic times are at lower levels of unemployment, it is always critical to find highly skilled and motivated new talent.

Employee Referrals

Another large and successful source of employees for many hospitality organizations is referrals by current employees. A great way to get the kind of new employees you want is to ask your star employees to find them. Your good employees know what

EXHIBIT 5.2

Sample Internship Programs From Major Hotel Companies

Four Seasons Internships

Four Seasons offers global internship opportunities to undergraduates and graduates who want to get a head start in their career. Four Seasons is a growing organization. Commencing the search for the right people at an early stage helps to identify the right people for the future. Internships offer students first-hand experience in what a career would be like with Four Seasons through exposure to various areas of a hotel, resort, or our corporate office.

Source: http://jobs.fourseasons.com/home/students/internships/

Hyatt Hotels Internships

Hyatt offers a paid internship program that provides practical work experience and an introduction to Hyatt's culture and management philosophy. Hyatt internships are offered in a variety of disciplines and may vary slightly by country as described in the specific job descriptions of the available internship postings. The Hyatt Internship Program builds the foundation to becoming successful in the hospitality industry. We recognize the value of our interns, which is why many top performers transition into Hyatt's Management Training program, which focuses on management development.

Source: http://www.hyatt.jobs/university-recruiting/internships/

Choice Hotels Internships

Choice internships provide real-world experience. Summer interns work on a variety of initiatives, shadowing the best in the hospitality and technology industry. Projects include marketing research, analytics, sales tracking, upscale, technology, brand development, public relations writing, and more.

Source: https://careers.choicehotels.com/interns-grads/

your organization is like, perform well in it, obviously like working for you, and can therefore be your best recruiters and spokespersons in the labor market. A bonus of this strategy is that existing employees who bring in their friends feel responsible for them and their performance. They exert positive peer pressure and encourage the new employees they sponsored to do well, which acts to the organization's benefit. Some organizations pay a bonus to their existing employees if they bring in a job candidate who is hired and stays through a probationary period. The reward might be monetary, or it could be something else that has value to employees, such as a free weekend trip to a nice resort area, dinner at a special place, or some other inducement. A common characteristic of *Fortune*'s "Best Companies to Work For" is the presence of an employee referral program.[29]

Professional Networks

Many occupations have professional associations that both hold meetings (state, regional, or national) and communicate with their members (such as with a newsletters, listserv, or website). Professional organizations frequently have career services, which typically take the form of a forum where organizations can post job openings and individuals can post resumes and apply to posted openings. Professional

[29] Timothy R. Hinkin and J. Bruce Tracey, "What Makes It So Great? An Analysis of Human Resources Practices among Fortune's Best Companies to Work for," *Cornell Hospitality Quarterly* 51, no. 2 (2010): 158–170.

networks held target recruitment efforts because only members of the occupation join such associations.

Employment Events, Job Fairs, Career Fairs

Sometimes, specific events are organized in order to attract a large number of potential candidates to a specific location on a certain day. These events may include a collection of employers, looking to both publicize their opening and provide an initial screening of applicants; alternatively, they may be held by a single organization seeking to fill a large number of positions. Job fairs are commonplace on university campuses, as multiple employers can come to one location to be exposed to a large number of people interested in gaining employment. Job fairs are also increasingly being held in central business-district locations, where any potential employee can talk to recruiters from sponsoring organizations.

Employers of Choice

A company's reputation can also aid in recruitment. Publications like *Fortune* magazine, *Fortune Small Business,* and *HR Magazine* list companies that they evaluate to be Employers of Choice. These employers are characterized as being good places to work, where the organization makes efforts to create and maintain a humane and respectful workplace. Says one employee of Kimpton Hotels and Restaurants—rated as a *Fortune* "Best Company to Work For"—"Since day one, everyone in this company has treated me with respect and made me feel special. Everyone in management has always made me feel like family. Companies often say that 'there is room for growth' for their employees, but this company really delivers, and they make sure that you are ready when that opportunity comes! I always look forward to coming in to work no matter what is going on in my life!"[30] These companies hold out for the best employees, invest in those people so they grow and develop, provide challenges and keep them motivated in their current jobs, and offer them future opportunities with the organization. These companies see higher average returns on investment than those not on the list. In 2017, six hospitality companies were on *Fortune's 100 Best Companies to Work For,* listing Kimpton Hotel and Restaurants at #14, Hilton at #26, Hyatt at #32, Marriott International at #33, Cheesecake Factory at #48, Delta Airlines at #63, and Four Seasons Hotels & Resorts at #79.[31]

Of course, there are many other such lists—such as "Best Company to Work for Women," "Best Companies for Minorities," "Best Small and Medium Companies to Work For," and even many local surveys within specific cities—and many different companies fill these lists. The best hospitality companies know the way management treats its employees will be directly reflected in the way the employees treat the customers. Some companies try to enhance their reputation as an employer of choice by building a positive image in the community. Southwest Airlines provides an excellent example of how a company can establish an exceptional community reputation. In addition to providing multiple educational programs and opportunities that have earned it the reputation for growing and developing its people, Southwest has spent much time and money making itself into a good neighbor. Each year, Southwest details its charitable contributions[32] and regularly updates its web page with details about its efforts in disaster recovery, community outreach, national giving, and local giving. Details are provided about activities related to environmental conservation, dona-

[30] "The 25 Best Workplaces in the Bay Area," *Fortune*, last modified April 26, 2017, accessed January 3, 2018. http://fortune.com/2017/04/26/best-companies-bay-area-large/.

[31] "100 Best Companies to Work for 2017," *Fortune*, accessed January 3, 2018. http://fortune.com/best-companies/.

[32] "Charitable Giving," Southwest Airlines, accessed January 3, 2018. https://www.southwest.com/html/southwest-difference/southwest-citizenship/charitableGiving.html.

Courtesy of Southwest Airlines

More than 140 Southwest employees from across the country gathered in Oklahoma to help clear debris after a tornado.

tions of money and tickets to charitable causes, number of employee hours devoted to charitable causes, and so forth.

The quality of the workplace is becoming a more important characteristic in the modern workplace, and is particularly important for Millennials entering the workplace. Even when the labor market is tight, Southwest and Marriott have a talented and deep labor pool. Being a good neighbor is good public relations, enhancing the company's positive reputation among potential employees and motivating satisfied employees to tell their friends that this is a great place to work.

Walk-Ins

Some hospitality organizations rely extensively on walk-ins. Here, they have a significant advantage over the manufacturing and industrial sector. A prospective employee curious about what goes on cannot casually walk into a General Motors assembly plant in Arlington, Texas, to see and feel what it is like. Almost anyone can casually walk into a hotel or restaurant and get a pretty good idea of what it might be like to work there. Indeed, many Disney employees are people who fell in love with the place after visiting with family or friends. One employee said that, after visiting the Magic Kingdom with her family, she planned for twenty years to work there. After her children grew up, she sold her home and moved to Orlando to work in the parks because she wanted to be one of the people who made other people happy. Students in hospitality management programs tell similar tales of a great experience in a hotel, restaurant, or other hospitality organization that excited them about the industry. As a result of that experience, they found out what they wanted to do when they grew up.

Recruiting From the Competition

Organizations can also use a more aggressive recruitment strategy: seek out excellent employees in similar service jobs elsewhere. Again, unlike the manufacturing sector, where a potential employer is not going to be able to walk in and watch the best workers on a competitor's factory assembly line, watching customer-contact employees do their jobs in the hospitality industry is easy. Every time you receive service or watch someone receiving service, you can evaluate the server as a potential employee in your own organization. Prospective employers can hand their business cards to those who really impress them, inviting them for a visit if they are interested in another job. Hiring people because you saw them working well elsewhere has the advantage of starting off the new relationship on the right footing: new employees found in this way will be flattered that you sought them out and asked. Everyone likes to be recognized, and if, by asking people to consider a job opportunity, you do a better job of recognizing them than their bosses have done, you may very well land some excellent candidates. A variation on this strategy is to ask good people, whether they work for you or not, if they know about other good people. A surprisingly large part of the existing workforce is networked with people who are like themselves or have similar jobs. Using the network to build a candidate pool can be a rewarding strategy.

Call-Back File

Usually, there are more applicants than positions. Companies can call unsuccessful applicants back several months later to see if they are still interested. Even applicants who dropped out because they found other jobs might now be interested if the positions they took didn't turn out to be what they hoped for. They were once interested and might be again. It is prudent to keep records of applicants, even if they did not get hired when first considered. An organization can then use this information to enhance future recruitment efforts.

The Final Applicant Pool

No matter how the set of applicants is acquired—through internal selection, via a job posting system, using the internet, or through public advertising—the selection decision will come down to two factors: first, how choosy the company can be in the selection process, and second, how well the employee's performance can be predicted.

Being choosy means having enough applicants apply for a position so that you can select the better ones and not hire others. Obviously, to make a decision you need at least two applicants for a given position. But companies want much more than that. United Airlines interviewed 9,914 candidates from a pool of 102,897 applicants, and ultimately 2,322 people graduated from the mandatory training program to begin work as flight attendants.[33] Similarly, when it opened its new hotel, the Gaylord Palms hired 1,400 full-time employees from a pool of 14,000 applicants.[34] The point is if you have not built a sufficiently large labor pool to select from, you cannot be picky; you cannot choose to hire better people.

But being picky is not enough. You also need to be able to predict who will be better employees. Companies must be able to collect information on each applicant that can be used to identify good performers—and ideally the best performers. This process of gathering information on applicants constitutes the third step in the selection process.

THE THIRD STEP: SELECT THE BEST CANDIDATE

With a pool of applicants assembled, the next step is to determine who will be hired into the company. The selection process sounds disarmingly simple: figure out what an ideal candidate looks like, collect information on potential candidates, and then select the person who best matches the ideal. The people hired should be able to offer the quality of service that guests expect and that makes hospitality experiences memorable. They should be able to handle the stress of providing service, especially when a service failure occurs. They must be able to connect with guests and respond to their individual needs in a positive way without regard for their own emotional state. They must handle service failures and fix them smoothly and successfully enough to satisfy the guest. Finally, they must act in such a way that each and every guest feels specially treated, safe, and secure. Anyone who has had both good and bad service experiences knows that companies perform the selection function with varying degrees of success.

Screening and Evaluating Applicants

Once you know what you want in a candidate, you must collect information on your applicants to make the best hiring decision. Many tools are available to help collect

---

[33] Andrea Rumbaugh, "After 6 Weeks of Training."

[34] Robert C. Ford, Celeste P. M. Wilderom, and John Caparella, "Strategically Crafting a Customer-Focused Culture: An Inductive Case Study," *Journal of Strategy and Management* 1, no. 2 (2008): 143–167.

this information efficiently so as to make accurate hiring decisions. There is, of course, a trade-off. The more information collected, the better the decision can be; however, collecting more information takes both time and money. Companies must therefore carefully consider how they evaluate applicants in order to make efficient and effective hiring decisions.

The Application Form

Application forms are the first screen an employer should use in deciding whom to hire. Application forms are now commonly electronic, and represent the first step an applicant must take to apply for a job. While some companies still use paper and pencil forms, a typical application form is completed by the applicant online or on a cell phone,[35] and includes the applicant's employment history, education level, and conviction record if any. The form should be designed such that responses provide enough information to permit reasonable decisions about whom to keep in the pool and whom to drop. Obviously, a major trade-off is involved here. The recruitment strategy should be designed to bring in as many legitimate candidates as possible but also screen out unsuitable candidates. The advertising should state what qualifications, work experience, or training are minimum requirements for employment. The application form serves as a preliminary check on whether or not the candidates do in fact have the appropriate occupational qualifications. Job requirements should be clearly stated, so they do not inadvertently amount to discriminatory hiring practices or eliminate candidates who could perform superbly in the role.

Application systems allow applicants to browse through the opportunities available at a company and apply for those that interest them, and it allows the company a means to begin collecting information with which to make a selection decision. For some companies, if the information it collects matches the organization's predetermined criteria, the system itself requests further information from the candidate or even schedules an interview. Some companies use optical character recognition systems to quickly scan résumés, which are then evaluated based on identifying and finding key words. These systems allow applications to be processed in larger numbers and with greater speed. They also allow organizations to be more flexible with their résumé screening, searching their database of résumés for applicants to see if any fit with the job openings on hand. These automated systems allow organizations to use computerized screening programs that save a great deal of time and money when compared to manually screening the many candidates who apply.

The use of technology in the application process allows people to apply for jobs at any time of any day or night. These 24/7 automated recruiting systems—just a phone call or click away for most potential applicants—are particularly useful for people who may not be able to call or come in during the usual work day. These sorts of systems thus also help employers broaden their recruitment efforts.

The Interview

If the applicant passes the initial screen, the organization will most likely schedule an interview by phone, SKYPE, or in person to determine if the information on the application checks out. That is, they will seek to determine if the applicant seems to fit the organization, see if the candidate is really committed to service excellence, and tell the candidate what the job is actually like. The interview is the most common method used by employers to help select employees. Research, however, has also shown it is often the least accurate.

Not surprisingly, the accuracy of an interview is largely determined by how well it is planned and how consistently it is used. When interviewers make up questions

[35] "SHRM Survey Findings."

as they go along, have no predetermined way to score applicants, or rely purely on their memory, they are conducting what is called an **unstructured interview**. Probing questions (e.g., "Tell me about yourself and why you're interested in or qualified for this job") can sometimes add valuable information, but they can also yield information that differs in quality and amount from candidate to candidate because of interviewer differences in ability to ask and interpret appropriate questions. Without training, interviewers can be overly influenced by their own mood, the attractiveness of the candidate, personal biases, and the quality of the candidate interviewed just before.

unstructured interview A selection technique in which interviewers make up questions as they go along, have no predetermined way to score applicants, and rely on memory and intuition to evaluate candidates.

Most writers believe that interviewing should follow a structured pattern. **Structured interviews** increase the likelihood that interviewers will assess all candidates according to the same, job-related criteria. When large numbers of interviewers interview large numbers of candidates, consistency becomes both organizationally and legally important. A structured array of questions ensures the interviewer collects the necessary personal and job-related data. A properly designed and administered structured interview ensures the questions are job-related, consistently scored, and asked of all candidates. Research shows that such interviews can be valid predictors of job performance.[36] Typically, a structured interview will include questions that address past experiences, work competencies, willingness to do the job as designed, and commitment to service.

structured interview A job interview conducted according to a set plan, usually involving a standard set of questions designed to gather relevant personal and job-related data, providing a standardized method to evaluate candidates, and ensuring that all candidates are evaluated in a comparable way.

Because past performance is often the best predictor of future performance, one would ideally assess an applicant's prior performance in order to make a hiring decision. Unfortunately, that information is generally not available, or perhaps the person has actually never performed the job before. A valuable way to assess a candidate, though, is to see how he or she has or would have responded to particular situations. In the hospitality industry, **behavioral interviews** are often the most effective way to assess applicant's qualifications on critical criteria. Behavioral interviewing is based on trying to specifically evaluate some instances of past performance to help predict future performance. So, unlike most interviews, in which applicants get questions like "Tell me about yourself" and "What are your strengths and weaknesses?" behavioral interviews try to capture past behaviors and performance. They might include questions like "Give me an example of how you helped to resolve a customer's problem," or "Tell me about a time when you had to make an unpopular decision and the consequences of your choice."

behavioral interview A form of structured interview where applicants give specific examples of how they handled a specific problem or performance of a specific task in the past.

Behavioral interviews, though, may not always be applicable. Sometimes, and particularly for entry-level positions, applicants simply do not have the experience to answer the questions typically asked in a behavioral interview. Depending on the pool of applicants, companies may want to employ **situational interviews**. Like behavioral interviews, situational interviews aim to assess performance, but they involve hypothetical situations rather than actual past experiences. So, questions might include "How would you handle a guest whose reservation cannot be found and the hotel is full?"

situational interview A form of structured interview where applicants explain how they would handle a specific problem or task.

A structured interview involves more than just giving interviewers the same set of questions and the same scoring sheet. For a structured interview to be successful—be it behavioral or situational—the key is to develop interview questions based upon a careful job analysis. The questions should be clearly related to specific KSAs that are required for successful performance of the job. Then, careful attention must be given to develop a method for evaluating answers to those questions. Not only must each candidate be given the same questions, but the way those questions are evaluated must also be the same. Then, those conducting the interviews must be trained to use the system. When these steps are all followed, the result is a highly valid selection device that can truly help find those who are qualified for the job in question.

[36] For an extensive review of research on employment interviews, see Therese Macan, "The Employment Interview: A Review of Current Studies and Directions for Future Research," *Human Resource Management Review* 19, no. 3 (2009): 203–218.

Work Competencies. The second group of questions that should be included in a structured interview are those related to work competencies. A good structured interview should be closely connected to the job analysis as defined in step one described earlier in this chapter, so the questions clearly help evaluate the characteristics of an applicant that are relevant to the job in question. For example, the interviewer assesses the competence of an applicant for a hotel front desk position by asking specific questions about check-in and check-out procedures and processes. Although hotels use customized systems and vary the routine, the steps of checking guests in and out are basically the same across all hotels. This part of the interview can be objectively scored, based on the candidate's correct and incorrect responses to job-related questions.

Doing the Job as Designed. The third part of a structured interview should assess the candidate's willingness to do the job as it is designed. The interviewer might ask questions about such aspects of the job as the applicant's willingness to work overtime, long shifts, or weekends. Many hospitality workers have to work when others do not. If candidates can't or won't be available when needed, they are probably not a good fit.

Commitment to Service

For positions with customer contact, interviewers will want to include questions that help to assess each applicant's commitment to service. The reality is the successful hospitality employee is different from the successful traditional manufacturing employee, and the interview must take the difference into account. Frontline hospitality employees must be able to do the task assigned to them, but they also need interpersonal skills to relate to the guests and creative decision-making skills to fix service problems when they occur. Service employees perform a wide array of tasks, both physical and mental, and yet throughout all of it, they must demonstrate a sincere and genuine sense of concern for their guests. Since applicants may try to hide their true feelings during an interview to get the job offer, interviewers must try to determine which of the candidates are the true service naturals,[37] who genuinely want to deliver exceptional customer service. Interviewers can try to assess this service orientation by asking situational-stress-type questions that focus on the service experience, and in particular, guest service problems. Employees must respond quickly, appropriately, and creatively when the organization fails the guest in some way. The nature and critical importance of each aspect of service delivery make it essential to assess the applicant's attitude and personality before that person is hired and put out in front of guests.

The best hospitality companies also know that commitment to service is not limited to frontline employees. Indeed, ensuring that managerial candidates possess a high commitment to service may be more important because the commitment of managers to service quality positively affects those around them, and especially those they supervise. Even when managers do not interact much with guests, their commitment to service influences their team members' behaviors and helps define the company's commitment to deliver excellent customer service.

Psychological Tests

Psychologists have developed a variety of tests to distinguish one person from another along different dimensions. Tests of mental ability measure logical reasoning, intelligence, conceptual foresight, ability to spot semantic relationships, spatial organization, memory, and a number of other cognitive factors. Some measures of personality traits and behavioral predispositions have also been developed and validated for use

---

[37] Scott T. Gross, Andrew Szabo, and Michael Hoffman, *Positively Outrageous Service: How to Delight and Astound Your Customers and Win Them for Life*, 3rd ed. New York: Allworth Press, 2016.

in the selection process. For example, service orientation is associated with gregarious and outgoing personalities who make a conscientious effort to help others. Psychological tests have also been used to assess applicant integrity, such as how likely they are to engage in theft or risky behaviors at work.

Personality Traits. Managers often talk about hiring the right type of person for a job, or someone with the right disposition. So it should be no surprise that some employers try to assess the personalities of applicants in order to make better hiring decisions.

Research indicates that personality can be reliably measured and summarized along five dimensions:

1. *Extroversion.* The degree to which someone is talkative, sociable, active, aggressive, and excitable.
2. *Agreeableness.* The degree to which someone is trusting, amiable, generous, tolerant, honest, cooperative, and flexible.
3. *Conscientiousness.* The degree to which someone is dependable and organized, conforms to the needs of the job, and perseveres on tasks.
4. *Emotional stability.* The degree to which someone is secure, calm, independent, and autonomous.
5. *Openness to experience.* The degree to which someone is intellectual, philosophical, insightful, creative, artistic, and curious.

Of these five, conscientiousness is generally considered to be the most valid predictor of job performance.[38] Common sense suggests that people who are more organized, thorough, and dependable are likely to be better-performing employees.

Emotional stability has also been shown to be associated with job performance. Since the quality and value of hospitality experiences exist only in the minds and memories of guests, hospitality employees are often uncertain about whether they are delivering the experience as guests expect them to. Emotionally stable servers are much more likely to deal with this uncertainty in a positive, confident way. If the service turns out to be less than the guest expects and the guest complains, emotionally stable employees are more able to deal with the stress of complaints and work to resolve the complaints quickly, fairly, and with a smile. Those high in emotional stability are also more likely to engage in deep acting emotional labor rather than surface acting.[39]

While conscientiousness and emotional stability are correlated with job performance across jobs, extroversion has been shown to be an effective predictor of job performance in occupations where interactions with others are a major job component. Extroverts tend to be sociable, gregarious, assertive, and energetic. They are therefore more likely to get along well with others and seek out relationships and interpersonal interactions. Research suggests that extroverts are better at socializing or initiating contacts with others (e.g., customers, co-workers, and supervisors). They enjoy interacting with the customer and are more likely to perform better in service jobs, where interaction is a critical component of successful performance. Extraverts are also more likely to engage in deep acting rather than surface acting.[40]

Of course, the five personality dimensions described above are just one way of classifying personality. Many companies sell different sorts of personality tests, all aimed at providing insights to a person's character that can help a company determine the fit between the applicant and the job. Technology is even emerging that scans a

---

[38] Bruce J Tracey, Michael C. Sturman, and Michael J. Tews, "Ability Versus Personality: Factors That Predict Employee Job Performance," *Cornell Hotel and Restaurant Administration Quarterly* 48, no. 3 (2007): 313–322.

[39] Ronald H. Humphrey, Blake E. Ashforth, and James M. Diefendorff, "The Bright Side of Emotional Labor," *Journal of Organizational Behavior* 36, no. 6 (2015): 749–769.

[40] Humphrey, Ashforth, and Diefendorff.

person's social media postings and uses that information to provide an assessment of the individual's personality. Personality testing can also provide information on how to manage an individual once he or she is hired.

Ultimately, whatever sort of test or technology is used, companies want to know about the person they want to hire. It is clear that someone's personality affects how they work, and learning more about the candidate can help make a better hiring decision.

Cognitive Ability Tests. While many managers think personality is the best predictor of job performance, decades of research have shown that cognitive ability may in fact be the best predictor.[41] This finding has been replicated across a wide variety of settings and occupational groups. Research has shown that general mental ability (GMA) can account for up to one third of the variance in performance ratings for complex, managerial jobs, and up to 16% of the variance in performance for less complex, semiskilled positions.[42] These results have led some to argue that GMA should be used as the primary basis on which to make selection decisions. As Norman Brinker states, "Look for people . . . who are smart. Remember, sinners can repent, but stupidity is forever."[43]

GMA is the ability to learn and process information. In part, GMA influences performance because it affects how quickly one can acquire the knowledge and skills needed to perform the requirements of the position. Given that modern jobs change frequently—in duties, responsibilities, and technology—smarter employees, on average, perform better. GMA also helps employees process more information simultaneously. For a server waiting on multiple tables; for a front desk agent juggling check-ins, questions, and phone calls; or an amusement ride attendant paying attention to the line, safety apparatus, and customer questions, higher GMA gives the capability to perform better. Although GMA is not the only predictor of success, it is a good predictor of performance and an important criterion to use in selection decisions.

Integrity Tests. Integrity tests predict the predisposition of job applicants to engage in theft, drug taking, and dishonest or otherwise disruptive work behaviors. They include questions like "Excluding pills you got from a doctor (prescriptions), which of the following drugs do you use? A: Cocaine, Coke, Snow, Crack; B: LSD, Acid, Mescaline, Peyote; C: Heroin, Opium; D: None." It might seem that some applicants would not answer questions on an integrity test honestly, if they do indeed steal, take drugs, or drink at work. But the evidence is strong that many people will indicate their misbehavior. In two separate uses of integrity testing in actual hiring in two hotel companies, roughly 30% of applicants indicated that they engaged in such risky behaviors.[44] Research shows that integrity tests can predict theft, illegal activities, drug use, absenteeism, tardiness, performance ratings, violence, and workers' compensation claims.[45] They have also predicted these behaviors for various types of jobs and for both current employees and job applicants.

---

[41] See, for example, Linda S. Gottfredson, "Why G Matters: The Complexity of Everyday Life," *Intelligence* 24, no. 1 (1997): 79–132; Frank L. Schmidt, "The Role of General Cognitive Ability and Job Performance: Why There Cannot Be a Debate," *Human Performance* 15, no. 1–2 (2002): 187–210.

[42] See John E. Hunter, "Cognitive Ability, Cognitive Aptitudes, Job Knowledge, and Job Performance," *Journal of Vocational Behavior* 29, no. 3 (1986): 340–362; John E. Hunter and Ronda F. Hunter, "Validity and Utility of Alternative Predictors of Job Performance," *Psychological Bulletin* 96, no. 1 (1984): 72–98; Malcolm James Ree and James A. Earles, "Intelligence Is the Best Predictor of Job Performance," *Current Directions in Psychological Science* 1, no. 3 (1992): 86–89; Neal Schmitt, Richard Z. Gooding, Raymond A. Noe, and Michael Kirsch, "Meta-analyses of Validity Studies Published Between 1964 and 1982 and the Investigation of Study Characteristics," *Personnel Psychology* 37, no. 3 (1984): 407–422.

[43] Norman Brinker and Donald Thomas Phillips, *On the Brink: The Life and Leadership of Norman Brinker* (Arlington, TX: The Summit Publishing Group, 1996), 191.

[44] Michael C. Sturman and David Sherwyn, "The Utility of Integrity Testing for Controlling Workers' Compensation Costs," *Cornell Hospitality Quarterly* 50, no. 4 (2009): 432–445.

[45] Chockalingam Viswesvaran and Deniz S. Ones, "Integrity Tests: Alternate Conceptualizations and Some Measurement and Practical Issues," in *The Wiley Handbook of Personality Assessment*, ed. Updesh Kumar (Wiley-Blackwell, 2016), 59–73.

Despite the research evidence, integrity tests are not commonly used in the hospitality industry or elsewhere. But since they are relatively inexpensive and show evidence of ability to screen out undesirable candidates, they seem to be a promising tool in selecting the best candidate.

Assessment Centers

An **assessment center** is a place where an array of tests are administered to measure the KSAs of individuals. This can be used either for the purpose of selecting individuals for higher level positions or as a tool to help develop the participants' careers. Assessment centers often include interviews, psychological testing, and a variety of exercises involving administrative tasks, group exercises, cases analyses, and managerial exercises. While assessment centers can come in many forms, they typically measure seven key sets of KSAs: organizing and planning, problem solving, drive, influencing others, consideration and awareness of others, stress tolerance, and communication.[46]

assessment center A place where an array of tests is administered to measure the KSAs of individuals.

Assessment centers require a significant time and resource commitment from organizations. Because of the large number of people involved and the types of devices used as part of the assessment center, the participants must be able to devote a significant amount of time to the process, and the organization must provide the necessary space over this time. Furthermore, assessment centers require trained assessors to help score performance on all the measuring tools and provide feedback to participants. This investment, though, can have a substantial payoff. Assessment centers typically have high validity and help predict performance beyond even cognitive ability and personality tests.[47]

References, Background Checks, and Drug Tests

It is also a fairly common practice to check a candidate's references. This may involve soliciting letters of recommendation, calling former employers, or requesting from candidates names of individuals who can attest to their character. Since most people are sensible enough to provide references from individuals who will write nice things about them, reference checks don't usually provide much useful information. Nonetheless, it is generally worthwhile to follow up on these references. If a given reference doesn't have good things to say, or worse, if the name given in the reference is fake, it clearly indicates a potential problem. Although many candidates can provide glowing references that may not really predict much, the skilled manager will still look for specific examples in the references that can attest to the KSAs and competencies needed for the job.

Once a candidate gets to the point of hiring, a criminal or background check and drug tests are often conducted. Most hospitality organizations do these checks routinely to protect themselves and their guests. Obviously, a hotel's baby-sitting service must avoid hiring convicted child molesters. Indeed, no organization that sends its employees out unsupervised to provide a service can afford to employ someone who has not been thoroughly checked out before the hire is made. Similarly, hotel employees may have easy access to guests' belongings because some jobs require that they have keys to their rooms. Many services also involve handling cash. For all these reasons, a background check is critical when employees are dealing directly with customers or valuables. Learning that you hired a person who could damage your organization's reputation is very embarrassing; much worse are the legal cases that can arise if a customer sues you for not exercising due diligence in your hiring practices.

---

[46] Winfred Arthur et al., "A Metaanalysis of the Criterion-Related Validity of Assessment Center Dimensions," *Personnel Psychology* 56, no. 1 (2003): 125–154.

[47] Natalia Merkulova et al., "A Test of the Generalizability of a Recently Suggested Conceptual Model for Assessment Center Ratings," *Human Performance* 29, no. 3 (2016): 226–250.

Companies also want to screen out those who use illegal drugs, as drug use leads to greater absenteeism and greater likelihood of being fired or being in accidents, which results in higher medical expenses. Furthermore, because many drugs are by definition illegal, courts have generally accepted the use of drug tests in hiring, even if employers cannot provide a clear link between drug use and job requirements. The growing trend of legalizing marijuana complicates drug testing for cannabis, but other drugs are regularly screened for in various employment contexts.

New Technologies for Screening and Evaluating Applicants

Technology

Like all parts of the modern workplace, the recruitment and selection process is also changing with technologies. The vast amount of data that exist on people, from social media to credit card transactions, are increasingly monitored and used by big data or artificial intelligence platforms to find patterns that can enhance the quality of hiring decisions. Technology can also automate parts of the selection and evaluation process.

For example, some companies provide technology to help conduct reference checks on applicants. Other technology is emerging that scours the internet to help verify the individual's background or find unreported criminal backgrounds. Technology can also examine individuals' social media pages and, based on posts, provide an assessment of the person's personality and thus the potential fit with the organization.

There is even a program, called "Robot Vera," which is an artificially intelligent recruiter. The program uses machine learning to refine its communication skills as well as learn how to hire better people. A company simply provides the program with a job description and interview questions tailored to the job, and the program reviews online resumes and cover letters, calls the candidate, interviews them, and answers questions. Promising candidates are passed along to human recruiters. Vera can engage in as many as 1,500 interviews a day, and is particularly useful for weeding out people who have online applications but are no longer looking for a job. More broadly, it is another example of how technology is changing the face of modern business.[48]

THE FOURTH STEP: HIRE THE BEST APPLICANT

After all the information has been collected on potential applicants, selecting the right people from the applicants becomes the next critical step. The goal is to ensure the company gets the employees who will provide the level of service the organization expects. While finding and hiring the right people is challenging for all organizations, it is especially difficult for the hospitality industry. Although many jobs require definable skills that can be identified, measured, and tested, the hospitality industry has the extra challenge of ensuring that the guest-contact employees they hire not only have the competency to perform the task skills but also have the interpersonal skills necessary to interact successfully with the guests and the creative skills to fix the inevitable service failures. The difference between a good and a great guest experience is so often the indefinable *extra* the employee adds to the experience. Finding, hiring, training, and rewarding the employee who happily and naturally gives that extra effort is one of the biggest challenges for hospitality organizations.

The hiring decision must thus be made while balancing a number of factors. Does the person have the right personality and attitude to be successful in a service-based role? Is the person smart enough and emotionally equipped to handle a dynamic environment, master the training, and learn the job efficiently? Does the person's experience suggest that he or she will perform effectively in creating memorable guest

[48] Peter Holley, "A Robot That Functions 'Like Uber for Job Recruitment,'" *Orlando Sentinel*, May 2, 2018: A8.

experiences? Does this person have the potential to grow into greater roles in the future? In short, is there a good fit between the person and the work environment? There is no simple way to collect information to definitively answer all these questions, but the previous step provides many tools that can shed some light on these issues. Nonetheless, all of these issues should be kept in mind when using the information that was collected to make the hiring decision. The purpose of all the different selection devices—the application blank, the interview, and the various psychological tests—is to collect information to answer these questions and help companies hire the kind of employee who can make the company's service experience truly stand out.

Robert C. Ford

Walt Disney World's Casting Center

Of course, most applicants for a given position will not be hired. Even so, those making hiring decisions should try to show respect, appreciate the applicants' efforts, and seek to build good relationships with all applicants. Someone not hired today may be offered a job tomorrow. The hospitality industry has very high turnover, so although there may not be an opportunity for a given candidate on Friday, the job could be vacant on Monday. Additionally, prospective applicants can also be prospective customers. If you treat applicants badly, they may not only refuse to work for you, they and their friends may not want to stay in your hotel or eat at your restaurant or apply for any future job openings. Word of mouth is a powerful force in the service industry, and negative comments can hurt a business even more than positive ones can help. All applicants should be treated courteously and with respect. Even if they are not selected as employees today, they might become good employees or valued customers tomorrow.

Disney offers an example of how guestologists think about hiring. It knows that meeting its very large labor needs will require it to process a very large number of applicants. The Casting Center is not only designed to handle this volume of people but is an impressive reminder of the culture and values of Disney itself. Even if applicants do not get a job offer (and most will not), everyone leaves the Casting Center with a positive impression of how they were treated by the process and a strong reminder of Disney's commitment to guest service. The experience not only pays off in how those that are hired feel about working for an organization with this strong culture of customer service, but it also impresses the many who are not hired but may be future customers.

THE FIFTH STEP: MAKE THE NEW HIRE FEEL WELCOME

Once the job offer is made and the selected applicant accepts the position, the staffing process may seem to be complete. Indeed, many companies think and act this way too. However, the staffing process is not done until the organization has "on-boarded" the new employee. **On-boarding** is the process of integrating a new employee into an organization and its culture. It should be designed to ensure the new hire feels genuinely welcomed. After all, the organization spent a lot of time and money finding the right person to hire and convincing that applicant to accept the job offer. Now the organization should find ways to tell its new employees how welcome they are. The way the employees feel welcomed on their first day of employment may well set the tone for the rest of their career with that company.

on-boarding The process of integrating a new employee into an organization and its culture.

Kiyoshi Ota/Bloomberg via Getty Images

New employees celebrate at Japan Airlines Initiation Ceremony, part of the on-boarding process for all new JAP employees.

Much of on-boarding is just common sense: people, especially the new supervisor, should be ready to greet the new person, the necessary paperwork should be complete, the office—if there is one for the position—should be ready with a computer, telephone, and other equipment and supplies. Many companies have formal orientation programs, and everything should be set up for the new employee to participate in one. While this process may all seem logical, surprisingly, many companies do not thoughtfully prepare for the arrival of new employees, and the result can be unpleasant. You only get one chance to make a first impression, and the best companies don't miss that chance.

As we discussed in Chapter 4, culture is critically important to most companies, and so communicating this culture to new employees is an absolute necessity for properly on-boarding a new employee. Since a lot of time and money have gone into the selection process, it is important to ensure this investment is solidified by giving the new employee a sincere welcome to show that the company is as excited about the employee joining it as the employee is in accepting the job.

Because Gaylord's Opryland needs to employ a large number of people, it has developed a Convention of the STARS as an innovative way to on-board its new hires in groups. Since Opryland's primary business is as a convention hotel, it sets up its on-boarding process to resemble a convention. It gives new hires name badges with lanyards and tote bags, has keynote speakers, breakout sessions by functional area, a trade show floor with booth displays, entertainment, and even a banquet. This event not only makes the new employees feel very welcome but also effectively introduces them to how Opryland delivers the convention experience.

THE SIXTH STEP: TURNOVER—RETAINING THE BEST AND SELECTING PEOPLE OUT OF AN ORGANIZATION

Although you must expend significant time, money, and effort to hire people into your company, turnover is an inevitable part of business, particularly in the hospitality industry. While selection is usually considered as the process of choosing employees from a pool of applicants, turnover can also be seen as selection of a sort. While those acquired are selected into the company, those leaving the company are essentially "selected out" of the company's workforce. While many companies give a lot of attention to the process of selecting people into the company, the process of turnover is often less strategically managed. But if you know it isn't a good idea to hire randomly, why would you leave the process of turnover up to chance?

The hospitality industry is known for having high turnover. This can be voluntary, where employees choose to leave, or involuntary, where the choice is made for them by the organization. Hospitality jobs often involve working in unpleasant conditions (such as hot kitchens) or during undesirable hours (holidays, nights, weekends). The hospitality industry also often pays less than other industries and attracts turnover-prone applicants who see it as a short-term job commitment or an industry where their career aspirations cannot be met.[49] High turnover is the result.

Turnover can be costly for organizations. Direct costs are associated with the selection of a replacement for a departing employee, namely the cost of advertising for an opening, processing applications, collecting information on candidates, and conducting background checks. Additionally, because new people must be trained in skills that departing people already had, turnover also increases training costs. These turnover, selection, and training costs show why organizations are frequently torn between designing a job task in a way that makes it challenging, complicated, and interesting (to reduce turnover) and designing the task to be quickly learned and easy to do (to reduce training costs). In the former situation, if the strategy does not reduce the turnover typically found in the hospitality industry, the organization will be constantly investing heavily in new employees who won't stay long enough to justify the cost of training. On the other hand, the simple, boring, and repetitive jobs are the ones that tend to have high levels of turnover. Obviously, this is something of a chicken-and-egg problem: more interesting jobs might lead to lower turnover, but most organizations are unwilling to pay the costs to find out.

Turnover also has an important indirect cost: the cost of disappointed customers. Guests frequently build relationships with servers, and being served again and again by the same person is part of the value they receive from an organization's guest experience. If turnover is high, these relationships are destroyed or don't get built at all, and a powerful means for retaining repeat guests is lost. New employees are also less productive than experienced employees, and it takes time for them to learn their new tasks as efficiently. Turnover can also create morale problems. As Jerry Newman describes his experiences in the fast-food industry, where turnover is very high, the other employees don't even bother to learn your name when you begin your job. Because turnover is so high, it isn't worth the effort. Instead, they will learn your name only after you have come back to work a few times.[50]

Because of the direct and indirect costs, turnover can be quite harmful. For entry-level positions in the hotel industry, some estimate that replacing a single departing employee costs 30% of that individual's annual pay.[51] For positions of greater complexity, some estimate the cost of turnover to be upwards of two times an individual's salary.[52] Clearly, if turnover is high, a company risks being at a significant competitive disadvantage.

On the other hand, turnover is not always a bad thing. While turnover always involves costs, it can actually benefit an organization. For example, the selection process is never going to be perfect, no matter how carefully planned and implemented it is. So, if the poor performers leave and are replaced by better employees, the organization will benefit in the long run. Customer service can be improved by shedding the employees who do not embrace the company's mission. Morale can be improved as the people that are unable or unwilling to do their jobs make more work for everyone else. Turnover also creates the opportunity to take advantage of the benefits of external selection. If the size of the company's workforce is not growing, turnover provides a means to hire employees from the outside with new ideas, new education, and different skills and perspectives, possibly from backgrounds that will enhance the company's diversity. Finally, if turnover occurs at upper levels, the

---

[49] Michael C. Sturman, "The Compensation Conundrum: Does the Hospitality Industry Shortchange Its Employees—and Itself?" *Cornell Hotel and Restaurant Administration Quarterly* 42, no. 4 (2001): 70–76.

[50] Jerry Newman, *My Secret Life on the McJob: Lessons from Behind the Counter Guaranteed to Supersize Any Management Style* (McGraw Hill Professional, 2007).

[51] Timothy R. Hinkin and J. Bruce Tracey, "The Cost of Turnover: Putting a Price on the Learning Curve," *Cornell Hotel and Restaurant Administration Quarterly* 41, no. 3 (2000): 14–21.

[52] Wayne F. Casio and John W Boudreau, *Investing in People: Financial Impact of Human Resource Initiatives* (Upper Saddle River, NJ: FT Press, 2011).

door is opened for junior talent to move up. Talented junior people who see openings filled from within may stay, rather than moving to other firms that give them such opportunities.

Every company has turnover, but before assuming all turnover is bad, the causes and consequences of this turnover should be investigated. Why are people leaving? Is it because of higher pay at competitors' firms, an unpleasant work environment, a poor manager, or something out of the company's control? Who is leaving? Is it high performers, low performers, new employees, long-tenured employees, a specific demographic group, or does it seem random? Once a company understands who is leaving and why, it can begin to manage the turnover process effectively. Seeing who leaves and who stays, who succeeds and who fails, helps provide a better understanding of what you are looking for in a candidate. Thus, this sixth step leads back into the first step—study the job—and the selection process becomes an ongoing cycle with the potential for continuous improvement.

Employing the Best to Serve Your Guests

To provide excellent service, the organization needs employees with the right knowledge, skills, abilities, and attitudes. To get the right people, the company needs to know what to look for, where to look to recruit talented workers, and the right ways to collect the information on job applicants. Successful staffing depends on a clear understanding of what the jobs require and of the personal characteristics that lead to success in these positions.

The best hospitality companies use a consistent and rigorous method to find, select, and hire the best talent. They also know that staffing does not just stop once an applicant is hired. Selection can continue as new positions and promotion opportunities open up within the company, and internal candidates may make the best hires for these positions. Also, sometimes employees need to be "selected out" of the company, and this turnover process should be monitored and maintained with as much care and thought as the processes that bring people into the company.

Staffing is the first step in having the right human resources within your company to provide the level of service you want to give your customers. But it is only the beginning. Hiring the best does not necessarily mean that employees will perform the best (although it certainly does help). Employees need to be trained in how to do their jobs, and they need to be motivated to perform their jobs well. These two steps are the focus of our next two chapters.

LESSONS LEARNED

LO 5.1 Explain the importance of staffing for an organization to be able to deliver an exceptional service product.

- The person providing the service can make or break the service experience.
- The organization that can attract and select the best service-oriented employees will have a significant advantage over those organizations that do not systematically seek out and find these guest-focused people.

LO 5.2 Describe why it is critical to study the job before efforts are made to fill it.

- Know not just what skills the job requires, but also the attitudes possessed by successful employees.
- An organization should be able to articulate the KSAs a job requires before it determines how it will recruit and select people for the job.

LO 5.3 Describe the process of recruiting employees who will give excellent guest service.

- Build a large candidate pool; it will improve the odds of finding good people.
- Recruit creatively: Use the major search strategies, but try to think of new ones.

LO 5.4 Recognize internal and external recruitment strategies that organizations use.

- Carefully consider whether you should look inside or outside your company for new talent.
- Looking at internal candidates first sends a positive message to all employees about the kind of company they are working for; look at external candidates to get individuals with new insights and special skills.

LO 5.5 Express the importance of a diversified workforce to hospitality organizations.

- Seek diverse candidates to fit with the diverse clientele, as well as to enhance awareness of new ideas and trends.

LO 5.6 Explain the standard approaches and techniques for screening and interviewing job candidates.

- Carefully check applicants; are they the people you want serving your guests?
- Organizations have many different tools at their disposal that they can use to evaluate applicants.
- Look for technical competence, strong interpersonal skills, and creative problem-solving ability.

LO 5.7 Describe how and why organizations need to balance all of the information gathered in the selection process to hire the right person.

- The selection process yields a lot of information about the job candidates; know what factors to focus on in order to hire the best possible employee.
- Focus on the information that differentiates a good employee from a great employee.

LO 5.8 Explain why organizations need to treat job applicants professionally and with respect, even those they end up not hiring.

- The person not hired today could be the employee you want to hire tomorrow, or perhaps even a future customer.

LO 5.9 Describe the process of on-boarding and why it is important.

- You only get one chance to make a first impression with your new employees; make it a good one.

LO 5.10 Discuss why managing turnover is just as important as managing who is hired.

- The quality of employees who leave is just as important as the quality of employees you hire.
- Manage turnover with as much rigor as you manage the selection process.

KEY TERMS AND CONCEPTS

assessment center 175
behavioral interview 171
deep acting 147
emotional labor 146
hiring from within 154
human resource management 144
human resource planning 152
job analysis 149
on-boarding 177
recruitment 149
selection 149
service naturals 148
situational interview 171
structured interview 171
succession plans 157
surface acting 147
unstructured interview 171

REVIEW QUESTIONS

1. Why are employees so critical for success in the experience economy?
2. Why is job analysis called the foundation of human resources?
3. Assume you are in a tight labor market for entry-level employees.
   A. Do any of the recruitment strategies described in the chapter seem more or less appropriate under those circumstances?
   B. What innovative ideas do you have that might improve your ability to recruit outstanding entry-level employees?
4. Why are hiring and promoting from within so popular in the hospitality industry? What are the disadvantages of this strategy?
5. When Scott Gross meets good employees in other hospitality organizations, he gives them his business card as a means of suggesting that they might want to give him a call for a job interview.
   A. Do you have any problems with the ethics of this method, which is not uncommon in the business world?
   B. Suppose that a competitor sent someone into your employee parking lot to put job-interview invitations under the windshields. Would you view this situation differently? Why or why not?
6. When Lone Star Steakhouse & Saloon needs staff, they print a large announcement on guest checks: Now Hiring Energetic Outgoing Servers! What do you think of this technique?
7. Explain why having a diverse workforce can be a source of competitive advantage.
8. Recruiting applicants is only half the task.
   A. Indicate several techniques you would use to select those you want to hire.
   B. Assume that you are hiring a server for a casual-dining restaurant. What KSAs would you look for?
   C. Assume that you are hiring a hotel front desk agent. What KSAs would you look for?
   D. Are the front desk agent KSAs different from those for the restaurant server?
   E. What problem-solving skills would you look for in either type of candidate?
9. Assume that you are interviewing candidates for a position that involves selling your hotel as a convention site. What questions would you ask of candidates?
10. Do certain personality traits seem to be typical of the best hospitality employees who have served you as a guest? How do these traits compare with those mentioned in the chapter?
11. Assume you are hiring an assistant front desk manager. You collect information on candidates' grades (GPA), experience (zero to five years), and service orientation (low, moderate, or high). You have three finalists:

    Candidate 1: 3.12 GPA; 5 years of experience; moderate service orientation;

    Candidate 2: 3.95 GPA; 3 years of experience; moderate service orientation;

    Candidate 3: 3.06 GPA; 2.5 years of experience; high service orientation.

    How would you rank the three candidates? Why?
12. Most people who apply for a given job don't get it. How can an organization best handle rejecting all of these candidates in a way that would allow them to consider these same candidates in the future, and not lose these candidates as potential future customers?
13. Think about a first day you had on a job (or at a school). Did the organization do good on-boarding?
14. When a company does not manage its turnover process, what sorts of employees do you think are most likely to leave the company? What are some steps you think companies should take to help manage turnover?

ACTIVITY

Find a hospitality organization that will tell you about its employee selection processes and procedures. How does the organization determine which recruits are likely to succeed as hospitality employees? What selection methods do they use? How well are the organization's predictors of employee success working?

ETHICS IN BUSINESS

As part of its screening process, after candidates fill out an application, the Family-Happy Hotel and Restaurant scours the internet looking for blogs and Facebook entries for these prospective employees. Often, it discovers a job candidate looking drunk in a Facebook photo or acting in a way that would be embarrassing if a customer saw that person once employed. Typically, these photos aren't on the candidate's social networking site but are posted on various sites of his or her friends and acquaintances. Family-Happy's management has decided that these behaviors are not consistent with the image they want to project of the organization, and so they remove from consideration any individuals for whom they discover such images. Besides, there are enough people looking for jobs that they can be picky when hiring, and in any case, they need some way to narrow down the pool of applicants.

Do you feel the company's policy is ethically defensible?

CASE STUDY

Case 1: Choosing a Manager

The director of management development for the Long Stay Suites was required to recommend someone for a high-level management position in the company. Careful screening of all present employees narrowed the selection to two men: John Jarvis and Satya Patel. After lengthy interviews, the following information was accumulated.

John Jarvis had a tenure of three years with the company. He was very seldom absent from work and had obtained a college degree in hospitality administration by taking evening courses. His superiors rated his management potential as promising. The one complaint voiced against him was that he appeared impatient and overly ambitious. During his interview with the director of management development, Jarvis indicated that promotions had not come along fast enough for him and that unless he received this promotion he would seek employment with another major hospitality organization. He hinted that he had received offers.

Satya Patel was several years older than Jarvis. He had been with the company since graduation from a nearby university six years previously. He was rated by his superiors as a steady, dependable employee, apparently very intelligent, but he had been given little opportunity to display his talent. Three years ago, he had turned down a more responsible position at one of the organization's branches in another city. He said he didn't want to relocate, and the job required some traveling. Since that time he had not been given another opportunity to move upward in the organization.

In considering the recommendation he would make, the director of managerial development recalled a comment Patel had made during his interview: "I'm confident that you will recognize the importance of seniority when you make your final recommendation."

1. Weigh the pros and cons of promoting Jarvis or Patel.
2. Which one would you recommend for the position, and why?
3. Ideally, what additional information would you like to have before making a recommendation?

Case 2: Regal Five-Star Hotel

During her first year as personnel manager of the Regal Five-Star Hotel, Margarita Gonzalez became increasingly aware of a possible morale problem among the housekeeping staff. Employee absenteeism and tardiness were rising. Coffee breaks were being extended beyond the allowed fifteen minutes. According to the grapevine, employees were not happy with working conditions or with the workload.

Although Gonzalez was aware that turnover had been rising, she was surprised to receive data indicating that it had exceeded 50% among the housekeeping staff over the past year. She reviewed the year's resignations. They accounted for 95% of the turnover. The other 5% were workers who had been terminated as unsatisfactory. Approximately 25% of the resignations were women, whose stated reasons for resigning were "husband being transferred to another city" and "leaving to devote more time to home and family." Gonzalez viewed these resignations as beyond the hotel's control and ignored them. The remaining resignations occurred for four reasons, in the following frequency of occurrence: (1) left to get salary increase, (2) left to get greater opportunity for advancement, (3) left to get different type of work, (4) personal reasons.

Margarita Gonzalez reviewed the criteria for hiring housekeepers, from desirable to undesirable in the hotel's view: under 25; single or newly married without children; husband in armed forces or for other reasons temporarily in the area; divorced with children; early twenties to early thirties; family fully established; husband permanently employed in the area; children fully grown. The hiring policy was obviously designed to appeal to women who seriously needed an income but who did not need a high income.

How should Gonzalez change the Regal Five-Star Hotel hiring policies, if at all?

Case 3: Cruising Travel Agency

Ho-Chien Lee is a manager at a travel agency that specializes in cruises. Among his other administrative duties at Cruising Travel Agency, he hires and trains entry-level employees.

The typical agency job applicant is fresh out of college, excited about the future of travel, and confident that some of the world's problems can be relieved if hard-working people have a chance to relax on a cruise. Most applicants understand that travel-agency jobs are at the entry level. In return for these ideals and this ambition, the agency offers minimal training, little chance for advancement, considerable job security, low pay, and long working hours at night and on weekends.

For several years, job applicants have been plentiful. In recent months, the number of applications has dwindled.

Lee recently expressed his concern to Mary Ammerman, sitting at the next desk. "Where are we going to get fresh new employees? How can we keep the good people we have at the lower levels? I can't for the life of me see why so many stay on at Cruising Travel. Of course, the best ones go somewhere else for more money and faster promotions. But I'm surprised that any of them stay at all. I wonder what they get out of it. And how can we help them to get more out of their jobs?"

Mary Ammerman said she didn't know. As a matter of fact, she thought to herself, she wasn't getting all that much out of her own job.

1. How would you describe the staffing situation at Cruising Travel Agency?
2. Do you think hospitality-related organizations like this agency make a mistake in hiring college graduates at the entry level?

Further readings on the topics in this chapter are listed in "Additional Readings" on pages 504–507.

Get the tools you need to sharpen your study skills. SAGE edge offers a robust online environment featuring an impressive array of free tools and resources.

Access practice quizzes, eFlashcards, video, and multimedia at **edge.sagepub.com/Ford2e**.

Visit **edge.sagepub.com/Ford2e** to help you accomplish your coursework goals in an easy-to-use learning environment.

©iStock.com/skynesher

6 Training and Developing Employees to Serve

Hospitality Principle: Train Your Employees, then Train Them Some More

The how and why of every operation may be clear as day to you, but it's clear as mud to a brand-new employee. You wouldn't believe the number of employees who say "I never could figure out exactly what they wanted me to do." They usually say that on their way out the door.

—T. Scott Gross, *Positively Outrageous Service*

Learning Objectives

After reading this chapter, you should be able to:

6.1 Explain the importance of training and development to hospitality organizations.

6.2 Evaluate the need for training.

6.3 Determine what a training program is supposed to accomplish.

6.4 Describe the types of training.

6.5 Examine training methods.

6.6 Discuss the methods used by hospitality organizations to measure the effectiveness of training.

6.7 Explain the importance of training in long-term development.

INTRODUCTION

Micah Solomon—an author, speaker, and consultant in customer services—relayed an experience about how an employee took it on himself to go the extra mile (literally) to provide an exceptional experience.[1] A couple arrived at *The Inn from Pittsburgh* after a several hour trip to celebrate their anniversary with a three-night stay. While getting unloaded, the husband realized he had left his wife's bag beside the car in their garage. She was checking into one of the fanciest hotels in the world, and all she had was what she was wearing. Understandably, she was quite distraught. But an experienced employee simply drove up in the company car and said, "Get me their keys and the address. I'll be back before dinner." And that's what he did. He drove eight hours straight, got the bag, and was back when promised. He ultimately provided the sort of exceptional experience that many businesses could learn from. The employee's effort, provided without being asked and without hesitation, turned what was shaping up to be a potential ordeal into an exceptional and memorable experience.

Teaching such resourcefulness to new employees is difficult, but every new employee in the hotel learned from this employee's example of what exceptional service looks like when solving a guest's problem. That employee saw the big picture: He knew that a creative solution could solve a problem for a guest, and he delivered one.

Leonard Berry and colleagues identified in their extensive research five key factors customers use to judge the overall quality of service.[2] Of these five, four are directly related to the ability of the service employee to deliver service in the way the customer expects. They include reliability (the ability of the organization and its employees to deliver service consistently, reliably, and accurately), responsiveness (the willingness of the organization's employees to provide prompt service and help customers), assurance (the employee's knowledge, courtesy, and ability to convey trust),

[1] Solomon, M. 2017, "5 Wow Customer Service Stories From 5-star Hotels: Examples Any Business Can Learn From," *Fortune*, July 29, 2017, accessed 1/2/2018. https://www.forbes.com/sites/micahsolomon/2017/07/29/5-wow-customer-service-stories-from-5-star-hotels-examples-any-business-can-learn-from/#7e578cd633e6.

[2] Arun Parasuraman, Valarie A. Zeithaml, and Leonard L. Berry, "Servqual: A Multiple-Item Scale for Measuring Consumer Perc," *Journal of Retailing* 64, no. 1 (1988): 12–40.

and empathy (the employee's willingness to provide caring and individualized attention to each customer). The fifth, tangibles, includes the appearance of the service employee.

While the hospitality organization's service product, environment, and nonhuman components of the delivery system are clearly important in forming the guest's impression of the guest experience, guestologists know that the individual hospitality employee delivering the service can make or break the organization's relationship with the guest in each and every encounter, or moment of truth. Disney, for example, estimates that each guest has seventy-four service encounters in a single visit to its theme parks.[3] Disney managers know how important it is to manage every one of these moments of truth, by selecting and training the right people to provide the consistent quality of guest service customers expect. Everyone remembers a truly bad service experience that was caused by an indifferent, uncaring, discourteous, or ignorant employee. One awful experience can overshadow the rest of the outstanding experiences the customer may have had with the organization. The customer may never return. In addition, that customer may tell everyone within hearing (both literally and virtually) about the bad experience.

The impact of a negative experience on the organization's reputation can be devastating. The disappointed guest won't come back and will spread the bad word. Excellent hospitality organizations recognize the value of investing time and money on employee training and development to prevent service disasters. Engineers can design an efficient service delivery system for a great service product, and the human resources department can select the right people, but those efforts are not enough. Companies that consistently deliver high-quality guest experiences also extensively and continuously train their employees.

EMPLOYEE TRAINING

In the United States alone, nearly $100 billion is spent annually directly on organizational training.[4] This figure translates to almost $800 per employee on average, and countless more hours are devoted to on-the-job training. Yet, even with this amount of time spent on training on average, the best organizations spend a lot more. The Cheesecake Factory, for example, provides 320 hours of training and professional development each year to its full-time salaried staff, and 150 hours to its full-time hourly staff.[5] The Cheesecake Factory mission is "to create an environment where absolute guest satisfaction is our highest priority."[6] To accomplish this, they know that employees have the ability, skills, and knowledge to deliver exceptional service. Similarly, at Four Seasons, their training is focused on ensuring that employees feel empowered to deliver the best guest experience. There is a strong emphasis on business, management, and on-the-job functional training, as well as fostering a deep understanding of the company's service culture. On average, management employees receive at least 40 hours of formal training per year with hundreds of hours of on-the-job and cross-training integrated into everyday work. All levels of management understand that constant coaching, experiential training, and business exposure are required to develop the necessary skills to provide guests with the exceptional level of service that is expected of Four Seasons.

[3] Mary Jo Bitner, "Building Service Relationships: It's All About Promises," *Journal of the Academy of Marketing Science* 23, no. 4 (1995): 246–251.

[4] "2017 Training Industry Report," *Training Magazine*, accessed on January 4, 2018. https://trainingmag.com/trgmag-article/2017-training-industry-report.

[5] https://www.greatplacetowork.com/.

[6] http://investors.thecheesecakefactory.com/phoenix.zhtml?c=109258&p=irol-mission, accessed February 16, 2018.

Patrick T. Fallon/Bloomberg via Getty Images

©iStock.com/Denis Linine

Cheesecake Factory and Four Seasons Hotels and Resorts, companies regularly recognized in *Fortune's* 100 Best Companies to Work For, both provide extensive training to managers and line-level employees

Hospitality organizations face the special challenge of training not just the required job or task skills, they must also teach the server how to interact positively with guests and solve the inevitable problems creatively. An inanimate product going down an assembly line doesn't care if the factory worker has a bad attitude; however, the customer facing the bartender at a private club, the front desk agent at a hotel, or the ticket seller at an amusement park certainly does. Guest service employees must be trained to do the required job task consistently for each guest in real time with a sense of sincere caring, with many people looking over their shoulders. This is a major training task. It goes far beyond the simple requirements of training someone to mix a martini, check in a guest to the proper hotel room, or receive money and make change. Of course, employees must possess the ability to perform their tasks, but they must also be able to establish a connection with the guest and be capable of finding and fixing potential problems that might arise in the service delivery process. Quality training makes it easier for the employee to perform the task and thus have the time and energy to devote to the other critical issues associated with the service job. Says Christoph Schmidinger, Regional Vice President and General Manager of the Four Seasons Hotel New York, "If the basic standards become your second nature, then you free up your mind to the more important aspects of the service, which is connecting with the customer, having an emotional interaction with the customer."[7]

Berry's Five Training Principles for an Effective Training Strategy

Leonard Berry recommends that service companies, including hospitality organizations, should follow five key principles in developing an effective training strategy[8]:

1. Focus on critical skills and knowledge.
2. Start strong and teach the big picture.
3. Formalize learning as a process.

[7] "Forbes Travel Guide Global Star Rating Awards," *Forbes Travel Guide*, last modified January 31, 2014. https://www.youtube.com/watch?v=J-0ou24Hlpw.

[8] Leonard Berry, *Discovering the Soul of Service–The Nine Drivers of Sustainable Business Success* (New York, New York: Free Press, 1999), 191.

4. Use multiple learning approaches.
5. Seek continuous improvement.

We shall discuss each of these in turn.

Critical Skills

Berry's first principle involves identifying the skills that service employees simply must have. A hospitality organization can identify these critical skills through a systematic analysis of the service, delivery systems, and staff. They can also determine them by asking their guests and employees. The guests will tell you what employee skills are related to their own satisfaction, and employees can be trained to ask the guests what it takes. The organization can survey regular customers who know the business well. Employees should also be involved in the design of training as they have a good idea of what critical skills they need for their positions. Ask the best service providers in the organization. Study the servers who do things well to understand what everyone else needs to learn. Study what the best do and what they know.

The Big Picture

In Chapter 4, we stressed the importance of teaching the organization's culture to give employees a way to make sense out of their jobs and how they do them. The best organizations do this consistently and well to show employees the big picture. Teaching the big picture means teaching employees the organization's overall values, purposes, and culture, and how what they do helps the organization succeed. Four Seasons wants to ensure their new employees fully understand the big picture. After new employees complete their initial training and their 90-day probationary period, they receive a complimentary stay at the hotel, so they can fully appreciate what a guest at Four Seasons experiences.

New employees in any organization are usually eager to learn the organization's core values and what the organization is all about, so they can see how their jobs fit into the big picture. When an employee is later confronted with a problem situation that doesn't exist in a handbook or training manual, the core values learned and accepted during training should lead that employee to do the right thing for the customer. Because so many situations in services are unplanned and unplannable, teaching the big picture and the culture's core values is especially critical. People who are taught the values and beliefs from the first day are far more likely to make the right choice for the customer and the organization when the situation calls for both personal judgment and decisive action. For JetBlue, the first employee value is safety. Employees know from their training that safety is their highest priority from day one. But after safety, the values of caring, integrity, passion, and fun help employees know how to behave and interact with guests to provide JetBlue's desired service experience.

Formalized Learning

Formalizing learning refers to the process of building learning into the job, making learning mandatory for everyone, and institutionalizing that expectation. Give employees learning opportunities, and do it on company time. By putting their money where their values are, the best hospitality organizations send a strong message to employees that learning is vital to the organization and everyone must participate.

Gaylord Palms has made a strong commitment to employee learning and linked formal training programs to the company's mission and strategic objectives. For example, it set an objective of promoting from within and designed a curriculum to teach its employees how to achieve that objective.

Varied Approaches

Different employees will learn differently; therefore, using a variety of learning approaches is also important. Berry recommends leaving no opportunity unexplored. In addition to traditional methods, he suggests that organizations sponsor book clubs, send employees out to observe exceptional organizations in the service industry to benchmark against the best, and encourage the employee to constantly practice the necessary skills through a variety of means.

Continuous Improvement

A commitment to continuous improvement is essential. The initial training found at most organizations provides the KSAs that enable employees to begin doing their jobs. But training shouldn't stop there. The best service organizations and their employees want continuing employee improvement through on-the-job training and supervision, special training sessions, video demonstrations, online courses, and the full range of training methods available to modern organizations. At Ritz-Carlton, every shift at each property begins with what they call the "Daily Line-Up." Each Daily Line-Up is a brief training session designed to reinforce the Gold Standards upon which Ritz-Carlton service is based as well as communicate important information to all of the employees. At Ritz-Carlton, every shift is an opportunity to emphasize the company's values and to reinforce continuous improvement.

DEVELOPING A TRAINING PROGRAM

Training programs have great potential to help an organization provide exceptional service; at the same time, however, they are a significant investment in an organization's employees. A valuable training program requires proper planning. Ultimately, an organization needs to determine what needs to be improved and if a training program provides the right solution to the problem.

What Do We Need to Improve?

Training should always be preceded by a **needs assessment** to determine if perceived organizational problems or weaknesses should be addressed by training or by some other strategy. For example, a service problem might be initially identified as a training issue, to be solved by offering servers a short training session. Upon closer examination, however, the issue might turn out to be a fault in the nonhuman part of the service delivery system. For example, constant guest complaints about slow beverage service at a local restaurant might seem at first to require training for the servers. But maybe the coolers in the beverage service area are too small. Or perhaps there are simply not enough servers on staff to manage the volume of orders. All the server training in the world cannot correct a flaw in some other part of the service delivery system.

needs assessment A process used to determine if perceved organizational problems or weaknesses should be addressed by training or by some other strategy.

Needs assessment takes place at three levels: organizational, task, and individual. The organizational analysis seeks to identify which skills and competencies the organization needs and whether or not it has them already. If, for example, the organizational analysis reveals a need for several new restaurant managers in the Boston market and people to fill that need are not available, the organization would initiate a training program to prepare either existing employees or new entrants to be restaurant managers in that market. Hilton Hotels, for example, when planning its expansion in China, recognized the need to train and develop employees to serve in key leadership roles in the hotels that would be eventually opening several years in the future. In addition to planning for the financial and real estate needs of their expansion plans,

Hilton also carefully planned how they would develop employees so they would have the requisite human capital needed to open their hotels on schedule.

The second level of analysis is the task. What tasks need to be performed? Are they being done well, or is training needed? Most training in the hospitality industry is at the task level, either to prepare new or newly promoted employees to perform the necessary job tasks or to retrain existing employees when existing task requirements change. Four Seasons, for example, uses its Manager in Training (MIT) program to prepare participants for Assistant Manager positions. Four Seasons carefully considered what it wants from its future managers and leaders, and the training program is designed to help prepare these employees for their careers with the organization.

At the third level of analysis, that of the individual, the organization reviews the performance of people doing tasks to determine if they are performing up to job standards. For example, a manager may realize the revenue manager is not sufficiently proficient with the new software. Or a particular housekeeper may need refreshing on the specified protocol and procedures for the job after having been away on a leave. Looking for ways to help employees do their jobs more effectively is a continuous task for effective managers.

Once the organization has assessed its needs at these three levels, it can use training programs to meet them. Exhibit 6.1 shows examples of training programs commonly found in the hospitality industry.

Solving the Guest's Problem

The needs assessment also identifies what the training should accomplish. If the needs analysis reveals a lack of some important employee skill, the training objective would be to ensure each employee needing that specific skill to perform effectively has it. La Quinta recognized its hotels were having difficulty providing the level of service that

EXHIBIT 6.1

Examples of the Types of Training Programs Offered in the Hospitality Industry

Mandatory training
EEO/diversity training
Orientation
Safety training
Skills-oriented training
Basic skills training
Computer training
Crisis training
Cross-functional training
Language training
Retraining
Specialized skills training

Competency-oriented training
Customer service training Communications training
Diversity training Ethics/values training
Remedial/basic education
Team training
Wellness/health training
Managerial training
Change-management training
Cross-cultural training
Leadership training
Performance feedback and management training

was expected during the busy summer season. The needs assessment revealed a need to improve its operational performance and improve customer service. La Quinta deployed 102 corporate office employees to 20 of the company's highest-occupancy hotels, who then cross-trained employees on a variety of operational tasks. As a result of the training, the company saw an increase in both positive online reviews as well as increases in employee morale. The training provided by the corporate office also strengthened the relationship between the property teams and the corporate office.[9]

With the objectives known, clear learning goals should be specified.[10] It should be apparent to both the trainer and trainee what is supposed to be learned during the training process. Continuing the above example, what do front desk agents need to learn in order to improve their mastery of the check-in and check-out procedures? Depending on the situation, it could require better customer service skills, or perhaps better knowledge of the organization's information systems. Once you are clear on your learning goals, it is much more straightforward to design a training program to accomplish those specific needs. This is what is ultimately needed for a training program in order to improve employee job performance.

Guest feedback about service problems or failures should serve as an important trigger for evaluating relevant parts of the service delivery system and for considering training as one way to solve the problems. It should concern you if your guests are dissatisfied with your employees' performance, whether your needs assessment has revealed a problem or not. Training may or may not be the answer.

Service failure could be a result of strategic issues (misidentifying the needs of the market), inadequate staffing (providing an insufficient quantity of staff to deliver services in expected time frames), poor selection (hiring people without the right skills or capability to learn the job), or delivery service issues (not having the right equipment to do the job correctly). The environment may cause a service failure (such as an approaching hurricane or a major earthquake that forces a resort to evacuate), and a poorly designed service delivery system can lead to poor service (e.g., the layout of the hotel kitchen and the hotel's rooms makes it impossible for room service to deliver food while still hot). Consider a hotel dealing with a problem of long check-in times. It is possible the problem could be resolved by better training of staff, but there may be a host of other causes. The company may not have recognized the expectations of the guests (a strategic issue), insufficient people staffing the front desk (inadequate staffing), individuals who simply cannot master the computer system needed to check in guests (poor selection), a slow computer system (delivery service issues), or perhaps a storm caused an unexpected number of guests to suddenly show up at the hotel at a specific moment (an environmental cause). Certainly, it is possible slow check-in could be caused by inadequate training of front desk employees, but a careful assessment of the causes of service failures is needed to ensure that training would be the appropriate solution.

In short, it needs to be very clear that training cannot fix all of the inadequacies that lead to service failures. Training is just one tool in the human resource management toolbox, and human resource solutions are only one set of solutions available to an organization. Yet training is what may make the difference between an acceptable service experience and an exceptional one. If you have enough employees to handle the demand, if your systems are properly designed, if the environment or setting doesn't interfere, if employees are ready and willing to perform, and if they have the capability to learn, training can give them the specific skills they need to provide the desired service quality and value to the customer.

---

[9] "Training Top 125," *Training Magazine*, January/February 2017, 60–95.

[10] Robert C. Ford, "Combining Performance, Learning, and Behavioral Goals to Match Job with Person: Three Steps to Enhance Employee Performance with Goal Setting," *Business Horizons* 60, no. 3 (2017): 345–352.; Gary P. Latham and Gerard H. Seijts, "Distinguished Scholar Invited Essay: Similarities and Differences Among Performance, Behavioral, and Learning Goals," *Journal of Leadership & Organizational Studies* 23, no. 3 (2016): 225–233.

Data-Driven Approaches to Identifying Training Needs

Effective hospitality organizations constantly measure and monitor the performance of their staff, systems, and service products to identify problems. Many problems in delivering the guest experience are caused by the people comprising the delivery system. If managers learn about these problems quickly—either from surveying guests, from their own observations, or comparisons of performance metrics to established service standards—and identify their connection to training issues, they can quickly institute corrective training to address the issue before other guests have the same problems.

The use of this approach can even be extended to look at the mix of talents in entire departments. If an analysis of a particular department shows the current composition of people does not include some vital talent for departmental success, individuals can be selected to receive specialized training to supply the missing ingredient.

The identification of training needs, however, is moving beyond this manual identification of training needs. Increasingly, companies are using data-driven analytics to identify employee effectiveness and training needs. These companies are capturing and structuring data that allow them to identify problems and training opportunities in the workplace. This use of "big data" can identify where employees lack particular skills, and which training programs can be used to fill the gap.[11] These data-driven efforts can identify training needs that might otherwise go undetected or misdirected. As these data driven tools gain widespread acceptance, the identification of training needs will not only come from organizational policy and managerial identification of problems, but by big data driven human resource systems that identify precisely where training can help improve organizational effectiveness.

TYPES OF TRAINING

Once an organization determines it needs to offer training, the next step is to begin considering how the training will be delivered. The first question that needs to be resolved is, is the organization going to provide its own training, or will it use the services of another organization? The focus of the training also needs to be clear. Will the training help employees learn new skills, will it help employees with broader educational needs, or will it be used to help keep employees fresh and up-to-date with their current skills?

Internal Training

internal training Training provided for organizational members by persons or groups within the organization itself.

Most training occurs within an organization. That is, most organizations provide **internal training**, where a person or people within the organization itself provide the training to the employees. This can take the form of formal on-the-job training, less formal coaching, or even specific classes provided by organizational personnel. Larger hospitality organizations often possess specific in-house training departments. For example, Four Seasons, Mövenpick, Hyatt, Marriott, McDonald's, Holiday Inn Worldwide, Darden, and Disney are just a few multi-unit organizations that have extensive and elaborate internal training departments.

As just one particular example, Hilton seeks to support its 300,000 team members across 91 countries with *Hilton Worldwide University*.[12] With this venture, Hilton provides more than five million hours of training each year, delivered through over

[11] "Four Ways to Use Big Data in Employee Training," InsideBIGDATA, last modified December 22, 2017, https://insidebigdata.com/2017/12/22/4-ways-use-big-data-employee-training/.

[12] "Hilton Worldwide University," Hilton Hotels, accessed February 16, 2018, http://www.hwu-overview.com/introduction/university.html.

2,500 courses. The courses also come in a variety of training formats, including classroom training, e-books, webinars, and online courses. Hilton sees this extensive training endeavor as an investment in their team members that helps them achieve their organizational mission.

External Training

Sometimes, companies don't have the resources or expertise to provide their own training on a particular topic. In such instances, companies may take advantage of **external training**, where they employ training consultants or independent training organizations to provide particular training needs. These external training companies range from independent consultants providing specialized training courses, to small organizations with a few experts in some specialized area of a particular industry, to large multinationals that offer training programs on just about any skill, area, or topic imaginable. If the required training is in a highly specialized area or if only a few people need it, a company-specific program would probably not be worth the expenditure, so employees needing training are sent outside to get it.

external training Training provided for organizational members by persons or institutions outside the organization.

Recognizing both the power of their own training knowledge and other organizations' needs for high-quality customer service training, Ritz-Carlton set up its own training school, called *The Ritz-Carlton's Leadership Center.*[13] The Leadership Center leverages the systems and processes of the Ritz-Carlton brand to deliver high-quality external training to other companies interested in learning about The Ritz-Carlton's approach to customer service and employee development. Participants come not just from hospitality, but from all sectors in the economy, including finance, retail, education, healthcare, insurance, and technology. For example, the course *Creating an Exceptional Patient Experience* is designed to help companies in the healthcare industry apply the Ritz-Carlton Gold Standards to issues associated with patient care. Similarly, the *Disney Institute*[14] offers training to other organizations, helping others learn from Disney's core competencies in leadership, employee engagement, and exceptional service.

Skills Training

Most training is designed to teach employees how to do their jobs. As Bill Marriott Jr. emphasized, "'Hire friendly, train technical' is the most important mantra in our HR manual. I want passionate associates who go the extra difference to help a guest."[15] Once you have hired people with the right attitudes (per Chapter 5), **skills training** provides employees with the knowledge they need to do their jobs. It may include organizational policies, how to use particular equipment, or the specified procedures to engage in a particular task. Hiring people with great attitudes can be very effective and can get you the *service naturals* discussed in the previous chapter. But this approach will only work if you also provide the skills training so that employees who want to provide exceptional service have the KSAs they need to do so.

skills training Training designed to give employees the knowledge they need to do their jobs.

Training the Very Basics

Companies sometimes find it necessary to provide the most basic training to its employees. According to the U.S. Department of Education, 21% of those at the end of high school lack basic writing skills, 38% lack basic reading skills, and 39% lack basic

[13] "The Ritz-Carlton Leadership Center," The Ritz-Carlton, accessed January 4, 2018, http://ritzcarltonleadershipcenter.com/.
[14] "About Us," Disney Institute, accessed February 12, 2018. https://disneyinstitute.com/about/.
[15] J.W. "Bill" Marriott, Jr. "Hire Friendly, Train Technical," Marriott, last modified January 27, 2014, http://www.blogs.marriott.com/marriott-on-the-move/2014/01/hire-friendly-train-technical.html.

mathematics skills;[16] and this does not even count the 16% of students who drop out of high school. Hilton Hotels offers "Career Online High School," where Hilton employees can use an online system to earn an accredited high school diploma.[17] Some restaurateurs even find it necessary to teach employees basic hygiene, including teaching food handlers how to wash their hands.

Large hotels may need to provide training just to teach new employees their way around the property. The Wynn hotel and resort complex in Las Vegas has a novel training program for new employees. The resort is so large—with dozens of places to eat, an extensive casino environment, many shops, a nightclub, a theatre, and so on—that new employees must be taught where everything is in the hotel. To help acquaint them with the entire property, they are asked to participate in a scavenger hunt, searching the property for artwork, items, landmarks, and so forth. As a result of the hunt, they learn where all the resort's important landmarks can be found and become prepared to answer any guest's questions about where something is located.

Using Training to Refresh Employee Skills

retraining Training designed to reinforce fundamental messages about the organization's mission while preparing employees for possible promotion and development.

Even employees who have been doing the job for a while can benefit from training. **Retraining** is used to reinforce fundamental messages about the organization's mission while preparing them for possible promotion and development. Mövenpick, for example, offers its "Business Academy" several times a year. This training program is designed to enhance employees' innovation by facilitating a process where employees from many different locations can share new ideas and best practices that have worked at their home locations; they also designed the program to develop participants' business and leadership skills. Peter Michell, Mövenpick's Vice President of Talent & Organizational Development, described the Business Academy as "a valuable training that continuously drives our commitment towards training and development, career progression and brings our key leaders together. This training is what sets Mövenpick Hotels & Resorts apart as one of the world's leading and most progressive hospitality firms."[18]

Retraining is often made available to employees who have burned out, have become unable to perform their current jobs because of technological developments, or whose jobs have been eliminated. Disney has operated a retraining program for many years that tries to sprinkle "Pixie Dust" on employees who have become disenchanted with their present jobs or have otherwise lost their enthusiasm for delivering magical moments for guests. The program retrains such employees for new jobs that might help them recapture their enthusiasm or rethink why they are unhappy with their existing jobs and to regain the spirit of doing it the way the guests expect.

To encourage employees to be more effective and responsive to guests, outstanding hospitality organizations also offer training in particular competencies, such as working as a team, creative problem solving, communications, relationships, leadership, and guest service orientation. These organizations realize that performing the basic job skills is only one part of the service requirement for delivering excellent service.

Companies have learned that even after having received initial customer service training, diversity training, attitudinal training, and other efforts to change how people consider others can have significant payoffs in improving the way their service

---

[16] "How Did U.S. Students Perform on the Most Recent Assessments?," The Nation's Report Card, accessed January 4, 2018, https://www.nationsreportcard.gov/.

[17] Elliott Mest, "Hilton Partners with Cengage to Offer Employees High School Diplomas, Training," *Hotel Management*, last modified November 14, 2017, https://www.hotelmanagement.net/human-resources/hilton-partners-cengage-to-offer-employees-high-school-diplomas-training.

[18] Diane Fermin Roeder, "Mövenpick Hotels & Resorts Hosts 'Business Academy' Leadership Training in Dubai," HotelierMiddleEast.com, last modified July 1, 2017, http://www.hoteliermiddleeast.com/30746-movenpick-hotels-resorts-hosts-business-academy-leadership-training-in-dubai/.

employees interact with each other and with the many different types of guests they see. The great diversity in the modern workforce, particularly in the hospitality industry, makes this training essential. There are more than fifty languages spoken by employees at the Waldorf Astoria in New York City, and guests come from an even greater number of different cultural backgrounds. In today's diverse environment, organizations need to train employees in how to get along with and understand each other and their guests.

Starbucks found out the hard way that a lack of this sort of training can have massive negative consequences. Although well known for their training programs,[19] after an incident when two black men at a Starbucks in Philadelphia were improperly treated by frontline employees, the coffee chain closed 8,000 U.S. company-owned stores to provide anti-bias training to 175,000 employees to try to prevent any future racial discrimination.[20] The incident at the store became a public relations nightmare. It also revealed that, despite extensive training aimed at providing a superior product, there existed an individual-level customer-service problem that the organization felt needed to be addressed, at least in part, through widespread mandatory retraining.

With the globalization of both travel and hospitality organizations, there is a growing need to provide training that helps employees understand and appreciate other cultures. When the Gaylord Opryland Hotel was preparing to host a large international meeting, it gave its 7,000 employees special training in international guest service. The grand training finale was an all-day international marketplace; employees won prizes by participating in games while dining on international foods.

TRAINING METHODS

The most common internal training method is on-the-job training. Other methods commonly used are coaching, apprenticeships, cross-functional training, classroom training, simulations, e-learning, executive education, and mentoring. These different training methods deliver their content in varied ways. Several methods rely on extensive interpersonal contact, such as through coaching and mentoring. Other training methods use technology to deliver content, as web-based methods and e-courses become more widely available. Exhibit 6.2 shows a variety of training methods, ranging from those with high personal contact to those with high reliance on technology and no or little personal contact. We now discuss the characteristics of each of these programs.

On-the-Job Training

One of the best ways to learn something is to actually do it. **On-the-job training** involves having an experienced employee instruct a new employee how to actually do the job. One-on-one supervised experiences are a typical on-the-job training method. The trainee may attend a short classroom introduction and then go to a work station, where a supervisor or trainer can demonstrate, observe, correct, and review the employee performing the required tasks. Because the skills required to do some jobs are often unique, learning by doing (under close supervision) is often the only cost-effective training method.

on-the-job training Training where an experienced employee instructs a new employee on how to actually do the job while the trainee is actually performing the job.

Hospitality organizations use the on-the-job training technique extensively because many tasks are best learned by doing, while supervisors or co-workers with

[19] Aimee Groth and Gus Lubin, "11 Things Starbucks Does Better than Almost Any Competitor," *Business Insider*, July 29, 2011.

[20] Christopher Chabris and Matthew Brown, "Review—A Big Anti-bias Experiment for Starbucks—After an Ugly Incident, the Coffee Chain Has a Chance to Test Whether Training Programs Produce Less Prejudiced Behavior," *Wall Street Journal*, April 28, 2018, C3.

EXHIBIT 6.2

Different Methods of Employee Training

On-the-job training	The employee learns the job by doing. The individual is placed in the work situation and a supervisor or co-worker instructs the employee on how the job is done directly at the work station.
Coaching	One person who has necessary knowledge instructs other individuals on a one-to-one or small group basis.
Apprenticeship	Trainees spend a set period of time learning a craft or trade under the guidance of an experienced master.
Internship	This is a short-term work experience, designed to give individuals experience in an industry or field, while also providing an opportunity for an organization to evaluate a perspective employee.
Cross-functional training	The trainee moves through a series of job assignments over specific time frames.
Classroom training	Content is delivered to trainees using a lecture-based format.
Simulation	The employee practices the job in a simulated work environment.
Online and electronic learning	Online resources and videos—typically usable 24/7; accessible from phones, tablets, or computers; available at home, on the move, or at work—are used to meet a wide range of teaching needs.
Executive education	These are non-credit and non-degree granting programs, often (but not always) offered by universities or colleges, designed to help in the development of higher-level managers and leaders in the organization.
Mentoring	This involves a formal relationship between junior and senior colleagues. The mentor gives advice regarding functioning in the organization and career development.

When learning on the job, an employee engages in productive work, but does so while under the guidance of a supervisor or a more experienced employee.

more experience are standing by to assist. Veteran servers help new ones; a new front desk clerk will often quickly find himself checking guests into the hotel, but with an experienced employee standing close by to ensure that all procedures are properly followed. Many small organizations, like Ralph's Restaurant on the corner, do the same thing. If Ralph can't hire someone with the experience he needs for one of the restaurant's many jobs, or can't afford to send a new employee to an external training course, then the most efficient and cost-effective training method is for Ralph to teach the new employee "Ralph's Way" of washing dishes, making spaghetti, or serving meals.

If managers are conducting the training, they themselves may benefit from on-the-job training as the specialists can coach them while instructing their employees. Jenny Lucas, director of education and development for Loews Hotels, says, "Our training managers are out there, watching training being delivered, watching managers in action, doing spot checks, and giving feedback afterward."[21]

Besides sometimes being the only way to train an employee in a job with varied and changing duties, on-the-job training has added advantages. First, employees find out directly what the job requires because they are actually doing it. There is no question about how well the training carries over to the actual task, because the trainee is *doing* the actual task. Another advantage is the organization is actually getting some productivity out of new employees, whereas if they were in classrooms, they would not be contributing to achieving organizational goals.

Of course, on-the-job training has its drawbacks. Because the trainee is actually doing the job, errors due to lack of experience may directly affect the customer and the organization's reputation for service. The impact of poor service delivered by untrained new employees can be compounded if management does not take its commitment to on-the-job training seriously. Jerry Newman describes his first day on the job at a cash register in a fast-food restaurant.[22] At first, a manager stood with him and gave him some guidance, but once the lunch rush started, the manager disappeared to do other tasks. Although he had told Jerry "I'll be here if you need me," Jerry was left totally on his own. Customers noticed his poor performance and were not favorably impressed.

On-the-job training can be a very effective way to help employees learn a new job, but it needs to be carefully planned and implemented. Is the job one that can actually be learned by doing? Are experienced employees ready, willing, and able to provide the necessary assistance? What are the business- and service-related consequences of having a new employee learn by doing on the job? In short, learning by doing can be a great way to learn, but companies that want to preserve their reputation for providing excellent customer service do not use it to force new employees to "sink or swim."

Coaching

Coaching involves a relationship between an individual (a teacher, supervisor, or trainer) and either an individual or a team of employees. Coaching requires opportunities for the coach to both observe the employees and provide feedback. Coaches also need to be able to explain appropriate behaviors, articulate why certain actions need to be taken, provide suggestions to improve performance, and reinforce desired behaviors. Coaches need to be skilled both on the task at hand, as well as on how to communicate what they know. Just because someone is a good performer does not mean the person will be a good coach. Coaching may be conducted by outside consultants, specialists within the organization, supervisors, or by particularly skilled peers.

coaching Training where there is a relationship between an individual (teacher, supervisor, or trainer) and an individual or a team, and the coach teaches how to perform the job, provides feedback, and reinforces desired behaviors.

Apprenticeships

An **apprenticeship** is a training program that combines on-the-job training with related one-on-one coaching-like instruction so that a worker learns how to perform a highly skilled craft or trade. In exchange for the instruction, the apprentice works for the trainer or training organization for an agreed period of time. Apprenticeship programs can be run by individual employees, trade groups, unions, or employer associations.

apprenticeship A training program that combines on-the-job training with related one-on-one coaching-like instruction so that a worker learns how to perform a highly skilled craft or trade.

Apprenticeships are historically and most typically found in construction or related jobs (e.g., carpenter, electrician, plumbing). In the hospitality industry, though, apprenticeships are still common in food-related occupations (e.g., baker, butcher, chef,

[21] Holly Dolezalek, "We Train to Please," *Training* 45, no. 3 (2008): 34–35.

[22] Jerry Newman, *My Secret Life on the McJob: Lessons from Behind the Counter Guaranteed to Supersize Any Management Style* (McGraw-Hill Professional, 2007).

George Rinhart/Corbis via Getty Images

Circa 1930, Cornell Hotel School students being trained on how to carry luggage.

pastry chef). Apprenticeships, though, are much more common outside of the United States, particularly in Europe. The Celtic Manor Resort, for example, is a leading hotel in Wales. It recently launched a new two-year apprenticeship program, where participants learn everything about the hospitality industry including both operational components (food and beverage, housekeeping, conferences and banqueting) and interpersonal development (teamwork, guest relations, and even interview skills).[23]

Internships

internship A short-term work experience designed to familiarize employees with a particular role or career.

An **internship** is a short-term work experience that an organization offers. We already discussed the role internships play in helping organizations decide who to hire (in Chapter 5). While internships give an organization the opportunity to evaluate potential employees, they also provide a way for individuals to gain experience in a given industry or field. Internships are typically of short duration, often some period of time between a few weeks and a few months. Internships are generally less formal and less rigorous than apprenticeships, and they range extensively in terms of how much supervision, training, and coaching is provided to the intern.

Internships provide essentially a blend of selection and training programs. The experience they provide helps individuals learn about a given job, company, and/or profession; companies meanwhile can assess how well the individual may perform if they were to become a full-time employee. Furthermore, if an intern is selected for full-time employment, the individual requires less training than others because the former intern is already familiar with aspects of the organization. Even if the individual is not given a job offer from the organization, internships are beneficial to individuals seeking to gain experience in a field, typically as a way of complementing formal education.

Cross-Functional Training

cross-functional training A training program that teaches employees how to do other jobs, thus enlarging the workforce's capabilities.

Cross-functional training enlarges the workforce's capabilities to do different jobs. Gaylord's Opryland Hotel cross-trains its front desk personnel and telephone-reservation agents so that each can help out the other. The front desk often needs help when many people wish to check in or check out within a short period of time. The hotel has set up a separate registration desk in the lobby, and when the lines at the front desk begin to reach unacceptable levels, these cross-trained agents are called to the separate desk to help serve guests. Some hotels cross-train employees from many departments on how to provide banquet service. On banquet days, current employees can be temporarily redistributed rather than hiring more employees. Because all hospitality organizations have similar variability in their demand patterns, cross-functional training is often necessary to handle the sudden surge in guests at different points in the service delivery system. At the same time, it provides task variety and higher interest levels for employees, which has significant benefits in employee motivation and morale. Cross-functional training is often a win-win-win for guests, hospitality organizations, and employees.

[23] Sion Barry, "Celtic Manor Resort Recruiting for New Hospitality Apprentices," *WalesOnline*, last modified July 24, 2017, http://www.walesonline.co.uk/business/appointments/one-wales-leading-hotels-launches-13376752.

Cross-functional training also provides a benefit even if employees won't have the opportunity to perform different duties: it helps employees better understand how all the parts of the operations work together. Employees often work in their own silos, so just getting to know and understand employees from other parts of the organization can improve cooperation. Marriott's management trainee program provides participants with training in a wide variety of disciplines, including accounting and finance, culinary, engineering, event management, food and beverage, human resources, revenue management, rooms operations, and sales. The diverse cross-functional training helps give participants a comprehensive understanding of all that Marriott does, and how all the different parts of the hotel work together to provide an exceptional customer experience.

Classroom Training

Another common training method is training in a classroom environment. **Classroom training** can follow a variety of formats. The most usual is the lecture presentation. A knowledgeable expert speaks to employees so they will learn the necessary skill or knowledge in the available lecture time. This listen-and-learn approach is based on the assumption that an expert can train the uninformed by speaking to them. That this assumption has been questioned by research on how people actually learn doesn't seem to deter its continued use. University teachers and students alike know that not everyone listens and not everyone can learn by listening.

classroom training Training provided to employees in a classroom setting, typically where an expert uses a lecture format to teach to employees.

Nonetheless, the method has advantages: it is inexpensive, time efficient, and to the point. If a top performer in the organization stands up and tells you what she knows, she may not feel the need to develop elaborate visual aids, instructional screens, or anything else that takes time and money to produce. She and the organization may assume that since she has been there, done that, and done it well, she is obviously worth listening to and will have great credibility with employees. Most of the time, these assumptions prove accurate. This strategy should be combined with on-the-job training and coaching to help reinforce the important points made in the classroom presentation. Hospitality programs, for example, frequently use demonstration kitchens as a way for a chef to provide classroom training to perspective chefs. The classroom presents an efficient way for the chef to demonstrate the proper cooking steps and cooking method to the students. The demonstration can then be followed up by practice in a classroom kitchen (i.e., simulation) or in the program's student-run restaurant (i.e., on-the-job training).

Another basic classroom technique is the interactive case study. Here, the organization provides learners with case material for discussion. The material may be related to the skill they need to learn, or it may be material to teach the more general skills of decision-making or problem solving. This technique requires a skilled facilitator, to keep the discussion focused and the learners engaged.

More recently, with the increasing organizational emphasis on teams and leadership, team-based training has become popular. Leaderless groups may be given a problem to solve or an issue to address and asked to form collaborative problem-solving teams to tackle it. People learn to work together, but they also learn about discovering and sharing the tremendous amount of knowledge that often exists within a team. Smart managers believe in training their people to take advantage of the wisdom of teams; other managers never discover their value.

The modern approach to classroom learning emphasizes learner involvement and frequently uses a mixture of educational formats to reach as many types of learners as possible. While some can learn from listening or watching, others can learn only by doing. Those facilitating classroom experiences mix short lectures or videos with case or problem discussions with role playing to engage and retain active learner interest.

YOSHIKAZU TSUNO/AFP/Getty Images

Simulation training provides a way to help employees prepare for potential emergencies. Flight crews practice methods for an emergency landing and evacuation; a flight simulator is used to train pilots.

Simulation

simulation A training program that provides a realistic but controlled and safe environment for employees to learn or practice new skills.

While learning by doing is often the most effective way to train new employees in certain areas, the consequences of failure may be too great or expensive to allow the employee to fail in real time with real guests and equipment. Sometimes, employees should learn by practicing a task in a controlled and safe environment: a **simulation.**

Airlines provide the clearest example. They use sophisticated flight simulators to teach their pilots how to fly different airplanes into different airports and how to prepare for emergency situations. They create a virtual airplane with all the controls, physical layout of a real cockpit, and simulated motions so that pilots flying the simulator feel like they really are flying an aircraft. Clearly, you do not want to use on-the-job training to teach a pilot what to do if two of the airplane's four engines fail or if the airplane flies into a flock of birds and has to ditch in New York's Hudson River!

Simulation can be used in a variety of settings. Some hotel companies use employees to act as guests with a complaint in a mock check-in scenario. Often based on real experiences at the hotel, the simulation lets the new employee learn by doing without the risk of mishandling a real situation and losing a real guest's business. One luxury hotel chain uses a simulation for its new bartenders. A preset number of orders come in, and the new bartender has to make the drinks in precise proportions within a certain length of time. To help prepare everyone for the real opening night, new restaurants will often have a mock opening, with chefs making meals and servers taking orders from each other or from local residents who are served a free meal.

Success in a simulation does not automatically mean success in a real situation. Simulations can also be a very expensive way to train employees, even if they are not as sophisticated as flight simulators. But in situations where employees need hands-on experience to truly learn how to do their jobs and service failures are too costly to risk in real time, simulations can be an effective way to teach employees the skills they need.

Online and Electronic Learning

Technology

e-learning Training that uses online resources and videos to deliver training content.

Another major training technique involves using online resources and videos, collectively referred to as **e-learning.** E-learning can be used by itself or in conjunction with a live presentation as a way to bring in new material beyond the expertise of the classroom presenter, add variety to the presentation, or allow the learning to take place at the trainee's own pace. For many hospitality organizations, e-learning is a highly cost-effective strategy. A centralized training department can make or buy video and mixed media presentations and host them on a website, or if necessary distribute them electronically over the world. Smaller, independent hospitality organizations can obtain a wealth of online learning instruction through either commercial retailers or their trade associations. Larger organizations often create their own.

Marriott wanted to find a way to better bring together new employees. Doing this physically for a multinational organization would clearly be cost-prohibitive. So they developed a 12- to 18-month on-boarding program, called *Voyage*. Designed to supplement the physical on-boarding they still provide, *Voyage* provides webinars, speeches, social media venues, and activities that employees can access 24/7 via mobile devices, tablets, or desktop computers. The technology allows Marriott to provide key expertise and testimonials to all new employees in a highly efficient manner. Speeches include content from the CEO, as well as the company's continental presidents and various HR professionals. The platform provides a cost-effective way to get consistency, connections, and better communication across a global workforce.[24]

In view of the traditionally high turnover in the hotel industry and the constant need to train new employees, an on-demand video is useful and practical. New employees can watch it by themselves anytime and learn the basics of how to engage in key tasks. The e-learning can be integrated into training while at work; alternatively, employees can improve their skills or refresh their knowledge at home or on their commute into work. E-learning allows you to put your entire curriculum online. Training modules can even be plugged into motion-capture performance tracking stations, providing trainees with guidance and feedback to learn the necessary job.[25]

Darden's restaurants uses a series of online videos to educate new employees about its various restaurant brands, including Olive Garden, Seasons 52, and Bahama Breeze. New servers learn how the different menu items are to be prepared and served, how guests are to be greeted, and how the wait staff are supposed to do their job. Darden's goal for its standardized training is to teach its people to provide the same high-quality restaurant experience in every facility throughout the entire chain.

Indeed, one of e-learning's many advantages is to standardize the presentation of the material so everyone learns from the same source of information and learns how to do the required tasks in the same way. Being able to offer the same high-quality experience every time in every location is quite important for a multi-unit operation like a chain, franchised restaurant, or branded hotel where guests have standardized expectations about what the organization is supposed to do, how it provides its service, and what it looks like.

E-learning is also relatively cost effective when organizational locations are numerous and widely dispersed. The cost and logistics to send a corporate trainer to every location of a brand every time a new employee is hired would be prohibitive, but providing access to streaming video through the web is easy. A well-designed and well-produced video can do an excellent job of holding the new employee's attention, portraying outstanding role models of expected service behavior and stressing important points. With professional actors or star employees in a video showing the correct means of providing guest service, a new employee can see far more easily what the expected behavior is than if an instructor spoke for several hours.

Videos can also overcome language barriers. Homewood Suites created a training video to meet the needs of its multilingual housekeeping staff. The videos demonstrate procedures, but no words are used.[26] Truly, a picture is worth a thousand words when it comes to training in the highly diverse hospitality industry. Technology also makes it easy for videos to include options for other languages to be spoken in

---

[24] Adriana Scott, "Virtual Onboarding: A Close Look," Society for Human Resource Management, last modified August 28, 2013, https://www.shrm.org/resourcesandtools/hr-topics/talent-acquisition/pages/virtual-onboarding.aspx.

[25] "Novility Launches Hospitality Training," *Hotel Management*, last modified May 14, 2015, https://www.hotelmanagement.net/tech/novility-launches-hospitality-training.

[26] "Acculturate, Educate and Motivate," *Training* 41, no. 12 (2004): 10–11.

New technologies are providing previously unimagined ways to facilitate employee training.

the video, and even more options for captioning additional languages. The making of online learning sources can itself be used as a training technique. The organization can call upon its best employees in the training video's subject area to provide the content for the course and star in the production of the video. Such an approach lets the participants see that the organization appreciates the quality of their job performance, gives them ownership in the training role, and provides live role models for the new employees to follow, but ensures the video is presented in a highly professional manner. Other times, organizations will choose to use professional actors to ensure the performance of individuals in the videos best captures exactly how the organization wants to present and illustrate its training methods.

Video streaming, video conferencing, and webinars are often used to conduct training simultaneously in multiple locations. Live transmissions allow participants from around the world to ask questions and interact with the instructor. Most webinars allow participants to type in questions, which a facilitator can then choose from and pose to the instructor to enable discussion. Some facilities allow for virtual classrooms, where the instructor can see the student participants and call on them in a way that replicates a physical classroom. Video conferencing allows small groups to interact, allowing coaching sessions to occur across the globe in real time.

Technology also allows the content from e-learning sessions to be saved and downloaded as desired by employees who need the training but could not participate in the live session. Employees may be able to participate in the webinar at work, ask questions of the instructor, and refresh their knowledge at a later date. Others may be able to catch the webinar later at home, or when it otherwise fits into their schedule. Online classes frequently combine recorded lectures, which participants can watch when convenient, with discussion boards, which allow interactions amongst participants and an opportunity for the trainer to provide input and facilitate peer learning.

The widespread use and availability of e-learning means that colleges and universities no longer have a monopoly on education in their geographical areas. These developments are a boon to the hospitality industry, as many organizations are multi-unit and geographically dispersed, and so getting their people to an educational center or a centralized training program is costly, difficult, and sometimes impossible. Getting these same people to use their phones, tablets, or computers to participate in a training course when it fits conveniently into their schedule is far easier, and the amount of information, knowledge, and training they can obtain through this medium is enormous. Hyatt has created its own Hyatt Leadership Network, which makes hundreds of training modules available to any Hyatt employee anywhere and anytime. Employees are enrolled into the modules according to their job description. The training content is organized into four schools: The School of General Studies (which provides fundamentals for all employees, designed to support Hyatt's mission, goals, and values to reinforce Hyatt's culture), the School of Hospitality (which provides operations standards of performance, including service expectations and operational knowledge required for daily hotel operations), the School of Management (which provides training to support management skills), and the Leadership Institute (which provides formal and informal development opportunities intended to help develop the future leaders of Hyatt). If a manager needs refresher training on how to conduct a performance appraisal, a training module in the School of Management can help with that. If a new property management system requires employee training on its use, there is a module for that in the School of Hospitality. The network is a formal part of each employee's development plan, and doesn't just help employees learn the skills they need at any particular moment, but gives employees greater confidence to do their jobs, which leads to greater employee motivation and commitment. E-learning capabilities make just-in-time education a reality as the people needing training can log on to the appropriate site at exactly the time they need it.

The cost of creating and disseminating e-training to employees throughout the world is declining rapidly. Once the organization has acquired the technology to deliver this sort of training, the incremental cost of additional training sessions can be minimal. After the technology is in place, organizations can have their own experts easily share their knowledge, and both present and future employees can learn from the content. The increasing availability of video conference and teleconference facilities, reduced costs and increased availability of online tools for presentations, program development, and telecommunications applicants, and the escalating costs of sending people to central training locations are making e-learning an increasingly desirable training option, especially when employees and service units are geographically dispersed. In fact, e-learning is coming quite close to providing the just-in-time education and training that is needed in industries like hospitality where organizational requirements, guest expectations, available technologies, and employees are diverse and change rapidly.

Of course, e-learning has its limitations. The key issue is the extent to which managers and new employees take them seriously. Jerry Newman describes one example of being "trained" in the fast-food industry. He was sent into a back closet with a video player and told to come out after he had watched a training video. No one emphasized the video was important; no one checked to see if Jerry had learned anything; no one even checked to be sure he watched the video. It was simply something that "had to get done" to satisfy a corporate policy. As is true of all forms of training, e-learning will work only if management is committed to their use and if trainees take them seriously.

Executive Education

Most training is targeted at new employees who are learning a job, managers in training, or to employees needing to refresh their skills or to have the culture reinforced. It is also true, however, that higher level leaders in organizations can benefit greatly from training. **Executive education** programs are typically non-credit, non-degree-granting programs offered by universities and colleges that provide training for managers, leaders, and executives in organizations.

executive education Training programs targeted at higher level leaders in organization.

Executive education programs are important sources of training, as the faculty members of universities and colleges frequently have job or industry expertise and the teaching experience and ability to convey it. Many universities offer night, weekend, or online classes to accommodate the busy schedules of those in critical leadership positions within companies, as well as short courses during the summer and at periodic times over the year. Executive education programs also typically offer customized programs, which are tailor-made for corporate customers. Using executive education programs to train one or two key employees may be much less expensive than developing and implementing a specially tailored in-house leadership development program.

Executive education offers a lot of potential options for delivering training to organizational leadership who are looking to learn the newest approaches in business, develop their personal skills, or gain a fresh perspective on the sorts of problems they face in the workplace. The executive education classroom can also be a highly challenging environment, as the high-level participants in the program typically challenge each other as much as they challenge the instructor of the course.

Courtesy of Cornell School of Hotel Administration, Executive Education Dept.

Executive education courses provide a way for more senior-level employees to learn the newest approaches to business and develop their personal skills.

Frequently, trade associations also offer programs that focus on topics of interest to their experienced members, such as working with unions, new purchasing techniques, sanitation in food-service organizations, and the rules and regulations defined by newly passed laws. The common benefit of membership in trade associations is that the organizations can collectively hire an expert consultant, or use someone from a member organization who has mastered a topic, to educate and train others in the industry. Trade associations also frequently offer certification programs in topic areas of interest to their members, typically including coursework that is required to get the certification as a means to help members gain new knowledge. The Educational Institute of the American Hotel and Lodging Association, Educational Foundation of the National Restaurant Association, the Professional Convention Management Association, and the Destination Marketing Association International have all developed training products for their members.

Mentoring

mentoring A relationship in which an experienced manager is paired up with an individual early in the latter's career or when new to the organization.

Mentoring is a relationship in which an experienced manager is paired up with an individual early in the latter's career or new to the organization. Unlike the forms of training above, mentoring is not really used to provide employees with specific job-related skills. Whereas training like coaching or on-the job training focuses on building skills or competencies, mentoring focuses on providing career advice.

The purpose of the mentoring relationship is for the experienced employee to convey interpersonal, organizational, and developmental skills to the junior employee. Mentoring can help employees acclimate to a new organization quicker and allow employees to better develop their own careers within the organization by using the advice of their more experienced mentors. Research has shown mentoring to be associated with a number of beneficial outcomes, including higher job performance, motivation, satisfaction, helping of others, and lower turnover, and stress.[27]

CHALLENGES AND PITFALLS OF TRAINING

While training can help an organization prepare its employees to provide excellent service, problems often arise. Common causes are a failure to establish training objectives, measure results, and analyze training costs and benefits.

Know Your Training Objectives

Training programs can run into trouble if the precise nature and objective of the training are unknown or imperfectly defined, or if the expected outcome of the training is hard to define or measure. Such programs are hard to justify or defend when senior management reviews the training budgets. Typical examples of areas in which the effectiveness of training is difficult to measure are *human relations, interpersonal*

[27] Bob Garvey, Paul Stokes, and David Megginson, *Coaching and Mentoring* (Thousand Oaks, CA: Sage Publishing, 2018).

skills, and *supervisory skills.* Since these terms are vague and situationally defined, knowing what and how much training to offer to improve trainees in these areas and how to measure results is difficult. Hospitality organizations quite naturally want their employees to have a service orientation, but the concept is as hard to define as it is to know whether the training has resulted in such an outcome. Such training is important, without question. What exactly that training should be and how to measure its effectiveness are much more difficult to determine.

Measuring Training Effectiveness

If you don't know what your training is or is not accomplishing, you cannot know whether it is making your organization more effective. Four basic measurement methods—participant reactions, content mastery, behavioral change, and organizational performance—are available to assess training's effectiveness.[28] As illustrated in exhibit 6.3, these approaches range in complexity as well as value.

Participant Reactions

The easiest, cheapest, and most commonly used method for assessing training effectiveness is to simply ask the participants what they think about it. They fill out a questionnaire based on general evaluation criteria and respond to questions such as "How valuable was this training?" Although asking such questions has merit, responses to these questionnaires tend to reflect the entertainment value of the training rather than its effectiveness for the organization. Such evaluations, therefore, have relatively little usefulness for accurate program evaluation. They tell you if the participants enjoyed the training, but not much more.

EXHIBIT 6.3

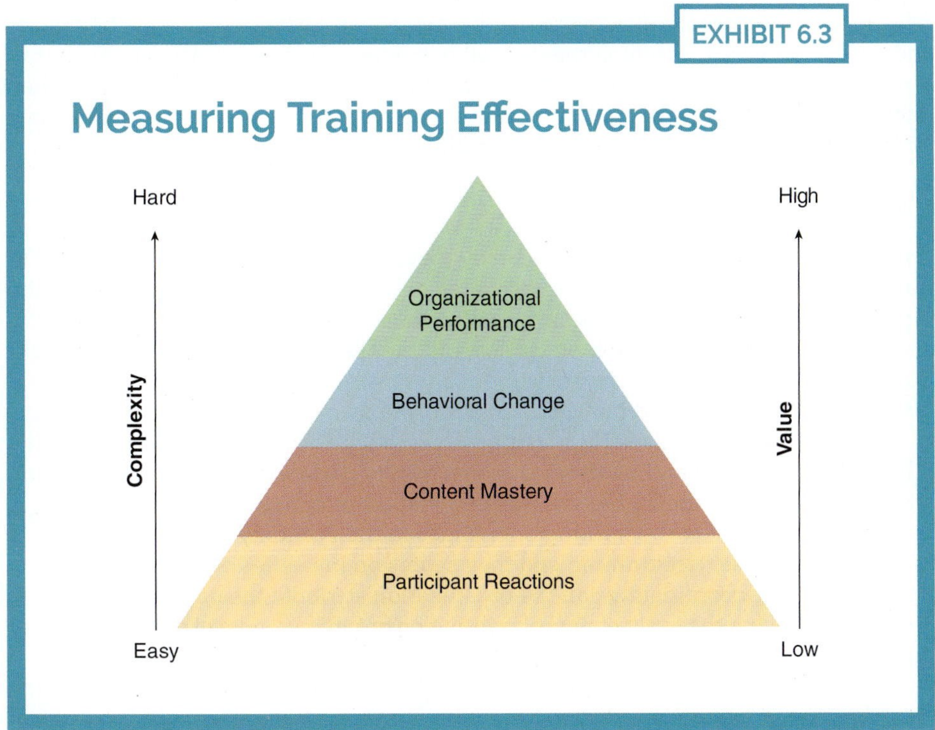

[28] Donald L. Kirkpatrick, *Evaluating Training Programs: The Four Levels* (San Francisco, CA: Berrett-Koehler Publishers, 1994).

Content Mastery

Another way to assess a training program is to test participants for content mastery. After all, if the point of the training was to learn a specific skill, competency, or content area, it should be possible to design a test to determine whether participants learned what they were supposed to learn. These measures can be as simple as paper-and-pencil tests similar to academic exams or as elaborate as on-the-job demonstrations of how well participants mastered the skill.

Of course, doing well on a test does not mean the employee will retain that knowledge or use it on the job. Such evaluations also run the risk of having instructors "teach to the test," essentially training people how to do well on the final exam and not necessarily how to be better performing employees. Employees may also learn a lot from a training course, but if they are not given the opportunity to use these new skills when back on the job, then the training will have been a waste.

Behavioral Change

A more advanced level of training evaluation is to assess the behavioral change in the participant. That is, do employees actually behave differently as a result of the training? Many people quickly forget what they learn in classroom settings, especially if they don't apply it. "Use it or lose it," as the saying goes. College students often say they learn a subject well enough to get through the final exam and then flush all the information out of their brains. To be effective, training must be followed by real and lasting behavioral changes when the employee returns to the job. If the training is well designed and connected to mastering specific service-related behaviors that are reinforced by positive results on the job, then positive, measurable behavioral changes should result.

One function of supervisors is to evaluate the behaviors of their subordinates. If the training affects subordinate behaviors, then the training results should be reflected by supervisory evaluations. Supervisors can observe employee behaviors and assess the extent to which the desired behaviors are exhibited. Companies can also use mystery shoppers to find out what behaviors their employees exhibit when interacting with guests. Feedback from actual customers concerning employee behavior is also a valuable way to learn if the training was effective.

Organizational Performance

The ultimate and most sophisticated level of evaluating training effectiveness is to watch what happens to the measures of overall organizational performance. The training may be well received, the employees may remember most of it upon completion, and they may continue to use it on the job, but the training is useless unless it eventually contributes to overall organizational effectiveness. In short, does the training result in improvements to organizational performance?

The problem with this sort of training evaluation is that it is usually extremely difficult to know precisely how organizational results change due to a specific training program. If booking agents receive training and then room occupancy increases, is this increase a result of the training or changes in the economy? If front desk agents receive customer service training and then scores on measures of customer satisfaction improve, how confidently can the organization attribute the gain to the training program? Knowing the exact effects of training on organization-level outcomes is very difficult.[29]

training control group A group of individuals that are similar to those being trained, except that they do not receive the training.

Yet no matter how difficult it may be to evaluate the results of a training program, organizations must try. The ideal is to contrast a trained group to a **training control group**. A control group is a group of individuals that are similar to those being trained,

[29] Jack J. Phillips, *Handbook of Training Evaluation and Measurement Methods* (New York, NY: Routledge, 2016).

except that they do not receive the training. In scientific studies, individuals are randomly assigned to either the treatment group (i.e., those being trained) or the control group. The random assignment creates a situation where any differences observed between the trained group and the control group are attributable to the training program. Unfortunately, companies often cannot assign people randomly to training to assess its impact, and so other methods must often be used to try to determine the effectiveness of training. One other way to approach this is to measure changes in key outcomes, like the number of guest complaints before and after training or customer satisfaction ratings. Alternatively, an organization could use mystery shoppers to sample the level of service before and after the training. The point of any such technique is to measure the value added by training.

Without being able to compare performance to that of a control group, or to contrast effects before and after the training, the organization has little way to know if the measurement after the training represents any actual improvement. Here, larger organizations have an advantage as they can use people from different parts of their organization as well as contrasting before and after outcome measures to test different types of training. Having data from the trained group as well from comparable employees who did not receive the training allows an organization to statistically determine whether a training program produced desired results.

While measuring the impact of training on the organization as a whole is quite challenging, all training programs should nonetheless be implemented with the goal of increasing organizational effectiveness. Training should help make your employees more effective, which should ultimately result in greater customer satisfaction, greater market share, higher profits, and other key results.

When a Great Training Program Can Hurt You

Sometimes, even when a training program is well-received by participants, leads to learning, changes behaviors on the job, and can be delivered in a cost-effective manner, the ultimate results of the training may still be negative. Even though, on average, training employees does improve employees' performance and reduces turnover, sometimes companies find that hiring trained employees away from competitors is easier and less expensive than developing their own training programs. For example, employees from The Ritz-Carlton are very marketable, as competing luxury hotels know these employees have been given excellent preparation and training in their jobs. Similarly, one chain of Japanese steak houses spends almost no money on training its chefs; instead, the owners travel to competing restaurants and try to find chefs who are already excellent at what they do. This restaurant chain finds that providing higher pay to attract another organization's experienced chefs is more cost effective than training new chefs and paying them until they become as proficient as desired. The same sort of "hunting" or "poaching" of employees occurs in many sectors of the service industry, for both customer facing positions (including casino dealers, restaurant servers, and tour guides) and even non-customer facing jobs (such as revenue managers, technology employees, and general managers).

Four Seasons Hotel and Resorts knows it risks losing its investment in well-trained employees. Its strategy is to not only provide exceptional training on how to deliver the top-level service in which it takes pride but also to select employees who find their fit into The Four Seasons culture to be so strong that they will stay. The Four Seasons also knows that showing employees opportunities for growth in the company is another way to help retain their highly trained employees. No matter what retention strategies an organization uses, the fact remains that it is not only the guests who can recognize exceptional training. Competitors can see it too, and so the risks associated with providing such training should be kept in mind.

However, employers should not over-estimate this risk. The fear of losing trained employees to competitors has led to some companies cutting back on their training investment.[30] If no organization wants to be the one that incurs the costs of training, the industry suffers as it runs the risk of having inadequately trained employees. The point is, when evaluating the value an organization can gain from training its employees, hospitality managers need to consider carefully both the costs and the benefits associated with it.

Training Costs

Although some organizations keep all training in-house to preserve organizational security and culture, the cost of providing training certainly plays a critical role in determining whether to use in-house or outside training. The number and location of employees who need training and the level of expertise they need to acquire determines the cost. If only a few employees need highly technical training, it will be expensive for the organization to deliver it. If the employees are scattered at multiple locations, the training will cost even more. If there are a large number of employees who need fairly consistent and standardized training, the organization will probably offer it internally. If many employees at a single location need training, the organization will probably find a way to do its own training. The high employee turnover that is a basic problem for many hospitality organizations can influence the decision. An organization of 2,500 employees with an annual employee turnover rate of 80% has the same basic training requirements for new employees as an organization of 20,000 employees with a 10% turnover.

Likewise, the level of expertise the training must develop has an important impact on the training cost. If considerable employee expertise will be required, training costs will be high. Offering 100 training hours to 10 employees who will be responsible for operating a sophisticated revenue management system, might cost about as much as offering 5 training hours to 200 employees hired to work at a fast-food drive-through window.

It is also crucial to take into account all of the costs associated with a training program. Clearly, training programs have obvious direct costs, and hopefully the organization can estimate the benefits of a training program. But when determining the net results of a training program, it is critical to factor in not only the direct costs, but the indirect costs as well.

In addition to the direct costs of training, training programs also involve opportunity costs. All the time that trainees and instructors spend away from their regular jobs costs money. Training is too expensive for the organization to train everybody in everything, so it must try to get the best value for its money by using those training programs that give the greatest positive results for the training dollar expended. Too many organizations fall victim to consultants selling programs of unproven usefulness and value. Organizations should make the effort to ascertain the value of each training program, and they should assess if each training program provides the desired results and greater guest satisfaction.

Training Return on Investment

Of course, training cost is only half of the equation when determining if training should be offered. The best approach to training evaluation is to consider training as an investment, and therefore estimate the return on this investment.

[30] C. Jeffrey Waddoups, "Did Employers in the United States Back Away from Skills Training during the Early 2000s?," *ILR Review* 69, no. 2 (2016): 405–434.

The hardest part in evaluating the return on investment for training is to quantify the benefits. You've already put a value on employee skills in general, as evidenced by how much you pay them; but what improvements can be gained because of your training investment? Is it employees can upsell guests more effectively? Do you experience a reduction in turnover, either by fewer people quitting or having to fire fewer people? Are customer satisfaction scores increasing? Does the training save managers' time?

It is a challenging task, and one that is being made easier with greater access to "big data." The key is not to offer a particular training course just because you have always offered that course, or because your competitors offer it. You need to focus on what you get from the training, and how it makes your employees, and ultimately your organization, more effective. Companies like Hilton, Hyatt, Marriott, McDonalds, and Wyndham, just to name a few, have people in human resource data analytics who examine company and customer information to find out exactly what impact training investments yield. This level of data assessment allows these companies to evaluate the effectiveness of their training programs, know which specific training modules are more effective, which methods of delivery work best, and how to better design and target training content in the future.

Training Exemplars

As we have seen throughout the book so far, some companies are exceptional in their efforts. For training, Starwood Hotels, Disney, and Scandinavian Airline Services are three great examples of how to use training to enhance the overall service experience.

Training at Starwood Hotels

Starwood Hotels and Resorts Worldwide has an extensive portfolio of hotel brands—Sheraton, Le Méridien, Four Points by Sheraton, The Luxury Collection, Westin, Element, W Hotels, Aloft Hotels, and St. Regis—and uses a correspondingly extensive training program to ensure they deliver the proper service product for each distinctive brand. For Starwood Hotels, the service product is all about being "on brand," and so employees must fully understand what that means.

As with most companies, new Starwood employees receive an orientation. They learn about the brand of the hotel for which they now work, the history of that specific brand and Starwood Hotels in general, and an overview of the entire line of Starwood brands. This general orientation sets up the next three phases of training which are delivered over roughly the next two years. These phases are designed to build and shape employee attitudes, skills, and behaviors while teaching employees the Starwood Culture in *service culture training.*

The phases are designed to teach employees what it means to be "on brand." While the overall content coverage may be universal for all Starwood Hotels, the programs are customized to each specific hotel brand. The first phase, delivered within the first few months of employment, lays the foundation. It emphasizes the unique nature of the hotel brand and its link to customer loyalty. Through classroom content, shared experiences, and storytelling, new employees learn each brand's core values. They also learn the brand's success profile, which describes what success looks like for an employee of that brand.

The second phase of training, delivered a few months later, emphasizes how the employee can bring the brand's core values to life. Again, all the training is aimed at making every aspect of employee and customer experiences on brand, including specific words (e.g., employees at Westin are called "associates"; employees at W Hotels are called "talent"), conversational tone, background music, customer interactions, and so on.

The third phase of the training emphasizes how employees should be "living the brand." While the first two phases are delivered mainly through classroom instruction, the third phase takes place in a variety of non-classroom settings. It includes activities in pre-shift meetings, e-learning modules, video content, and self-learning exercises.

Overall, Starwood sees training as essential to its success. In their effort to build world-class brands, Starwood's management recognizes that all employees need to understand the unique culture, approach, and attitude associated with the brands for which they work. They believe delivering an exceptional service experience unique to each brand will build customer loyalty to the brand, and ultimately financial success.

Training at Disney

Disney uses an extensive training program to teach new employees how to do their assigned jobs and how to deal with guests in a manner consistent with guest expectations about what the Disney experience should be and how employees who deliver it should act. Visitors to Walt Disney World Resort not only assume employees will be competent at the technical aspects of their jobs but also have high expectations about the level of employee caring, consistency, and enthusiasm. While a street cleaner inside the Magic Kingdom can quickly learn the mechanics of operating a pickup broom and dustpan, learning how to do it the Disney way takes more time. The street sweeper is to many guests the always-handy expert on where everything is, the available extra person to snap a group photo, or the symbol of continuing reassurance that the park is clean, safe, and friendly for all. To prepare that person properly for those multiple roles is an essential training task.

Disney's innovative *Traditions* training program is made mandatory for all new employees from street sweepers to senior management. The program teaches everyone the company's history, achievements, quality standards, and philosophy; details the responsibilities of new cast members in creating the Disney show; and provides a tour of the property. It becomes the first exposure for new employees to the culture that unites all Disney cast members in a common bond. Here, they are taught the four parts of the Disney mission in their order of importance: safety, courtesy, show, and efficiency. They also receive an introduction to company policies and procedures, a summary of recreational and social benefits available, and an introduction and orientation to each cast member's new work area. Above all, and regardless of their job assignments, cast members learn their foremost job requirement is creating happiness in guests. A supervisor or coach then teaches the new employee the necessary job skills. The *Traditions* training is a combination of classroom experiences, with both instructors and interactive videos at Disney University, which is later followed by on-the-job training. After a set period of time, the new cast members are evaluated to ensure the training provided was sufficient to teach them the Disney way and their individual job responsibilities.

Wall-to-Wall Training at Scandinavian Airline Services

Other organizations also appreciate the value of including every employee in a training program. When Jan Carlzon took over the ailing Scandinavian Airline Services (SAS) in 1980, he immediately recognized the deficiencies in the airline's strategy and in its employees' understanding of the airline's mission. He launched a service quality training program for all 20,000 employees that eventually cost several million dollars at a time when SAS was losing $17 million a year. Because it involved training every employee throughout the airline, this concept became known as wall-to-wall training. Karl Albrecht, the author of *At America's Service,* says, "He [Jan Carlzon] wanted the message [of service quality importance] presented in its original, compelling, unfiltered, undiminished form to every SAS employee."[31] Albrecht suggests this was the

---

[31] Karl Albrecht, *At America's Service: How Your Company Can Join the Customer Service Revolution* (New York: Warner Books, 1988), 185.

first time a major corporation used a 100% training process to help create an organization-wide cultural change. Every employee, from shop workers to top managers, went through a two-day workshop entitled The New SAS.

This program was so successful in creating a total organizational enthusiasm for service excellence that Carlzon initiated a second program in 1983. This follow-up was designed to teach everyone in the organization how to read the company's financial statements. Carlzon believed that if employees could understand these statements, they would better understand where the revenues came from, where the money went, how much it cost to run the company, and how much each employee could influence profit. Carlzon said, "I didn't think I could get a 1,000% improvement, but I knew I could get 1% from 1,000 smaller things." The success of these wall-to-wall training efforts at SAS encouraged other organizations to train their entire workforce, including British Airways, which trained all its 37,000 employees.[32]

Hospitality service providers should be trained not only in the skills necessary to deliver the service and interaction expected; they should also be taught the organization's cultural values, practices, strategies, products, and policies. This knowledge helps them figure out how to fix a problem when a customer is unhappy. Unless they understand the fundamental values and beliefs, they cannot know what the organization expects them to do. Because the guest defines the quality and value of the guest experience, hospitality service providers should also learn about their customers' expectations, competitors' services and strategies, industry trends and developments, and the general business environment. Even a cab driver needs to know more than how to drive a car to meet the service expectations of the rider in the back seat.

EMPLOYEE DEVELOPMENT

Employee development involves a combination of work experience, education, and training, all of which combine to improve employee capabilities over time. Training typically focuses on teaching people how to do the new jobs for which they have been hired or to overcome deficiencies they may have in performing their current jobs. Employee development, on the other hand, is typically focused on getting people ready for their future. Training tends to look at the present to identify and correct employee deficiencies in performing the job today. Development looks forward to identify the skills, competencies, and areas of knowledge the employee will need in order to be successful tomorrow.

employee development A combination of work experience, education, and training, all of which combine to improve employee KSAs over time.

The greatest challenge with providing the right employee development opportunities and training is that knowing exactly what will be needed to be successful in the future is impossible. Therefore, employee development programs tend to emphasize more general managerial, problem-solving, and leadership skills. Measuring these general development programs and evaluating their effectiveness is difficult. Companies like Four Seasons, which have a strong commitment to promoting employees from within the organization, work to retain their employees and develop them over time in order to meet whatever future business needs they may encounter.

Career Paths and the Right Experience

Norman Brinker of Chili's said, "People either shrivel or grow. Commit to helping people help themselves."[33] Walt Disney said, "Get in. Be part of it and then move up."[34] CEOs of the best hospitality organizations agree. They provide many opportunities

[32] Albrecht, *At America's Service*, 185.

[33] Norman Brinker and Donald Thomas Phillips, *On the Brink: The Life and Leadership of Norman Brinker* (Irving, TX: Tapestry Press, 1999), 194.

[34] Walt Disney, *Walt Disney Famous Quotes*, Disney's Kingdom Editions (Lake Buena Vista, FL: The Walt Disney Company, 1994): 55.

for employees to grow and develop, and they give employees the opportunity to work their way up through their individual efforts. Satisfying employees' need for growth, discussed in Chapter 7, can be facilitated by means of the many techniques covered in this chapter. Organizations should make it possible for employees with ambition, ability, and a willingness to expend the effort to rise as high as they want to. Career paths should be made available and visible, and these paths should provide employees with the experiences they need to continue their advancement. The current leaders of many hospitality organizations took advantage of the educational opportunities and the promotional paths available and worked their way to the top. When each entry-level employee can see the same possibility, it provides a general feeling of opportunity for all. The desire to learn, the encouragement of learning, and the assumption that learning can lead to advancement should be an important part of the organization's culture.

Preparing for Organizational Needs

In spite of the challenges in predicting what the future will bring, organizations need to prepare for how they will meet those challenges. Many companies plan to grow and they need to have people who are ready to rise to higher-level positions as that expansion occurs. Current economic growth in China and India, for example, will see the opening of thousands of new hotels over the next twenty years as the growing numbers of leisure and business travelers seek accommodations. These hotels will need general managers, executive teams, trainers, managers, supervisors, and staff. You cannot prepare for this sort of expansion without giving careful consideration to where the people will come from and what KSAs they will need in order to perform well in those positions. Preparing for these future global opportunities is part of the planning of those hospitality companies known for strong employee development. Says Bill Marriott Jr., "And, as our JW Marriott brand continues to expand globally, we are focusing our efforts on ensuring that associates at each, individual hotel around the world complete rigorous cultural and functional training based on their location so they can deliver perfectly orchestrated experiences and exceed the expectations of our guests."[35]

Companies often want employees to follow certain preferred career paths that will effectively prepare them to move up into future assignments. For example, some hotel chains require their employees to have a full range of experiences—in the front-of-house, back-of-house, marketing, sales, food and beverage, and rooms divisions—before they can be considered for general manager positions. Ensuring these experiences are provided for potential managers in a chain with dozens of hotels takes careful planning and career tracking of employees.

The most effective organizations know they cannot simply promote someone from a functional task into a management position and hope for the best. Training must be designed to help newly promoted managers make the transition, but the employee must already possess at least some of the necessary knowledge and skills that turning a "super doer" into a supervisor will require.

Giving Employees the Chance to Advance

Employees tend to believe the longer a person is with an organization, the more that person is worth to the organization. This belief is often supported by celebrating anniversary dates with parties and pins to show the organization recognizes and appreciates the employee's commitment.

Pins and parties, however, are not enough. The outstanding service organizations recognize that most, but not always all, individuals' need for personal growth and development must also be satisfied in well-designed career development paths. The

---

[35] "Good Training Leads to Service Excellence," Marriott, last modified April 8, 2011, http://www.blogs.marriott.com/marriott-on-the-move/2011/04/good-training-leads-to-service-excellence.html.

hotel housekeeper should be able to see a path upward through the organization that can be successfully traveled with hard work, dedication, and effort. Too many organizations typecast their employees, and these people know no one expects them to go very far. Indeed, some employees lack the ability or even the desire to move up, and some employees may be quite satisfied to stay in their present positions. Trying to convince a successful bellman at a resort hotel to abandon his tip money and move up as front desk manager is a tough sell because many bellmen are not willing to give up their higher income (much of it in tips) for the lower salary of an entry-level manager with only the hope of long-term career growth prospects.

On the other hand, very few people picture themselves doing in the far future the same thing they are doing today. Humans have a need to grow and develop. People who are helping the organization succeed today should also be getting prepared to help it succeed in the future, and most of them want to. The outstanding organizations provide career paths with development support that give talented people the opportunity to realize their dreams.

The opportunity is symbolically important, even if employees don't choose to take it. For example, the Gaylord Palms Resort sets as a goal to get much of its leadership from internal promotions and includes employee development in its managers' evaluation. To accomplish this, it offers three levels of leadership training. The first and most basic level is offered to all its employees (STARS). The second is for individuals who have been promoted into leadership positions and is designed to give them the tools and skills to help them be effective in their new roles. The third level, for those in positions above entry leadership, provides advanced training in the core processes and procedures needed to operate the hotel, with a special emphasis on the finance and people sides of the business.[36] Even those Gaylord employees who do not enter the leadership program appreciate the fact that their organization makes the opportunity available to any who aspire to lead.

Education

While experience and in-house training are clearly valuable in the preparation for some tasks, certain jobs require formal education. For example, knowledge of accounting, finance, human resources, information systems, marketing, and organizational behavior is necessary for taking on many managerial roles in modern businesses. Chefs are often required to have formalized instruction. Academics, such as the authors of this book, strongly believe that formalized education can help train people to perform well in new areas, think critically, and communicate more effectively. These skills, available primarily through formal education, may be the best way to prepare today's employee for the unknown challenges of tomorrow's competitive environment. Some companies make sure to provide opportunities for employees to get the education they need to grow and develop within the organization.

Tuition Assistance

A good example of how to provide formal education is the traditional employee tuition assistance policy that many organizations use to encourage employee development. Companies may pay all or a portion of tuition in advance for certain programs, or they may reimburse employees upon the successful completion of a course. Recognizing the challenges in attracting and retaining employees with the right attitudes and skills, companies like Starbucks and McDonalds have expanded tuition-assistance programs in recent years to foster employee loyalty and help employees overcome the escalating costs of higher education.[37]

---

[36] Robert C. Ford, Celeste PM Wilderom, and John Caparella, "Strategically Crafting a Customer-focused Culture: An Inductive Case Study," *Journal of Strategy and Management* 1, no. 2 (2008): 143–167.

[37] Vanessa Fuhrmans, "Hotels, Pearson Team for Tuition Program," *Wall Street Journal*, March 1, 2018, B6.

A recent initiative has been launched between the American Hotel and Lodging Association and Pearson AcceleratED Pathways that will allow employees to pursue higher education at no cost to the employees. Ten hotel companies—including Hersha Hospitality Management, Red Roof Inns, and Wyndham Hotels and Resorts—involving 1,500 hotel properties were initial participants of the venture. The program allows employees to get a high school diploma, a cost-free Associate degree, or a low-cost Bachelor's degree.[38]

Of course, any sort of tuition reimbursement program needs to be thought out in advance. Will employees have to reimburse the organization for education payments if they leave the organization within a certain length of time? What is *successful* completion of a course? A? A or B? Not failing? And what courses should employees be allowed to take?

Companies may want to reimburse only for courses directly related to the employee's existing job. This limitation controls the potential tuition expense and makes it more likely the organization will receive some direct business value for the expense. On the other hand, it might be better for both the organization and the employees if the organization pays for any course regardless of field. Doing so expands the total pool of knowledge available to the organization. Consider what could happen if a group of people who are studying different topics in different majors are brought together in a quality circle or problem-solving group session to work on an organizational matter. A variety of learning experiences expands the creative potential of both the employees and the organization and, therefore, increases the possibility of finding new and innovative ways to perform existing jobs and prepare for the future.

Supporting General Education

Supporting any legitimate employee effort to improve, grow, and learn is in the employer's interest. Such support lets employees know the organization values their potential as much as it values their current contributions. Even more important is employee awareness that the organization supports a learning environment. An organization that actively promotes learning of all kinds sends a powerful message to its employees that it believes the only way it will stay competitive is to learn continuously. These learning organizations promote the active seeking of new knowledge that not only benefits the individual but the entire organization by building its total pool of knowledge. No matter how irrelevant the material may seem, the creative employee will use it to connect to organizational needs.

The organization will eventually benefit from whatever creativity the educational experience spurred and from the increased loyalty and feeling of support any employee gets from working for an organization that supports employee learning. Forward-looking organizations understand that most of their profits in ten years will come from products or services they don't even know about today. Restricting educational reimbursement programs to those courses the organization thinks are important today may be as erroneous as trying to predict which products will be around ten years from now.

On the other hand, companies are in business to make money, and the present needs of the business must often be put ahead of the employee's needs for long-term growth and development, important though they may be. Obviously, not all employers can afford to let all employees take time off for tuition-paid courses, nor can many employers even pay partial subsidies for classes taken on an employee's own time. In difficult economic periods, companies may have to worry more about which

[38] "Hotel Industry Partners with Pearson to Offer Debt-free College Degrees to Employees," American Hotel & Lodging Association, last modified February 28, 2018, https://www.ahla.com/press-release/hotel-industry-partners-pearson-offer-debt-free-college-degrees-employees.

employees to lay off than about funding coursework that may have some return in the future. Employee development, like any business cost, must be considered in the context of the broader business picture. While supporting employee growth needs is desirable and beneficial, business needs must come first if the organization hopes to survive in the long run.

The Competition Is Watching

While paying attention to immediate business needs is critically important, many organizations are too short-sighted and don't offer any development programs. Their employees may feel permanently stuck where they are and, as a result, may feel the only path to career advancement lies in opportunities outside their present organization. Some organizations seem to think that keeping their best service employees at the guest-contact level is smart. These employees, however, are likely targets for competitors, who seek out stuck people and invite them to join an opportunity to grow and develop.

They Want Your Best

At least some of your competitors will always seek to hire your best people. Some of your competitors are out in your restaurant or resort right now, handing their business cards to your best employees. Ignoring the needs of the employee to grow and develop may be a money-saving short-run strategy, but it will be a long-run expense. Not giving employees opportunities to grow means the hospitality organization itself may not grow and develop either. The best employees you need for your future can always find opportunities elsewhere to use their talents if you don't give them the chance. The key idea behind organization development is that everyone must continue to grow and develop. Skill and knowledge development is a continuous process. It must be ongoing to meet the ongoing changes in the guest's expectations. It is a never-ending journey.

LESSONS LEARNED

LO 6.1 Explain the importance of training and development to hospitality organizations.

- Develop your people for your organization's future.
- Do more than just believe in your people; champion their training and development.

LO 6.2 Evaluate the need for training.

- Before training people, check the delivery system technology; the problem may lie there.

LO 6.3 Determine what a training program is supposed to accomplish.

- Do not train just to do training; know what outcomes you expect from your training dollars.

LO 6.4 Describe the types of training.

- Training can be provided by content experts or training experts.
- Training teaches more than just new skills to new employees.

LO 6.5 Examine training methods.

- Training comes in many different forms, and they can be delivered in many different ways.
- Use the training method that best accomplishes your goals.

LO 6.6 Discuss the methods used by hospitality organizations to measure the effectiveness of training.

- Training is an investment in your employees; know how you are going to evaluate the effectiveness of this investment.

LO 6.7 Explain the importance of training in long-term development.

- Training is just one part of employee development, which includes helping employees grow professionally and personally over their careers.

KEY TERMS AND CONCEPTS

apprenticeship 199
classroom training 201
coaching 199
cross-functional training 200
e-learning 202
employee development 213
executive education 205
external training 195
internal training 194
internship 200
mentoring 206
needs assessment 191
on-the-job training 197
retraining 196
simulation 202
skills training 195
training control group 208

REVIEW QUESTIONS

1. Virtually all organizations give their employees some training.
   A. "Training frontline employees is more important to hospitality organizations than to manufacturing organizations, because hospitality employees are dealing with people, not widgets." Do you agree or disagree? Discuss.
   B. How can organizations try to find out if the training they provided was effective? Can they ever be sure?
2. This chapter presents Berry's five principles of training. How would you set up a training program to apply these principles to restaurant servers?
3. How should a training program for fine dining and casual dining wait staff be different?
4. The chapter presents several types of training. Match several of those training types to employee types and job types. For example, which techniques described in the chapter might be most effective with restaurant servers? Ride operators at a theme park? Agents at an information booth on a cruise ship?
   A. How do you like to be trained or instructed? Which method or methods work best for you, and why?
   B. If the class shares responses to that last question, how do you account for the differences among students?
   C. How does all that relate to managing the guest experience in hospitality organizations?
5. What does it mean to *develop* employees anyway? Why is it particularly important to develop employees in hospitality organizations?
6. Some types of hospitality organizations typically experience (and accept) a high rate of entry-level employee turnover. Do you think these organizations should develop their entry-level employees to reduce turnover? Or would they simply be spending money to develop employees who will be moving on anyway, possibly to competitors?

ACTIVITIES

1. Interview three friends who have held jobs. Find out which of the chapter's training methods were used to train them. To what extent were any of your friends "developed" as well?
2. Divide into groups. For the group members who have held jobs, make a list of the different training methods that their organizations used. How are they similar to or different from the methods described in the text?

3. The next few times you visit a service provider, take particular notice of your servers. Although you did not see the training they received, do they seem to be conforming to some training and doing the job as it was designed to be done? If not, where are they going wrong, and why?
4. Interview four employees at a restaurant or hotel to discuss their training. Report your findings to the class.

ETHICS IN BUSINESS

In service jobs, training often involves in some ways "manipulating" the customer. This could be training a service worker how to calm down an angry customer, or might go as far as how to manipulate a customer to purchase a product even if the customer may not really need it. Ethically, when does this sort of training go too far? Servers can be trained to perform certain actions in order to increase tips. This may not improve the level of service, but creates subtle changes that research has shown have led to larger tip sizes. Is this appropriate? Salespeople can be trained to identify psychological characteristics of a potential customer and make a sales pitch in a way that evidence suggests is more likely to get that customer to agree to a purchase. Some employees are trained in high pressure sales techniques, based on the evidence that some customers are effectively manipulated in this way, resulting in sales of products the customer may not really need. What level of customer "manipulation" is ethically appropriate? Can anything be justified in terms of increasing organizational profits as long as it is not illegal, or should companies have additional standards?

CASE STUDY

Case 1: The Beef and Reef Mystery Guest

Sally Salkind has worked for two years as a server at the Beef and Reef Restaurant while getting her degree in hospitality management. As a national restaurant chain, the Beef and Reef has specific written standards about how guest service should be provided and posts those standards in the kitchen, where all employees can see them. The chain also allows local managers considerable latitude in training employees and providing service, so long as unit financial results are satisfactory. Most of the servers go "by the book" in serving guests, figuring the company knows best and they can't go wrong by following company standards. But Sally has developed her own very successful way of opening the service encounter and delivering service thereafter. Since manager Bill Gordy has had nothing but good things to say about her performance, she has continued to serve guests in her own style. Apparently, the guests like it; her tips are among the highest and her average check is the highest in the restaurant.

Early one evening, the manager, Bill Gordy, informed the servers of a rumor he heard at a national meeting: corporate headquarters intended to use more mystery shoppers in the following month. He said, "I know you all do the best job possible, and I appreciate it, but next month, let's all lift our service to a new level." About two weeks later, as Sally Salkind started to walk to greet a couple who had just been seated, Bill Gordy whispered to her, "Mystery shoppers. I can tell them a mile away. Do it by the book, Sally, and you'll be fine."

Sally tried to do it by the book: "Good evening. I'm Sally and I'm going to be your server tonight." But then she got tongue-tied. She couldn't remember if the procedure called for her to solicit a beverage order, recite the specials, or encourage the party to choose an appetizer. The rest of the meal went the same way. The party of two had to ask for information Sally usually related in her comfortable, natural way. But when called upon to do it by the numbers, she couldn't remember what the numbers were. She had never been so happy to see two people leave.

Several days later, Bill Gordy called Sally into his office and reprimanded her for not following standard serving procedures at the very time when following procedures was most important.

"Sally, I had been considering promoting you to head server, but I can't promote somebody who can't follow simple instructions."

Sally went quickly from surprise, to shock, to anger. She asked Bill Gordy why, if the procedures posted on the kitchen wall were so important, he had never said anything about them in her two years with the restaurant.

"I'm not dumb, Bill. I can learn as well as anyone. But you never told me that I had to learn that stuff, much less taught me how to do it. You threw me in the water, and, fortunately, I could swim. I did darn well on my own, using my own talents plus some things I learned in my hospitality courses. How can you expect me to change my whole way of doing things with 20 seconds notice?"

Bill Gordy didn't have an answer for Sally's question. He simply reiterated his criticism, told her she had embarrassed him and the restaurant in front of "a big shot from headquarters," and sent her back to her station.

Sally had been thinking of trying to get a permanent position with the Beef and Reef organization after she finished her studies, but she decided she didn't want to work for an outfit that gave her little training in how to do the job, complimented her for the way she did it, then criticized her because she didn't follow formal procedures and memorize the silly little phrases. She would stick around for now because the tip income was good, but she would be looking.

1. What went wrong? Who was at fault?
2. Discuss the pros and cons of a strict set of serving standards for everybody.

Case 2: Flint Hill Beef and Lamb

Just before graduating with a degree in hospitality management, Barbara Hopper interviewed with several hospitality organizations. She was most impressed with Beef and Lamb, a medium-sized restaurant chain founded by Bob Beef and Larry Lamb. She was particularly impressed that Bob and Larry had come to campus to do the interviewing themselves.

Barbara got along well with Bob and Larry. They invited her to corporate headquarters for further interviews, and the impression she made on other Beef and Lamb executives was exceeded only by the impression they made on her. On the second day of her interview series, she was surprised to be offered a selection of several assistant manager positions in different cities. She had relatives and friends in central North Carolina, so she picked Flint Hill, NC, a growing community near Charlotte. The week after her college graduation, she headed for Flint Hill exuberant with optimism.

Smith Hamilton, manager of the Flint Hill Beef and Lamb, had only the day before been told he was being sent an assistant manager. When Barbara entered the restaurant, eager to begin the career she had trained for, make a good impression, and justify the faith that Larry and Bob had shown in her, Smith Hamilton barely gave her the time of day. He told her he was busy but said that she should "make herself useful." Barbara was quite surprised to receive such a reception at the local level, since she had been treated so beautifully by the company founders, but she resolved not to be down about it.

Barbara spent her first day walking around in the restaurant, meeting people, taking notes, asking questions of employees and guests, and generally getting the lay of the land. Since Smith Hamilton was too busy to talk to her on the second day, she spent it in much the same way. By the end of the week, with no help from Hamilton, Barbara had gathered valuable information, given it much thought, and saw numerous ways in which the already successful operation of the restaurant could be improved.

The next day, she made her presentation to manager Smith Hamilton. She was too excited to notice he kept looking at his watch. When she finished, he said: "Young lady, I have made money with this Beef and Lamb restaurant every year since I have been here. I have 18 years of experience in the business, and I've got this restaurant set up just like I want it. Sure, I never went to college, but I know the food business. All you have is book learning. These ideas of yours might look good on a homework assignment, but they will not work in Flint Hill, North Carolina. I don't want all these 'point of sale' machines you talk about; they aren't worth the money. Neither are any of your other ideas. Maybe you ought to interview with Beef and Reef; your highfalutin college notions might be just what that outfit needs. Or you can stick with me and learn something about the restaurant business."

1. How did things go so wrong?
2. Should Barbara bear any part of the blame? Should the institution where she received her training in hospitality bear some blame?
3. If you were Barbara, what would you say to Smith Hamilton, and what would you do? Would you "stick with him and learn something about the restaurant business"?

Further readings on the topics in this chapter are listed in "Additional Readings" on pages 507–509.

Get the tools you need to sharpen your study skills. SAGE edge offers a robust online environment featuring an impressive array of free tools and resources.

Access practice quizzes, eFlashcards, video, and multimedia at **edge.sagepub.com/Ford2e.**

Visit **edge.sagepub.com/Ford2e** to help you accomplish your coursework goals in an easy-to-use learning environment.

Jon Feingersh via Getty Images

7 Serving With a Smile: Motivating Exceptional Service

Hospitality Principle: Motivate and Empower Your Employees

People often say that motivation doesn't last. Well, neither does bathing—that's why we recommend it daily.

—Zig Ziglar, author, salesperson, and motivational speaker

Learning Objectives

After reading this chapter, you should be able to

7.1 Discuss how motivating your employees is just as critical as how you select and train them.

7.2 Describe the different needs employees possess that drive their behaviors.

7.3 Explain how hospitality organizations motivate their employees to provide outstanding guest service.

7.4 Express how empowering employees can make them more motivated and more effective.

7.5 Describe how setting SMART goals can be a powerful way to motivate employees.

7.6 Review the role of teams in changing the way work is done and improving organizational effectiveness.

7.7 Relate the importance of fairness and ethical leadership for maintaining employee motivation.

7.8 State how authority and leadership work in organizations and why employees accept authority.

INTRODUCTION

The service setting is superb, the best employees have been hired and trained, and all the mechanical and back-of-the-house aspects of the delivery system are flawless—so far, so good. Now it's up to that frontline employee you've worked so hard to hire and train to deliver. In almost all guest experiences, the guest-contact employee can make the difference between a satisfied guest and a dissatisfied guest. This employee is also the one who can turn a satisfied guest into a "wowed" guest, who then returns as a loyal customer, ultimately making the exceptional culture, staffing, and training pay off on the bottom line. In the manufacturing sector, the automobile or toaster being assembled doesn't really care about the scowl on the employee's face, the sarcastic comments, or the bad attitude. But people who seek guest experiences are very aware of how employees treat them, and how important this treatment is in the guest's decision to return again to that establishment or even re-patronize any establishment associated with that brand. If the hotel gift-shop clerk makes a comment that offends a guest, the guest will obviously be angry at the employee. Yet, in all likelihood, the guest will also be angry at the hotel that hired and trained the employee, and perhaps even at the brand the hotel represents. Because the guest service employee is so important in the guest's determination of value and quality, hospitality organizations that strive for *positively outrageous service*[1] take great care, as we have seen in previous chapters, in the hiring, training, and development of their employees. But this is not enough to ensure the exceptional service that helps hospitality organizations to succeed.

[1] Scott T. Gross, Andrew Szabo, and Michael Hoffman, *Positively Outrageous Service: How to Delight and Astound Your Customers and Win Them for Life*, 3rd ed. (New York, NY: Allworth Press, 2016), 147.

This chapter focuses on motivating and empowering the hospitality employee to provide a high-quality guest experience. Since quality and value are defined by the guest, the employee who provides the guest experience must be not only well-trained, but highly motivated to meet the guest's quality and value expectations and do so consistently. And, if the role of the hospitality service provider is this important to the organization, the role of the hospitality manager—whose leadership and managerial skills are the most important influence on employee work attitudes and job behaviors—is vital.

MOTIVATING EMPLOYEES

A family was checking in at the Hyatt Grand Cypress on a busy night. The hotel was full, the family's reservation had not been properly handled, and the husband, wife, and three tired children were upset. The front desk employee assessed the situation and acted promptly. She took some quarters out of the petty cash drawer and gave them to the kids to go and play the video games and gave the parents vouchers for free drinks in the lobby bar while she went to find a manager to straighten out the problem. The parents were happy, the kids were happy, and the front desk person had defused a tense situation.

In contrast, consider the experiences of Tom Farmer and Shane Atchison in 2007. They had a confirmed reservation at a hotel, which was held for late arrival with a major credit card. Yet, when they arrived at 2 a.m., they were refused rooms. Tom and Shane publicized their service experience with an open complaint to the hotel called "Yours is a Very Bad Hotel" that went viral.[2] They reported that "Mike the Night Clerk" was "deeply unapologetic," "had done nothing about finding them accommodation elsewhere," and when they suggested that he should have lined up other rooms in advance, Mike the Night Clerk "bristled!" Maintaining the customers were wrong to be upset that their "guaranteed" room was not saved for them, Mike told them, "I have nothing to apologize to you for." After the internet posting, representatives of the hotel did apologize and reportedly improved their training and overbooking policies, but the damage was done: Over ten years later a Google search in 2018 of "Yours is a Very Bad Hotel" still yields reposts of the story, PowerPoint presentations, discussions, press coverage, magazine articles, and many other related links! This bad hotel story is only one of many. Customers and even employees have set up thousands of protest sites to complain about how companies have treated them. These days, through the power of the internet and social media, one unhappy guest or employee can create a public relations disaster for a company.

Both of the above cases began in a similar way: A reservation was not properly handled. But because of the employees' actions, the results were markedly different. The Hyatt employee took a creative path to solve a guest problem, not because she had to, but because she wanted to. Something or someone motivated this employee to act to satisfy a customer despite a problem that was not of her making. On the other hand, Mike the Night Clerk could not have cared less. The challenge for hospitality managers is to discover what makes employees do not only what is in their job descriptions efficiently and competently, but also the extra things that can make the difference for guests and organizations.

The best hospitality organizations have learned the importance of using their employees from the neck up as well as from the neck down. Every guest experience is unique, and any manager who believes it is possible to predefine policies and procedures for handling any and all guest experiences is mistaken. Employees should

[2] There are many web pages that present the entire slideshow. See, for example, "Yours is a Very Bad Hotel," SlideShare, last modified March 30, 2007. https://www.slideshare.net/politicsjunkie/yours-is-a-very-bad-hotel/.

know they are encouraged, empowered, and trusted to handle all of the many and varied situations that come up in the guest service areas for which they are responsible. Even if employees were properly selected and trained, management must continue to encourage them do their jobs with responsibility, skill, enthusiasm, and fun. But how?

The fundamental managerial task employers face is creating the policies, displaying the leadership style, and offering the incentives that get the employees they worked so hard to recruit, select, and train to not only perform their jobs but to do so with a smiling enthusiasm and authentic commitment to serving guests and each other. Although managers often hear that "a happy employee is a good worker," the research doesn't support this. Employees' happiness with their jobs explains less than 10% of their performance. We have all known employees who love their jobs but don't do them very well. Conversely, we have also known very unhappy employees who take enough pride in their work that they provide excellent customer service; or they are so competitive they refuse to let others do better than they do; or they are afraid to do poor work because they need the job. The challenge then is to get the right employees with the right training in the right jobs with the right attitudes. This is the lesson of the service-profit chain—develop organizational and managerial strategies and processes that encourage the employees so effectively that they "wow" the guests so the customers repeatedly return and, thereby, make the hospitality organization successful.

Employee **motivation** is the drive or compelling force that energizes people to do what they do in a given situation. Highly motivated employees are not just working for a paycheck; they are engaged so much with the organization's mission they are willing to work hard to help reach it. Whether the mission is to be a place where guests can have a fun experience, to create a world class lodging experience, or to provide a memorable dining experience, if employees are committed to the organization's mission to the point that its mission is also theirs, they are willing and even inspired to provide extraordinary effort to obtain it. Disney, Four Seasons, and Southwest employees are not only employees, they are fully motivated to fulfill their company's mission.

motivation The drive or compelling force that energizes people to do what they do in a given situation.

The Service-Profit Chain

One of the fundamental concepts of why the role of the hospitality manager is critical can be traced to the classic logic developed by Heskett, Jones, Loveman, Sasser, and Schlesinger in 1994.[3] In their article, they modeled in their **service-profit chain** what they were seeing in the practices of excellent service organizations. The service-profit chain argues that managerial and organizational practices influence employee attitudes, which influence customer satisfaction, which results in customer loyalty, and then ultimately results in profitability.[4] Certainly, you need a good product as well as employees who have been hired and trained appropriately so they have the KSAs needed to perform the job. But, creating the customer satisfaction that leads to a profitable outcome starts with the way in which managers encourage their employees to use their capabilities to perform at their best.[5] This means, in addition to having employees with the right knowledge, skills, abilities, and attitudes—many of which were obtained through selection and developed through training—managers need to motivate their employees to achieve high performance.

service-profit chain The idea that organizational practices affect employee motivation, which affects customer satisfaction, which ultimately affects profitability.

[3] James L. Heskett, Thomas O. Jones, Gary W. Loveman, W. Earl Sasser, and Leonard A. Schlesinger, "Putting the Service-Profit Chain to Work," *Harvard Business Review* 72: 2 (1994): 164–174.

[4] Jens Hogreve, Anja Iseke, Klaus Derfuss, and Tönnjes Eller, "The Service-Profit Chain: A Meta-analytic Test of a Comprehensive Theoretical Framework," *Journal of Marketing* 81, no. 3 (2017): 41–61.

[5] David Solnet, Robert Ford, and Char-Lee McLennan, "What Matters Most in the Service-Profit chain? An Empirical Test in a Restaurant Company," *International Journal of Contemporary Hospitality Management* 30, no. 1 (2018): 260–285.

What Motivates People?

Motivation is a simple idea that is difficult to put into practice. To motivate means to instill a desire within a person that encourages the person to act. In the organizational setting, motivation rests on the idea that people are driven to achieve their own ends and satisfy their own needs. They will give up some control over their own behavior to organizations they join because they believe they will have greater opportunities to achieve their goals and meet their needs by joining an organization than by not joining.

Organizations offer all kinds of inducements for individuals to join them and provide incentives and rewards for employees to stay with them. In return, the companies expect employees to make organizational contributions. Not all of the inducements, rewards, and incentives, though, are necessarily monetary.

Clearly, most people look for employment to satisfy economic needs. That is, they need money to pay bills, feed their families, and buy goods, services, and luxuries. But people join hospitality organizations seeking a wide variety of incentives and rewards—not all of them financial—for which they will, in return, contribute their knowledge, skills, abilities, loyalty, and effort. For example, individuals may join a company to satisfy their needs for friendship and belonging. People may take jobs to satisfy social needs (a great group to work with), recognition needs (being recognized by managers, peers, or customers for their performance), growth needs (challenging work assignments), and achievement needs (a job that lets them exercise their talents). The challenge for the hospitality manager is to discover what incentives and rewards each employee requires as reasons to give up at least some personal control to the organization and exert effort on its behalf. Finding the right combination of incentives and rewards is the hard part of instilling motivation, as employees—like guests—are highly individual persons with their own sets of needs, wants, expectations, capabilities, and behaviors. Managers of hospitality employees need to use the same guestology principles with their internal guests—employees—that they use with their external guest—customers.

In motivating employees, the role of the manager is critical. Managers must (1) understand what employees need and want so that rewards can be aligned with these interests, (2) know what tools are at their disposal to help motivate employees, (3) understand how employees react to both financial and nonfinancial rewards and how these rewards motivate employees to perform, and (4) understand how their roles as managers and leaders are critical for doing all of this effectively and in a way that is seen as fair. This is no easy task, as employees' needs, personal circumstances, and environmental conditions are always changing. Precisely because of these difficulties, a manager's effectiveness as a leader can be judged by how well that person performs in each of these four roles.

THE NEEDS PEOPLE HAVE

Before managers can know how to create systems to motivate and reward employees, they need to figure out what their employees need and want. Theories that try to explain people's needs are numerous.[6] In general, they suggest that people seek to fulfill five levels of needs when joining organizations. The five needs are economic, social, recognition, growth, and achievement. Of course, the degree to which these needs drive behavior will differ from person to person, for any given person at different times, from organization to organization, and from country to country. The task of hospitality managers is to identify which needs are driving the behavior of each of

[6] Gary P. Latham, *Work Motivation: History, Theory, Research, and Practice* (Thousand Oaks, CA: Sage Publications, 2012).

their employees and then to offer each the combination of incentives and rewards that will satisfy or help satisfy those needs. Offering the most effective combination will best motivate employees to exert effort.

Economic Needs

In general, the most basic employee need is for a steady and sufficient stream of income. To meet employee **economic needs**, the most obvious inducement is money provided though a paycheck. While people join organizations for a wide variety of reasons, most people who seek to work for an organization do so in large part because they need to earn a living. For many people across the world, the primary need satisfied by employment is earning enough to pay rent, buy food, and acquire the other basics of living. People do not worry much about their social, recognition, growth, or achievement needs if they are concerned about how they are going to get their next meal, feed their family, find a safe place to stay, or buy warm clothes in the winter. Before offering employees incentives or rewards that can help satisfy their other needs, companies must ensure their employees are paid enough to meet their most basic needs.

economic needs The needs of individuals for a steady and sufficient stream of income, necessary for purchasing the essentials in life (food, housing, and other necessities).

This issue is especially salient for entry-level employees who are at the bottom of the pay scale. If they are to be the first—and sometimes the only—point of contact with the organization's guests, they must not be worried that they may be unable to meet their basic needs. To help ensure they stay focused on the guests and not their economic needs means managers must first attend to these basic needs such as scheduling enough hours, working around child or elder care responsibilities, and helping employees find affordable health care and housing for their families. If Fred Yang is the first person the guest sees when entering your hotel, restaurant, or casino, a first impression by a worried Fred, as he thinks about how long it will be until he has to start his second job or where he and his children are going to sleep tonight, may not be the positive encounter the organization wants the guest to have.

Of course, economic needs go beyond that of just basic survival. Making money allows people to buy luxuries, take a vacation, afford nice housing, raise a family, send kids to college, retire comfortably, and have the sort of freedom and flexibility that having "enough" money provides. A difficulty, though, is when people get more, they often get used to their new circumstances and end up wanting more. This is referred to as the **hedonic treadmill**: the tendency of people to return to a relatively stable level of happiness despite positive (or negative) events, purchases, or life changes. In short, employees will almost always have economic needs. Therefore, no matter how much a given employee makes, economic considerations will always be a major consideration in employment.

hedonic treadmill The tendency of people to return to a relatively stable level of happiness despite positive (or negative) events, purchases, or life changes.

Social Needs

While money is clearly a major motivation for work, it is not the only reason. Most people enjoy being a part of a group or team, and thus have **social needs**. This sense of belonging can be helpful in managing employee direction and behavior in the workplace. Indeed, as studies at the Hawthorne Plant of the Western Electric Company showed nearly a century ago, whether employees feel they do or don't belong greatly influences what they will or won't do in the workplace. Having a "best friend" at work not only makes employees happier and healthier, they are seven times more likely to be engaged in their jobs.[7] Although the main purpose of a work group, obviously, is to work, the group often fulfills the need of members to *belong*.

social needs The needs of individuals to be part of a group.

[7] Emma Seppala and Marissa King, "Having Work Friends Can Be Tricky, but It's Worth It," *Harvard Business Review Digital Articles* (August 8, 2017): 2–4. https://hbr.org/2017/08/having-work-friends-can-be-tricky-but-its-worth-it.

formal group A group of employees that exists because of the formal structure of an organization (a company, a shift, a team, etc.).

informal group A social group that forms without guidance from the organization.

When employees join any organization, they join a **formal group.** This includes the company as a whole, but may also be the team they join or the shift they work. In addition, employees may belong to an **informal group** at the workplace. An informal group refers to a social group that forms without guidance from the organization. The managerial focus here, therefore, should be to establish an environment where employees can work in harmony with informal and formal work groups to support each employee's effort to achieve group goals which will—directly or indirectly—help achieve the organizational goal.

The first managerial challenge in meeting employee belonging needs, then, is to identify those informal groups, in addition to the formal work groups, to which employees belong. This is not always obvious or easy to do. The second challenge is to discover those informal groups' goals. The last is to develop a path to fit the informal groups' goals and the organizations' work group goals together to ensure the satisfaction of both groups' goals, and, ultimately, the satisfaction of the employees in their informal groups and in their organizational groups.

Courtesy of Hilton Hotels

Joining an organization also helps satisfy social needs. Here, employees worked together as part of Hilton's Global Week of Service at the Thuzanna Kari Monastery in Myanmar.

Social groups form alongside or as part of work groups for a variety of reasons. People who work together tend to have things in common: what they do, when they do it, and who they do it with. They not only work together on the job every day but also may end up associating off the job. They have things in common to talk about, shared experiences, and constant reminders of their common basis for acquaintance, which serve as reasons to continue their on-the-job relationships. Since the best hospitality organizations use careful hiring criteria, these people tend to share even more commonalities, which bind them as a group. They frequently share similar values and beliefs, and have many personality traits in common. When you take similar people and put them together in a work setting, where they can talk and work together constantly, you have the basis for forming a work group that is also a friendship group.

Another benefit of formal and informal groups in the workplace is they provide the opportunity to share. Sharing thoughts and ideas about the job has obvious organizational benefits. But being able to share the dreams, ambitions, challenges, joys, and problems of life with someone has great benefits to most people. Groups give the individual a sympathetic ear, reassurance of self-worth, and help and assistance in times of challenges to the individual. The more that group members identify with their group, the more they will look to their groups to affirm their worth, acknowledge their successes, and recognize their achievements. Research shows that the more employees identify with their groups, the more they are willing to engage in helping behaviors, both with co-workers and with the company as a whole.[8] Organizations benefit by finding ways to incorporate informal group goals into the organizational goals.

[8] Steven L. Blader and Tom R. Tyler, "Testing and Extending the Group Engagement Model: Linkages between Social Identity, Procedural Justice, Economic Outcomes, and Extrarole Behavior," *Journal of Applied Psychology 94*, no. 2 (2009): 445–464.

Recognition Needs

Although the need for recognition is stronger in some people than others, everybody likes to be appreciated. **Recognition needs** refer to employees' desire for praise and attention from customers, colleagues, and/or superiors.

recognition needs The needs of individuals for praise and attention from customers, colleagues, and/or superiors.

Recognition needs can be satisfied in a number of ways. Most obviously, a formal recognition program is one way to acknowledge and appreciate stellar performance. But recognition need not always be formalized. It can be conducted on a specified schedule or ad hoc, formal or informal, individual or collective, private or public, and monetary or nonmonetary. Letting employees know they did a good job has a number of advantages. It lets employees know that what they did is indeed desired behavior, and it demonstrates to employees that management is aware of their behaviors and likes what they see. Employee recognition, be it formal or informal, is key to preserving and building the desired organizational culture. Valoir Borland, Corporate Director of Culture Transformation at the Ritz Carlton Leadership Center, emphasized that two important things you can say to an employee are "Thank you" and "That means a lot."[9]

Certainly, the level of employee needs for recognition varies. Some employees desire public recognition, while others are embarrassed by it. Individual recognition may also be more effective in individualistic cultures like the United States and the Netherlands, than in more collectivist cultures like China and Indonesia. Recognition needs also vary by generation, with younger employees desiring more formal and informal recognition than their Baby-Boomer-generation counterparts. Once again, it is important for a manager to identify the level and form of recognition that different employees want so that this need can be filled appropriately.

Growth Needs

Humans possess an almost insatiable desire to learn and grow. An individual's **growth needs** represent the degree to which that person is motivated by learning and challenging work assignments. Many individuals take a job, at least in part, to improve the skills they have worked so hard to develop through prior jobs, experience, and/or education. Individuals with high growth needs want their jobs to contribute to their personal growth, and so they pay particular attention to what they can learn on the job, the nature of the tasks undertaken by the job, and opportunities for promotion.

growth needs The needs of individuals for learning and growing.

Opportunities for personal growth and development is a recurring theme when you examine the characteristics of the Fortune *100 Best Companies to Work For*. Hyatt hotels, for example, touts that its "benefits include basic business networking, mentoring each other and others in their communities and developing professionally"; Cheesecake Factory offers roles as "Designated Trainers" to staff interested in professional growth opportunities; Hilton Hotels touts its Leadership Development Framework, helping develop new leaders and facilitate the growth of existing leaders; Marriott provides an "Emerging Leader Program" designed to provide growth opportunities for women and minorities, providing one-on-one interactions with senior leaders, in-person networking and development sessions, online collaboration with leaders and peers, and challenging "stretch assignments" to expose participants to new and stimulating experiences.[10] These are just a few of the hospitality-specific examples provided by these highly reputed organizations. Nearly all of the companies in the list discuss in some way the opportunities they provide to employees for personal development and growth.

Growth opportunities, however, can be a two-edged sword. The same characteristics—challenge, high job demands, task variety, risk-taking, role

[9] Dawn Bailey, "Is the Customer Really Always Right? A Hotel Company Invests in Its Employees First," NIST, last modified July 27, 2017. https://www.nist.gov/blogs/blogrige/customer-really-always-right-hotel-company-invests-its-employees-first.

[10] "Homepage," Great Place to Work. Great Place to Work Institute, 2017, https://www.greatplacetowork.com/.

ambiguity—that satisfy growth needs can also be a source of stress.[11] Opportunities for personal growth must be balanced with careful employee development. The best managers know that employees have to have the capabilities to succeed if they are to be given the opportunities to grow and develop.

Achievement Needs

achievement needs The needs of individuals for significant accomplishments, setting and meeting high standards, and excelling in what they do.

Individuals also vary in the degree of their **achievement needs**. Employees like to believe that what they do is important and the companies they work for do important things. If employees think their level of service really makes a difference to their customers, their profession, or their community, they will feel a legitimate sense of importance. They will have pride in the jobs they do and in the organization for which they do those jobs. If the employees believe what they are doing is important, they will be highly energized to give incredible effort to make that important task happen. Ritz-Carlton emphasizes this idea with their credo: "The Ritz-Carlton is a place where the genuine care and comfort of our guests is our highest mission."[12]

Tales of Disney's early days report employees who worked incredibly long hours with energy and enthusiasm because they were so committed to what the organization was trying to accomplish. Everyone wanted so badly for Walt's wonderland to work they gave it their all. "I ran my ass off," says one veteran. "I lost fifteen pounds in the first sixty days. You never walked; you got behind the scenes and ran. There was always a fire to put out. I went fourteen months straight without a day off."[13]

Seeing a new establishment—a new hotel, restaurant, amusement park, or any other facility—open and succeed creates an incredibly good feeling of success and achievement in those who made it happen. Additionally, if the community thinks the hotel, restaurant, theme park, or convention center plays a major role in its economic health, all the employees who work there will feel good about their contributions to their community. They will have pride in the jobs they do and in the organization for which they do them. Finding ways to show employees they are contributing to making a real difference in something they feel is important and valued is a key talent of managers in successful hospitality firms. They know how to get the spark of enthusiasm, extra effort, and the strong commitment that a dedicated missionary feels and a clock watcher never does.

Achievement needs can also be fulfilled while satisfying social needs. Since groups offer members the opportunity to achieve something greater by being a part of the group than would have been possible individually, the value of the group becomes greater than merely helping to satisfy social needs. Employment in organizations with strong corporate cultures, whose objectives are respected by the society as a whole, is valuable to both the group and individual. Asking the group to help accomplish the valued, respected organizational purpose becomes a powerful motivational tool for the organization and a potent means for keeping the individual and the group positively involved in the organization's mission. When employees strongly identify with the company and share in the goal of providing exceptional service, they are highly motivated to achieve exemplary customer satisfaction.

THE REWARDS MANAGERS CAN PROVIDE

Once managers know what employees need, they can begin to develop ways to meet those needs. To do so, managers have a variety of financial and nonfinancial tools at

[11] Emin Babakus, Ugur Yavas, and Osman M. Karatepe, "Work Engagement and Turnover Intentions: Correlates and Customer Orientation as a Moderator," *International Journal of Contemporary Hospitality Management* 29, 6 (2017): 1580–1598.

[12] "The Ritz-Carlton Legacy," Marriott, accessed January 9, 2018, http://www.marriott.com/ritz-carlton-careers/history.mi.

[13] David Koenig, *Mouse Tales: A Behind-the-Ears Look at Disneyland* (Irvine, CA: Bonaventure Press, 2012), 27.

their disposal. These tools include financial rewards like wages, bonuses, and group incentives; the most effective hospitality companies also use nonfinancial rewards, like formal recognition programs, to motivate exceptional performance. The best managers also restructure jobs for employees to make the work more rewarding, including making the job itself more fun and empowering employees to more effectively use their knowledge and skills to achieve superb performance.

Financial Rewards

Money serves different purposes for different people. As noted earlier, employees need money for purchasing basic necessities; yet individuals often want to purchase more than what they need to survive, and regularly want to acquire various sorts of luxuries. For all employees, money plays some role in motivating them to perform, but because different people have different needs, desires, and preferences, the best managers realize that money and paychecks are a tricky incentive or reward to manage effectively.

As seen in Exhibit 7.1, money can be offered as an incentive or a reward for employee performance in a variety of ways, and can be used to satisfy a variety of needs. For example, annual performance bonuses reward individual performance. Group financial incentives reward team success and focus employees on working in a group to achieve common goals. Individual tips can encourage high-quality customer service, while pooled tips can encourage servers to work together. Ownership in the company (through stock) helps employees realize that their own success depends on the company's overall success. Depending on how almost any financial reward is presented, it can help satisfy employees' needs, reinforce what is expected from employees, and encourage certain future behaviors. In these ways, various pay methods can be designed to help focus employees on achieving high performance and lowering employee turnover.[14] However, because financial incentives change behaviors, managers need to ensure the performance measures they are using will focus employees on what they want them to do.

Although most people need a job for the income it provides, money alone can go only so far in helping to create the type of personal and emotional attachment to a company that motivates its employees to provide customers with a "wow" experience. Some of this is because of the hedonic treadmill: the positive attitudinal and motivational effects of a raise or bonus diminishes with time, but it is also because many of the reasons people behave as they do are unrelated to money (e.g., being with people they like, joining civic and religious organizations, raising children, helping a stranger, volunteering in the community, caring for parents). Smart managers know that in addition to monetary incentives, nonfinancial incentives—like friendship, fun working environment, altruism, recognition, praise, personal growth, and achievement—can often produce individual effort that money could never buy.

The point is this: managers must discover what needs each employee is seeking to fulfill in the employment relationship and then offer different incentives for different employees that make it possible for each to meet those needs. Managers also need to think beyond incentives, on the way jobs are designed and the authority granted to employees, as a means to motivate exceptional performance.

Recognizing a Job Well Done

The purpose of a **recognition program** is to say, publicly and officially, "thank you" for a job well done. A survey of U.S. firms revealed that nearly 90% of companies have recognition programs, and about 76% of firms have both formal and informal recognition

recognition program A program designed to provide a reward (financial and/or symbolic) to individuals who achieve a notable goal.

[14] Sanghee Park and Michael C. Sturman, "How and What You Pay Matters: The Relative Effectiveness of Merit Pay, Bonuses and Long-Term Incentives on Future Job Performance," *Compensation & Benefits Review* 44, no. 2 (2012): 80–85.

EXHIBIT 7.1

Financial Incentives and Reward Options

PAY FORM	DEFINITION	HOW PERFORMANCE IS ASSESSED	EXAMPLE
Merit raise	An increase in base pay (i.e., a raise) that is tied to individual performance.	Individual performance review	Being rated as an exceptional performer, and so receiving a 5% raise.
Annual performance bonus	A one-time lump sum payment made to an individual based on a performance evaluation.	Individual performance review	Being rated as an exceptional performer, and so receiving a lump-sum bonus that year of $10,000.
Spot bonus	A one-time payment made to an employee who exhibited great performance through some specific act.	Observing a specific incident of exceptional performance	Handling a difficult guest complaint so well that the guest was fully satisfied, so the manager gives the employee a $100 bonus for how she handled the incident.
Individual tips	Voluntary payments given to service providers by the customer after the provider delivered service.	Each service encounter, as judged by the customer	A server who receives a 20% tip from a customer.
Pooled tips	When all customer tips are put into a common "collection" and are then divided evenly between the servers on duty.	Customer rewards for service over all the instances of performance on a given night, and for all servers in the restaurant.	At the end of a shift, all the tips received from customers are divided evenly by the servers on duty that evening.
Recognition program	A program designed to provide a reward (financial and/or symbolic) to employees who make some notable achievement.	Some period of performance (monthly, annual, etc.)	The rooms agent who takes the most reservations in a year is publicly recognized in a ceremony, given a plaque by the CEO and a check for $5,000.
Group incentive plan	A bonus paid to all employees of a group for successfully meeting a specific goal.	Team or company-wide performance	A $100 bonus is paid to employees each month if customer satisfaction ratings exceed a certain level.
Compensation through ownership	When employees actually own a portion of the company.	Stock market performance	Employees are given the option to purchase 500 shares of stock at $20. If the stock price goes above $20, then the employees will benefit from this stock option.

programs.[15] They recognize not only exceptional performance but a variety of other accomplishments—like length of service, innovative suggestions, safety performance, and attendance—as well as providing a means for employees to recognize outstanding

[15] "Trends in Employee Recognition: A Report by World-at-Work," WorldatWork, last modified May 2017. https://www.worldatwork.org/dA/d0815e4c41/trends-in-employee-recognition-2017.pdf.

performance by their peers.[16] The recognition reinforces behaviors that represent the company's cultural values and achievement of the service mission. In the service industry, these awards show employees that their efforts to deliver a "wow" experience to customers are desired, valued, and appreciated.

Courtesy of Hilton Hotels

Hilton's Light and Warmth Award is the company's most prestigious employee recognition.

Fairmont Hotels & Resorts launched a recognition program designed to reinforce the company's service culture. The program featured different award levels, such as *Memory Maker* for outstanding demonstrations of thoughtfulness and creativity, and *Star of the Month* for employees, nominated by their peers, who have consistently demonstrated superior performance. Each Fairmont property recognizes three employees per month for outstanding service: one in front-of-house, one in heart-of-house, and one manager. The nominating committee includes managers and one executive, but is composed mostly of hotel staff.[17] This sort of recognition program helps support the organizational culture of appreciation and recognition for everyone, from housekeepers to senior management, and for all Fairmont employees around the world. Winners received gift certificates in small denominations (typically $10–$50 in value) that could be redeemed with thousands of merchants around the world. Surveys of Fairmont's employees after the program was implemented revealed that employees felt more recognition for a job well done, that the best performers were more likely to receive recognition, and that they were being recognized in a way that was personally meaningful. Surveys also showed employee levels of motivation increased significantly following the program's inception.

While many programs offer cash awards alone, many others offer symbolic, non-cash rewards or gifts—like plaques or certificates, merchandise with the company logo, jewelry, electronics, food, travel, office accessories, household items, recreational items, and electronic goods.[18] A key advantage of these non-cash awards is that they often create a lasting memory of the experience for the employee, which proves more effective in achieving employee satisfaction than cash awards. While cash is usually spent immediately on things that people may or may not remember (often, for such things as paying bills), non-cash rewards tend to serve as long-lasting reminders of company appreciation. Moreover, the cost of non-cash awards—from the plaque on the wall, to the trophy on the desk, to photos from the special vacation—is often insignificant when compared to the high level of recognition. For example, a special pin that announces an employee's outstanding service may cost only $20, but its emotional impact on the employee, wearing it for all to see and perhaps keeping it for a lifetime, is far greater than the impact of simply receiving a twenty-dollar bill. The way the reward is presented can also be a powerful symbol. Having the CEO of the company personally recognize excellent performance sends a clear signal that indeed the company values stellar performance.

Making the Job Fun

Not all rewards for working well have to come in the form of cash, an incentive, a plaque, or a prize item. Sometimes, the work itself can be its own reward. Chili's Norman Brinker said, "If you have fun at what you do, you'll never work a day in

[16] "Trends in Employee Recognition," 2017.

[17] "Fairmont Stands Out with Employee Recognition Programs," GO2 Tourism HR Society, accessed January 9, 2018. https://www.go2hr.ca/articles/fairmont-stands-out-employee-recognition-programs.

[18] "Trends in Employee Recognition," 2017.

your life. Make work like play—and play like hell."[19] Southwest Airlines specifically embraces "Fun" as part of its values, emphasizing the "Southwest Way" includes having a "Fun-LUVing Attitude."[20]

Courtesy of Southwest Airlines

Making work fun is one way to help keep employees motivated. As just one example, Southwest employees compete each year in a "plane pull."

Some jobs may never be completely fun, but to whatever extent managers can establish an enjoyable atmosphere, the organization will benefit. Fun is contagious. People having fun at work tend to infect peers as well as guest-customers. Customers of hospitality organizations expect to deal with happy people; they expect to be greeted with a smile. A happy work setting can not only enhance sales but can improve employee retention, morale, and recruitment.[21] It is simply more enjoyable to go to work in an organization that is fun than in one that is not. Of course, the fun has to help achieve the organization's goals. As one manager stated, "We don't take ourselves seriously, but we take what we do very seriously." You want the job to be fun but not in ways that employees are just playing around and ignoring their job duties and customer service responsibilities.

Minimizing the Negatives

Another way to make a job enjoyable is to eliminate or minimize the things that make it uninteresting or unpleasant. In all jobs, there exist some parts that are never fun or interesting or challenging, but they must be done. Managers can motivate employees by providing fun ways to minimize these less attractive aspects. Good managers add fun elements to jobs to break the monotony, boredom, or annoyances. Anyone operating the *It's a Small World* attraction at the Magic Kingdom must receive some relief from the constant repetition of the attraction's distinctive theme song. Likewise, anyone walking backward loading a constant stream of guests on Epcot's Spaceship Earth while ensuring the guests are properly seated needs a break from this repetitive task. If employees have jobs like these, managers should consider rotating them to other jobs in other locations from time to time, or find other fun ways to break the routine or escape the monotony.

Motivating employees whose jobs contain monotony and boredom is hard enough. Motivating employees whose jobs have downright unpleasant aspects is even more difficult. As we mentioned in Chapter 5, service jobs often require significant emotional labor, which can be just as fatiguing as physical labor. Imagine being an airline lost-baggage representative, a customer service representative dealing with passengers of late or cancelled flights, or a front desk agent who has to listen politely while an angry customer lodges a complaint. As comedian Bill Engvil put it, "Who applies for that job? Who says 'I want to work in lost luggage?' You don't have a good day."[22] The demands of emotional labor for jobs that require polite and reasonable interactions in the face of angry or difficult customers are extremely taxing, but they must be done by someone. Helping reduce the impact of negative situations will help keep employees more motivated overall.

---

[19] Norman Brinker and Donald Thomas Phillips, *On the Brink: The Life and Leadership of Norman Brinker* (Irving, TX: Tapestry Press, 2002), 195.

[20] "Culture," Southwest Airlines, accessed on January 9, 2018, https://www.southwest.com/html/about-southwest/careers/culture.html.

[21] Robert C. Ford, Frank S. McLaughlin, and John W. Newstrom, "Questions and Answers about Fun at Work," *People and Strategy* 26, no. 4 (2003): 18–33.

[22] "Blue Collar Comedy Tour: The Movie," directed by C.B. Harding (2003; Burbank, CA: Warner Home video, 2007), DVD.

Managers of the best organizations appreciate the emotional price these employees pay and seek to minimize or compensate for the negative aspects of all jobs. Some organizations offer stress-reduction programs, such as physical exercise and time off from the stressful aspects of jobs. Others offer counseling. The most common approach is to encourage employees to apply their professional standards (e.g., a nurse dealing with a dying infant), use scripted behaviors (e.g., "Welcome to McDonalds, how may I serve you?"), or use a variety of other strategies that allow the employee to cope with the stress-creating situation.

Mark Wilson/Getty Images

Some jobs really can't be made fun. It is hard to imagine a good day working in Lost Luggage.

Angry and unhappy guests present a challenge. Managers must find ways to help employees who have to deal with such guests so they don't lose their ability to do their jobs or angrily retaliate against an angry customer. But, as we shall discuss later in this book (Chapter 13), dissatisfied guests are also an opportunity for the company, and the people who interact with these guests must be skilled, emotionally ready to deal with them, and effective at maintaining their professional poise while solving the problems that caused the dissatisfaction.

Empowering the Employee

In addition to motivating employees by means of an incentive plan, through recognition, and by making the work environment more enjoyable, organizations can change the responsibilities associated with a job to help fulfill the company's mission. One important strategy for accomplishing this is **empowerment.**

empowerment Giving employees authority and responsibility to make decisions and gain greater control over their work.

What Is Empowerment?

Empowerment is the assignment of decision-making authority and responsibility to an individual. It requires sharing information and organizational knowledge that enables empowered employees to understand and contribute to organizational performance. It is best accomplished by giving employees the authority to make decisions that influence organizational outcomes and rewarding them based on the organization's performance. When organizations empower their employees, they often find the employees become more motivated to fulfill the company's mission. As Norman Brinker said, "If I tell you what to do, then the task is my responsibility, not yours. But if I inspire you to act on your own, the responsibility and results are yours. The difference in dedication is phenomenal."[23]

The concept of empowerment is broader than the traditional concepts of delegation, decentralization, and participatory management. Empowerment can stretch responsibility for decision-making beyond a specific decision area within a job to include decision responsibility for the entire job and for knowing how performing on that job fits within the organization's overall purpose and mission. It sends a powerful message to the employee that he or she is trusted. Empowered employees know their managers trust them to make the right decision at the right time to enable the guest to get the service expected. Because no one can predict everything that can happen

[23] Brinker and Phillips, 194.

when a guest has a moment of truth with an employee, it is impossible to prescribe in advance how to deal with all guest encounters. Empowered employees know what to do, know what their company expects of them, have the ability to do it, and can make the difference in turning an "ow" situation into a "wow" situation.

One of the most widely known examples of empowerment in hospitality is the approach used by The Ritz-Carlton. Empowerment there extends beyond simply planning how work is done: it is a core component of The Ritz-Carlton culture. Indeed, empowerment is number three in the company's twelve service values: "I am empowered to create unique, memorable, and personal experiences for our guests." If guests are unhappy, The Ritz-Carlton employee is authorized to spend up to $2,000 to make them happy again without approval from upper management. Actually spending the money, though, is typically a last resort. Ritz-Carlton employees often pride themselves on resolving a guest's issue without having to resort to financial recompense. The size of the amount was chosen to send a clear message that the employee owns the problem and is supposed to find a way to ensure the guest is happy. As Joseph A. Michelli describes it, "This financial authority is the living embodiment of trust and power conferred to each staff member at The Ritz-Carlton."[24]

Rick Eglinton/Toronto Star via Getty Images

The Ritz-Carlton is famed for its employee empowerment.

While empowerment may make the job more fun and interesting for employees, it also presents them with an opportunity for growth and development, which makes the job itself more interesting. The organization also benefits from employees who are not only well trained, but also authorized to use their skills and capabilities to provide an outstanding guest experience. As the legendary restaurateur Norman Brinker said, "You can achieve so much more by empowering people to achieve on their own. Don't be too hands-on."[25] The empowered server can personalize the service experience to meet or exceed each guest's expectations and can take whatever steps are necessary to prevent or recover from service failure.

Some organizations talk the talk of employee empowerment without giving employees any real power or authority to implement decisions. The purpose of employee empowerment is not only to ensure that effective decisions are made by the right employees, but to make sure these employees actually have the authority and responsibility to make those decisions. Empowerment also means that management is willing to share relevant information about and control over factors related to effective job performance. While management still needs to provide job performance guidelines, define the mission, and set goals, empowerment sends a powerful signal of sharing with employees the responsibility and authority to find ways to deliver excellent service and resolve customer problems.

In the short-run, empowerment changes how decisions are made; in the long run, empowerment helps achieve an organization's mission. For example, Hyatt felt it was not doing enough to provide an authentic hospitality experience to its most loyal customers: its Gold Passport Members. Hyatt decided to empower employees to perform what it called *random acts of generosity*. Gold Passport Members started to find their bar tab paid, or they might receive a complimentary massage, or their family's breakfast might be paid for by the hotel—all because an empowered employee saw a way to enhance a loyal customer's hotel stay by doing

[24] Joseph A. Michelli, *The New Gold Standard: 5 Leadership Principles for Creating a Legendary Customer Experience Courtesy of the Ritz-Carlton Hotel Company* (New York, NY: McGraw-Hill, 2008), 110.
[25] Brinker and Phillips, 192.

something special. The company could have dictated a set of policies that told employees how to surprise and delight guests (such as, if guests do X, then give them Y). Instead, Hyatt empowered their employees to find a situation and then decide on how to provide a "wow" element to a customer's experience.

When successfully implemented, empowerment has several benefits for both employees and managers. It tells employees the organization trusts them to know what to do, how to do it, and trusts them to do it well. Nothing frustrates people more than being hired and trained to do a job, and then having the manager constantly look over their shoulders to be sure they are doing it right. Empowerment treats employees as respected adults. Managerial unwillingness to allow employees to make the decisions they are both capable of making and willing to make can lead to a loss of employee self-respect, a loss of self-confidence that they can do their jobs, and a loss of interest in doing them. Empowerment builds self-respect, self-confidence, and interest.

Empowerment also benefits the hospitality manager. No one can be everywhere all the time. How employees behave when an overly controlling manager is away or unavailable can be a problem. Employees can be either helpless or empowered. Those who cannot make decisions on their own become helpless, and ultimately useless (or worse) when their boss is not present, but the empowered do their jobs as their managers hoped they would even without managerial oversight. Another benefit is that organizations simply cannot train people to solve every problem that may occur in their jobs. But if employees know the organization's mission and goals and understand and believe in the organization's culture, they can be empowered to make the right decisions. Former Southwest Airlines CEO Herb Kelleher said, "I can't anticipate all of the situations that will arise at the stations across our system. So what we tell our people is, 'Hey, we can't anticipate all these things; you handle them the best way possible. You make a judgment and use your discretion; we trust you'll do the right thing. If we think you've done something erroneous, we'll let you know—without criticism, without backbiting.'"[26] Saying the same thing with fewer words, John Caparella, opening manager of the Gaylord Palms, told his employees, "Do the right thing."[27] No one can anticipate, train, and prepare for every possible problem, outcome, or customer request. Empowerment enables employees to act when the circumstances are new, unique, or unexpected.

Empowerment Implementation

Successful implementation of employee empowerment requires organizations to take some key steps. Empowerment cannot simply be decreed; it requires an investment in training employees so that they know how to use their new decision-making freedom effectively, training managers so they know what types of decision responsibility should be given to those trained employees, and ensuring systems are in place so employees are provided the information they will need to make those decisions. Of course, organizations must also recognize that not every employee can be empowered to solve all problems, so it should be implemented only where the key prerequisites are present.

The five keys to implementing an effective empowerment program are as follows:

1. *Managerial buy-in.* Management must be willing to empower employees, let them make their own decisions, and not interfere. An empowerment program will not work if managers cannot learn to trust the capabilities of empowered employees. If managers who let their people make decisions end up changing,

[26] Kevin Freiberg and Jackie Freiberg, *Nuts! Southwest Airlines' Crazy Recipe for Business and Personal Success* (Austin, TX: Bard Press, 1996), 289.

[27] Duncan Dickson and Robert Ford, "'We only need one rule.' Growing a Service Culture: An Interview with John Caparella, President and Chief Operating Officer The Venetian Las Vegas, The Palazzo Las Vegas, and Sands Expo and Convention Center." *Journal of Applied Management and Entrepreneurship* 17, (2012): 98–114.

overriding, or otherwise not using these decisions, employees were not really empowered in the first place. A commitment to empowerment must begin at the top of the organization.

2. *Training.* Empowerment requires an investment in employee training. Employees must learn to understand their areas of responsibility thoroughly. Then they must learn how to make sound decisions within their areas.
3. *Willingness.* Empowerment requires employees to not only be ready and able to make decisions about their jobs, but also be willing to do so. If the employees are uninterested in the company and its future, empowering them to make decisions will be risky.
4. *Measurement.* Employees must have goals or standards against which the results of their decisions can be measured. Otherwise, they will not know either what they should do or if their decisions were good or bad.
5. *Incentives.* Rewards need to be attached to successful performance. To be most effective, an incentive system rewards employees for making good decisions. Rewards help reinforce the goals of the program and make it clear to employees that using their empowerment appropriately is worthwhile.

Limitations and Potential of Empowerment

Of course, not all organizations can benefit equally from employee empowerment. Empowerment may be less appropriate if (1) the basic business strategy emphasizes low-cost, high-volume operations, (2) the tie to most customers is short term, (3) the business environment is highly predictable, and (4) employees have low growth needs, low social needs, a poor ability to communicate, and/or weak interpersonal skills. Alternatively, employee empowerment can be highly successful and rewarding if (1) service is customized or personalized, (2) customer relationships are long term, (3) the environment is unpredictable, and (4) employees have high social, growth, and recognition needs, a good ability to communicate, and strong interpersonal skills. Under these circumstances, the potential gains from employee empowerment are significant. Although the hospitality industry generally does not use complex technology, nearly every guest-contact situation is customized and unique. If you have selected and trained the right employees, employee empowerment will lead to most guest-contact decisions benefiting the organization.

Degrees of Empowerment

Of course, empowerment is not an absolute; it has degrees. Managers may find that more is not necessarily better. Employees need to be capable of making appropriate decisions. Robert Teerlink, former head of Harley-Davidson, said, "If you empower idiots, you get dumb decisions faster." A manager may choose to provide higher degrees of empowerment for some individuals and teams doing certain tasks than for others. Indeed, even within a given employee's job or a given group's task responsibilities, different decision areas can be empowered to different degrees. A restaurant chain, for example, may empower its restaurant managers with complete authority to resolve customer complaints, but it may not let the same managers make even minor modifications to the menu.

Since the workforce is so diverse, some employees will be better suited for empowerment than others. Part-time employees or contract (temporary) employees may not be interested enough in the goals of the organization or in a long-term relationship with it to be good candidates for empowerment programs. One aspect of good management is to determine what degree of empowerment to extend to different employees based on an assessment of the five keys discussed earlier.

Unintended Consequences of Empowerment

Organizations must be careful to ensure empowerment is accompanied by good communication. Empowerment can lead to problems if empowered employees make decisions that are disadvantageous to other employees or to the organization as a whole if one empowered employee does not know what another empowered employee is doing. For example, if a desk agent allows guests to check out two hours late, the housekeeping staff may have difficulty in preparing the room for the next guests, especially if another empowered desk agent allows them to check in early. The actions or decisions of an empowered employee must not be allowed to affect other employees negatively in the performance of their jobs as that will in turn affect the organization's ability to deliver a service experience that meets their guests' expectations.

WAYS REWARDS CAN MOTIVATE

Once you have hired qualified people, trained them, and have identified their various needs, you have the challenge of keeping them interested in the specifics of their jobs. Knowing what employees need and want is only half the battle; you need to figure out how you are going to connect rewards and behaviors. As we have now discussed, there are many different motivational forces: individuals' needs (economic, social, recognition, growth, and achievement), as well as rewards the organization can provide (financial, recognition, fun, and empowerment). At the same time, every person is unique, and the exact needs and wants of employees will vary considerably.

Individual, Generational, and Cultural Differences

While all people are different, and we expect that there will be some variation across all individuals in terms of what they want and what motivates them, there are some general differences in needs and wants that are a function of individuals' backgrounds, including their generation and culture. Younger workers, for example, tend to place a greater emphasis on feedback, recognition, and growth; older workers place more emphasis on economic needs and financial rewards.[28] There are also notable differences in preferences across cultures (national, but also organizational). For example, cultures that are more individualistic favor individual-based rewards (e.g., raises, individual bonuses, individual recognition), whereas group-oriented cultures favor broader rewards systems (e.g., team rewards, profit sharing, employee ownership).[29] Cultures that are more risk seeking prefer pay-for-performance plans.[30]

Depending on where your organization is located, the characteristics of your organizational culture, and the demographics and other characteristics of your workforce, you need to determine the connection between rewards and behaviors so that, in the process of fulfilling your employees' needs, you can elicit from them the exceptional performance that you desire. You may satisfy these needs through financial incentives, job restructuring, recognition programs, and empowerment. The key issue is to understand how these motivational tools work to produce the desired behaviors.

---

[28] Mohammad Faraz Naim and Usha Lenka, "Development and Retention of Generation Y Employees: A Conceptual Framework," *Employee Relations: The International Journal* (2018).

[29] Nemanja Berber, Michael J. Morley, Agnes Slavić, and József Poór, "Management Compensation Systems in Central and Eastern Europe: A Comparative Analysis," *The International Journal of Human Resource Management* 28, no. 12 (2017): 1661–1689.

[30] Nicholas R. Prince, J. Bruce Prince, Bradley R. Skousen, and Rüediger Kabst, "Incentive Pay Configurations: Bundle Options and Country-Level Adoption," *Evidence-Based HRM: A Global Forum for Empirical Scholarship* 4, no. 1 (2016): 49–66.

The Power of Positive Reinforcement

positive reinforcement Providing rewards to employees for organizationally approved behaviors—namely, those associated with high levels of guest satisfaction—to encourages repetition of those behaviors.

A well-accepted psychological principle is that if you reward desired behaviors and don't reward undesired behaviors, you will get more of the desired behaviors and fewer of the undesired ones. Rewarding desired behaviors is called **positive reinforcement**. While the idea seems simple enough, providing appropriate positive reinforcement is no simple task. Rewarding the wrong behavior can create as many problems as not rewarding the right behavior. Managers need to review their words and actions constantly and carefully to ensure the behaviors being rewarded are the behaviors they and the organization really want. If the proverbial "squeaky wheel" employee who constantly complains is the one who seems to get the manager's attention, it won't be long before the other employees realize the way to get their manager's attention is to complain. Behavior that is rewarded with the manager's attention will not only be repeated by the complainer but copied by everyone else as well. Managers need to think carefully about their actions and what they are rewarding with those actions.

All rewards need to be scrutinized carefully to determine exactly what is being incentivized. GuestFirst Hotels, for example, may tell its employees they should make every effort to satisfy the guest, but employees will quickly realize customer satisfaction is not really the priority if GuestFirst managers actually evaluate and reward only according to whether employees meet the budget numbers. This type of managerial misdirection is called *the folly of rewarding A while hoping for B*[31] and it is folly for any organization whose managers engage in it. Depending on how the reward systems are constructed, individual bonuses may discourage teamwork; a reward plan based on customer satisfaction ratings may cause employees to provide too many free upgrades; a profit-sharing plan may focus employees on short-term cost-cutting rather than long-term exceptional customer service. Over time, everyone figures out exactly what behaviors are being rewarded. As a result, most employees will focus on management's actions and not their words about the importance of customer service.

At the Buffet

A popular buffet restaurant decided to add a greeter position to welcome guests as they entered the restaurant. Manager Gail Bowman told newly hired Charles Jones explicitly that his primary responsibility was to greet and welcome the guests. As time went on, however, to keep Jones busy when guests were not entering the restaurant, Bowman added responsibilities to the position—such as checking periodically to make sure there were enough trays or that the butter dish was always full. Jones quickly realized that Bowman never complimented him for properly greeting the guests, nor did she ever say anything to him when he missed a guest because he was too busy with his other duties. However, if he ever let the buffet line run out of trays or butter, Bowman strongly reprimanded him. By both her actions and lack of action, Bowman implicitly redefined the job description. She made her real priorities clear (in the mind of Charles Jones, at least), and therefore he adjusted his actions accordingly.

The point is that *what gets rewarded tends to be what gets done*. Managers must remember to reinforce preferred behaviors by providing the right incentives in the right amounts at the right times. If you want your employees to exert appropriate effort, you must be clear and consistent about what you reward.

Linking Performance and Rewards

A critical part of the manager's job, in addition to identifying the mix of incentives or rewards that each employee needs, wants, and expects, is to define how each employee

[31] Steven Kerr, "On the Folly of Rewarding A, While Hoping for B," *Academy of Management Journal* 18 no., 4 (1975): 769–783.

can get those rewards. **Expectancy theory** maintains that organizations need to relate rewards directly to performance. If employees believe or expect (1) that they can achieve a certain performance level by putting in a certain level of effort, (2) that achieving this performance level will most likely lead to promised rewards, and (3) if employees value these rewards sufficiently, they will be motivated to put in the effort necessary to get the rewards. While employees must of course have the right knowledge, skills, and abilities and be given specific goals so they clearly know their job responsibilities, offering desired rewards and establishing expectations that effort will lead to receiving those rewards is a critical managerial responsibility for motivating excellent performance.

expectancy theory The idea that organizations need to relate employee rewards directly to performance. If employees believe or expect that they can achieve a certain performance level by putting in a certain level of effort, that achieving this performance will lead to promised rewards, and if employees value these rewards sufficiently, then they will be motivated to put in the effort necessary to get the rewards.

Based on expectancy theory, managers must take several essential steps in order to motivate employees to perform effectively. First, they must give their employees the confidence that their skills, training, and capabilities are adequate for doing what is necessary to receive rewards if they put in the effort. That is, employees must possess sufficient **self-efficacy.** Second, managers must ensure employees believe that if they exert effort and perform their jobs well, management will deliver the rewards as promised. The rewards can be financial, but could also include personal growth opportunities, recognition, or even time doing more enjoyable tasks. If employees do not trust management to deliver the promised rewards, they will not be motivated to exert any effort to obtain them. Third, they must provide the array of rewards that employees believe are important and worthwhile to satisfying their needs. Whether it is the value or recognition the reward provides or opportunities for growth or achievement, employees must want the reward to motivate high performance.

self-efficacy The belief of employees that their knowledge, skills, and abilities are sufficient to perform at the desired level.

This theory puts a major burden on managers to *manage*. Managers need to ensure their employees are properly trained; that they have the right people in the right jobs to do the work; that they carefully detail the job's requirements; that they identify, offer, and then deliver the rewards that have value to their employees; and that they behave fairly toward them. If Mary is told she will get the trip to Hawaii she has always wanted if she books the big convention she has been working on and she succeeds, then management had better give her the trip to Hawaii. Otherwise, she and everyone she talks to will not be very motivated to give the job much effort in the future as they will not believe that management will deliver on its promises. A manager who fails to meet an internal customer's expectations will need to find and fix that failure with the same commitment and effort the manager would use to find and fix a failure in meeting the expectations of an external guest.

Managing Fairly

Employees also want to be treated fairly by their managers and the organization, and successful managers seek ways to ensure they are. According to **equity theory,** we compare what we get out of an endeavor (the outputs) to what we put into it (our inputs) and draw a conclusion as to the fairness of the ratio of the two. We may have an internal standard of comparison, or we may compare ourselves to other people both inside and outside our organizations. If we think we are getting a fair deal, we are satisfied. If we think we are getting less than we deserve, we feel unfairly treated. According to the theory, research, and common sense, employees who feel fairly treated are more motivated to perform on behalf of their organization than employees who feel unfairly treated. Employees who feel unfairly treated will seek to restore their sense of what is fair by reducing their motivation to perform to a level they feel is fair.

equity theory The theory that people consider what they get out of an endeavor (the outputs) and what they put into it (the inputs) and draw conclusions as to the fairness of the endeavor by comparing their ratio of outputs to inputs to the perceived ratio of others.

The challenge when trying to manage fairly lies in figuring out how or with whom your employees are comparing their inputs and outputs and, if the comparison is external, in trying to understand how employees value the inputs and outputs of both parties. Managers who seek the superior performance that distinguishes excellent organizations from the merely average must be alert to the equity comparisons their employees make. Employees are, ultimately, volunteers. They can choose to leave their jobs whenever they want to. And nothing undermines voluntary performance faster than a feeling of being treated inequitably. Employee feelings of inequity lead to lower performance, less positive customer interactions, greater dissatisfaction, and increased turnover.

Justice in the Workplace

In the last few decades, research on equity theory has expanded into consideration of organizational justice to examine how fair and unfair treatment by managers, supervisors, and co-workers affects employee behaviors. Regarding employee reactions to how fairly or justly they are treated, three forms of justice have been examined: distributive justice (i.e., fairness of decision-making outcomes), procedural justice (i.e., fairness of decision-making processes), and interactional justice (i.e., the extent to which the individual is treated with dignity and respect in the decision process). A multitude of studies confirm what common sense suggests: When employees feel treated fairly by their organization and other organizational members, they tend to be more committed to their organization, have higher levels of job satisfaction and performance, and engage in more helpful behaviors and fewer harmful behaviors.[32] Employees who feel unjustly treated tend to be absent or call in sick more often, have poor morale, and may even steal from the company. They also do not sound or act happy with their customers.

Of most interest to a hospitality manager is the relative importance of these three types of justice in influencing employee outcomes. Procedural justice plays the largest role. Surprisingly, it isn't fairness in the rewards that employees receive that most determines their feelings of fairness. Instead, when employees feel the process that led to the reward decisions was fair, they will have more positive perceptions of their companies. Yet it is also critical that, in this process, they are treated respectfully. Ultimately, just like with customers, when there is a problem, it is often the process used to address the problem and the treatment of the employee in the process that matters more than the actual compensation that may or may not be received.

At the other extreme, employees who initially feel they got more than others in similar situations eventually conclude they deserve what they got. For a short time they may feel guilty they were overly rewarded and may work harder to justify what they got, especially in the eyes of their fellow workers. For example, an employee who has received an apparently unjustified pay increase may come to work earlier and stay later—but only for a few weeks, if that long. Employees inevitably talk with each other about how fairly they are treated in rewards and especially their pay. Given that employees talk anyway about such things, it may be in the managers' interest to publicly disclose how pay, promotion, and other rewards are decided. When employees don't know the actual process by which these outcomes are awarded, they assume unfairness.

Pay Secrecy

Whether to keep salary figures (and really any sort of rewards information) private or make them public is increasingly an organizational fairness concern that the leaders of many organizations discuss. On one hand, many employees (and employers) feel pay is a private issue and don't want that sort of information made public. Employers also often feel making pay information public leads to comparisons and discontent that can be avoided by keeping pay information secret. On the other hand, when people do not know what others are getting paid, they tend to assume wider salary disparities than actually exist. These assumptions can lead to feelings of inequity.

[32] For example, Jason A. Colquitt, Donald E. Conlon, Michael J. Wesson, Christopher OLH Porter, and K. Yee Ng , "Justice at the Millennium: a Meta-analytic Review of 25 Years of Organizational Justice Research," *Journal of Applied Psychology* 86: 3 (2001): 425–445; Yochi Cohen-Charash and Paul E. Spector, "The Role of Justice in Organizations: A Meta-analysis," *Organizational Behavior and Human Decision* Processes 86, no. 2 (2001): 278–321.

Some academics advocate publishing everyone's salary, in the hope that accurate information will reduce feelings of inequity, if in fact salaries are equitable. When everyone's pay is published, no one has to guess what someone else is being paid. In this case, everyone can see what behavior gets the highest rewards. However, since organizations realize that equity is in the eyes of the beholder, many of them are reluctant to publish actual payroll data because of privacy concerns and because they fear raising equity concerns in the minds of employees who might have thought their salaries were fair until they saw the full salary figures. Although pay secrecy rules are generally illegal in the United States, most companies still keep pay information confidential, and many employers still actively discourage employees from discussing pay.[33]

Setting Goals

Another way managers can clarify their expectations for employees, and at the same time motivate better performance, is by setting goals. Goals can not only be set for an employee's performance outcomes, but also for learning needs and behavioral expectations.[34] Most managers are familiar with the motivational effects of **goal setting** for individual employees and units. Research has repeatedly shown that setting specific and challenging (but attainable) goals lead to higher performance levels than expressing vague goals or simply telling people to "do their best."[35] Organizations should seek to create **SMART goals**; that is, goals that are **S**pecific, **M**easurable, **A**ttainable, **R**esults oriented, and **T**ime bound.[36] Specific and measurable goals allow people to know where they are supposed to be heading and what it will look like when they get there. They are a powerful means to achieve attainable, result-oriented, and time-bound outcomes. Goal setting that follows these SMART rules is an excellent motivational tool. Most employees want to do the job for which they were hired and are frustrated when they don't have SMART goals set. Moreover, SMART goals allow people to self-manage since they can show clearly and objectively whether behaviors at work are leading toward or away from the set goals. They provide a means to keep everyone's efforts aligned with the organizational purpose since the goals are directly connected to the organization's mission. Finally, specific and measurable goals are a way to keep people from wasting time doing things that do not need doing. When goal setting is used in conjunction with a clear mission statement, a strong organizational culture, the right incentives, and appropriate training, people will be more productive, more satisfied, and happier.

goal setting Setting goals for individual employees and units for the purpose of motivating higher performance. Setting specific and challenging goals can lead to higher performance levels than merely setting vague goals or telling people to do their best.

SMART goals Goals that are Specific, Measurable, Attainable, Results-oriented, and Time-bound.

The goal-setting process has two desirable organizational outcomes. First, it produces a logical and complete plan of how each part of the organization will contribute to the overall success of the hotel, convention bureau, restaurant, resort, or local attraction. Second, it demonstrates to all members of the organization how what they do adds value to the organization's ability to achieve its mission. Employees perform more effectively when they know how they are contributing to organizational success, and the goal-setting process communicates in specific terms what they need to do in order to make their contribution.

An Example: Management by Objectives

Organizations often make their goal-setting process systematic by incorporating Peter Drucker's **Management by Objectives (MBO).**[37] MBO is a process of having each employee set specific and measurable goals, and then using the achievement of

Management by Objectives (MBO) A process of having each employee set specific and measurable goals, and then using the achievement of those goals as a key driver for that employee's performance assessment.

[33] Jake Rosenfeld, "Don't Ask or Tell: Pay Secrecy Policies in US Workplaces," *Social Science Research* 65 (2017): 1–16.
[34] Robert C. Ford, "Combining Performance, Learning, and Behavioral Goals to Match Job with Person: Three Steps to Enhance Employee Performance with Goal Setting," *Business Horizons* 60, 3 (2017): 345–352.
[35] Ruth Kanfer, Michael Frese, and Russell E. Johnson, "Motivation Related to Work: A Century of Progress," *Journal of Applied Psychology* 102, 3 (2017): 338–355.
[36] Ford, "Combining Performance, Learning," 345–352.
[37] Peter F. Drucker, *The Practice of Management* (New York: Harper, 1954).

those goals as a key driver for that employee's performance assessment. It's a great value to both the organization and employees because it forces specification of job responsibilities in a contract-like written document that allows everyone to know exactly what they are supposed to do and how they will be evaluated on it.

The heart of traditional MBO is the *manager's letter,* written by employees to managers and not vice versa. In the letter, employees express their understanding of their own job objectives and the manager's job objectives, their own goals for the coming period (e.g., the following quarter or year), the obstacles to meeting them, the standards by which they expect to be evaluated, and the specifics of what they plan to do to meet the goals. The employee and manager discuss the letter until they reach an agreement about its contents.

The manager's letter is a valuable tool that can be used to engage the manager and employee in a collaborative process. The letter engages the employee in the goal-setting process, forces the manager to think carefully through the goals the employee is setting, and provides a document for both the manager and employee to track and ultimately assess the progress toward goal achievement.[38] Preparation of the letter involves a rich discussion by employee and supervisor about the employee's goals and job objectives, with a breakdown of job responsibilities into detailed sub-objectives and specific activities. The letter opens up communication between supervisor and employee about how each contributes to the overall organizational mission. Employees should leave the final discussion of a properly done manager's letter with a full understanding of what their tasks are for the coming period, how their performance is going to be evaluated, and how their performance fits into the fulfillment of their supervisor's job responsibilities, the supervisor's goals, and the overall organizational mission. The letter represents a formal agreement between employee and supervisor that tells the employee what to do during the forthcoming period and how the supervisor will evaluate the employee at the end of the period.

As a communication tool, the letter is exceptional. As a performance-measurement and employee-direction tool, it is as good as management theory can offer, because the standards against which performance will be measured are mutually determined and clearly understood by managers and employees. Combining the advantages of solid communication about employee expectations with the benefits of specific goal setting makes these letters a powerful device for aligning everyone in the organization with the mission and motivates them to perform.[39] As a means for telling the right people the right things to do, MBO can play a large part in organizational success—placing the right people in the right jobs, exhibiting the desired behaviors in the right tasks in the right ways, with sufficient commitment and effort to get the mission accomplished.

Of course, MBO and goal setting are not perfect, and doing them well can be a challenge for the hospitality manager. Managers have to estimate correctly what goals to emphasize, for themselves and their employees, or run the risk of being wrong at the end of the period. Also, if the manager does not know what employees are doing, should be doing, and what they are capable of doing, having a thoughtful discussion about the contents of the manager's letter will be difficult or pointless. Furthermore, because they can be spaced out as far as a year, the periodic nature of performance reviews can lead to inflexibility in responding to rapid changes in the organization's environment.

Setting clear and measurable goals is an important but difficult managerial responsibility. Doing it well takes time and effort, especially for tasks whose performance outcomes are difficult to measure. However, the benefits achieved by working

---

[38] Ford, "Combining Performance, Learning," 345–352.

[39] John C. Crotts, Duncan R. Dickson, and Robert C. Ford, "Aligning Organizational Processes with Mission: The Case of Service Excellence," *The Academy of Management Executive* 19, no. 3 (2005): 54–68.

with employees to set goals make the effort worthwhile. Even if organizations do not want to use a formal MBO approach, they should have some sort of goal-setting process in place to create SMART goals that focus employee performance, learning, and behavior on delivering excellent guest-focused service.

Working in Teams

While people are hired and paid as individuals, increasingly, hospitality organizations are relying on their employees working in teams. A **team** is two or more individuals, working together (either face-to-face or, increasingly, virtually), who are performing organizationally relevant tasks to achieve one or more common goals.[40] Teams typically bring together people with diverse and complementary skills to complete a project or task within a specified time period. They are especially important in hospitality as so many guest experiences are time limited while involving many different parts of the organization. A hotel's convention coordinator, for example, serves as a project team leader who assembles a temporary team consisting of members of every functional area across the hotel whose collective task is to do whatever it takes to produce a terrific convention. Teamwork is crucial to deliver an overall exceptional experience as the rooms division, food service, and all the hotel's support employees have to work together to provide what the meeting planner or conference organizer sees as a seamless experience.

team Two or more individuals, working together (either face-to-face or virtually), who are performing organizationally relevant tasks to achieve one or more common goals.

Working in teams can be motivating because they can provide for employees' social needs. By bringing together a diverse set of skills, teams can also be more effective, thus helping satisfy individuals' achievement needs. Teams are also typically used to deal with challenging tasks, and thus can satisfy growth needs. Furthermore, because organizations care about team effectiveness, they often provide team-level financial and non-financial rewards based on team performance, thus also providing the potential for recognition needs and economic needs. In short, teams have the great potential to improve organizational effectiveness by motivating individual employee's effectiveness. Teams can also increase employee motivation.[41]

For teams to be effective, though, it is critical that the team be capable of coordinating decision processes, efforts, and behaviors. A team leader will often have responsibility for leading and coordinating the team's efforts. It is also critical that the company's culture and incentives encourage teamwork. Teams rarely work effectively in overly bureaucratic organizations or in companies with highly individualistic cultures because such environments don't encourage cooperation or commitment to the team's goals. When teamwork is fostered, however, employees are motivated not just to perform their own jobs, but they are further motivated to perform well because they want the team to succeed. In highly effective teams, team members work particularly hard because no one wants to let the other team members down. Teams work best when team members have a high

Photo by Jake Chessum

Servers at Eleven Madison Park work together as a team to provide the level of service that helped get the restaurant rated as the best restaurant in the world.

[40] John E. Mathieu, "A Century of Work Teams in the *Journal of Applied Psychology*," *Journal of Applied Psychology* 102, 3 (2017): 452–467.

[41] Sharon K. Parker, Frederick P. Morgeson, and Gary Johns, "One Hundred Years of Work Design Research: Looking Back and Looking Forward," *Journal of Applied Psychology* 102, no. 3 (2017): 403–420.

level of confidence in the team leader, but also when the team leader develops and empowers team members.[42]

An example of the use of teams in hospitality is Hyatt Hotel's "Thrive Teams." Thrive teams are cross-functional teams charged with finding ways to reduce environmental impact, as well as organize employee training and engagement initiatives. Each hotel's Thrive Team is led by the general manager, the director of engineering, or a similarly highly ranked employee, but consists of managers and associates from various departments within the hotel. Hyatt's Thrive Teams bring together expertise from across the hotel to help find ways to fulfill the organization's commitment to global corporate responsibility. Outstanding performance by Thrive Teams is recognized quarterly through a company-wide newsletter, as well as on Hyatt's global intranet.

self-managed team A team that is empowered to control its own task behaviors with relatively little external control.

An increasingly common management technique is the use of self-managed teams. A **self-managed team** is a team that is empowered to control its own task behaviors with relatively little external control. Developing self-managed teams represents a concerted effort by organizations to reduce formal and informal hierarchy, while simultaneously giving employees greater autonomy and influence.[43] Self-managed teams determine on their own how they will accomplish their goals, as well as how to evaluate their members' performance. Self-managed teams are thought to have the potential to achieve better results—higher performance, better cost-control, higher customer satisfaction, and greater profitability—than regular teams, yet their success is not universal. The removal of leadership from a team can sometimes leave the team feeling abandoned.[44]

Larry Sternberg, former General Manager for the Ritz-Carlton at Tysons Corner, implemented self-managed teams at his hotel. While he is a strong advocate of self-managed teams and has seen them be successful, he cautions people not to underestimate how significant a change the implementation of self-managed teams entails. "Whenever people ask me about self-managed teams, the first thing I do is start really challenging them to make sure there's not a misconception about what this is. It's really radical. And even if you understand exactly what it is, it's so hard to do that unless a leader wants that kind of a culture for its own sake and not just for the improved business results, it won't stick because other strategies can drive similar business results."[45]

While management will still play a role in how it selects members for self-managed teams and by assigning their tasks or setting SMART goals, management's role tends to be more focused on providing the team members with the information, resources, organizational support, authority, and autonomy they need to perform, rather than supervising what they do and how they do it. Sternberg emphasizes this point: Self-managed teams represent "a genuine transfer of power from the leader to other people, not just participatory management."[46]

Team effectiveness depends on many characteristics of the team itself, particularly for self-managed teams. This includes personality characteristics of team members, how well the team understands and shares its vision of what it is supposed to accomplish, the communication abilities of those in the team, and the level of trust between team members. It also depends on the organizational culture, employee selection, and the availability of external coaching.[47]

---

[42] Allan Lee, Sara Willis, and Amy Wei Tian, "Empowering Leadership: A Meta-Analytic Examination of Incremental Contribution, Mediation, and Moderation," *Journal of Organizational Behavior* 39, no. 3 (2017): 306–325.

[43] Michael Y. Lee and Amy C. Edmondson, "Self-managing Organizations: Exploring the Limits of Less-Hierarchical Organizing," *Research in Organizational Behavior* 37 (2017): 35–58.

[44] Lee, Willis, and Tian, "Empowering Leadership," 306–325.

[45] Kim Turnage, "Self-Directed Teams: Beyond Empowerment to 51%," *Talent Plus*, 2015, http://talentplus.com/talent-plus-viewpoint-blog/35-leadership/745-self-directed-teams-beyond-empowerment-to-51.

[46] Turnage, 2015.

[47] Lee and Edmondson, 35–58.

Organizations seeking to improve their teams' effectiveness, especially virtual teams, often engage in teambuilding exercises that build team member trust, communications skills, and shared mission. Because of the typically high levels of turnover in the hospitality industry, these team building efforts require organizations to spend extra time and effort to make sure new team members are prepared to perform in teams. A company culture that emphasizes the importance of the skills used in teamwork will help ensure that teams retain their effectiveness in spite of changes in team members. Ritz-Carlton emphasizes this cultural value with their seventh value: "I create a work environment of teamwork and lateral service so that the needs of our guests and each other are met."

Just as for individuals to be successful, you need a high level of team motivation for the team to succeed. For regular teams, the motivation of a team is largely driven by the leadership skills of the team's manager. Effective team leaders let team members work together by playing the role of facilitator. Facilitators encourage every member of the team to communicate and participate in the decision-making and implementation of action plans. Developing leaders for self-managed teams can be challenging. With no formal leader, it is critical that the organization have a culture that supports the team's efforts, and the level of empowerment in the company is already high so that the team's efforts fit with the company's culture rather than work against it.[48]

HOW MANAGERS AND LEADERS PROVIDE THE RIGHT DIRECTION

We have emphasized in this chapter the critical role managers play in motivating employees. Managers not only have to find and train the right employees and instruct them carefully on their job roles, but they need to know what processes cause motivation, what needs their employees have, and what rewards they can offer. Managers need to be able to determine which employees are capable of handling some degree of empowerment, and if an employee has sufficient belief in his or her abilities to perform those tasks or needs encouragement and support. The best managers have learned whether an employee needs merely encouragement, close supervision, or specialized training to do the job well. Managers also need to have sufficient administrative or transactional skills to take care of the basic job-related requirements of their employees. They must be able to handle the paperwork, administrative procedures, and policies that directly influence each employee's ability to perform the job. A manager who forgets to submit the proper payroll, doesn't get the computer fixed, or schedules too few people to work on a shift creates situations in which even the most enthused, energetic employee can't succeed. Good managers are those who also thoroughly and competently attend to these basic and routine requirements.

Managers have another critical tool to manage their employees. By the nature of their role, managers are given formal authority to help run the company. How they use this authority, and how employees respond to it, is another important mechanism to understand for directing employee behaviors.

Managers and Authority

To many managers, authority is the power to yell at someone because the manager is the boss. These managers are still comfortable with the outmoded idea that the boss tells subordinates to jump and expects them to ask "how high?" "I don't have to motivate my people. I tell them what to do, and they do it." Such

[48] Lee, Willis, and Tian, 306–325.

managers are less comfortable with the fact that, in the contemporary working environment, they may get little or no cooperation, high turnover, low morale, and a hostile work force. Employees working for these managers are not usually motivated to provide the exceptional service for which hospitality organizations strive.

Why do managers behave this way? One reason is that people "learn" how managers behave by watching their own managers. When promoted, new managers often do the same things they remember seeing. Learning from an abusive manager often leads to adopting an abusive management style. Other managers may become abusive because they fear their subordinates will not listen unless they are abusive to them. They feel the only way to achieve their performance goals is to abuse their subordinates, or they are being abusive as a learned behavior because they were abused by their own managers.[49]

While no one wants to work for an abusive manager, most people generally also prefer not to work for authoritarian managers. Such managers lower employee morale, increase turnover, and hurt the company culture. And yet, hospitality managers and supervisors need to get people to accept direction and work hard on behalf of the organization. Organizations must therefore pay as much attention to the selection, training, and motivation of their managers as they do for line-level employees. Ultimately, they must teach their managers how to *exercise their authority* without being *authoritarian*.

Authority-Acceptance Theory

authority-acceptance theory Chester Barnard's theory of what authority is and why people do or do not accept it.

While not all managers have the characteristics of great leaders, they all possess the power and responsibility to direct subordinate behaviors because of the very nature of the managerial job. Managers who wish others to work well for them have to understand why people follow (or don't follow) directions and do (or don't do) what managers ask them to do. According to classic management writer Chester Barnard's **authority-acceptance theory,** authority is the quality of a directive that causes someone else to accept the directive and to do as directed.[50] If someone instructs you to bring a keg of beer from the cooler and you do it, that directive has authority for you. If you do not do it, that directive does not have authority for you. So, whether a directive has authority or not is determined by the directive receiver, not the sender or person in authority. That is, the organization gives the manager formal powers; the individual gives the manager authority. Yet, in much the same way that value is defined by the guest and rewards defined by the employee, authority has to be accepted by the employee or there is no authority.

The factors influencing the acceptance of managerial authority lie in the nature of the sender and receiver, their relationships to the organization and to each other, and in the nature of the communication itself. The manager must understand and pay attention to these factors that influence employee acceptance of direction. Just as governments must ultimately rely on the consent of the governed, so too must hospitality organizations.

Preconditions for Employee Acceptance of Authority

Four preconditions must be met before an employee will accept managerial authority. Even if the preconditions are met, however, the employee may still not accept the directive. But if they are not met, the employee either will not or cannot accept the directive.

[49] Bennett J. Tepper, Lauren Simon, and Hee Man Park, "Abusive Supervision," *Annual Review of Organizational Psychology and Organizational Behavior* 4 (2017): 123–152.

[50] See Chester I. Barnard, *The Functions of the Executive* (Cambridge, MA: Harvard University Press, 1968), Chapter 12.

1. *The employee must understand the directive.* If the employee does not understand the directive, compliance is impossible. Many employees have listened carefully and then later wondered what the manager was talking about or what the manager wanted done. Many employees thought they understood a directive and then found they did not because the communication was too confusing or too general. For example, Area Regional Supervisor Jones tells Store Manager Smith, "Get rid of the trouble with the refrigerator at the Garden Grill Restaurant." Smith removes the troublesome refrigerator, scraps it, and replaces it with a new one, but Jones really wanted the old one repaired. The two employees had different meanings for "get rid of the trouble." Even though they both "understood" the communication, their understandings were different. A manager who has not checked to see if the communication was understood has not exercised authority. Employees who are supposed to comply with a directive cannot do what they do not understand.
2. *The employee must believe the directive is consistent with the organization's goals.* An airline flight attendant notices the exit to a plane has oil on the floor, which might endanger the safety of deplaning passengers. The pilot tells the attendant to allow the passengers off the plane anyway. Because so many training sessions have stressed the primary importance of passenger safety, the attendant may well ignore the pilot and keep the passengers on the plane until the oil is cleaned up. Without a reasonable explanation for departing from safety standards, the attendant would not see the directive as consistent with the organization's goals. All experienced managers know that employees hesitate to follow such directives. If a directive appears to conflict with an organizational goal, accepted policy, tradition, or past practice, the manager must spend the time to explain why this time it is different.
3. A special violation of this precondition is the role conflict caused by conflicting directives from two or more managers. Both directives are sent down, but they cannot both support the organization's effort. The employee will either accept one and reject the other or do nothing.
4. *The employee must believe the directive is consistent with the employee's own goals.* This precondition is related to whatever motivated the employee to affiliate with the organization in the first place. If carrying out the directive will result in the employee having to do something that will make the organization less attractive to the employee, the directive may be disobeyed or (more usually) evaded. Such directives are inconsistent with the employee's personal motives, beliefs, or values which are the basis for accepting any directives at all. If the directive is totally inconsistent with goals or principles that are important to the employee, and the directive cannot be ignored or avoided, the employee may resign. Accepting or rejecting managerial or supervisory authority is a result of the employee carefully weighing the balance between the inducements offered and the contributions expected in return. If inducements offered are equal to or more than the contributions expected, directives will be accepted. If required contributions outweigh inducements, directives will not be carried out. While there are survival situations where there is no realistic choice but to accept a boss's authority (as discussed later in this chapter), even that decision to comply will result from an employee's careful weighing of the personal costs of complying with the benefits of accepting even the most offensive exercises of authority.
5. *The employee must be physically and mentally able to carry out the directive.* This precondition may seem too obvious to mention; yet, we are sometimes asked to do the impossible. A woman with a bad back is told to carry heavy cases of liquor. An employee allergic to detergent is told to take a temporary

assignment in the hotel laundry. The manager who gives directives without knowing each employee's capabilities soon finds out that if it can't be done, it won't.

Securing Employee Compliance with Directives

Once the preconditions to the acceptance of authority are understood, how do managers actually secure compliance with their directives? When you are a manager, what will you need to do to ensure your subordinates do what you ask of them? The compliance necessary for a smoothly functioning organization comes about for four reasons.

1. Effective managers issue directives that comply with the four preconditions. The effective managers communicate directives that are accepted. Directives that do not comply with the preconditions are not obeyed. Poor managers ignore the preconditions primarily for one reason: They don't know any better. They think their formal organizational positions give them the right to issue commands of all types. Many managers believe they have absolute authority over their subordinates. This belief is confirmed by many organizational experiences in which managers' subordinates do indeed comply with their commands, but it can also lead to those managers having subordinates leave for more fulfilling positions. Effective managers know that "absolute" authority is absolute only as long as the four preconditions are not violated. If managers meet the preconditions, employees allow them to use their authority. Once the manager begins to ignore the preconditions, employees begin to ignore the directives.
2. Effective managers ensure not just clear communication from the manager to the subordinate, but also from the subordinate to the manager and between subordinates. Managers may forget that the organizational view and knowledge they have is different from those of their subordinates. It is easy to forget that information you have frequent and easy access to is not available to your employees. Managers who know what their subordinates don't know often forget to share what they know, and the resulting communication gap can lead to employee misunderstandings and failure to do what needs to be done. A manager needs to make sure that all employees have the information they need to do their jobs correctly and that the information can flow freely among the employees who need it to effectively deliver the service product.
3. People joining an organization expect to do job-related tasks. Another reason for compliance is that people expect to be given directions, instructions, and sometimes commands regarding certain aspects of their behavior in organizations. They obey directives within these "zones of acceptance" without question. Directives fall into one of three classes: clearly acceptable, clearly unacceptable, and questionable.

   If Lois Evans tells her assistant, Bill Elliot, to come into her office to install a new spreadsheet program on her computer, the order would fall within Elliot's zone of acceptance. Elliot knew when he took the job that Evans might tell him to do software installations. On the other hand, if Evans asks Elliot to come over to her apartment for drinks and software installation, Elliot would probably be very uncomfortable with that request. He would not consider such overtime work outside the office to be an acceptable part of the job.

   Many directives fall into a third area: the questionable zone. If Evans asks Elliot to make the coffee, or get a birthday card for Mr. Evans, or do some other task that is not part of the job but is not really outrageous, Elliot may be unsure about whether to follow the directive and might have to think about it.

The width of the acceptance zone depends on the extent to which the organization fulfills the member's needs. The fanatical member of a cult might literally be willing to do anything to advance the cult's cause. Most organizational members, however loyal and hard-working they may be, are not nearly so fanatical.

An employees' acceptance zone will be influenced by the goals of that employee. If continuing affiliation with the organization is necessary (as would be the case of the fanatic above) for achieving a personal goal then securing that person's compliance with authority is more likely regardless of what the contribution is that is expected.

4. Members enforce each other's compliance. Most members want "their" organization to run smoothly. If it does, they can gain the benefits they anticipated when they joined. Therefore, group members will bring social pressure to bear on any member unwilling to accept authority. Employees realize they cannot achieve their own personal goals if the organization fails. An organization cannot succeed if its members will not accept authority and take direction. Therefore, any member who denies a directive or will not cooperate represents a threat to those members who identify with and work toward organizational goals for their own reasons. Accordingly, the group takes an active interest in maintaining every member's compliance with organizational directives.

The informal group plays this important enforcement role in support of the formal organization's authority structure. If the informal group wants a decision implemented, it is usually implemented. If a decision is not agreeable to the informal group, its members can find many effective ways of holding up implementation.

Organizations promote their best and most expert employees, give them titles to remind everyone of their rank, and give them control over information and resources—among which are rewards. The more important the rewards a manager controls are to an employee, the more able the manager will be to get the employee to accept authority. Determining which resources are important to employees is a key responsibility of managers seeking to retain the enthusiastic commitment of their employees. Managers able to provide these rewards can elicit effort, productivity, enthusiasm, and other contributions that the hospitality organization seeks from employees—all without unduly exercising their authority. The essential point here is that the greater the benefits or inducements (intrinsic or extrinsic) the organization provides to its members, the more willing they are to accept orders from the organizational leadership. Effective managers find ways to keep the inducements/contributions balance tilted heavily in favor of the employee. They know what inducements are available, try to identify those that are important to the employee, and provide that array of inducements.

Sexual Harassment in the Hospitality Industry

There are many times when employees will not accept the authority of managers, and either avoid or outright refuse to follow the specified directive. There are many times, however, when employees are so concerned over the risk of losing their jobs that they simply do not feel they can ignore what is asked of them, even when it is clearly outside of the zone of acceptance. When the employee's goal is survival, the boss's power to hire and fire can be a powerful influence on an employee's willingness to comply with authority, especially if the alternative is to become unemployed and putting the employee and family at risk of homelessness. Subordinates who simply do not have the economic means to quit their jobs, if confronted with a boss's authority directives, may have to accept them. With many young, and often lower-paid employees in the hospitality industry, some managers will take advantage of their power and threaten subordinates with job loss to secure their compliance with directives that are inappropriate, unethical, or outright illegal.

An increasingly discussed example of this in the work force in general, but in hospitality in particular, is sexual harassment. Employees in the hospitality industry experience sexual harassment on average more than other industry employees. For many of these employees, putting up with harassment or worse is their only real choice as they fear the loss of income if they quit or lose their jobs.[51] Unfortunately, the problem is quite widespread. In a survey conducted by a union of hospitality workers, 89% of workers said they had experienced one or more incidents of sexual harassment in their working life; of those reporting harassment, 56.3% said they had been targeted by a member of the public, and 22.7% said they had been harassed by a manager.[52] The hospitality industry has been criticized for being very slow to recognize these issues[53] and is increasingly called upon to prevent abusive supervision and remedy inappropriate and illegal behaviors when they occur. While harassment frequently results from inappropriate guest behavior, it is often a result of an abusive supervisor or manager who is misusing power to gain employee compliance with inappropriate use of authority.

Ronen Tivony/NurPhoto via Getty Images

Sexual harassment is a dangerous and unlawful exhibition of power by those in authority. Employees are increasingly speaking up against such acts.

The best hospitality organizations recognize the importance in attracting the best job candidates by protecting their employees, as well as complying with the law. Employers of choice know they are responsible for the actions their managers take. If they fail to prevent or remedy abusive supervision, their brand as an employer and their legal position will suffer.

The Council of Hotel and Restaurant Trainers suggests companies follow seven best practices to prevent, thwart, and remedy sexual harassment in the industry:[54]

1. Make a sexual harassment policy part of the team member handbook, with a zero-tolerance policy in place against harassment and discrimination.
2. Make it a non-negotiable topic to discuss on orientation day.
3. Ensure managers go through in-depth training on their first day. Include how to prevent and recognize harassment and discrimination, and make sure managers know how to report and investigate any claims that are made. Also make sure managers know the disciplinary process.
4. Ensure non-management team members are trained regarding harassment during their orientation.
5. Ensure team members understand why sexual harassment and discrimination is wrong, and what effects it can have on people.
6. Create an anonymous hotline or specific e-mail address to report issues.
7. Ensure the human resource department is able to better handle complaints from a diverse (often multilingual) workforce.

---

[51] Shekina Tuahene, "Sexual Harassment: A Hospitality Problem," *Hotel Owner*, last modified January 10, 2018. https://www.hotelowner.co.uk/13209-sexual-harassment-and-the-hotel-industry/.

[52] Alexandra Topping, "Sexual Harassment Rampant in Hospitality Industry, Survey Finds," *The Guardian*, last modified January 24, 2018. https://www.theguardian.com/world/2018/jan/24/sexual-harassment-rampant-hospitality-industry-unite-survey-finds.

[53] Clark Wolf, "Restaurant Business' 'Excruciatingly Slow' Reckoning on Sexual Harassment Just Won't Do," *Forbes*, last modified January 4, 2018. https://www.forbes.com/sites/clarkwolf/2018/01/04/excruciatingly-slow-reckoning-in-restaurant-business-just-wont-do/#5f84ee14215a.

[54] Ron Ruggless, "7 Best Practices for Sexual Harassment Training," *Nation's Restaurant News*, last modified December 13, 2017. http://www.nrn.com/workforce/7-best-practices-sexual-harassment-training.

Managers and Leaders

Managers must take care of the administrative duties, but managers can do more than exercise their authority to direct the way work is done. Managers who are also leaders can transform the organization and the people working in it. Ken Blanchard defines **leadership** as a process to influence others. "Anytime you are trying to influence the thinking, beliefs, or development of another person, you are engaging in leadership. Of course, there are traditional organizational leadership responsibilities that involve goals and objectives, but if you think beyond those confines, you'll realize that everyone is a leader—you are a leader—unless you're stranded on an island by yourself!"[55]

leadership A process to influence others.

Effective leaders possess a combination of qualities allowing them to influence others. These include negotiating ability, a willingness to cooperate, diplomatic skills, knowledge of effective team building, and the traits of inspiring and nurturing others.[56] In short, effective leaders have the ability to identify and provide the kinds and amount of inducements that motivate the individual employee because they are the inducements the employee wants, needs, and expects from contributing effort to the organization. Although fear and the threat of punishment may be powerful short-term motivators, it is the ability of leaders to fulfill employee wants, needs, and expectations that invokes energetic employee commitment to organizational goals in the long run. Employee expectations must be identified and met if managers are to lead enthusiastic, committed, and effective employees. While a manager may simply tell subordinates what to do, a leader inspires employees not only to complete their job tasks, but to make the extra effort needed to provide exceptional service.

The power of effective leadership is undeniable. Kerry Miller, former Vice President of People Development for Bertucci's Restaurants, explains, "I think that when you get behind a true leader, you're more jazzed up to get into work every day because you know that person is supportive of what you're doing."[57] Effective leadership motivates employees to focus their efforts on achieving the organization's goals. Great leaders *get the job done* because others want to help them achieve the goals and objectives they have mutually set. Great leadership obviously includes results-oriented achievements, but it also involves employee development and engagement so that employees are motivated and capable of achieving their own long-term goals, as well as helping to achieve organizational goals.[58]

Ethical Leadership

A leader's responsibilities are many: to inspire, challenge, and create a shared purpose among employees. This entails promoting employee motivation, establishing goals, providing feedback, offering inspiration, and setting the example that motivates employees to go the extra mile. There have been many instances, however, of major ethical lapses, only some of which gain extensive media attention.[59] Most people actually see business executives as having poor ethics.[60] As discussed earlier in this chapter, of particular note, there have been growing concerns about the prevalence of sexual harassment in the hospitality industry.[61] A key effort that must be made to address this issue is for leadership to play a much more substantial role, exhibiting and enforcing a greater level of ethics in the workplace.

[55] Ken Blanchard, "Are You a Leader? Here's How to Tell," *Ken Blanchard Blog*, June 2014, https://www.kenblanchardbooks.com/2014/06/.

[56] John Antonakis and David V. Day, Eds., *The Nature of Leadership* (Thousand Oaks, CA: Sage Publications, 2018).

[57] Tony Simons, *The Integrity Dividend* (San Francisco, CA: Jossey-Bass, 2008), 25.

[58] Ken Blanchard and Spencer Johnson, *The New One Minute Manager* (New York, NY: HarperCollins, 2015).

[59] See, for example, Lucinda Shen, "The 10 Biggest Business Scandals of 2017," *Fortune*, last modified December 31, 2017, http://fortune.com/2017/12/31/biggest-corporate-scandals-misconduct-2017-pr/.

[60] Bruce Weinstein, "Business Leaders Get an 'F' in Ethics, Yet Again," *Fortune*, last modified January 9, 2016, http://fortune.com/2016/01/09/ethics-business-leaders-gallup/.

[61] Stefanie K. Johnson and Juan M. Madera, "Sexual Harassment Is Pervasive in the Restaurant Industry. Here's What Needs to Change," *Harvard Business Review Digital Articles* (January 18, 2018): 2–6.

ethical leadership Leadership that is directed and driven by a respect for ethical beliefs and values, and respectful for the beliefs, dignity, and rights of others.

Ethical leadership is defined as "the demonstration of normatively appropriate conduct through personal actions and interpersonal relationships, and the promotion of such conduct to followers through two-way communication, reinforcement, and decision-making."[62] More generally, it is leadership that is directed and driven by a respect for ethical beliefs and values. At the same time, the leadership is respectful for the beliefs, dignity, and rights of others. Exhibiting ethical leadership has a number of benefits. Not only do ethical leaders generate better ethical behaviors of their subordinates,[63] but they also inspire better motivation, task performance, helping behaviors, and a variety of job attitudes.[64]

Organizations can be proactive to obtain ethical leaders. As with all key competencies, it begins with selection, can be developed, and can be encouraged. For hiring, pay particular attention to individuals' resumes and references. As past performance is the best predictor of future performance, individuals who exaggerate or outright lie on their resumes or include questionable or even fake references, will likely exhibit that sort of behavior in the workplace.[65] With regard to development, employees can be trained to be more sensitive to ethical issues. This includes active listening and role playing, imagining from others' perspectives, providing exercises that encourage people to step back from a situation to determine whether it has moral implications, and actively practicing humility and openness to other points of view.[66] Finally, ensure that the organization promotes ethical behavior. Encourage employees to voice ethical concerns; avoid creating win-at-all-cost environments which may encourage people to engage in questionable behaviors to obtain desired results.[67]

Leaders and the Changing Environment

As hospitality leaders try to strike the inducements-contributions balance that will motivate employees to perform at their best, they must remain responsive to the ever-changing environment: increased diversity, more work teams, greater global competition, cultural shifts, new technologies—the list goes on. As a result, future leaders will need to be more culturally aware and be able to incorporate multiple perspectives, appreciate cross-cultural and cross-generational differences, understand both individual and team needs, and function effectively in complex environments.[68] All these factors will make determining rewards that fulfill employee needs and exercising authority more difficult.

Solving the Leadership Challenge of Motivating Exceptional Guest Service

People are complex and, as a result, there is no simple way for a leader to motivate everybody. While realizing the critical role of financial rewards in the world of work, managers must also realize that money will not solve all motivational

[62] Michael E. Brown, Linda K. Treviño, and David A. Harrison, "Ethical Leadership: A Social Learning Perspective for Construct Development and Testing," *Organizational Behavior and Human Decision Processes* 97, no. 2 (2005): 120.

[63] See, for example, Lei Huang and Ted A. Paterson, "Group Ethical Voice: Influence of Ethical Leadership and Impact on Ethical Performance," *Journal of Management* 43, no. 4 (2017): 1157–1184.

[64] Thomas W.H. Ng and Daniel C. Feldman, "Ethical Leadership: Meta-analytic Evidence of Criterion-related and Incremental Validity," *Journal of Applied Psychology* 100, no. 3 (2015): 948–965.

[65] Denis Collins, *Essentials of Business Ethics: Creating an Organization of High Integrity and Superior Performance* (Hoboken, NJ: John Wiley & Sons, 2009), 33–57.

[66] Craig E. Johnson, *Meeting the Ethical Challenges of Leadership: Casting Light or Shadow* (Thousand Oaks, CA: Sage Publications, 2012).

[67] Ng and Feldman, "Ethical Leadership," 948–965.

[68] Bruce J. Avolio, John J. Sosik, Dong I. Jung, and Yair Berson, "Leadership Models, Methods, and Applications," in *Handbook of Psychology*, eds. Walter C. Borman, Daniel R. Ilgen, and Richard J. Klimoski (New York: Wiley, 2003), 277–307.

problems. Recognition and feedback are effective motivators, but only if managers have the leadership and management skills to provide these nonfinancial rewards effectively. The work itself can be highly motivating if designed appropriately. A complicating factor is that jobs cannot be designed only to motivate employees. Jobs must be designed while also keeping in mind the company's culture, the types of employees selected, the training they receive, and the way the service product is delivered.

Ideally, the manager gets it all right. Employees are offered the incentives that best fit their needs, managers structure jobs to make them motivating, employees understand their roles and have SMART goals to direct them on how their behaviors can lead to rewards, and managers provide clear leadership, exercise managerial authority effectively and appropriately, and lead ethically. All parties to the "contract" do their jobs—employer contributions match the incentives that employees seek. The result (ideally) is a satisfied, skilled, and motivated workforce.

LESSONS LEARNED

LO 7.1 Discuss how motivating your employees is just as critical as how you select and train them.

- Your frontline employees are heroes; make their jobs fair, fun, interesting, and important.

LO 7.2 Describe the different needs employees possess that drive their behaviors.

- While money is an essential part of the employment relationship, employees also have needs for social interactions, recognition, growth, and achievement.
- Use the financial rewards that employees want, emphasize the desired behaviors, and fit with your organizational mission.

LO 7.3 Explain how hospitality organizations motivate their employees to provide outstanding guest service.

- Reward behaviors you want, and don't reward behaviors you don't want.
- Praise, praise, praise. Look for reasons to reinforce people doing the right things. Privately re-educate and coach those doing the wrong things.

LO 7.4 Express how empowering employees can make them more motivated and more effective.

- Give people a chance to grow and get better, and then reward them for it.
- Show employees the relationships between their personal goals, group goals, and organizational goals. Find win-win-wins.

LO 7.5 Describe how setting SMART goals can be a powerful way to motivate employees.

- Set clear, measurable standards that define expectations for job performance. Constantly reinforce these standards by setting examples; let employees know that the standards are important; reward employees when they meet these standards.

LO 7.6 Review the role of teams in changing the way work is done and improving organizational effectiveness.

- Putting people into teams can make the set of people more effective than the sum of their individual inputs.

LO 7.7 Relate the importance of fairness and ethical leadership for maintaining employee motivation.

- Be fair, ethical, and equitable. People need to feel they are being treated equitably. If you don't show people why reward differentials are made between employees, they will assume the worst.

- Establish clear connections between performance and rewards, so that employees know that if they work hard they will receive the rewards they expect.
- Don't just support your frontline employees; trust them as well.

LO 7.8 State how authority and leadership work in organizations and why employees accept authority.

- Pay attention to communication; people can't do what they don't know about or don't understand.
- People give you the right to direct them. Know how to earn that right.
- As a leader, you must set the example. Employees respond more to what you do than to what you say.

KEY TERMS AND CONCEPTS

achievement needs 230
authority-acceptance theory 248
economic needs 227
empowerment 235
equity theory 241
ethical leadership 254
expectancy theory 241
formal group 228
goal setting 243
growth needs 229
hedonic treadmill 227
informal group 228
leadership 253
Management by Objectives (MBO) 243
motivation 225
positive reinforcement 240
recognition needs 229
recognition program 231
self-efficacy 241
self-managed team 246
service-profit chain 225
SMART goals 243
social needs 227
team 245

REVIEW QUESTIONS

1. If you have ever been employed, what if anything did you want from your job other than a paycheck?
   A. If you are employed now, have your job expectations changed from those of the past?
   B. What are your job expectations from the position you hope to hold in ten years?
2. If you have been employed, can you recall times when you were upset due to the boss ignoring your good work because the boss was giving complete attention to another employee who was complaining or doing a bad job? If so, what managerial lesson did this teach you? How would you use that lesson to determine or change your own managerial style?
3. What does it mean to be empowered? Give some situations in which you were empowered.
   A. How did you handle empowerment? How did you feel?
   B. Compare those situations to a few in which you were not empowered. How did you handle the latter, and how did you feel?
   C. If you were a hotel or restaurant manager, can you think of some job functions that you would hesitate to empower your employees to perform? Why?
   D. Why is it particularly important to empower the frontline people who interact with hospitality guests? Or is it?
4. Consider a restaurant meal in which much of the service is provided one on one, server to guest. How important is teamwork to the success of this guest experience?
5. The authority-acceptance theory suggests that people must accept authority or it does not really exist. Do you agree or disagree?
   A. Give examples of situations you have been in where people did not follow direct orders. Did they refuse because the conditions for authority acceptance detailed in the chapter were not met, or for other reasons?

B. What do managers need to know to ensure that their authority is accepted?

C. How does all that relate to managing the guest experience in hospitality organizations?

D. Does authority-acceptance theory seem to you to have more or less relevance to the hospitality industry as compared to most industries?

ACTIVITIES

1. Find a hospitality organization that seems to have succeeded in motivating its frontline employees to give outstanding service. How do they do it? If you work for an organization that does not sufficiently motivate you, what is the organization doing or not doing that causes you to be unmotivated?
2. Find an organization that seems to try to make its hospitality jobs fun and interesting. What do they do, and how well does it work? If you or your friends have jobs that do not provide fun and are not interesting, why is that so? Does the organization seem to care whether you are interested and having fun? Why or why not?
3. Interview three line employees from two hospitality organizations and find out what motivates them to perform well.

ETHICS IN BUSINESS

Rewards can change behavior, but you need to design your pay system carefully to be sure you want the behaviors your pay plan is actually encouraging. Below is a list of pay plans and their desired goals. What might be the unintended consequences of each system? How might each form of pay inadvertently motivate employees to behave inappropriately?

GOAL	PAY SYSTEM
To encourage teamwork among servers	Change from individual tips to pooled tips
To encourage front desk agents to "up-sell" customers to more expensive rooms	Provide a bonus for each luxury suite sold
To achieve higher customer satisfaction	Provide bonuses if customer satisfaction ratings average above 4 on a 5-point feedback card given to all guests
To improve the hotel's financial performance	Give company stock to all employees
To encourage employees to get higher performance evaluations	Provide raises and bonuses for higher evaluations
To encourage employee retention	Implement a recognition program to reward employees on their five-, ten-, fifteen-, and twenty-year anniversaries

CASE STUDY

Case 1: Hartsell Hotels

While he was still in college, Bill Hartsell decided he wanted to own hotels. When he graduated, he borrowed some money, bought a bankrupt property, and created the first Hartsell Hotel. The hotel presented constant problems, but Bill was highly motivated and worked twelve to sixteen hours a day, six or seven days a week. He did as much of the work as he could himself, from making beds to preparing light meals in the hotel coffee shop.

The hard work paid off. Bill succeeded with his original hotel, bought two more, and increased his staff accordingly. He made a determined effort to hire young people, old people, women, minorities, and the disabled, and he paid them as well as he could. Bill felt a genuine sense of responsibility to his employees and to the community. After five years, Bill had 300 employees.

Bill hired three recent hospitality graduates, intending to move them into responsible management positions after a training period. At his first meeting with them, Bill made his position plain: "No one at Hartsell Hotels works harder than I do. I'm the first to arrive and the last to leave. I work most weekends. I'm paying you well. I'm offering you a chance for rapid advancement. But don't think in terms of a 40-hour work week. I want you to work as hard as I do and act as if this business were your own. Is that clear?" In unison the three responded, "Yes, sir, Mr. Hartsell."

Three months later, they had all left to take jobs with Marriott, Hilton, and Hyatt.

1. What, if anything, was wrong with Mr. Hartsell's approach? Why did the new employees leave, and what might have motivated them to stay?
2. Were Mr. Hartsell's expectations for his new employees unrealistic? If so, why?
3. What inconsistencies, if any, do you see between the goals of the three new employees and Mr. Hartsell's goals?
4. Could those inconsistencies have been resolved? How?

Case 2: Farney Spa and Fish Camp

Farney Spa and Fish Camp has found its niche; it caters to women who want to combine the facilities of a luxury spa with fishing opportunities. Sally Blade, supervisor in charge of fishing guides at Farney Spa and Fish Camp, has a problem with one of the fishing guides. All guides are supposed to be at work by 5:30 a.m. They must have their skiffs ready for operation by 6:30 a.m. But Mary Lou Day is almost always late for work. She arrives any time between 5:40 and 6:15 a.m. Once she gets to work, she is excellent. She is easily the best guide in the camp and always gets her boat prepared early, even after arriving late. She is qualified for a promotion except that she has not been in her present position long enough. She understands and accepts that situation, but she hopes to move up into management someday.

Day's frequent tardiness is causing problems. Other guides, without Day's willingness or ability, are using Day's lateness to justify their own. Sally Blade feels she cannot crack down on the other guides without cracking down on Day as well. Sally has had several talks with Mary Lou. She always promises to do better, but she never does. Sally has even suggested a different reporting and leaving time for Mary Lou, to accommodate fishing parties that don't like to head out onto the lake so early, but Mary Lou does not like the idea of being treated differently. "After all," she says, "I always get my skiff ready on time, my guests like the service I provide, and I always get my boat back and cleaned up by quitting time, don't I?" Mary Lou has even suggested she may quit if the organization cannot be "flexible enough to let one good employee be a few minutes late every so often, without bugging me about it. There are other fish camps on this lake, you know."

1. Mary Lou Day is Sally Blade's best fishing guide. Is Mary Lou justified in asking that Sally "cut her some slack"? Should Sally comply?
2. If you think Mary Lou should meet the same work requirements that are imposed on the other guides, how would you motivate her to do so?

Case 3: Jubilee Hotels Corp.

Jubilee Hotels Corp. was having problems with negative worker attitudes and low productivity at its Hartwell, Alabama, hotel. To turn things around, JHC decided in 2015 to change the operation of the Hartwell hotel completely. The hotel would be run with a minimum of supervision. The employees themselves would take over such traditional management prerogatives as making job assignments, scheduling coffee breaks, interviewing prospective employees, and even deciding on pay raises.

The new system eliminated several layers of management and supervisory personnel and assigned three primary areas of responsibility—front desk, housekeeping, and office duties—to self-managing teams of seven to fourteen workers per shift. The former middle managers, divided among the primary areas, retained some supervisory authority but had not nearly as much as before. The workers rotated between the dull and the interesting jobs. The teams made all necessary management decisions.

For several years, the new system was a success in many ways. Unit costs decreased by 10% compared to costs under the old system, translating into a savings of $2 million per year. Turnover dropped to only 5%. Quality of work life and economic results were good.

Notwithstanding the plan's success, in 2018 the hotel began the transition back to a traditional organizational and management system, as an accompaniment to a major expansion. JHC introduced more specialized job classifications and more supervisors, and they reduced opportunities for employee participation. The company added seven management positions to the hotel, including controller, engineering manager, and services manager. Management took back the right to make decisions about pay raises.

Professor Andrew Stubbs analyzed what had happened at Hartwell for his hospitality class: "The basic problem was that in this functional organization, many managers became nervous about what functions they could perform after the hotel workers themselves were given so many responsibilities. In addition, they resented being left out of things; upper-level management's enthusiasm for enriching the jobs of the workers didn't take into account the feelings of the middle managers. Where was their enrichment?"

1. Do you agree with the professor's assessment of what went wrong?
2. What does the Jubilee Hotels experience tell you about applying work team, enrichment, and incentives principles in real life?
3. What do you think will happen to the hotel once it fully returns to a "traditional" management system?

Further readings on the topics in this chapter are listed in "Additional Readings" on pages 509–511.

Get the tools you need to sharpen your study skills. SAGE edge offers a robust online environment featuring an impressive array of free tools and resources.

Access practice quizzes, eFlashcards, video, and multimedia at **edge.sagepub.com/Ford2e.**

Visit **edge.sagepub.com/Ford2e** to help you accomplish your coursework goals in an easy-to-use learning environment.

©iStockphoto.com/sumnersgraphicsinc

8 Involving the Guest: The Co-Creation of Value

Hospitality Principle: Empower Guests to Co-Create Their Experiences

If you can't get it for yourself, who's going to get it for you?

—Fritz Perls, father of gestalt psychology

Learning Objectives

After reading this chapter, you should be able to

8.1 Recognize that there are parts of all service experiences that require co-production.

8.2 Describe how, when, and why hospitality organizations encourage or empower guests to help provide their own guest experiences.

8.3 Discuss the advantages and disadvantages of guest involvement for the organization and guest.

8.4 Explain what organizations must do to make co-creation successful.

8.5 Explain why hospitality organizations must sometimes "fire the guest" and how to do it.

INTRODUCTION

In the traditional firm-centric view of organizations, management decides what the guests want and designs a delivery product, setting, and delivery system to provide it. The guest-centric view is that the guestologist seeks to identify what the customers want and involves them in the co-creation of the experience, before, during, or after the actual experience itself. Co-creation is based on the logic that the interactive process of joint production can be of value for both customers and firms.[1] Guests' involvement and engagement lead to their **co-creating** the value and quality of that experience.

co-creating Guest involvement in creating the value and quality of the guest experience.

If guests are involved in the design of the experience, through focus groups or by providing feedback on their prior experiences, they have the opportunity to co-create the experience before it happens. For example, a prepare-a-meal franchise will offer busy people the opportunity to come to a location where ingredients, recipes, utensils, and expertise are available for customers to co-create a week's worth of meals to take home and freeze. They cook their own meals. On a more complex level, guestologists at Disney use guest feedback to determine what aspects of the Disney experience are working well and which need to be redesigned. In today's instant-access-to-information environment, the hospitality organization can access guest comments via a designated complaint web page, blogs (e.g., Marriot's blogs.marriott website), and social networking sites to find out what its guests are saying about things that make them satisfied and dissatisfied or even by collecting tweets of their opinions while they are still co-creating the service. Exhibit 8.1 lists some popular social networking and blog websites. Guests can also co-create knowledge by posting reviews about their travel experiences, on sites like those listed in Exhibit 8.2.

During the hospitality experience, management can use a variety of strategies to engage the guests in the **co-production** of that experience so they co-create quality and value. In this chapter we will talk about co-creation of value by a guest's participation in the co-production of an experience. While there is much discussion in the

co-production The active producing or helping to produce and deliver the guest experience by guests themselves, ideally to the mutual benefit of guests and the organization.

[1] This idea is based on the work by Robert Lusch and Stephen Vargo, on what they termed the Service Dominant Logic. See Robert F. Lusch and Stephen L. Vargo, *The Service-Dominant Logic of Marketing: Dialog, Debate, and Direction* (New York: Routledge, 2014), 2014, and Stephen L. Vargo and Robert F. Lusch, "Evolving to a New Dominant Logic for Marketing," *Journal of Marketing* 68: 1 (2004): 1–17. See also Prakash K. Chathoth, Levent Altinay, Robert James Harrington, Fevzi Okumus, and Eric SW Chan, "Co-production versus Co-creation: A Process Based Continuum in the Hotel Service Context," *International Journal of Hospitality Management* 32 (2013): 11–20; Prakash K. Chathoth, Gerardo R. Ungson, Robert J. Harrington, and Eric SW Chan, "Co-creation and Higher Order Customer Engagement in Hospitality and Tourism Services: A Critical Review," *International Journal of Contemporary Hospitality Management* 28, no. 2 (2016): 222–245.

EXHIBIT 8.1

Popular Social Networking and Blog Sites

WEBSITE	WHAT IT IS OR DOES
BlackCareerZone	A career and job search site for black professionals
Doostang	By invitation only, chiefly for financial services
85Broads	For female professionals and executives
Facebook	A social networking giant
GoogleGroups	A wide array of easily created shared interest groups
Jigsaw	A social network for business contacts with profiles
LatPro	For bilingual or Hispanic professionals
LinkedIn	A social network targeting professionals
Meetup	Helps groups of people with shared interests plan meetings and form offline clubs in local communities around the world
CareerBuilder.com	One of the largest online job sites in the United States
My.Monster.com	Networks of Monster help-wanted opportunities
MyWorkster.com	Connects students, alumni, employers, companies, and the university community to foster professional growth and interconnectivity for college communities
Plaxo.com	A business and professional network; tailored to family, friends, or business
QuintCareers.com	Job search site with expert advice
Ryze.com	Business networking; member-created, themed networks
Saludos.com	Hispanic employment service for jobs promotes work force diversity and offers free résumé postings to qualified bilingual and college-trained professionals
Vault.com	A career information website, providing employee surveys of top employers, career advice, job listings, and career guides to individual industries; networks allowing anonymity
Windows Live Groups	A service that allows users to form their own community groups; an online service provided by Microsoft as part of its Windows Live services
YouTube.com	Site to watch, share, upload, and discover videos
Ziggs.com	White pages and free people search for professionals; for job data and profile sharing

academic literature about the unique meanings of these two terms,[2] we will offer a simple distinction and use it throughout this chapter. Since all services require both a customer and an organization to do something to make the experience happen, the way in which this co-production is managed and engages the guest will influence the guest's determination of its value.[3] The more engaged, generally, the more the guest feels a sense of value gained from performing the tasks required in co-production, especially when the resulting experience was memorable.

Exemplar hospitality organizations carefully manage their own co-production responsibilities and monitor their guests' performance of their co-production tasks to make sure the guest experience at least meets, if not exceeds expectations.[4] Co-production is how guests co-create the value of their experience. As a result,

[2] See, for example: Janet R. McColl-Kennedy, Stephen L. Vargo, Tracey S. Dagger, Jillian C. Sweeney, and Yasmin van Kasteren, "Health Care Customer Value Cocreation Practice Styles," *Journal of Service Research* 15, no. 4 (2012): 370–389.

[3] Elina Jaakkola and Matthew Alexander, "The Role of Customer Engagement Behavior in Value Co-creation: A Service System Perspective," *Journal of Service Research* 17, no. 3 (2014): 247–261.

[4] Robert C. Ford and Janet R. McColl-Kennedy, "Organizational Strategies for Filling the Customer Can-do/Must-do Gap," *Business Horizons* 58, no. 4 (2015): 459–468.

EXHIBIT 8.2

Websites for Finding and Posting Reviews Related to Travel and Hospitality Services

WEBSITE	WHAT IT IS OR DOES
Consumersearch	Reviews mostly consumer goods, but also includes reviews related to travel.
Epinions	Reviews mostly consumer goods, but also includes reviews related to travel.
Fodors	Allows members to read and write reviews about travel experiences, share tips, and ask travel-related questions.
IgoUgo	Allows users to plan trips, read and write reviews, create travel journals, and share photos.
TripAdvisor	Offers advice from travelers and a variety of travel planning tools.
Virtualtourist	Provides user-generated travel content from around the world. Includes tips, reviews, and photos from travelers sharing their experiences.
Yelp	A social networking site that provides reviews of businesses and services. Includes travel-related reviews, such as for hotels and restaurants, but also of other businesses and nonbusiness locations.

customers can learn what organizations are really doing in dealing with their guests by talking to others, on social networks or information-sharing websites (e.g., TripAdvisor); what they should pay, by visiting product comparison websites (e.g., shopzilla, pricegrabber); and what the quality and value of the service product is.[5] These websites give guests the opportunity to interact directly with the hospitality organization and tell it what they, the guests, really want. It is up to the organization to find ways to listen, and guestologists always find ways. The point is that today's guests expect to co-produce the experience and co-create its value and quality in some way, and hospitality organizations need to find the means to fulfill that expectation.

There are several processes that can be used to engage the guests with the organization before, during, and after the hospitality experience. Some writers categorize the types of guest engagement into marketers, information providers, and co-producers. The discussion below will use a more elaborate categorization.

THE GUEST CAN HELP!

In the traditional manufacturing organization, the people involved in the core production tasks are insulated from external interruptions by layers of strategic planners and middle managers. The people providing many hospitality services, in contrast, are right out in the open where the guests can see and even interact with them. In many circumstances, the guests will take the primary role in co-producing the service themselves. Obvious examples are salad bars in restaurants and self-service check-ins at airports. Other obvious examples are the growing number of self-service technologies like web-based restaurant, airline, and hotel reservation sites.

[5] Coimbatore K. Prahalad and Venkat Ramaswamy, "Cocreation Experiences: The Next Practice in Value Creation," *Journal of Interactive Marketing* 18, no. 3 (2004): 5–14; Stephen L. Vargo and Robert F. Lusch, "Evolving to a New Dominant Logic for Marketing," *Journal of Marketing* 68, no. 1 (2004): 1–17.

A crucial implication for hospitality organizations when they involve guests in co-producing the guest experience, either indirectly as observers or directly as participants, is that they must remain constantly aware that a server, smartphone, or web screen is likely to be the point of contact between the organization and the guest. Instead of relying on highly paid, experienced, and loyal executives or well-trained sales representatives serving as the point of contact with customers and the outside world, the hospitality organization must rely on its frontline servers, a phone app, or a website to represent the company. Both the server and the technologies represent the initial moments of truth for creating the guest's first impression of the organization. Each year—for millions of Disney park visitors, Southwest Airlines passengers, Olive Garden restaurant diners, and Marriott hotel guests—the visible, frontline employees answer questions, solve problems, co-produce experiences, and keep their organizations operating smoothly and efficiently. These employees not only produce the magic that guests expect, but they do it while the guests are watching, participating, and asking a million questions about everything. Unlike the automobile assembly-line production employee who can work undistracted in a controlled and structured environment, these employees must produce the guest experience consistently and flawlessly while coping with the many uncertainties that interacting constantly with guests can create.

Guests as Quasi-Employees

Hospitality organizations know they must help manage the confusion, stress, and uncertainty guests can create for their employees while on their jobs. One way is by training the employees in both job skills and the management of guest co-production. Another effective strategy for managing this confusion is to think of guests as **quasi-employees** and "manage" them accordingly.[6]

quasi-employees
Term used to define the many different ways customers can help an organization be effective. Roles include not only co-producing their own experiences but also supervising, rewarding and motivating employees, training and supervising other guests, being quality control consultants, being part of other guests' experiences, and marketing.

These unpaid "employees" must have the knowledge, skills, and abilities (KSAs) to successfully co-produce the service experience. This means organizations need to design a service product, an environment, and a delivery system that match the KSAs the customers bring to the experience. It may also mean that companies need to "train" the customers on how to take advantage of the service product. If it is to the advantage of both guests and organization to involve guests in the experience, the organization must take on the responsibility of figuring out how best to enable these quasi-employees to succeed in doing their tasks within the experience. Unlike customers of the typical manufacturing organization, guests are actually paying the hospitality organization to be successfully managed—putting an extra burden on management to manage them effectively.

Benjamin Schneider and David Bowen recommend a three-step strategy for managing these quasi-employees:[7]

1. Carefully and completely define the tasks in which you want guests to engage. In effect, do a job analysis, similar to that developed in Chapter 5 for employees. Define the knowledge, skills, and abilities required to perform the jobs identified as desirable and appropriate for guests.
2. Make sure guests know exactly what you expect them to do and that they are physically able, mentally prepared, and sufficiently skilled to do those tasks.

[6] Robert C. Ford and John T. Bowen, "Getting Guests to Work for You," *Journal of Foodservice Business Research* 6, no. 3 (2004): 37–53; David E. Bowen, "Managing Customers as Human Resources in Service Organizations," *Human Resource Management* 25, no. 3 (1986): 371–383; Jonathon R.B. Halbesleben and Oliver K. Stoutner, "Developing Customers as Partial Employees: Predictors and Outcomes of Customer Performance in a Services Context," *Human Resource Development Quarterly* 24, no. 3 (2013): 313–335.
[7] Benjamin Schneider and David Earl Bowen, *Winning the Service Game* (Boston, MA: Harvard Business Review Press), 88–89.

Show guests that performing the tasks is to their benefit. Give them a reason to do the tasks well.

3. Once task performance is underway, evaluate the guest's ability and willingness to perform well. In effect, conduct a performance appraisal on the guest to ensure the experience being co-produced is meeting the guest's expectations. If it is not, identify what needs to be fixed. Does the guest need further training? Is something about the setting or delivery system impeding the guest's success?

Of course, the customers should not co-produce those parts of the experience where their performance may be too dangerous for them, time consuming, or when it would be too difficult for the customer to master the necessary skills in the time available. Airline passengers don't help fly the plane, although they may be asked to make sure they pick up their trash so the plane can be prepared for its next flight more quickly. By assessing each component of the entire guest experience carefully, the hospitality provider can identify those parts of it that might be designed to discourage, encourage, or even require guest co-production. A restaurant could offer a low-price self-service buffet to *discourage* patrons requesting expensive waitstaff, a hotel might provide self-service check-in kiosks to *encourage* its guests to avoid waiting for an available front desk agent, or an airline might *require* self-check-ins with a kiosk assistant available only to help when guests have problems. In each of these instances, customers can choose to have an employee serve them (and wait for service) or they can produce their own service product: go get their salads, access their hotel rooms, or print their own boarding passes.

The Organization Decides

Some hospitality organizations do not offer the guest any choice; they either design parts of the experience in ways that make co-production impossible or structure it so that the guest must participate to some extent. A quick-serve restaurant is quick-serve and inexpensive because it requires customers to serve as their own order-takers, servers, and table clearers. Without the cost of servers bustling about taking a variety of customized orders, filling glasses, and picking up dirty dishes, McDonald's and Burger King can save money and offer a quick, less expensive food product than a fine-dining restaurant can. In the fast-food service setting, the customer must participate somewhat but cannot be allowed to take over completely. The efficiency of the quick-serve process is based on a carefully engineered food-production system that ensures a consistent quality and safe food product. Allowing customers to cook their own burgers and fries would significantly interfere with production efficiency while creating substantial food safety and sanitation problems. The quick-serve restaurant gains efficiency by letting the customers serve themselves in the part of the service delivery system that takes place in front of the counter. They do not allow customers behind the counter, where they can slow down the production process or jeopardize food safety.

Organizations need to think through when and where to let guests co-produce their own experience and how much co-production there should be. Sometimes co-production makes sense for the organization and the guest, and sometimes it does not. The challenge is to identify which situation is best regarding the amount of co-production that leads to the greatest value for the guest.[8]

[8] Christopher Mims, "The Customer-Service Quandary: Touchy Feely or Do It Yourself: Some Companies Want to Make You Their Friend; Others Make It Hard to Phone Them," *Wall Street Journal*, November 2, 2015, https://www.wsj.com/articles/the-customer-service-quandary-touchy-feely-or-do-it-yourself-1446440460; Michael Etgar, "A Descriptive Model of the Consumer Co-production Process," *Journal of the Academy of Marketing Science* 36, no. 1 (2008): 97–108.

STRATEGIES FOR INVOLVING THE GUEST

A guest can be involved with a hospitality organization in several ways: as a consultant or source of expertise and quality information, as a marketer, as part of the environment for other guests, as co-producer of the experience, or as a manager of the service providers and systems. Some of these involvements may sound unlikely, but they are all common.

Guests as Unpaid Consultants

When the hospitality organization asks its guests what they like or dislike about the guest experience, they become unpaid consultants and act as quality control inspectors. Because their input regarding their experiences will become part of the information that management uses to review and adjust the service product, environment, and delivery system, the guests are acting as expert consultants in giving this important feedback to the organization. Using outsiders in this way is not unique to hospitality firms; many other types of organizations systematically invite their suppliers, customers, and even communities to provide feedback about how they are doing. Uber and Lyft both rely heavily on the idea of using customer feedback to evaluate and manage their drivers. For both companies, if customer ratings of a driver fall below a certain point, the drivers can be put on warning or even be "deactivated." Both companies also try to get customers to explain ratings so that drivers can understand why they did not receive the top ratings from a given customer which can help drivers to improve their service experiences. After all, who is better to judge whether a driver was friendly and efficient than the actual customers of the company?

Organizations also frequently invite customers to participate as members of focus groups. As discussed in a later chapter on assessing service quality, these groups are designed to give expert feedback about the service experience to the service provider, and no one can be more expert on that experience or its quality and value than the customers themselves.

Technology

Some hospitality organizations are creating ways for guests to help discover new ways of delivering a service experience through crowdsourcing.[9] Crowdsourcing allows these organizations to open up their innovation processes to guests across the world. By posting on its own web page or some commercial crowdsourcing platform a question (e.g., "What do you think our next flavor of ice cream should be?") or request for opinions (e.g., "Tell us three reasons you like our restaurant.") with rewards for the best contribution, organizations are turning their feedback and idea generation processes into contests open to anyone anywhere with internet access. Since no one really knows where the next great idea will come from or who will suggest it, crowdsourcing offers organizations the ability to access everyone's ideas and suggestions wherever they may be.

Guests as Marketers

Everyone has asked a friend or colleague about a hospitality experience. The person who just came back from a terrific meal, a resort stay that was beyond expectations, or an amazing cruise, is eager to talk about it. Likewise, the person who just returned from a ruined dining experience, terrible hotel stay, or the cruise with bad food and service, is equally eager to talk about it—perhaps more so. Guests are excellent marketers for good or bad service. They are asked by their friends and acquaintances for their opinion in both face-to-face communications and through web-based social

[9] Robert C. Ford, Brendan Richard, and Michael P. Ciuchta, "Crowdsourcing: A New Way of Employing Non-employees?," *Business Horizons* 58, no. 4 (2015): 377–388.

networking, and this "word of mouth" can make or break a hospitality organization. Recognizing the power of this marketing medium—the customer—especially when the service experience is bad, is an important part of the manager's responsibility and will be covered in greater detail in the chapter on fixing service failures (Chapter 13).

Technology

A more recent development in using guests to co-produce marketing is the group coupon sites. The basic idea is to get people to organize into large enough groups so they can qualify for a discount or special rate on a service. Websites like Groupon and LivingSocial negotiate with retailers for a special price on items like spa services, paintball, or specialty restaurants. The Groupon site lists one retailer a day but the deal becomes official only when a fixed number of people sign up for it. These sites reward people for their help in marketing. With LivingSocial, a person can get a specific deal free if he or she gets three others to sign up for it. Both sites give dollar rewards to users who recruit friends. In other words, these sites utilize guests to market to other guests using their social networks in a powerful way. The communications technology used today in combination with the existing social networking sites offer amazing opportunities to use guests as active marketers for a wide variety of hospitality organizations.

Guests as Part of Each Other's Experience

If you enjoy simply watching other guests, you may think of them as part of the service environment. If other guests are especially important to your enjoyment of your experience, you might even consider them a part of the service product itself. The line is not always clear. For example, most people don't like to go to an empty restaurant or movie theatre; enjoying the experience along with other people, even strangers, is part of the package. Going to a water park when it is comfortably full and when it is almost empty are very different experiences. Water parks, like many other service situations where the emphasis is on "having fun," rely to some extent on other customers being part of the fun. Thus, many people get great enjoyment out of watching other people, ordinary folks just like themselves, act as bit players in a Universal or Disney Hollywood Studios film-making demonstration. For those doing the acting, the guest experience obviously includes the opportunity to participate in the movie simulation. For observers, however, those customers doing something unusual are perhaps best considered as part of the service ecosystem.[10] Though interesting, unusual, or amusing, watching them is not really the reason why you came to the amusement park, water park, or casino.

This principle of encouraging customers to be either directly or indirectly part of other guests' experiences is evident in new web-sharing technologies—for example, video clips on YouTube—but it has been a practice in hospitality for quite a while. For example, at one of Coney Island's earliest amusement parks, Steeplechase, there was a stadium set up next to a rotating Barrel of Love so the customers could watch others fall down in a tangle with complete strangers and look foolish. For them, the opportunity to watch other people falling down awkwardly was an important part of the amusement experience. Indeed, the founder of Steeplechase Park early in the twentieth century, George Tilyou, was one of the first to recognize that a successful amusement park provided its customers the opportunity to observe the most entertaining experience of all: other people. In his park, the visitors were the main show. According to amusement parks authority Gary Kyriazi, "Tilyou felt that people will pay any price in order to provide their own entertainment."[11]

After couples had finished the Steeplechase ride, they would walk down a corridor and then find themselves on a brightly lit stage called the Insanitarium. Unknown to them, crowds of people would be sitting in bleachers watching them. As Kyriazi

[10] Pennie Frow, Janet R. McColl-Kennedy, Toni Hilton, Anthony Davidson, Adrian Payne, and Danilo Brozovic, "Value Propositions: A Service Ecosystems Perspective," *Marketing Theory* 14, no. 3 (2014): 327–351.

[11] Gary Kyriazi, *The Great American Amusement Parks: A Pictorial History* (Secaucus, NJ: Citadel Press, 1976), 82.

Welgos/Getty Images

Bettmann via Getty Images

At Coney Island, Brooklyn, New York City, children race against each other in the Steeplechase ride. On the Spinning Disk, two women try to remain on the wheel before being flung off to the side. For a long time at amusement parks, both watching others and participating have been part of the experience.

describes the scene, "Suddenly, strong air jets would lift the women's dresses (exposed ankles were rare at the time) and blow the men's hats off. A clown would prod the men with an electric stinger. When they tried to escape, piles of barrels on either side of the exit gangway would begin to sway and appear to tumble down on them as they made their escape." They could then join the crowd beyond the glare of the stage lights and laugh at others going through what Kyriazi calls "the same light, humorous torment."[12]

Although standards have changed, and modern hospitality organizations do not see torment, even if "light and humorous," as a service they want to provide outside of Halloween "fright nights," the principle that guests enjoy watching guests is as true today as it was then. Successful operators make sure to offer plenty of opportunities for guests to observe other guests.

Although a case can be made for considering other guests as part of the service product itself or as supervisors under certain circumstances, they are most often a part of the service environment. Like any other environmental element, they can be a neutral influence, they can damage the experience for others, or they can enhance it. Movies, concerts, and Broadway plays all rely on the audience to help create the mood. All these entertainments are more enjoyable with a full house than they are when empty. The laughter and other reactions of people surrounding the customer become an important part of the customer's environment. Indeed, some attractions rely on paid professionals or electronically created cues to generate applause, laughter, or other emotional responses that create the right setting for the service experience. At the other extreme, everyone has had an experience ruined by a crying baby, a person at a concert that won't sit down, or a thoughtless bunch of loud talkers on cell phones. The reason the three-ring circus was invented by William C. Coup was to increase the ability for all spectators to see the performances without leaving their seats and blocking the view of others.[13] For better or worse, other guests are part of the hospitality servicescape and, therefore, need to be managed like any other environmental element.

Guests as Co-Producers

Perhaps the most important way in which guests can participate, other than simply being there, is as active co-producers of the guest experience. During all or parts of

[12] Kyriazi, 87.

[13] Keenan D. Yoho, Robert Ford, Bo Edvardsson, and Fred Dahlinger, "Moving 'The Greatest Show on Earth': WC Coup as an Innovation Champion," *Journal of Management History* 24, no. 1 (2018): 76–98.

the service experience, they can actually become participants in the production and delivery system. This participation can be as simple as having guests serve themselves at a fast-food restaurant, preparing their own salads at the salad bar, or carrying their own bags at the golf course to substitute for the job of a paid employee. The value of guest co-production can be substantial for the organization. While this may be a more costly strategy under some circumstances, in general, every time guests co-produce at least some of their own experiences, they are replacing some or all of the labor the organization would otherwise have to pay to do the same thing, while often improving the quality and value of their own experience.

©iStockphoto.com/Alina555

Guests are often part of each other's experience in casino gaming.

Marriott is an example of one company that looks for interesting and fun ways to help guests reduce the environmental impact of their hotels. For example, in 2017, Marriott introduced its *Marriott Towel Origami Promotion* at over 100 hotels across Europe. Guests were invited to reuse their towels, and use them to make origami sculptures in their rooms. Guests could then post their creations to Tumblr, Instagram, or Twitter and be entered into a drawing for a free weekend stay.[14]

Sustainability

Marriott created a way to encourage guests to help them reduce their environmental impact while also getting some positive social media exposure. By giving guests a fun way to help Marriott reduce its laundry expenses, it met its goals of saving energy, reducing water consumption and operating in a more environmentally friendly way.

Advantages of Co-production for the Organization

The organization gains several advantages by having the guests co-produce their experience. First, co-production may reduce employee costs.[15] Generally, the more guests do for themselves, the fewer employees the organization needs to employ. In addition to being an obvious labor-saving strategy, co-production allows the organization to use the talents of its employees better. If guests are allowed, encouraged, or required to take care of some of their own basic requirements or perform routine tasks, employees are freed up to do more elaborate or complicated tasks that the guests would not enjoy or do successfully, and tasks that would simply not be suitable for guests. For example, at many restaurants, patrons can make their own reservations on the web or with a phone app. Maitre d's and hosts take fewer reservation phone calls, which permits them to spend more time responding to guests who need information or advice. In effect, by letting the guests schedule themselves, the quality of the restaurant service goes up with no increase in costs.

In a similar fashion, the strategy of offering buffets at lunch is an effective way for restaurants to stay open at lunch time without overextending their waitstaff. Many servers are unhappy working at lunch time, because the check sizes (and tips) are lower. People tired out from working at lunch cannot work as efficiently at the dinner

---

[14] Planet Marriot Europe, "You Create, You Post, We Donate," planetmarrioteurope.tumbler, Tumblr, 2016, http://planetmarriotteurope.tumblr.com/post/115122877560/you-create-you-post-we-donate.

[15] Ming-Hui Huang and Roland T. Rust, "Technology-Driven Service Strategy," *Journal of the Academy of Marketing Science* 45, no. 6 (2017): 906–924.

©iStockphoto.com/zoranm

A buffet is a common method of co-production, allowing guests to select what and how much they want, while also allowing the company to hire fewer service personnel, thereby saving money.

hour. A buffet provides meals with a minimal use of waitstaff, the diner gets a good price on the meal, the restaurant gets more utilization of its physical plant and increases total revenue by being open more hours and serving more diners, and the restaurant provides a better work situation for its servers.

Advantages of Co-production for the Guest

For the guest, co-production has a number of advantages. First, it can decrease the opportunity for service failure while increasing the perception, and perhaps the actuality, of service quality. Since the guests themselves define value and quality, handling production themselves means they can produce exactly what they want. If guests fix their own salads at the salad bar in exactly the way they want them, how can they complain if the salads aren't perfect? Guests can pile on their favorite salad items in their favorite quantities and avoid the items they dislike. They end up feeling they got the very salad they wanted. This opportunity creates the perception of real value. This can range from the obvious examples like simply telling the server what you wish to eat or taking the initiative to enter the desired restaurant in the first place to less obvious examples—like walking to enough attractions to get full value from a theme park visit or abstaining from texting long enough to enjoy the concert.

Second, the opportunity for self-service typically reduces the time required for service. A simple example is the customer at the airport who chooses to use the self-check-in kiosk instead of standing in line to wait for a counter clerk. Fast-food, fast-casual, and fast-fine restaurants make their reputations and define their market niches on the basis of both the nature of their food *and* saving time for their customers who are too busy to eat in a full-service restaurant.

Third, self-service reduces the risk of unpleasant surprises for guests. If diners walk through a cafeteria's buffet line, they can see exactly what the food products are, instead of ordering off a menu and hoping for the best. While not everything tastes as good as it looks, choosing one's own meal from a cafeteria line or buffet can reduce the perception of risk in comparison with ordering meals unseen from a menu.

©iStockphoto.com/anouchka

Self-serve kiosks at airports allow guests to save time.

Disadvantages of Co-production for the Organization

Permitting or requiring co-production may also have disadvantages for the organization. First, in this litigious society, participation exposes the organization to legal risk. Having a guest handle a hot pot in a cook-your-own fondue restaurant could lead to a major burn and lawsuit. Second, the organization may have to spend extra money to train the customer contact employees so they can add to their usual serving jobs the task of both recognizing when guests are ready to co-produce and when they are not and, then, communicating effectively and easily about what guests are supposed to do. These employees are responsible for instructing the guests in how to provide the service for themselves and for monitoring the experience to prevent the guests from creating any disasters. Every guest is different and comes to the guest experience with different skills, knowledge, abilities, and expectations for the service itself. Servers who train and oversee guests must be alert, observant, and skilled in recognizing guests' capabilities to co-produce and in how to coach all types of guests through the experience. This training cost increases as guest use of self-service technologies increases. Hiring and training people to perform the necessary job skills at, say, a modern copy center is one thing, but to allow or encourage self-service, the organization must go beyond basic job skills to hire and train people who can successfully teach customers to use computers, scanners, and copy machines. One of the most interesting challenges of self-service technologies is to ensure that customers do not fail while using it or get confused and discouraged to the point they abandon the use of the technology and the company offering it.[16]

This means that successful hospitality organizations must not only train their guest-contact employees to recognize when guests are ready, willing, and able to participate in the co-production of their experiences, but they must also carefully design their service systems and service setting to accommodate the variations in guest capabilities. Teaching employees to recognize the difference between customers who are able to co-produce and those who are not is important.[17]

If guests co-produce their experience, the service delivery system and the service environment must be user friendly. If the organization wants the guest to follow a predetermined sequence of operations to create the desired experience, it must have people to guide them, excellent directional signs, or, for online or phone-based services, an interface that is intuitively obvious to people from varied cultures. Only then can the organization be reasonably sure that all types of guests will do what they are supposed to do when and where they are supposed to do it. Signs in a self-serve cafeteria must indicate clearly where the entry point is, where the trays, silverware, and napkins are, and how the diner is supposed to proceed through the food selection and payment procedure. Someone unfamiliar with a cafeteria restaurant may have no idea how to navigate this service delivery process. The cafeteria workers must be alert to confused-looking people wandering around looking for signs, directions, and instructions on how to participate successfully in this food delivery process.

Involving guests in the service delivery system also has an impact on the cost and layout of the environment. Most hospitality organizations already spend time and energy ensuring that the traditional front-of-the-house areas meet guests' expectations in terms of appearance and quality, but those organizations that involve guests in the service delivery system spend the money to ensure that back-of-the-house areas meet their expectations as well. Making the back of the house a part of the "show" has an obvious impact on how the equipment is laid out, what it looks like, how shiny and clean it is kept, how the personnel are dressed, and what skills they must have to work alongside the guests in service co-production. Instead of having not particularly articulate cooks in greasy aprons producing meals in an out-of-sight kitchen, involvement of the guest in a food-production system means that the organization must hire employees who can communicate easily with diners, maintain a neat appearance,

[16] Mary Jo Bitner, Amy L. Ostrom, and Matthew L. Meuter, "Implementing Successful Self-Service Technologies," *The Academy of Management Executive* 16, no. 4 (2002): 96–108; Joel E. Collier and Sheryl E. Kimes, "Only If It Is Convenient: Understanding How Convenience Influences Self-Service Technology Evaluation," *Journal of Service Research* 16, no. 1 (2013): 39–51.

[17] John Bateson, "Are Your Customers Good Enough for Your Service Business?," *The Academy of Management Executive* 16, no. 4 (2002): 110–120; Robert C. Ford and Duncan R. Dickson, "Enhancing Customer Self-efficacy in Co-producing Service Experiences," *Business Horizons* 55, no. 2 (2012): 179–188.

and ensure the kitchen and other visible food preparation areas are always clean and healthy looking to meet the guest's expectations. All this is expensive because the costs of the uniforms, the extra interpersonal skills required of the employees, and the rearrangement of the food-production area to allow the guest to be involved in the food-production process will add to the costs of the production system.

Guest involvement expands the role of the guest-contact employee. Now the employee must have the skills and abilities to be a coach, trainer, teacher, standard setter, fixer of problems, and manager of the guest flow through the delivery system. Hospitality employees must know how to get guests engaged in co-production and also how to get them to disengage. If guests enjoy co-production and are reluctant to disengage, the organization that does not want to hurry its guests may have to add extra capacity.

Clearly, when guests become co-producers, the traditional role of server in the guest experience requires redefinition, and servers need additional training in the new roles they must play if co-production is to work to the organization's advantage.

Disadvantages of Co-production for the Guest

From the guest's perspective, co-production can have disadvantages.[18] The most obvious one is that paying guests may resent having to produce any part of that for which they are paying. Some task-oriented guests don't particularly want much guest-server interaction; they just want, for example, a quick meal. A production-line approach suits them just fine. Other guests insist and thrive on close personal attention and are willing to pay for it, or they may be uncomfortable with the technology used in place of the personal service. If shifting part of the guest-experience production to guests themselves results in a perception of less TLC, some guests will be dissatisfied.

Another possible disadvantage is that guests may fail to co-produce the service properly. If they find the items they assembled from the salad bar don't taste as good as they thought they would, or if they experiment with some new food selections from the buffet and it turns out it was not a success, the guest will not have co-produced a "wow" experience. Similarly, a customer may mistakenly select the wrong option when using an automated kiosk or telephone tree, be frustrated by the experience, and perhaps may not be able to figure out how to fix the error. While hospitality organizations that seek to provide excellent service may want to utilize the advantages of guest co-production, when problems occur, they can't blame the guest for the unsatisfactory experience. Hospitality organizations know that people tend to take credit for their successes and attribute failures to someone else—usually the company.[19] Excellent providers of customer service try to protect guests against self-service failures and create opportunities for their success. They want the guest to have the satisfying experience expected when they chose the organization rather than a competitor. The organization may let the guest try again or offer to help. The risk is nonetheless present that the guest may not be able, ready, or willing to co-produce a desired experience.

The High Cost of Failure

While unsatisfactory or unsuccessful co-production can be a minor annoyance to a restaurant patron, it can be disastrous if the cost of failure is great. If you run a dude ranch and let inexperienced riders go off alone on horseback, the result may be humiliation, broken bones, or worse—plus a lawsuit. Or imagine a situation in which you co-produce a fondue meal with a peer, boss, or significant other—and fail. The best hospitality organizations make every effort to ensure that guests succeed

[18] Sven Heidenreich et al., "The Dark Side of Customer Co-creation: Exploring the Consequences of Failed Co-created Services," *Journal of the Academy of Marketing Science* 43, no. 3 (2015): 279–296; Tina Harrison and Kathryn Waite, "Impact of Co-production on Consumer Perception of Empowerment," *The Service Industries Journal* 35, no. 10 (2015): 502–520.
[19] Neeli Bendapudi and Robert P. Leone, "Psychological Implications of Customer Participation in Co-production," *Journal of Marketing* 67, no. 1 (2003): 14–28.

as co-producers, but the risk of failure is always there. If the costs of failure are too high, the organization must tactfully intervene to keep the guest from failing. The server must be sensitive and aware enough to recognize when a guest is about to fail, must take over before the failure occurs, or fix the failure, and be able to do all these things with sufficient grace that the guest is not embarrassed by failing when others all around are succeeding. These requirements add up to high expectations for a low paid, entry-level employee.

Motivating Guests to Co-Produce

Guests can safely participate when they have the necessary knowledge, skills, and abilities to create the service product, but guests must be both motivated to participate in the process and confident they can do what is required. Like employees, guests will be motivated to "perform" when they can see some economic, psychological, or social benefits in participation.[20] Some experiences can be completed only if co-produced. Psychiatric treatment will fail if the patient refuses to be involved. In any large geographically spread service setting—like a zoo, museum, food court, cruise ship, or national park—customers who want a particular array of experiences must schedule them for themselves. If customers don't plan out their time and physically move themselves around, they are unlikely to enjoy the experience.

Many guests are motivated to participate because of the economic incentives available to those who take a role in their own guest experience. Others are motivated by their personalities or their familiarity with the experience being offered, or they are simply looking for something to do while waiting for the other parts of the guest experience to take place. Some guests just want to be a part of whatever it is they're involved in at the moment, no matter what, and constantly look for such opportunities. Some people always park their own cars, carry their own luggage, or walk up the stairs for the benefit of the exercise, or because they like to demonstrate for themselves (and anyone else who may watch) that they are physically fit enough to do these things. Others like to show how mentally fit or technically adept they are by doing things for themselves—whether it be by making their own online travel reservations or baiting their own hooks on a deep-sea fishing trip. Of course, some people also think they do a better job than an employee could do.

Finally, some people just like to be the center of attention and seek opportunities to be "on stage." In a simple situation, Joe wants to show his friends how well known he is at Ralph's Restaurant, so he goes and gets his own coffee or refills his partner's ice water instead of waiting for the server. Even more on stage is the couple who volunteers to sing in a karaoke bar, the woman who volunteers to be the magician's assistant, or the man who sits where he will be drenched in a SeaWorld demonstration. Many people enjoy showing off, and hospitality organizations should try to provide appropriate opportunities for them somewhere in the service delivery system.

On the other hand, some guests need reminders that they are able to perform the tasks required in co-production. This means the organization needs to provide confidence building cues to guests. Not everyone reaching the front of the bungee cord line, ski slope, or roller coaster is ready to actually do what they need to do to enjoy the experience. Even though the organization has made sure that those they admit to the experience will be safe, some guests won't believe they can do it. The hospitality organization can implement strategies to build guests' self-efficacy or confidence in their ability to perform the required co-production tasks. As seen in Exhibit 8.3, these can include training employees to be encouraging when seeing a guest showing doubt, providing video screens that show other guests enjoying the experience,

[20] Mekhai Mustak et al., "Customer Participation Management: Developing a Comprehensive Framework and a Research Agenda," *Journal of Service Management* 27, no. 3 (2016): 250–275; Janet R. McColl-Kennedy et al., "Fresh Perspectives on Customer Experience," *Journal of Services Marketing* 29, no. 6/7 (2015): 430–435.

EXHIBIT 8.3

Organizational Strategies to Enhance Customer Self-Efficacy to Co-Produce Experiences

STRATEGY	EXAMPLES
Enactive Mastery	• Videos of self in successful task performance (e.g., golfers, skiers, athletes) • Self-imagery to imagine self succeeding at task • Extensions of past successful performance (e.g., iPad, selection of seats on airplane) • No-risk trials (e.g., dance studios, investment advisors) • Employee stationed to failsafe (e.g., FASTPASS, airline check-in) • Organizational memory of customer capabilities (Customer Relationship Management: CRM) • Simple task design (e.g., McDonald's)
Vicarious Experience	• Modeling by friends and intimates (e.g., watching a friend or group of friends perform task) • Modeling by demographic similars (e.g., advertisements, videos, live performances, group therapy, online tutorials, volunteers from audience) • Fictitious models (e.g., tales and stories about exemplars)
Verbal Persuasion	• Encouragement from friends and intimates (e.g., "You can do it, honey!") • Verbal support from boss and co-workers (e.g., employee coaching) • Self-talk (e.g., talking oneself into performing task) • Audience/strangers (e.g., listening to audience encouraging one to bungee jump) • Computer-generated encouragement on task performance
Physiological Arousal	• Appeal to senses (e.g., smells good, up-tempo music gets you going) • Adrenalin rush to heighten performance

Source: Robert C. Ford and Duncan R. Dickson, "Enhancing Customer Self-Efficacy in Co-producing Service Experiences," *Business Horizons* 55, no. 2 (2012), p. 182.

or displaying inspiring slogans and getting other guests to cheer. All these strategies are designed to boost the guest's confidence in successfully performing the tasks required in co-producing the experience.[21]

The Guest as a Substitute for Management

Guests can serve in a quasi-managerial role as unofficial supervisors and motivators of employees; they can even supervise and train other guests.

Guests as Supervisors

Guests have more contact with the service personnel, speak with them more often, and see more of their job performance than the organization's supervisors do. Guests have the opportunity and the motivation to act as supervisors and provide immediate feedback as to whether an employee is making them happy or unhappy. After all, the guest is paying for the service and is, therefore, motivated to tell the server (who to the guest receiving the service is the organization) what the guest thinks about the service, the server, and the organization. Hospitality employees are trying to produce memorable guest experiences; the guests themselves will let the employees know how well they have succeeded. The more familiar guests are with the organization, the more they know about what level of service should be provided and the more qualified they are to provide technical feedback. All these guest activities and functions are in a sense

[21] Robert C. Ford and Duncan R. Dickson, "Enhancing Customer Self-Efficacy in Co-producing Service Experiences," *Business Horizons* 55, no. 2 (2012): 179–188; Jinyoung Im and Hailin Qu, "Drivers and Resources of Customer Co-creation: A Scenario-based Case in the Restaurant Industry," *International Journal of Hospitality Management* 64 (2017): 31–40.

supervisory because the guests are observing, guiding, and motivating employees and, in many cases, "paying" them for good or poor service with a large or small tip.

Everyone has watched an unhappy guest tell an employee that the employee is not providing the service properly. That guest is in effect performing a supervisory function: providing feedback to the employee. Anyone watching characters in the Magic Kingdom interact with the children will soon see that the children are supervising the actions and behavior of the characters better than any supervisor ever could. The children will immediately respond to any deviation from character or any flaw in the character performance. They give constant feedback to cast members to let them know if they are not doing something right. Although supervisors also monitor the behavior of cast members as they perform their character roles, their job is, in a sense, much simpler than that of supervisors in the manufacturing sector. The typical auto assembly-line worker never has a car talk to him, smile at him when he installs the brakes correctly, participate as a co-producer in the installation, or complain when he fails to do it correctly. The hospitality supervisor must worry about guests doing all these things. In the hospitality organization, guests talk, smile, co-produce, give directions, and complain. They assess the performance of servers and, through tips, compensate certain employees for the services they provide. Having guests constantly monitoring and responding to the employee's job performance is a substantial aid to the supervisory responsibility.

Guests as Motivators

Having guests participate in supervision can be highly motivating to employees when guests tell them in both verbal and nonverbal ways what a good job they are doing. The classic example of guests serving in a quasi-supervisory role is seen in the practice of guest tipping. Many trace the origin of the term, TIPS, to its use as a guest provided incentive, "To Insure Prompt Service," given in advance of a service to motivate the server to provide excellent service. While the term has taken on broader use today, the idea behind tipping is still for the guest to help motivate servers to provide excellent service. This monetary incentive, in addition to the use of customer feedback in rewarding and recognizing customer facing employees, makes guests quasi-supervisors as they influence the employee's rewards for service performance.

Guests can provide supervisory feedback in other ways as well. Most hospitality employees find great enjoyment in meeting and exceeding the expectations of guests. Chefs often love to be challenged by guests who are knowledgeable about the culinary arts. Hospitality employees usually enjoy the opportunity to be challenged by a guest who shares an interest or expertise in the subject of the experience. College professors often find the students who ask the most difficult questions to be the most fun to have in class. Most hospitality employees are constantly tested by the variety in guest expectations and ability to perform their responsibilities in the service delivery process. In the Magic Kingdom, the challenge of making all children happy by responding to their unique needs and personalities makes the job of playing a Disney character a high-status and highly sought-after job. It's fun to show off what you can really do when you have an appreciative audience.

Guests as Supervisors and Trainers for Other Guests

Guests can also supervise and train each other. Learning how to stand in line seems like an obvious skill until one encounters people from other cultures who do not believe in standing in line. Someone has to train the untrained to stand in line in an orderly way, and the people already in line will do that. Watch the customers already standing in line the next time you see someone break into a line and you'll witness a training session in line standing. Most guests of hospitality organizations, like most employees, are anxious to fulfill their responsibilities and do their jobs well. They can be seen watching other people in order to learn what their own behavior should be in the various tasks of the co-production process. Waiting lines are often located to allow guests not being served to observe guests who are being served; by the time the guests in the airport security line get to the screener, they know pretty much what they are supposed to do.

We all learn from watching others, and with so many people in most hospitality situations on a typical day or occasion, we can learn what we're supposed to do to enjoy the experience by observing others. The first-time guest at a basketball game learns from others when to chant "airball" and enjoys the game all the more for chanting.

The organization can also use videos of experienced guests to show waiting guests what they are supposed to do. At most amusement parks, television monitors are set up so waiting guests can see what role will be expected of them when their turn comes to participate in the attraction or get on the ride. If the organization can use its guests to train at least some of the other guests, it can save itself the cost of those employees who would be required to train those guests and minimize the time spent explaining to the next guest what the last guest just did. The cost and time savings can be substantial.

Likewise, guests can supervise other guests in the performance of the roles they need to successfully perform to be satisfied with the experience. Many guests are more than willing to tell other guests where to go or not go, when they are behaving inappropriately, or doing something that might be dangerous or detrimental to both their own and others' experiences. Managing guests as they manage other guests is a tricky task as there are costs and benefits of letting guests train and supervise one another that must be carefully balanced to avoid guest dissatisfaction.

DETERMINING WHERE CO-PRODUCTION MAKES SENSE

Sometimes, both the organization and the guest benefit from co-production and sometimes not. Distinguishing when, where, and how much the guest should or should not be involved in any specific part of the overall guest experience depends on a variety of factors. Generally speaking, co-producing specific aspects of the service is in the interest of guests when they can gain value, reduce risk, or improve the quality of the overall experience by their engagement. Co-production is in the organization's interest when it can save money, increase production efficiency, or differentiate its service from that of competitors in a key way. Each opportunity for co-production should be assessed on these criteria and designed into the hospitality organization when the factors are favorable and designed out to the extent possible when they are not.

Enriching the Wait

Sometimes, situations encouraging co-production evolve when guests are required to wait for service. Organizations should try to decrease the feeling that the wait is too long by giving guests something to do, ideally something that will enrich the overall experience. A good example is getting a group of people sitting on a delayed flight to participate in a singalong, a technique frequently attributed to Southwest Airlines. Passengers get the opportunity to keep active while they are waiting for their flight to take off, and the singing may even enhance the experience by providing a pleasant way to pass the time.

Co-Producing Value

While all hospitality situations require some participation and some guests look for opportunities to participate no matter what, almost everyone is happy with opportunities to co-produce if doing so adds value to their experience. By definition, value can be added by reducing costs (for the same quality), increasing quality (for the same costs), or both. Costs include not only the price but also the other costs incurred by being involved in the guest experience. For example, if a potential guest sees a long line outside her favorite restaurant, the time cost of waiting for the next available table may be so great that she willingly goes to a nearby cafeteria or fast-food restaurant—to reduce the time cost of getting a meal. The guest may experience a decrease in quality but expects the greater decrease in overall cost to compensate for it. Similarly, guests who want to be sure of service quality may want to participate in providing service. Those guests derive additional value from knowing that they are getting the service "their way." Even non-hospitality organizations like Lowes have learned they can make a lot of money serving customers who want to co-create the quality and value of their home repair by doing it themselves. Customers look to Lowes not only to provide a fair price on the building products, but also to give the necessary instruction or help to do the job correctly.

Another cost of co-production for the guest is risk, the risk that the service may not meet expectations. Guests who take on more of the co-production of their experiences minimize the risk that a hospitality employee will not provide exactly what is wanted. Most travelers now go online to look for hotel accommodations and flight reservations instead of relying on travel or airline agents. They believe they will be able to find the best options to fit their needs, whereas a travel agent or airline may be more interested in selling them the most profitable travel package or simply won't make the effort to find the price, times, or routes they want.

Key Factors: Time and Control

Besides the obvious factors of having the necessary knowledge, skills, abilities, and motivation (and self-efficacy) to participate, two other dimensions of providing service can help distinguish between situations where guests can beneficially be involved in co-production and where they should not. The two other important factors are: time and control. Each of these is of two kinds: real and perceived.[22]

With respect to time, the *feeling* of how long something takes is as important to the guest as how long it *actually* takes. In Chapter 11, on waiting lines, these real and perceived factors are discussed in detail. The same is true for control. The amount of control over the quality of, value of, risk involved in, or efficiency of the experience that guests think they acquire by participating is as important in determining the value of participation as the actual control guests have. As an example, many resort facilities offer a climbing wall for their guests to enjoy the feeling of rock climbing. The walls are designed to allow climbers to choose their own path up the wall and experience the exhilaration of a successful rock climb. On the other hand, every climber is required to wear a safety harness to ensure that the occasional slips and falls do not turn into a disastrous experience. Climbers enjoy the illusion they are in control of the situation, when in reality the harnesses cover up any mistakes.

Cutting Costs, Increasing Capacity

From the organization's point of view, the most obvious reason to incorporate the guest into the guest experience is to save money. As noted earlier, whenever the guest

[22] John E. Bateson, "Self-service Consumer: An Exploratory Study," *Journal of Retailing* 61, no. 3 (1985): 49–76.

produces some or all of the service experience, the guest is providing labor the organization would otherwise have to hire. The second reason is to increase production efficiency or increase capacity utilization. If a restaurant offers a buffet at lunch, it provides a meal product at a time of day when waitstaff are sometimes unavailable or unwilling to work. The restaurant still has the opportunity to derive income from its physical plant and food-production capacity without overusing its human resources. In a similar sense, many other organizations can add self-service capacity to handle surges or unevenness in guest demand. A hotel can offer its check-in and check-out guests an automated option if they don't want to wait in line, or a rental-car agency can offer automated check-in/check-out service for its regular customers. In this way, the organization can maintain a constant staffing level while still being able to accommodate the variability in customer demand for this service. Letting customers co-produce this part of the service experience increases the number of customers who can be handled without increasing labor costs.

Co-Production as a Differentiation Strategy

Organizations can also use co-production as part of a product differentiation strategy. The obvious example is the cook-your-own restaurant that sells the experience of doing it yourself to distinguish itself from other restaurants. While the physical part of the service product is food, the entire service product also includes the experience. These restaurants, and increasingly grocery stores, often try to make the cooking a social experience, making reservations for groups of friends, and providing the environment that produces not only food people want and the opportunity to enjoy cooking their own meals, but also the fun of the social experience. These co-production experiences are also used by organizations seeking to build stronger teams by having their employees work together to create a meal as a team building exercise. Other examples abound, such as self-service gas stations, car-rental agencies, cafeterias, and banking services. Boston Market offers a take-home product but no delivery service. This combination distinguishes it from both the quick-serve drive-through and home-delivery restaurants. Having the customer come inside gives Boston Market the opportunity to sell more products than it could if the customer was ordering over the phone or reading off the menu at the drive-through window. This co-production strategy helps Boston Market position itself as a quick and convenient stop for busy people.

Building Commitment

A final reason for letting guests participate is to build guest commitment and repeat business. If a guest feels the organization trusts her enough to let her provide her own service, the guest feels a bond and a commitment to this place where everybody knows her name. Getting the guest involved in the guest experience is a positive way for the guest to feel ownership in that experience and a loyalty to the organization that provides this opportunity.[23] Pouring one's own coffee at the coffee shop may be a way of getting a coffee cup filled fast, but it also may be a way for that guest and the organization to express their tie to each other. Many organizations try hard to build such relationships because they recognize the lifetime value of a loyal repeat customer. Loyalty programs such as frequent-flyer and frequent-guest programs are designed to build this attachment so that customers come back time after time to the organization that "knows" them.

---

[23] Neeli Bendapudi and Leonard L. Berry, "Customers' Motivations for Maintaining Relationships with Service Providers," *Journal of Retailing* 73, no. 1 (1997): 15–37.

The Bottom Line: Costs Versus Benefits

The key to deciding when to offer the guest the opportunity to participate is to do a simple cost-benefit analysis (e.g., see Exhibit 8.4). The organization needs to be sure, for both itself and the guest, that the benefits of participation outweigh the costs. The organization will want to look closely at the costs it will incur: the costs of extra training or more elaborate skill requirements for employees, extra or simpler equipment necessary for guest use, and extra effort to lay out the service delivery system in a way that is user friendly. In essence, these are the costs of training a guest to be a quasi-employee.

Help Wanted: Co-Producer

As it would in assessing any job position it wants to fill, the organization must ask itself the following questions: What are the KSAs necessary for a guest to perform successfully as a quasi-employee? Are we likely to find these KSAs in our job candidates/guests? What is the motivation of guests to participate, and how do we appeal to that motivation? What are the training requirements for successful performance in the guest-employee role, and do we have the time and personnel necessary to train guests in the proper performance of that role? Will guests come back and use that skill if we spend the time and money to train them? If so, the expenditure of time and money may be worthwhile. Is it cheaper, faster, or more efficient for the organization to take on a larger part of the responsibility for co-production of the service or to allow the guest to do most of it? Do we have procedures in place that allow us to identify those guests that can do what is required to co-produce from those that can't or won't? Are role models (especially other guests) available to help with the training, and how can we physically structure the service environment to use these models? Are there interactions with other guests or other parts of the organization that letting guests provide their own experience will interfere with or harm?

EXHIBIT 8.4

Advantages and Disadvantages of Guests Co-Producing Service

FOR GUEST		FOR ORGANIZATION	
ADVANTAGES	DISADVANTAGES	ADVANTAGES	DISADVANTAGES
Reduces service costs	May frustrate guest	Reduces labor costs	Increases liability risk
Increases interest	May diminish service level	Improves quality	Guest training costs
Saves service time	May not have needed KSAs	Reduces service failures	Increases needs for employee training
Improves quality	Requires a learning-curve period	New market niche	Increases design costs
Reduces risk		Enriches employee jobs	May interfere with other units
Chance to show off			Variability in guests

To employ guests effectively in the guest experience, they must have the ability to participate, the knowledge of how to participate, and the motivation to help produce their own service experience at a level that meets or exceeds their expectations. Since the guests have come to your place to receive some service, they must see a reason to do something for themselves. Thus, the role they perform in the guest experience must be clearly defined. In addition, some guests just want to do things for themselves and will do so if given the opportunity. These people get satisfaction out of serving themselves and being in control of the situation. Some people, on the other hand, do not want to do anything to help provide their own experience. If they are paying for it, why should they provide it? Organizations that see mutual benefits to co-production and try to encourage it must always have a backup plan to accommodate the fact that some guests will and some guests won't want to (or are unable to) participate in the experience. Those organizations that find ways of enabling guests to participate as much as possible in co-producing their own experiences will, however, decrease their costs and increase the value and quality of the service for those guests.[24]

Inviting Guests to Participate: Guidelines

The basic point is that all situations lend themselves to using some self-service or co-production for all guests. Two strategies are available to the hospitality organization to gain the advantages of using co-production while not incurring the disadvantages. First, they can let customers in their targeted market segment know that everyone entering the service setting must provide some of the service themselves. No one goes into a McDonald's expecting table service. The second strategy is to segment the service process so that guests entering the service setting can choose the extent to which they can or will participate. Some restaurants have learned that some guests wish to gain the advantages of serving themselves while others come to the restaurant expecting service and are willing to pay for it. To accommodate this, guests can decide whether to order off the menu or choose from the buffet.

Other ideas about when to include the guest in the experience are suggested in Exhibit 8.5. It describes several situations in which both the guest and the organization may benefit. Obviously, the ideal is when both benefit in some meaningful way so that the experience is at least what the guest expected, and perhaps more.

ONE LAST POINT: FIRING THE GUEST

In a sense, all guests co-produce—or have the potential to co-produce—the hospitality experience for others simply by being in each other's company. If a well-mannered, well-dressed guest sits quietly and passively within the service setting, that guest may be no more than a minor enhancement, an adornment, to the experience of other guests. Unfortunately, despite the old saying that the customer is always right, all organizations know the customer is sometimes wrong by any reasonable standard: certain extreme behaviors are unacceptable in any hospitality setting. Guests sometimes make outrageous demands, refuse to comply with reasonable organizational rules and policies, get drunk, and may even become verbally or physically abusive.[25]

Not all employees work out; not all guests work out either. Sometimes, the guest's "job performance" as a co-producing quasi-employee is so unsatisfactory that the organization must—as a last resort and employing clearly defined procedures—**fire the guest.**

fire the guest A relatively recent concept involving the refusal to serve certain guests who engage in unacceptable extreme behaviors; a philosophy contrary to "the guest is always right."

[24] Alicia A. Grandey, David N. Dickter, and HockPeng Sin, "The Customer Is *Not* Always Right: Customer Aggression and Emotion Regulation of Service Employees," *Journal of Organizational Behavior* 25, no. 3 (2004): 397–418.

[25] Janet R. McColl-Kennedy et al., "Customer Rage Episodes: Emotions, Expressions and Behaviors," *Journal of Retailing* 85, no. 2 (2009): 222–237.

Firing Airline Passengers

Customer aggression is an unfortunate part of a service employee's workday that can impact employees causing such negative outcomes as emotional exhaustion and absenteeism.[26] The best hospitality companies recognize this reality and will intervene to support their employees when necessary. Southwest Airlines, while always committed to customer service, has also worked diligently to protect its employees from such customers. Herb Kelleher, cofounder of Southwest Airlines, has said, "When we encounter a customer like that, we say to him, 'We don't want to see you again because of the way you treat our people.'" Kelleher made the point that the customer is not always right. If a passenger is abusive to a Southwest employee, Kelleher is known to have called the passenger on the phone. Customer complaints to management are common; management complaints to customers are unusual. Employees appreciate this kind of support.[27]

The airlines in particular have trouble with guests. Airlines reported 10,854 incidents during 2015, up from 9,316 in 2014—or one for every 1,205 flights. By comparison there were 5,416 in 1997 and just 1,132 in 1994.[28] The interesting statistic is that only 23% of these incidents were alcohol related. In a study by Katy DeCelles and Michael Norton, they reported that the existence of a first-class cabin made an incident four times more probable, while loading from the front doubled the odds of air rage over boarding from the middle. The loading effect was more pronounced among first class passengers who, when having economy class passengers walk through their section, were 12 times more likely to exhibit air rage.[29]

EXHIBIT 8.5

Guidelines for Deciding Whether Guests Should Participate in Co-Production

1. Would guests derive value or satisfaction from participating in the co-production of the service experience? Are they ready, willing, and able to co-produce their service experience?
2. Can you clearly communicate to guests when and how they are expected to participate in the service experience, and can you make it clear to guests when and why they may not participate?
3. Can you make it advantageous for guests to co-produce, thereby replacing employees and reducing labor costs?
4. Are your employees doing routine, repetitive, easy-to-learn tasks that could be performed by guests or guest-friendly equipment? Can guests participate in co-creating the service experience with little or no training?
5. Can guest participation speed the delivery of the service experience and eliminate waits?
6. Are your guests trying to avoid your service personnel (to avoid giving tips, perhaps) in a way that shows that some guests prefer to co-produce their service experience?
7. Can guests participate in the service experience without being a risk to themselves, other guests, or employees?
8. Are your customer-contact employees ready, willing, and able to help guests co-produce?
9. Can you design your service experience to permit those guests who can and want to co-produce to do so, and so that guests who do not want to co-produce do not have to?

---

[26] Rebecca L. Greenbaum et al., "When the Customer Is Unethical: The Explanatory Role of Employee Emotional Exhaustion onto Work–Family Conflict, Relationship Conflict with Coworkers, and Job Neglect," *Journal of Applied Psychology* 99, no. 6 (2014): 1188–1203.

[27] James L. Heskett, W. Earl Sasser, and Leonard A. Schlesinger, *The Service Profit Chain: How Leading Companies Link Profit and Growth to Loyalty, Satisfaction, and Value* (New York, NY: Free Press, 1997), 238.

[28] Oliver Smith, "Air Rage Is on the Rise—and Sober Passengers Are Usually to Blame," *The Telegraph*, September 29, 2016, http://www.telegraph.co.uk/travel/news/air-rage-on-the-rise-sober-passengers-to-blame/.

[29] Katherine A. DeCelles and Michael I. Norton, "Physical and Situational Inequality on Airplanes Predicts Air Rage," *Proceedings of the National Academy of Sciences* 113: 20 (2016): 5588–5591.

Airlines are taking actions to reduce and address air rage. The central government in India was the first country to try to help airlines prevent incidents of air rage by creating a "no fly" list of unruly passengers. The list has three levels of severity, which determines how long the passenger is banned from flying. The first level includes verbal harassment, being intoxicated and unruly, or physical gestures; this can lead to a ban of three months. The second level is for physically abusive passengers, which leads to a ban of up to six months. The third level includes any sort of life-threatening assaults or damage to the aircraft that would put others at risk. This can lead to a ban of a minimum of two years.[30]

The causes of these air rage incidents appear to include the record numbers of people wanting to fly, more passengers per plane with less room to stretch and move around, the increased frequency of airline delays, free liquor in first and business classes, and people breaking the smoking ban. Some passengers think the airlines have, to some extent, brought the unpleasant incidents upon themselves.

Other organizations fire customers too. When an Uber driver picked up two white supremacist passengers who made disparaging remarks about African Americans, she pulled over and ordered the two men out. One of the men was then permanently banned from using Uber. Uber then reiterated to its drivers its willingness to ban users who engage in discriminatory behavior.[31]

Abrupt Firings

The termination of the hospitality relationship must occasionally be dramatic and abrupt, perhaps even implemented by a security guard, a large person wearing an "Events Staff" t-shirt, or a "bouncer." Dramatic "firings" should occur when customers threaten the well-being or safety of other customers, employees, or themselves. No organization should tolerate customers who are threatening, excessively rude, loud, or dangerous to others or themselves. If any customer threatens or endangers the physical and mental health of an employee, that employee should be empowered to tell the offender to go elsewhere for the service, as this organization is unable to continue rendering it. Employees should also be trained on how to recognize such situations and the procedures involved to get the assistance necessary to conduct the abrupt firing.

Subtle Firings

Customers can also be fired subtly. Everyone realizes that organizations place their advertising so that their target markets will see it, as in beer commercials accompanying televised athletic events. But organizational advertising can also be carefully placed so that some customers never see the ads for a service, never get promotional mailings, or are never offered premiums for using the service. Sometimes, this strategy is more overt, such as a cruise line's refusal to allow unaccompanied children under eighteen to book passage, car companies that refuse to allow drivers under age 25, or a sign in a restaurant saying "No Shoes, No Shirt, No Service."

Maintaining Guest Dignity

Not even hospitality organizations are required to extend unlimited hospitality. They should, of course, give guests the benefit of the doubt. However, in the case of those few guests who are demonstrably unable to participate appropriately in the experience that all have come to the hospitality provider to enjoy, the organization should

[30] Kara Godfrey, "Passenger Ban: Airlines to Create 'No Fly' List as Drunken Arrests SOAR," *Express*, September 8, 2017, https://www.express.co.uk/travel/articles/851781/airline-drunk-passengers-banned.

[31] David Z. Morris, "Uber Says It Can and Will Ban Passengers for Hate," *Fortune*, August 18, 2017, http://fortune.com/2017/08/18/uber-ban-white-supremacists/.

not hesitate to show them the exit. If at all possible, however, the dismissal should be accomplished with minimal harm to the guest's physical or mental well-being and dignity. The guest, like any employee, who feels unfairly treated and who is really angry about being dismissed or fired, can become a source of long-term negative publicity, bad-mouthing, and even litigation.

Although the firing of a guest is a response to a guest failure of some kind, the organization must realize that it has also failed in some way. The rude, troublesome guest had expectations—whether reasonable and realistic or not—and the organization failed to meet them.

LESSONS LEARNED

LO 8.1 Recognize that there are parts of all service experiences that require co-production.

- Co-production is how guests participate in their experiences.

LO 8.2 Describe how, when, and why hospitality organizations encourage or empower guests to help provide their own guest experiences.

- Co-creation of guest experiences adds value to the experience.
- Motivate guests to derive value from participation in co-creation and co-production, and prevent guests from engaging in behaviors that could harm themselves or others.
- Guests must be selected, trained, and motivated to co-produce the experience correctly.
- Encourage guests to help monitor the service behavior of your employees.
- Structure guest experiences in ways that encourage other guests to train your guests; provide preshow videos or otherwise prepare your guests on how to engage in the experience.

LO 8.3 Discuss the advantages and disadvantages of guest involvement for the organization and guest.

- The more guests do for themselves, the less you have to do for them.
- Guest involvement can reduce costs by improving efficiency and capacity utilization, especially at peak demand times.

LO 8.4 Explain what organizations must do to make co-creation successful.

- Train your service personnel to coach, monitor, and supervise the co-production of guests, and hire people who enjoy this kind of activity.
- Train your guests to participate before you let them do so; be sure they have the necessary KSAs to successfully co-produce.

LO 8.5 Explain why hospitality organizations must sometimes "fire the guest" and how to do it.

- If you have to fire a guest, try to preserve the guest's dignity.

KEY TERMS AND CONCEPTS

co-creating 261
co-production 261
fire the guest 280
quasi-employees 264

REVIEW QUESTIONS

1. Name some ways or situations in which guest involvement in the co-production of a restaurant experience can be useful to the organization.

   A. Name some ways in which it can be useful to the restaurant guest.
   B. What KSAs should restaurant guests have to be successful co-producers?
   C. "Train them if they need it; motivate them if they need it; and keep it simple, undemanding." Would that formula promote successful guest co-production?

2. Name some ways or situations in which guest involvement in the co-production of a restaurant experience would not be useful or might be harmful to the organization.
   A. When might co-production in a restaurant not be useful to guests? When might it be harmful?
   B. What can the organization do to discourage co-production in those situations?
3. Suggest some ways in which a restaurant, a hotel, a theme park, a tour bus, and a travel agent might achieve a higher level of guest co-production that would benefit both the organization and the guest. Was it more difficult to apply the co-production idea to some of those hospitality or hospitality-related organizations than to others? If so, why?
4. Under what circumstances do you think the organization is justified in firing a guest? Think of a hospitality situation in which you would almost but not quite fire a guest. See whether your classmates agree with you or whether they would fire the guest.
5. Some hospitality authors suggest that guests should be managed as if they were quasi-employees.
   A. Who do you suppose these authors think should do this managing?
   B. Whoever these managers are, should they be selected differently for their jobs because of the type of "management responsibilities" their jobs will entail?
   C. Should they be trained differently?

ACTIVITIES

1. Find a hospitality situation in which the guest is required to co-produce the service experience. Try to find something more challenging than a salad bar or receptacle labeled "Trash." Describe and evaluate how the organization prepares its employees and its guests for successful co-production. How effective is the co-production strategy? What incentives are offered to guests to encourage their participation? In what ways is this co-production beneficial for the guest, the organization, or both?
2. Interview a manager or supervisor within a hospitality organization to find out what the organization will and will not let guests do regarding co-producing the guest experience. Try to get some examples of guests co-producing excessively—trying to do more for themselves than the organization wants them to—and find out how the manager, supervisor, or server handled those situations. Report your findings to the class.
3. Interview a teacher who seems to believe in classroom "co-production," even if not under that term, and find out why the teacher does so and how the teacher got that way. Bring back your findings for discussion in groups. Discuss the extent to which you are required or invited to co-produce your own education, and how you feel about it.

ETHICS IN BUSINESS

By definition, the co-production process requires certain actions on the part of the customer. But how much is the customer obligated to do? A fast-food restaurant uses co-production to facilitate efficiency. In order to provide cheaper prices, individuals clear their own tables. What if a customer does not clear his or her own table? At a buffet, co-production occurs when customers go up to the buffet and serve themselves. For health reasons, each time you visit a buffet you are to take a new plate. What if a customer does not want to do this? At the buffet, customers can take what they want. Typically, buffets do not allow customers to take leftovers home. So if any remaining food cannot be brought home, what responsibility does a customer have to not waste food? At a fine-dining establishment, part of the co-production is that others in the restaurant dress and act the part appropriate for that establishment. What responsibility does a customer have to dress appropriately? What if a customer chooses to be loud, talk on a cell phone, or otherwise act in a way that others typically deem inappropriate for that environment? In short, what are the ethical responsibilities of consumers in the co-production process to engage in the expected behaviors that enable the service experience?

CASE STUDY

Over the Bounding Main

Luke Dwyer and Sue Mayes met when they were both crewing on a yacht in a round-the-world sailing race. They married, started a software business on a shoestring budget, came up with several innovative ideas that enabled them to attain financial security, and then started looking for a way of life that would be more fun if perhaps not as profitable. Running a bed and breakfast was one possibility, but it seemed rather tame.

Then Sue saw an article in a shipping magazine about the *Shingo Maru*, a small 1920s-vintage freighter for sale. Luke and Sue sent off for a set of the freighter's plans, looked them over with a maritime architect, and decided to convert the ship into a kind of floating wilderness experience. They figured that a certain part of the cruise clientele must be tired of the typical big-boat cruise, where all you did was sit around on deck or by the pool all day, eat huge fattening meals, and drink all night while watching mediocre entertainment and waiting for the midnight buffet. Luke and Sue would give guests an opportunity not to be pampered but to take part in an experience they would remember for the rest of their lives: helping to sail a ship around the world or, for the less committed, some part of it.

About a million dollars and four years later, the conversion was complete, and Sue was breaking a bottle of champagne against the prow of the now-christened *Windenwaves*, a classic square-rigged, three-masted sailing ship with a top mast five stories high. The ports of call on its maiden voyage were going to be romantic-sounding, faraway places that most people experienced only through the novels of Joseph Conrad and Robert Louis Stevenson: Bali, Zanzibar, Bora Bora, Fiji, the Galapagos Islands, Tahiti, Samoa, Barbados, and Antigua. About half the time would be spent sightseeing in these ports and about half the time at sea. The hired crew of twelve, all of them veteran sailors, would help the three dozen paying guests learn to climb the masts, stand proper watch, navigate by the stars, steer, repair sails, and all the other standard shipboard activities. For the privilege of co-producing their own sailing experience, the guests were to pay anywhere from $4,500 for a one-month onboard stay to $60,000 for the full eighteen-month round-the-world trip.

After about six months, approximately half of the passenger-guests had experienced the thrill of a lifetime. The other half wanted their money back. They didn't enjoy sleeping in bunks in one big dorm-type room, getting seasick, using a hose for a shower, being without TV, eating canned and dried foods (the ship had no refrigeration), and having little privacy. Some guests just couldn't "learn the ropes" (literally), and the experienced sailors among the crew didn't seem to be able to teach them how. One guest, who later claimed that he had been forced to climb the five-story mainmast, curled up into a paralyzed ball and had to be airlifted by helicopter to shore. He later sued the Dwyers and Windenwaves Partners Ltd. for $750,000 and won; the Dwyers had not thought to get insurance protection against such an action.

The delighted guests thought their trip on the *Windenwaves* was a high point in their lives, and not just because of the climb up that five-story mast. Said one, "Everybody who's been on a sailboat dreams of a trip like this. We saw places and things we would never get to see in any other way." The disappointed guests were really disappointed. They saw no reason why they should pay so much money and have to do so much of the work themselves. Said one, "I wanted a relaxing cruise. They treated me like a common sailor; made me scrub the decks and empty the slop. At those prices, who needs it? Next time, I'm going on the Disney Magic."

1. Which dangers of co-production became realities for Luke and Sue?
2. How might they have headed off those dangers by planning more thoroughly?

Further readings on the topics in this chapter are listed in "Additional Readings" on pages 512–514.

SECTION 3

The Hospitality Service Delivery System

Design systems that allow you to do the job right the first time. All the smiles in the world are not going to help you if your service is not what the participant wants.

—Joseph J. Bannon, Hospitality academic, educator, and author.

Fairfax Media via Getty Images

Communicating for Service

Hospitality Principle: Glue the Guest Experience Elements Together With Information

If you make customers unhappy in the physical world, they might each tell 6 friends. If you make customers unhappy on the internet, they can each tell 6,000 friends.

—Jeff Bezos, founder, Amazon.com

Learning Objectives

After reading this chapter, you should be able to:

9.1 Recognize the importance of information to your guests.

9.2 Describe ways in which information embedded in the service product, setting, and delivery system provides value to the guests.

9.3 Explain how the service setting communicates information about the quality and value of the service experience.

9.4 Discuss the impact of the internet on communication with customers and employees.

9.5 Recognize the benefits of data analytics to cope with information overload.

9.6 State the types of problems that can occur when there is too much data.

9.7 Explain how the hospitality organization itself can be considered a large information-processing system.

INTRODUCTION

A traveler was waiting for her breakfast to be served at a business hotel. Within a reasonable time, the server brought her eggs and bacon. She looked at the bacon and realized it was too undercooked to eat. She moved it to the side and proceeded to eat the rest of her meal. During a routine visit to the tables, the manager asked how the breakfast was. All right, she said, except the bacon was not cooked properly. The manager apologized and went on to another table. A short time later, the server appeared and asked the same question. The second time the traveler was annoyed. Not only did the restaurant do nothing about the poorly cooked bacon, the manager didn't even share the information with the server so that he would know of a problem with one of his customers.

At another restaurant, a guest wants to order a bottle of wine and is presented with a wine menu longer than some novels. Hundreds of options are provided, choices of different varietals from regions around the world. After pretending to study the list for a period of time, the guest simply gives up. Frustrated, he decides to just have water with his dinner. The frustration and embarrassment of not knowing what to do with the information available diminishes the quality of the dining experience and, at the same time, the restaurant loses a profitable sale.

At yet another restaurant, the manager makes sure every guest gets a ten-item guest satisfaction survey after dining and every employee gets an internal customer satisfaction survey after each shift. Upon reviewing the daily reports and their comparisons with weekly, monthly, and annual trends, she has no idea what all those data mean or how to use the information to change her leadership, service products, environment, or delivery systems to improve the numbers.

All three situations illustrate the challenge of **managing information.** In the first case, the manager did not convey important information to the server to alert him about a possible problem with one of his customers. The manager had the information but did not communicate it, so the server was unable to make the dining experience better. In the second illustration, the guest was provided with a near encyclopedia of wine, but he could not use any of it. In the third example, the manager had information, but had no idea how to translate this large volume of data into actions that might improve either the guest or the employee experience.

managing information Using information systems to get the right information to the right person in the right format at the right time.

THE CHALLENGE OF MANAGING INFORMATION

information system A system, often computerized, designed to get the right information to the right person in the right format at the right time so that it adds value to that person's decisions.

Creating a system that manages information effectively is one of the most important and challenging issues facing any hospitality organization. Information is data that informs, and an **information system** is a method to capture data that inform those who need to be informed. A well-designed information system gets the right information to the right person in the right format at the right time so it adds value to that person's decisions. The right person in hospitality organizations could be an employee, a manager, a guest, a supplier, a combination of all these people, or many others. Information that does not add value to either the guest's or the organization's decisions is useless. Informing a guest standing in line waiting for a table at a Ralph's Restaurant that they had plenty of empty tables last night is not only useless, it is infuriating. Similarly, receiving a free-beverage coupon in the mail the day after the offer expires does not enhance the potential guest's fondness for the sending organization.

Informing the Guest

Since service is by definition intangible, the information the hospitality organization provides to help the guest make the intangible tangible is a critical concern of the information system. What information should the organization provide, where, in what format, and in what quantity, in order to help create the experience that the customer expects? If the experience is a formal dinner, the restaurant should organize all the information it provides to the patron to cue the perception that this is a formal-dining environment, and an excellent one at that. The restaurant should be set up to look appropriate for a formal-dining experience. The chef should have the clean white coat and chef's hat that announce, "I am a chef, not just a cook; I create a fine-dining experience, not merely cook food." The silverware and plates should be elegant, and the rest of the environment should communicate the message *fine-dining experience*. While the focus of a fine-dining experience is usually the food, the total experience includes everything from the food, to the environment, to the delivery system that provides the service. The restaurant must manage the many bits of information the guest tastes, touches, hears, sees, and smells to be sure that each one contributes to helping the guest define the intangible elegance of a fine-dining experience in the way the restaurant wants the guest to define it.

Cues Communicate

Regardless of the hospitality experience being offered, all informational cues in the service setting should be carefully thought out to communicate what the organization wants to communicate to the guest about the quality and value of the experience.[1] If the experience is themed, all cues should support the theme and none contradict or detract from it. The less tangible the service, the more important consistent communication will be. By recognizing that information is the glue connecting the service product, the service environment, and the delivery system together to make a *whole* experience for the guest, the organization should use information to make the guest experience seamless. The organization can manage its information and use the available information technology to tie together all the elements of the

[1] Leonard L. Berry and Neeli Bendapudi, "Clueing in Customers," *Harvard Business Review* 81, no. 2 (2003): 100–106.

guest experience to ensure the guest enjoys it and will want to come back. Similarly, an organization that looks at each manager and employee as a customer for its information can design the organization's information system to facilitate the optimal flow of useful information to those people. Information systems can even connect all parts of the industry supply chain so that vendors, suppliers, and distributors can know what they need to provide, in what quantities, and when, all to ensure that the organization can deliver a seamless guest experience.

Courtesy of Elite Events Catering

Courtesy of Elite Events Catering

Cues help communicate the setting. A catering company changes a functioning hanger into a stylish reception for an airline company.

Adding Quality and Value Through Information

Organizations can use information in many ways to add quality and value to the service experience. Occasionally, information technology becomes so important that it can even transform the organization itself.

Information can help employees personalize the service to make each customer, client, or guest feel special. For example, having caller ID allows the service representative to address the customer by name when answering the customer's phone call and allows adding a special touch to the experience. Information and information technology can improve the service. While a barcode on a retail product or an RFID (radio frequency information device) on a gaming chip provides the basis for recording the transaction, it also provides a wealth of other information that enhances the service experience for both the organization and the customer. For casinos, having a real-time record of which customers are betting what amounts provides for more accurate player tracking, better bettor recognition, and labor-cost savings.

Technology

With an RFID reader at each table, casinos can track bets, check the flow of money on the casino floor, ensure that customers get the comped meals and rooms they deserve, and check to see if any player is using a banned betting technique.[2] Just as retail stores can track inventory and sales patterns with these information systems, casinos can track players. Even more interesting is the opportunity to keep track of what types of products or bets the customer is buying or making so that options can be suggested or offered accordingly as an enhanced service. If you buy a book online from Amazon.com, the online retailer will track previous searches, make subsequent book suggestions based on choices of others who have also purchased the same book, or even offer new books on the same subject the next time you visit its website. Also, cross-selling between organizations is possible.

[2] Mary Branscombe, "How Technology Is Transforming The Casino and Gaming Industry," dinCloud (blog), dinCloud, accessed January 21, 2018, https://www.dincloud.com/blog/how-technology-transforming-the-casino-and-gaming-industry.

If you purchase an airplane ticket using any of the many internet retailers, you will be presented with opportunities to purchase an array of other services, including hotel rooms and car rentals.

Finally, information technology can transform an organization or even an industry. Amazon, Zappos, travel websites, customized print-on-demand book publishers, e-book readers, social networking sites, and the amazing array of applications on smartphones are all transforming their respective industries in important ways. The easier, cheaper, and faster provision of information and services for customers made possible by advancing information technology has rapidly changed the dynamics of many industries. When Google became a verb, it meant the end of the encyclopedia business. When Amazon bought Whole Foods to enable it to deliver food to individual homes, traditional grocery stores were challenged to remain competitive. And, when JetBlue offers those whom it tweets special discounts on airfares, the rest of the airlines will have to respond to this competitive initiative or risk losing contact with an entire segment of customers.

New Information From Virtual Worlds

Technology

Even more dramatic has been the technology that enhances information quality through the creation of virtual worlds, where customers can have an experience without leaving their homes. Rather than look at a two-dimensional picture, guests can take virtual tours on websites like synthtravels, a virtual-reality travel agency.[3] It, and others like it, can arrange virtual tours of art museums, VIP homes, and even other planets. Massive multiplayer online games offer a window into online virtual worlds, where people can gather, buy, sell, and generally do the same things they do in the real world. Starwood used Second Life to test market the design of a new concept hotel, Aloft, and to observe how avatar visitors used the space and furniture.[4] Additionally, Lifewire reviewed eight virtual reality experiences that it found very "mind blowing."[5] These included kayaking through the Grand Canyon, climbing Mt. Everest, and swimming underwater. Perhaps the most impressive is a VR experience developed by Google Earth. Livewire reports, "Google dropped Google Earth VR on the world and blew our collective minds. Google Earth VR lets everyone not only see their house from Space, but allows you to virtually fly to it and stand in your front yard or on your rooftop (if that's your thing). Google Earth VR gives you god-like powers such as the ability to change the sun's position at will or to scale things to pretty much any size and fly around. Feel like stabbing yourself in the eye with the top of the Eiffel Tower? Google Earth VR can make that happen for you. There are hours of fun to be had flying all over the globe like you're Superman."

Getting Information Where It Needs to Go

The challenge for hospitality managers, then, is to gather the data that can inform, organize the data into information, and distribute that information to the people—both customers and employees—who need it just when they need it. Hospitality organizations that are effective in getting information to where it needs to be recognize that

---

[3] Emily Flynn Vecant, "Window Seats: Virtual Tours Provide Exploration Without Jet Lag, Hassles, or Crowds," *Newsweek*, May 28, 2007, https://www.highbeam.com/doc/1G1-163800104.html.

[4] Henry M. Kim, Kelly Lyons, and Mary Ann Cunningham, "Towards a Theoretically-Grounded Framework for Evaluating Immersive Business Models and Applications: Analysis of Ventures in Second Life," *Journal for Virtual Worlds Research* 1, no. 1 (2008): 1–19.

[5] Andy O'Donnell, "8 Virtual Reality Travel Experiences That Will Blow Your Mind: See the World Without Ever Leaving Your Couch," *Lifewire*, May 23, 2017, https://www.lifewire.com/virtual-reality-tourism-4129394.

Timothy Fadek/Corbis via Getty Images

A woman uses a virtual reality headset to take a museum tour.

providing information is in itself a service to guests, often as important as the primary service itself, and a necessity for employees.

Just as it is important to develop information systems that get the right information to the right person at the right time, it is equally important to develop systems and procedures to prevent the wrong information from getting to the wrong person at the wrong time. Every organization needs a plan that not only protects sensitive information from unauthorized employee or outsider access but also details other information rules, such as who can say what to whom when a major disaster strikes, who will talk to the press when a guest complains publicly, or who is the spokesperson for the organization on key decisions and policy. When information is not managed well, the information that is in the public domain will confuse and not inform. When statements that shouldn't have been made are made, they may even lead to lawsuits. Employees need to be taught what not to say as much as what to say. In this era of instant communication and online connections, they also need to be reminded of what information they have that should not be shared on their social networking sites and how to protect the organization from hacking.

The whole challenge of information systems is to figure out exactly how to provide only the required information just when and where it is required. Designers of information systems must, therefore, identify the information needs of both guests and hospitality employees in regard to all three components of the guest experience: the service product itself, the service setting, and the delivery system. Let's talk about information as it relates to each of these elements.

INFORMATION AND THE SERVICE PRODUCT

Information about services offered is usually found within the environment rather than as part of the service product itself. Chapter 3 showed the many ways in which the hospitality organization can plant cues or information in the service setting. Such "tangibilizing" leads guests to favorable judgments about the quality and value of the guest experience. Just as doctors hang diploma certificates on the wall, restaurants display food reviews, and hotels display American Automobile Association ratings, all in the effort to say to guests, "This experience will definitely be good and may even be a wow." Similarly, sensory information can communicate a message about the guest experience. The smell of bread baking, fresh flowers, or even antiseptic will communicate information to guests that can help make an intangible experience tangible. We shall presently speak in more detail about information in the service setting.

With the dramatic growth of the web and its use by hospitality guests for making reservations, co-producing experiences, and giving feedback, there is increasing concern with ensuring that the self-service capabilities of web-based services meet customers' expectations. After all, it can be just as frustrating for a guest to wait for a web page to load as it is to wait for the phone to be answered or to be served in a restaurant. There are many aspects of guests' use of self-service technologies for hospitality organizations to plan for and manage. Besides the obvious things like "do they work?" "will they work fast enough?" or "will they work consistently?" managers must think through and plan for the different users' needs, wants, expectations, and capabilities just as they would with any aspect of the hospitality experience.[6]

Information as Product: FreshPoint

Technology

A good illustration of a sophisticated information and decision system properly used is that developed by Sysco's FreshPoint in Orlando. FreshPoint sells more fresh fruits and vegetables to central Florida restaurants, hotels, theme parks, and other hospitality customers than all its competition combined, and its information system is one of the big reasons why. FreshPoint has developed its information system so that it can accurately predict what all its customers will need and when they will need it. In effect, FreshPoint has moved beyond the business of supplying fruits and vegetables into the business of managing its customer inventories through data analytics. Its computerized models are so accurate that FreshPoint frequently knows better than its customers what they need, how much, and when. This is important to FreshPoint because its Orlando location is about a week away from its suppliers, and fruits and vegetables are extremely perishable. Since freshness is critical to most chefs, effective inventory management is a competitive advantage. Through the capabilities of its information system, FreshPoint is able to become responsible for the freshness and adequacy of fruits and vegetables for its foodservice customers. For one large customer, FreshPoint manages more than 50% of its inventory, and its purchasers are no longer required to physically place those orders.

economic ordering quantity (EOQ) model
A formula for calculating the optimum reorder size (number of units) of an item once the reorder point is reached; designed to minimize annual order and holding costs.

FreshPoint uses what is called an **economic ordering quantity (EOQ) model** to determine the optimum number of units to reorder. Based on the EOQ model, the customer's inventory is monitored, future demand estimated, and orders generated automatically via EDI (Electronic Data Interchange) for next-day delivery. Although most of its customers do not have the technical capability to connect to its inventory management system through its EDI, FreshPoint predicts demand patterns for them anyway and uses its decision models to monitor called-in or web orders for accuracy and completeness. When customers call in or log onto its online ordering system, they are prompted to order items they typically request, alerted when their orders are not large enough to accommodate a big weekend or large convention, advised when they made a mistake on quantity, and made aware of special deals and products. With this information in its database, FreshPoint can call and help its customers avoid a problem before it happens. One of its divisions has developed a system that allows users to simply select menu items, and the system

Courtesy of FreshPoint

FreshPoint uses an inventory management system to help its customers get the products they need.

[6] Mary J. Bitner, Amy L. Ostrom, and Matthew L. Meuter, "Implementing Successful Self-service Technologies," *The Academy of Management Executive* 16, no. 4 (2002): 96–108.

will both determine what ingredients they need *and* determine the most efficient way for the customers to receive the product. FreshPoint's market share attests to the appreciation its restaurants have for the help FreshPoint's information system provides.

Giving Employees the Information They Need

Employees also need relevant, timely, and accurate information to do their jobs effectively. When you consider information to be a service product, the employee is an internal customer for that product. For this internal customer, the service provided is the delivery of the information that the employee needs for making decisions about how to satisfy external customers. This information-as-product is provided to the internal customer by an employee or information-gathering unit acting as an internal "service organization."

For example, if your hotel is hosting a conference with more than 10,000 attendees, and they are all ready for dinner, your employees need up-to-date information to deliver exceptional service. The Gaylord Opryland Resort and Convention Center uses an **integrated information system** to help employees serve guests at their four full-service restaurants more effectively. Using a small hand-held wireless device, employees find out what tables are available, can clear and close any table, or can update seating arrangements from anywhere in the four restaurants. Employees can get immediate information on wait times, can find out if a table's food has been ordered, if a quoted wait time is about to expire, or even if it is a repeat customer's birthday. All this information allows employees to be more efficient, as well as deliver better service. The information provided to employees allows them to fulfill the company's mission. As Rickie Hall, the senior vice president and chief information officer says, "It's all about the guest service."[7]

integrated information system A system designed to bring together diverse sources of organizational information to enable managerial decisions.

Providing information is the service product for many internal employees/customers, and all hospitality organizations seek to provide it as effectively and efficiently as possible. Indeed, the entire movement toward frontline employee empowerment that characterizes benchmark hospitality organizations depends upon employees having easy access to needed information. Without some systematic way to provide it, empowerment would be impossible. Managers and empowered employees alike must have information to make good decisions and to measure the results of their decision-making activity.

INFORMATION AND THE SERVICE SETTING

The service setting and its features and aspects can provide several kinds of useful information for guests.

The Environment and the Service

First, the service setting can be a source of information related to the service itself, and that information must be efficiently and effectively provided. If the tangible product in the guest experience is a quick-service meal, the patron needs to know how to get quick service, which quick-service meals are available, and when the meal is ready. Signs are therefore placed in the service environment to facilitate quick customer access to the order taker, menus are posted in easy-to-find places to aid the diner in selecting the meal, a picture of what the meal looks like may be located next to each

[7] E. Rubinstein, "Gaylord Hotels Extends Reservations, Table Seating Systems to Increase Customer Service Quotients with Solutions from NTN," *Nation's Restaurant News* 39, no. 26 (2005): 29–30.

Photograph provided courtesy of the Dolder Grande Hotel

Nearly all hotels allow guests to look at prospective rooms before making a reservation.

menu item so that the diner knows what the menu item is, and the customer order number may be displayed on an overhead video screen to let the customer know as soon as the order is ready.

Many hotels have attractive graphics on their websites showing room interiors or offering panoramic 360-degree views of a sleeping room or other places in and around the hotel. Some even allow the site visitor to take a virtual tour of the hotel and the surrounding destination. These are especially valuable to convention planners who want to see what the meeting rooms look like. Some conference hotels now offer trade show and event planners an interactive experience so they can move tables, chairs, and exhibits around to see how various seating and display configurations might look. Tourist destinations are also increasingly using virtual tours to give potential visitors a visual representation of what it's like to be in that destination. These visuals of the setting help to make the service tangible for potential guests.

The Environment as Information System

In a larger sense, the service environment itself can be thought of as an information system of sorts by the way it is themed and laid out. Not only does the environment provide information on the location of various points of interest, but the environment itself becomes part of the service and therefore influences the customer's perception of the service's quality and value.[8]

The information embedded in the environment can enhance or detract from the service experience. This information can be in the form of carefully located walls and shrubbery that tell guests where they should not go and paths that tell them where they should. Simple orientation maps located properly tell customers where they are, and arrows and signs allow customers to obtain the information they need to fully enjoy the service experience.

Casinos have long known this, and their environments are carefully designed to send the desired messages to the customers. Interiors of casinos are full of information. Signs are carefully located to quickly show where different restaurants, bars, the theatre, and the night club are located. In addition to signage, casinos use environmental stimuli—such as architectural design, colors, furnishings, textures, lighting, ceiling height, and aromas—for both functional and marketing purposes.[9] Of course, casinos also set up their environment so that to get anywhere, customers must pass by the games offered on the casino gaming floor. Casinos know that the longer they can keep customers inside their establishment near the various gambling opportunities, the laws of probability will ultimately lead to financial success. Casinos are designed not only to enhance the customers' experience, but also to present information that keeps them there longer.

---

[8] Lesley Johnson, Karl J. Mayer, and Elena Champaner, "Casino Atmospherics from a Customer's Perspective: A Re-Examination," *UNLV Gaming Research & Review Journal* 8, no. 2 (2004): 1–10.

[9] Karl J. Mayer and Lesley Johnson, "A Customer-based Assessment of Casino Atmospherics," *UNLV Gaming Research & Review Journal* 7, no. 1 (2003): 21–23.

Customer-Provided Information

Technology

Guests do not need to wait for companies to provide information to them. There are now many sources of information available to customers to help evaluate a hospitality experience before they decide to have it. In the previous chapter, we listed a number of websites where customers post information about their experiences to share with anyone who wants it. There are numerous other online sources for customers to post reviews and find information on nearly any hospitality organization that exists in any part of the world: their prices, service quality, quality of destination attractions, and anything else the inquiring visitor might wish to know. New sites and phone apps are being created all the time in response to customers' demands for this sort of information. Exhibit 9.1 provides a list of some—but certainly not all—of these information sources.

EXHIBIT 9.1

Examples of Websites for Hospitality and Brief Descriptions of Use

Guests Sharing Information with Other Guests

- **www.Consumeraffairs.com:** Consumers can vent and try to get needs met
- **www.consumerist.com:** Spotlights poor customer service
- **www.Cruisecritic.com:** Reviews boat by boat and port by port
- **www.foursquare.com:** Recommendations by locals on destination's restaurants and attractions
- **www.ripoffreport.com:** Gives consumers a chance to fight back
- **www.TripAdvisor.com:** Reviews lodging places, travel packages, and other travel services
- **www.wayz.com:** Shares travel information on roads, congestion, and delays
- **www.zagat.com:** Information and reviews of restaurants

Websites for Finding Deals or Comparing Prices

- **www.airbnb.com:** Booking site to find shared accommodations
- **www.AirlineConsolidator.com:** Sells unsold seats from airlines at steep discounts
- **www.backroads.com:** Website for walking tours
- **www.bedandbreakfast.com:** Search engine for bed and breakfasts
- **www.Ctrip.com:** Search engine for hotels, flights, and cars in China
- **www.Cheaptickets.com:** Website for plane tickets, hotel rooms, car rentals, events, and cruises
- **www.countrywalkers.com:** Website for upscale walking tours
- **www.ebookers.com:** Website for flights, hotels, car rental, cruises, and travel insurance
- **www.eLong.com:** Search engine for flights and hotels in China
- **www.Expedia.com:** Travel agency for airlines, rental cars and lodging
- **www.FareCompare.com:** Search for discounted first-class seats, historical data
- **www.homeaway.com:** Booking site for shared home accommodations
- **www.hotels.com:** Search to find airfares, hotel deals, and vacation packages.
- **www.Hotwire.com:** Offers discounts, supplier not disclosed until after purchase
- **www.jetsetter.com:** Locates and evaluates luxury travel deals
- **www.Kayak.com:** Searches both online agencies and suppliers
- **www.lastminute.com:** Search for last-minute deals
- **www.momondo.com:** Search engine for finding and booking travel
- **www.Opodo.com:** Travel agent search site
- **www.Orbitz.com:** Travel agency for airlines, rental cars, and lodging
- **www.Priceline.com:** Allows travelers to bid on fares
- **www.skiplagged.com:** Search websites for hidden deals on flights and hotels
- **www.toursbylocals.com:** Search engine to find local tour guides in destinations
- **www.travelocity.com:** Travel agency for airlines, rental cars, and lodging

(Continued)

(Continued)

- **www.travelzoo.com:** Search to find best air fares from other search engines
- **www.trivago.com:** Searches all hotel booking sites for best rates
- **www.Shoretrips.com:** Links and reviews of shore trips
- **www.Yapta.com:** Notifies of price drops and refund possibilities
- **www.zuji.com:** Travel guide and engine for flights, hotels, rail travel, cruises, and packages in a number of Asia Pacific countries

Information Tools for Guests

- **maps.google.com:** Provides information and driving directions
- **www.cdc.gov:** Centers for Disease Control and Prevention post cruise ship inspection scores
- **www.DisneyFamilyTravel.com:** Go to source of family-oriented travel
- **www.Flightstats.com:** Notice of flight changes, cancellations, or delays
- **www.Foders.com:** User-generated reviews of hotels and restaurants
- **www.goby.com:** Search engine to help find friends, their locations, and GPS on how to find them
- **www.HotelShark.com:** Composite summary of reviews
- **www.iglta.org:** Travel-friendly information for LBGTQ community
- **www.IgoUgo.com:** Provides background information on person writing review
- **www.maps.com:** Provides information and driving directions
- **www.loneyplanet.com:** A site providing reviews and information for "responsible tourism"
- **www.OpenTable.com:** Finds restaurants and makes booking
- **www.Roadfood.com:** Lists memorable eateries along highways and back roads of America
- **www.seatguru.com:** Displays seating locations for all flights
- **www.travel.sygic.com:** International trip planning with maps
- **www.travelandleisure.com:** Provides recommendations on travel and trip plus booking engine
- **www.TripIt.com:** Puts all confirmation numbers in one document
- **www.triphobo.com:** Travel planning with user-generated itineraries
- **www.utrip.com:** Travel planning concierge creates daily itinerary
- **www.Walkscore.com:** Walkability of over 2,500 neighborhoods
- **www.Wayn.com:** Lifestyle and travel social network
- **www.Zoomandgo.com:** Reviews and video clips of hotels and vacations

Companies definitely need to pay attention to guest-provided content. Because potential customers are making purchase decisions in part (and sometimes entirely) based on this information, technology has allowed "word of mouth" to travel far beyond what it ever could even just one decade ago. Some people habitually evaluate anything they do. Others only post comments when something particularly good or, more often, particularly bad happens. A bad customer experience can hurt a company more than losing a customer or those friends whom the customer tells about the experience: It will likely lose many potential guests with internet access who are trying to find information about the quality of its service. In this information-rich environment, many hospitality organizations have created new monitoring units whose only responsibility is to track and correct, if necessary, what is being said about the company on the web.

With the increasing use of guests posting on social media sites while still engaged in the experience, those hospitality organizations that have invested in real-time monitoring of what their guests are saying have created the incredible opportunity to respond to and fix customer problems while those customers are still on the premises. As we will discuss later, one of the great challenges for hospitality organizations is to find and fix their guest's sense of disappointment with the service experience (a service failure) before they leave and take their disappointment with them.

If an employee is monitoring social media for guests telling friends of their disappointment, many times they can be found still in the restaurant, event, or theme park and have their concerns addressed before they leave. It is always better to fix a failure quickly, and finding the guest by monitoring a social media posting while still present makes it easier to turn an "ow" into a "wow."

INFORMATION AND THE DELIVERY SYSTEM

Finally, and perhaps most obviously, information is required to make the service delivery system work. That system includes both people and the processes by which the service and any accompanying tangible product are delivered to the customer. Here again, the nature of the service product and the delivery system unique to that product and guest will determine what the information system ideally should be. If the end result of the service is a properly prepared hotel room, the information system needs to be set up in a way that communicates to the front desk agent that the room is properly serviced and ready for a guest. Such an information system could be as simple as having the housekeeper bring the room key back to the front desk only after the room has been cleaned. In this way, no guest could be checked into a dirty, unprepared room because the key wouldn't be at the desk.

Really Knowing Your Customers

Many hotels seek to provide more than just a simple clean room, and their information systems are designed to provide this extra level of guest service. The Wyndham Hotels and Resorts use data warehousing applications to allow customers enrolled in its frequent-guest programs to use its website to configure rooms to their liking. Members of Wyndham ByRequest can log on and create a detailed guest profile of their preferences (what floor they like, nearness to elevator, pillows, drinks, etc.). This information is combined with members' guest history data to customize and thereby enhance their experience at any Wyndham hotel. This technology allows frontline employees to access comprehensive guest information stored in Wyndham's database. Housekeepers are empowered and enabled, for example, to customize rooms and amenities for individual guests without the need of supervisory intervention or direction.[10]

The Ritz-Carlton Hotels also has a similar database, called Mystique, for its guests. It goes further, however, as it asks its employees to listen for and record any information that can be used to help The Ritz-Carlton Hotels improve or add value to a guest's experience. For example, if a floor sweeper overhears guests talking about celebrating their anniversary, the sweeper is supposed to pass the information along so that the hotel can take some notice of this special event. The employees help deliver the wow Ritz-Carlton experience by inputting useful information into the organization's information system.[11]

Technology

One example of accessing the web to find data that improves service quality for customers is a call center that is using powerful data analysis techniques to mine the internet for information about customers calling in. When its customers call into its call center, they search the web to find information about them that allows the person answering the call to know a lot about those callers. From the web, this call center's employees can discover not only your credit history and buying behavior but can also scour your Facebook, Twitter, Tumblr, Instagram, and LinkedIn pages

[10] Gabriele Piccoli, Luis D. Anglada, and Richard T. Watson, "Using Information Technology to Improve Customer Service: Evaluating the Impact of Strategic Opportunities," *Journal of Quality Assurance in Hospitality & Tourism* 5, no. 1 (2005): 3–26.
[11] Joseph Michelli, *The New Gold Standard: 5 Leadership Principles for Creating a Legendary Customer Experience Courtesy of The Ritz-Carlton Hotel Company* (New York, NY: McGraw Hill, 2008).

to learn a lot about who you are—for instance, where you live informs your likely income and social status, your past buying and social behavior, and even your personality. This information not only helps the employee answering the phone but also helps select which call center employee gets your call. Data analytics allow the call center to track the success of individual call center employees with different customer profiles so it matches each caller to an employee who is most likely to have success with that type of person. One agent, for example, might have demonstrated success with Spanish speaking callers from Hartford who post frequently about traveling to Orlando[12] so if that is who you are when you call in, you will be switched to that employee. Using data analytics is a win-win as it provides a match that enhances the service experience for the guest and business performance for the hospitality organization.

Delivering Freshness

In restaurants, the information system can improve service delivery by including in the database information about the freshness of the food products used to prepare the meals. Chefs could know how fresh an ingredient is on the basis of its freshness date. Labels with date of production or purchase on food products, "day dots" on fresh-food items, and online inventory systems are all examples of how an information system can be designed to ensure the chefs have the information they need to make the right decisions about using or not using the available ingredients to produce the fresh meals they are responsible for preparing. Though the information is related to the product—the ingredients—and to the service delivery system, its primary purpose is to ensure that product delivery is "just-in-time"—available fresh when the chef needs it.[13]

Technology

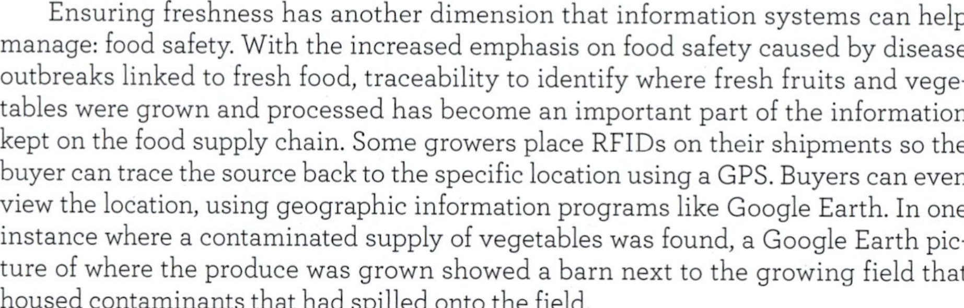

Ensuring freshness has another dimension that information systems can help manage: food safety. With the increased emphasis on food safety caused by disease outbreaks linked to fresh food, traceability to identify where fresh fruits and vegetables were grown and processed has become an important part of the information kept on the food supply chain. Some growers place RFIDs on their shipments so the buyer can trace the source back to the specific location using a GPS. Buyers can even view the location, using geographic information programs like Google Earth. In one instance where a contaminated supply of vegetables was found, a Google Earth picture of where the produce was grown showed a barn next to the growing field that housed contaminants that had spilled onto the field.

Information on Service Quality

Perhaps one of the more important uses of service delivery information systems is in the systematic gathering of information on service quality. Acquiring this information, organizing it into a usable form, and disseminating it to managers and service providers is critical to ensuring that service delivery and other problems are identified and resolved. Inputting the fact into the information system that a guest is annoyed because she is allergic to the feather pillows typically used in the rooms is important, but the information is worthless unless the manager and other employees responsible for guest satisfaction are able to access that same information promptly. Finally, the information system must be designed so that the person concerned follows up on this information to ensure high service quality in the future.

[12] Ryan Knutson, "Call Centers May Know a Surprising Amount About You," *Wall Street Journal*, January 6, 2017, https://www.wsj.com/articles/that-anonymous-voice-at-the-call-center-they-may-know-a-lot-about-you-1483698608.

[13] E. W. T. Ngai, F. F. C. Suk, and S. Y. Y. Lo, "Development of an RFID-based Sushi Management System: The Case of a Conveyor-Belt Sushi Restaurant," *International Journal of Production Economics* 112, no. 2 (2008): 630–645.

Information to the People

The information system can be used to ensure that all the people involved in delivering the service have the information they need to do their jobs in the best possible way. Here is where the most powerful applications of modern information technology have been developed. Providing the hospitality employee with the information necessary to satisfy and even wow the guest is an effective way to add value to the guest experience.

At Hyatt

Every employee phone at the Hyatt hotels has a caller ID system that allows any employee to greet the caller by name when answering the phone. To a hotel manager, this information "allows the guest to experience a higher level of guest satisfaction and find greater value in the hotel's service." To the guest, it's "a nice personal touch." The technology provides information that was previously unavailable; it gives the service delivery employee the opportunity to add quality and value to the guest experience. The system should be designed to accommodate multiple users who want the same information at the same time. If simultaneously (1) a telephone operator is attempting to find a particular guest for a telephone caller, (2) the front desk agent is trying to find the name of the same guest on the database, and (3) the restaurant is trying to bill the same guest for tonight's meal, the need for multiple access to databases becomes obvious. As the Wyndham example showed, even the frontline housekeepers need access to the database to do their part in providing a guest experience that exceeds expectations.

At United

United Airlines was confronted with considerable customer dissatisfaction because of overbooking. When overbooking occurred, the frontline United employees were faced with the challenges of denying a seat to someone who thought he or she had one. In one case, they even forcibly removed a customer from a flight.[14] When the media put the story on the nightly news, it focused on the passenger being injured while dragged from the plane. United responded to the negative publicity by using its data analytics capabilities to find a way to eliminate its overbooking problem. By studying the travel patterns of its flyers, it learned that some flights would frequently have no-shows and empty seats while other flights would seldom have anyone missing. Moreover, they learned that most overbookings were created by weather problems or equipment problems that caused either a reduction in capacity or a different configuration (and capacity) when malfunctioning airplanes were replaced. By communicating these changes quickly to their ground attendants, the impacted flyer could be helped to find other flights and rebooked quickly. By reconstructing its app, United was able to reduce overbooking problems in three ways. Its use of data analytics allowed it to more accurately predict which flights would have no-shows and how many. Its communications system allowed it to better inform ground personnel so they could better help passengers impacted by weather and equipment issues. And, the app enabled many impacted passengers to rebook themselves thereby reducing the long lines of frustrated passengers seeking new flights.

High Tech Becomes High Touch

Technology

In many other situations, information systems make it possible for the organization and its employees to provide service to customers quickly and efficiently. Customers

[14] Steven Norton, "United's Strategy to Reduce Overbookings," *Wall Street Journal*, August 13, 2017, https://www.wsj.com/articles/uniteds-strategy-to-reduce-overbookings-1502676300.

now expect immediate access to information about their service experience. Domino's created an app that lets customers track their pizza by providing a real-time status report of their pizza's preparation, complete with the name of the employee handling the pie.[15] While this information system still has some problems to work out, the benefit of offering this service to pizza customers is the same as already enjoyed by users of the UPS and FedEx tracking systems.

As technology has advanced and customers have become accustomed to self-service kiosks in various venues (e.g., airports, rental cars, retail stores), self-serve devices have become increasingly accepted in hotel environments and even in some of the luxury establishments. Hospitality organizations are continuing to expand their technology applications to increase access to information through smartphones and other handheld devices. A growing number of Hilton Hotels are using hotel door keys that are sent to personal phones, building on the success airlines have had with this technology. Disney provides its guests with a "Magic Band" that each guest wears on the wrist. The Magic Band not only opens hotel doors but can also be used to gain admission to the parks, as a fast pass, a point of purchase device, and identification. Once a guest puts on the band, no other identification, credit card, or admission ticket is needed. This trend in technology use will only continue to increase in the future as the Internet of Things continues to expand and **big data** gets bigger.

big data A massive volume of structured and unstructured data that is so large as to make traditional approaches to its analysis difficult or even impossible.

The use of technology is a challenging issue for hospitality organizations, as they want to capture the benefits and economies that technology offers without losing the human contact that is so vital to the guest experience. The key, not surprisingly, is giving guests what they want, need, and expect.

Says Pierre-Louis Giacotto, General Manager of the Sofitel Chicago O'Hare, "I believe that self-service in luxury and higher end establishments can dilute customer service if that is the only method offered. However, if technology is in addition to the traditional way of checking in, I don't see a problem at all." Walter Brindell, Vice President of Rooms for Hyatt Hotels and Resorts, echoes the point: "You have to have both, depending on your market. Some customers need personal interaction and others prefer the availability of technology that they can control, select, and orchestrate themselves." Hospitality organizations therefore try to use as much technology behind the scenes as they can, primarily to save on back-of-the-house labor costs and give the customer a choice of service options in the front of the house.[16]

A great example of high-tech high-touch technology that stays behind the scenes but adds to the customer experience is used at the Ocean House in Rhode Island. The hotel has microchips in the room service carts as well as the door frames. When a guest is done with a meal and places the cart in the hallway, the chips register this movement and sets off an alarm for the floor valet until the cart is removed. This use of technology helps the Ocean House avoid unsightly carts and food in the hallway, and contributes to their continuing effort to provide luxurious customer service.[17]

Technology for Expertise

Technology

In many ways, information technology now allows the hospitality organization to provide expert skills without paying experts to provide them. A concierge who knows every good restaurant in town or how to get last-minute tickets to a sold-out play is a valuable hotel asset and is generally paid accordingly. Acquiring this level of expertise takes time and experience, and the organization and the guest pay for that expertise.

[15] Katherine Bindley, "Domino's Tracking App Tells You Who Made Your Pizza–Or Does It?," *Wall Street Journal*, November 28, 2017, https://www.wsj.com/articles/dominos-tracking-app-tells-you-who-made-your-pizzaor-does-it-1511889445.

[16] Mary L. Carlin, "High Touch V.S. Touch Screen," hospitalitytech, EnsembleIQ, February 19, 2008, https://hospitalitytech.com/high-touch-vs-touch-screen.

[17] Micah Solomon, "What in the World is Triple Five-Star Customer Service? Ocean House's Daniel Hostettler Spills the Beans," *Inc.*, January 16, 2018, https://www.inc.com/micah-solomon/what-in-world-is-triple-five-star-customer-service-ocean-houses-daniel-hostettler-spills-beans.html.

On the other hand, if this knowledge is online, through the guest's own phone, a Google search, a touch-screen device in the lobby, or an employee who can easily find it in a computerized database, the cost to the guest and the organization of accessing that information is reduced while the quality of the information and the ease of access are increased.

The web also makes it possible for customers to provide expertise to each other, and guests increasingly want to get this information for themselves. Rather than asking a concierge for the information, they prefer to do a Google search for nearby restaurants and walking tours themselves, ask for suggestions from other guests on sites like TripAdvisor and Yelp, search blogs, or text their friends for suggestions. With billions of text messages sent every day, there is a lot of communication going on besides what the organization itself offers. Guests may use avatars or access virtual customer environments, which can range from discussion blogs about the organization's ability to deliver the guest experience to product prototyping.[18] This trend has resulted in hotels reducing costs as they do not need to staff as many people at the concierge desk while still providing the service their guests want and expect. Further, it provides an opportunity for hotels that traditionally do not offer this level of service to provide their guests with this information via the web, thereby increasing customer satisfaction. There are a growing number of opportunities for hospitality organizations to use information and information technology to enhance the hospitality experience as a whole, or enhance the guest experience directly by providing the guest with easy access to information. The best organizations are constantly seeking these opportunities in order to do this.

Centralized Reservations at Hyatt

Like most hotel chains, Hyatt has a centralized reservation system that all callers reach when calling in for rooms or access via their phone or the web. Hyatt's reservationists have access to the entire inventory of rooms available in all Hyatt properties and can help the caller find a room that best matches the desired price point and time when the caller wants to come. Instead of calling each Hyatt hotel, the person needing a room calls the centralized reservation system and speaks to a reservationist, who offers complete information about how best to meet that person's lodging needs.

Cross-Selling

Even better, from an organizational perspective, is that having the information system set up in this manner allows the organization to **cross-sell** its other products and services. A potential guest calling the Hyatt reservation number for a hotel room can also be offered a room upgrade or other available products or services. The net result of this integrated reservation information system is to ensure the guest becomes aware of the many options that Hyatt provides. The reservationist can not only sell a room in one location for one hotel, but is empowered with the expertise to offer hotel rooms for every night at every location the traveler will visit. Travel agents, phone apps, and websites do the same type of cross-selling when they book hotel rooms, arrange for rental cars, and offer other services when people call in or log in to make airplane reservations.

cross-sell Using an interaction with a guest who has come to the organization for one service as an opportunity to sell the guest another product or service.

The Front and the Back of the House

The hospitality service delivery information system ties together front-of-the-house operations with back-of-the-house operations. Coordination between those people

[18] Satish Nambisan and Priya Nambisan, "How to Profit from a Better 'Virtual Customer Environment,'" *MIT Sloan Management Review* 49, no. 3 (2008): 53–61.

Joe Amon/The Denver Post via Getty Images

A bartender enters a customer's order into the restaurant point-of-sale system.

and systems serving the guest and those people and systems serving those who serve the guest is critical in providing a seamless experience. The guest does not care that the communications system between the cook and the server is faulty. The guest cares only about the quality of the overall restaurant experience, and the organization is responsible for serving the ordered food in a timely and appropriate manner.

Point-of-Sale Systems

Point-of-sale (POS) systems have been developed to help managers, servers, and cooks do their jobs better. The server enters the order on a touchscreen or handheld wireless touch screen device, and it is transmitted back to the cook station for preparation. POS systems ensure that the orders are entered in the proper sequence so the hot foods are served hot and the cold foods are served cold and not the other way around.

Some systems help the cooks do their jobs more effectively, such as by accompanying each order with a display of the recipe and a picture of the final plated meal so the cook can verify if the meal being produced matches the standard. This extra informational feature lets cooks self-monitor their work; they can review the proper preparation procedures for the meals they are producing to assure a consistent, high-quality meal.

Modern POS systems are so powerful they can provide information that influences almost any dimension of the business. For example, some POS systems can produce financial reports that can be accessed from any mobile device anywhere in the world, track individual server performance, determine which menu items are big sellers, track inventory, provide more accurate estimates of wait times, allow online orders and reservations, and identify returning customers.[19] They can also be combined with customer relationship management systems (CRMs) to support strategic decision-making. A CRM system collects and analyzes information designed for sales and marketing insights to enable the organization to understand and support existing and potential customer needs. CRMs include account management, catalog and order entry, payment processing, credits and adjustments, and other functions.

For example, by tracking coupon use and sales, a CRM system can determine whether a promotional campaign is profitable. A CRM system combined with POS systems also can collect and analyze data to make sales forecasts, provide inventory recommendations, and create employee schedules that meet employee preferences and reduce labor costs. Some systems help with guest retention by identifying lapsed customers and sending them a coupon. In short, advances in these systems are allowing managers to gather and use vast amounts of information quickly and easily. The information they provide can then help managers improve nearly every operational and strategic decision they make.[20]

[19] Warner Seibert, "How to Choose the Right Point of Sale System For Your Full-Service Restaurant," *Modern Restaurant Management*, January 12, 2018, https://www.modernrestaurantmanagement.com/how-to-choose-the-right-point-of-sale-system-for-your-full-service-restaurant/.

[20] Roger L. Baran and Robert J. Galka, *Customer Relationship Management: The Foundation of Contemporary Marketing Strategy* (New York: Taylor & Francis, 2016).

The Daily Count

Another illustration of how an information system can improve experiences for customers and performance results for the company is a **daily count** system, like the one used at Disney. Every guest entering the park is counted and added to the total in the park at that time. Based upon its extensive attendance database and knowledge of arrival-rate distributions, Disney can accurately predict after the first hour of operation how many guests will come into the park during the whole day. This information can then be used to inform the food and beverage people how much food needs to be taken from central storage facilities and brought into the park's various restaurant and foodservice locations, and how many salads, soups, and other prepared food items need to be on hand.

daily count A prediction arrived at by an information system after a relatively short period of time (e.g., an hour), and based on a combination of actual count, an attendance database, and knowledge of arrival-rate distributions, of how many guests will come into the service location during the whole day.

Further, the same data are made available to human resources managers to ensure an appropriate number of employees are scheduled to handle the total number of guests Disney now knows will be coming into the park that day. Similarly, the supervisors and area managers of the various attractions can access these data to know how many cars, boats, and trains need to be available for their attractions. The first-hour guest count can be used in a number of important decision areas to ensure the park is prepared to serve all of the day's guests with the level of service quality that Disney strives to provide. This one data source flowing through the information system can be used simultaneously across the entire service experience to improve the quality of the service delivery system, the service setting, and the service itself. The information generated by the system will make the many different experiences a guest will have of higher quality than would otherwise be possible and enables Disney to deliver these experiences with high efficiency and consistency.

The Information Flow Between Levels

The last major requirement of the information system, as it relates to the service delivery system, is providing for information flows across organizational levels. This level-to-level flow can be as simple as an employee newsletter or a routing slip, or as complicated as an online, real-time, data-retrieval and decision system. Information can also be provided through a centralized database or intranet made available through computer connections to all employees, so they can access the specific information they need to interpret corporate policy, identify the dates and places of training opportunities, or the availability of alternative jobs.

All these methods are ways in which hospitality managers can reinforce the organizational culture, motivate employees, and educate them to enhance the guest experience. Of course, many other communication channels flow up and down between management and employees. For example, employee-of-the-month programs allow the organization to communicate to all employees by example what types of behavior are desired and rewarded. Employee suggestion programs are another way for management to pick up new ideas and other types of information from their employees that let them quickly identify problem areas in the service delivery system. Building an efficient two-way information system into the design, structure, and operation of the hospitality organization is vital to gather and share the necessary information in a timely way. This allows managers to supervise and monitor the contribution of all parts of the organization to the quality and value of each guest's experience and for employees to inform managers about what guests are saying and doing.

DECISION SUPPORT SYSTEMS

With computerized data bases collecting so much information across so many aspects of the hospitality business, many companies are finding that they now have vast databases with information on customers and their behaviors. Data come from centralized reservation, POS, CRM, and Mystique-type customer relationship management systems, as well as from credit card databases or even systems that scan the web for information about a particular customer. Imagine how impressed you would be if the desk agent not only greeted you by name but also congratulated you on the award you had traveled to her hotel to receive. As discussed earlier in the Wyndham and The Ritz-Carlton Hotels examples, data also come from customers who voluntarily provide information that can be entered into a database for future reference. It is also possible for companies to purchase consumer data containing demographic information and information on past purchasing behavior. Organizations like National Demographics, Lifestyles Company, and Google make a business of collecting and providing such data, and some state driver-license bureaus make money by selling information about their licensed drivers. In order to sell targeted advertising, some companies have added "history sniffing" capabilities to their websites so they can surreptitiously track what other sites their users are visiting. All these data clearly have the potential to provide more information about one's guests, and what they want and expect from the hospitality organization. But having a lot of data does not mean you have good information. You have to use the data to change how you make decisions, and there are a number of ways technology can help accomplish this task.

decision support system (DSS) An information system that, in addition to providing information, has the capability of responding to information, choosing between alternatives, and either making or helping to make a decision.

Systems that go beyond getting information to the right person at the right time, and actually help improve business decisions, are called **decision support systems (DSSs).** Built into these systems are analytical methods and decision rules that either help a decision maker make a decision or, in some cases, replace the decision maker altogether. Examples of a decision system that supports a decision maker would be an automatic warning that signals a manager when the temperature goes below a critical level on a refrigeration system, a computer icon that flashes on a computer screen to warn a cruise-ship engineer that a piece of equipment is heating up or malfunctioning, or a computer-generated e-mail that alerts a manager if a worker has not received mandatory training within a specified amount of time since being hired.

A DSS can help support decision-making in a number of ways. Most obviously, it can help collect, synthesize, and present data in meaningful ways. DSSs frequently generate reports that help in both tactical and strategic decision-making. DSSs can also provide recommendations. One way to generate recommendations is to model how experts make decisions. That is, a DSS can be programmed to mimic the process used by a recognized expert; once captured in a computer program, this expertise can be shared with anyone who uses the system. DSSs can use sophisticated algorithms and statistical methods to analyze data and present recommendations based on these models' results but it is still up to the manager getting these recommendations to make the decision.

Using Data to Drive Decisions

In general, DSSs collect and present information, and sometimes even recommendations. It is up to the user to ask the right questions and carefully weigh the value of these recommendations. Capturing the power of information systems and DSSs to improve an organization's decision-making capabilities requires gathering the right data, organizing it in the right way, gathering expert knowledge from the right experts, and using the right models. DSSs can support organizational decision-making using a variety of approaches.

Technology

Most recently the systematic use of data is expanding through artificial intelligence (AI). AI allows computers to be programmed to imitate human decision-making. What makes AI different is the ability of computers to learn in the same way humans do so they not only can be programmed to make smarter decisions but can learn from their mistakes and improve. Machine learning has evolved from its early applications in simple chess games to the ability of IBM's AI system, Watson, to solve complex problems to the recent development of autonomous self-driving vehicles. Hilton Hotels has partnered with IBM Watson to develop "Connie" the Hotel Concierge. Creating computers that can learn, think, or drive vehicles offers the potential to replace employees in a variety of routine and even non-routine jobs.[21]

The June Oven, for example, is an example of AI in the kitchen. By using cameras to identify what is on a plate, it then accesses the internet through a wi-fi connection to gather the relevant knowledge on how to cook what it sees. A person using this oven will stick a probe into the dish and close the microwave door, and the oven will tell you when it's ready to eat.[22] While this may still be in the developmental stage, as is also true for self-driving trucks and cars, the possibilities these innovations suggest for other applications are exciting. Hospitality managers will increasingly be required to understand and use this evolving technology. The challenge will be to continue to offer the personal touch desired by guests while gaining the efficiencies of the technology.

Modeling Decisions

Some decisions can be modeled because the environment in which they occur is generally predictable. Since situations that call for such decisions recur frequently, it is worth the organization's time and trouble to develop a mathematical model describing the situation and to discover the appropriate decision rule. For example, if a pressure sensor in a Tunnel of Love ride registers a change in the weight of the car carrying guests, the DSS that monitors the ride makes the "decision" to shut the ride down because past experience has shown that someone has probably left the car and started walking on the track. Since this behavior is dangerous, the DSS is programmed to check the weight sensor continuously to ensure that no person is walking where people shouldn't be. If someone is out of place, the system shuts the ride down until the operator can check. Other illustrations of automatic decision-making can be seen in recommended staffing and preparation levels of certain food items based on statistical projections, prepositioning taxis in locations and at times that match demand patterns, and rerouting airplanes based on analysis of real-time load factors.

As is true of any procedure designed to improve service to customers, the organization needs to assess the relationship between the value and the cost of the information before it establishes such a system. Because professional chefs are artists and not accountants, they may not get around to gathering and organizing data about ingredient supplies often enough to justify the expense and sophistication of an online system. Just because a company has a lot of data does not mean its systems necessarily support the types of decisions it needs to make. If the input of data is haphazard, or the available data irrelevant, the value of the frequently out-of-date or inaccurate information would be low and the expense of installing a sophisticated system unjustified.

Statistical Analysis

Another way to use available data is to statistically analyze it to detect relationships. Statistical data analysis can either be used to test certain expectations (e.g., test to see if prepositioning taxis led to quicker response times to customer calls) or be exploratory in nature (e.g., looking to see what customer characteristics are related to greater spending at the hotel casino). Statistical analysis is relatively easy to use. Microsoft Excel has a Data Analysis tool, and there are many statistical packages available in the

[21] D. Temin, B. Molloy, and J. Kolla, "For The Hype: What Every Business Leaders Needs To Know About Artificial Intelligence Now," *Forbes*, December 6, 2017, https://www.forbes.com/sites/daviatemin/2017/12/06/forget-the-hype-what-every-business-leader-needs-to-know-about-artificial-intelligence-now/.

[22] Geoffry A. Fowler, " June Oven Review: Can Artificial Intelligence Beat Mom's Home Cooking?," *Wall Street Journal*, December 14, 2016, https://www.wsj.com/articles/june-oven-review-can-artificial-intelligence-beat-moms-home-cooking-1481729982.

market or on the web. The challenge is that the person conducting the analysis must understand the basics of how to use and interpret statistics. Someone must also be willing and able to devote the time to organize the data and perform the desired analyses. While this may be a task the authors of this book, professors that they are, enjoy, it is not a task many others may relish. Furthermore, as companies gain more data, it is possible the sheer size of the database will make it unmanageable for statistical analysis on a single computer. So, while statistical analysis is actually within the reach of many hotels, restaurants, casinos, and other service providers, many are unable to drill down into their data to take full advantage of the large amount they collect.

Big Data Analytics

Technology

data analytics A largely automated process that uses statistical analyses to search large datasets for useful and meaningful patterns to support decision-making.

When companies have massive datasets, completely analyzing the data is simply not feasible. Often, companies do not have the time or expertise to conduct sophisticated statistical analyses to take advantage of the true potential their huge data stores may provide. The process of **data analytics** has emerged to help resolve these issues.

Data analytics is a largely automated process that uses statistical analyses to search massive datasets for useful and meaningful patterns. The process is user friendly as it does not require complete understanding of the underlying analytical methods. The system identifies relationships and trends in the data that can then be used in a variety of ways to improve the ability of the organization to satisfy its customers. In hotel marketing, for example, mining large quantities of customer data allows the hotel to create more focused direct-mail campaigns, offer more effective seasonal promotions, time and place its ad campaigns better, quickly define which market segments are growing most rapidly, and determine the number of rooms to reserve for wholesale customers and business travelers.[23]

Synthesizing large amounts of data to search for useful information through data analytics, however, can be expensive, requiring sophisticated software and hardware. Nonetheless, it is a technology being employed by most companies today including many large hospitality companies like Hilton, Marriott, Wyndham, and Harrah's. Because these large companies can combine information from many properties, they have the potential to track their best customers and create highly targeted promotional campaigns. For instance, Harrah's Hotels and Casinos combine information from every customer transaction, including which casino games the customer prefers as well as psychographic and demographic information on the customer. Analyzing these data, the system can determine which customers are potentially the most profitable, and then provide appropriately customized incentives to attract repeat business. Customers who live outside the Las Vegas area, for example, received complimentary hotel rooms or transportation, while drive-in customers received food, entertainment, or cash incentives.[24] Harrah's also estimates that it has saved over $20 million by not offering incentives to customers who were unlikely to return.

In a more sophisticated use of data analytics, Harrah's has used data analytics to analyze behaviors of large numbers of people allowing them to identify the trigger points where people lose enough money that it diminishes their desire to gamble. The goal is to allow people to lose up to that amount but not beyond it. By analyzing large amounts of data on similar people, Harrah's can identify when a guest might be at that point and will send an employee to offer that guest a free dinner or show, or find some diversion so that person does not go over the tipping point where he or she will give up on gambling.[25] This process is called doppelganger

[23] Vincent P. Magnini, Earl D. Honeycutt Jr. and Sharon K. Hodge, "Data Mining for Hotel Firms: Use and Limitations," *Cornell Hotel and Restaurant Administration Quarterly* 44, no. 2 (2003): 94–105.

[24] Joe A. Nickell, "WELCOME TO Harrah's," *Business 2.0* 3, no.4 (2002): 48–54. See also Gary Loveman, "Diamonds in the Data Mine," *Harvard Business Review* 81, no. 5 (2003): 109–113.

[25] Seth Stephens-Davidowitz and Steven Pinker, *Everybody Lies: Big Data, New Data, and What the Internet Can Tell Us about Who We Really Are* (New York, NY: Harper Luxe, 2017).

research and is designed to find patterns of behavior on people like you (your doppelgangers), similar to how Amazon analyzes your purchasing behavior and offers you products that others like you have purchased. These sophisticated analytical tools allow organizations to match you against others similar to you in an effort to provide suggested purchases that might not have otherwise occurred to you. In hospitality, this tool may have applications in restaurants ("May I suggest a wine that you might like with that menu item?"), event planning ("May I suggest an amenity that other event planners have found their attendees liked?"), or other guest services. The point is that data analytics provides new ways to be a successful guestologist by offering service options that wow the guest who had not been aware of them before they were offered.

Data analytics, of course, does not guarantee finding information that will help improve either business success or the guest experience. Although it generally requires a substantial investment, it is a technology that many companies with large amounts of data can turn into synthesized information that will enable them to get a better idea of what guests want, how they behave, and perhaps how they can be influenced to become more loyal, profitable, and satisfied.

Using Information

Once data has been converted into information, hospitality organizations can use that information in a variety of ways to make better decisions. Having clear and specific information on what customers want, knowing what makes a profitable customer, and knowing how to communicate with those customers will improve the organization's ability to provide guests with the experiences they desire.

Market Segmentation

By finding out more about individual customers, companies have found they can customize their products to serve customers more personally. Rather than treating all customers the same, there is an increased emphasis on relationship marketing, or the *market-segment-of-one* concept, which has been made possible through the increasing power of computers to store, analyze, and interpret large quantities of information. The idea is to find out so much about customers that the organization can treat each person as a separate "market." When customers return warranty cards on products, fill out the online customer feedback surveys, send in for discount coupons, or wear Disney's Magic Bands, they provide information that companies can use to gain a better understanding of their customers and their unique needs. As discussed earlier in the Wyndham and The Ritz-Carlton Hotels examples, customers themselves may voluntarily provide information when they know it will enhance their experience or employees may be asked to listen, learn more about their customers, and enter what they hear and learn into the database for future reference. Knowing the individual customers better allows the company to customize and target its marketing campaigns, offer the services they know specific individuals want, and, ultimately, best meet the guests' needs with the goal of providing a "wow" experience.

Identifying and Targeting Your Best and Worst Customers

Just as market segmentation helps identify the different preferences and purchasing behaviors of customers, gathering customer information can be used to identify how profitable each customer is. The fact is that not all customers are equally profitable. In truth, some are simply unprofitable. Instead of taking a "come one, come all" approach to customers and guests, more and more organizations are using information to determine customer value. Organizations use this information to establish closer relationships with their best guests. These customers are targeted to encourage their repeat business and continued loyalty. At the other extreme, companies can use information technology to identify unprofitable customers, allowing the company to change how it markets to this segment, and sometimes even severing relationships with them.

Using information on purchasing behavior, Dorothy Lane Market, a small supermarket chain that offers gourmet food and attentive customer service, identifies its best and worst customers with sophisticated technology. It knows that 30% of its customers generate 80% of its profits, and 1% of its customers are responsible for 11%of its profits.[26] Instead of advertising in newspapers and providing coupons to everyone, the market uses the internet and direct mailing to provide specific incentives to its best customers. For example, during a milk price war, select customers received coupons to purchase milk at $1.49 per gallon; those who simply stopped in off the street paid $3.89.[27]

Harrah's Casino developed a loyalty program to track and reward its customers. Called *TotalRewards,* the program tracks both the customer's profitability and value to the casino, as well as room, leisure, drink, and many other preferences and habits of the customer. Harrah's will use the information on customer value to determine if a guest may be given a discounted rate on a room, or have it comped altogether. Harrah's uses this information about customer value to keep its most profitable customers happy and coming back.[28] Customers who aren't as profitable pay higher rates. While a few customers are often responsible for much of a company's profits, it is also true that some customers actually cost a company more than it gains. These customers demand more attention than they may be warranted given their spending and profitability.[29] Companies may want to get rid of these customers to become more profitable. The danger, of course, is that the organization may be cutting loose presently unprofitable customers who might generate large future profits or who might, if treated well, recommend the organization to potentially profitable friends.[30]

Collaborative Filters

Technology

Internet-based programs allow customers to make information about themselves available to companies and each other through collaborative filtering and social networking sites.[31] Collaborative filters can be found with many online vendors—like Amazon, eBay, iTunes, Netflix, and Spotify—where customer patterns are gathered and organized. This allows the customers to see what others searching in similar ways have purchased (Amazon), watched (Netflix), or listened to (iTunes) while also adding their information to the database. Agent programs, like Apple Music and Spotify, organize and categorize individual's judgments about music and then compares them with those of others like that person in a single database. These programs learn what you like and can, therefore act as your personal assistant. They will recommend new products and services based on what people like you are buying or using. In effect, they allow the powerful influence of informal word-of-mouth marketing to be used even from strangers whose recommendations you'd never heard before. These filters offer powerful tools for providing experiences and products to targeted customers whose database histories indicate their specific preferences.

---

[26] *CIO Insight*, "Fire the Worst Customers: Dorothy Lane Market Inc," *CIO Insight* 1: 34 (2006): 51.
[27] CIO Insight, 51.
[28] Michael Bush, "Why Harra's Loyalty Effort Is Industry's Gold Standard," *Ad Age*, published October 5, 2009, http://adage.com/article/news/harrah-s-loyalty-program-industry-s-gold-standard/139424/.
[29] Valarie A. Zeithaml, Roland T. Rust, and Katherine N. Lemon, "The Customer Pyramid: Creating and Serving Profitable Customers," *California Management Review* 43, no. 4 (2001): 118–142.
[30] Werner Reinartz and V. Kumar, "The Mismanagement of Customer Loyalty," *Harvard Business Review* 80, no. 7 (2002): 86–95.
[31] Gediminas Adomavicius and Alexander Tuzhilin, "Toward the Next Generation of Recommender Systems: A Survey of the State-of-the-Art and Possible Extensions," *IEEE Transactions on Knowledge and Data Engineering* 17, no. 6 (2005): 734–749.

Social networking sites, on the other hand, reduce the concerns with privacy as they are created by the people themselves. People willingly share their data and personal information to any who find their website and view their public profile. While some restrict access to more personal information, it is surprising how many do not. With the widespread use of smartphones and their ever-increasing information-sharing applications like Facebook, Instagram, and Twitter, more people (and companies) can learn more about other people than ever before. Geosocial networking platforms have evolved to enable users to interact with others based on sharing their locations. Web mapping services with geocoding data for places (streets, buildings, and parks) can be used with geotagged information (meetups, concert events, nightclubs, or restaurant reviews) to match users with a place, event, or local groups with which to socialize. Popular geosocial applications like Yelp, Gowalla, and Facebook Places are ways for users to share their locations as well as preferences for locations or venues. Even Snapchat has integrated geosocial capabilities into its platform, allowing users to see where their friends are, wherever in the world they may be. One interesting application, CitySense, is offered by Sense Network, which has found a way to track people through their devices, whether they want to be tracked or not. This company avoids privacy concerns by not identifying the specific people holding the phones and instead tracks electronic dots representing individual cell phone users as they move in a geographical area. Observing customer behaviors by tracking the movement of cell-based communicators by day and time across their maps allows the company to see what people are really doing and where they are.[32]

Problems With Information Systems

Although no hospitality organization is going to give up its information system, these systems have potential and actual problems associated with them. One is **information overload,** the tendency of the system to produce and transmit too much data. A second is the creation of a false sense of information preciseness. Since these systems produce such apparently accurate numbers, managers tend to focus on the numbers instead of on less definite but often more important qualitative and human factors. Another problem is that an information system can produce bad information that looks good. Still another major concern is that organizations have crucial and sometimes proprietary information within their system, so maintaining security is an issue. Finally, the costs of installing, safeguarding, updating, and learning the systems must be matched against the benefits those systems can confer. These points will be discussed in turn.

information overload Literally, too much information; generally referring to a tendency of information systems and their users to generate and send too much information or non-useful information to guests and employees.

Information Overload

Information systems are helpful and have revolutionized business, but they are far from perfect. The most obvious problem in the hospitality industry is the possibility of creating information overload for both guests and employees. As anyone who has ever done a Google search knows, too much information is just as bad as not enough. While sophisticated systems are designed to provide only the right information to the right person when that person needs it, many information systems (and search engines) provide a lot of raw data, and leave it to the recipients to discover whatever information they need in the pile. Indeed, many systems are designed by having systems planners ask users what information they need. Human nature being what it is, most users will ask for as much information as they can get, instead of only as much as they really need. Most people believe having too much is better than not having enough; their proof is that they have seen people disciplined for having too little information but never for having too much. Another aspect of this same issue is that when asked,

[32] Loannis Krontiris, Marc Langheinrich, and Katie Shilton, "Trust and Privacy in Mobile Experience Sharing: Future Challenges and Avenues for Research." *IEEE Communications Magazine* 52, no. 8 (2014): 50–55.

Michael Williamson/The Washington Post/Getty Images

Employees answer phones at Travelocity's call center in Clintwood, Virginia. The call center was phased out as Travelocity placed greater emphasis on text analytics and other technology solutions to handle its large information flow.

most people indicate that they use many informational data sources, instead of mentioning the one or two they actually use. Not wanting to admit ignorance or own up to how little information they use, they ask for a lot and then get lost in the pile.

Travelocity offers an example of how a company dealt with a very large information overload problem. Every month, Travelocity received 30,000 customer survey results, 50,000 e-mails, and notes sent by a half-million calls that it did not have enough employee time to read and respond to. Its managers knew that in this large pile of information, however, was important information about customer problems, sources of dissatisfaction, and issues that needed their response and resolution. Their solution was to turn to software based on **text analytics**.[33] This term describes *linguistic, statistical,* and *machine learning* techniques that can capture the information content of textual sources for use in *business intelligence, exploratory data analysis, research,* or investigation. These programs are similar to the use of analytical techniques for large volumes of data in that they can scrutinize large volumes of text documents, quickly identify crucial terms and concepts they contain, and then put this information into an easily understood format. Companies have used this big data type of technology to keep track of blogs and other online communications that may mention the company's name. This customer-created information on the internet can be a gold mine of useful data about how its customers view the company and the service it provides. Data analytics offer one promising way for organizations to dig out from under this information overload.[34] As Domino's Pizza found out much to their surprise, a practical joke by two employees in North Carolina, who put a fictitious video on YouTube showing them putting cheese sticks up their nose and then sneezing the sticks into a sandwich they were making, can become a national marketing problem requiring quick reaction.[35] If an organization has no way of sorting through the large volume of information that is on the web to know that something like the Domino's video is out there, then it has no opportunity to get the right information to the right person at the right time in the right format so that the person can fix it.

text analytics Linguistic, statistical, and machine learning techniques that can capture the information content of textual sources for use in business intelligence, exploratory data analysis, research, or investigation.

Focusing on the Numbers

A second problem with information systems is the tendency to get tied up in numbers. Since computers excel in transmitting, organizing, and analyzing numbers, much information is provided in numeric form. While this aids accurate conversion of data into information, it does tend to focus attention on only those things that can be quantified or somehow expressed in numerical terms. Unfortunately, much of a manager's job focuses on subjective, qualitative information and not quantitative data. The availability of numerical information creates an overemphasis in decision-making on such information and an under-emphasis on qualitative information. If you have one

---

[33] Scott Morrison, "So Many, Many Words," *Wall Street Journal*, January 28, 2008, https://www.wsj.com/articles/SB120129801401017897.

[34] A. De Mauro, M. Greco, and M. Grimaldi, "What Is Big Data? A Consensual Definition and a Review of Key Research Topics," in *AIP Conference Proceedings*, vol. 1644, no. 1 (2015): 97–104; Steven Rosenbush and Michael Totty, "How Big Data Is Changing the Whole Equation for Business," *Wall Street Journal*, March 10, 2013, https://www.wsj.com/articles/SB10001424127887324178904578340071261396666.

[35] B. Levinsohn and E. Gibson, "An Unwelcome Delivery," *Business Week*, May 4 2009, http://www.mtpspin.ca/picture_library/Dominos_pizza.pdf.

hand in the oven and the other in the freezer, it does not mean that on average you are comfortable at room temperature any more than a high customer satisfaction rating of 4.5 on a website means a business is doing a good job when only two customers have rated your restaurant.

Bad Information

Related to the problem of falling in love with numbers is the third problem with information systems: assuming that the numbers are accurate when they may not be. The saying "garbage in, garbage out" is quite true. A sophisticated information system can quickly get a lot of bad data to a lot of people. If bad data get into the organization's decision-making structure, those bad data will be used in many decision situations. The results can be worse than garbage: they can be catastrophic. Bad information leads to bad decisions. A ship captain who gets a false reading of crossing traffic in a narrow ship channel can make a steering error that collides with rather than avoids another ship. Likewise, bad information widely circulated by means of a sophisticated information and decision system can lead to disaster.

Maintaining Security

A fourth potential problem with information systems is security, or maintaining the integrity of the database. An organization's information system must be protected so that another person or organization cannot hack into it and access its confidential or proprietary data, or worse yet, crash the system, hold it for ransom, or destroy the stored data. In this era of virtual employees and managers working at home or on the road with wireless connections to the information system, protecting the integrity of the database from unauthorized or inappropriate access is an important concern. As the newspaper headlines often report, when employees are able to download sensitive information on personal laptops or flash drives, they can also misplace it, sell it, or leak it to the press while potentially providing hackers access to install malware, worms, or ransomware. Moreover, if the increasingly sophisticated hackers can get into Defense Department and CIA computers—as they have—hackers or competitors may find ways to get into your corporate database or personal computer as well. Protecting against such unauthorized entry is a big problem and big expense for organizations. Uber only realized that its information on 57 million driver and rider accounts were vulnerable after a hacker told the company about it. Uber paid the hacker $100,000 for exposing the vulnerability, but the fact that the security risk was so large became a public relations disaster for the company.[36] HEI Hotels and Resorts, a hotel management company, reported a data breach that could have exposed the names, card account numbers, expiration dates and verification codes of thousands of customers from at least 20 of their 43 Hyatt, Intercontinental, Marriott, and Starwood hotels.[37] Unfortunately, these are increasingly common incidents. Companies like Chipotle, Hard Rock Hotels and Casinos, Hilton, Hyatt, Intercontinental Hotels, Kimpton Hotels, Mandarin Oriental, the travel services company Sabre, and the management company White Lodging have all reported security breaches of their systems.

The problem isn't only outside hackers. Database managers need to ensure that unauthorized persons inside the organization cannot obtain confidential employee data or business secrets. Both outsiders and company insiders need to be prevented from unauthorized access to the organization's database.

[36] Nicole Perlroth and Mike Isaac, "Inside Uber's $100,000 Payment to a Hacker, and the Fallout," *New York Times*, January 12, 2018, https://www.nytimes.com/2018/01/12/technology/uber-hacker-payment-100000.html.

[37] Brittany Jones-Cooper, "Starwood, Marriott, Hyatt Got Hacked: What You Need to Know," *Yahoo Finance*, Yahoo, published August 15, 2016, https://finance.yahoo.com/news/starwood-marriott-hyatt-got-hacked-what-you-need-to-know-163947160.html.

Value Versus Cost

Another problem is determining the true value and true cost of the information. Even though it often seems like it in this era of instant access to endless amounts of information on the web, information is not really free. Buying computers, routers, and servers; hiring programmers, web designers, and data analysts; operating a network; and maintaining an accurate and user-friendly information system are hugely expensive. On the other side of the expense are the largely intangible benefits of employees having access to the right information at the right time in the right format to do their jobs. How does one measure the value of an employee being able to instantaneously access a guest database so that the guest is identified by name, a piece of information the guest wants is immediately available, and the guest's unique expectations are known so that they can be met? United Airlines, which built its computer systems over 20 years ago, estimated in 2016 that its dated technology is costing the company nearly $1 billion a year in lost revenue.[38]

Obviously, the difference in price between a hotel room at the Four Seasons and the Econolodge is one way to estimate the presumed value of these information-driven services to a guest. If guests didn't think these amenities were worth the price, they wouldn't select the Four Seasons. Since many guests do, they must place a value on these services, but their exact value in relation to their cost is usually impossible to establish. Deciding how much better a decision was because the manager had the right information available is all but impossible. Yet, most organizations believe their systems are worth the cost and give them a competitive advantage over others that do not have the same capabilities. The problem is that when budget time comes and paybacks on investments are calculated, defending information system upgrades and improvements is difficult because evaluating the exact contribution of the system is so challenging.

Though determining costs and benefits of information systems is complex, companies can make estimates. Consider how Google has forged its entire business model and financial success on understanding the value of information. In part, Google computes what it calls Page Rank to estimate the relevance of information on web pages to over 2 billion search terms. Google factors in a wide variety of information (over 200 components, or "signals"), including such factors as links to the page, quality of linked pages, content, page speed, click-through rates, and many others.[39] At the same time, Google uses data collected from every search and advertising click (millions a day) to estimate a host of metrics, all aimed at helping estimate the value of information to users and advertisers.[40] The result is a completely different way of doing business than nearly all other companies: Google gives away its best services, doesn't set prices for the advertisements it sells to support its business, makes businesses bid for advertising, and even turns away advertisers if its algorithms determining value and relevance suggest the ad has a poor fit.

Learning the System

The final problem with information systems involves the costs of learning how to use the new system and evolving tools that become available. People with decision-making responsibilities are the very group who need to learn how to use the organization's information system. At the same time, because these individuals are often those who have been out of school the longest, they frequently are the very people who are

[38] John Pletz, "How Outmoded Technology Is Clipping United's Wings," *Crain's Chicago Business*, Crain Communication, published 10, 2016, http://www.chicagobusiness.com/article/20161210/ISSUE01/312109994/how-outmoded-technology-is-clipping-uniteds-wings.

[39] SEO PowerSuite, "8 Major Google Ranking Signals in 2017," Search Engine Land, Third Door Media, published July 11, 2017, https://searchengineland.com/8-major-google-ranking-signals-2017-278450.

[40] Steven Levy, "Secret of Googlenomics: Data-Fueled Recipe Brews Profitability," *Wired Magazine*, May 22, 2009, https://www.wired.com/2009/05/nep-googlenomics/.

most uncomfortable and unfamiliar with the new technologies. Worse yet, given the problems in quantifying the value of the technology, these are the same people who make the decisions about buying the equipment and investing in the system. Obviously, a lot of learning has to take place before those who are uncomfortable with new technology—such as those who don't regularly tweet about their day or don't know the difference between MMSs, SMSs, and RSSs—are at ease when using the new systems. Nonetheless, it is critical to get employees familiar with the technology necessary for them to make high-quality decisions. Even though increasingly user-friendly software has made it easier for these managers to learn and use the powerful technology available to them, the challenge for them will be that as soon as they master one technology, a newer and more powerful one will come along and they will need to learn that one. The rapid changes in what technology can do in managing information will require managers to rapidly adapt to new situations. With so many other things to worry about in performing their jobs, many managers' use of technology can be predicted by what was available when they were growing up rather than what is available to them now. This can cause a challenge when trying to communicate needed information to people from different technological generations.

THE HOSPITALITY ORGANIZATION AS AN INFORMATION SYSTEM

Perhaps the easiest way to understand how information ties the hospitality organization together is by considering the organization itself as a big information system. The main purpose of the information network is to provide each person with whatever information that person needs to serve the customer when that person needs it. Looking at the organization in that way, everyone becomes a transmission point on the organizational network—gathering, sending, and processing information into a user-friendly format. Those responsible for designing the **organization as an information system** must consider how all these network participants are linked together along with what information each participant needs to provide to others and what information each participant needs to have provided by others. If a Delta Airlines customer service representative is responsible for telling an inquiring customer about an alternative set of flights to get the customer to the same destination after the scheduled flight was canceled, the information system had better be designed to obtain and provide that information to the representative when the phone rings. Likewise, if the Delta customer service desk needs to know that Flight 1582 is arriving late and will have to rebook passengers with missed connections, the late arriving pilot needs to communicate that information to the person scheduling staff at the customer service desk. The Delta information system design will therefore require communication linkages, across all members and departments of the organization, providing access to all information needed by the customer service representatives so that the person responsible can solve customer problems. Reengineering the organization and its information system around the customer's needs is a necessity in our present-day competitive marketplace.

organization as an information system The idea that the organization itself should be considered as and structured as an integrated information network or system that connects all the departments and people that deliver the guest experience.

Integrated Systems

Retail stores illustrate how organizations can design their entire physical and record-keeping setup around an integrated information system. The system has a structure and, to gain the full benefit of the information system and its database, the organization designs its other functions to accommodate the requirements of that structure. Here's how it might work at a Cracker Barrel gift shop. The shop's POS system uses barcodes on the items similar to the way in which restaurants use their POS systems.

When a customer brings an item to the counter to pay for it, the employee responsible for registering the sale runs a scanner wand over its barcode to gather the price and quantity information from a central database and then register that information on the customer's receipt. At the same time, the inventory of that product is adjusted to reflect the sale of one unit, and the customer payment is added to the daily sales cash or credit ledger, the gift shop's daily profit-and-loss figures, the particular salesperson's record of sales for the day, and other corporate databases that collect information about how the shop's operations are doing. This simple act of running scanners over product barcodes ultimately leads to information that tells Cracker Barrel management how the product is selling, how the store is doing, and how the salespersons are producing.

When all the parts of an organization are connected via technology, the company collects a wealth of data over time. The best hospitality companies use this integrated information system philosophy to determine how well all parts of their service operations are working, and what can be done to better meet customer needs, improve efficiency, and continuously improve their service product.

The Primacy of Information

The logic of organizing around the availability and flow of information changes the way in which jobs are organized and tasks are performed. It may even drive changes in the sequence of operations and the organization of departmental units. The organization should be designed in a way that responds to information requirements. Jobs and departments dealing with uncertain, ever-changing, ambiguous situations require a lot of information to ensure that the managers, employees, and co-producing guests making decisions in those units can get all the information they need to create a successful service product. Jobs or units that are relatively insulated from uncertainty, ambiguity, and changing circumstance may not require the same volume or quality of information; they can anticipate that whatever happened or was true yesterday will pretty much be the same today and tomorrow. In either case, though, the final goal—to create a great service product—remains the same.

Organizational units facing uncertainty need to add the information capacity that will allow the necessary information to be gathered, or they must find ways to reduce the need for that information. Both strategies involve integrating the organizational design into the information system and vice versa. We shall now take a more detailed look at these two strategies.

Increasing Capacity

When the organization must increase its information-handling capacity to cope with the greater amounts of information managers need when dealing with uncertain situations (e.g., rerouting passengers when weather may impact multiple airports), its system designers must consider the ways in which information is transmitted across the organization. The system will need to be designed in a way to filter and analyze large volumes of data to eliminate unnecessary or distracting information while ensuring the essential information is presented in a clear and readily usable format. Furthermore, the system will have to create redundant sources of critical information. Information that a decision maker absolutely must not miss should be provided in more than one channel of communication to ensure that the manager has it when it is needed. That way, if one channel breaks down or fails to get the information to the person needing it, it can be provided through another means. A simple example would be sending someone an e-mail, followed by a text message, followed by a mailed hard copy, with the same information in all three communications. Building in this redundancy obviously creates additional demand upon the information system, and organizations should carefully consider what information is so important that it needs to be sent in more than one way.

Reducing Need

An alternative to building additional information-processing capacity into the organization is reducing the need to handle information. One major way to do this is to create self-contained decision-making units with employees who are empowered and enabled to make decisions about their areas of responsibility. By increasing the number of decisions made at the point where the information is generated, usage of the information channels is reduced. This is the classic strategy of decentralized decision-making or, in the more current literature, the growing use of individual or group empowerment. The idea here is that with proper training in asking for job-related data and turning it into information used for decision-making, the individual employee or department can make many decisions that would otherwise have been routed up the administrative chain of command. If a furious guest is standing in front of the employee, that guest does not want to wait until some unseen manager gives approval for resolving a problem. This is why The Ritz-Carlton Hotels gives its employees the authority to use up to $2,000 to resolve a customer's problem without seeking permission from a supervisor. As a Ritz-Carlton manager once stated, "I've come to learn that the least costly solution is the one that happens immediately. The longer and higher a customer complaint lives in an organization, the more it grows."[41] The time and effort it takes to check with a supervisor or higher-level organizational unit can use up information channel capacity, but even worse for a hospitality organization, it also slows down the response to the problem and makes the already unhappy guest even more unhappy.

Everybody Connected

The most effective strategy for increasing the information flow is to give all employees access to a company intranet with immediate and easy access to the relevant information in the corporate database plus access to the web where answers can be found with a Google search of the entire internet. Increasingly, rather than sending masses of hard copy information through the traditional communication channels, organizations are putting information online so that any employee with an internet connection and a password can ask for it. Many organizations have an expanded intranet that allows any employee to ask any manager any relevant question over the internal e-mail, by text, or even through a tweet. The flow of information back and forth across all levels of the organization is incredibly enhanced by this technique. The recent move by many organizations to connect to external websites with the amazing databases and informational resources available on the internet means that even more information is available to anyone who needs it whenever they need it. By simply asking Google, frontline employees now have access to much the same information that their bosses do and, with proper education about corporate goals and training in decision-making, can make decisions in specified job-related areas of the same quality that their bosses could in previous eras. Of course, this clearly underscores the importance of hiring the right people, training them, and motivating them in a way that leads to the effective use of this information and improved decision-making and service.

Implications for Service

The impact these communication systems have on empowering frontline employees to do their jobs better, faster, and cheaper is astonishing, and it will only grow even more so in the future. These changes have important implications for middle managers and supervisors in the hospitality organization, who historically were responsible

[41] Michelli, 111.

for transmitting information from senior managers to frontline employees. The impact these technological trends have on organizational design, frontline-employee responsibilities, and need for middle managers is profound. When a frontline employee can obtain any information needed, training required, or questions answered via the web, the information-processing responsibilities and requirements of the traditional middle manager and supervisor are greatly changed. Information technology has changed and will continue to change the way organizations are managed, responsibilities are organized, and the reporting relationships are structured; it has also changed in a fundamental way the nature and role of hospitality employees who are concerned with delivering high-quality guest experiences.

Designers of the information systems for hospitality organizations must be aware of the three components of the guest experience—service product, service setting, and service delivery system—and the best information system would integrate all three. Such a total information system would simultaneously be providing information to guests, management, guest-contact servers, and back-of-the-house staff, just when they need it 24/7. Achieving this end requires system designers to pay close attention to the needs of users, their capabilities, and the time available to them to find and use the information provided. It would not do any good to provide thirty pages of statistical output to a person who doesn't understand statistics or who doesn't have the time to sort through the pile of data to find the necessary information. If you're out of food in your restaurant, you don't want to review statistical predictions of how much food you were supposed to use this week, the sales forecast for next week, or the summary data for last week. You simply want to connect with somebody who can get some more food to you. You need all that other information, but not right now. When you're in the weeds, you don't care what the chemical composition of the weed killer is, as long as you have some. The list of chemicals may be data, but it is not information.

LESSONS LEARNED

LO 9.1 Recognize the importance of information to your guests.

- Each internal and external customer has unique informational needs. You need to know them in order to ensure customer satisfaction.

LO 9.2 Describe ways in which information embedded in the service product, setting, and delivery system provides value to the guests.

- Information has value to each customer, internal and external.

LO 9.3 Explain how the service setting communicates information about the quality and value of the service experience.

- What people see in the service setting communicates a great deal about the quality and value of the hospitality.

LO 9.4 Discuss the impact of the internet on communication with customers and employees.

- Information should be made available in a format that each customer expects, can use, and will use.
- Ensure access to information to all in the organization who need it, and exclude access to those who do not.
- Make organizational information available online, but make sure it is secure.

LO 9.5 Recognize the benefits of data analytics to cope with information overload.

- Data analytics can provide substantial value for processing large amounts of information.

LO 9.6 State the types of problems that can occur when there is too much data.

- Beware information overload—more data does not always mean more information.

LO 9.7 Explain how the hospitality organization itself can be considered a large information-processing system.

- The way the organization is designed helps to enhance the flow of information to enable the right people at the right time to get the right information for decision-making.

KEY TERMS AND CONCEPTS

big data 302
cross-sell 303
daily count 305
data analytics 308
decision support system (DSS) 306
economic ordering quantity (EOQ) model 294
information overload 311
information system 290
integrated information system 295
managing information 289
organization as an information system 315
text analytics 312

REVIEW QUESTIONS

1. What is the difference between providing a guest with information and actually communicating with that guest? Give an example of each. How can hospitality organizations know if information has been communicated effectively to both guests and employees?
2. How is this chapter on communications related to meeting or exceeding the expectations of guests? Is an effective organizational information system important for providing quality to guests, providing value, or both equally, and why?
3. Think about a restaurant you go to frequently. The server probably listened to you place your order and then wrote the information down on a pad or entered it into a POS terminal. What decisions and activities might this order then trigger or affect throughout the entire restaurant organization? (Hint: Think about immediate, on-the-spot matters, but also about inventory, staffing, menu selection, profit and loss calculations, etc.)
4. Think of several different hospitality organizations with which you are familiar.
   A. What are some significant decisions that those organizations must make?
   B. Which of those decisions should perhaps be made by computer systems and which by a well-informed manager?
   C. What differences do you note between the two types of decisions?
5. Some think of organizations as big information systems. According to that idea, the only function and responsibility of a hospitality organization is getting the right information to the right person at the right time so people can make the right decisions that will enable the providing of outstanding guest service.
   A. To what extent does that kind of thinking make sense to you?
   B. Does this idea of the organization as information system correspond to what you yourself have actually experienced in organizations?

ACTIVITIES

1. Interview a local hospitality manager. Find out what information technologies at that hospitality location are the most advanced and most basic. Does the manager want any technology that is not available? Find out which technology the manager thinks the organization could least afford to do without. Report back to the class.
2. Interview service employees at four levels within an organization. Ask them how they learn what's going on in the organization. What communication devices, channels, and sources do they use or have access to? Then compare the differences between information sources of the different levels. If any of the employees don't seem to be getting the adequate, timely information that they need or want, what strategies or devices could be used to improve the information flow?

ETHICS IN BUSINESS

Many restaurants now use the internet to communicate with customers. This includes providing background information on the restaurant, menu items, contact information, and so forth. Some restaurants also allow customers to provide comments about the restaurant. Imagine you are a restaurant owner and have such a site. Most of the time, the site provides complimentary information and that helps business. But once in a while, someone complains. Because it is your own website, you have the power to delete the comment. Would you? Would any of the following factors affect your decision?

1. What if the post is anonymous versus signed?
2. What if the post complains about a specific server and gives the name?
3. What if the post uses profanity?
4. What if you think, but don't know for sure, that the post is possibly fictitious?
5. What if you simply disagree with the posting? Would you delete it? Would you respond?

CASE STUDY

Case 1: At the Country Club

While waiting to tee off at the country club, Lillian Hollowell and Sarah Dinsmore were arguing about emerging technological trends in the restaurant industry.

Hollowell, president of Conglomerate Restaurants, spoke this way: "Sarah, I don't know how I got along before our restaurants purchased point-of-sale handheld units. I got them to improve communication between the servers and the kitchen, but they have really made my job easier, too. They instantly give me sales data I can combine with other databases. I can convert reams of numbers into colorful charts and graphs that my managers can easily understand. These units have enabled me to get more useful information, make decisions, and have more time for golf. I don't have to depend any longer on summary reports from the branch restaurants. I have instant access to my company's database, so I can call up info on current and past performance of any of my units, along with comparative industry and economic information from outside databases. If I see something out of the ordinary, I can get right to the restaurant manager responsible and check it out, or hold a teleconference with several managers."

Sarah Dinsmore was president of International Restaurants. Although the chain had 1,400 units, it specialized in friendly, personal attention. Sarah thought of her organization as high touch, as opposed to her high-tech rival: "I want no part of those POS units. You don't see the fine restaurants in Europe cluttered up with those machines. The blasted things churn out a ton of data, but I still can't get much information. I've tried three different POS systems and I despised them all. If you want to do anything beyond the simplest operation, then you need to be very familiar with the system. I don't have the time to gain that familiarity, so I've turned my link in our current system over to my executive assistant. She knows how to run it and I don't think I'll ever need to learn. Besides, when I go to a restaurant with handheld POS terminals, the servers are often so busy punching in my order that they forget to make eye contact and they fail to give me the personal attention I expect. I think they spend too much time with the technology and not enough with me."

1. Will Sarah Dinsmore be able to function effectively for very long with this attitude, or will she eventually have to learn how to use the data that the POS units make available?
2. How can she gain the advantages of high tech without losing the high touch she believes is a differentiating hallmark of her restaurants? Or is this a trade-off situation in which you can't do both?

Case 2: Fine Family Motels

The reservation agents at the 105 units of the Fine Family Motels chain worked hard, but the chain's occupancy rate seemed to keep drifting lower. When that rate hit 58% management realized something had to be done.

While most locations had an acceptable occupancy rate, a few low-occupancy locations pulled down the overall rate. Unfortunately, the low-occupancy properties seemed to shift around from month to month. The local reservation agents, travel agents, and airline reservation networks weren't notified of the low-occupancy areas until the problem became acute. The company was willing to offer discounts of up to 50% in the low-occupancy properties to fill rooms, if it could identify them promptly and get the information out to tour organizations, online distributors, travel wholesalers, and other client sources.

1. What technological changes would benefit Fine Family Motels?
2. What structural changes might they make necessary?
3. How might Fine Family Motels use the web to improve its occupancy rates?

Further readings on the topics in this chapter are listed in "Additional Readings" on pages 514–516.

Get the tools you need to sharpen your study skills. SAGE edge offers a robust online environment featuring an impressive array of free tools and resources.

Access practice quizzes, eFlashcards, video, and multimedia at **edge.sagepub.com/Ford2e**.

Visit **edge.sagepub.com/Ford2e** to help you accomplish your coursework goals in an easy-to-use learning environment.

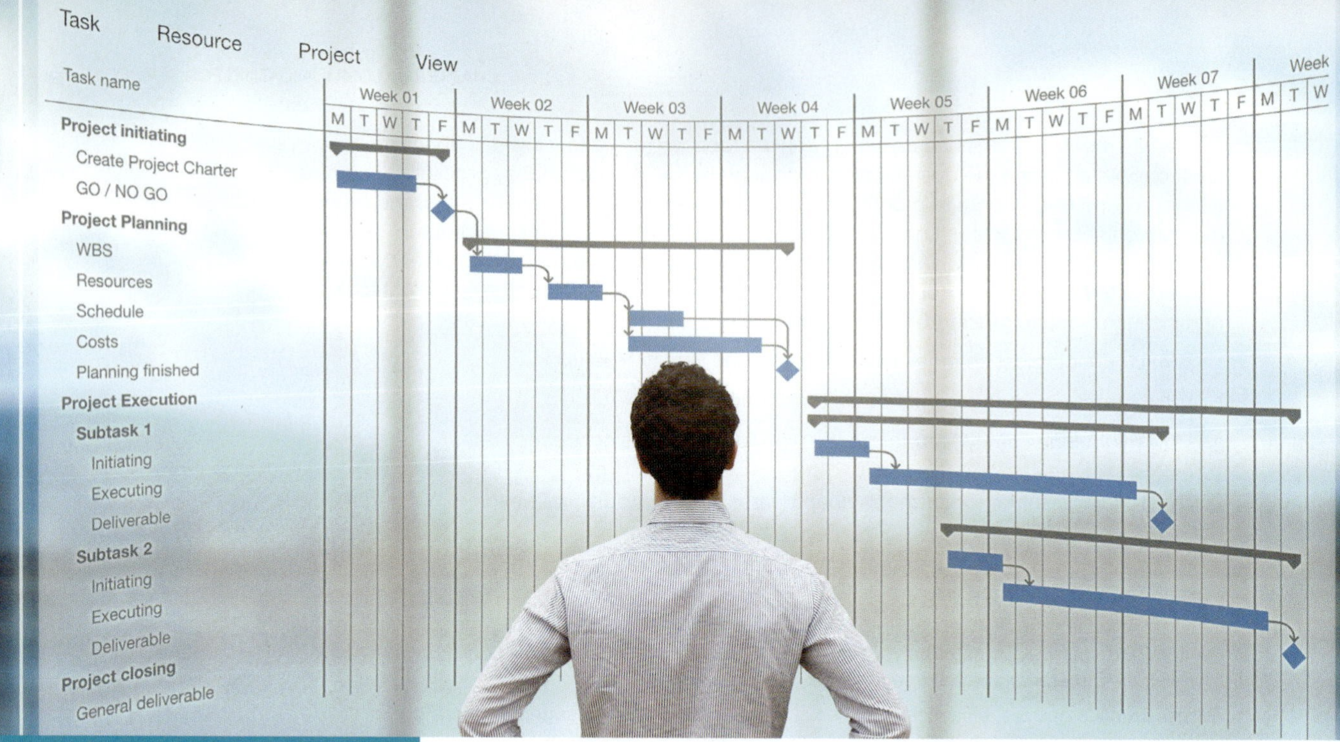

©iStockphoto.com/NicoElNino

10 Planning the Service Delivery System

Hospitality Principle: Provide Seamless Service Delivery

> Being nice to people is just 20% of providing good customer service. The important part is designing systems that allow you to do the job right the first time.
>
> —Carl Sewell, Customers for Life

Learning Objectives

After reading this chapter, you should be able to:

10.1 Describe why it is critical for organizations to fully plan their service delivery system.

10.2 Describe how organizations plan, design, analyze, and check the hospitality organization's service delivery system.

10.3 Demonstrate how to design a delivery system using several methods, such as flow-charting, blueprinting, the universal service map, and PERT/CPM.

10.4 Explain how to use fishbone analysis, poka-yokes, and other methods to locate the source of problems and prevent their occurrence or reoccurrence.

10.5 Discuss how to use a cross-functional organizational design to deliver a service product.

INTRODUCTION

Horst Schulze, former chief operating officer of The Ritz-Carlton Hotels, liked to tell the story of how one hotel manager solved the problem of delays in serving room-service breakfasts. After several guests complained to the manager about their breakfasts being brought to the rooms both slow and cold, the manager knew he had to investigate. The traditional managerial solution to the problem would have been to call in and loudly criticize the offending room-service manager for technical incompetence and poor supervisory skills. The then properly disciplined manager would return to the kitchen, gather the room-service staff around, and yell at them. After all, in most organizations, blame rolls downhill to the lowest-level employee.

Schulze used the example to illustrate a different problem-solving approach. The manager organized a team of room-service people and asked them to study the problem, find out why the meals were not getting to guests within a reasonable time, and suggest ways to solve whatever problem they found. The team did exactly that. They studied the problem at great length and found that the cause was the unavailability of service elevators needed by the room-service people to get the meals quickly to their guests. They studied why the elevators were unavailable and even had a room-service employee spend an entire morning in the elevators with a stopwatch to see where the elevators were, what they were being used for, and why they were unavailable when the room-service people needed them.

What the team found astonished Schulze and the manager. The whole problem could be traced to a faulty management decision about how many bed sheets the housekeepers were allowed to stock on each floor (called the "par"). The decision had left some floors with too few sheets, and the housekeepers were using the elevators in order to hunt for extra sheets and finish cleaning the rooms on their floors. The elevators were therefore unavailable to the room-service delivery people when they needed them, cold meals intended to be hot were delivered late, and guests got angry. Because a manager trying to save on the cost of sheets stocked too few, the rest of the system was disrupted. This cost-saving move drove up the costs of room service (because the hotel did not charge for meals when guests complained) and housekeeping labor (because housekeepers were spending their time in elevators instead of making beds). Trying to solve a problem in one part of the service delivery system created problems for another part. The total impact was an increase in costs as well as guest dissatisfaction.

PLANNING AND DESIGNING THE SERVICE DELIVERY SYSTEM

What manager would ever have thought the late-breakfast problem would be solved by adding more bed sheets to the available supply on each floor? Schulze drew three lessons from this story. First, managers aren't smart enough, or do not have enough time or information, to prevent or solve all the problems by themselves. Therefore, they tend to find the simplest, quickest solution, which is frequently based on their assumption that a subordinate lacks sufficient motivation, training, or supervision. These managers rely on the traditional theory that "if you correct the person, you correct the problem." Second, employees may have a better chance of finding the root causes of a problem than the manager. After all, those in the middle of the situation often know more about what is really going on than the manager. According to Schulze, not using the talents, intelligence, and job-related knowledge of these people is simply foolish. Finally, the most important lesson is that every problem should be addressed first from the perspective of the entire service delivery system. Although a person may end up being the cause of a service failure, Schulze believed that the fault is frequently found in the system and not the person. Simply putting out one small fire ("we are spending too much money on sheets") without thinking about the system-wide effect can cause big problems elsewhere.

Designing and Checkin g the Service Delivery System

We have said all along that the service delivery system includes all aspects of the service experience—service product, service setting, and service delivery—and hospitality managers need to think about the entire process that delivers the service to the guest and about the systems that are needed to make the process work flawlessly. Developing a service product that meets guests' needs and having well-trained, motivated, and enthusiastic employees using the right information, equipment, and tools to deliver the product to guests within a well-designed service environment, are all necessary, but these are not sufficient. The key component of a flawless service experience is making sure the entire service delivery system, the process by which the service is delivered to the guest, is designed so that it effectively integrates the many elements of the experience to make it happen in the way the customer expects.

Achieving guest delight and avoiding service failure can both be greatly affected by the delivery system design. Every hospitality organization should spend whatever studying and planning time and energy it takes to get the system right. It is a crucially important topic.

The total quality management movement, which emphasized that everyone is responsible for quality—not just the quality control department—has taught organizational leaders several important lessons. First, achieving total quality requires consideration of the entire system—from initial design, to using whatever raw materials and inputs are needed, to the finished product. Second, everyone is responsible for delivering and monitoring quality; in hospitality, everyone is responsible for the quality of the guest experience. Third, the system needs to be proactively checked for problems before people are blamed. Hospitality managers must determine *root causes* of problems and implement solutions to avoid future problems; these root causes often lie in the system.

Too many times, hospitality managers assume an employee has made an error when in reality the fault lies in a bad system, which makes it difficult, if not impossible, for the employee to deliver the service experience with the excellence that the organization, the employee, and the guest would like. Talk with frontline servers at hotels, restaurants, or any hospitality organization, and they will tell you how frustrated they become when the service systems get in their way of doing the jobs they are hired, trained, and paid to do, and which they really want to do well. When the service delivery system fails, everyone loses. The guest is unhappy, the employee is frustrated, and the organization may lose a guest and all the profits the guest's future business represents.

Neville Elder/Corbis via Getty Images

Behind the scenes at a busy restaurant, a service delivery system must be carefully planned to ensure that every guest is delighted by both the service and the service product.

The Goal: Fail No Guest; Delight Every Guest

The hospitality manager must spend the extra time and effort to plan and organize the service delivery system so that it works right every time. To achieve the companion goals of failing no guest and delighting every guest, successfully planning the entire guest experience (the cycle of service) and focusing on an effective delivery system are critical. While we don't want to downplay the contributions of production management techniques and the solutions that industrial engineers have found for problems in manufacturing organizations, these tools cannot guarantee the success of any hospitality organization's service delivery system because *the guest* is always the ultimate judge of the quality and value of the guest experience. Service delivery system designers must, therefore, ensure that they design the experience from the guest's point of view and not their own. Too many organizations design their service production processes for employee convenience or efficiency. Although the system should be user-friendly for employees, the outstanding hospitality guestologists organize their service experience around the guest's needs, expectations, capabilities, and actual behaviors. The delivery of any service should always be smooth, seamless, and transparent from the guest's point of view.

Some Guiding Principles

Given the goal of providing exceptional customer service, and learning from the lessons of Horst Schulze and The Ritz-Carlton example (and indeed, all the examples in this book), here are some principles to keep in mind. Study your customers in minute detail; build a service delivery system that will provide the experience they expect from your organization; monitor the system closely; create accurate early-warning measures for each possible failure point; engage everyone in the organization in watching those measures; and keep records of and follow up on everything that doesn't meet your guests' expectations for whatever reason. If the records show failures occur repeatedly at certain points, change the system design. If service standards are frequently unmet, find out why. If the organization has a service guarantee, be sure the delivery system can meet and exceed that guarantee. Track the times and reasons guests invoke the guarantee so system flaws can be found and fixed.

Although excellent hospitality organizations do their best to keep service failures from happening by keeping a careful eye on all the places where the system might fail, they know that failures are inevitable. Therefore, they plan for how to recover from the inevitable failures. They design systems that ensure success, avoid failure, and are able to track and recover from inadequacies based on the key drivers of guest satisfaction.

DEVELOPING THE SERVICE DELIVERY SYSTEM

Juran Trilogy Joseph Juran's model of quality: planning, control, and improvement.

After almost fifty years of research, Joseph Juran published the **Juran Trilogy**[1] in 1986. It defined the three management processes that Juran thought were required by all organizations to improve: quality planning, quality control, and quality improvement. Quality planning involves identifying customers, determining their needs, creating a product or service to meet those needs, and then developing a system to deliver the product or service. Quality control with respect to the hospitality industry means making sure the system has a way to measure that the service is being delivered in the most effective way. Errors as the product or service is being delivered, whether due to inadequate planning or faulty execution, are prevented or minimized through quality control. Quality improvement involves after-the-fact analysis of the errors and failures that have contributed to poor quality and improving the delivery process to reduce or eliminate future errors based on the quality control measures.

The influence of Juran's Trilogy can be seen in Exhibit 10.1. It shows the when, what, who, and how of a comprehensive service delivery system and the service experience that it provides. It reminds us that an exceptional customer service experience begins with the planning that takes place even before the guest walks through the door. It also reminds us that knowing the needs, wants, expectations, capabilities, and behaviors of the targeted guests is the starting point of any delivery system. The exhibit shows that the overall process consists of three phases: planning, monitoring, and assessing/improving the service delivery system. These three phases are the focus of this final section of the book. If the process was well planned and designed, then the organization is ready to deliver the desired service, in a way that should elicit a wow reaction.

This chapter focuses on carefully planning the service experience. The next chapter focuses on a special case of planning—managing waits—because waits and queues are so pervasive in hospitality experiences. Chapter 12 describes how companies can better manage the delivery of each guest's experience by monitoring, measuring, and evaluating the quality of their service delivery as it is being delivered. Chapter 13 describes the process of service recovery, and how fixing service problems and learning from service errors after the service has been delivered can both help recover unsatisfied guests and lead to improvements in the entire service delivery system. No service system is foolproof, but the best managers take the time to plan out the guest experience with all available planning tools, monitor it while it is happening, and fix it when they find that it did not meet guest expectations. Since no one can manage what isn't measured, we will focus on tools that measure the service delivery system so that a flawless experience can be delivered to every guest every time.

Planning the System

Any good delivery system begins with careful planning. Careful analysis and detailing of every step in the entire service delivery process will make the difference between having it mostly right and reaching the level of excellence that the very best service organizations deliver.

service standards The company's explicit expectations for how the different aspects of the service experience should be delivered every time to every guest.

Service standards should be established early in the planning process. Blaine Sweatt, former President of New Product Development for Darden Restaurants, strongly believes that service standards are the backbone of delivering service excellence. He says that unless management carefully defines measurable standards for each element of its service experience, there is no way to know if it is providing the

[1] Joseph M. Juran, "The Quality Trilogy," *Quality Progress* 19, no. 8 (1986): 19–24.

EXHIBIT 10.1

Planning the Delivery System, Monitoring the Service Experience, and Assessing the Experience to Improve the System

	PHASE I: PLANNING THE SERVICE DELIVERY SYSTEM	PHASE II: MONITORING THE SERVICE EXPERIENCE	PHASE III: ASSESSING THE EXPERIENCE TO IMPROVE THE SYSTEM
When	**Before** the guest arrives, and while the guest is waiting for the service experience	**During** the guest's experience	**After** the guest's experience
What	Experience expected	Experience realized	Experience remembered
Who	Target customers	Actual customers	Past, current, and potential future customers
How	Setting service standards; blueprinting; universal service map; fishbone analysis; PERT/ CPM; simulations; forecasting demand; designing waits (queues); training; quality teams; poka-yokes; cross-functional organizational design	Applying service standards and job performance standards; managerial observation (MBWA); employee observation meeting terms of service guarantees; personal interviews and encounters with guests	**Guest assessment:** Comment cards; toll-free 800 numbers; surveys (mail and web, phone, critical incidents); SERVQUAL; guest focus groups; mystery shoppers **Other data review:** Service failure reports; service guarantee utilization; interviews; customer complaints by category and type; employee feedback; sales and revenue reports; market share/ capacity utilization **Further review:** Organizational design; service standards; training methods **Refer findings back to system planners**

excellent service customers expect. Service standards are the company's expectations for how the different aspects of the service experience should be delivered every time to every guest. And, as is true when setting individual goals (discussed in Chapter 7), the criteria for service standards should be SMART: specific, measurable, attainable, results oriented, and time bound.

Some standards are widely used in the hospitality industry: twenty minutes to get a room-service breakfast, six minutes to check-in including waiting time, and less than that to get the first cup of morning coffee in the hotel restaurant. Special types of service standards (see Exhibit 10.2) are those set by industry associations or other agencies that establish certification, accreditation, and recognition standards. Organizations or individuals are assessed on the degree to which they meet these standards and those

EXHIBIT 10.2

Externally Developed Standards

Some organizations test the accuracy of their internally developed standards by seeking external affirmation of their service quality. They do so in three basic ways: certifications, accreditations, and recognition by ranking organizations.

Certifications

The National Institute of Standards and Technology's Malcolm Baldrige Award and ISO 9000:2015 series certification are the external evaluations generally seen by hospitality and other service organizations as the best affirmation of their service quality. Many are now also seeking environmental certifications such as Leadership in Energy and Environmental Design (LEED), Green Lodging, BigGreenG, and various state-level certifications. Those organizations seeking to be ISO 9000-certified develop the supporting materials for showing their compliance with each standard and apply for a review. If the review finds that the firm meets the standards, the firm can advertise itself as being ISO 9000 certified. The International Organization for Standardization details its requirements on its website. These certifications may have little meaning to most guests, but to both employees and external business partners, the certifications are marks of quality that can be displayed proudly. Individuals can earn a Six Sigma Black Belt Quality certification from the American Society for Quality (ASQ) to affirm their mastery of the quality-improvement principles defined by the Design, Measure, Analyze, Improve, Control (DMAIC) methodology. A variety of other certifications are designed either for a specific employee category, such as those for cruise line counselors, meeting professionals, and sommeliers, or for specific industry groups, which in some cases are required by law to affirm compliance with quality standards such as the National Restaurant Association's ServSafe Food Safety Manager and the Hazardous Analysis and Critical Control Point (HACCP) certification.

Accreditations

Accreditation provides public notice that an organization has met standards of quality established by the accrediting group. Several professional organizations related to hospitality offer accreditation as a way for their members to affirm to their key stakeholders that they are of high quality. Examples are the Destination Management Accreditation Program (DMAP) initiated by Destination Marketing Association International (DMAI), the International Air Transport Association (IATA) accreditation for travel agents, and the International Cruise Council of Australia's (ICCA) Cruise Accreditation Program.

Recognitions

The various hospitality recognition programs are generally the most visible and important affirmations of quality to guests. They include evaluations and ratings by magazines like *Consumer Reports* and *Wine Spectator*, quality-rating organizations like J.D. Power and American Automobile Association, and print or online travel guides such as Michelin, Fodor, Rick Steves, Lonely Planet, and TripAdvisor. These external organizations create and then apply service standards to evaluate hospitality organizations. Knowing that these standards and ratings exist and may be used by guests, hospitality organizations can use them as blueprints for developing a set of more detailed internal service standards that focus organization members on key drivers of guest satisfaction. Knowing that the guests using these external reviews are seeking a specific level of service when they arrive at a hotel, restaurant, cruise line, or an attraction not only gives the organization's management a set of standards to meet but also provides an opportunity and motivation to exceed those expectations and provide a wow experience, instead of merely meeting the standards.

Achieving these certifications, accreditations, and recognitions provides visible evidence to key customers and stakeholders of the organization's commitment to service excellence. A concierge who is a member of the Les Clefs d'Or proudly wears her crossed gold keys to show her mastery of the profession and commitment to high levels of guest service quality.

The external evaluations also provide an excellent means for organizations that have not yet developed internal service standards to begin the process of identifying what service factors are most important to their guests.

assessments are then made public. Most standards, however, are specific to the organizations setting them and are designed to meet or beat the expectations of their targeted guests and often the competition as well. McDonald's sets standards for every task including the creation of an "Operating Report" that their more than 950 field inspectors use to evaluate each location.[2] Airlines define how many minutes it should take for bags to get from the parked aircraft to the baggage-claim area. If they are not on the conveyor belts in that time, the service-quality standard has not been met. Many organizations measure the number of rings it takes to answer the phone in a call center responsible for responding to guest inquiries. If a reservationist, for example, hasn't picked up the phone within three rings, the service-quality standard has not been met. These are service-quality standards, established during the planning phase, that guide employees in what quality and kind of experience they are expected to deliver to guests.

Service standards are one of the most important tools that hospitality managers have to ensure that the service expectations of guests are at least being met, if not exceeded. Service standards need to be established in the planning stage, before the guest is present. As we will discuss in subsequent chapters, they also need to be checked when the guest is present to be sure they are being met, and again after the guest leaves to determine the degree to which the service experience was delivered the way it was planned.

Monitoring the Service Experience

Phase II in Exhibit 10.1 involves monitoring the experience through measurement as the experience is happening, to be discussed in Chapter 12. We have said before that you can't manage what you don't measure, and this is especially true of service situations. Industrial engineers in manufacturing have taken measurement methods to the level of a precise science. The service industry in general, and the hospitality industry in particular, have lagged behind in understanding how to apply measurements to the largely intangible services they offer. However, the need to find ways to measure what is happening to the guest in every step of service delivery, especially for moments of truth, is critical in assuring continued guest satisfaction. Furthermore, if problems arise, measurement is critical for recognizing them, applying solutions, and determining if those solutions were sufficient.

Organizations should measure the quality of service delivery against service standards whenever possible. Such standards help to make the intangible experience tangible for the purposes of measurement and control. These standards, carefully created during the planning stage, are an excellent way to focus everyone on what is important to the guest. Saying to a server "I think you ought to work faster" is easy and might (or might not) improve the service experience of tonight's guests. However, in the long run, comparing a server's performance from last month against target levels for standards like "time until initial greeting," "time for delivery of food or drink," and "time to bring the bill" can be much more helpful. Indeed, in the best circumstances, when the measures are clear, fair, connected to providing excellence, and completely understood by the employees whose performance is being measured, employees will be able to measure and manage themselves more effectively on those certain performance measurements. If done well, *self-management through self-measurement* is to everyone's benefit. If you teach employees what is important to their individual job success and then train them to measure how they are performing on those critical factors, you have the beginnings of a self-managing workforce and, when things go wrong, a self-healing system. Ideally, performance measures make it possible for employees to monitor their own delivery effectiveness while actually providing the

[2] Paul Facella and Adina Genn, *Everything I Know About Business I Learned at McDonalds: The 7 Leadership Principles that Drive Break Out Success* (New York, NY: McGraw Hill Professional, 2008).

service. If Kris Smith knows that the organizational maximum for answering her phone is three rings, and a computerized device displays a running record of how many average rings it takes Kris to answer a call, then she knows at all times where she stands in relation to the company standard.

Standards can be set for departments and organizational units as well. At Gaylord Palms, management has asked each department to create Wildly Important Goals (WIGs) that become their unit's performance standards. The idea is based on their application of the first discipline of execution developed by McChesney, Covey and Hurling.[3] This discipline requires a leader to focus attention on only one or two goals that will have a great impact toward the organization's success rather than focusing on multiple goals that will only have a mediocre impact.

Gaylord Palms applies this goal setting discipline to not only the overall hotel but also for each department. An example of an overall hotel WIG was to increase the STARS engagement. Setting this as a Wildly Important Goal caused leadership to put a laser-like focus on identifying behaviors and taking actions that would increase employee engagement. As a result, Gaylord's management team decided to add new methods of employee communications such as the publication of the daily "Know Your Stuff" (KYS) newspaper that STARS were asked to pick up each day as they arrived at the hotel. Leaders were asked to use the information in this daily newspaper in pre-shift meetings to recognize employee events and accomplishments, remind all STARS of the Gaylord values, and provide information about what customer groups were in the hotel that day. STARS were asked to keep the KYS with them at all times in order to have the information to answer any guest questions. Gaylord also created a weekly newsletter, "The STAR Weekly" that communicated the Gaylord Culture and shared other information about the company and its STARS. As another new way to improve communications, Gaylord updated the STARS Guarantee Wall to spotlight both its commitment to the STARS Guarantee and to provide specific evidence of what departments were doing to live up to it. At the end of two years, the management focus caused by adopting this WIG led to an increase in the employee engagement metric of 19%.

Assessing the Experience and Improving the System

After planning the system and monitoring the experience through measurement comes the last step: assessment and improvement. Collecting and analyzing information about what has actually occurred drives system improvement. Once the plan is clearly laid out and results of the implementation are adequately measured regarding system operations, both management and employees have the information needed to redesign the system and fix the problems to continue the improvement of the guest experience.

In Exhibit 10.1, in the "How" block of Phase III: Assessing the Experience to Improve the System, sales and revenue reports and market share/capacity utilization are included. The overall health of the business is a good indicator of whether or not guest service quality is where it should be. If the business is losing money, market share, capacity utilization, and so forth, these measures may indicate problems with the service product, setting, or delivery system. In other words, gathering and reviewing data generated by the tools described in the chapters to follow are important, but the overall success of the business itself is an indicator of whether or not you are providing the guest experience on which you built your business model.

The Blurred Lines

Exhibit 10.3 shows that the lines between the different phases of service are not sharply drawn. This exhibit helps us to organize across the following chapters what

[3] Chris McChesney, Sean Covey, and Jim Huling, *The 4 Disciplines of Execution: Achieving Your Wildly Important Goals* (New York, NY: Free Press, 2012).

EXHIBIT 10.3

The Phases of Service Delivery

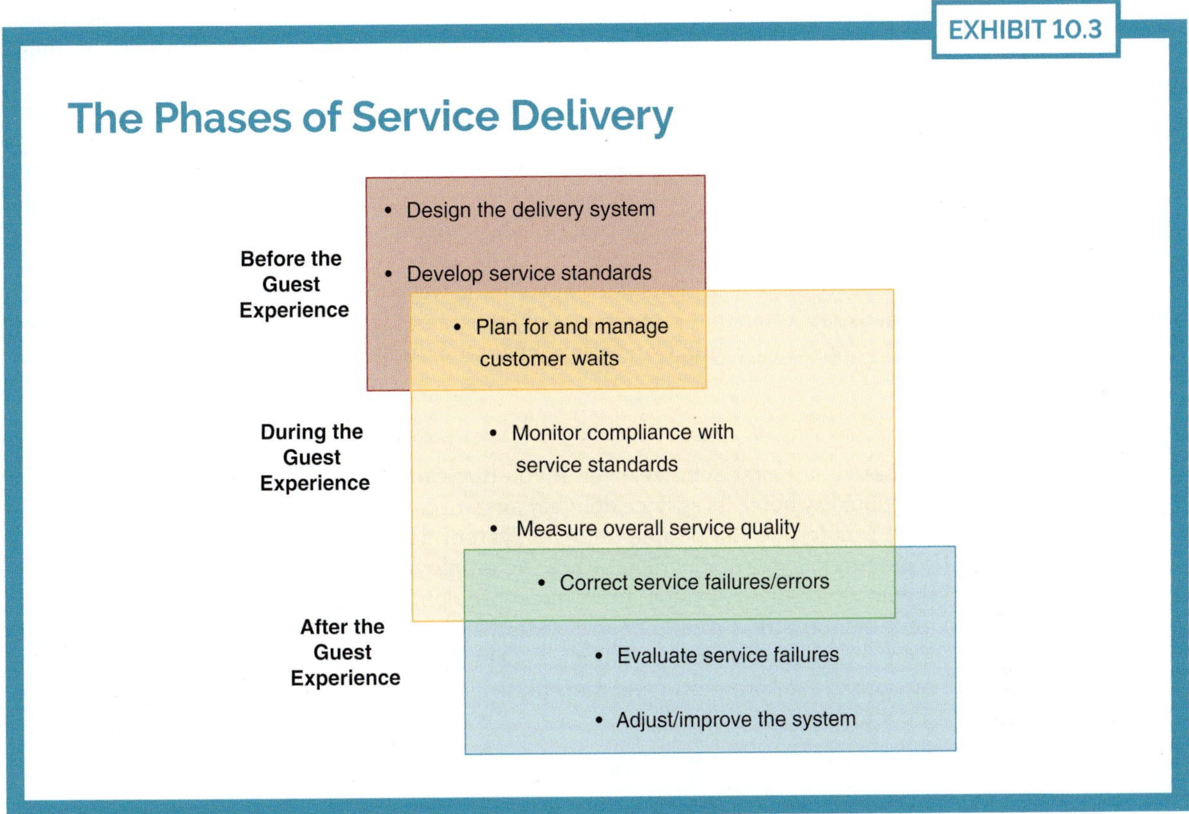

we know about managing a service delivery system so as to provide an exceptional service experience. In reality, the distinctions between the phases of producing intangible services like hospitality experiences are not clear. A refrigerator is built in a distant factory, delivered to a store, and then purchased in that store. Each stage of the production and delivery system is clearly distinct. The borders between the phases of service delivery, however, represent overlapping areas and are not distinct.

As noted above, planning for the service experience begins even before the guest walks through the door, and part of this planning involves preparing for the inevitable customer waits, represented by the top area in Exhibit 10.3. The customer perceives the wait as part of the service experience, and if it is mismanaged or too short or too long, then the guest may feel that, overall, the entire service experience was disappointing. Another blurred line, represented by the lower area in Exhibit 10.3, represents service recovery or the correction of errors. They can be corrected either during the service or after the service. Obviously, the best time to catch, fix, apologize, and possibly compensate for failures is before the guest actually leaves. Once the guest leaves the service setting, whether a physical location or on the web, the likelihood of being able to again contact with that person to fix a failure is greatly diminished or even impossible.

Although organizations are not happy about guest complaints, all should welcome them as valuable feedback on how well they are meeting their guests' needs and expectations. Janelle Barlow and Claus Møller titled their book *A Complaint Is a Gift*, and guestologists agree.[4] Bill Marriott Jr. urged his employees, "I challenge you to not give up on the picky customer. I actually think they can do our business a lot of good. These

[4] Janelle Barlow and Claus Møller, *A Complaint Is a Gift: Recovering Customer Loyalty When Things Go Wrong*, 2nd ed. (San Francisco, CA: Berrett-Koehler Publishers, 2008).

customers point out the little flaws that others may not notice.... Picky customers force us to pursue excellence, to not give up until we get it right.... The way I see it, we have two choices... we can let them anger us... maybe even scare us... or we can learn how and where we can improve... striving to be better, listen to what they have to say and act on it."[5] Complaining guests give a clear indication that their service experience was in some way not a success. Because research shows that most dissatisfied guests do not complain, organizations need methods for measuring the success of all service experiences, not just experiences that guests complain about. Only in that way can organizations ensure they are delivering the expected service, to every guest, every time.

Because organizations need systematic ways to learn how well they are doing in order to get better, they survey not only the guests who came, but also the ones in their target market who didn't, and even those who didn't come back.

The Self-Healing System

As noted by Horst Schulze, even if you have all the characteristics and features of a high-quality hotel, its service delivery system can still fail from time to time. Schulze's goal was to use the people and the system designers to create what he termed a *self-healing system,* in which either the employees or the system itself can override the normal delivery system to fix guest problems when it fails. The employees are the built-in monitors in a self-healing system and are also responsible for telling management where the system has failed so that together they can fix it. Just as everyone is responsible for providing and maintaining quality, everyone is responsible for avoiding and fixing service failures.

The Cycle Goes On

The cycle of planning, monitoring, and assessing/improving should never stop. The service plan lays out what you think your service delivery system should do for the guest; the control measures tell you if what you planned is in fact happening; and the commitment to improvement focuses everyone's attention on analyzing the data collected to fix any identified problems and move toward a flawless guest experience. The measures used should be able to trigger recognition of "exceptions," variations from the plan.

In addition to including ways to measure how well the service is being rendered at every step of the delivery process, a good plan must also include ways to measure how the overall plan is succeeding. When guests are asked about their experience, most of them evaluate it holistically. They are often unable to identify how any one part of the experience influenced their determination of the total experience's value and their degree of satisfaction. They can, however, give an overall impression of service quality that can trigger managerial investigations. The guest may be unhappy with the dining experience at the restaurant, but until management sits down and carefully analyzes the data measuring each step in the entire guest experience, it may not recognize whether the dissatisfaction was caused by a long wait, a dirty bathroom, a cold appetizer, a rude server, or a messy entrance littered with cigarette butts. Knowing what the delivery system is supposed to do and analyzing data collected from the measures should trigger the necessary corrective actions.

PLANNING TECHNIQUES

The first step in service delivery system design is planning out the steps and processes in the entire system. Planning techniques focus on constructing or *diagramming*

[5] Marriot International, "Learn To Love The Pickiest Customer," *Marriot: On The Move* (blog), May 31, 2016, http://www.blogs.marriott.com/marriott-on-the-move/2016/05/learn-to-love-the-pickiest-customer.html.

a thoroughly detailed step-by-step description of what the service delivery process involves and the service standards that must be met. Planning always starts with the guest and frequently begins with the moment when the guest becomes aware of the organization's ability to satisfy some need. The guest's expectations begin to build from that moment, long before the guest ever arrives at your front door. Since we know that what the guest expects forms the basis or criterion for determining how well the experience satisfies the guest, understanding those expectations becomes the first step in planning for and then providing any guest experience. This understanding forms the basis for the beginning of delivery system planning.

Detailing the delivery system by diagramming it has several immediate benefits to managers seeking to fail-safe the delivery of their service.[6] First, by writing it down and creating a flow chart, either on paper or on a computer screen, they are able to easily understand and study how all the parts of the system work. Second, the process of creating a diagram allows managers a visual means to show the service delivery process to others and how the various parts of the organization must work together. Third, having a visual representation of the service delivery system allows for thoughtful consideration of what processes guests should see and what should occur out of their line of vision. Fourth, it provides a means for comparing the ideal service experience, as embodied in the diagram, with the actual experience to identify aspects of the process that need improvement. Fifth, and perhaps most importantly, by focusing attention on component elements of the service delivery process, diagramming illustrates areas where problems are occurring and which areas need improvement.

Of the many planning techniques available, four basic ones are commonly used to develop a detailed plan for delivering the guest experience. These techniques are blueprinting and the related concept of a universal service map, fishbone analysis, PERT/CPM (Program Evaluation Review Technique/Critical Path Method), and simulation. Each has its own advantages, but all are premised on the idea that a detailed written plan leads to a better system for managing the people, organization, and production processes that deliver the total guest experience. These tools are especially useful because they can readily incorporate the measurements necessary for control and analysis of problems that may appear in the system. After the plan is devised, managers can also use these techniques to focus on any part that guest feedback indicates might be a problem area. If effort and care are devoted to the plan, failures should be minimized. This is important because if situations are regularly permitted to get to the point where problem-solving and failure-recovery techniques become necessary, some guests will inevitably be lost to competitors.

Blueprinting

The most commonly discussed type of service diagramming is **blueprinting**. The entire service delivery process and its sub-processes are described in blueprint format as if one were building a house and needed a plan of what went where. In effect, a good blueprint defines every component part and activity, not just of the delivery system, but of the entire guest experience from the moment when the guest sees the front door or greeting sign to the time the guest departs and moves out of sight.

blueprinting A flowchart diagram of the events and contingencies in the service process, on paper or digitally, in blueprint format.

A typical blueprint has five parts[7]:

1. *Physical evidence.* The tangible physical parts of the service experience that can impact customer assessment of quality and value.
2. *Customer actions.* The actions and behaviors of customers, which drive the creation of a blueprint.

[6] Mary J. Bitner, Amy L. Ostrom, and Felicia N. Morgan, "Service Blueprinting: A Practical Technique for Service Innovation," *California Management Review* 50, no. 3 (2008): 66–94.

[7] Bitner, Ostrom, and Morgan, 66–94.

3. *Onstage/visible contact-employee actions.* Things that customer-contact employees do as part of the face-to-face encounter and which customers see.
4. *Backstage/nonvisible contact-employee actions.* Things that customer-contact employees do out of sight of customers but that must happen for the experience to take place; this part of the blueprint also includes nonvisible interaction with customers (e.g., a customer's telephone call to make a reservation).
5. *Support processes.* Activities essential to providing the service but carried out by individuals and units that do not have direct contact with the customer (e.g., maintaining the company's information systems, food delivery, managing payroll).

Every event that is scheduled to happen from the start to the finish of the experience is laid out on a blueprint, as is every contingency that can reasonably be projected. Those points at which service failures are most likely to occur should be identified and early-warning mechanisms included.

The blueprint should attach times to the activities and processes involved in providing the service and the time for the entire guest experience. If an excellent service product in a compatible environment is provided in twenty minutes, a guest may feel rushed; if the service is provided within an hour, satisfied; if the service takes two hours to deliver, the guest may never return.

Finally, the purpose of blueprinting is not only to satisfy the guest but also to enable the organization to achieve its profit goal. Providing the service according to a well-designed blueprint will permit the organization to show a profit while maximizing the quality and value of guest experiences.

©iStockphoto.com/Juanmonino

Even for a business that provides a simple service product, such as a hot dog stand, a service blueprint can identify how long service should take, potential fail points, and the complexity that can exist in the service delivery system.

The Hot Dog Stand

Exhibit 10.4 details the complete service cycle for a street vendor's hot dog stand.[8] As diagrammed in the exhibit, the service begins with the vendor greeting the potential customer. The vendor takes the order, assembles a heated dog-and-bun combination, applies condiments and dressings, delivers the hot dog to the guest, and finally collects payment. The blueprint of the service also shows an arrow dropping from the application-of-condiments step to represent a potential area of failure where the vendor might incorrectly select and use the wrong condiment—kraut instead of relish, for example. If this happens, the next step shown in the exhibit is for the server to fix the problem by cleaning off the wrong condiment and returning to the application-of-condiments step. The blueprint also contains some other useful information. It provides time estimates for each step so the total time of the service experience can be calculated. A "line of visibility" separates the events the customer can see from those that can't be seen. Finally, the blueprint shows the customer tolerance time of the entire cycle.

The work-cycle times are calculated from carefully studying the process. The customer time tolerance is calculated by carefully studying the customers. The entire

[8] Jane Kingman-Brundage and Lynn G. Shostack, "How to Design a Service," in *The AMA Handbook of Marketing for the Service Industries*, eds. C. A. Congram and M. L. Friedman (New York, NY: American Marketing Association, 1991): 243–261.

EXHIBIT 10.4

Blueprint for a Hot Dog Stand

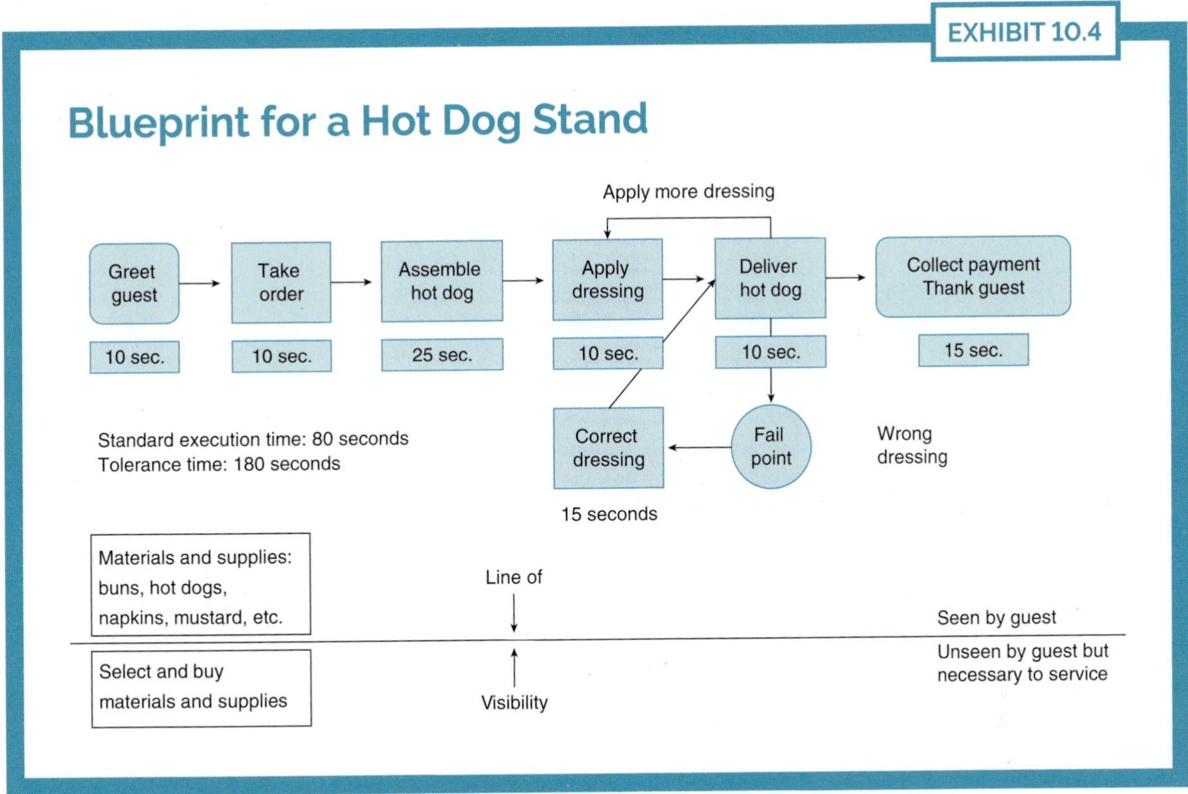

finished schematic clearly shows the planned sequence of activities and the measures for each step in the cycle of service. The blueprint becomes an easily communicated picture for analysis of the entire service cycle.

Obviously, this example is both simple and incomplete. The excellent regional manager or staff guestologist for a string of hot dog stands would want to extend this schematic to include the events that happen before the hungry customer arrives. The regional manager might start at the point where the overall strategy for the hot dog stand was established in the first place. Doing so would allow the manager to see all the other influences that have an impact on the total hot dog purchase experience, from establishing the nature and appearance of the sign that initially attracts the customer to the hot dog stand, to the many other intangible and tangible aspects of the actual hot dog experience. Smart managers start off their planning of the service delivery system by surveying their customers to determine the key elements of the experience from the customer's perspective. Once those key drivers are determined, the delivery system can be designed to ensure the customer's expectations regarding those key drivers are met or exceeded. Once again, the customer drives system design.

One final factor necessary for a complete delivery system plan is the point at which customers may fail to do their part in co-producing the experience. A complete delivery system plan needs to account for the possibility that some customers may decline or be unable to participate at those points of the service delivery process where guest participation had been designed into the blueprint.

Adding Detail to Blueprints

Extending the simple example by incorporating all the fine points of hot dog vending would make for a more complicated but more complete process diagram. The blueprint could go into even greater detail by breaking down each step into even more specific subroutines (e.g., how long each hot dog should cook, ounces of condiments and their order of application). The blueprint for the hot dog stand would become even more complex if complimentary products were added, such as sandwiches, sodas, or ice cream desserts.

Of course, more detail isn't always better. The level of detail should be sufficient to help improve decision-making and service quality but should not go so far as to produce a document too extensive and overwhelming to be of any use. For example, Albrecht tells the story in his book, *Service America!,* about a service blueprint for a frontline bank employee so detailed that it covered thirty-six 11-by-18 pages.[9]

Although the level of detail seen in Albrecht's bank employee blueprint may seem excessive, extensive detail is necessary in some situations. When an organization serves huge numbers of people at once, it may have to make extensive use of sophisticated production techniques as well as a systemization and routinization of the service delivery system, even if the hospitality organization would prefer to deliver the service in a more personalized way. The need to load thousands of people a day onto an amusement park's roller coaster or respond to countless phone calls at a reservations center could require that the service delivery steps be broken down into highly specialized and routinized jobs in order to make the process as efficient as possible, or make the process work at all.

The challenging question about those jobs is how to retain the human interaction component in the hospitality experience. The numbers of customers are so large and the service must take place so rapidly that even the most personable employee will find it difficult to achieve a wow interaction with customers each time.

The Universal Service Map

universal service map An elaborate and detailed blueprint that can be generally applied to a variety of service situations.

Exhibit 10.5 shows a **universal service map,** a variant (and, typically, more elaborate version) of a blueprint that can be generally applied to a variety of service situations.[10] It begins, appropriately, with the guest making a reservation. In Chapter 2, on strategic planning, we discussed the importance of a customer-focused strategy, representing the managerial commitment to service excellence that drives everything the organization does, including the service delivery system. Therefore, the process shown in Exhibit 10.5 reflects a hotel stay from the guest's perspective and not the hotel's.

A quick overview of Exhibit 10.5 shows that the customer is at the top, and the business processes and management are at the bottom. This arrangement is more than symbolic; it shows that the satisfied customer is the ultimate outcome of the process. All the boxes and the lines connecting them merely represent how the organization gets from the initial determination of management strategy to the final outcome of customer satisfaction.

The Line of Internal Interactions

In the universal service map, three horizontal dotted lines divide groups of boxes. The bottom line is the line of internal interactions, representing all the things that must happen inside the organization to produce the service experience. In this group of boxes are the organizational back-of-the-house functions that supply and support the frontline service employee with the product part of the service experience. These would include the reservation system of a hotel, the kitchen for a restaurant, and the underground trash-removal system at the Magic Kingdom. The customer doesn't usually see these activities being performed, but their impact on the service experience is nonetheless considerable. Moving trash in the Disney theme parks is a

[9] Karl Albrecht and Ron Zemke, *Service America!: Doing Business in the New Economy* (Homewood, IL: Dow Jones-Irwin, 1985).

[10] Kingman-Brundage Shostack, 244. For more information on service blueprinting and service mapping, see G. Lynn Shostack, "Designing Services That Deliver," *Harvard Business Review* 62, no. 1 (1984): 133–139; Jane Kingman-Brundage, "Technology, Design, and Service Quality," *International Journal of Service Industry Management* 2, no. 3 (1991): 47–59.

EXHIBIT 10.5

This Universal Service Map, Essentially a Blueprint of the Entire Service Delivery System, Provides a Detailed Analysis of a Customer's Overnight Stay at a Hotel

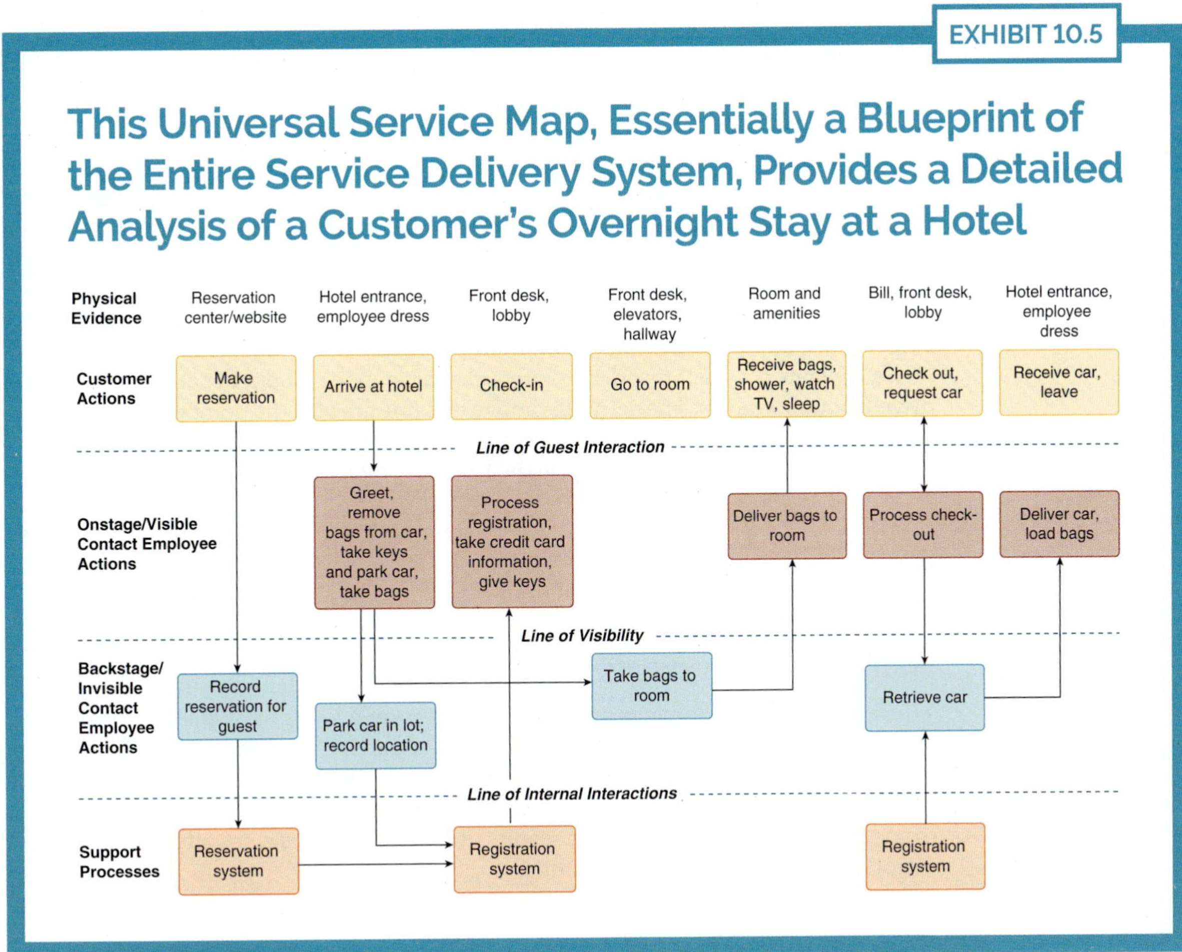

good illustration. Since dirt, trash, and clutter interfere with the fantasy, Disney has designed a way to remove it without customers noticing. All trash produced in the Magic Kingdom is dumped into vacuum stations located strategically throughout the park. The trash is then whisked away beyond sight of the customers.

The Line of Visibility

Next is the line of visibility. This line separates activities that are visible to the customer from those the customer cannot see. The service employee disappears beyond this line from the view of the customer to interact with the back-of-the-house operations. After the server at a restaurant takes an order from the guest, she disappears from view to deliver it to the line cook in the kitchen. Although this part of the service delivery process occurs out of sight of the customer, recognizing this interaction between server and cook as a category of activities is important because service failures at this point are frequent. Problems arise when the server does not take the time to write down the entire order and assumes that the cook will know what to do, or when the convention manager forgets to tell the food and beverage department all the details about the time and length of the convention food break. In effect, the back-of-the-house people must think of the servers as their guests or customers, and vice versa, and do the best they can to serve their needs just as the front-of-the-house people serve the guests. In these interactions between servers and support staff lie many opportunities for communication problems and system breakdowns. They require as much managerial time and attention as the encounters between the guests and the front-of-the-house servers.

The Line of Guest Interaction

The uppermost dotted line is the line of guest or customer interaction. It separates those things the customer does in the service experience from those that the service employee does. These are the points of interaction between the provider and the customer at which the customer becomes, in effect, the co-producer of the service experience. It is the point where passengers respond to the flight attendant's instruction of looking around and picking up all their personal belongings before they leave the plane, or where the customer drives forward to pick up the food order at the McDonald's drive-through window. The activities above this line are also the point where customers decide about the value of the experience, which in turn decides whether or not they will return. By noting the activities above the line of guest interaction, the service manager can identify the critical events—the *moments of truth*—that influence this all-important decision process by the customer. By focusing on these actions (making the reservation, arriving at the hotel, checking in, checking out, etc.), the manager can do whatever is possible to influence the customers' experiences so that they decide to return.

Fishbone Analysis

fishbone diagram
A diagram, shaped like a fish skeleton, used in problem solving with the problem represented by the fish spine and the possible causes of the problem attached to the spine.

fishbone analysis
An approach to problem solving that involves drawing a diagram, shaped like a fishbone, of the problem and its possible causes.

While planning the delivery system, if a widespread and possibly system-wide service delivery problem is foreseen, as opposed to a more localized service failure, one technique that may be used is a cause-and-effect analysis, in the form of a **fishbone diagram.**[11] It provides a way to concentrate on the problem areas to avoid or recover from faulty service outcomes. The results of fishbone analysis are often used to make major changes in the delivery system.

Late Departures at Quickconnect Airlines

Exhibit 10.6 shows an application of **fishbone analysis** to a problem at a hypothetical regional connector airline, Quickconnect Airlines: too many planes departing late. That problem becomes the spine of the fish in the diagram. The general areas within which problems that could delay flights might arise are attached as bones to the spine. For example, "equipment" is required to get the planes off the ground on time and so becomes a potential source of delay. All the possible contributors to an equipment failure then become bones attached to the equipment bone, and so on with each resource and potential problems with it. The potential contributors to failure are typically identified through group discussion in which employees are involved; they should know the reasons for late departures. Quickconnect's employees should be able to readily identify the possible trouble spots.

Resource Categories

Pareto analysis
A problem-solving technique based on arranging the potential causes of an organizational problem in their order of frequency, from most to least.

The resources required for airplane takeoff can be categorized as equipment, personnel, procedures, ground support, and other. They are attached to the spine of the diagram. Within any one of them, a problem might arise that could cause the undesirable effect: late departures. Proceeding with the fishbone construction, the potential problems associated with each resource would then be identified, listed, and prioritized by the employee group working on this problem. This prioritizing technique, known as **Pareto analysis,** calls for arranging the potential causes of the problem based on the frequency in which they occur.

[11] D. Daryl Wyckoff, "New Tools for Achieving Service Quality: A Cornell Quarterly Classic," *Cornell Hotel and Restaurant Administration Quarterly* 42, no. 4 (2001): 25–38.

EXHIBIT 10.6

Fishbone Analysis—Reasons for Departure Delays for Quickconnect Airlines

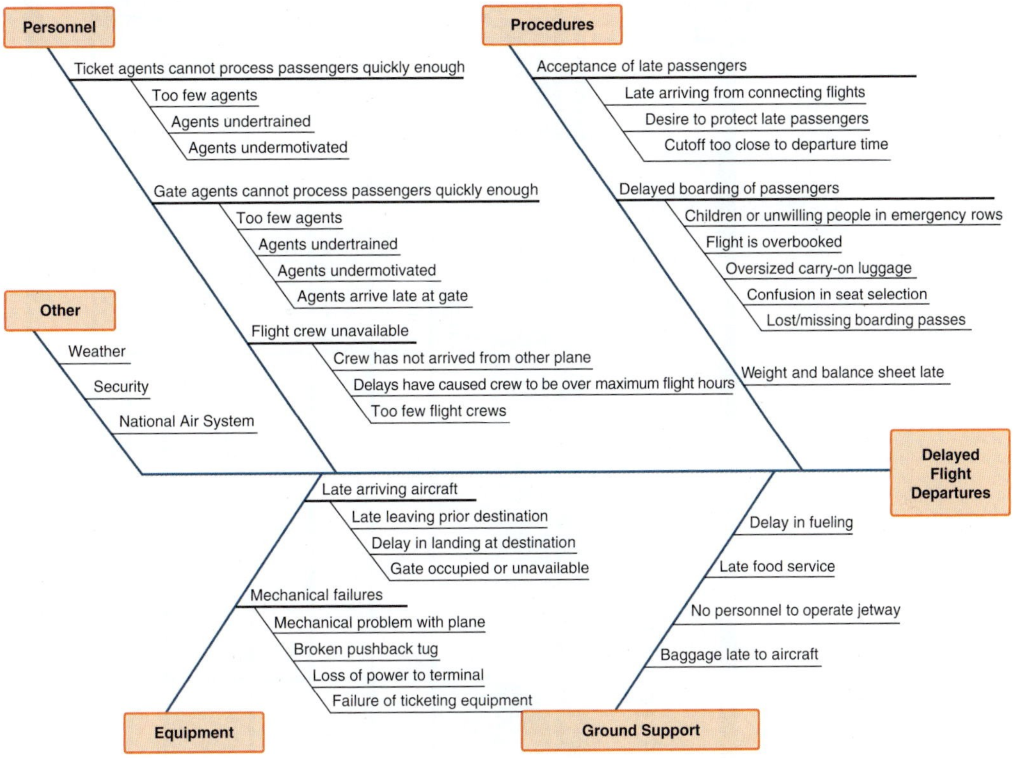

Personnel
- Ticket agents cannot process passengers quickly enough
  - Too few agents
  - Agents undertrained
  - Agents undermotivated
- Gate agents cannot process passengers quickly enough
  - Too few agents
  - Agents undertrained
  - Agents undermotivated
  - Agents arrive late at gate
- Flight crew unavailable
  - Crew has not arrived from other plane
  - Delays have caused crew to be over maximum flight hours
  - Too few flight crews

Procedures
- Acceptance of late passengers
  - Late arriving from connecting flights
  - Desire to protect late passengers
  - Cutoff too close to departure time
- Delayed boarding of passengers
  - Children or unwilling people in emergency rows
  - Flight is overbooked
  - Oversized carry-on luggage
  - Confusion in seat selection
  - Lost/missing boarding passes
- Weight and balance sheet late

Other
- Weather
- Security
- National Air System

Delayed Flight Departures

Equipment
- Late arriving aircraft
  - Late leaving prior destination
  - Delay in landing at destination
  - Gate occupied or unavailable
- Mechanical failures
  - Mechanical problem with plane
  - Broken pushback tug
  - Loss of power to terminal
  - Failure of ticketing equipment

Ground Support
- Delay in fueling
- Late food service
- No personnel to operate jetway
- Baggage late to aircraft

Exhibit 10.7 presents an example based on actual transportation statistics from the Federal Aviation Administration (FAA), but for our hypothetical airline. The data representing the percentages of late flights associated with each cause are listed next to the cause in their order of frequency. The Pareto analysis reveals that about 90% of all late takeoffs are caused by only five of the approximately thirty possible causes listed by the FAA. The most frequent reason for delay at all airports combined was late arriving aircraft, at 36.2%, followed by late arriving passengers (at 30.7%). The remaining causes, all contributing to fewer than 10% of the delays, include waiting for pushback, waiting for fueling, and mechanical problems with planes. These results revealed that the second leading cause of delays was due to giving preferential treatment to the passengers who least deserved it: those who arrived late for flights.

Airport Data

The data can also be analyzed by individual airports to see if the overall problems are the same as those found in each individual airport. As the data show, both the percentages and the reasons for delay at the Newark airport are different from those seen at the other airports. The fifth most frequent factor at Newark, "no personnel to operate jetway," does not appear as a problem for Washington Reagan, where

EXHIBIT 10.7

Pareto Analysis of Flight Departure Delays

ALL STATIONS EXCEPT HUB			NEWARK			WASHINGTON (REAGAN NATIONAL)		
Cause Of Delay	Percentage of Incidences	Cumulative Percentage	Cause of Delay	Percentage of Incidences	Cumulative Percentage	Cause of Delay	Percentage of Incidences	Cumulative Percentage
Late arriving aircraft	36.2%	36.2%	Late arriving aircraft	41.7%	47.1%	Late arriving aircraft	32.9%	32.9%
Late passengers	30.7%	66.9%	Late passengers	10.7%	52.4%	Late passengers	19.0%	51.9%
Waiting for pushback	8.8%	75.7%	Waiting for pushback	10.6%	73.7%	Waiting for pushback	19.0%	70.9%
Waiting for fueling	6.6%	82.3%	Waiting for fueling	10.7%	63.0%	Waiting for fueling	5.4%	87.2%
Mechanical problem with plane	5.1%	87.4%	No personnel to operate jetway	7.2%	80.9%	Mechanical problem with plane	10.9%	81.8%
Weather	5.0%	92.4%	Weather	5.2%	92.8%	Weather	9.8%	97.0%
Security delay	0.4%	92.8%	Security delay	6.7%	87.6%	Security delay	0.1%	97.1%

"mechanical problem with plane" is a problem, one not found at Newark. By arranging the information in this way, managers looking for causes of service delivery failures have an easy-to-use analytical tool. For each potential failure point, they merely collect and arrange the data that the fishbone categories tell them to gather. Recognizing the problem—delayed flight departures—is the first step in improving the service delivery system, but then you must find out what caused the problem—late arriving aircraft and late passengers. You can't fix a problem if you don't know what caused it.

No More Waiting

Once the impact of late-arriving passengers was identified, the airline could decide that flights would no longer wait for them simply because they couldn't get to the airport on time. While this solution might contradict the airline's commitment to service, and gate agents naturally would want to help out late-arriving passengers, the airline was denying on-time service to the many passengers who made sure to get to the airport on time. By setting up this fishbone and comparing the survey data against the key factors, the airline could identify the problem and discover a solution that worked: don't wait on anybody. Of course, that solution might cause a customer-relations problem with late arrivals, but the airline might be willing to pay that price. Indeed, it is likely when the word gets out that the airline will not wait any more for late passengers, fewer passengers will arrive late. Furthermore, given that late passengers were a notable problem at non-hub airports, eliminating this cause of delays could actually lead to more on-time aircraft at hub airports, and thus a decline in the primary cause for late departures at these airports as well.

The individual parts of any delivery system can be broken down in the same way to discover the equipment, people, procedures, supporting services, and other factors that contribute to a service problem. Once managers measure each factor's contribution to the problem, finding a solution is relatively straightforward.

PERT/CPM

Let's say you want to build a backyard patio for your new barbeque grill. You could design the patio with pencil and paper, go buy some bricks and landscaping timber, go out back to dig the foundation, realize you don't have a shovel, go buy one at the hardware store, start digging the foundation, and, while you are doing that, have a chat with a neighbor who tells you that you need permission from the Neighborhood Homeowners Association before you can build a structure of that size on your property. Hospitality organizations obviously cannot operate that way. They cannot afford to start building a hotel and then find out that the county zoning ordinance will not allow it. When the planning and delivery of the service product involve different activities, and especially when those activities recur in a repeating cycle (like planning a convention or golf tournament or building multiple units for a restaurant or hotel chain), a helpful technique to use is PERT/CPM.

PERT/CPM Defined

The **PERT/CPM** planning technique, frequently used in the construction industry and the military, has many points of application in the hospitality industry as well. PERT stands for Program Evaluation Review Technique and CPM for Critical Path Method. Because these two techniques are similar, they have been merged into a single planning strategy and device referred to as *PERT/CPM*. PERT/CPM offers the benefits of any good planning tool. It provides the manager with a detailed, well-organized plan combined with a control measurement process for analyzing how well the plan is being executed. PERT/CPM is useful in planning major projects such as hosting a

PERT/CPM PERT stands for Program Evaluation Review Technique, and CPM stands for Critical Path Method.

convention, building a convention center,[12] or opening a new hotel. PERT/CPM can also be used to plan a wide variety of smaller repetitive projects that have a beginning, an end, and a whole lot of things that must happen in between.

The steps in the PERT/CPM process are (1) identifying the activities that must be done to complete the project, (2) determining the sequence of activities, (3) estimating how long each activity will take, (4) creating and diagramming the network of activities, and (5) finding the **critical path,** which highlights the sequence of activities where no slack time is available and everything has to happen as planned or else the project will be delayed. The successful use of the process may depend on the accuracy of the estimates made in Step (3), and they are not always easy to make.

critical path The sequence of activities from the start of a project to its completion having the greatest cumulative elapsed time, thereby determining how long the entire project will take.

The Diagrams

Using a PERT/CPM diagram like that seen in Exhibit 10.8 allows the service manager to achieve several important objectives. First, the manager gains all the usual advantages of planning. Unforeseen events and activities can be identified. How long something will take to do is readily estimated. Everyone involved in the project has an easily understood picture, in the form of the PERT/CPM chart, that shows all the pieces of the project, the sequence in which they are laid out and must be accomplished, time estimates for finishing each project step, and the total time for completing the entire project. Finally, the PERT/CPM chart shows the items that must be done on time to get the project accomplished as scheduled, which activities can be done at the same time as other activities, and which must happen before others. PERT/CPM can be used to plan any activity that takes time, and it would be hard to find any service experience that doesn't take time.

EXHIBIT 10.8

A Simple PERT/CPM Chart

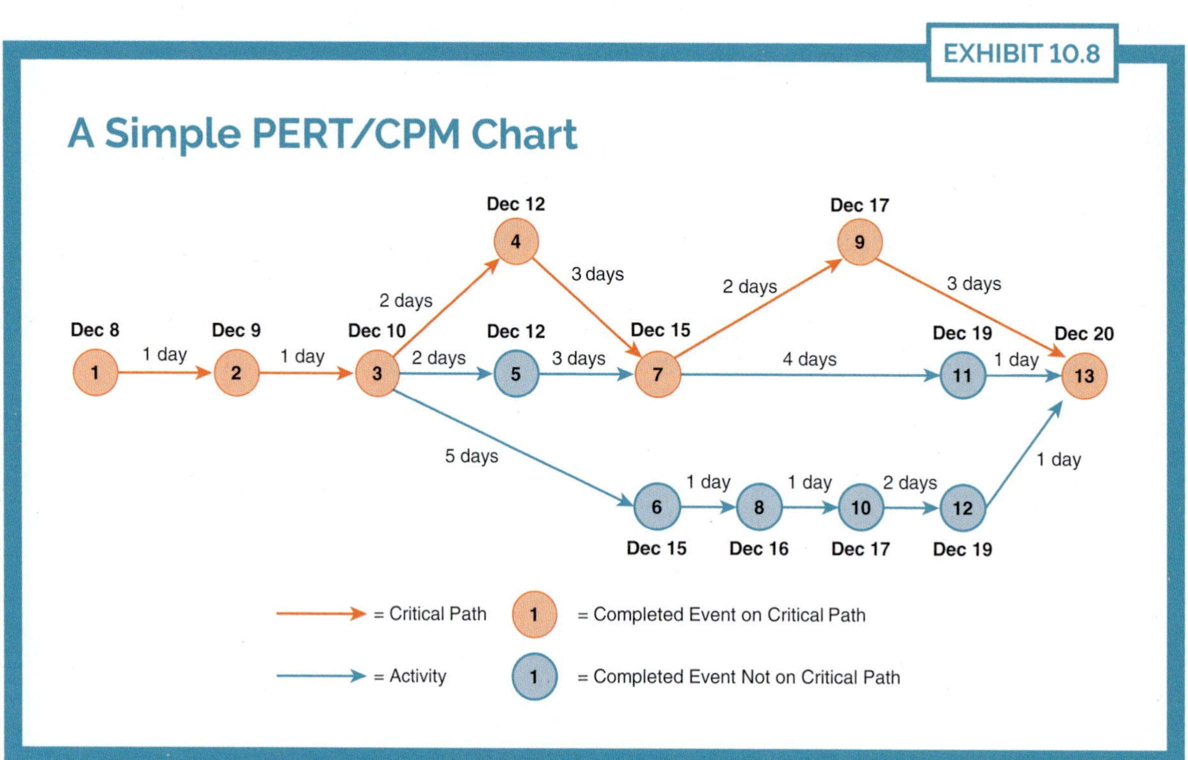

[12] Richard G. McNeill and Ronald A. Evans, "So You Want to Build a Convention Center: The Case of Hope Versus Reality," *Journal of Convention & Event Tourism* 6, no. 1-2, (2005): 23–43.

Circles and Arrows

PERT/CPM diagrams are simple to create. They consist of circles or bubbles, representing completed events, and arrows representing the activities that must be done before an event can be considered completed. The arrows connect the circles, and the arrow points to the event for completion of which the activity is necessary. In Exhibit 10.8, Event 1 must be completed before work can begin on activities leading to completing Event 2, and the same is true of Event 3. Only after completing Event 3 can work begin on Events 4, 5, and 6, which can be worked on independently of each other. Event 13 has three arrows pointing toward it, signifying that completion of Event 13 will first require completing Events 9, 10, and 12, and then completing the activities following them and leading up to Event 13. As the chart shows, Events 9, 10, and 12 themselves require that prior activities and events must be completed before their own completion. The critical path indicated in the chart will be explained in more detail below, but, briefly, it is the sequence of events that must occur on time if the project is to be completed on time. It has no "slack" time (i.e., any time difference between when an event is scheduled for completion and when it must be completed for the entire project to end on time) in it as the other two paths do.

PERT/CPM chart A diagram, usually used in the planning of major projects, consisting of circles representing completed events, arrows representing the activities that must be done before an event can be considered completed, and includes a critical path indicating the sequence of events that must occur on time if the project is to be completed on time.

Tony's Deli

Let's leave abstract events and think about the new delicatessen Tony wants to open. The final event in the sequence, the final circle on his **PERT/CPM chart**, will be "Opening Day." One activity arrow leading up to that circle might be labeled "Hold three staff training sessions." But before those training sessions can be held, several other activities and events must take place. Tony must find a place to hold training, order training materials, hire and prepare a trainer, and hire the new deli personnel. Some of those activities can be done simultaneously. Their conclusion might be indicated in the diagram by a circle labeled "Preparations for training sessions finished." Also included in the diagram would be estimates of how long each activity will take. Summing the activity times will give Tony a pretty good estimate of how long it will take to have his delicatessen staff trained and available.

Technology

Complicated PERT/CPM networks are usually done on a computer or by accessing an online program. If organizations cannot afford to do their own programming, they can use online or off-the-shelf PERT/CPM computer programs. Owners of smaller service organizations can plug in their service delivery system's essential elements, and the program will figure out the math and draw a PERT chart for them. There are also literally hundreds of instructional videos on YouTube that make it easy for anyone to use this powerful planning tool.

Building the Network

Five steps are required to build a PERT/CPM network.

Step 1: Activity-event analysis. The manager defines all events that must occur for the project to be completed, and all activities leading up to those events are listed. The real fruits of the planning process occur at this step. By taking the time and making the effort to plan, the manager can detail every activity in the project and uncover every step that must be taken.

Step 2: Activity-event sequencing. Once the manager has defined the activities and events that must at some time occur, they can be placed in their proper sequence. Developing the sequence of activities in this step has the added benefit of revealing previously undiscovered or unknown events that must be scheduled. If you are describing how to tie a shoelace, you may have forgotten Event 1—that you must first have a shoelace—unless you sequence the process step by step.

Step 3: Activity time estimates. The next step is for the manager to estimate how much time each activity will take so that an expected time for completing each event and the entire project can be calculated. The manager can use a simple and often-used formula to arrive at a weighted-average time estimate for each activity:

Expected time = (optimistic time + 4 times most likely time + pessimistic time) divided by 6.

Step 4: Diagramming the project. After all the events are sequenced, the activities detailed, and time estimates for each activity made, the pieces can be put together into the total-project PERT diagram. As seen in Exhibit 10.8, each activity and event is set out in the diagrammed network along with the expected times.

Step 5: Identifying the critical path. By summing up the activity times across the paths leading to the project completion, the manager can estimate the total time for completing the project and can identify the *critical path,* the CP of PERT/CPM, the sequence of activities that leaves no slack time. If these events don't happen on time, the project won't be finished as scheduled. Other paths in the network may have a time difference between when the events must happen and when they are scheduled to happen based on the calculation of activity times. In Exhibit 10.8, Event 6 must happen on December 15 or the entire project will get behind schedule, but Event 6 is scheduled for completion on December 12, so the project manager has some slack time. Even if Event 6 takes five days to complete instead of two, the delay won't affect the project completion date. Slack time also represents an opportunity to shift resources and attention away from events that finish earlier than they must and toward activities that need help.

The Big PERT/CPM Picture

In addition to showing the critical path, the projected completion time for the project, and the complete sequencing of activities needed to get the project done, the PERT/CPM network diagram provides a terrific visual of what is involved in the project. Using the diagram, the manager can show everyone what the whole project looks like, what each person's part in the project is, when each activity needs to be done, which activities are critical, and which events precede or follow each person's job. Even more helpful is that the manager now has a complete model that can be used to test what might happen under a different array of assumptions. What will happen, for example, if some of the pessimistic time estimates come true (whatever that could go wrong, did go wrong)? The PERT/CPM network diagram gives the manager an easy and quick way to substitute new numbers and revise the time schedule for total project completion if necessary. Obviously, every major project involves a whole lot of uncertainties. With this tool, however, the manager can plug in the uncertainties and refigure their impact on the project as they occur.

Holding a Convention

The PERT/CPM diagram in Exhibit 10.9 represents the steps necessary to prepare for and hold a convention. Convention manager Dorothy Barker went through all the steps noted above to determine the activities, their sequence, and the time estimates. Then she set up the PERT/CPM network to show the customer, the hotel staff members who will be critically involved in providing convention services, and herself all the things that must happen to complete a successful convention. This diagram can serve as a daily planning guide; it can be hung on the wall to show everyone what activities they need to accomplish each day. Since most convention managers have responsibility for more than one convention at a time, having these pictorial representations for each convention can help tremendously in keeping track of all the activities that each convention requires. A well-constructed and complete PERT/CPM chart can be used repeatedly because conventions generally have the same events and follow the same sequence of

EXHIBIT 10.9

PERT/CPM Chart of the Steps Needed to Hold an Annual Convention

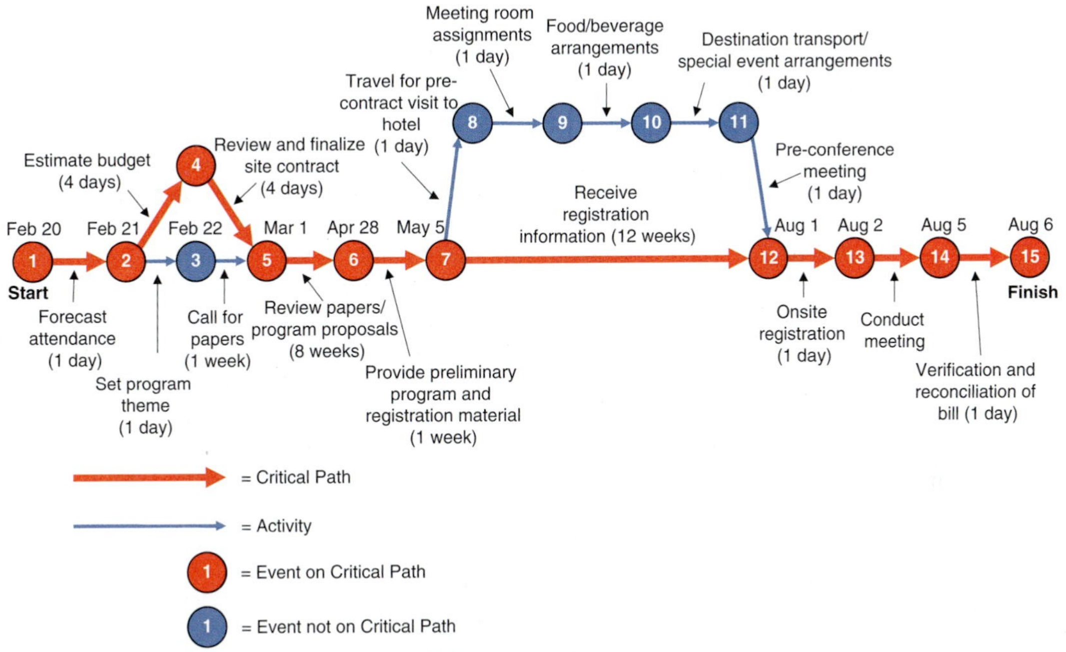

Meeting room assignments (1 day)
Food/beverage arrangements (1 day)
Destination transport/ special event arrangements (1 day)
Travel for pre-contract visit to hotel (1 day)
Estimate budget (4 days)
Review and finalize site contract (4 days)
Pre-conference meeting (1 day)
Receive registration information (12 weeks)
Feb 20 | Feb 21 | Feb 22 | Mar 1 | Apr 28 | May 5 | Aug 1 | Aug 2 | Aug 5 | Aug 6
1 2 3 4 5 6 7 8 9 10 11 12 13 14 15
Start
Finish
Forecast attendance (1 day)
Call for papers (1 week)
Review papers/ program proposals (8 weeks)
Set program theme (1 day)
Provide preliminary program and registration material (1 week)
Onsite registration (1 day)
Conduct meeting
Verification and reconciliation of bill (1 day)

= Critical Path
= Activity
1 = Event on Critical Path
1 = Event not on Critical Path

activities. The same would be true for servicing an airplane, for planning a restaurant or hotel opening, or a particular cruise in a cruise ship's annual schedule.

PERT/CPM can be used for any event, process, or experience that has a definable beginning and end to describe and detail the sequence of activities that must occur to complete all steps on schedule. Since the activities of hospitality organizations are often sequences or processes with a beginning and an end—from cooking and serving a meal, to cleaning and preparing a room for the next day's guests, to the entire guest experience itself—there are many possible applications of PERT/CPM to service situations.

Isaac Brekken/Getty Images for Nightclub & Bar Media Group

While each convention is of course unique, the common elements to planning a convention make the use of a tool like a PERT/CPM diagram helpful for planning purposes.

Potential Disadvantages

The PERT/CPM process assumes the activities leading to a project's completion are independent and can be clearly defined. That is not always the case. Also, the process depends on the accuracy of the time estimates. Since time estimates are made by fallible human beings, they may be incorrect, and it does not take many incorrect time estimates to throw off an entire project.

Simulations

simulation An imitation of a real or potential problem or organizational situation.

A **simulation** is an imitation of the real thing. It may be doodled on a piece of paper with a pencil, or it may be done on a computer. Some simulations are big, like a computerized simulation of Epcot, and some are small, like a role-playing exercise at a company training session. Some simulations can consist of professional actors simulating the guest experience to show the observing employees and managers where problems in service delivery can occur. These simulations can reveal problems that the people who work there may not have thought about. They can also improvise customer mistakes to see if the system has safeguards built in to keep the customer from failing in the co-production experience or, if a failure does occur, to keep the customer from irreparably harming the value and quality of the experience. Organizations can use a wide variety of simulations when planning the service delivery system.

Computerized simulation techniques are typically the most sophisticated. They allow incredibly detailed simulation of a service delivery system and provide ways to measure and manipulate the system to see what might happen under different assumptions. Computers can also simulate behaviors of customers—with their infinite needs and ranges of behavior—on the receiving end of the system. The unique challenge in service delivery is that each customer is different. Because predicting exactly how any one customer will behave within the service experience is almost impossible, the opportunities for system failures are tremendous. Simulating customer behavior allows for a better comprehension of how that variability in customers affects the system's ability to deliver the service consistently at the expected level. Across the entire service experience, simulation can identify problems created by both the organization—in service design, environment, and delivery systems—and the customer.

At Epcot

Walt Disney World Resort used a computerized simulation model of Epcot during the planning and design of the park. Different patterns of guest behavior were modeled to make decisions about park capacity and where individual attractions, rest rooms, foodservice facilities, and retail stores should be located. After the park opened, refinement and adjustment of the simulation model continued.

No one can know what any single guest might do inside the park during the course of a day, but knowledge of guest behaviors and statistical probabilities can yield relatively accurate predictions of how large groups of guests will behave. Probability distributions for all possible Epcot guest behaviors were developed and then built into the model. The resulting simulation accurately reflected the movements and behavior of a day's guests as they progressed through the park. The simulation model was then used to test and optimize such planning decisions as the location, size, and capacity of the attractions, restaurants, merchandise shops, and other facilities.

The Odyssey Restaurant

Here is a specific example of how the Epcot simulation led to a surprising discovery. In the early days of the park's construction, simulation runs were done to predict how guests would use the Odyssey Restaurant, a large fast-food facility being built on an island in the lake between the Future World attractions section and the World Showcase section of the park. Studies had clearly shown that guests look for food near the exits of whatever attraction they happen to be leaving during peak mealtime periods. Since the Odyssey Restaurant was somewhat remote from the exit of any attraction, the model predicted that rather than go to Odyssey, guests would head for the nearest fast-food locations placed at the exits of the Future World and World Showcase attractions. Unfortunately, there was not enough time to use the results of the simulation and relocate Odyssey. It opened and even though a bridge was constructed to make Odyssey more accessible, few guests used it—exactly as the simulation had predicted. Today, the facility is used for other purposes.

Computer Simulations for All

Technology

Not every organization will have the volume of customers to justify or pay for the creation of a full-scale computer model to study the service delivery system in detail. Nonetheless, with the increasing availability of online programs and smaller, more user-friendly software packages, even a Ralph's Restaurant on the corner may have economical access to a computerized simulation package. Simulations can be used for a variety of decisions, such as determining whether to offer "early bird" or "night owl" specials,[13] scheduling labor hours,[14] scheduling tasks in a cafeteria,[15] or determining how many allergy-friendly rooms a hotel should have in its rooms inventory.[16] Already available is a computer program called a general purpose system simulator (GPSS), which organizations can use to simulate their delivery systems. Even more widely available is Microsoft's Excel program, which can be used to create some types of simulations. As is true for so many other products and services, a Google search will find customer reviews of simulation programs on the web. Many simulations are focused on modeling and predicting waiting lines or queues, which is the subject of Chapter 11.

TARGETING SPECIFIC PROBLEM AREAS IN SERVICE DELIVERY SYSTEMS

Much of the planning process we have discussed in this chapter is designed to *make something good happen:* a "wow" service experience. Such planning addresses the entire service system and how the functional components work together to deliver the guest experience that customers want and expect. This planning is indeed critical to deliver an exceptional service experience by integrating all elements of the process. An equally important part of planning is to *keep something bad from happening:* problems and service failures. Such techniques as a fishbone analysis and PERT/CPM charts can identify actual or potential problem areas in the system. In this section, we address some of the tools to plan for common delivery-system problems before they occur since the best way to keep something bad from happening is to prevent it.

"A sandwich tossed is better than a customer lost." Arby's knows that their standard for tossing out sandwiches after they sit for a specific number of minutes not only prevents problems from occurring but also is less costly than recovering from an unhappy customer who got the poor-quality sandwich. Successful organizations use such strategies to identify and fix trouble spots before they become a problem for their guests.

---

[13] Gary M. Thompson, "Deciding Whether to Offer 'Early-Bird' or 'Night-Owl' Specials in Restaurants: A Cross-Functional View," *Journal of Service Research* 18, no. 4 (2015): 498–512.

[14] Seifedine Kadry, Aremn Bagdasaryan, and Mohammad Kadhum, "Simulation and Analysis of Staff Scheduling in Hospitality Management," *7th International Conference on Modeling, Simulation, and Applied Optimization (ICMSAO)* (2017): 1–6.

[15] Chen-Feng Kuo and Douglas C. Nelson, "A Simulation Study of Production Task Scheduling for a University Cafeteria," *Cornell Hospitality Quarterly* 50, no. 4 (2009): 540–552.

[16] David A. Dittman and James W. Hesford, "A Simulation-based Optimization Approach for Investment Decisions: A Case Study of Pure Allergy-Friendly Rooms," *Cornell Hotel and Restaurant Administration Quarterly* 48, no. 1 (2007): 48, 88–100.

Forecasting Demand to Prevent Problems

A major function of planning is to prevent problems. One strategy is forecasting and managing demand, which we will discuss in greater detail in Chapter 11. For example, if an analysis of the service delivery system indicates a potential service problem caused by excessive waits, a statistical analysis that forecasts demand might be an effective tool for discovering how much of a problem the waits might be and what can be done to address them before the doors open for the first customer. If a statistical prediction of the customer demand for a theme park on a particular day indicates the park will be full, a preventive strategy will lead to the park's management calling in full staff, preparing extra food supplies, and having available the full capacity of each attraction. Restaurants may require reservations when the projected guest demand is high. Having a reservation system means that customer demand can be better matched with restaurant capacity and guests will not be disappointed with waiting when they come to the restaurant. In addition, the restaurant can know the number of diners to expect so that it can staff appropriately and have sufficient amounts of prepared items in order to ensure that the dining experience is enjoyable and trouble free. If the restaurant fails to plan and customers are disappointed with a long wait, slow service, or out-of-stock menu items, then their perception of the quality of the overall service experience will be poor, and a service failure will result. It is not uncommon to see Internet posts like "Good dinner, fair price, but I had to wait too long. I don't think it's worth the wait and don't see what all the hype's about. I'd suggest you go somewhere else." Keeping the wait down avoids that type of failure.

If the demand can be forecasted for a longer period of time, other proactive strategies can be implemented. If demand for the next quarter or next year, for example, is expected to increase by 20%, new capacity can be built, new employees hired and trained, and merchandise inventories increased to ensure that customers are not disappointed by long lines, unavailable souvenirs, or untrained and inadequate staff.

Training

Properly training employees before they ever get the chance to serve a customer can prevent many service failures. We discussed training in depth in Chapter 6, but the importance of training is worth repeating, not just for delivering the service product, but also for preventing service problems before they occur. For example, Rich Ungaro, the Senior Vice President of Operations during the time of Wendy's rapid expansion, developed a "people plan" for training new managers. New management trainees were sent to designated training stores for six weeks where they were instructed in the proper preparation of menu items, standards of service, product offerings, and "the Wendy's Way" to deliver guest service by a small group of employees known as "Ambassadors." After the six weeks, these ambassadors would travel with the newly trained manager to the assigned new store for four weeks (two weeks prior to opening and two weeks after opening). This people plan ensured that whenever a new Wendy's opened, the newly trained manager supported by the "Ambassadors" knew the products being served, the systems for providing the Wendy's quality experience to the guest, the Wendy's service setting, and the other members of the opening team. The ambassador program allowed Wendy's to effectively develop leaders to support its exponential growth at a rate that ensured it would never open stores faster than its ability to manage them. As an additional benefit of this innovative training plan, the ambassadors were, upon returning to their certified training store, themselves trained for a promotion to the next level of management.

The people who deliver any service need to know exactly what the total experience should consist of and need to be motivated to ensure that the guest experience happens in the way it is supposed to, every time, for every guest. Just as hospitals run disaster drills in conjunction with fire departments and rescue teams to prepare for unexpected, randomly occurring disasters, so can hospitality staff be trained, through practice, to handle both the expected and the unexpected.

Quality Teams

The use of quality teams is another preventive strategy. Recall how the Ritz-Carlton employees solved their service delivery system problem of late room-service breakfasts and how quality teams at the Quickconnect Airlines used a fishbone analysis to solve departure delays. Both show the value of letting the people directly involved in the service experience get together to identify service delivery system problems and recommend solutions to prevent their recurrence. Quite often, no one is in a better position to foresee and prevent problems than the employees who have already experienced a wide range of problems and seen first-hand guest frustration with those problems.

Poka-Yokes

Trying to fix a problem once a customer has experienced it may be too late, so any devices or processes that can fail-safe the service delivery system or any part of it against human error are extremely desirable. Conceived by the late Shigeo Shingo, a Japanese quality improvement expert, **poka-yoke** (POH-kah YOH-kay)—the name Shingo gave these failure-preventing devices or procedures—means "mistake proofing" or "avoid mistakes" in Japanese.[17] A poka-yoke basically involves inspection of the system for possible failure points and then finding or developing simple means to prevent, or immediately detect and correct, mistakes at those points. A poka-yoke is a proactive or preventive strategy for avoiding mistakes. Although it originated in the manufacturing sector, it can be used in planning and monitoring the service experience to keep it operating as flawlessly as possible.

poka-yoke A device or procedure designed to prevent or immediately correct mistakes "mistake-proofing" in Japanese.

Poka-yoke techniques can be of several forms, such as mechanical, electrical, or human. Since both the server and the customer can make mistakes during the service experience, both parties need to be mistake-proofed to the extent possible.

Here are some simple poka-yoke examples. Automobiles have many poka-yokes. To ensure that cars don't start moving when the ignition is turned on, the car is designed to not start unless the driver has a foot on the brake. Likewise, there are devices that prevent you from shifting a car into reverse when it is moving forward and devices that keep intoxicated drivers from starting their cars. Everywhere you look, you can see examples. To ensure equity of service order and avoid disagreements, organizations ask customers to "take a number" or make a reservation. A surgeon's tray and a mechanic's wrench-set box may have a unique indentation for each item to ensure that no instrument is left inside a patient following surgery or wrench in an engine. Restaurants buy different colored knives and cutting boards to prevent cross-contamination of food: Blue for fish, yellow for fowl, green for vegetables, and red for meat make it immediately apparent to all what should be on the cutting board and which knife should be used to cut it.

Types of Inspections

Shingo identified three types of inspections. In the services industry, they would be *source inspections,* in which potential mistakes are located at their source and fixed before they can get into the delivery system, *self-inspections,* in which people check their own work, and *successive inspections,* in which the person next in the service delivery system checks the quality and accuracy of the previous person's work. Mistakes can occur and poka-yokes can be used in all these inspection types.

An example of a source inspection is the chef monitoring the prepared foods—such as salads, boned chicken, or whatever must be assembled in advance of the rush

[17] Shigeo Shingo, *Zero Quality Control: Source Inspection and the Poka-Yoke System* (Portland, OR: Productivity Press, 1986), 45.

hour—to ensure that sufficient quantities of the items are available. An example of a self-inspection is the line cook personally comparing the order he has prepared against a picture of what the food display should look like before putting it on the service counter. An example of a successive inspection is the food server in a restaurant checking the food order on the counter before taking it out of the kitchen. Obviously, the closer to the source that errors or potential errors can be detected, the better.

Warnings and Controls

Poka-yokes are either "warnings that signal the existence of a problem or controls that stop production until the problem is resolved."[18] The *warning poka-yoke* occurs before an error is made. The *control poka-yoke* keeps a process from beginning or continuing after an error is made. A warning poka-yoke would be a light that flashes when the fries are ready to come out of the fryer. It signals the operator to remove the fries before they become overcooked. A control poka-yoke would be a device that turns a microwave oven off whenever the door is opened.

Warning and control poka-yokes can each be of three types. *Contact* poka-yokes monitor the item's physical characteristics to determine if they meet predefined specifications. Some restaurants cut their meats on scales to ensure that each cut is of the right weight before cooking. The second type of poka-yoke is based on the use of *fixed values* or constant numbers. It is used when a certain step is repeated—such as frying French fries—to ensure that the step is done the same way every time. McDonald's knows that a certain poundage of fries must be put in the fryer to make the fries taste the way McDonald's wants them to, so it designed a prepackaged bag containing a fixed value of potato pieces to ensure the right quantity is placed in the fryer every time. The third type of poka-yoke is the *motion step,* or sequence method, used when more than one step is involved. This poka-yoke is useful in processes where an error-prone step must be completed correctly before the next step can take place. A simple example is the pop-up temperature gauge found in many turkeys. If the red button doesn't pop up, the turkey isn't done to the right temperature, and the turkey cannot move a step forward for further preparation until it does.

The tangible parts of the service experience can be mistake-proofed by poka-yokes just as readily as the tangibles in a manufacturing process. Preventing and quickly correcting service failures in the intangible aspects of service delivery is more challenging. Many service organizations try to avoid server errors during interactions with customers by standardizing or scripting what servers say and do during the service experience. These standards or scripts are poka-yokes designed to fail-safe the service delivery process. To whatever extent the servers can be prevented from making mistakes in routine aspects of the service by poke-yokes, it will reduce failure rates, and allow the servers to focus their efforts on the more creative, individualized aspects of guest service.

Poka-Yokes for Customers

Customers add a further complication to the service delivery process. They are frequently right in the middle of it and responsible for co-producing some or most of the service experience. Poka-yokes can be designed to enable customers to prevent their own problems. For example, customers are irritated by a frequent fast-food service failure: leaving the drive-through only to find that they were served the wrong order. To avoid these failures, Burger King has installed poka-yoke video displays, called order confirmation units, at its drive-through windows so customers can verify the accuracy of the orders they are about to receive.

Customers can be prepared to do their part without error even before the service experience begins. The popular sign "No Shirt, No Shoes, No Service" prevents a

[18] Richard B. Chase and Douglas M. Stewart, "Make Your Service Fail-Safe," *Sloan Management Review* 35, no. 3 (1994): 35.

customer error relating to attire and avoids the embarrassment for the customer and the organization of asking an improperly dressed customer to leave. During the service experience, the organization can develop poka-yokes to signal customers to do the right thing and avoid doing the wrong thing while co-producing their experience.

Speed Parking

Another example of a poka-yoke designed to help customers avoid failure is the speed-parking technique. Often seen at events where a lot of cars arrive at the same time, this system has the drivers line their cars up and park in a row of successive spaces under the direction of a parking attendant. Each row is filled before cars are directed to the next row. This parking method is fast; it keeps all cars facing the same way and in line to park in the next available space. The method has led to the creation of a poka-yoke at some theme parks and other large attractions. When guests stream into the park every morning, the parking attendant writes down the time each row is filled. When evening comes and a family shows up lost and uncertain as to where their car might be, the attendant pulls out the poka-yoke, a list of what sections were parked at what time. The attendant asks the family about what time they arrived at the parking area, then uses the list to locate the car. The poka-yoke prevents a guest-caused failure that could ruin the day's experience.

All poka-yokes should be simple, easy to use, and inexpensive. Human error can occur at many points in most service delivery systems, so poka-yoke is a useful concept in identifying something wrong and halting delivery until it is made right. Even if organizations do not use the term *poka-yoke,* they should keep the concept in mind. They should look for potential error sources as they plan the delivery system and should introduce means of preventing errors, if possible, and detecting errors quickly if they do occur.

A final point, emphasized by Shigeo Shingo, is that the end purpose of poka-yokes is not simply to find and prevent errors, valuable though that may be, but *to use error detection to improve the system.* If the causes of service errors are not located and the system not improved, their number may not be substantially reduced in the future, regardless of how many poka-yokes are introduced.

Cross-Functional Project and Matrix Organizations

Sometimes, the problems in delivering a service experience can be traced back to the design or structure of the organization itself. A functionally organized hotel, for example, may not consistently provide the service experience defined by its mission if its individual departments focus on their own individual goals and objectives rather than on guest satisfaction across the entire experience. A guest doesn't care about the rooms division manager's goals and challenges or the food and beverage manager's problems and concerns. Guests care about the quality and value of the entire experience they are paying for, and the individual organizational components need to be effectively connected in ways that unite them to focus everyone on ensuring guest satisfaction.

It may be helpful to consider the organization itself as an element of the service delivery process that effectively integrates and coordinates the activities of people working in different departments performing different functions. Is the organization designed so that individual departments perform their functions smoothly, or is it designed so that the overall service delivery system functions smoothly? The two are often not the same.

One method of organizing people and groups to enable them to focus on the guest's needs, wants, and expectations across the boundaries of functional organizational units is by creating a temporary **cross-functional structure.** This term is also used to refer to a matrix structure where a group or project team is overlaid on the traditional functional organizational structure to work on a specific task or serve a

cross-functional structure A method of organizing people and groups so as to enable them to work temporarily across the boundaries or functional units in which organizations are traditionally structured; also, an overlaying of a group or project team upon the traditional functional organizational structure to work on a task for a limited time, which creates multiple lines of authority.

particular customer for a limited time. Traditional organizational structures are characterized by a single line of authority running from top to bottom: You report to one person; that person reports to somebody else. This also tends to mean information flows in one direction: from the top down. A cross-functional organization is characterized by multiple lines of authority. You may temporarily report to more than one person; that person may do the same.

In hospitality organizations, many situations arise that call for focusing everyone's functional skills on solving a guest's problem or meeting a guest's expectation right now. Because so many functional areas must work in coordination with each other to deliver a whole service experience, information must flow between different functional groups. For example, a hotel's convention coordinator has to bring together all the functional areas of a hotel to meet the needs and expectations of the convention's meeting planner. In such a case, the convention coordinator acts as a project manager temporarily responsible for ensuring that everyone who needs to serve the customer is available and ready to do so. She will have the authority to direct people in the rooms division, food and beverage, or any other function in the hotel she needs to satisfy a guest's request. Cross-functional structures are especially useful in the hospitality industry, and, in fact, in any service-driven industry.

At the Ritz-Carlton

While discussing how The Ritz-Carlton Hotels won the Malcolm Baldrige Quality Award, Horst Schulze spoke about finding a cross-functional organizational solution to identify and correct delivery system flaws. The Ritz-Carlton had used guest surveys to identify eighteen key guest-satisfaction measures. The Ritz-Carlton then hired a process manager for each hotel whose responsibility was to eliminate flaws and reduce work-cycle times by 50% in the systems that delivered the eighteen keys leading to guest satisfaction. The keys were deemed so important that this specific person was hired to ensure that someone worried about them all the time, no matter which functional units were responsible for the different keys. The Ritz-Carlton thereby avoided the potential limitations of the functional orientation that come naturally to departments by authorizing the process manager to cross all functional areas to ensure that someone was focused on the hotel's guests and what satisfies them.

Advantages and Disadvantages of Cross-Functional Project and Matrix Structures

To ensure maintaining the same focus on guest satisfaction as the Ritz-Carlton, other hospitality organizations use project teams, matrix structures, and other cross-functional structures. Because these structures generally involve people working under more than one line of authority, some traditional managers who believe that strict lines of authority are important have problems working in cross-functional structures. On the other hand, crossing functional areas and getting everyone focused on the guest can offer some important benefits. Exhibit 10.10 compares the advantages and disadvantages of these organizational structures.

The Real Boss

Here is the bottom line on organizational design: Use whatever organizational design best enables every unit and every person to focus on the guest's needs, wants, and expectations. The Ritz-Carlton knows this and major convention hotels know this. While the organization chart may show functional divisions with different people responsible for different areas like maintenance, front office, and housekeeping, everyone in these excellent hospitality organizations knows that *their real boss is the guest* and that their real organizational function is ensuring that their guest experience meets or exceeds their guest's expectations. They are guestologists.

EXHIBIT 10.10

Advantages and Disadvantages of Cross-Functional Project and Matrix Structures

ADVANTAGES	DISADVANTAGES
1. Makes the guest, not the function, the focus. If one person or team is responsible for satisfying guest needs, the focus of the organization is placed directly on the overall service needs of the guest, rather than the specific element of the experience delivered by any one functional department.	**1. Violates traditional "single line of authority."** Most companies are still organized to have a single and clear chain of command. Implementing a cross-functional structure changes this traditional form of management.
2. Improved lateral exchange of information. If multiple functional areas work together, different providers of services will communicate more with each other.	**2. Ambiguity about control.** Because different functional areas are involved, it can be unclear who is ultimately in charge or responsible for certain decisions, either for technical issues or human resource management issues.
3. Improved vertical exchange of information. The interactive process needed for cross-functional teams means that information will flow to, from, and through an organization's hierarchy more quickly. Cross-functional structures also lead to flatter (less hierarchical) organizations, with fewer levels through which information must pass.	**3. Creates organizational conflict between functional and project managers.** Even when units work together for certain projects, there are still functional activities that must be completed. Having cross-functional groups can create a conflict between managers of cross-functional teams and managers of functional areas, because they may have different, even conflicting, goals.
4. Increased flexibility in use of human capital. When different functional areas work together, it becomes easier to determine where there may be too many people, and where there are not enough employees. A cross-functional structure facilitates the ability of people to work in different areas.	**4. Creates interpersonal conflict.** Cross-functional structures require that individuals with different backgrounds, perspectives on work, time horizons, and goals work together. Such differences can lead to greater interpersonal conflict.
5. Increased individual motivation and attitudes. Through a cross-functional structure, individuals have a better sense of the entire service product being delivered. When employees see the entire product, as opposed to just a piece of it, they tend to be more motivated to perform better and have higher job satisfaction, organizational commitment, and morale.	**5. Creates insecurity and loss of status.** With a different organizational structure, some managers will lose some authority as more responsibility is given to cross-functional groups and project managers. This can reduce the perceived status of functional managerial roles and make some managers insecure with their reduced authority.
	6. More costly for organization. Cross-functional structures can lead to increased overhead and staff, more meetings, delayed decisions, and more information processing. All this can add to organizational costs.
	7. More difficult for individuals. Individuals working in cross-functional structures will face greater role ambiguity. Potentially conflicting instructions or orders may lead to personal stress.

LESSONS LEARNED

LO 10.1 Describe why it is critical for organizations to fully plan their service delivery system.

- A bad system can defeat a good employee. Check for system failure (e.g., not enough elevators; too many monorail trains) before blaming people.
- Detailed planning can avoid most service failures. The goal: Fail no guest; "wow" every guest.
- Problems will recur if you can't or don't find out the source of the cause.

LO 10.2 Describe how organizations plan, design, analyze, and check the hospitality organization's service delivery system.

- Detail and analyze every step in the entire service delivery process.
- Measurement is crucial: you can't manage what you don't measure.
- Develop a *self-healing system:* the system itself should be able to override the normal delivery system to fix guest problems when it fails.

LO 10.3 Demonstrate how to design a delivery system using several methods, such as flow-charting, blueprinting, the universal service map, and PERT/CPM.

- There are many planning tools to help deliver excellent guest experiences. Use them as much as possible.

LO 10.4 Explain how to use fishbone analysis, poka-yokes, and other methods to locate the source of problems and prevent their occurrence or reoccurrence.

- Everyone is responsible for monitoring and maintaining the quality of the service delivery system; everyone is responsible for avoiding service failures.
- There are many tools to help diagnose problems with delivering excellent guest experiences. Use them to prevent failures as much as possible.

LO 10.5 Discuss how to use a cross-functional organizational design to deliver a service product.

- Use cross-functional design and employee cross-training to match guest demand patterns.
- The organization itself is an element of the service delivery process, integrating and coordinating the activities of employees in different departments performing different functions
- Allow information to flow between different functional groups.

KEY TERMS AND CONCEPTS

blueprinting 333
critical path 342
cross-functional structure 351
fishbone analysis 338
fishbone diagram 338
Juran Trilogy 326
Pareto analysis 338
PERT/CPM 341
PERT/CPM chart 343
poka-yoke 349
service standards 326
simulation 346
universal service map 336

REVIEW QUESTIONS

1. Why is it important to check the delivery system first before checking to see whether employees are to blame for service failures?
2. Recall two types of hospitality organizations with which you are familiar.
   A. What people and non-people parts of each organization's service delivery system can you see? Not see?
   B. What steps does each organization take to ensure that you cannot see certain parts of the delivery system, and why does it take those steps?

   C. Are any parts of these two organizations' service delivery systems (e.g., the frontline server) more important than other parts? Or are all equally important because a service delivery system is only as strong as its weakest link?

3. If you opened a new restaurant, would you bother to blueprint your service delivery system? Why or why not?
   A. If you did a blueprint, would you show it to your employees and discuss it with them, which would take time and money, or simply teach them their jobs on a need-to-know basis? Or would you leave it up to them whether they studied the blueprint or not?
   B. The chapter referred to a service blueprint for a frontline bank employee that covered thirty-six 11-by-18 pages. How long would your restaurant blueprint be? Compare the relative usefulness of your blueprint with the bank-employee blueprint.
4. You have been asked to manage a local music festival.
   A. How would a PERT/CPM chart help you do this?
   B. What would its essential elements, the individual circles in the chart, be?
   C. What would your PERT/CPM chart look like? Sketch it out, indicating the critical path.
5. Describe several situations in which hospitality managers could use cross-functional project and matrix teams to improve the quality and/or value of the guest experience.
6. Providing a wow service and preventing service problems are two sides of the same coin. Discuss.

ACTIVITIES

1. Apply a PERT/CPM chart to a guest service situation in a hospitality organization with which you are familiar.
2. Blueprint the service experience provided by a hospitality organization with which you are familiar, with emphasis on the delivery system.
3. Find a potential problem area in that blueprint and draw a simple fishbone diagram that you might use to prevent or resolve the problem.

ETHICS IN BUSINESS

Airlines, in essence, provide the service of getting guests from point A to point B safely. While there are clearly many parts to this service product, safety is a critical component that gets significant attention in the planning process. Fail-safes and various forms of security have been added to provide greater security for guests, but all of these come at a cost. The U.S. government has recommended the use of cost-benefit analysis for assessing potential new regulations. The regulatory safety goal is roughly $10 million per life saved,[19] meaning that a regulation costing this amount or less per life saved is worthwhile to implement. So, by these standards, hardened cockpit doors, which are estimated to cost $800,000 per life saved, seem like a good investment; however, the Federal Air Marshal Service, estimated to cost $180 million per life saved, seems a poor investment.

Safety is an issue for all parts of the hospitality industry. Measures could include maintaining heightened security at hotels and restaurants, having trained medical staff on hand, and putting more safety measures into all aspects of the service system. Hotels could hire a full-time doctor, have extensive security teams, hire dozens of more people to inspect and test all food products coming into the kitchen, and many, many more.

How should decisions about implementing greater safety measures be made? What ethical issues are involved? Can you put a value, or a budget, on a human life? Should a safety decision be made this way? If so, how do you estimate the value to put on a human

[19] Office of Secretary of Transportation, "Revised Departmental Guidance 2016: Treatment of the Value of Preventing Fatalities and Injuries in Preparing Economic Analyses," transportation.gov, U.S. Department of Transportation, accessed January 2018, https://www.transportation.gov/sites/dot.gov/files/docs/2016%20Revised%20Value%20of%20a%20Statistical%20Life%20Guidance.pdf.

life to help determine if an investment is worthwhile? Is approximately $10 million the "right" value? If you should not make a formal calculation using a value for a human life, what measures should you use to make these sorts of decisions?

CASE STUDY

Room for Improvement

Monique Kazer spends quite a bit of time on the road in her job as a salesperson for a company specializing in audiovisual equipment for convention hotels and centers. She works long hours, often dines late at night, and returns to her lodging place late, often after midnight. Monique has asthma and is very sensitive to cigarette smoke, so she always requests a nonsmoking room at her hotel or motel.

Several weeks ago, tired after visiting three convention hotels, in Newark, Jersey City, and Hoboken, in one day, Monique arrived a few minutes after midnight at the Hospitality Inn, where she had a guaranteed reservation. The Hospitality Inn was a unit of the major chain with which her firm did business because of the deep discounts offered. She checked in and headed for Room 315, looking forward to a hot shower and good night's sleep; tomorrow was going to be even busier. As always, she checked the door for a no-smoking sign. When she entered, the smell of cigarettes, or possibly cigars, mixed with air-freshener spray, almost made her sick. She began to cough, and her throat started to close up.

She quickly backed out, shut the door, and returned to the front desk. At least she didn't have to wait in line at that time of night, thank goodness for that. Desk agent Hyun Cho had a magazine open on the area beneath the counter that she used as her desk, but she was not reading it because—as Monique saw it—she was obviously talking to a friend on the phone. She glanced at Monique a couple of times but continued to talk on the phone, making it clear that Monique would have to wait her turn. Ordinarily, Monique would have waited a few moments, but tonight she was not in the mood so she employed her last-ditch technique for gaining attention in such a situation: She reached over the counter, took the phone out of Cho's hand, and hung it up. The service encounter went downhill from there.

Monique didn't even give a red-faced Hyun Cho a chance to mention the phone hang-up: "I made a reservation for a nonsmoking room, and you people put me in a room full of smoking fumes. Just change my room and we'll let it go at that."

Cho was a fairly conscientious night desk agent, and she had actually been talking with her babysitter, but she was still steaming from having the phone taken from her in mid-sentence. Hyun said nothing, checked the hotel records with a glance, and then said to Monique: "That *is* a nonsmoking room!"

"Check again, Ms. . . . (looking at her name tag). . . . Cho. The room smells like a pre-war stag party."

"I don't care if it smells like hell warmed over. I don't need to check again, Ms. . . . (looking at the registration card). . . . Ka-Zer. I can read and I know my rooms and I can tell you that Room 315 is for nonsmokers." She concluded triumphantly, "We changed it over last week!"

Monique whispered the first curse she had uttered in a year or two, and then said, "Just move me to a nonsmoking room that has been a nonsmoking room as long as you have been open."

"No, problem, Ms. Ka-Zer. (pause) Usually. But tonight, I'm sorry, we're filled up."

Monique tried to have the room fee canceled, but Hyun refused. "If you don't show up until after midnight, it's actually the next day. No cancellations or refunds under any circumstances after midnight." She played her hole card: "Company policy." Then she added, "You ought to do something about that cough."

Monique left—tired, defeated, and still coughing—and headed out into the night to find another room, if she could. If not, there was always the back seat of the rented Crown Vic.

1. How would you have handled this situation if you were Monique Kazer?
2. How would you have handled this situation if you were Hyun Cho?

3. What devices described in the chapter might system planners have used to prevent this service failure, and how might they have used them?

Room for More Improvement

As Monique Kazer rushed through the exit of the Hospitality Inn lobby, she almost knocked manager Roberta Morales down. Morales recognized Monique from previous visits and knew that Monique's firm gave Hospitality Inns across the region a lot of business. Morales realized that something was wrong and suspected that the something was a service failure.

"I'm the inn manager. Is there something I can do for you?" she said to Monique. She heard Monique's side of the story, took her to the cocktail lounge, bought her the beverage of her choice, and asked an assistant manager to chat with Monique while she went back to the front desk. After hearing Hyun Cho's side of the story ("she yanked the phone out of my hand and hung it up!"), Roberta Morales headed back to the lounge. She would speak further with Hyun Cho later.

1. In a later chapter, you will be reading about some techniques for handling service failures. For now, what steps might you take to retain the patronage of Monique Kazer (and her entire organization)?
2. What steps would you take with regard to Hyun Cho and the failure at the front desk?
3. Using some hypothetical but realistic numbers, how much do you think it might end up costing Hospitality Inns if manager Roberta Morales is unable to recover from this failure and ends up losing the patronage of not only Monique Kazer but her entire firm?

Further readings on the topics in this chapter are listed in "Additional Readings" on pages 516–518.

Get the tools you need to sharpen your study skills. SAGE edge offers a robust online environment featuring an impressive array of free tools and resources.

Access practice quizzes, eFlashcards, video, and multimedia at **edge.sagepub.com/Ford2e**.

Visit **edge.sagepub.com/Ford2e** to help you accomplish your coursework goals in an easy-to-use learning environment.

©iStockphoto.com/MariusLtu

11 Waiting for Service

Hospitality Principle: Manage the Guest's Wait

All things come to him who waits—provided he knows what he is waiting for.

—Woodrow T. Wilson

Learning Objectives

After reading this chapter, you should be able to:

11.1 Explain why it is critical to make any wait for service as short and pleasant as possible.

11.2 Discuss how to plan for capacity shortages.

11.3 Demonstrate how to use queuing theory to plan the wait.

11.4 Describe how to create virtual waits.

11.5 Describe how organizations can manage a guest's perception of the wait.

11.6 Explain how to offset the wait's negative effects by managing the value of the experience provided to the guest.

INTRODUCTION

How long we wait and how long we are willing to wait are fascinating subjects. While solid scientific evidence is hard to find, various estimates suggest that we wait in line about two to three years in a lifetime. To see a cardiologist in Boston, you'll need to wait, on average, forty-five days. To get a table for two at Noma, in Copenhagen, you may need to wait nearly three months for your reservation. Some parents put their children on the waiting lists for exclusive preparatory schools before their children are born. And, if you want season tickets for the Green Bay Packers or the Philadelphia Eagles, at the present rate the "line" is moving, you may need to wait thirty years.

Nobody likes to wait in line. Yet, almost every hospitality organization relies on waiting lines or **queues** to match its serving capacity with the number of guests who want service. Planning and managing the wait of the customers are among all service provider's fundamental concerns. Guestologists have learned that waits can be designed to improve the level of guest satisfaction with an experience through the careful management of time spent waiting. By providing entertaining or informative diversions that engage and divert the guest while waiting, it is possible to refocus their attention to a pleasant anticipation of an experience and away from an unpleasant wait.

queues Waiting lines.

This chapter presents some strategies for planning and managing the reality and the perception of the guest's wait for service. These include both quantitative and perceptual strategies. The secret to managing the guest's wait effectively is to use all available techniques, in the right combination, to make a seemingly endless wait acceptable, perhaps even enjoyable. Since nearly every service experience, whether in an actual queue or online, has a wait in it somewhere, planning for and **managing the wait** are sufficiently important to merit their own chapter.

managing the wait The organization's use of queuing theory and psychological techniques to minimize the negative impact on guests of inevitable waits.

In some respects, the wait is an inevitable part of the service experience since no organization can perfectly prepare itself to serve all guests, whenever and whatever they want. In another respect a wait is a service failure. When the wait between courses at a fine-dining restaurant is too short, because guests have anticipated a more leisurely experience, or a wait at a quick-serve drive-thru window is too long, the guest is disappointed. Even when the wait at a popular attraction is no surprise and, therefore, "meets the guest's expectations," the guest generally doesn't like it.

CAPACITY AND PSYCHOLOGY: KEYS TO MANAGING LINES

The guest experience often starts off not with a "wow," but a wait. The wait for service begins at the entrance to the restaurant, the automated message on the phone, the log-on to a website, or the line in front of Pandora—The World of Avatar at Walt Disney World Resort. The prospective guest or customer assesses the Pandora line, the number of cars in the restaurant's parking lot, the time to wait estimate in the automated message on the help-line, or the turning hourglass on the computer screen, and decides whether to walk to the next attraction, drive on to the next restaurant, hang up the phone, click to another website—or to wait. What makes that guest wait or leave can be anticipated and managed—if waiting lines are understood. If no other eating places are within eyesight, or the exceedingly hungry guest does not know what other restaurants are available nearby and doesn't have a smartphone to find out, or the guest is absolutely convinced that he must eat in that restaurant because the quality or uniqueness of the dining experience is said to be unsurpassed, he will probably pull into the parking lot, walk inside, and wait in line.

When the Wait Begins

High expectations of guests explain the large crowds usually standing outside a P.F. Chang's or a Cheesecake Factory. The people waiting believe the quality or the value of the dining experience will outweigh the costs to them of waiting, despite the full parking lot and the crowd standing in line outside the restaurant waiting to be served. In fact, sometimes guests view a line as a signal of quality. If there are two restaurants next to each other, one with a line and one without, a person might actually prefer the restaurant with the line, thinking that the one where people are waiting must be worth a wait. The same high expectations can explain the lines waiting to enter The Wizarding World of Harry Potter—Hogsmeade and the other popular attractions throughout the Universal Orlando Resort. In effect, each person makes an opportunity-cost judgment. If the expected benefits of the wait outweigh the costs (boredom and impatience, to name just two) of idly standing around, then the guest will wait. If they don't, the guest will leave and go elsewhere for the service.

For those customers who decide to wait rather than leave, how can planners be sure that the wait will be as short and as pleasant as possible? No matter how good the Pandora-The World of Avatar attraction or the Cheesecake Factory meal is, if the customer begins the experience angry, distressed, or unhappy about having to wait for service, then that customer's expectations will be much harder to meet thereafter.

Designing the Service to Manage the Wait

Managing the wait has two major components. First is to keep the wait as short as possible by planning for and building the appropriate capacity into the service facility to minimize the wait for the anticipated number of guests arriving at the anticipated rate at a particular time. Second is to ensure that the guests who are waiting have their physiological and psychological needs and expectations met while they wait.

The capacity decision results from careful study of the expected demand pattern. Whether one is trying to plan for how many two-top versus four-top tables to place in a restaurant, how many registration booths to open at a convention, how many reservation agents to staff at a call center, or how many blackjack tables to put in a casino, the need to make an accurate capacity estimate is the same. Planners must predict three factors that drive the capacity decision: how many people will arrive for the service at a particular time, at what rate they will arrive, and how long the service will take.

If, on every day that the organization is open for business, the same number of people were to arrive for service every day, their arrivals were evenly spaced throughout the day, and serving each person took the same length of time, the capacity decision would be easy. For example, a psychiatrist can schedule eight patients per day, schedule them to arrive on the hour, then serve each patient for forty-five minutes and use the remaining fifteen minutes to write up notes on that patient and prepare for the next. The psychiatrist has an easy capacity decision (assuming no emergencies occur and everyone is on time): one service facility (an office) containing one chair for the psychiatrist and one couch for the patient, plus other furnishings and equipment for one office. If the service is a guided tour through a museum, the service provider knows how long it will take, but the museum's planning staff must predict how many people will arrive for service. If the service experience has a less definite beginning and ending time, like a meal or a day at a ski resort, both the number of persons arriving for service and the average time taken to deliver each part of the network of events that make up a service experience will have to be estimated or predicted.[1] We will discuss several methods for making these predictions later in this chapter.

Capacity designs can affect perceptions of service quality. While a restaurant with too little capacity will fail to meet guest expectations for prompt service and short waits, a restaurant with too much capacity can also fail to meet guest expectations. A restaurant with too many seats will appear empty to diners and may lead them to conclude that the food or service is not up to par. This assumption predisposes guests to expect a poor experience. Further, they may feel foolish for choosing a restaurant that is so obviously unpopular. The chefs and the servers have two strikes against them, just because the restaurant designers put in too many seats.

Of course, from the restaurant owner's point of view, the excess capacity costs money! Fixed costs are tied up in unused tables, silverware, equipment, rent, and so forth. Too much capacity may mean higher variable costs as well. The manager may schedule too many servers and cooks who end up being paid simply to wait around.

Capacity

In an ideal world, planners would be able to determine the exact capacity required to serve each guest at the moment when the guest expects service. Each customer for Cheesecake Factory or Pandora—The World of Avatar would arrive just when a table or the next flight was available to receive the desired experience. Guests want that kind of service, and organizations want to provide it. Both are frequently disappointed.

What to Do?

Because people do not arrive at service operations in neat, ordered patterns, they sometimes have to wait for service. When hospitality managers see that waiting lines are becoming long, they have several choices. Customer-focused research can identify the best options. The goal is to find the decision that ensures customer satisfaction with the lowest capital cost. Managers should choose the option that allows both customers and the organization to come out ahead.

1. ***Close the Doors to Further Customers.*** This choice is highly undesirable, but sometimes the movie theater manager, cruise ship booking agent, or rock show entrepreneur must tell those waiting, "Sorry, we're sold out."
2. ***Add Capacity.*** Because this alternative is usually expensive, organizations do not usually choose it unless they believe the high demand causing the waiting

[1] For an interesting example of a ski resort network of waits, see Madeleine E. Pullman and Gary M. Thompson, "Evaluating Capacity- and Demand-Management Decisions at a Ski Resort," *Cornell Hotel and Restaurant Administration Quarterly* 43, no. 6 (2002): 25–36.

Construction at Denver's International Airport added capacity to the airport through a new hotel and transit center.

lines will continue. The organization will be particularly hesitant to add capacity if its design-day capacity is already at a high percent level, meaning that the organization is already at or below capacity most of the time. Stopgap measures for adding capacity temporarily are sometimes available. For example, employees can be asked to work overtime or on flexible schedules, cross-trained employees can be reassigned from their normal areas to help unclog a service bottleneck, temporary help can be hired, or temporary changes in physical facilities can be made, like adding tents to provide additional exhibit space at a convention hotel or busses for increasing capacity to move people at special events.

3. ***Manage Demand.*** Simply informing guests of when the busy and slack times occur may smooth out demand. Service providers can also schedule appointments or offer inducements to customers to use capacity at nonpeak demand times.

   Requiring reservations at a restaurant is an example of the first method, and early-bird specials or discounts on airline travel or hotel rooms at off-peak times are examples of the second.

   Some organizations, such as airlines and hotels, can ask that guests make reservations, even guaranteed reservations in some cases, to help manage demand. Customers are often willing to call for reservations with such organizations because they do not want to take a chance on not getting a flight or a room. No one wants to arrive at the cruise-ship dock only to find that all rooms are occupied. But many hospitality organizations do not have the market stature or have too many similar competitors for most customers to help them in their capacity decisions by requiring reservations. Guests will make reservations when the alternatives are few or they do not have the flexibility regarding time, desire, or distance to do something different if their primary choice is at capacity. Thus, guests are willing to pay for a guaranteed hotel-room reservation at Phantom Ranch, located at the bottom of the Grand Canyon, more than a year in advance to ensure that the room will be waiting for them after they walk to the end of the Bright Angel Trail. But, they may not see any value in making a reservation at the nearby Carrabba's since, if that restaurant is at capacity, many similar alternatives are probably available near Carrabba's.

   arrival patterns The patterns describing the number of customers arriving or entering a system in a given period of time.

   Another way to manage demand is by shifting demand from peak-capacity use times to off-peak times by offering guests inducements to change their **arrival patterns**. When the wait times for popular attractions became excessive, Disney shifted demand by creating a special after-hours ticket called "Magic Kingdom's E-Ride Nights." The tickets were sold for under $15 and provided guests with unlimited access to the nine most popular attractions for an additional three hours after the normal park closing. To guarantee the guests minimal wait times on the nine attractions, the tickets sold each night were limited to a fixed number of guests and were sold in advance at the Disney resorts on a first-come, first-served basis. The actual number of tickets sold was limited to match the capacity of the nine attractions.

   The guests who paid less than $15 for the right to spend an extra three hours after normal closing time to ride their favorite rides as many times as they wanted were happy and thought they got a great deal. They did not have to stand in long lines with everybody else waiting for these rides during the day. Regular daytime guests were also happier; their lines were shorter because the E-Ride Nights guests were no longer in the lines during the day. In effect, Disney expanded park capacity by shifting demand, but unlike the power company that gives customers a lower rate at off-peak times or the restaurant that offers low-cost early-bird specials, Disney was able to charge more and guests were happy to pay; they felt they got good value for their money.

Disney provides information to its guests that enables them to manage their own time to wait. One guest, for example, analyzed daily crowd predictions available at the WDW Prep School website to plan out the optimal schedule for visiting attractions on the days her family planned to visit the parks.[2] She inputted that data to build a schedule on Trello, an online project management app, to plan how to visit the parks' attractions on each of their six days at Walt Disney World. The result from having access to this self-management of demand was minimal waits for this family.

Technology

Another way to manage demand is to use technology to decrease the time it takes to access or engage with the service capacity. The obvious example is smartphone apps that allow the online placement of orders so that when the guests arrive at the service location there is no time required to order the service. Panera, for example, created a mobile app that allows customers to place an order by phone ahead of their arrival. This increased online orders to represent one fourth of their sales and reduced the average wait of customers to one minute.[3] The increasing popularity of online ordering reflects the value customers place on this time saving way to get their desired services, benefiting both them and the companies offering them.

4. ***Allow the Line to Form and Then Manage the Line by Diverting Customers.*** When lines are unavoidable, one way to keep customers happy is by offering people waiting in line something else to do. Having a gift shop in a Cracker Barrel or Rainforest Cafe gives patrons an opportunity to go and do something while they wait for their table to be ready. These diversions not only benefit the guest by creating the perception that the experience has begun, but they can be highly profitable, sometimes more profitable than the service product itself. Rainforest Cafe even calls itself "A wild place to shop and eat." An organization may go so far as to close down some available capacity to ensure that people wait long enough to become "diverted" to the gift shop, with its high-margin items for sale. Or an organization may keep a phone caller on hold longer than absolutely necessary to present a recorded message promoting other services. Many restaurants suggest guests wait in the bar, where they can order drinks (typically a high profit-margin item) until their table is ready. A related strategy is to upgrade a low-demand aspect of the organization's service to divert customers toward it and away from high-demand features. For example, a resort hotel could upgrade its pool bar to attract people away from the main lobby bar at peak times. A cruise ship could upgrade a currently underutilized restaurant to be family friendly so it takes pressure off the main dining facility. A golf course could upgrade its practice area with computerized swing-analysis equipment, to take pressure off the course during the most popular tee times.

   Many call centers divert customers waiting on hold by suggesting they visit a website for desired services rather than wait for the next available operator. Others offer a "call back" service where the customer who wants to do something else

[2] Erin G. Smith, "Listen to the Disney Ninjas," *Wall Street Journal*, May 4, 2016.

[3] Julie Jargon, "Panera Slices Lines with Mobile," *Wall Street Journal*, June 3–4, 2017.

besides waiting on hold can leave a name and phone number, hang up, and be placed in a virtual queue to be called back when an operator becomes available.

From their own daily experience, most people can cite numerous examples of organizations that planned and managed the wait well or poorly. The best organizations know what steps they need to take when lines start to form.

5. ***Do Nothing.*** The organization can accept the fact that it will make customers unhappy with a wait and hope that they aren't so unhappy that they leave and vow never to return. Maybe lines form only rarely, and so the organization is not willing to spend money to address an occasional problem. Some establishments actually seem to benefit from doing nothing. For example, the long lines at some night clubs or restaurants signal an establishment that is trendy, in demand, and exclusive.

Design Day

Whether they realize it or not, or whether they do it consciously or not, all hospitality organizations use the design-day concept (also discussed in Chapter 2). The design day is the hypothetical day the facility, attraction, or service was designed to handle comfortably, but not too comfortably. Planners set the design-day capacity to handle a predetermined amount of demand without compromising guest satisfaction. If demand is less than the design-day capacity, then guests are happy, but the facility is underutilized. If demand exceeds the design-day capacity, then some guests will probably be unhappy. Planners know that waiting lines may form on design days, but they should not become so long that guests perceive a decline in the quality or value of their experience.

Benchmark organizations know just how long the lines can be and still remain within limits acceptable to guests. Some, like restaurants, even know how long a wait can be in each phase of the experience before guests become dissatisfied.[4] Others, such as a major theme park with a network of rides and events, may use a fifteen-minute average wait as a criterion across the entire park experience. On the design day, the park doesn't want anyone to wait longer than this average time in any queue because guest surveys have shown that the quality and value of the experience decline sharply beyond this time length. Because fifteen minutes is an average, it may take much longer for guests to get on a popular ride. However, based on the accumulated data, a fifteen-minute average may be the best balance between having too much capacity and not enough. A truly guest-focused theme park may set its design day at a very high level, say 80 to 90%—meaning that supply will be adequate for demand on 80 to 90% of the days of the year—because it appreciates the fact that most guests have traveled a long way, have limited vacation time, and have no choice but to wait once inside the park. To provide a guest experience with as little waiting as possible, the planners will set the design-day percentile high and build more capacity than might otherwise be practical. The cost of an unhappy guest to a major theme park that relies on return guest visits must be carefully balanced against the costs of building capacity.

capacity day The maximum number of guests allowed, by law or by the organization, in a service facility in a day or at one time, used like the design day to balance the costs to the organization of excess capacity and the costs to the guest (in terms of quality and value) of inadequate capacity.

The Capacity Day

Design days are the times when capacity is the best trade-off for both the guest and the facility—not ideal for either one, but satisfactory. Many organizational planners also calculate and use a **capacity day**, the maximum number of customers allowed in the facility in a day or at one time. This number is often set by the fire marshal based on the number of square feet each customer must have available. The capacity day may be set by the organization itself, to represent a point beyond which overall customer dissatisfaction with crowds, lines, or delays in service is unacceptable. Hospitality

[4] See, for example, Johye Hwang and Carolyn U. Lambert, "The Interaction of Major Resources and Their Influence on Waiting Times in a Multi-Stage Restaurant," *International Journal of Hospitality Management* 27, no. 4 (2008): 541–551.

organizations know that guests disappointed because they did not have the guest experience at all are preferable to dissatisfied, angry ones who did.

QUEUING THEORY: MANAGING THE REALITY OF THE WAIT

Few organizations in any industry have the luxury of adjusting capacity quickly or managing demand by getting customers to show up when the organization wants them to, instead of when customers want to come. Most hospitality organizations must, therefore, rely on predicting and managing the inevitable waiting lines that are created when customers arrive looking for service.

The general problem for planners is that adding capacity costs money, such as by hiring more servers, but reduces the wait, which improves guest-experience quality, guest satisfaction, and guest loyalty. Reducing capacity saves money but increases the wait, which decreases guest-experience quality, guest satisfaction, and guest loyalty. How is the hospitality organization to find the proper cost-benefit balance?

The place to begin is in the use of **queuing theory**, sometimes called **waiting-line theory**, and the mathematical solutions this technique offers. A typical queuing theory problem facing an organizational planner might be: If an average of forty cars arrive per hour at a drive-thru window with a single server, and if the server takes an average of two minutes to fill an order, how long does the average car spend in line? During an average hour, how many minutes will the server be working and how many minutes idle? Most applications of waiting-line theory in the hospitality industry are based on the idea that people do not arrive in neat patterns. The typical approach is to sample the arrival and service patterns of guests and use this information to simulate the distribution that best matches the reality for the particular organization's guests. A restaurant might actually count all its guests over a period of time or sample them over a longer period using some appropriate sampling methodology and let the actual guest patterns represent the distribution of both arrival and service times.

queuing theory The theory of how waiting lines behave; same as waiting-line theory.

waiting-line theory The theory of how waiting lines behave; same as queuing theory.

Characteristics of Waiting Lines

All waiting lines have three characteristics that any model must include:

1. ***Arrival Patterns: The Numbers of Guests Arriving and the Manner in Which They Enter the Waiting Line.*** The arrivals could be random such as patrons to a restaurant, in bulk such as a busload of tourists, or in some other distribution that is difficult to describe, such as patients coming to a hospital emergency room in varying but not completely random intervals. Queue management is easiest when customer arrivals can be scheduled through reservations. Even if arrivals cannot be strictly scheduled, they may be controlled. Charging extra at peak times and offering discounts during the off-season would be examples of arrival-control strategies.
2. ***Queue Discipline: How the Arriving Guests Are Served.*** Options are first-come, first-served; last-come, first-served (not a formula for hospitality success), or some other set of service rules. For example, guests with reservations or wanting takeout food only may be served first, or restaurant parties of two may be served when a two-seat table is available regardless of how many parties of three or more are in line ahead of them. Guests understand such a service rule.[5] They don't understand service rules that seem unfair to them or have

[5] See Kelly A. McGuire and Sheryl E. Kimes, "The Perceived Fairness of Waitlist-Management Techniques for Restaurants," *Cornell Hotel and Restaurant Administration Quarterly* 47, no. 2 (2006): 121–134.

no explanation. And, they really don't understand an implicit rule such as the following, which seems to be in effect at numerous service locations: "Answer a phone call from someone sitting at home before serving the customer or guest standing right in front of you who may have traveled miles to do business with you." The point is that a **queue discipline** must be obvious and familiar, or managers must find ways to carefully explain what the rules are and why they are fair.

queue discipline In hospitality settings, the organization's pattern or plan for how arriving guests are served; usually first-come, first-served.

The guests themselves can usually be counted on to maintain the discipline of the first-come, first-served queue. If someone breaks into the line in front of you, queue etiquette requires you to object and those in line behind you to support you. If the queue discipline in a certain grocery store line is first-come, first-served, no more than ten items, customers count each other's items and may forcefully object to a number over ten.

3. ***Time for Service: How Long It Takes to Serve Guests.*** The time boundaries of some service experiences can be carefully planned, like a flight from Boston to Atlanta, or a ride on a roller coaster car. But customers in most service settings vary, voluntarily or involuntarily, in the time it takes them to receive the service. Some diners want to eat and run; others wish to savor the meal. Likewise, some hospital emergency-room patients suffer from severe injuries while others have trivial problems. The amount of time it takes to serve the different customers can be as unpredictable as the people themselves. If the waiting-line model is to be an aid in managing the line, planners must take this variation into account. Although the previous examples involve people, waiting-line theory can be applied to anything that waits in line for something to happen to it. An automobile waiting in a fully automated painting line or a meal waiting to be served is as queued up and in need of managing as the newly arriving guest at the hotel front desk.

single-channel, single-phase queue A type of queue where there is a single server and a single step.

Line Types

Organizational planners must decide what line types will best meet customer needs and expectations. In the following discussion, "channel" refers to a *server,* and "phase" refers to a *step* in the service experience once it is underway.

PATRICK KOVARIK/AFP/Getty Images

Tourists line up in a single-channel, single-phase queue to enter the Elysee Palace in Paris.

Single-Channel, Single-Phase Queue

The basic line type is the **single-channel, single-phase queue**—one server, one step. This queue type is represented at the top in Exhibit 11.1. Mary Blaine has a one-chair hair salon. Customers come in, wait their turn, and have their hair cut in the single service phase. Indoor customers at some quick-serve restaurants stand in any one of several single-channel, single-phase queues. The customer looks the lines over, chooses one, stands in it waiting for service, and eventually reaches the counter to begin the single service phase. In that phase, the counter person takes

EXHIBIT 11.1

Some Basic Queue Types

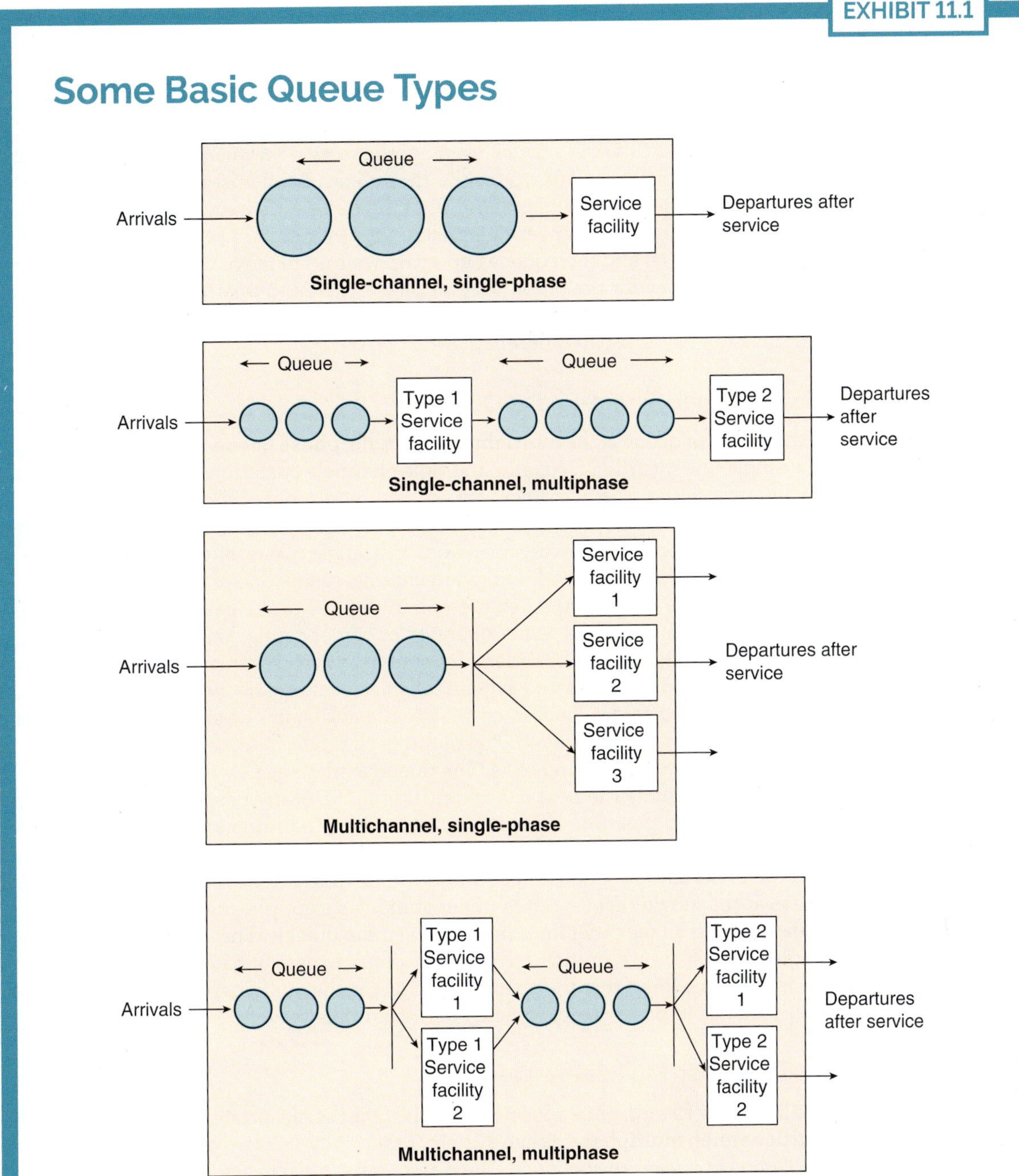

the order, assembles and delivers it, and collects the money. Highway toll plazas and McDonald's counters are not the sites of multichannel queues, even though they may have multiple servers. They consist of a group of single-channel, single-phase queues, with one server per queue.

Single-Channel, Multiphase Queue

single-channel, multiphase queue Two or more single-channel, single-phase queues in a sequence. The guest waits in one queue for service from a single server, and then moves on to wait in another queue for another phase of service from another single server.

The second queue type in the exhibit is the **single-channel, multiphase queue**, such as a cafeteria line or the drive-thru at a limited-menu, quick-serve facility. Essentially, it is two or more single-channel, single-phase queues in sequence. The guest waits in one queue for service from a single server, and then moves on to wait in another queue for another phase of service from another single server. At a typical drive-thru restaurant, customers queue up for the first phase. Each customer drives up to the order microphone, tries to understand what the person (the server, the single channel providing the first phase of service) inside the restaurant is saying, places an order (end of first phase) and then queues up again waiting to move forward to the window to receive and pay for the order (second phase, meaning another single channel for service with a single server). In this guest experience, the customer interacts with the organization twice, at two different places.

Multichannel, Single-Phase Queue

multichannel, single-phase queue The customer begins in a single line that then feeds into multiple channels or stations for the service, each staffed by a server. The customer waits to get to the front of the single line, and then goes to the next available channel (server) for service.

A third type of queue is the **multichannel, single-phase queue**. The customer begins in a single line that then feeds into multiple channels or stations for the service, each staffed by a server. The customer waits to get to the front of the single line, and then goes to the next available channel (server) for service. An example would be a bank or airport waiting line where everyone stands in a single queue, often snake-shaped to fit into available space, waiting for an open channel to any one of multiple servers. The queue discipline is to call the next person in the line to the next available teller, airline-counter attendant, call center operator, or career counselor, who renders a single service in a single phase. The Federal Personnel Office uses this method for incoming telephone calls. The automated system tells each caller how many callers are ahead, so the caller can decide whether to wait or call back later. The single phase of service is to have a phone call answered. The multiple channels for obtaining this service are the many operators handling calls. The queue is managed by having the next available operator handle the next caller waiting in line. Many hospitality organizations find this method the most efficient way to manage their lines as it accounts well for the varying lengths of time that it takes to serve different customers. Everyone has had the experience of choosing to stand in one of several available single-channel lines—at the movie-theater refreshment stand, for example, or the hotel front desk—then watching all the other lines move much more quickly. The use of a multichannel, single-phase system eliminates this feeling of unfairness or bad luck; everyone starts out in the same line. From the guest's perspective, the multichannel, single-phase line feels faster as it moves people quickly to the multiple servers.[6]

Multichannel, Multiphase Queue

multichannel, multiphase queue Two or more multichannel, single-phase queues in sequence. The guest waits to get to the front of one line, and then goes to the next available server. After receiving the first phase of service, the guest then gets into another line, wait to arrive at the front, then goes to the next available server/channel to receive the next phase of service.

The last type of waiting line shown in Exhibit 11.1 is the most complicated to manage the **multichannel, multiphase queue** system. Essentially, it is two or more multichannel, single-phase queues in sequence. The guest waits to get to the front of one line, then goes to the next available server. After receiving the first phase of service, the guest then gets in another line, waits to arrive at the front, then goes to the next available server/channel to receive the next phase of service. Most airports use this queue type for security screening where the line for the first phase checks passenger documents and the second screens people and carry-ons. Vapiano, a European fast-casual restaurant serving Italian foods, uses this pattern between its single-channel entry and exit points. At the entry point, the guest lines up to receive a "charge card" to be used at the different food stations. The guest then sees lines leading to each of several entrées

[6] See, for example, Anat Rafaeli, Greg Barron, and Keren Haber, "The Effects of Queue Sructure on Attitudes," *Journal of Service Research* 5, no. 2 (2002): 125–139.

and takes a place at the end of, say, the pizza line or the pasta line. The guest waits to become first in line, then orders his or her desired meal. The guest follows the same procedure for pasta, antipasto, salad and soups, dessert, and so forth. The guest then gets in a checkout line and turns the charge card in to a cashier, who totals up all the purchases.

A hospitality organization will often have numerous queues linked in various combinations. For example, a restaurant will have a line for people waiting to be seated, a wait time while the server serves other customers in a queue ahead of you before taking your order, a line of orders queued up for processing by the cook, a queue of servers waiting while the food is being prepared, and a line of people at the checkout. To consider just the line of people waiting to be seated, it is a multichannel, single-phase queue, if the restaurant tables are considered to be channels and being seated is considered to be a phase. Managing the wait times associated with single and multiple channels and phases is difficult, but it is critical for ensuring excellent guest service and minimizing service failures.

Virtual Queues

A final type of queue that has become increasingly popular is the **virtual queue**, or the line that isn't visible. Most people don't like to stand in line, and the virtual queue enables them to avoid doing so. This type of queue, based on the idea underlying Disney's FASTPASS™[7], was first introduced at Walt Disney World Resort in 1998 in response to a need to better manage waiting times to allow more efficient time use for guests and more efficient capacity use by the company. Disney found that guests using this virtual queue system spent significantly less time in lines, spent more per capita, saw significantly more attractions, and as a result had significantly higher overall levels of satisfaction. After a series of initial tests and refinements, FASTPASS™ was expanded to all Disney Parks worldwide and is now used by millions of its guests annually. Its success has led to the FASTPASS technology being offered to guests in a wide variety of applications from managing waits at other theme parks, to waiting to sit on Santa Claus's lap, to waiting for the next available operator.

virtual queue A line that is not visible and allows consumers to be "in line" without actually having to stand in a line. Allows customers to engage in other activities while waiting for service.

This virtual queue system is quite different from the waiting-line experience of most guests. Although the introduction of the FASTPASS+ on "Magic Bands" in 2014 has changed the way it works today, the original technology was ticket based. When guests approached a FASTPASS™ attraction, they were instructed to insert their park admission ticket into a specially designated FASTPASS™ turnstile to enter a virtual queue in the computer. Based upon how many guests were in front of the ones who were just joining the virtual queue and the current flow of guests at the attraction, the computer estimated how long it would take for the newly arriving guest's space in the virtual queue to get to the front of the line. This estimated time was automatically printed out on each guest's FASTPASS™ ticket and became the designated time for the guest to return and gain immediate entry into the attraction with no wait. Both FASTPASS and FASTPASS+ allowed the computer to hold guests' space in the virtual line while they visited other attractions, ate, shopped, or whatever they wanted to do throughout the park before returning at any time within the assigned sixty-minute window. This sixty-minute flexibility was created to ensure that guests had the opportunity to engage in other activities during the wait time without worrying that they might be late for a specific entry time. They knew that if they arrived back at the attraction within the sixty-minute window, they could walk right in.

A key point in making the FASTPASS™ and FASTRPASS+ systems work was that guests always had a choice between a FASTPASS™ virtual line and the actual "stand by" line. It turned out that most of the guests in the standby line were people who also held a FASTPASS™ ticket for another attraction and were using their extra time to

[7] Duncan Dickson, Robert C. Ford, and Bruce Laval, "Managing Real and Virtual Waits in Hospitality and Service Organizations," *Cornell Hotel and Restaurant Administration Quarterly* 46, no. 1 (2005): 52–68.

Robert C. Ford

Early example of FASTPASS™ use at Disney's Jungle Cruise

experience a second attraction by physically standing in line for it. Since seeing attractions is a key driver for guest satisfaction, these guests were usually very satisfied because they were able to see two attractions during the time they would have previously only been able to see one.

In addition to the primary benefits already described, the innovation of the FASTPASS™ virtual queue system provided many secondary benefits. During peak days, many guests previously waited in line as many as three to four hours in a day for the most popular attractions. The use of FASTPASS™ resulted in guests seeing more attractions during the day as well as greatly increasing the utilization of the other secondary attractions in the park, which previously had little or no wait times. Another secondary benefit was that guests also used some of the time "freed up" from lines to engage in other revenue-producing activities, such as dining and shopping, without taking time away from visiting other attractions. Lower perceived wait times led to higher customer satisfaction levels, and at the same time, Disney officials saw increased revenues on food and merchandise per person in the parks.[8] Helping people to avoid standing in line benefits both Disney and its guests.

The virtual-queue concept has many potential applications in hospitality. Cruise ships and resorts are similar to theme parks in that guests have many activities from which to choose, so virtual queues could be used in the same way. Restaurants that hand out paging devices to indicate to guests when capacity is available can keep queued-up guests from having to stand in actual lines. These guests can spend time (and money) in nearby retail shopping or bar areas. Any free-standing attraction that experiences long lines for admission and entry is also a potential site for creating a virtual queue.

Which Queue to Use?

Guest preferences drive planners' decisions about queue types at the best organizations. McDonald's believes that using multiple single-channel, single-phase lines meets customer desires for quick service. Wendy's, Burger King, and most other quick-serve and fast casual restaurants have a different opinion: They use the single-channel, multiphase queue, with customers placing an order with a server at one location and moving to another server to pick it up. At some other quick-serve restaurants and many airline counters, all customers get into one line, often a "serpentine" line that snakes between posts and velvet ropes. Once customers reach the head of the line, they wait to enter whichever channel leads to the next available server or attendant. These different queue choices by company planners are based on their studies of what guests want in particular situations.

Common sense suggests the best queue type for an organization to use is the one that guests perceive as enabling them to begin receiving service as quickly as possible. The guest-focused planner knows the best line type is the one that customers prefer, and that may not be the type suggested by common sense. For example, guests

[8] B. J. Wolfston, "Disney Chief Financial Officer Sees Changes Raising Customer Satisfaction," *Orange County Register*, April 11, 2000, www.ocregister.com; E. S. Reckard, "More Disneyland Rides to Get Shortcut System," *Los Angeles Times*, May 26, 2000, www.latimes.com.

may prefer to stand in a certain type of line because they think they will be served faster, even if they won't.

Anat Rafaeli and her research colleagues suggest that planners need to consider at least four factors when choosing a queue type for a given situation.[9] Planners should select the queue that best provides customers with all the following:

1. A sense of progress toward their goal or service experience.
2. A sense of control over what is happening.
3. Activity.
4. A sense of fairness with how their wait was managed.

People generally seem to prefer the single serpentine queue—with several channels at the end of it, each leading to a server—even though the length of the single line can be intimidating. They don't have to think or worry about which line to choose, whether to change lines if the present line seems slow or another line seems to have gotten shorter, or whether someone joining the next line over will be unfairly served more quickly.

In short, while a single serpentine line may yield the same average wait as multiple lines, the variance in wait times is much smaller. With multiple lines, you have the chance to get through much quicker than customers in other lines, but you also run the risk of being much slower. The serpentine line guarantees first-come, first-served. It is also becoming more widely adopted—at hotels, banks, by Wendy's and Burger King, Panera Bread, and many others. McDonald's, Walmart, Target, and most grocery stores continue to employ multiple lines.

Line Simulation: A Gift Shop

While planners can use a statistical distribution to describe the arrival and service patterns of many standard queues, in some situations only a simulation will yield the quality of data necessary to explain and predict the reality of a particular queue. Here is how a simulation might work.

The Christmas Tree is an extremely successful Christmas-themed restaurant; its slogan, "Make every day like Christmas!" appeals to young and old. Because Christmas-related items are available in regular stores only during Christmas season, Rudolph's Gift Shop attached to the Christmas Tree does a huge business during the rest of the year. In fact, many customers shop at Rudolph's rather than dine at the Christmas Tree.

Rudolph's has twenty checkout counters, which if fully staffed would require two people at each, for a total of forty people. If on an average day only fifty customers are typically in the shop at any one time, then full staffing of the checkout counters would be an obvious waste of money because the probability of all fifty people moving to the checkout lines at the same time is extremely small. But, if Rudolph's opens only one checkout counter, a long line will soon form. Planners must decide what staffing level best balances the cost of staffing Rudolph's checkouts against the cost of lost customers who vow never to return because of the long lines or lost sales as customers abandon their carts full of Christmas items and walk out. How might planners help the shop manager to make this decision?

Observing the Flow

Over several weeks the shop manager can observe the flow of customers and time how long they are in the shop. If sufficient observations are made, the shop manager

[9] Rafaeli, Barron, and Haber,125–139.

can create distributions that accurately describe customer arrival patterns, the quantity of items that they bring to the checkout stand, and their time spent in Rudolph's shopping for those items. With this information the manager can then simulate the shopping experiences of Rudolph's customers to determine how to staff the checkout counters appropriately at different times and on different days of the week. Here is how that might be done.

Allocation Wheels

In her office, the manager could set up the two roulette type wheels in what is frequently termed the Monte Carlo method as shown in Exhibit 11.2. Spaces are allocated on the first wheel to represent, in percentage form, the time between customer arrivals at the checkout counters. From the observations already made, the shop knows that for 15% of their observations, the time between arrivals at checkout was zero minutes; people arrived simultaneously. For 20%, the time between arrivals was one minute; for 25%, the time was two minutes; for 10%, the time was three minutes. For another 10%, the time was four minutes; for 12%, five minutes; and for 8%, six minutes. The wheel has spaces reflecting the likelihood of each arrival time. To simulate the arrival patterns of the customers at checkout, the manager would merely spin the wheel and write on a chart the arrival interval noted in the section of the wheel when it stopped.

The second wheel in Exhibit 11.2 is, in similar fashion, portioned off to represent the observations about how long the customers took to go through the checkout process. This total would include the time to scan the purchased items, write the checks or pay cash, and wrap or bag the purchases. Since people vary in both quantity of purchases and speed of writing checks or making payment, the time for service and the proportions on the wheel representing those times would likewise vary. The

EXHIBIT 11.2

Wheels Representing Time Between Arrivals and Time for Service at Checkout

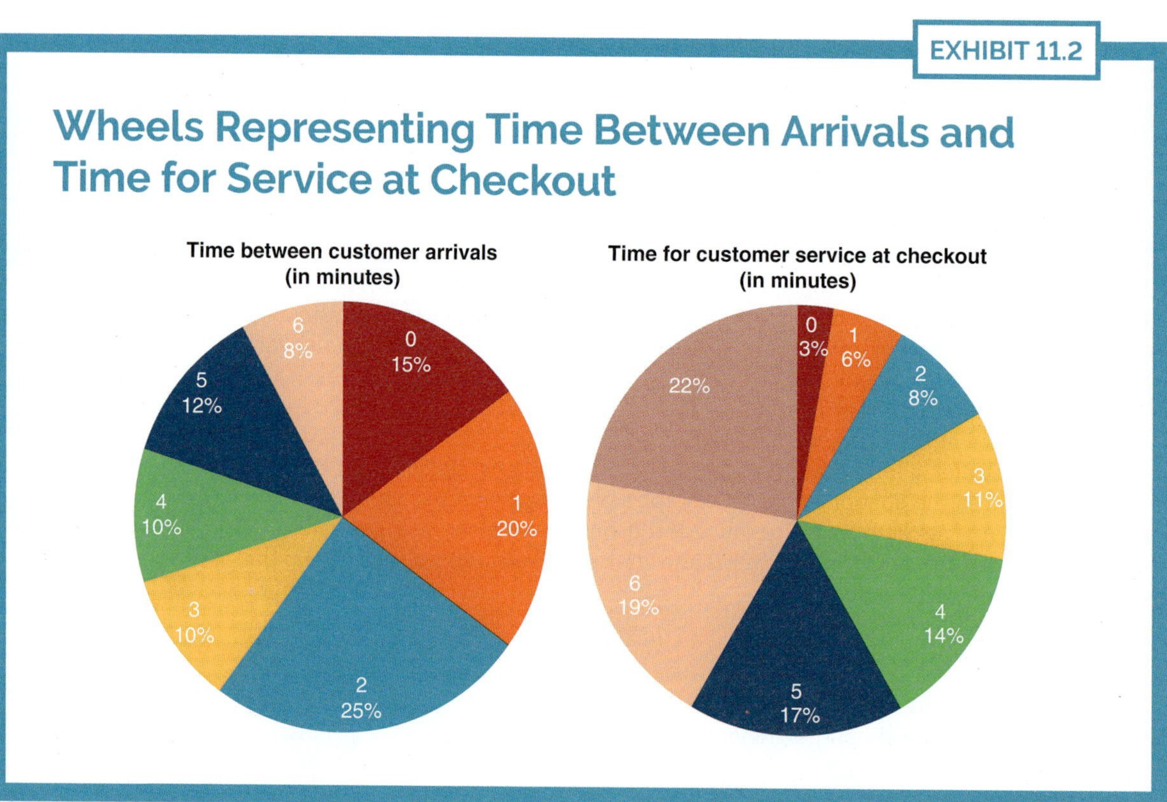

observations might reveal that customers were served with no wait 3% of the time, had a one-minute wait 6% of the time, a two-minute wait 8% of the time, a three-minute wait 11% of the time, a four-minute wait 14% of the time, a five-minute wait 17% of the time, a six-minute wait 19% of the time, and a seven-minute wait 22% of the time.

Now the manager can execute the simulation by spinning the first wheel to randomly determine the time between customer arrivals and spinning the second wheel to determine how long each guest took to be served once in a checkout line. By recording the numbers on a simple chart that notes the time between arrivals, times for service and, finally, the time customers were waiting, the entire day's activities can be simulated to determine the maximum, minimum, and average length of time customers waited for service plus the total waiting time for all the customers. The chart would simulate a day's activities by beginning when the shop opens and recording the arrivals throughout the day until it closes. Running this simulation many times (typically more than 1,000 on a computerized model) would allow Rudolph's manager and planning staff to draw some statistical conclusions about the length of waiting time, checkout capacity utilization, and the impact on waiting (and guest perception of the quality and value of the experience) that opening up more checkout stands and adding more capacity would have.

Although this is a fairly simple illustration and, in all likelihood, the entire simulation would be conducted on a computer, it does show the usefulness of mathematically determining the relationship between the service provider's capacity and the average waiting time for guests in a way that allows the hospitality organization to find the ideal balance between the two. This same technique can be used to determine the ideal number of monorails in a theme park, toll booths on a turnpike, front desk people in a hotel, servers and cooks in a restaurant, spaces in a parking lot, ski lifts on a ski slope, taxis waiting at the airport, or any other application where an organization needs to balance the costs of providing capacity with the quality of the service experience.

Certain basic forces affect waiting lines, and they can be expressed mathematically. An explanation of the mathematics of waiting lines appears in the chapter appendix.

Balancing Capacity and Demand

Determining the proper balance between supply and demand requires more calculations than just the basics. The gift shop planners in the earlier example should gather more data about customer behaviors and expectations. If, for example, they find in interviewing or by simply observing customers that when the wait is longer than five minutes they will put down their selections and leave the shop without buying anything, then a wait longer than five minutes is unacceptable no matter what the remaining data might reveal. On the other hand, if the surveyed customers reveal that the uniqueness of the shop or the nature of the clientele makes waiting time an insignificant issue, then planners might recommend letting the lines grow without much adjustment. The essential feature of the calculation is to determine that point beyond which the length of the wait damages the quality of the guest experience beyond the level acceptable to the guest and the organization.

Once the capacity-and-demand balance decision has been made, planners must determine how to accommodate the inevitable lines created by uneven demand patterns. Here the challenge is to plan and manage the wait in such a way that the guest is satisfied with it. Two major dimensions are involved. The first is the way the time spent waiting *feels* to the guest, and the second dimension is how to minimize the negative effects of the wait by managing the *value* of the experience to the guest. The organization wants each guest to conclude that the experience was well worth the wait.

Robert C. Ford

Occupied waits feel shorter than unoccupied waits. At Legoland in Orlando Florida, children can play with legos in the hotel lobby while their parents wait to check into the hotel.

MANAGING THE PERCEPTION OF THE WAIT

Understanding what makes time fly while guests wait in line is a fundamental concern for planners seeking to improve the quality of the wait. Guestologists have found that time flies not only when they're having fun but also under other circumstances. Hospitality planners must remember that everyone is different, and these differences will influence how people feel about waiting in line. How customers feel about the wait is at least as important as how long the wait is.

1. ***Occupied Time Feels Shorter Than Unoccupied Time.*** If you are busy doing something while you are waiting, the time seems to go by faster. Most line waits can be made more enjoyable and made to feel less lengthy if guests can be distracted or diverted in some way.

   Disney planners are the masters of managing time waits by giving their guests something to divert them from thinking about the wait. If the line for a particular Walt Disney World Resort attraction has become extraordinarily long and a service failure is imminent, a strolling band or acrobats or some other distraction arrives to entertain and occupy the guests while they wait. For long lines, Universal Orlando Resort spaces television sets throughout the time which show a video or movie. People can watch an interesting program while moving toward the entrance to the attraction.

2. ***Time Spent Waiting to Begin the Service Experience Feels Longer Than Time Actually Spent in the Experience Itself.*** Hospitality planners, therefore, try to find ways to minimize how long the wait "feels." Theme parks and other entertainment attractions may offer pre-attraction features, termed the *preshow*. Preshows make guests feel that they are already in the attraction, though they are mainly still standing in line. For example, people standing in line to get into Walt Disney's Enchanted Tiki Room hear a caged Audio-Animatronics bird telling bad jokes. Time seems to pass more quickly for guests when they are watching a preshow or a preview of the main attraction—almost as if the attraction itself has started.

   Some airlines send roving people down long lines waiting to check in, to begin the contact with people and make them feel that someone is finally taking care of them. Avis Rental Car quickly gathers up people at the airport terminal contact point and shuttles them to an off-site facility where the line may be quite long and the wait substantial, but customers feel that Avis is at least doing something to take care of them. This strategy has the additional benefit of getting customers away from competing rental counters. Out at the off-site facility, they will wait longer in line because they cannot simply move to the competitor at the next counter.

   Another way to make guests feel as if the experience has begun before it actually does is to use this "pre-experience" time to teach customers what they are supposed to do once they reach the actual event or attraction. The education provided during the wait can improve or enhance the service experience and actually becomes part of the experience. Many customers waiting in a fast-food line use their time to evaluate the menu items to select what they want. If they could walk right up to the counter, they would still need the time to review the menu options; they would then feel awkward about being at the front of a forming line unprepared to be served. For these customers having time to stand in a line is an advantage.

Many restaurants give patrons standing in line a menu to look over while awaiting their table. This gives customers something to do and not only speeds up the ordering process once customers are seated but also gives them the impression that the service experience has begun. Providing a complimentary beverage or snack if the wait is unusually long accomplishes the same purpose. Having a cocktail waitress serve waiting guests generally achieves the same goal and creates an additional revenue source.

3. ***Anxious Waits Feel Longer Than More Relaxed Waits.*** If people are afraid of what will happen to them once the service experience begins, the wait will seem longer. If people are sitting in an airplane that is obviously waiting for something to be fixed before it takes off, people may become quite anxious about what is wrong with the plane or what malfunction is holding it up, and the wait will feel long. If you are waiting in a hospital room, perhaps to receive the results of a diagnostic procedure, the wait will seem to drag. Sometimes, organizations want to create a little anxiety. The school principal may let the ill-behaved child waiting for punishment wait a little longer than necessary. Waiting to enter a scary ride at an amusement park can enhance the effect of the ride.

4. ***Waits of Uncertain Length Feel Longer Than Certain Ones.*** Anyone who has been at an airport waiting on a flight that is delayed for an unknown reason will know that such a wait feels endless. Waiting without knowing when the delay will be over causes any wait to feel much longer. Let your guests know what to expect. A time estimate can help the customer set a mental clock to let time pass more quickly until that preset time is reached. Telling phone callers how many callers are ahead of them in the phone queue serves the same purpose.

Norwegian Cruise Lines uses TV monitors throughout their ships to provide information on how full their various restaurants are. These "Restaurant Seating Guides" let guests know in real time how full each dining venue currently is, so they can decide which restaurant to go to with full knowledge of how long the wait, if any, will be.

Matthew Staver/Bloomberg via Getty Images

Uncertain, anxious, uncomfortable, and boring waits feel longer than certain, relaxed, comfortable, and entertaining waits.

Disney uses sign boards to tell guests how long before they will enter the attraction from that point in line. Generally, they overestimate the time because guests are always happy when they get to the ride faster than they thought they would but are never happy when they get there later. This is one reason patients want doctors to be on time for scheduled appointments. Once the appointment time is reached, in the patient's mind it is time to be served, and any time spent after that is uncertain and long.

5. ***Unexplained Waits Feel Longer Than Explained Waits.*** When you don't know what is holding up the line or causing the delay, the wait will feel longer than if you know the reason. If traffic stops and your view ahead is blocked so you can't see why, the wait will feel longer. If service is delayed, customers want to know why. Effective managers of waits will tell them or provide a visual cue that can explain the wait.

   For example, a line at a restaurant can be structured so customers can see that all the tables are full, or at a bank so one can see that all the tellers are busy. On the other hand, effective managers of queues will ensure that front desk attendants or airline check-in staff doing something other than attending to waiting customers are kept out of sight of customers, so they do not have to explain why their personnel are not serving customers. Restaurant managers try to keep empty tables out of sight; otherwise people queued up for a meal will think their wait does not have a legitimate explanation, and it will feel long. Restaurant guests do not buy the explanation, "That section is closed."

   One author describes an airline experience that is familiar to many travelers.[10] He boarded a plane in San Francisco heading for Chicago. A broken toilet delayed the departure. The pilot and crew made an announcement about the problem and said that the flight would leave as soon as it was fixed. The pilot and crew gave frequent updates to the passengers and told them that the pilot was seeking permission to leave without one toilet operating. Every twenty minutes the author-passenger received a text message on his cell phone updating the departure time. After an hour of unsuccessful effort to repair the toilet, the pilot announced that he had decided the plane would not fly with only one toilet working. Instead, he told the passengers that they would have to disembark and leave later on another plane. Despite the uncertainty and annoyance over the broken fixture, the passengers were calm and understanding. The writer's seatmate said he found it reassuring that the captain himself had made the final announcement and explained his reasoning.

   If this was the end of this story, it would be an excellent illustration of the value of explaining waits to customers, but the author went on to describe the chaos, anger, and frustration that occurred to these same passengers once they were back inside the terminal where no one would tell them anything and no one seemed to know what to do next. The contrast between the attitudes and reactions of guests who know why the wait is occurring and those who are uninformed is striking and serves as an important lesson to practitioners of guestology: Keep your guests informed as to why a wait is happening and what this means to them.

6. ***Unfair Waits Feel Longer Than Fair Ones.*** If customers feel that the queue discipline is consistently followed and fairly used, then the wait seems shorter than it does when people are allowed to get away with cutting in line, or people are served out of the apparent sequence of service order, violating the perceived queue discipline. Good organizations recognize this truth and manage their lines with this knowledge in mind. At times, VIP guests or some other special category of guest requires that the line discipline be broken. Airlines usually have a separate line for customers paying for first-class tickets. Passengers flying coach usually don't object to that special treatment since they know that the first-class passengers are paying for it. For VIPs, sometimes the layout of waiting lines into twisting maze patterns enables VIPs to be integrated into the line flow so smoothly that those waiting do not usually notice that the discipline has been interrupted. But if they do notice, the airline personnel had better be prepared to hear about it.

[10] Donald A. Norman, "Designing Waits that Work," *MIT Sloan Management Review* 50, no. 4 (2009): 23.

When an organization needs to break the queue discipline, it must find some way to communicate a reason for the apparent unfairness that customers will accept after hearing it. Time-honored reasons are "Lady with a baby!" and "Women and children first!" Passengers needing assistance go onto planes first, and nobody minds. No one complains if a disabled person goes to the front of the line. Seating a party of four at a restaurant before seating waiting parties of six or more seldom creates guest complaints or problems for the restaurant; everyone knows that almost all tables are set up for smaller parties and that some juggling must be done to accommodate the larger group.

7. ***Solo Waits Feel Longer Than Group Waits.*** Waiting by yourself feels longer than waiting in a group of friends, or even in a group you don't know. Planners recognizing this perceptual issue try to organize their lines in such a way that people are grouped with other people. Under this logic, a double line would feel shorter than a single line, and a line structure that encourages people to interact so they feel like members of a group feels shorter than one in which the people are allowed to stay inside their own personal and highly individual spaces. Planners can arrange the seating in waiting room areas so as to promote interaction and a sense of being part of a group.
8. ***Uncomfortable Waits Feel Longer Than Comfortable Ones.*** All hospitality organizations dread seeing guests queued up in the hot sun, rain, or other uncomfortable conditions. Finding a way to keep people comfortable in outdoor queues while they wait to enter an air-conditioned environment is a real managerial challenge. Obviously, such devices as paddle fans, awnings, or artificially created shade can be useful for making the wait feel more comfortable and less lengthy.
9. ***Interesting Waits Feel Shorter Than Uninteresting Ones.*** We have already said that occupied waits are shorter than unoccupied waits. This principle is true even if the activity in which one is occupied is only "busy work." But if you are occupied in doing something interesting while you wait, the time will seem even shorter. Bank of America found that when they provided television monitors in the bank lobby, customer perceptions of wait times decreased significantly.[11] Restaurants frequently have a bar with entertainment so that guests waiting for a table can have a drink and listen to some music. The time seems to pass more quickly that way.
10. ***Happy Waits Feel Shorter Than Sad Ones.*** While this goes without saying in most situations, it is part of the perception of the waiting experience. Customers who are having fun, enjoying themselves, and feeling positive about the wait itself and the service experience to come will find the wait to be shorter than those who are unhappy, sullen, or feeling negative about waiting. Planners need to think of ways to keep happy customers happy and make unhappy customers feel better about waiting. Using clowns or people dressed in character costumes are ways to turn unhappy children into happy ones. Professional comics warm up their audiences; the comics get them laughing during the wait, to make sure that when the television cameras come on, the guests are ready to have fun and laugh.

The Emotional Wait State

In all these waiting situations and especially the last one, the customer's emotional state will significantly impact the wait for service. Different people react differently to anxiety, uncertainty, discomfort, and other perceptual influences on the waiting

[11] T. Stefan, "R&D Comes to Services: Bank of America's Pathbreaking Experiments," *Harvard Business Review* 81, no. 4 (2003).

time. Planners should keep these different reactions in mind as they structure organizational queues.

Crowds and Clientele

If the waiting line to be managed is large and diverse, then the "typical customer" drives the design of the line and the associated wait. While planners should consider individual differences as much as possible in designing and managing waits, the line for large crowds must be designed to accommodate what the average guest expects when entering the wait process.

If the people in line are a more select clientele with identifiable features, such as a queue at an upscale restaurant or hotel, then variability in treatment of the waiting guests may be possible and even necessary to ensure that the quality of the entire experience, including the wait, meets the guest expectations for that upscale level of service. You want to make the wait enjoyable or at least less irritating, and that is harder to do with a mass-market audience than with a select, known clientele, for reasons other than the size of the crowd.

Waits in Contrast

In all these waiting situations, the contrast effect will also influence the perception of the wait. If a customer has just had a comfortable, totally explained, predictable wait, followed by a subsequent wait that is unpredictable, anxiety producing, and of uncertain length, the second wait will seem longer than if a well-managed wait had not just occurred. Similarly, if a customer has just had a long wait, a short one will feel even shorter in contrast. If the guest has just been waiting where employees were friendly and all servers were busy, that wait will seem shorter than a wait in which employees pay minimal attention to guests and some are engaged in activities other than serving people in line.

The key for planners is to remember that the customer, client, or guest perceives the wait. If the objective data say the average wait at your place should be acceptable to customers or the wait at your company is actually shorter than it is at a competitor's, that doesn't matter to customers who think they have waited too long for your service. Customers have mental clocks in their minds that tell them when the wait is too long or just right and extremely well managed. Managing the perception is as effective a technique as managing the actual waiting time, and if the organization is particularly good at managing perceptions, it can make even very long waits acceptable and tolerable to customers.

SERVICE VALUE AND THE WAIT

The more value the customer receives or expects to receive from the service, the more patiently the customer will wait. Since the customer defines the value of services rendered, the second major strategy for managing the perception of the wait is to manage the perceived value of the service for which the customer is waiting. This strategy can be implemented before, during, or even after the service is delivered.

Before Service

Before receiving the service, waiting customers can be provided with information (or even with some other service) that will enhance the value of the service that motivated them to enter the queue in the first place. A hotel, for example, can enhance the perceived value of the guest experience by offering guests waiting in line some sparkling water or champagne, or they may be entertained by a chamber-music group. Such thoughtful touches not only distract and occupy the guest, they also add value to the experiences that the hotel and restaurant are selling (and for which the guest must wait in line).

ANDY BUCHANAN/AFP/Getty Images

A tight-rope walker entertains the crowd as they wait in line to enter the Glastonbury Festival of Music and Performing Arts.

During Service

During the performance of the service itself, its value (to the customer and as defined by the customer) can be enhanced over the customer's expectations by many strategies. The organization will want to employ these strategies in any event, but the idea here is that if the service meets or exceeds expectations when the customer gets it, the wait was worth it.

In addition to providing customers with a service that is beyond their expectations in the first place, some more subtle actions can enhance the value of the service experience or increase the perceived cost of abandoning the wait. Some restaurants believe in hanging signed photographs of celebrities who have eaten in the restaurant; doctors display diplomas from their medical schools to indicate the high quality of their training. These touches tend to encourage the guest or patient to think that the meal or the medical treatment is worth the wait. As a more direct response to the wait, the server could apologize for it and offer a free desert, which adds a personal touch that may increase the value of the experience for the guest. These are all examples of how the value of the service to the customer can be enhanced even as it is being delivered. These enhancements all make the wait seem shorter in retrospect; an excellent service experience diminishes the ill effects of the wait.

After Service

After the service, the value of the experience in the eyes of customers can sometimes be enhanced, so they feel better about having taken the time to wait on the service in the first place. Although advertising is generally used to attract the attention of potential customers, people who have already purchased services are even more attentive to ads than those who have not. The ads reinforce the wisdom of purchasing the service as well as waiting in line to do so. Of course, ads seen ahead of time can also reduce the effects of the wait while it is in progress; the ads have convinced customers that the experience will be good, so they wait more patiently. A phone call to a customer after the service experience, asking for feedback on it, can enhance the value of the experience and reduce the negative effects of the wait. Once Honda dealers started calling up customers after they left the dealership to ask about the quality of the service experiences, to remain competitive, other dealers had to make the calls, too. This type of personal attention after the experience can help compensate for the wait before the experience.

Managing Waits in an Imperfect World

Planning and managing the waiting line are fundamental challenges for managers in the hospitality industry. The service cannot be stockpiled or inventoried, and planners must find the right balance between having enough capacity to fill demand and having so much capacity that some sits idle most of the time. In a perfect world, the flow of customers matches the supply exactly. When one guest leaves the restaurant, another walks in for lunch. When one guest finishes with the concierge, another arrives to ask a question, and so on across the entire range of services offered by organizations. In our less-than-perfect world, getting customers into the service setting and meeting their time expectations require effective queue planning and management. The critical point is to make it visibly clear to guests by everything that everyone in the organization does and says that they respect their customers' time, appreciate their tolerance of any waits, and are doing everything they can to make waits fair, fast, comfortable, and as enjoyable as possible.

LESSONS LEARNED

LO 11.1 Explain why it is critical to make any wait for service as short and pleasant as possible.

- Find out how much a dissatisfied guest costs you; that will motivate you to manage the wait for your guests more carefully.
- Try to minimize the negative effects of the wait before, during, and after the guest experience.

LO 11.2 Discuss how to plan for capacity shortages.

- Know how long or whether your guests are willing to wait.
- Make design-day decisions that best balance the costs of providing capacity with the costs of guest dissatisfaction from waits.

LO 11.3 Demonstrate how to use queuing theory to plan the wait.

- Design queues to best meet guest expectations.
- Know the arrival rates, queue discipline, and service rates for each wait and use the knowledge to calculate the length of each.
- Use waiting-line models to understand how your queues work.

LO 11.4 Describe how to create virtual waits.

- Use virtual waits whenever possible.

LO 11.5 Describe how organizations can manage a guest's perception of the wait.

- Know the psychology of managing waiting lines.
- How long a wait feel depends on what the guest is doing, feeling, or experiencing during the wait.
- Communicating information to the guest can affect how long the wait feels.

LO 11.6 Explain how to offset the wait's negative effects by managing the value of the experience provided to the guest.

- Plan for and manage the guest waits across their entire experience; don't just let them happen.

KEY TERMS AND CONCEPTS

arrival patterns 362
capacity day 364
managing the wait 359
multichannel, multiphase queue 368
multichannel, single-phase queue 368
queue discipline 366
queuing theory 365
queues 359
single-channel, multiphase queue 368
single-channel, single-phase queue 366
virtual queue 369
waiting-line theory 365

REVIEW QUESTIONS

1. "Just about every full-fledged guest experience has at least one wait somewhere within it." True or false?

   A. If false, name some guest experiences that do not involve a wait.

   B. Indicate some common front-of-the-house waits (as opposed to out-of-sight waits such as queued-up food orders) during a typical guest's experience at a casual restaurant such as Chili's or Olive Garden. Which ones should be managed, and which ones can be left alone to take care of themselves?

   C. Indicate some common back-of-the-house waits, unseen by the guest, during a typical guest's experience at such a casual restaurant. Which ones should be managed, and which ones can be left alone to take care of themselves?

2. Think of a pleasant or an enjoyable wait you have experienced within a hospitality setting. Think of an unpleasant or annoying wait.

   A. What strategies described in this chapter did the organization's managers use or fail to use that caused your wait to be one kind or the other?

   B. Did the managers employ any strategies not covered in the chapter?

3. What strategies are available to match the capacity of a hospitality organization with the demand for its services? Which strategies work best and under what circumstances?

4. This chapter explained how a theme park might use the design-day concept.

   A. How might the concept be used by a hotel, a restaurant, and an airline?

   B. Is the concept as applicable to those other organizations as to a theme park?

   C. If so, what are the common elements that facilitate applicability? If not, why is that?

5. Give some examples from your own experience of the different queue types shown in Exhibit 11.1. Did the queue type used seem to fit the situation? Was it readily apparent why the organization chose it? If you have to wait, which line type do you prefer and why?

6. You are the front desk manager of a popular hotel, and you are frustrated by the number of guests you see waiting impatiently in line to check in and check out. Compare the advantages and disadvantages (and the costs and benefits, if you can) of relieving this situation by considering the following alternatives.

   A. Set up and use simulation wheels like those in Exhibit 11.2.

   B. Use some of the techniques in the chapter for managing the feel of the wait.

   C. Cross-train some employees so they can help out at the front desk during busy times.

7. Some organizations, restaurants in particular, seem to take more interest in managing the wait in positive ways than others. How does an organization decide how much time and effort to place into managing the initial wait for service?

8. Although some academic people make a life's work out of queuing theory, many readers enjoy reading about the "psychological" methods for managing the wait more than they do studying "theory." Which is more important to manage the guest experience in hospitality organizations: the hard numbers of queuing theory or the softer psychological approach?

9. You may have heard someone say, or may have said yourself, "Whichever line I am in, the others always move faster." Can this be true?

ACTIVITIES

1. Find a situation in which a hospitality organization has found a way to control or shift guest demand. Why does the organization employ this strategy? How effective is the strategy? What incentives are offered to guests to encourage them to seek the hospitality service at one time rather than another? How profitable do you think the strategy might be?

2. Study the waiting-line situations (movies, athletic events, fast-food outlets, etc.) in which you find yourself over a period of time. Evaluate how well the lines are being managed. Which line-management strategies described in this chapter might have been used to improve these situations?

ETHICS IN BUSINESS

Generally, people feel that "first come, first served" is fair and that people should not violate the order in a queue. But sometimes exceptions are made. When is it appropriate to make these exceptions? Imagine that you are managing a fine-dining restaurant, several patrons are waiting for tables, and you estimate roughly a forty-five-minute wait. When do you think is it appropriate to allow a newly arriving patron to bypass the line and be seated immediately?

- A Supreme Court justice shows up, and her security detail says that for security reasons, she cannot wait in the lobby, so she must either be seated immediately or will have to leave.
- A famous movie star arrives wanting a table.
- The owner of the company that supplies your alcohol arrives wanting a table.
- Your mother surprises you and comes by wanting a table.
- Your first-grade teacher is in line.
- You recognize one of the authors of this book in line waiting for a table.
- Someone shows up, at the right time, with a reservation.
- Someone shows up fifteen minutes late for a reservation.
- Someone shows up thirty minutes late for a reservation.
- Someone shows up one hour late for a reservation.

What factors do you consider when making the decision to move someone to the head of the line? Why are some decisions "fair" and others "unfair"? Does a decision have to be fair for you to make the exception?

CASE STUDY

Case 1: The Front Desk

Jane Gianini, manager at the Thusly Manor, an upscale inn and golfing resort in the North Carolina Mountains, was becoming increasingly concerned about the situation at the front desk. On several occasions during the past week, she walked by the desk and saw a line of waiting guests. Several other times she walked by and saw no guests at all.

The dramatic rise in personal income and tourism during the first part of the new millennium had caused a boom in the number of guests wanting to combine a stay in a fine hotel with some golfing on a beautiful hilly course. But success also brought problems for Thusly Manor, how to handle the increased numbers at the front desk among them. Gianini thought she had controlled the situation by implementing a new staffing procedure.

If her calculations were correct, the new procedure should have just about eliminated both the waiting lines and the front desk server down time. Nevertheless, she had seen guests lined up several times, and idle desk agents quite frequently.

When she first analyzed the data, she computed simple averages. To construct her present staffing schedule, she had found out how many guests arrived during each eight-hour shift on average and had divided that number by eight, to arrive at guest load per hour during a shift. She then staffed the front desk accordingly. She pulled the following data for the 8 A.M. to 4 P.M. shift from her files to check on whether she had analyzed it correctly when she had set up her present system.

Type of Service and Percent of Service Time Used

SERVICE TYPE	AVERAGE SERVICE TIME	
I. Check-in/check-out	10 minutes	70%
II. Informational/misc. requests	5 minutes	30%

Frequency of Guest Arrivals at Front Desk

AVERAGE TIME BETWEEN ARRIVALS	
0 minutes	30%
5 minutes	40%
10 minutes	20%
20 minutes	10%

1. What was wrong with Gianini's original analysis?
2. How should she have analyzed this problem?

Case 2: Waiting for Gaudeaux

Grand Gaudeaux Cruise Lines specialized in taking passengers on luxury cruises to the Gaudeaux island chain in the Caribbean. Because of its financial success and good reputation in the industry, Grand Gaudeaux had recently been able to expand its passenger capacity by adding two brand-new, large ships to its fleet. The guest-satisfaction measurement team was meeting this morning with Steve Weitzman, CEO of Grand Gaudeaux, to discuss some surprisingly low guest-satisfaction ratings received from passengers on these two state-of-the-art ships. The company practice was to mail departing guests a survey about a week after their cruise, asking them a variety of questions. The recent data were troubling. Grand Gaudeaux had hoped to delight its guests by providing these new ships; instead, guests were reporting dissatisfaction.

The topic today was the dramatic downturn in the satisfaction scores. Knowing that this meeting was coming up and realizing the CEO's depth of concern, the measurement team had done some further investigation into guest opinions through a variety of means. The most interesting insight was gained from a series of focus groups in which guests from the newer, larger ships had indicated their frustration with the departure routine. It appeared that the larger the ship, the more difficult it was to get everyone ashore after the cruise ended. This long wait tended to give "cruisers" on the two newest ships an unsatisfactory last experience with Grand Gaudeaux Cruise Lines. Because of the "recency effect"—the psychological theory that the most recent events are best remembered and have greatest impact—the passenger problems in departing the ship were overshadowing the many excellent aspects of the cruise experience.

The team recognized some system solutions; for example, the port facility could be retrofitted with larger capacity to accommodate more departing passengers. Such a retrofit would involve significant expenditures. But even if the budget were available to make such improvements over the long run, the guest-satisfaction measurement team realized the acute need to improve the management of the passenger wait experience in the short run. The team knew of Weitzman's personal pride in and high hopes for the new ships. They knew he would want some answers as to what might be done to fix this source of guest dissatisfaction.

If you were on the guest-satisfaction measurement team, what steps would you recommend to Weitzman?

APPENDIX

The Mathematics of Waiting Lines

The mathematics are quite simple for a single-channel, single-phase line. An understanding of a few calculations will reveal much about the dynamics of waiting lines.

In the following example, we will use a single-channel line for a hotel's front desk, with one server/agent at the desk. We will calculate the average amount of time that a guest stands in line and stands in the system (time in line plus time being served). In addition, we will determine the idle time of the front desk staff. These figures would be useful to a hotel manager wishing to control the waiting time for guests and to reduce the idle time for service personnel.[12]

These calculations for a single-channel, single-phase line, to illustrate the underlying principles of waiting-line management, can be done manually. However, more complicated line systems requiring more complex formulae should be (and can easily be) analyzed by computer. A standard spreadsheet product such as Excel can be used to perform such waiting-line analysis.

The Single-Channel, Single-Phase Case

The Chelten Hotel has a simple front desk with one service station. Ben Blake, the front office manager, has been observing the line at the front desk for several weeks. Not wanting guests to wait in line too long, he wishes to calculate the average wait in line for his guests over a one-hour period. He also wants to know how much idle time his servers will have during that hour. Mr. Blake would like them to perform some routine tasks such as sort the mail and enter charges to guest accounts during their idle time.

Blake has compiled the following information for this one-hour period. For this example, we ignore variability and use averages to describe both arrival and service rates for the hotel guests:

The average time it takes to register a guest is four minutes; the hotel can register about fifteen guests per hour. This is the service rate, the units of server capacity per time period.

Ten guests are expected to arrive during the hour. This is the arrival rate.

The formulas use the following symbols:

$$A = \text{arrival rate per hour (10)}$$
$$r = \text{service rate per hour (15)}$$

1. Average time a guest waits in line:

$$W_q = A/r(A-r) \quad W_q = 10/15(15-10) \quad W_q = 0.133 \text{ hours or 8 minutes}$$

W_q means waiting time in the queue before being served. This calculation tells manager Blake that the average wait in the line for a guest is eight minutes. If that wait time is unacceptable to Blake, he may have to add another server.

2. Average time spent in system:

$$T_S = 1/(r-A) \quad T_S = 1/(15-10) \quad T_S = 0.2 \text{ hours or 12 minutes}$$

T_S means the average time a guest waits in the system. This equation tells manager Blake that the average guest spends twelve minutes in the system, including both waiting time and service time.

3. Average number of guests in line:

$$L_q = A^2/r(r-A) \quad L_q = 10^2/15(15-10) \quad L_q = 1.33 \text{ guests}$$

L_q means the average length of the queue, in number of guests. Knowing that only 1.33 guests are in line at any one time, on average, reveals to Blake that the line's space requirements are minimal.

---

[12]Although the following assumptions underlie these formulas, it is not necessary to understand them to follow the discussion: (1) Queue discipline is first-in, first-out; (2) No balking or reneging. Customers must accept service when it is offered, and no one quits or leaves the line; (3) Arrivals are accurately represented by a Poisson statistical distribution; (4) Service times must follow a negative exponential Poisson distribution; (5) Arrivals are independent; (6) Arrival rate does not change over time.

4. Percent of time the server is busy:

$$p = A/r \quad p = 10/15 \quad p = 67\%$$

p means the percentage of time the server is busy. The front desk registration procedure has one or more guests in it—either in line or being served—67% of the time, or about forty minutes out of every hour.

5. Probability that there is no one in the system:

$$P_0 = 1-(A/r) \quad P_0 = 1-(10/15) \quad P_0 = 33\%$$

P_0 means the probability that no one is in the system. This is obviously the inverse of the previous formula. If the wait-plus-registration system has someone in it about forty minutes out of each hour, it is empty for the other twenty minutes. Blake can use this information to assign other tasks to idle servers. Now that Blake has run his calculations, the registration agents can probably look forward to an expanded job description.

Further readings on the topics in this chapter are listed in "Additional Readings" on pages 518–519.

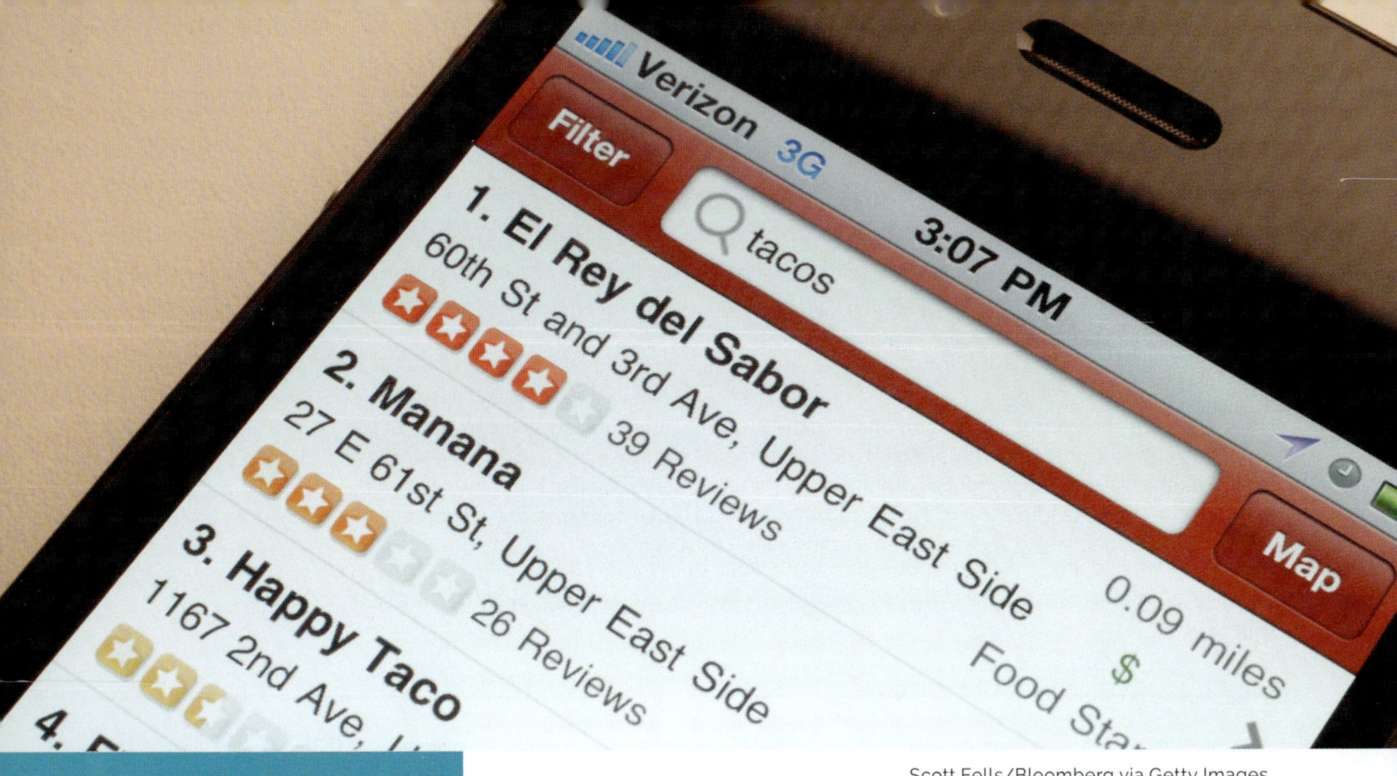

Scott Eells/Bloomberg via Getty Images

12 Measuring and Managing Service Delivery

Hospitality Principle: Pursue Perfection Relentlessly

Unless you have 100% customer satisfaction—and I mean that they are excited about what you are doing—you have to improve.

—Horst Schulze,
Former President, The Ritz-Carlton
Hotel Company, L.L.C.

Learning Objectives

After reading this chapter, you should be able to:

12.1 Measure the effectiveness of service delivery and of the overall guest experience.

12.2 Demonstrate how to use methods of measuring service effectiveness, including service standards, process strategies, managerial observation, and employee assessment.

12.3 Explain how to use service guarantees.

12.4 Demonstrate how to acquire guest opinions of service effectiveness using comment cards, surveys (mail, web, and phone), focus groups, and mystery shoppers.

12.5 Determine the costs and benefits of the different methods for acquiring guest opinions.

12.6 Discuss how to achieve continuous improvement in the experience provided to guests.

INTRODUCTION

The service has been planned and the guests have arrived. Now, you must deliver the expected service experience. You hope to provide great service, but how will you know whether you are succeeding? Accurately measuring what guests think about the quality and value of their cruise, hotel stay, restaurant meal, or any other service experience is a difficult challenge for hospitality organizations striving to achieve service excellence. Nevertheless, it must be done. All hospitality organizations face rising guest expectations and an increasing guest unwillingness to settle for less than they think they paid for. This new customer activism has made service quality more important than ever as managers strive to meet both heightened customer expectations and increasing competition.

This chapter focuses on finding out how the guest perceives the quality of the guest experience so that the hospitality manager can see, from the guest's perspective, where there are any problems. The critical challenge for hospitality managers seeking this information is to identify and implement the methods that best measure the quality of the experience from the guest's point of view *as the experience is occurring*. Measurements taken after the experience may be too late to enable recovery from failure, though they may be useful in improving the service experience for the future.

As we have stated throughout this text, each guest determines the quality and value of the service experience. Consequently, an acceptable experience for one guest might be a "wow" experience for another and totally unacceptable to a third. The subjective nature of the quality and value of a guest experience makes identifying and implementing the appropriate measurements particularly difficult.

One key to creating a flawless guest experience is that the organization must know what errors are being made or what failures are occurring. If you don't know it's broken, you can't fix it. Consequently, monitoring and measuring the quality of the guest experience with an eye out for flaws or failures is a crucial part of the hospitality organization's responsibility. Satisfied guests come back, and dissatisfied guests go elsewhere.

The best time to find out about possible service failures is before the guest ever arrives. The best mistake is one that never happens because the organization planned thoroughly to ensure that each part of the experience is flawless. But no matter how well the management planned the meal, scheduled the convention, or designed the hotel lobby, mistakes will happen. The organization wants to have measures in place to identify the mistakes as soon as possible—certainly before the guest leaves the service setting, while the information is still fresh in the guest's mind. Finding out about failure on the spot gives the organization the opportunity to recover. The worst time to learn of a service failure is after the guest has departed because the opportunity to fix it is substantially decreased once the guest has left the premises.

As we have discussed in prior chapters on planning the service experience with blueprinting, fishbone analysis, waiting-line simulations and other techniques, the most effective tool for ensuring quality is through planning to ensure that anything that might go wrong is anticipated and fail-safed to the extent humanly possible. In this chapter we look at techniques for assessing and monitoring how successful this planning has been. Since achieving perfection in hospitality experiences is impossible no matter how thoroughly you plan, we will discuss the art and science of finding and fixing service failures in Chapter 13.

TECHNIQUES AND METHODS FOR ASSESSING SERVICE QUALITY

Because service quality is so important to ensure the guest gets the hospitality experience expected, scholars have spent much time and energy devising ways to measure it. We divide those into (1) measures that can be made while the experience is occurring and (2) those that can be made after the experience took place. The point is that regardless of the timing, hospitality organizations must find ways to measure the quality of the experience because what isn't measured is generally unmanaged.

Process Strategies

process strategies Means of comparing what is happening in the service experience against what is supposed to happen, usually but not always expressed as a measurable service standard.

Process strategies include various ways in which organizations can avoid failing their guests by monitoring the delivery while it is taking place, while it is in process. A process strategy is a means of comparing what is happening against what is supposed to happen—usually, but not always, expressed as a measurable service standard. Sometimes process strategies are the experience and training that managers and employees have in delivering the high-quality service experience that organizations want their customers to have. The idea behind process strategies is to design monitoring mechanisms into the delivery system to find and fix failures before they affect the quality of the guest experience. A supervisor can monitor telephone calls, a server can check the food order against what is served, or a machine can control the frying time of French fries to get them perfect every time. The advantage of process strategies is that they can catch errors before or as they occur, enabling prevention or immediate correction before the errors impact guest satisfaction beyond repair. Of course, organizations need to devote the resources to create and maintain the error-prevention system, and that has costs.

Hard Rock Cafe, for example, hires an additional person to stand at the end of the food preparation line to match the order against the food on the plate to be served, in order to catch discrepancies before the guest ever sees the order. Even though the traditional job description for wait staff includes this checking responsibility, the additional person reduces the possibility of error even further. Carraba's believes this quality control process is so important that the front-of-house manager performs it. The Opryland Hotel in Nashville cross-trains some of its employees in front-desk service so they can be called upon in peak demand times when the front desk is extra busy. If line lengths threaten to exceed the service standard, this "swat team" staffs extra positions at the front desk to reduce the wait for the incoming or departing guests.

Service standards that can be applied while the service is in process provide employees with objective measures against which to monitor their own job performance while they are doing it. Specifying the maximum number of times the phone can ring before it is picked up is an example. Some hospitality organizations have created a group of stand-by employees who can answer calls when their volume exceeds their regular employees' ability to meet the answering standard. Other process-related measurements that allow the organization to minimize errors or catch them while the guest experience is underway include the number of times a server should revisit a table during the meal, or the number of people who stand in line before the manager adds extra personnel to the check-in. The point is simple—if service excellence is measured, it can be managed and, even better, it can be self-managed by the employees delivering the service.

management by walking around (MBWA) Managers walk around observing the operation firsthand, looking for problems or inefficiencies, talking to guests and employees, and offering suggestions; sometimes referred to as walking the front.

Rusty Pelican Standards

Restaurants know guests value prompt service. Exhibit 12.1 shows an example of some of the service standards from the Rusty Pelican restaurant. Although the full document is nine pages long, Exhibit 12.1 shows the portion describing how the server should "approach the table and seat the guests." Because the servers themselves determined the standards, several benefits resulted. They were eager to monitor their own performance and try to meet or surpass the standards. Service quality improved; increased server productivity meant that fewer servers were needed, which increased the tip income of servers; customers (to management's surprise) were willing to pay more to receive better service, and servers identified a couple of bottlenecks—potential failure points—that interfered with prompt, reliable service. Smoothing out those points improved service quality even more.[1]

Hoberman Collection/UIG via Getty Images

The Rusty Pelican restaurant has created explicit service standards both to inform servers of the quality of service expected from them and to motivate better service as servers try to beat the standards. The exhibit on the following page shows just one of nine pages of standards for the restaurant.

Continually checking the performance of organizational members against pre-established service standards while the service experience is in process is an excellent way to ensure a successful experience. Two other in-process methods of assessing the service quality of the experience while it is happening are managerial observation, sometimes called **management by walking around (MBWA)**, and employee

[1] D. Daryl Wyckoff, "New Tools for Achieving Service Quality," *Cornell Hotel and Restaurant Administration Quarterly* 25, no. 3 (1984): 78–91.

EXHIBIT 12.1

The Service Standards at the Rusty Pelican

Approach the Table and Seat the Guests

1. Server will approach the table and greet members by name within one (1) minute.

   Immediately after the guest is seated: "Good evening Mr. or Mrs. Jones, welcome to the Rusty Pelican." Do not memorize greeting for all tables. Use creativity, vary wording to guests. Do not slouch, but stand up straight. Smile. Hold your tray at the side and not in front of you.
   If guests appear to be rushed, find out what time they must leave and make a notation on top of the check. For guests in a hurry or at lunch, you will discuss the menu and attempt to take order immediately during the greeting. Suggest faster service items.
   Suggest and sell a specific cocktail, appetizer. Use a head nod when making suggestions.

2. Suggest a cocktail to all guests at the table. "May I bring you a fresh-lime margarita with Cuervo Gold and Grand Marnier, a glass, or perhaps a bottle of Kendall Jackson Chardonnay?"

   For non-drinkers, suggest "Mocktails" (virgin drinks such as virgin strawberry margaritas). Suggest bottled water. "May I bring you some water?" If response is yes . . ."we serve Pellegrino, Evian, and Perrier. Which would you prefer?" If exotic drinks are not requested, then you may suggest juice, soft drinks, iced tea or coffee. Create a "Drink Special for a Day." Tell your guests about the ingredients. Remember to garnish all drinks as specified in the Mr. Boston liquor guide. If your guest would like a cocktail, UPSELL. If he/she orders a scotch on the rocks, ask them "Would you prefer Johnnie Walker Black or Chivas Regal?" Always give two choices.

REMEMBER: Repeat back the order as the guest orders.

3. Suggest an appetizer:

   "and how about a delicious _____ made with mouth-watering _____ and a tangy _____ sauce, or my favorite _____ to begin your dinner?"
   Encourage guests to share an appetizer!!!
   Use buzz words to entice and describe food and beverages.
   At lunch, for the benefit of the guest, the total order should be taken at this time, IF GUEST DESIRES.

Source: Courtesy of Rusty Pelican.

observation and inquiry. If managers or employees ask a guest "how is it?" or see someone unhappy, they might be able to identify and fix a service failure immediately. Some standards of performance are embodied in service guarantees offered to guests, so organizations will want to keep the terms of these guarantees in mind while providing service. After providing the service experience to the guests but before they have left the premises, the organization may want to solicit their opinions about whether their expectations have been met.

The methods designed to assess quality while service is being provided are intended to ensure the success of individual service experiences. Also important for long-run organizational success is having methods in place for collecting data directly from guests after their experience. This allows an organization to identify the areas needing improvement to satisfy regular guests and attract new ones. Among these methods are comment cards; toll-free 800 numbers; e-mail, phone apps, and web surveys using various techniques; and **guest focus groups**. Mystery shopping is an additional widely used approach for gathering data about the quality of a service experience.

guest focus group A method of assessing service quality in which, typically, six to ten guests gather with a facilitator for several hours to discuss perceived problems and make suggestions. It provides in-depth information on how guests view the service they receive.

The various methods differ in cost, accuracy, degree of guest inconvenience, and at what point in the guest experience they are used. Measuring service quality can have many organizational benefits, but as usual, the benefits must be balanced against the costs of obtaining them. The organization must balance the information needed and the research expertise required to gather and interpret the information against the available funds. As a rule, the more accurate and precise the data, the more expensive it is to acquire.

Measures of Service Quality

Managers of outstanding hospitality organizations try to develop service standards and measures for every part of the guest experience so they can monitor where they are meeting or failing to meet their own definition of quality service. These measures are critical to ensure the service is delivered to the customer as it should be. According to Phil Crosby in *Quality Is Free,*[2] the price of not conforming to a quality standard can be calculated. That price is how much it costs to fix errors and failures that result from not meeting the quality standard in the first place. Although some may think that determining the cost of not answering phone calls within three rings is impossible, quality experts such as Crosby think it can and should be done.[3]

Some standards are built directly into the design of the service system. For example, a restaurant bar is designed to contain sufficient beer capacity and wine storage space to meet forecasted demand. Some standards are for employee use in anticipating guests coming in the door. To use the restaurant again as an example, if the restaurant has reliable predictions of how many customers come in on the different days of the week, those predictions can be used as a basis or standard for the number of servers scheduled, the number of salads that should be pre-prepared, the number of tables that should be pre-set, and the amount of silverware that should be rolled into napkins. If the prediction is correct and the standards for these aspects of the service are met, any service failure caused by poor preparation should not occur. A final group of standards is used after the guests have arrived and while the service is taking place, such as maximum number of minutes before greeting and number of visits to the table during the meal. Poka-yokes such as those described in Chapter 10 can be used to prevent failures in many of these activities.

Other examples of how performance standards can prevent failures might include annual hours of training required of service personnel, number of computer terminals to be purchased to serve anticipated demand, and number of banquet tables to be set up or other facilities to be available when the organization can reasonably predict requirements before the service experience ever begins.

Exhibit 12.2 provides a summary of the methods and techniques available to hospitality organizations for monitoring and assessing the quality of the service experience while it is being delivered. They all depend on careful planning to set service standards, careful training to prepare the employees to meet those standards, and rewards for employees when the guest experience meets or exceeds the set standards.

Use Many Measures or Just One Super Measure?

Most hospitality organizations measure quality by developing and using standards in as many ways as they can. Leading Hotels of the World (LHW) is a consortium of more than 375 luxury hotels and resorts, located in over 75 countries. All of the hotels and resorts in the consortium are five-star luxury establishments, but LHW doesn't take the property's word on that. LHW uses an 800+ point quality inspection. Explains Ted Tang, President and CEO, "The detailed 800+ point system is designed to cover all phases of the guest experience, from reservation to check out, including every

[2] Philip B. Crosby, *Quality Is Free: The Art of Making Quality Certain* (New York, NY: McGraw Hill, 1980).

[3] For a taxonomy of service standards, see Knut Blind, "A Taxonomy of Standards in the Service Sector: Theoretical Discussion and Empirical Test," *The Service Industries Journal* 26, no. 4 (2006): 397–420.

EXHIBIT 12.2

Techniques for Assessing Quality During the Service Experience

TECHNIQUE	ADVANTAGES	DISADVANTAGES
Job performance standards	• Translate service standards into behaviors that can be measured • Provide objective criteria for rewarding employees for doing what the standards require • Allow easy monitoring by supervisors and self-monitoring by employees of what they should be doing	• Can't cover all aspects of every service encounter • May discourage innovative solutions to customer requests falling outside of service standards and prescribed behaviors
Managerial observation (MBWA)	• Management knows business, policies, procedures, and service standards • No technology or up-front costs required • No inconvenience to customers • Opportunity to recover from service failure • Opportunity to collect direct, specific guest feedback • Opportunity to identify service problems • Opportunity for immediate coaching or reinforcing of service-providing employees	• Management presence may influence service providers • Lacks statistical validity and reliability • Objective observation requires specialized training • Management may not know enough about situation to gather all the facts • Takes management time away from other duties
Employee observation	• Employees have first-hand knowledge of service delivery system obstacles • Customers volunteer service-quality feedback to employees • No inconvenience to customers • Opportunity to find and fix service failures immediately • Employee empowerment improves morale • Opportunity to collect detailed guest feedback • Minimal cost for data gathering and documentation	• Objective observation requires specialized training • Employees disinclined to report problems they created • Lacks statistical validity and reliability • Employee trust of management will influence what feedback is shared • Organizational system for collecting/analyzing customer feedback is required
Service guarantees	• Allow customers to see service standards and monitor them • Send employees strong message about organizational commitment to service quality • Document service failures • Enhance likelihood of guest complaining to allow fixing service failures	• Employees try to avoid mentioning them or honoring them when invoked • Typical guarantee out of touch with actual service experience, not taken seriously • Managers may hide guarantee data to avoid negative performance implications
On-site personal interviews and encounters	• Opportunity to collect detailed guest feedback • Ability to gather representative and valid sample of targeted customers • Opportunity to recover from service failure • Suggest that company is interested in customer opinions of service quality	• Require a significant investment in training and time • May not be representative sample of guests • Difficult and expensive to collect a large sample of respondents • Recollection of specific service experience details may be lost • Memory of other service experiences may bias responses • Respondents tend to give socially desirable responses • Inconvenience makes incentives for participants necessary

aspect of the hotel product from reception, to back-of-house. A recent revamping of the standards criteria has strengthened the original system while integrating new, forward-thinking categories. Serving as the benchmark for the luxury hospitality industry, the meticulous criteria by which we judge and accept our members is periodically reviewed and revised to adapt to the changing landscape and guest expectations. These quality standards are the foundation of our collection."[4]

Others argue that a "super measure" capturing the most important factor in the experience is a better managerial strategy as it focuses everyone on that one important thing. At the other extreme from LHW, Continental Airlines, now part of United Airlines, returned to profitability in the mid-1990s by using just one of the BA quality indicators—on-time performance—as a single super measure: Be On Time. For every month that the airline was in the top three of Department of Transportation monthly rankings of on-time flight arrivals, all Continental employees received a bonus. The airline extended the on-time concept throughout its system; everything—from baggage handling to aircraft cleanup—had to be on time. By 2000 Continental had become not only number one in on-time flight arrivals but was also rated number one in customer satisfaction by J.D. Power.[5] Regardless of the number of standards, the best hospitality organizations seek to measure all of the guest's key drivers.

Planning, as described in Chapter 10, establishes a range of standards before and during the entire experience. If the standards are met, the experience should happen as it is supposed to happen. Now we need techniques and methods to assess how those plans work out in practice.

Service Standards

As discussed in Chapter 10, part of the process of planning a service delivery system is to develop service standards: the organization's expectations for how the different aspects of the service experience should be delivered every time to every guest. In a lot of ways, service standards in service organizations are the equivalent to quality-control standards in manufacturing organizations, except that no QC inspector can use calipers to measure the aspects of the service experience. Instead, service organizations try to invent surrogate measurement tools, such as service standards, to measure the essentially immeasurable service experience as it is being produced. The hope is that using such standards will enable catching and fixing bad experiences in a way similar to that in which the QC inspector catches and tosses bad ball bearings.

Job Performance Standards

The organization can help to ensure success by setting specific **job performance standards**. These standards for specific jobs, derived from the service standards, provide employees with clear and specific performance expectations for each major duty associated with their jobs. When guests are seated in a restaurant, they expect someone to attend to them within a reasonable time. Emeril Lagasse, famed chef, restaurateur, and television personality, tells how he implements his service standard that waiters must take a cocktail order within fifteen seconds of the guest being seated. Salt and pepper shakers are used to signal whether the standard has been met. The shakers are usually together. The person seating the guest subtly separates them, meaning that the drink order has not yet been taken. When servers take drink orders, they subtly put the shakers back together. This simple cue lets everyone see whether

job performance standards Standards that can help ensure success by providing employees with clear and specific performance expectations for each major duty associated with their jobs.

[4] CPP-LUXURY, "Ted Teng, CEO, Leading Hotels of the World to Create a New Business Model," CPPLUXURY: Business of Luxury, posted on July 29, 2015, accessed January 21, 2018, https://cpp-luxury.com/ted-teng-ceo-leading-hotels-of-the-world-to-create-a-new-business-model/.

[5] Ivor Morgan and Jay Rao, "Aligning Service Strategy through Super-Measure Management," *The Academy of Management Executive* 16, no. 4 (2002): 121–131.

the standard has been met.[6] One additional benefit of setting and monitoring standards is that they can encourage employees who seek to meet or beat the standards to develop innovative solutions. Some servers create partnerships with other servers to cover for them when delays keep them from meeting a standard. If they are busy taking an order at a table, the partner will make the initial greeting for them to beat the standard.

On the other hand, the potential benefits of job performance standards may not be realized, and in fact may even become a disadvantage if the performance standards are not carefully set. If standards are too limiting, employees may be reluctant to deviate from them if guests make unanticipated requests. Nonetheless, the potential benefits of well-designed standards can far outweigh the disadvantages. Performance standards make supervision easier (the manager can see if the employee is performing according to standards) and also facilitate self-management by employees (employees can see in clear terms what the organization's performance expectations are).

To help assess how well job performance standards are being met, employee performance can be monitored, by managers observing performance or by using technology such as a device that monitors how many rings it takes to answer each call, or by the employees self-monitoring their performance. One of the big challenges for managers here is to ensure that their employees do not feel they will be punished for reporting failures to meet standards because of something they did. While it's easy to report a failure someone else or the delivery system made, most people find it hard to report service failures they made. Managers must make it clear to employees that doing what they can to fix service failures is their first responsibility and that not telling someone who can fix a problem they caused will get them in more trouble than reporting their mistakes.

The keys to the use of job performance standards are that (1) the standards must be clear and relevant to the service being delivered, (2) employees must know what they need to do and how they must perform to meet those standards, and (3) the standards must be related to things the employee can control. To gain their benefits, though, managers must use job performance standards effectively. They must (1) ensure they observe enough of each employee's performance so the evaluation accurately represents how people actually perform, (2) differentiate between levels of service performance (don't just say everyone is great just to avoid confrontation), and (3) give honest feedback to employees of what they are doing effectively and ineffectively. By measuring the extent to which employees meet the standards, the organization will have a good indication of how well employees are doing their jobs in providing the service. By communicating these results to employees through performance feedback, good employees can maintain high performance levels and poorer performers know what they need to improve.

Managerial Observation of the Delivery Process

The simplest and least expensive technique for assessing the degree to which guest-service quality is meeting service standards while service is being delivered involves simply encouraging managers to keep their eyes open, especially to the interactions between employees and guests. Management by walking around, sometimes called in hospitality organizations "walking the front," means that managers are observing the operation first hand, looking for problems or inefficiencies, talking to both guests and employees to assess their reactions, and then recording and relaying any information that might improve service quality. Managers know their own business, its goals, capabilities, formal and informal service standards, and the job performance standards for their employees. They know when employees are delivering a high-quality experience. At their best, these observations do not interfere with

[6] Jonathan M. Tisch and Karl Weber, *The Power of We: Succeeding Through Partnerships* (Hoboken, NY: Wiley & Sons, 2004).

service delivery or do not cause inconvenience to guests, and they often permit immediate correction of guest service problems. Further, managerial observation gives the boss the opportunity to reward the excellent employee immediately or counsel the employee who might not be delivering the service as the organization wants it delivered. It provides a modeling situation, a "teaching moment," in which a supervisor observing a service failure can show the employee how to fix the problem. When managers walk the front to serve as coaches and not as spies, their presence favorably influences employee attitudes and performance, as well as guest satisfaction.

There are, of course, drawbacks to this approach. Some managers may not have enough experience or training to fully understand what they are observing, or they may have biases which influence their objectivity. More importantly, when employees know that managers are observing the service delivery process, they invariably perform it differently. Additionally, although managerial observation may ensure the quality of the experience for a particular guest, managers can't watch every guest-employee interaction. The unobserved guest's reactions to unobserved experiences remain unknown to the manager.

Of course, hiring and developing good managers can mitigate some of these drawbacks. Training them in methods of observing guest–server interactions and measuring servers' performance against quality standards can reduce both ignorance and personal bias. Unobtrusive observational techniques, random observations, and video cameras diminish employee awareness that the boss is watching. For example, many organizations tell their telephone operators and guests that all phone conversations may be "monitored for training purposes" to eliminate the observation bias by making it uncertain as to when management is actually listening in. The operators know that someone may always be listening, so they do the job by the book. Some larger companies use managers from one location to observe employees at another location as mystery shoppers for the same reason.

Employee Assessment of Guest Experiences

While valuable information can be obtained from managerial observation, employees themselves should be even more aware of how well they are delivering service. Just as managers can observe by walking around, service-providing employees can constantly monitor the guest experience and compare it against either formal standards set by management or informal standards set by their experience, training, and the organization's culture. The process of continuously comparing what they see against what they know they should be seeing enables them to find and fix guest problems, to improve the service as they are delivering it, and to report any findings or observations that might enable improvement of the delivery process.

Line employees are often the best people to find and fix service problems and innovatively adapt the service experience to meet each guest's expectations. They can also provide excellent feedback about the quality of guest experiences that supplements and adds detail to managerial observation and survey data. Line employees can provide input on issues such as cumbersome company policies and control procedures, managerial reporting structures, or other processes that inhibit effective service delivery. Because these employees are watching, talking, and listening to guests, they know firsthand about organizational impediments that prevent them from delivering a memorable service experience. As an added bonus, employees are often able to learn about new industry trends and service innovations when guests talk with them about how their expectations for service quality and value have been changed by their experiences with competing organizations. The challenge as noted earlier is to make sure that all employees feel safe in reporting all the errors including those they have made. This is a delicate managerial task to build the level of trust that encourages employees to report their own failures. They have to believe from managers' words and deeds that it is better to tell about their failures than to cover them up.

Employee work teams and quality service circles are another source of feedback. The Ritz-Carlton Hotels uses work teams to gather feedback to develop "zero-defect" guest service strategies. Such techniques foster an understanding and appreciation of how each employee can directly influence service quality. Employee awareness of management's strong commitment to service quality is affirmed through work teams. They show not only management trust in employee judgment to correct service problems but also that management is willing to put its money where its mission is by paying for work time lost to team participation and employee training. The entire process of the employee empowerment movement discussed in Chapter 7 depends on such trust.

The Service Guarantee

service guarantee
An organization's written promise either to satisfy guests or to compensate them for any failure to satisfy them regarding the overall service or particular aspects of it.

To make their service standards clear to customers, companies can offer service guarantees, which may be expressed in simple statements such as "Satisfaction guaranteed or your money back; no questions asked" or in complex documents resembling contracts. A **service guarantee** is a publicly expressed, usually written promise either to satisfy guests or to compensate them for any failure in part or all of the service.[7] If both guests and employees know the service standards expressed in the guarantee, both parties can measure quality levels against them as service is being delivered.

Service guarantees are often considered only a marketing tool, to persuade potential guests unsure about an organization's quality to give it a try. They have the potential, however, to do much more for management. That is, they provide a means to encourage guests to tell the organization what they think of its service quality while sending a strong message to employees about the organization's commitment to provide an experience so good that it can be guaranteed. The guarantee gives guests a strong incentive to tell the organization when a service experience is not meeting their expectations, and it gives the organization a strong incentive to fix whatever problems there may be with its service, staff, or delivery systems, so future guests don't have the same problems. Even better, it makes it possible to fix any problems the guarantee covers before the guest leaves and the organization loses the opportunity to recover from the failure. In 1989 Hampton Inn hotels were the first in the industry to offer an unconditional 100% satisfaction guarantee: "If you're not completely satisfied, we'll give you your night's stay for free." Every Hampton employee was empowered to approve this refund. According to Stephen Tax and Stephen Brown's research at the time, the Hampton Inn organization "realized $11 million in additional revenue from the implementation of its service guarantee and scored the highest customer retention rate in the industry."[8] Upon the celebration of the 25th anniversary of the Hampton Guarantee in 2014, the brand began researching ways to refine and refresh it. After evaluating data from hotel owners, operators, and guests globally, it moved to update its Hampton Guarantee to better meet guests' expectations, stay ahead of competition, and offer its teams more flexibility with service recovery. A number of other brands—including Premier Inn Hotels, Virgin America, Popeye's Louisiana Kitchen, and Jack in the Box—have modeled their own Guarantees after that of Hampton by Hilton.[9] Here are some examples of service guarantees:

> ***100% Hampton Inn Guarantee:*** "If you're not 100% satisfied, we don't expect you to pay. That's our promise and your guarantee."
>
> ***Premier Inn:*** "At Premier Inn, we're so confident you'll have a great night's sleep that if you don't, we'll give you your money back. If there's a problem, just have a

---

[7] For a thorough review of advantages and disadvantages of service guarantees, see Jens Hogreve and Dwayne D. Gremler, "Twenty Years of Service Guarantee Research: A Synthesis," *Journal of Service Research* 1, no. 4 (2009): 322–343.

[8] Stephen S. Tax and Stephen W. Brown, "Recovering and Learning from Service Failure," *MIT Sloan Management Review* 40, no. 1 (1998): 75.

[9] Hospitality Net, "Hampton by Hilton's New 100% Hampton Guarantee," Hospitality Net, posted January 19, 2017, accessed January 8, 2018, https://www.hospitalitynet.org/news/4080485.html.

chat with a member of our friendly reception team. They'll be happy to put things right. This is our Good Night Guarantee."

Hilton Garden Inn: "We promise to do whatever it takes to ensure you're satisfied, or you don't pay."

Embassy Suites Satisfaction Guarantee: "Embassy Suites Hotels offers an unconditional 100% Satisfaction Guarantee at all of its hotels. The unprecedented guarantee assures that guests will receive high-quality accommodations, clean, comfortable surroundings and friendly, efficient service. If guests are not completely satisfied, they are not expected to pay for that night."

Priceline's Sunshine Guarantee: "Travelers booking on Priceline will be refunded 100% of their air fare, hotel, and car rental if it rains more than 0.5 inches per day on half or more of the holiday. The policy is underwritten by WeatherBill which insures several destination guarantees of vacation perfect weather."

Organizational Advantages of Guarantees

A good service guarantee should meet several important criteria,[10] summarized in Exhibit 12.3. The value of a good guarantee to both guests and the organization is significant. The service guarantee can have a powerful effect on customer intent to return by signaling an organization's commitment to quality to both employees and guests. As described by Chris Hart,[11] service guarantees provide several important benefits for measuring and improving the effectiveness of the service delivery system:

- The guarantee forces everyone to think about the service from the customer's point of view since the customer decides whether to invoke it.
- It pinpoints where the service failed since the customer must give the reason for invoking the guarantee, and that reason then becomes measurement data on the service delivery system. As Chapter 13 will show, a guest complaint helps a hospitality organization become better. Guarantees are an incentive to get customers to complain if their expectations (and the guarantee's terms) have not been met. These complaints help the organization fix whatever is wrong before many more customers have problems.
- It gets everyone to focus quickly on the problem at hand since the costs of making good on guarantees can be quite large. Once a customer invokes the guarantee, the cost in lost revenue directs management's attention to correcting the problem.
- It enhances the likelihood of recovery from a service failure because the guest is encouraged to demand instant recovery, instead of sending in a negative guest comment card or saying nothing resolving to take the business to a competitor.
- It sends a strong message to employees and customers alike that the organization takes its service quality seriously and will stand behind it.

If the company has a strong and well-understood service guarantee that its customers can and do readily invoke, everyone in the organization can learn much about the service delivery system from its use. Embassy Suites, for example, takes its guarantee so seriously that it has created multiple ways to inform guests about the guarantee, such as posting it on a lobby sign and having it mentioned by the person

[10] Louis Fabien, "Design and Implementation of a Service Guarantee," *Journal of Services Marketing* 19, no. 1 (2005): 33–38.
[11] Christopher W.L. Hart, "The Power of Unconditional Service Guarantees," *Harvard Business Review* 66, no.4 (1988): 54–62.

EXHIBIT 12.3

The Characteristics of a Good Service Guarantee

1. ***Unconditional.*** The more asterisks attached to the bottom of the page and the more fine print, the less credible the guarantee will seem to both employees and customers. Few or no conditions should be required to use the guarantee.
2. ***Transparent.*** The guarantee must not appear to have any catches or special conditions. The guarantee should be clear and straightforward and all the "rules" should be known by the customer.
3. ***Credible with a high perceived value.*** If customers don't believe you will really make good, then they won't use the guarantee. They think "If it sounds too good to be true, it probably is." The classic illustration is Pizza Hut Delivery's 30-minutes-or-free guarantee which was changed partly because people thought it was too good to be true.
4. ***Focused on key features of the service.*** The guarantee should focus on the services that the guests are most concerned about or the core features of the service product.
5. ***Supported by significant compensation to the customer.*** The remedy or compensation should cover the guest's dissatisfaction completely. If invoking the guarantee only partially solves the customer's problem or is of little consequence to the organization, neither the customer nor the service people will value the guarantee.
6. ***Easy to understand and communicate.*** Follow the old KISS rule: Keep It Simple Stupid. The more complicated the guarantee is, the less likely anyone will believe or use it.
7. ***Easy for customers to invoke.*** Invoking the guarantee and receiving its benefits should be painless for the guest. The harder a guarantee is to use, the less credible it will be and the less likely it will help identify serious service problems. Don't ask customers to fill out a bunch of forms and talk to several different departments to have their problem solved. It wasn't their fault you messed up, so why should they have to do all the work to get it fixed?
8. ***Easy to implement.*** The policy must also be easy for the company to use. If employees do not have the authority to implement the guarantee or if internal bureaucratic hurdles unduly delay processing the guarantee the customer will not perceive the company to be taking its guarantee seriously.

taking the reservation, the van driver, and the front desk agent. Using multiple means increases the likelihood that the guest will know about the guarantee and its message of quality, believe that the guarantee is real, and use it when things go wrong. The guarantee gives Embassy Suites the opportunity to fix any service failures before the guest leaves and to solicit feedback from its guests about any dissatisfaction with the hotel experience.[12]

Potential Disadvantages of Service Guarantees

Service guarantees do have some downsides. Perhaps the most obvious one is that employees will not always honor a guarantee when it is invoked. Supervisory commitment to the guarantee must be shown to reinforce for employees that the organization wants to make the guarantee known to guests and honor it without qualification or quibbling when guests invoke it. However, some supervisors may believe that reporting service guarantee use may negatively impact their annual reviews. As a result, they may avoid reporting the data generated by the service guarantee that could help

[12] Mary Ann Hocutt and Michael R. Bowers, "The Impact of Service Guarantees on Consumer Responses in the Hotel Industry," *Journal of Hospitality & Leisure Marketing* 13, no. 1 (2005): 5–23.

to improve the service delivery system. Therefore, the organization must offer incentives to encourage managers, employees, as well as guests to invoke service guarantees. Companies must also be wary of guests who may inappropriately invoke the service guarantee. To avoid abuses of the guarantee, for example, Hampton keeps a database of customers who have invoked it and recommends another hotel to guests who repeatedly violate the company's trust. All parties must clearly understand what the guarantee covers in sufficiently specific terms so they all take it seriously and use it only when it is appropriate.

Asking Guests the Right Questions

One of the best ways to find something out is simply to ask. Besides the manager and employees' informal observations and inquiries mentioned earlier, there are three additional in-process methods for acquiring the opinions of guests before they leave the service setting: informal queries by employees, formal inquiries by employees, and structured guest interviews.

Informal Queries by Employees

The most basic way to discover a service problem is simply to ask the guest. The desk agent who asks about your stay as you check out is a good example. Asking "Was everything OK?" may be the simplest and most effective way to find out if there was a problem. Some hotels ask employees to act informally as "lobby lizards" by randomly approaching guests on the property and asking about their experience. Of course, employees should be able to respond if the answer is "no." Don't ask this question unless you are prepared for a negative answer. Studies show that whether customers seek redress of a problem or simply let it go is determined by their perception of whether the organization really wants to hear about it and will act on it. Even customers who are reluctant to complain are more likely to do so if they perceive the organization cares and will solve the problem.[13] Asking is a basic way to find out if your service has met the guest's standards.

Formal Inquiries by Employees

As noted earlier, employees are often in the best position to gather feedback from guests by just listening to them. But this role can be expanded in a more structured way. For example, rather than simply ask "How was your stay?" or "How was your meal?" a front desk agent or restaurant cashier can ask guests a series of carefully developed questions about their experience and then listen carefully to what they say and observe how they say it. Because guests may not always recall or report all the important details, employees recording guest reactions and responses in a systematic survey program can use questions that are professionally developed and validated, perhaps even scripted, to help ensure the information gathered is useful and accurate for both immediate recovery from service failure (if discovered) and for further analysis.

Acquiring feedback in this way, before guests leave the premises, may allow recovery from service failures that might otherwise go unnoticed or unreported. Guests who have not yet left can be offered some compensating benefit or at least an apology to try to offset any failure. Employee training for many hospitality positions should, therefore, include appropriate service-recovery techniques, since research confirms that the organization benefits greatly from soliciting and quickly resolving guest

[13] Jeffrey G. Blodgett, Donald H. Granbois, and Rockney G. Walters, "The Effects of Perceived Justice on Complainants' Negative Word-of-Mouth Behavior and Repatronage Intentions," *Journal of Retailing* 69, no. 4 (1993): 399–428.

complaints. As we shall discuss further in Chapter 13, effective hospitality managers know that recovering from service failures yields greater guest loyalty and repeat visits. In addition, because service quality information derived directly from the guest is highly believable to both employees and management, it motivates a quick recovery from service failures.

Structured Inquiries by Professional or Trained Interviewers

structured guest interview An interview conducted according to a set pattern, usually involving a standard set of professionally developed, validated questions designed to gather guest perceptions of service quality.

Face-to-face guest interviews provide rich information when trained interviewers, able to detect nuances in responses to open-ended questions, have the opportunity to probe guests for details about their experiences. These in-depth interviews can uncover previously unknown problems or new twists to known problems that might not be uncovered in a preprinted questionnaire or reflected well in numerical data. However, **structured guest interviews** are costly. The interviewers must be hired and trained, interview instruments must be custom designed, and they must be implemented on a clear and consistent schedule. Of course, it is impossible to conduct such in-depth interviews to all guests, so guests are typically selected at random. At theme parks and similar attractions, teams of interviewers roam the parks seeking guest responses. These conversations not only gather useful information about the guests' assessment of service quality but also enable the identification of any service failures that can be corrected while guests are still on the property.

As an alternative to hiring professional interviewers into your company, you may employ professionals skilled in customer intercepts to conduct the structured guest interviews. These consultants can design and implement the structured guest interview and provide a detailed report of the results to the organization. Because many businesses do not have the time, resources, or skills needed to design an appropriate structured interview, it is often more efficient to hire professionals to carry out this specialized task.

Regardless of who is conducting the interview, though, it is critical that accurate information is collected from guests. To get appropriate participation, inconvenienced guests must be compensated for participating. Without incentives, most guests see little personal benefit from participating in an interview unless, as with guest comment cards, they are motivated by being very satisfied or very dissatisfied with the service experience. Finally, for most experiences, the most desirable time to interview guests is at the conclusion when the experience is over but before the guest leaves in case there is a problem requiring resolution. Getting guests' attention and cooperation when they are most likely anxious to leave, however, can be a significant challenge. Some hospitality organizations solve this problem by identifying their guests' waiting times and surveying them then. For example, departing hotel, convention, cruise, and restaurant customers waiting for an Uber, a bus, a customs line, or a parking valet may be willing to fill some of their wait time by answering questions about their experience.

MEASURING SERVICE QUALITY AFTER THE EXPERIENCE

Companies need good information from their guests in order to evaluate service performance and to make any needed changes. The service experience must be measured carefully and continuously, to make sure it consistently meets guest expectations.

Service quality can be measured both during and after the service experience. Collecting information during the experience—by means of managers and employees comparing the actual service experience against service standards and other methods previously discussed—provides immediate information and may allow the company to repair the damage if service failures occur (again, service recovery is the topic of

Chapter 13). Collecting information after the service generally allows more data to be accumulated and can yield a more representative sample of the organization's entire customer base. This sampling process allows more thorough analysis of the service systems. Results can be fed back to service planners who can then make changes and continuously improve the service.

Techniques to collect data directly from guests vary in cost, convenience, objectivity, and statistical validity. Informal methods are quick and easy, but generally lack validity. Formal methods generally can offer statistically valid, reliable, and useful measures of guest opinion that informal options cannot. Yet, even formal methods can range in sophistication, precision, validity, reliability, complexity, and difficulty of administration. The formal methods are generally more expensive than the informal ones.

The previously described methods of monitoring and assessing quality during service delivery and before guests have left the service setting are critically important in meeting the expectations of guests receiving service. But, to meet the goal of continuous improvement and to plan for future service success, hospitality organizations need methods for obtaining data from guests who have already experienced the service. The following pages describe several of these methods: comment cards, toll-free 800 numbers, mail and web surveys, telephone surveys, critical-incidents surveys, the SERVQUAL instrument, and guest focus groups. A special service-assessment method called mystery shopping is also covered. Exhibit 12.4 summarizes the techniques that may be used to assess service after the service experience. In some cases, it may be possible to use an experimental design to gather very good data about the guest's evaluation of the experience.

Comment Cards

Other than asking guests the right questions before they leave, **comment cards** are the cheapest and easiest to use of all formal data collection methods. If properly designed, they are easy to tally and analyze. These advantages make them attractive for gathering guest-satisfaction data, especially for smaller organizations that cannot afford a quality assessment staff or consultants. Widely found throughout the hospitality industry, comment cards rely on voluntary guest participation. Guests rate the quality of the guest experience by responding to a few simple questions on a conveniently available form, typically a postcard. Guests deposit the form in a drop box, return it directly to the service provider, or mail it to the corporate office.

comment card A method for obtaining guest feedback, often in the form of a postcard, enabling guests to rate the quality of the guest experience by responding to a few simple questions.

Technology

Increasingly, companies are using the internet to implement the comment cards method often with an incentive to participate such as a chance to win a prize. Companies provide web addresses in visibly prominent areas on their printed material such as credit card receipts and bill copies; many post them in their ads, on their coupons, and any other place their customers might see them. Most organizations use a "contact us" link on their websites to provide a mailing address and contact names for those customers who prefer to write their comments to a specific person or functional area. Most websites also now include a space where a guest can write a comment. While many are not as customer friendly as they might be with "I am not a robot" check boxes or other security measures to prevent spamming, they do offer a quick and convenient way to tell an organization about an experience.

Many paper comment cards include a web address so that customers can complete the card online rather than on paper. Some companies such as Marriott and Olive Garden have completely replaced paper comment cards with electronic ones. The benefits of using the internet to collect comment cards are that the data can be easily monitored, sorted, and analyzed, and the technology usually offers an easy way for the company to respond to customer comments.

EXHIBIT 12.4

Techniques for Assessing Quality After the Service Experience

TECHNIQUE	ADVANTAGES	DISADVANTAGES
Comment cards	• Communicate company interest in customer opinions of service quality • Signed cards are an opportunity to recover from service failure • Low to moderate start-up cost • Minimal cost for data gathering and documentation • If printed in house, can be changed easily and often to evaluate needs or new service products	• Self-selected sample of customers not statistically representative • Comments generally reflect extreme guest dissatisfaction or extreme satisfaction • Limited in information provided • Employees can influence results • Time lag between filling out and reading of card • Lack of specifics may make it difficult to use information to find real problem
Toll-free 800 numbers	• Permit potential and prior customers to ask questions, volunteer opinions on service • Opportunity to recover from service failure • No cost to callers	• Self-selected sample of customers not statistically representative • Comments generally reflect extreme guest dissatisfaction or extreme satisfaction • Time lag between experience and making phone call may cause important feedback to get lost in memory
Surveys: mail and web, phone, critical incidents	• Gather info from potentially representative samples of targeted customers • Opportunity to recover from service failure • Allow follow-up discussion to probe into potential problems and opportunities in all parts of service experience • Send message that company cares enough about its service quality to spend money to ask customers what they think about it	• Recollection of details of a specific service experience can be inexact • Other service experiences may bias or confuse responses because of time lag • Inconvenience of participation makes offering incentives to participants necessary • Cost to construct questionnaire and then gather and analyze data from representative sample can be great • Still risks potential for only highly satisfied or dissatisfied guests to respond
Focus groups	• Permit potential and prior customers to ask questions, volunteer opinions on service • Gather info from potentially representative samples of targeted customers • Send message that company cares enough about its service quality to spend money to ask customers what they think about it • Allow follow-up discussion of potential problems and opportunities identified by group	• Are very expensive • Rely on facilitator skill to enable group participation and focus discussion • Small sample can lead to misidentification of important or overemphasis on unimportant opportunities and challenges in total service experience
Mystery shoppers	• Unannounced observation by seemingly typical guests allows sampling of typical experience, not "dressed up" • Can be scheduled to observe/test specific training outcomes, times of day, or problem areas • Can be used to observe competing organizations • Provide more detailed data on all elements of service experience • Can be very accurate on objectively measured elements of experience • Are more accurate than guest feedback on subjective aspects of experience • Employees see shopper feedback as less subjective than manager's performance review	• Are expensive • May not be used often enough to gather statistically accurate data • Shopper biases, other experiences, and preferences can over- or underemphasize quality assessments

What questions should appear on the comment cards? The organization studies its guests to determine their expectations and then embodies those expectations in the comment-card questions. If studies show a restaurant that its guests expect a friendly greeting, a properly setup table area, and overall cleanliness are key drivers, its comment card will ask guests about those specific elements of the guest experience. If an organization tries to differentiate itself from similar organizations, questions regarding the differentiating factors may appear on the comment card, so that the organization can gauge the success of its differentiation strategy.

Once the issues the comment card should address are known, it should then be carefully designed. To do this, according to Bartkus and colleagues,[14] comment cards should adhere to the following guidelines:

Courtesy of Maxie's Supper Club and Oyster Bar

Maxie's Supper Club, located in Ithaca, New York, strives to provide great New Orleans–style food and warm professional service.

1. Include a secure return mechanism (e.g., a secure web page, locked drop box, or postage-paid mail)
2. Make introductory statements brief and neutral, not leading
3. Provide an opportunity to complete the comment card using the internet
4. Limit the number of questions; don't make the survey too long
5. Provide enough writing space for responding to open-ended questions
6. Make questions concise, and ask about only one issue in each question
7. For closed-ended questions, use at least five clearly labeled response points
8. Make questions neutral (e.g., "How was your stay?") rather than containing positive cues (e.g., "What did we do especially well?") or negative ("Were there any problems with your stay?").

MAXIE'S SUPPER CLUB AND OYSTER BAR **comments & suggestions**

What do you like about Maxie's Supper Club?: ______

What would you change about Maxie's if you owned it?: ______

Name: ______

Address: ______

Email: ______ Phone: ______

☐ Check here to receive our e-newsletter "SUPPER CLUB LIFE" every two months

••• Your comment card will be entered into a monthly drawing for a free dinner for two •••

Courtesy of Maxie's Supper Club and Oyster Bar

Maxie's Supper Club's Comment Card courtesy of Maxie's Supper Club and Oyster Bar.

Of course, comment cards are available in many forms and styles. Consider the following examples:

- The West Inn and Suites[15] asks guests to evaluate the front desk, housekeeping, maintenance, and breakfast, in addition to providing general comments using a four-point scale (Excellent, Good, Fair, and Poor) with an opportunity to provide open-ended comments also.
- The Hilton Garden Inn at the Montreal Airport uses a ten-point scale to assess overall satisfaction and two questions related to the likelihood of return and overall value for price paid.
- The Rusty Pelican asks guests how often they visit, their favorite thing about the restaurant, what the restaurant should do to get them to visit more often, and whether they'd recommend the restaurant to a friend, and provides a place for "other comments."

Completed comment cards indicate whether the organization is meeting the general expectations of the guests who take the time to fill them out. Written remarks

[14] Kenneth R. Bartkus, Roy D. Howell, Stacey Barlow Hills, and Jeanette Blackham, "The Quality of Guest Comment Cards: An Empirical Study of US Lodging Chains," *Journal of Travel Research* 48, no. 2 (2009): 162–176.
[15] West Inn & Suites, "Guest Comment Card for West Inn & Suites," accessed January 21, 2018, http://www.westinnandsuites.com/guest-comments-en.html.

about long waits for food, long lines at the front desk, or housekeeping problems reveal the weaknesses of the service delivery system, the service environment, the personnel and their training, and the service product itself. Positive comments provide management with the opportunity to find and fix service delivery system problems, rework the service product, adjust the environment, and, importantly, recognize employee performance. Positive comments can be used to reinforce the behaviors that lead to good guest service and create role models and stories about how to provide outstanding service that other employees can use in shaping their own behavior in their jobs. Negative comments can be used for individual coaching, departmental training (without mentioning specific employees) to illustrate behaviors that caused negative guest experiences, and as input for reviewing employee training programs. Using comment cards in these ways allows managers to coach and train employees about how to provide excellent guest service through the voices of the guests themselves.

Comments accumulated from cards may be categorized and plotted as numerical values on bar graphs and charts that visually display how guests perceived their experience. The plots will suggest whether service failures are occurring occasionally and randomly, or whether overall service quality might be deteriorating. If comment cards increasingly report guest annoyance with worn and stained rugs, management knows it is time to replace them.

Disadvantages

The greatest disadvantage of comment cards is that many guests ignore them and don't fill them out, so the cards received are not likely to be a true general picture of guest perceptions. Typically, only 5% of customers are motivated to return comment cards, and they are usually either very satisfied or very dissatisfied with the service experience. Managers don't even know what percentage of the delighted total or the dissatisfied total these responses represent. The other 95% say nothing. Were they happy, unhappy, or indifferent? You might guess that they are indifferent, but there is a very good chance you would be wrong. A large percentage of dissatisfied guests fill out no cards, leave quietly, and never return. To help overcome the lack of response, some companies use incentives—like coupons or potential cash prizes—to encourage participation. These incentives do help increase participation, but of course they also cost additional money.

Another major disadvantage of comment cards, and in fact of many methods for acquiring feedback, is that the time lag between guest response and managerial review prevents on-the-spot correction of service gaps and failures. Once the moment of truth has passed and the angry or disappointed guest leaves after expressing negative responses on a comment card, the opportunity to recapture that guest's future business is diminished. Even worse, negative word-of-mouth advertising generated by dissatisfied guests cannot be corrected. Moreover, card usefulness can be impacted by employees themselves who may try to influence guests in filling them out. Some employees will watch guests while they fill out cards or even tell guests what to put down on the cards to influence the grades given, especially when scores may affect employees personally. If bonuses rest on comment-card scores, good comment cards will be kept and bad ones may disappear.

While guest comments and their visual representations are interesting and helpful to management, the information lacks statistical validity, one reason being that the random-sample requirement of most statistical techniques is not met because the guests who respond tend not to be representative of all customers that organization serves.

Because of the negatives associated with comment cards, some restaurants simply decide not to use them. For example, one of this book's authors asked the hostess at a Legal Sea Foods restaurant for a comment card. She said the restaurant no longer uses them, and then asked if he would like to speak to a manager. Such a procedure conveys a simple yet powerful message: don't fill out a card; instead, tell us about your experience, and, if there is a problem, let us hear directly from you in that moment so we can try to fix it immediately.

Call-in Feedback

Another way of measuring the quality of service is providing customer-service telephone numbers. This technique invites customers to say what's on their minds twenty-four hours a day. This method also allows companies to get back in touch with customers to let them know how they addressed problems and comments. Like the guest comment cards, the usefulness of this method for obtaining feedback depends upon the willingness of the guests to respond, and even the convenience of this method does not guarantee a representative response from all types of guests. Some companies also offer incentives such as coupons printed on receipts to encourage customers to call the numbers. Others enter the caller into a lottery to win cash or other prizes or incenting their customer facing employees to encourage their customers to call.

Web, Tablet, and Phone App Feedback

Technology

Companies are always looking for new ways to get new and better information from their customers. Companies increasingly rely on their web pages and phone apps to get more, faster, and better responses, so they can use the information more effectively.[16]

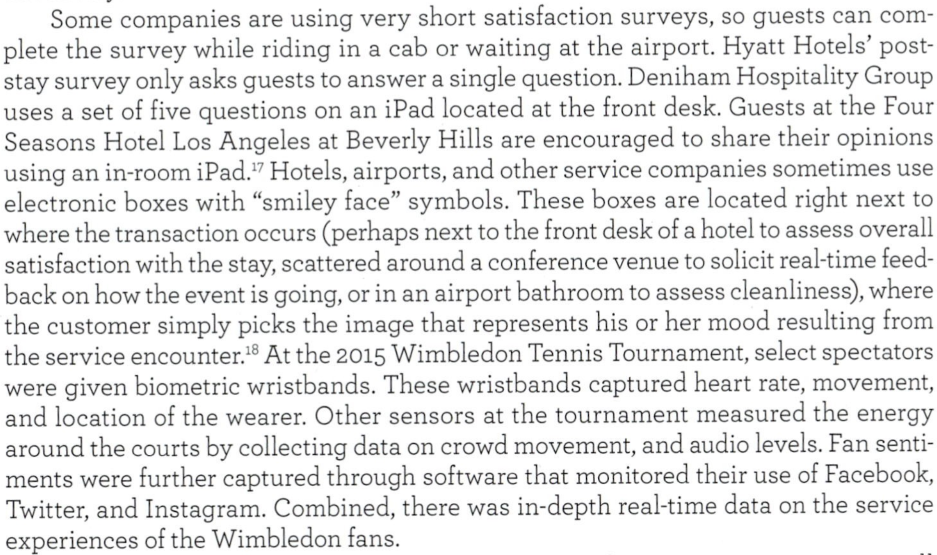

Some companies are using very short satisfaction surveys, so guests can complete the survey while riding in a cab or waiting at the airport. Hyatt Hotels' post-stay survey only asks guests to answer a single question. Deniham Hospitality Group uses a set of five questions on an iPad located at the front desk. Guests at the Four Seasons Hotel Los Angeles at Beverly Hills are encouraged to share their opinions using an in-room iPad.[17] Hotels, airports, and other service companies sometimes use electronic boxes with "smiley face" symbols. These boxes are located right next to where the transaction occurs (perhaps next to the front desk of a hotel to assess overall satisfaction with the stay, scattered around a conference venue to solicit real-time feedback on how the event is going, or in an airport bathroom to assess cleanliness), where the customer simply picks the image that represents his or her mood resulting from the service encounter.[18] At the 2015 Wimbledon Tennis Tournament, select spectators were given biometric wristbands. These wristbands captured heart rate, movement, and location of the wearer. Other sensors at the tournament measured the energy around the courts by collecting data on crowd movement, and audio levels. Fan sentiments were further captured through software that monitored their use of Facebook, Twitter, and Instagram. Combined, there was in-depth real-time data on the service experiences of the Wimbledon fans.

Hospitality organizations seeking feedback on their service experiences will find new methods to take advantage of the ways that technology has us connected. They are creating new software tools to capture their customers' tweets, Instagram posts, and Facebook likes, as well as sending them surveys on company phone apps and gathering their ratings on TripAdvisor or Travelocity. In general, the power of technology is being used to more efficiently and effectively gather useful customer feedback.

---

[16] Kesh Prasad, Philip W. Wirtz, and Larry Yu, "Measuring Hotel Guest Satisfaction by Using an Online Quality Management System," *Journal of Hospitality Marketing & Management* 23, no. 4 (2014): 445–463.

[17] Julie Weed, "Checking in After Checkout," *New York Times*, May 27, 2013, https://www.nytimes.com/2013/05/28/business/hotels-work-harder-to-collect-customer-responses.html.

[18] James Morgan, "5 Interactive Ways To Get Real-Time Feedback," Event Manager Blog, posted February 26, 2018, accessed January 21, 2018, https://www.eventmanagerblog.com/interactive-real-time-event-feedback.

Surveys

Surveys are a common technique to solicit feedback, and they are offered in a variety of formats and media.

Mail/Web Surveys

Well-developed mail or web-based surveys, sent to an appropriate and willing sample, can provide trustworthy information concerning guest satisfaction. Brinker International, the parent company of such restaurants as Chili's and Maggiano's Little Italy, has developed a variation that combines the mail survey and the frequent-diner card program. The feedback advantages of the survey join with the card's promotion of guest loyalty and return visits. Once Brinker obtains basic guest demographic information on an application form for the card, it not only can record the buying patterns for that customer whenever the card is used but it can use the guest's address information to follow up with mailed surveys that will collect valuable feedback on eating preferences and patterns.

Yet, while organizations can use mailed or web surveys to their benefit, many uncontrollable factors can influence guest responses to them. Inaccurate and incomplete mailing lists or e-mail addresses, or a simple lack of interest in responding, can produce a participation rate too small to provide useful information. In addition, the time lag between the experience and filling out a survey can blur a guest's memory of details. Further, many people have so many experiences across their lives that it is difficult to recall specifics of any one of them, especially when it was brief or unmemorable. Trying to learn why the experience you provided is not memorable is impossible when customers can't remember anything about it.

While these surveys are usually used to generate reports full of numbers, the subtleties of the guest experience and guest perceptions cannot be fully expressed numerically. Also, averages may not be sufficiently informative. If some guests remember an experience as terrific and give it a high rating while an equal number of other guests rate it low as terrible, the numerical average would suggest that guest expectations were met on average.

Finally, formal mail or web-based survey techniques require proper questionnaire development, validation, and data analysis, and therefore can be expensive.

Telephone Surveys and Interviews

Telephone surveys and interviews are another method for assessing customer perceptions of service. Car dealerships, for example, frequently use telephone surveys to measure customer satisfaction with a recent transaction. In the hospitality industry, some tour operators call their customers to obtain feedback about a recent vacation experience while paving the way for subsequent travel arrangements.

Telephone surveys and interviews are easy to conduct and can be inexpensive. If the company's own employees make the calls in their slack times, the only costs are for setting up a well-designed interview/questionnaire and a calling strategy/protocol that will yield the best possible statistical results. The data-collection process must ensure the data are captured into a database that will permit solid analysis of the responses. Moreover, a telephone survey allows the immediate identification of service failures (or successes). The guest being called might well tell the interviewer about a failure that would not otherwise have been reported to anyone who might be able to fix it or offer restitution. Finally, the telephone survey allows the company caller to probe deeper into issues raised by the respondent in ways that no online or mailed questionnaire can. Only a face-to-face encounter is a better way of digging deeper to capture the whole story behind either a service success or failure in sufficient detail to ensure that the service experience was provided in the way it was supposed to be or to find out why it wasn't.

Unfortunately, although telephone interviews eliminate the inconvenience to guests of gathering information while guests are still in the service location, they do present other challenges. Telephone interviews can be expensive when organizations use a trained interviewer who uses a sophisticated questionnaire to solicit feedback from guests. When data analysis and expert interpretation are included, the total cost for a statistically valid survey can become quite high. Moreover, in this era of increasing scam, phishing, and robo-calls, there is a growing reluctance to answer the phone for any caller, even those with caller IDs. This makes it even more difficult to gather a representative sample of respondents for any customer survey via phone.

Phone interviews, like surveys, also rely on retrospective information that can be blurred by the passage of time. If the service received was too brief or insignificant for guests to recall accurately, or if guests have no special motivation to participate, the information they provide is likely to be unreliable or incomplete. In addition, customers often regard telephone surveys as intrusions on their time and violations of their privacy. Annoyed respondents feeling resentment toward the organization for calling them at home are likely to bias the data with intentionally negative responses. Red Lobster, Captain D's, and others try to avoid some of these difficulties by building into their guest checks a code that asks every nth guest to call an 800 number to respond by pressing specific numbers to questions about their experience at the restaurant. In return for participation, the restaurant offers coupons for free desserts or "two entrées for the price of one" when the guest visits the next time.

Critical-Incidents Surveys

Another important survey tool is the critical-incidents technique. Through interviews or paper-and-pencil surveys, customers are asked to identify and evaluate numerous moments—classified as dissatisfiers, neutral, or satisfiers—in their interactions with the organization. The survey lets the organization know which moments are critical to customer satisfaction, and the critical dissatisfiers can be traced back to their root causes and rectified. In one study done by a cruise line, for example, passengers were asked to describe one positive and one negative aspect of their cruise either on board or at a port of call that might have impacted their decision to take another cruise with this company's ships. Analysis of the responses indicated that ten negative and eight positive categories or themes emerged as critical incidents and factors. Once the cruise line knew which incidents passengers viewed as most important in determining their post-cruise evaluations of satisfaction (e.g., service, staff, and food), it could concentrate on turning any incidents with negative ratings into positives.[19]

SERVQUAL

Of the many service quality measures that have been developed,[20] one well-accepted technique is **SERVQUAL** (short for "service quality"), developed by A. Parasuraman and his associates. An adaptation of the SERVQUAL survey instrument, designed to evaluate service quality at Belle's Restaurant, is presented in Exhibit 12.5. SERVQUAL has been extensively researched to validate its psychometric properties. It measures the way customers perceive the quality of service experiences in five categories: tangibles (the physical facilities, equipment, and personnel), reliability (the organization's ability to perform the desired service dependably, accurately, and consistently),

SERVQUAL Standing for "service quality," SERVQUAL is the best-known survey instrument within the services field; measures customer perceptions of service quality along five dimensions: reliability, responsiveness, assurance, empathy, and tangibles.

[19] James F. Petrick, Catherine Tonner, and Christina Quinn, "The Utilization of Critical Incident Technique to Examine Cruise Passengers' Repurchase Intentions," *Journal of Travel Research* 44, no. 3 (2006): 273–280.

[20] For a review and discussion of these alternative measures, see Ivan K. W. Lai, et al., "Literature Review on Service Quality in Hospitality and Tourism (1984–2014): Future Directions and Trends," *International Journal of Contemporary Hospitality Management* 30, no. 1 (2017): 114–159; and Riadh Ladhari, "Alternative Measures of Service Quality: A Review," *Managing Service Quality: An International Journal* 18, no. 1 (2008): 65–86.

EXHIBIT 12.5

Instrument for Measuring Guest Perceptions of Service Quality at Belle's Restaurant

Directions

Listed below are five features pertaining to Belle's Restaurant and the services they offer. We would like to know how important each of these features is to you when you evaluate a restaurant's quality. Please allocate a total of 100 points among the five features according to how important each feature is to you—the more important a feature is to you, the more points you should allocate to it. Please ensure that the points you allocate to the five features add up to 100.

1. The appearance of the restaurant's physical facilities, equipment, and personnel.______ points
2. The ability of the restaurant to perform the promised service dependably and accurately. ______ points
3. The willingness of the restaurant to help customers and provide prompt service.______ points
4. The knowledge and courtesy of the restaurant's employees and their ability to convey trust and confidence.______ points
5. The caring, individualized attention the restaurant provides to its customers.______ points

Directions

Based on your experience as a customer of restaurants, please think about the kind of restaurant that would deliver excellent service quality. Think about the kind of restaurant at which you would be pleased to eat. Please show the extent to which you think such a restaurant would possess the feature described by each statement. If you feel a feature is not at all essential for excellent restaurants such as the one you have in mind, circle the number "1" for Strongly Disagree. If you feel a feature is absolutely essential for excellent restaurants, circle "7" for Strongly Agree. If your feelings are less strong, circle one of the numbers in the middle. There are no right or wrong answers—all we are interested in is a number that truly reflects your feelings regarding restaurants that would deliver excellent service quality.

[The 22 survey items for this section are the same as those in the next section, but without any reference to Belle's Restaurant.]

Directions

The following set of statements relate to your feelings about the service at Belle's Restaurant. For each statement, please show the extent to which you believe Belle's Restaurant has the feature described by the statement. Once again, circling a "1" means that you Strongly Disagree that Belle's Restaurant has that feature, and circling a "7" means that you Strongly Agree. You may circle any of the numbers in the middle that show how strong your feelings are. There are no right or wrong answers—all we are interested in is a number that best shows your perceptions about the service at Belle's Restaurant. **[On the instrument itself, the five category labels (Tangibles, etc.) would be omitted.]**

Tangibles

1. Belle's Restaurant has modern-looking equipment.
2. Belle's Restaurant's physical facilities are visually appealing.
3. Belle's Restaurant's employees are neat-appearing.
4. Materials associated with the service (such as menus) are visually appealing at Belle's Restaurant.

Reliability

1. When Belle's Restaurant promises to do something by a certain time, it does so.
2. When you have a problem, Belle's Restaurant shows sincere interest in solving it.
3. Belle's Restaurant performs the service right the first time.
4. Belle's Restaurant provides its services in the way it promises to do so.
5. Belle's Restaurant insists on error-free service performance.

Responsiveness

1. Employees of Belle's Restaurant tell you exactly when services will be performed.
2. Employees of Belle's Restaurant give you prompt service.
3. Employees of Belle's Restaurant are always willing to help you.
4. Employees of Belle's Restaurant are never too busy to respond to your requests.

Assurance

1. The behavior of Belle's Restaurant employees instills confidence in customers.
2. You feel safe in going to Belle's Restaurant and doing business with them.
3. Employees of Belle's Restaurant are consistently courteous to you.
4. Employees of Belle's Restaurant have the knowledge to answer your questions.

Empathy

1. Belle's Restaurant gives you individual attention.
2. Belle's Restaurant has operating hours convenient to all its customers.
3. Belle's Restaurant has employees who give you personal attention.
4. Belle's Restaurant has your best interests at heart.
5. Employees of Belle's Restaurant try to learn your specific needs.

Source: Adapted from Arun Parasuraman, Leonard L. Berry, and Valarie A. Zeithaml, "SERVQUAL: A Multiple-Item Scale for Measuring Consumer Perception of Service Quality," Journal of Retailing 64 (1988):12–40.

responsiveness (willingness to provide prompt service and help customers), assurance (employee knowledge, courtesy, and ability to convey trust), and empathy (providing caring, individualized attention to customers).[21]

SERVQUAL also asks respondents to rate the relative importance of the five areas, so organizations can understand what matters most to customers. In each area SERVQUAL asks customers what they expected and what they actually have experienced, to identify service gaps at which organizations should direct attention. Exhibit 12.5 shows how the items on the SERVQUAL instrument might be adapted to a restaurant situation.

The SERVQUAL instrument reflects a point we have made throughout—the importance of the frontline server to service quality. While tangibles refer primarily to the setting and to the physical elements of the delivery system, and reliability reflects a combination of organizational ability and server ability, the remaining three elements—responsiveness, assurance, and empathy—are almost exclusively the responsibility of the frontline server.

If an organization's quality ratings on any of the SERVQUAL categories are unsatisfactory, it might consider setting up performance standards for the unsatisfactory items. For example, if the responsiveness ratings are unsatisfactory, standards could be established for promptness and helpfulness.

[21] Arun Parasuraman, Leonard L. Berry, and Valarie A. Zeithaml, "SERVQUAL: A Multiple-Item Scale for Measuring Consumer Perception of Service Quality," *Journal of Retailing* 64 (1988):12–40; just a few examples of hospitality applications of SERVQUAL may be found in Bekir Bora Dedeoğlu, and Halil Demirer, "Differences in Service Quality Perceptions of Stakeholders in the Hotel Industry," *International Journal of Contemporary Hospitality Management* 27, no. 1 (2015): 130–146; Ji-Eun Lee and Denver Severt, "The Role of Hospitality Service Quality in Third Places for the Elderly: An Exploratory Study," *Cornell Hospitality Quarterly* 58, no. 2 (2017): 214–221; Rebecca Milner and Adrian Furnham, "Measuring Customer Feedback, Response and Satisfaction," *Psychology* 8, no. 3 (2017): 350; Krishna Moorthy et al., "Customer Loyalty to Newly Opened Cafés and Restaurants in Malaysia," *Journal of Foodservice Business Research* 20, no. 5 (2017): 525–541; Jafar Rezaei et al., "Quality Assessment of Airline Baggage Handling Systems Using SERVQUAL and BWM," *Tourism Management* 66 (2018): 85–93.

Focus Groups

Focus groups provide in-depth information on how guests view the service they receive. Typically, six to ten guests gather with a facilitator for several hours to discuss perceived problems and make suggestions. Researchers Rawan Nimri, Anoop Patiar, and Sandra Kensbock used focus groups in Queensland, Australia, to discover the participants' beliefs about the importance of environmental concerns in their hotel selection decisions.[22] The researchers learned that the participants' beliefs in the importance of supporting environmental benefits were more important than their beliefs in the personal benefits in their hotel selection decision process. On the basis of this group's comments, the researchers concluded that environmentally friendly hotels should more heavily emphasize and publicize their hotels' commitment to green campaigns in their marketing.

Many hospitality organizations routinely invite current or former guests to participate in focus groups to discover their feelings about and perceptions of existing or potential service experiences. Current guests are especially valuable because they can share their reactions and insights before they leave the premises before they can forget the details of the service they just experienced. Focus-group guests are usually impressed that the company cares enough about their opinions to ask for them, and also tend to find the free return park admission, complimentary dinner, or other expression of appreciation that compensates them for their time as fair.

Focus groups are useful but also expensive, time consuming, and labor intensive. They require a group facilitator, a process for selecting participants, meeting space, recording equipment, transcription costs, travel, and sometimes lodging expenses for the facilitator and participants, and, typically, some compensation to the participants. Since focus groups should represent the targeted customer market, correct selection of participants is crucial in obtaining accurate information. If the customer sample is not accurate or doesn't match the desired customer profile, the resulting information can lead to inappropriate conclusions about customer experiences. A large hospitality organization like a theme park can pick ideal and representative groups from its thousands of customers; an individual restaurant, a hotel, or a travel agency will have much greater difficulty in assembling a focus group that accurately represents the targeted customer profile.

Alex Garcia/Chicago Tribune/MCT via Getty Images

Loyola University students participate in a focus group on attitudes toward department stores.

On the other hand, the growing use of social media websites such as Instagram, Twitter, Facebook, and Reddit have expanded the use of computer mediated discourse for conducting focus groups. In contrast to traditional in-person focus groups, online text-based focus groups are completely anonymous, allow members to be selected from any time zone as they can participate asynchronously, have virtually no size limitations in number of participants or ideas to discuss, and can be managed by a facilitator using multiple strings of thought to explore many different ideas. Perhaps most importantly, these methods allow a text record of the discussion that can be maintained for review and later analysis. In their most robust form, online focus

[22] Rawan Nimri, Anoop Patiar, and Sandra Kensbock, "A Green Step Forward: Eliciting Consumers' Purchasing Decisions Regarding Green Hotel Accommodation in Australia," *Journal of Hospitality and Tourism Management* 33 (2017): 43–50.

groups are crowdsourced where anyone anywhere can be allowed to contribute to the topic under discussion. A text-based focus group does, however, have limitations, such as a lack of social cues from body language and facial expressions or vocal intonation that are important influences in face-to-face discussions.

Because of focus groups' many advantages, researchers have tried to determine the effectiveness of online versus traditional focus groups. One study found that online focus groups generate more ideas at a lower cost per idea when compared with traditional focus groups.[23] A later study also showed that text-based online groups were able to generate as many ideas both in quantity and quality when compared to in-person focus groups.[24] These findings, as well as other studies, show that online focus groups have the potential to assist hospitality organizations in obtaining the best answers at a significantly lower cost.

Experiments

In some situations where guest responses to an experience are being researched, it may be possible to use randomized experiments to evaluate the impact different aspects of the guest experience have on guests' determinations of quality and value.

The Planet Hollywood in Orlando, largest in the chain, has three kitchens—one for each floor. It is therefore a nearly perfect experimental site for testing new menu items, portion sizes, and other service product features. Guests can be randomly distributed between the three dining levels. This randomization allows them to collect statistically valid information on how differences in plate presentations, menu design, portions, or any other aspect of the guests' restaurant experience the restaurant wants to know about impacts guest behaviors and satisfaction. The ability to constantly test and compare new ideas gives the food production people at Planet Hollywood a statistically valid approach to finding new and innovative ways to "wow" their guests. By comparing the results from tested options in their service product, service setting, and service delivery systems at the restaurants, they can learn which improve guest satisfaction.

Continental Airlines (now a part of United Airlines) wanted to test which service recovery strategy was most effective by randomly assigning those that complained to receive one of three responses: a letter of apology, an apology letter plus free membership for the airport lounge for six months, or nothing. The findings showed that just a letter of apology was enough to satisfy most of its complaining flyers. More interestingly, 30% of those also receiving the Lounge Membership paid to renew when their complimentary membership expired.[25] Websites can use the same experimental strategy by randomly assigning site visitors to different web pages to see which one yields more hits, purchases, or click-throughs.

Courtesy of Planet Hollywood Restaurant

Planet Hollywood in Orlando, Florida, has three separate floors with their own kitchens, making it an ideal environment for testing different service strategies or menu items.

[23] Fiona Maria Schweitzer, Walter Buchinger, Oliver Gassmann, and Marianna Obrist, "Crowdsourcing: Leveraging Innovation through Online Idea Competitions," *Research-Technology Management* 55, no. 3 (2012): 32–38.

[24] Brendan Richard, Stephen Sivo, Marissa Orlowski, Robert Ford, Jamie Purphy, David Boote, and Eleanor Witta, "Online Focus Groups: A Valuable Alternative for Hospitality Research?," *International Journal of Contemporary Hospitality Management* (2018).

[25] Ian Ayres, *Super Crunchers: Why Thinking-by-Numbers Is the New Way to Be Smart* (New York, NY: Bantam Books, 2007).

The point is that experiments can be designed and run that test all key aspects of the service experience. The quality of the information gained can be very high when the design is randomized and with a sufficiently large sample. The hospitality organization seeking to use this technique for assessing the contribution to quality and value by varying different aspects of their guests' experience should be careful, however, to avoid designing experiments where some of its guests have experiences that are intentionally lesser in quality and value to others. If, on the other hand, the intent is to discover what parts of the service product, setting, or delivery system can be changed to improve the guest experience, a creative and well-designed experiment can provide that information.

Customers Evaluating Services on Their Own

Technology

We have reviewed a number of ways in which companies can solicit feedback from customers. However, with the internet facilitating the spread of information, and with so much information available through social media sources, customers often don't wait for the company to ask them what they think. Individuals post blogs, post information to company sites, tweet their views, post their experiences to their Facebook page, or provide reviews on websites like TripAdvisor and Yelp. When researching where to stay or eat, many people look for these unsolicited ratings and reviews with the expectation that they will find useful information about the quality of various service products based on the experiences of other guests similar to them.

While customers posting information on their own is generally out of the company's control, some organizations proactively monitor this information to look for problems. Many hospitality organizations monitor guest comments on TripAdvisor to see if any complaints have been posted and provide responses accordingly. Some organizations use search tools to scan through social media for mentions of their establishments. Other companies hire consulting companies or employ search services like Reputology and eClincher that are specifically devoted to monitoring and tracking social media comments and trends. When considering unsolicited information, the company often has no idea of who made the comments, if they actually stayed or ate at the establishment, are expressing a typical problem, have some ulterior motives, or are actually real customers trying to give useful reviews. Nonetheless, this information is widely available and it does affect customer decisions, and so the best companies pay attention and seek to address problems that appear in these customer-generated sources.

Mystery Shoppers

mystery shopper Hired or in-house person who poses as a guest, methodically samples the service and its delivery, observes the overall guest service operation, and then submits a report to management.

Mystery shoppers or secret shoppers provide management with a relatively objective snapshot of the guest experience. While posing as guests, these sometimes trained and sometimes untrained observers methodically sample the service and its delivery, take note of the environment, and then send a systematic and detailed report of their experience back to management. They are often specifically instructed to determine if service standards were met (did the server introduce herself, did their drinks come in under three minutes, were they offered an appetizer, etc.). They can sample a restaurant meal, a trip on a cruise ship, a tour, a visit to an attraction, or an overnight stay at a full-service resort hotel. Almost any hospitality experience a guest might have, a mystery shopper can measure. Shopper reports generally include numerical ratings of their observations so that assessments of the guest experience can be compared over time and with other organizations. While employees usually know that their organization uses a mystery-shopper program, they don't know who the shoppers are or when they will shop. Owners of smaller organizations, such as independent restaurateurs or hoteliers, can hire an individual consultant or ask a personal friend or university class to conduct a mystery-shopper program. Larger organizations and national chains may employ a commercial service or use their own staff as shoppers.

Since visits by mystery shoppers are unannounced, employees cannot "dress up" their performance. Research shows that shoppers are especially accurate when reporting objective aspects of the service experience (e.g., Server uniforms clean? Paper towels/trash on rest room floors?) where service standards are clearly set. In addition, shoppers can be scheduled at specific times to assess the quality of service during various shifts, under diverse conditions, with different employees, and through the eyes of different types of shoppers.[26] For example, a hotel designed as a family resort employed a shopper and her children to assess the "family-friendly" factor at the property. The children said the front desk counters were too high and prevented them from seeing what was going on. As a result, a special registration desk was installed where young guests could check in and learn about the activities available for them at the hotel. Another hotel hired a mystery shopper in a wheelchair to learn how a person with this disability would experience the service product, environment, and delivery system. Based on that shopper's report, the hotel moved its directional and room signage to a lower eye level.

Brian Brainerd/The Denver Post via Getty Images

J.L. Barnes is a professional mystery shopper who tests customer services for companies.

Mystery shoppers can also observe competing organizations in a particular market and systematically gather information on a competitor's service level, facilities, prices, and special packages. Some hotels employ mystery shoppers to test the ability of their properties to respond to anticipated service problems and service delivery failures. For example, shoppers can create a problem or intensify a situation by asking certain questions or requesting unique services to assess employee responses under pressure.

Mystery shoppers can also gauge the effectiveness of a particular training or incentive program by shopping at a hospitality organization before and after the training occurs or incentive is implemented. They are more accurate than customer surveys when the experience or service encounter being assessed is too brief for most guests to recall accurately. Finally, and most importantly, mystery shoppers give managers third-party data to use in coaching employees identified by the mystery shopper as performing poorly or in praising those identified as performing well. Because the appraisal is provided not by a manager but by a real customer, employees are more likely to accept the assessment as objective and fair. A manager using shopper feedback is more likely to be seen as a coach helping employees working together to respond to a guest, rather than as a judge who is criticizing employees for their mistakes. Employees think the feedback is fairer when it comes from customers themselves.

The main disadvantage of using a mystery shopper is the small size of the sample from which the shopper generates reports. Since anyone can have a bad day or a bad shift, a mystery shopper may base conclusions on unusual or atypical experiences. One or two observations are not a statistically valid sample of anything, but hiring enough mystery shoppers to yield a valid sample is impractical and too expensive for many organizations. Further, the unique preferences, biases, or expectations of individual shoppers can unduly influence a report. Well-trained shoppers with specific

[26] Gallayanee Yaoyuneyong et al., "Resort Mystery Shopping: A Case Study of Hotel Service," *Journal of Quality Assurance in Hospitality & Tourism* (2018): 1–29.

information about the organization's service standards, instructions on what to observe, and guidelines for evaluating the experience avoid this pitfall.

One restaurant, however, found a way to not only pay for the cost of its mystery shopper program but believed it made money on its use. According to Blaine Sweatt, the former President of New Business Development for Darden, the use of daily mystery shoppers at Seasons 52 not only yielded important improvement in the quality of a restaurant's product quality and service, but also paid for itself because the mystery shoppers liked their experience so much that they returned at a higher rate than other guests. Their more frequent return rate more than offset the cost of the program. Seasons 52 employed nonprofessional mystery shoppers to make daily visits to each unit in the chain. Importantly, each shopper was selected on the basis of having made no prior visits to that restaurant. Further, each shopper was only allowed to evaluate a given restaurant one time. These restrictions insured that shopper evaluations were always the result of first-time shopper experiences and unbiased by prior visits. The reports generated were sent to the individual restaurants the following morning, and the managers were required to meet with the servers, hosts, and bartenders mentioned in the report to discuss the report and coach them on any performance problems noted. Further, the reports were posted for all employees to see. These postings created a competition and served as an incentive for employees to perform at high levels and improve, as well as a reminder of management's commitment to its service standards. Across each month, 80% of all employees were named in a report and, more importantly, had a one-on-one coaching experience with their manager.

The restaurant performance data confirmed that the benefits in improved customer service and headcount outweighed the costs of the daily shopper program. The mystery shoppers were reimbursed only up to a fixed amount, and they were required to bring at least one paying dinner partner. Not only did this approach generate positive revenues, but further analysis revealed that the shopper program had the effect of a free marketing campaign using coupons to get customers to try the restaurant, as the mystery shoppers liked the restaurant so much they were returning again and again to eat.[27] Sweatt's data confirmed his belief that the program not only paid for itself, it provided the customer feedback data that, because it arrived daily in a timely manner and was discussed with the mentioned servers, importantly influenced the performance outcomes for the restaurant in measures of customer satisfaction, profitability, and return visits.

FINDING AND USING THE TECHNIQUE THAT FITS

Exhibits 12.2 and 12.4 provide an overview of quality assessment methods and show some advantages and disadvantages of each. Organizations should choose the techniques that fit their particular purposes. A luxury resort hotel, for example, may require more elaborate and expensive strategies to measure feedback since any reports of poor service can harm the reputation and bottom line of the hotel, the brand with which the hotel is affiliated, and the livelihood of countless employees up and down the line. The value to such a hotel of finding and correcting service failures so that it can deliver the service quality its guests expect is tremendous. Failing to meet guest expectations will quickly make the hotel and all services and business affiliated with it uncompetitive in a dynamic marketplace. On the other hand, a small independent restaurant whose owner loves to "interview" his patrons will probably not require sophisticated quality assessment methods.

[27] Robert C. Ford, Gary P. Latham, and Gwen Lennox, "Mystery Shoppers: A New Tool for Coaching Employee Performance Improvement," *Organizational Dynamics* 40, no. 3 (2011): 157–164.

Costs and level of expertise used to gather data also vary. An important question to ask is who should collect data: line employees, managers, consultants, a company that monitors online content, or a professional survey research organization. Using line employees and managers is the least expensive alternative, but they also have the least expertise in research and may lack the communication skills to interview effectively. Consultants and survey organizations cost more, but they are better able to gather and interpret more detailed statistical data using more sophisticated techniques. Fortunately, with the increasing use of online search technologies and availability of companies that compile customers' online comments and social media postings, the costs of using more sophisticated methods of evaluation are getting lower, and it may indeed become a much more cost-effective way for even smaller organizations to gather customer feedback.

Finally, the organization must consider when to request feedback. Is information to be collected during or after the service is delivered? The best companies do not limit themselves to one approach and hope for the best; they do both. Information collected during the service experience (such as by talking to guests, using management by walking around, monitoring adherence to service standards and guarantees, using employee assessments of the guest experience, or having the technology to obtain immediate feedback from Twitter) allows companies to react immediately to any problems. This information, though, cannot be analyzed in depth (at least at that moment) because by its nature it requires quick decision-making to respond to immediate customer concerns. Information collected after the service experience (such as through analyzing comment cards, toll-free numbers, surveys, online review sites, e-mails, and gathering reports from mystery shoppers) gives companies much more detailed information about service quality. Taking the time to conduct detailed analysis provides valuable information on trends in guest services and issues, indicates where problems might be emerging, and helps spot service problems that can perhaps be fixed before they escalate into large service failures.

Your Best Evaluators: The Guests

Regardless of the evaluation technique selected to measure service quality, one thing is certain. Guests evaluate service every time it is delivered, forming distinct opinions about its quality and value. All hospitality organizations that aspire to excellence must constantly assess the quality of their guest experience through their guests' eyes—while planning the experience, during the experience, and after it is over. Although guests will usually offer an unsolicited opinion only if they are very satisfied or dissatisfied with their experience, most guests are happy to offer an opinion if they are asked in the right way at the right time. Telephone surveyors calling on Friday night at dinner time will get the rejection they deserve. Hospitality managers striving for excellence need to find appropriate methods to elicit from guests the information necessary to ensure service that meets and exceeds guest expectations.

The Improvement Cycle Continues

Once the systems for identifying service failures and delivery system flaws have been put in place, the data that they have generated have been collected systematically, and the customers who were the source of complaints have been contacted and offered an apology and, possibly, some form of restitution, the organization can now use all of this information to revisit its planning process for the entire service experience. Knowing what has failed, and even what has not failed, provides the knowledge needed to reassess all aspects of the service experience to ensure that where it has not met guest expectations, it will do so in the future; where it has only met expectations, it might be improved to exceed them; and where it has exceeded expectations, it can learn why and how to extend the features that led to success to other parts of the experience. In other words, the benchmark organizations in hospitality or any service industry use information to learn how to improve. A key element in the continuous-improvement philosophy—which the best organizations use to drive continual reassessment of what they do—is to learn from their own history how to improve their future. The tools and techniques covered across the past several chapters are the means by which they gather the information needed to drive continuous improvement. Using these tools and techniques consistently and effectively is how the best stay the best.

LESSONS LEARNED

LO 12.1 Measure the effectiveness of service delivery and of the overall guest experience.

- The quality of employee work and the quality of guest service can be different; manage the service product, environment, and delivery systems so as to achieve high quality in both.

LO 12.2 Demonstrate how to use methods of measuring service effectiveness, including service standards, process strategies, managerial observation, and employee assessment.

- Remember the importance of setting service standards as they should reflect the key drivers that guests use to determine service quality and value.
- Recognize the strengths and weaknesses of available assessment techniques.
- Find ways to measure guest satisfaction before, during, and after the experience.

LO 12.3 Explain how to use service guarantees.

- Offer service guarantees to show commitment to guests and to show staff your commitment to service quality.

LO 12.4 Demonstrate how to acquire guest opinions of service effectiveness using comment cards, surveys (mail, web, and phone), focus groups, and mystery shoppers.

- Pay attention to what your guests are saying on the internet.

LO 12.5 Determine the costs and benefits of the different methods for acquiring guest opinions.

- Balance the value of service information obtained from guests with the cost of obtaining it.
- The more sophisticated the information needed from guests, the more expensive it is to acquire.

LO 12.6 Discuss how to achieve continuous improvement in the experience provided to guests.

- If you don't measure it, you can't manage it; if you don't manage it, you can't improve it.
- If you want to become or stay the best, be proactive. Be driven to continuously learn and improve.

KEY TERMS AND CONCEPTS

comment cards 401
guest focus groups 390
job performance standards 393
management by walking around (MBWA) 389
mystery shopper 412
process strategies 388
service guarantee 396
SERVQUAL 407
structured guest interviews 400

REVIEW QUESTIONS

1. Is it critically important for hospitality organizations to measure how satisfied guests are with service quality and value? Or is it sometimes sufficient for organizations simply to offer the best service they can and hope for the best?
2. Regarding the strengths and weaknesses of different methods for measuring service quality:
   A. What are the strengths and weaknesses of managerial observation?
   B. What are the strengths and weaknesses of guest comment cards?
   C. Why is the comment card technique used so frequently in spite of its weaknesses?
   D. What randomized experiments could you invent for innovating guest experiences at a hotel?
3. What provisions would you expect to find in a typical service guarantee for a restaurant?
   A. What are the advantages and disadvantages to restaurants of offering such a guarantee?
   B. How might the service guarantee of a quick-serve restaurant and a fine-dining restaurant differ?
   C. Why would a hotel be more apt to use a guarantee than a restaurant, or a restaurant than a hotel? Do the restaurants with which you are familiar have guarantees?
4. What are the advantages and disadvantages to hospitality organizations of mystery shoppers? In which types of hospitality organizations do you think mystery shoppers would be most and least effective? How could you make a mystery shopper program pay for itself?
5. To what extent should managers use a cost/benefit analysis when trying to determine which techniques to use to measure the guest's perception of the guest experience's quality and value?

ACTIVITIES

1. Collect guest comment cards or examine web-based surveys from several hospitality organizations and compare the factors about which organizations solicit comments. What conclusions can you draw? If possible, interview the managers whose organizations make the cards or web surveys available to guests and ask how the managers use the results.
2. Imagine that you are a mystery shopper for a hotel. Write up a list of the activities in which you would engage, starting with deciding how long you will stay to do a thorough evaluation (twenty-four hours? forty-eight hours?). Develop service standards, such as for calling in to make a reservation. (What will your "number of rings" standard be? three rings? four rings? and so forth.) What evaluation system will you use for the different hotel areas? Pass/fail? An excellent-through-poor scale?
3. Go mystery shopping. If appropriate, use some of the activities from your hotel evaluation list created for question 2. Or do a quick evaluation or service audit using "the three Ts"—Task, Treatment, Tangibles. Write up a brief description of what you found and observed on your shopping trip and send it to the manager of the service location.
4. Either in groups or individually, use Hart's criteria for a good service guarantee as presented in this chapter and create a guarantee for a real or imaginary hospitality organization.

ETHICS IN BUSINESS

A national restaurant chain in the United States has an interesting policy to help detect service problems. If any tip to a server is particularly low, the server must immediately report it to the manager. The manager then inquires as to what problem there might have been. If there was a problem, the manager can perhaps take some steps to correct the situation. This policy raises some interesting questions:

1. Is it appropriate to require servers to report low tips? The requirement may place the server in a very uncomfortable position. A server may have to report a low tip knowing it is justified because of poor service, or the server may know that everything was fine and by reporting the low tip, the customer will be placed in an uncomfortable and embarrassing situation. On the other hand, failure to report a low tip can result in the server being fired. Is it appropriate to put servers in this position?
2. What responsibility, if any, does a restaurant have to inform customers as to what is an appropriate tip? Many tourists from other countries do not know the "norm" in the United States is to provide a tip of 15%–20% of check size. Even many Americans do not necessarily know this "norm." Should the company take steps to educate customers before causing them public embarrassment?

CASE STUDY

Case 1: Try Before You Buy: The Service Guarantee

Ed Jennings had never stayed at Super 10 Suites before, but he hadn't been very satisfied with the only other lodging establishment in Grover, Montana, a regular stop in his western sales territory, so he decided to try Super 10. The guarantee of service offered by Super 10 persuaded him to make the switch. It was basic, but it offered all that Ed wanted:

> "Try before you buy. We guarantee that your rooms will be cleaned, inspected and ready, with all amenities in place, or you pay nothing! No questions asked. We want you to be happy in your choice of Super 10 Suites, Grover's finest."

Ed checked in late in the evening after a hard day on the road, went to his room, and looked around. The room wasn't exactly dirty, but it wasn't exactly clean either. There were small scraps of paper on the floor, some hair in the sink, and mold in the shower. He sat down in a chair, opened the complimentary bag of pretzels, and chewed on one while he thought about whether to stay or to leave.

"Oh, well, if it doesn't get any worse than this, I guess I can take it."

Without going into all the details, it did get worse. The hot water didn't work, the bed was lumpy, and the air conditioner failed during the night. A screaming baby in the next room kept Ed awake for several hours. When Ed checked out the next day, he informed the clerk that he was exercising his service guarantee; he wasn't going to pay. Of course, the clerk asked why, and Ed explained the problems he had experienced.

"Your guarantee said the room would be clean and inspected, and it was not clean. There was hair in the sink, paper scraps on the floor, and mold in the shower."

"No," said the clerk. "The guarantee says that the room will be cleaned, and it was cleaned, last week. As for inspection, I inspected it myself."

Ed said, "When you inspected it, didn't you notice the scraps, the hair, and the mold?"

"This guarantee doesn't say anything about what I noticed or didn't notice. It just says the room was inspected. And before you even ask about the amenities, that's what the pretzels are—amenities."

"All that may be true," said Ed, "but this guarantee says 'No questions asked.'"

"Didn't you see the asterisk by that? Didn't you see the fine print?" asked the clerk. "The asterisk refers to our statement at the bottom that if you ask questions, this guarantee is null and void. This other asterisk, which apparently you didn't see either, says that 'This guarantee and the terms thereof shall be valid and its terms exercisable with respect to the cost of one night's room only, with all the covenants appertaining thereunto. Management shall retain its sole and exclusive right to interpret the terms of the guarantee.' In my opinion, and I'm the management this morning, we fulfilled our guarantee to you the guest, and then some."

Ed Jennings gave it up. He had sales calls to make. Mighty tired and upset, he headed out into the day.

What was wrong with this guarantee? Indicate as many faults as you can.

Case 2: Standard Times at Happy's Restaurant

The top management at Happy's Restaurants, Inc., had assigned its new Work Methods and Standards Department the task of establishing "standard times" for the chain's units. Work Methods personnel went out into the restaurants as mystery shoppers and observed operations carefully. Work Methods then reported to management that the speed and efficiency of service in virtually all of the restaurants needed improvement.

Laura Martin, manager of a very successful and profitable Happy's Restaurant in South Carolina, got the e-mailed memo about the new "standard times for food and cocktail service" late one afternoon. A highly experienced server herself and a respected manager, Martin just laughed at the proposed standards and set the memo aside. She thought she had noticed some mystery shoppers making secret notes, so she had expected some kind of ivory-tower memo like this. It might look good on paper, but it just couldn't be done.

Next day at the afternoon meeting, Martin told her servers: "If you hear anything about new standard times and methods for serving food and drinks, don't pay any attention. As you know, we have all committed ourselves to getting the entrées to guests within eighteen minutes of taking their orders, but our average is sixteen minutes. We've been averaging sixteen for all the years I've been here, and our comment-card results on promptness are excellent. Because you are all terrific at your jobs, I'd say fifteen minutes is the absolute best we could do. But those bozos at headquarters say the new standard is all entrées to guests within fourteen minutes of taking the order." The servers looked at each other with disbelief, then they started to laugh.

"And they also think we can have the drinks on the tables within three minutes of first guest contact." The servers just rolled their eyes and smiled. "Don't worry," said Laura Martin. "I'll straighten this out in a hurry." Martin sent her boss an e-mail telling him that the new standards had to be a mistake because they were entirely unrealistic.

Her boss soon called her and straightened her out in a hurry: "Laura, the new standards will go into effect tomorrow. Work Methods has achieved improved results in several of our other chains already, and now all Happy's branches must conform. Sure, servers always resist at first, but they can meet the standards if you lay down the law, and if they use more efficient methods."

"Maybe that's true elsewhere," said Laura, "but I know my restaurant, my kitchen staff, my servers, and my guests, and I know we can't make fourteen minutes, even with these new methods they want us to use. Things can only be done so fast."

"Martin, call a meeting of your staff, explain that the new standard times will be met, teach your people the new methods, stick to managing your unit, and leave methods and times to the Work Methods and Standards Department. That's what we pay you for, and that's what we pay them for."

Martin tried her best, but her restaurant knew how she felt about the situation. The servers at this South Carolina Happy's Restaurant failed to meet the new work standards, and the head of the Work Methods and Standards Department blamed Laura Martin. He recommended that new talent should be located for her position.

1. What is the problem here?
2. Under what circumstances can such "by the minute" standards be made to work?
3. How would you determine service standards at your restaurant?

Further readings on the topics in this chapter are listed in "Additional Readings" on pages 519–522.

Get the tools you need to sharpen your study skills. SAGE edge offers a robust online environment featuring an impressive array of free tools and resources.

Access practice quizzes, eFlashcards, video, and multimedia at **edge.sagepub.com/Ford2e**.

Visit **edge.sagepub.com/Ford2e** to help you accomplish your coursework goals in an easy-to-use learning environment.

©iStock.com/MachineHeadz

13 Fixing Service Failures

Hospitality Principle: Don't Fail the Guest Twice

You want your customers to tell you when you've screwed up, so that you can take care of the problem and take steps to ensure that it doesn't happen again—to them, or anybody. If they don't tell you they'll just walk away shaking their heads and they'll never come back. Worse, you're likely to alienate somebody in the future by doing exactly the same thing.

—Carl Sewell, ***Customers for Life***

Learning Objectives

After reading this chapter, you should be able to:

13.1 Explain how guests respond when the guest experience fails to meet their expectations.

13.2 Describe how organizations should respond when the experience fails to meet guest expectations.

13.3 Explain how organizations prepare their employees to find and fix failures.

13.4 Explain why positive word of mouth is so valuable and bad word of mouth so harmful.

13.5 Express why the recovery method for handling a service failure is so important.

13.6 State why fixing service failures quickly and fairly—on the spot, if possible—is so important.

13.7 Recognize how to learn from service failures.

13.8 Describe how guests evaluate the hospitality organization's recovery efforts.

13.9 Match the recovery strategy to the failure.

INTRODUCTION

As we first stated in Chapter 1 and have reiterated throughout the book, providing a service is not like making a refrigerator on an assembly line where you can bring in an industrial engineer to study the production process that makes the refrigerator, see the product as it is being built, and check it for flaws after it is completed. While parts of most guest experiences are tangible and produced by a similar production process, like a kitchen in a restaurant that produces a dinner, the service the guest experiences is only partially produced by a physical production process. The rest of the service product is intangible. Add the fact that the service product's value and quality are determined by the guest at the moment of or over the period of consumption, and you see why all the methods engineers in the world cannot build a 100% reliable, dependable service system. The guest sees, experiences, and evaluates the service. The guest decides what the experience was worth, whether it was worth returning for, whether to tell friends and neighbors that it was great or poor, and whether the overall experience met, or even exceeded, expectations. To succeed under these circumstances, any service delivery system has to be as nearly perfect as thoughtful planners can make it. The best systems must also have flexibility, allowing the appropriately trained and motivated employee to find and fix any problems to ensure customer satisfaction.

When something goes wrong in the delivery of a service, it is called a **service failure**. As noted earlier, the best way to handle a service failure is to prevent it before it occurs. This involves building proactive or preventive strategies into the design of the service experience and its delivery system. These techniques—such as blueprinting, PERT/CPM, simulations, and fishbone analysis—were covered in Chapter 10. Yet, despite the greatest of efforts during the planning phase, and no matter how many poka-yokes, service standard checks, or fail-safes are put in place,

service failure The organization's failure to deliver the promised service according to its own standards or the guest's expectations.

not all failures can be prevented. Indeed, whenever a server interacts with a guest, the potential for something to go wrong is present. Human beings are not perfect. Therefore, quality must be constantly monitored and measured during the delivery phase to minimize failure and ensure success. Measures can be used to collect information during the service delivery processes so that errors can be immediately identified and addressed, or after the service so that systems can be updated, corrected, or improved in such a way that future service is delivered more effectively. But when a failure does occur, steps should be taken to fix it quickly, ideally on the spot, for the guest.

Chapter 12 discussed various methods used to collect information to measure service delivery quality. When these methods indicate that a guest has experienced a service failure, organizations must find ways to both fix the failure and improve their systems to prevent a recurrence of the failure. In this chapter, we shall focus on strategies for finding and fixing service failures. The methods we discuss are the result of both process and outcome service quality assessment strategies. Although service failures should be rare, and for the best hospitality organizations they are, this is such an important topic to managers committed to providing a great experience for each and every guest that it merits its own chapter.

Here is another reason for studying service failures intensely. In Chapter 10 we discussed the importance of assessing the service experience to improve the system. Exhibits 12.1 and 12.3 listed numerous ways for measuring service quality during and after the service experience, such as guest surveys, comment cards, employee feedback, focus groups, mystery shoppers, and others. All of these are important, and they may reveal many interesting findings regarding the delivery of service. But the information most likely to lead to service-delivery improvement is data about service failures. If the organization wanted to, it could review and study every aspect of the delivery system; however, if it did so, it would probably be analyzing many aspects that "ain't broke." Information about the service failure shows where something went wrong. The best way to improve the system and deliver better service in the future is to determine, by studying service failures, how to minimize them and refer those findings back to the system planners.

Stuck in the Snow

Service failures in the airline industry are a commonplace discussion topic among travelers, on the internet, in newspapers, and on television. Compare the following two service failures by airlines and how they were handled.

Continental Flight 2816, operated by ExpressJet, was flying from Houston to Minneapolis. Weather conditions forced it to land in Rochester, Minnesota, at 12:28 A.M. on a Saturday where the passengers sat on the tarmac next to the terminal for the next 5½ hours with babies screaming, toilets overflowing, and the terminal tantalizingly near. The Express Jet spokesperson said no ground handlers were available to deplane the passengers at that hour of the morning. The airport stated this was not true and that Delta's still available ground handlers repeatedly contacted them to ask permission to deplane the stranded passengers. The passengers' agony did not end when morning came and they could finally get off the plane. ExpressJet said no buses were available to transport the stranded passengers to Minneapolis, their final destination. Moreover, the plane could not take off again as the crew was over its legal flying limit. When a relief crew finally got into Rochester to fly the plane to Minneapolis, the airline closed the toilets as no one had thought to get ground service to empty them. When the plane finally arrived in Minneapolis over nine hours after it landed in Rochester, the passengers stormed the ExpressJet counter to express their anger and dissatisfaction. As a last part of this story, the news media publicized this incident across the country as another example of an uncaring airline industry, causing Congressional leaders to call for an expansion of passenger rights and reimbursement amounts.[1]

©iStock.com/Socha

The original cause of a service failure may be beyond a company's control, such as a snow storm disrupting air travel. How an organization manages a service failure, however, can have dramatic effects on its reputation and future repatronage.

Negative articles about the airline industry appear frequently in the newspapers, and just about everybody can tell stories of lost bags, indifferent and unhelpful desk agents, missed connections, or long unexplained waits. It is little wonder that the general frustration has led to formal efforts to regulate the industry more tightly and to the development of websites offering informal airline passenger advice, ways to complain, and consumer advocacy. Websites such as refund.me, Euclaim, AirHelp, and Flight-Delayed for European travelers help fliers win penalty payments for long delays, cancelled flights, and being bumped against their will.[2]

Contrast this service with that delivered by the motivated, empowered Scandinavian Air Service (SAS) purser in the following example. A planeload of SAS passengers was stuck at an airport because of snow. Because the purser knew the SAS philosophy was to do whatever is necessary to satisfy the customers, or at least try to, she decided to offer them free coffee and biscuits. She went to the catering supervisor, a middle manager who outranked her, and asked for forty extra servings. Because each flight was allocated only so many cups of coffee and biscuits, the catering supervisor refused the request.

The purser could have let the system defeat her, but she noticed the plane at the next gate belonged to Finnair, an airline that purchased food and drink from the SAS catering department. The SAS purser asked the Finnair purser to order the coffee and biscuits, because the catering supervisor was required by SAS regulations to fill the order for Finnair. The SAS purser then bought the coffee and biscuits from the Finnair purser with petty cash, and the stranded customers received a welcome snack.[3]

The purser solved a problem by finding a way around regulations and the catering supervisor. Through the empowered purser, the system "healed itself" without managerial intervention to achieve the airline's primary goal: customer satisfaction. Everybody was happy—except perhaps the angry, confused, bypassed catering supervisor. The system failed once when it could not accommodate the purser's desire to satisfy the customers, recovered briefly by giving the frontline purser the autonomy to solve the customer problems, then failed again in not telling a middle manager how to deal with the autonomy that had been granted to a subordinate.

Service failures can vary considerably across the dimensions of frequency, timing, and severity. A guest can experience a service failure anytime during a single experience or across multiple experiences. Failures can happen to first-time guests or long-time customers. Errors are more noticeable to long-time friends than they are

[1] Gary Stoller, "Tarmac Ordeal Renews Push for Fliers' Rights," *USA Today*, Aug. 11, 2009.

[2] Brittany Shoot, "This Woman-led Startup Is Turning Flight Delays into Cash," *Fortune*, November 24, 2014, http://fortune.com/2014/11/24/airline-delays-cash/.

[3] Karl Albrecht, *At America's Service: How Your Company Can Join the Customer Service Revolution* (New York: Warner Books, 1988), 124–125.

to new customers. Since first impressions are so important, a failure occurring early may weigh more heavily than one occurring late. And obviously, big mistakes count more than little ones. Mistakes on key drivers that represent moments of truth for the guest are bigger mistakes.

No matter how hard the organization works to prevent service failures in the first place by using the tools and methods covered earlier in this book, they can't avoid them all. If the organization fails once by not providing the expected guest experience, then not fixing this failure is failing the guest twice. This chapter shows the importance of finding and fixing service failures, the reasons why failures happen, and the strategies available to recover from and avoid future service failures.

SERVICE FAILURES: TYPES, WHERE, AND WHY

Service failures are inevitable in hospitality, so the best organizations plan for them. They make the effort to anticipate the types of failures that can occur, where they will occur, and why. The best hospitality organizations know that even if service failures are inevitable, they can recover from almost any failure if they have a plan.

Types of Service Failures

A well-accepted categorization of service failures divides them into four types:

1. Service product failures: These include any failure in the core service products (e.g., cold or poorly prepared food, unavailable hotel room, or broken attraction), service settings (e.g., dirty or smelly rooms, no directional signs, or overly worn carpets), and service systems (e.g., out-of-stock items, inoperative credit card machines, or disorganized servers).

2. Failure to meet explicit or implicit customer requests: These include any inability to provide what guests expect and ask for, such as special requests on menu items, a nonsmoker being put in a smoking room, or not honoring a reservation.

3. Failures caused by employee actions or inactions: These include both intentional and unintentional acts such as showing rudeness or bad attitude or not presenting the expected service in a timely way.

4. Failures caused by other guests, random events, or circumstances beyond the control of the organization but which guests will still expect to be fixed such as a dropped ice cream cone, rained out concert, or break down of a theme park attraction.

Service failures can also occur for a combination of these four basic reasons. For example, a rude server may bring a salad that was poorly prepared by a supplier along with an entrée to a guest who asked that the salad come out first, thereby committing errors of the first three types. If the guest gets very angry, begins yelling and cursing at the server, and makes an unpleasant scene in the restaurant that ruins another party's evening, then the fourth type of service failure would occur. Regardless of the reason or combination of reasons, a service failure can dramatically reduce customer satisfaction and can have severe negative consequences for the business.

In a study that analyzed critical incidents during service encounters to identify the reasons for customers switching to other products or services, three common problems emerged[4]. The most influential critical problem that could explain why customers switched was due to failures in the service itself (such as mistakes committed by staff, technical failures, billing errors, or service catastrophes); they were mentioned by 44% of all respondents (noted by 11% as sole reason and 33% as one of two or more reasons). The second largest category of service failures involved employees' inappropriate actions, negative attitudes, or bad behaviors (noted by 34%). If employees were perceived as uncaring, impolite, rude, unresponsive, uncommunicative, or unknowledgeable (as in inexperienced, untrained, inept, out of date), they failed. The third largest category of reasons why people switched was unsatisfactory employee response to service failure (noted by 17%). When employees responded reluctantly, failed to respond with empathy or at all, or offered negative responses—for example, blaming the customer for service failure—customers understandably found those responses unsatisfactory and are more likely to switch even if the initial failure was not a sufficient motive to switch.[5] Summing those percentages reveals that when customers switch from one product or service to another, they do so more than half the time because of the way they were treated or spoken to by employees. In effect, the hospitality organization pushed them away.[6] Most of the time, service failures occur when the people part of the delivery system let customers down. The challenge this creates for managers is that often the servers who create a failure are the same ones that must not only admit they failed in order to fix it for the guests, but they must also trust their managers enough to tell them about their failure.

Customer Failure

Customer unhappiness is not always the hospitality organization's fault. Another source of failure is the customers themselves. The company may have done a perfect job of producing a meal to a customer's specifications, but the diner simply may not like the taste. For example, a diner might order halibut steak thinking it was a cut of beef; a guest may have ignored an "emergency exit only" sign and set off the alarm; or a guest may have lost a set of keys, a child, or money. Even though the organization does not create these problems—which are often beyond the organization's ability to manage no matter how much they train their people, perfect their systems and refine their services—the organization must still address them.

The organization should also be ready to handle those failures caused by other guests—the diner who sneezes on another diner's food, the sports bar Red Sox fan who tries to knock down the Yankee fan, the inconsiderate passenger who cuts in front of others at the airport security line, or loud talkers on cell phones in a movie theater or concert hall. However, while doing everything in its power to rectify such situations, the hospitality organization should not admit liability for unfortunate, unavoidable occurrences that are not its fault. The Red Sox fan would probably have gone after the Yankee fan in any venue.

---

[4] Susam M. Keaveney, "Customer switching behavior in service industries: An exploratory study." *The Journal of Marketing* (1995): 71–82.

[5] For more research on customers' responses to service failures, see Arne K. Albrecht, Gianfranco Walsh, and Sharon E. Beatty, "Perceptions of Group versus Individual Service failures and Their Effects on Customer Outcomes: The Role of Attributions and Customer Entitlement," *Journal of Service Research* 20, no. 2 (2017): 188–203; Katja Gelbrich, Jana Gäthke, and Yany Grégoire, "How a Firm's Best versus Normal Customers React to Compensation After a Service Failure," *Journal of Business Research* 69, no. 10 (2016): 4331–4339; Simon Hazée, Yves Van Vaerenbergh, and Vincent Armirotto, "Co-creating Service Recovery after Service Failure: The Role of Brand Equity," *Journal of Business Research* 74 (2017): 101–109; Heejung Ro, "Customer Dissatisfaction Responses to Restaurant Service Failures: Insights into Noncomplainers from a Relational Perspective," *Journal of Hospitality Marketing & Management* 24, no. 4 (2015): 435–456; Aditi Sarkar Sengupta, M. S. Balaji, and Balaji C. Krishnan, "How Customers Cope with Service Failure? A Study of Brand Reputation and Customer Satisfaction," *Journal of Business Research* 68, no. 3 (2015): 665–674.

[6] Jishim Jung, Heesup Han, and Mihae Oh, "Travelers' Switching Behavior in the Airline Industry from the Perspective of the Push-Pull-Mooring Framework," *Tourism Management* 59 (2017): 139–153.

Psychologists know that attributing one's successes to oneself and one's failures to others is human nature. Guestologists know that too. Hospitality organizations that want to keep guest-created service failures from destroying the guest experience and the guest's feelings about the organization build in strategies to help guests recover from their own failures so they can take a positive impression away from the service setting. Airlines have routines to help people who have lost their tickets complete their flights. Universal Studios has routines to help parents who have lost their children in the park find them again. The best organizations recognize the importance of helping guests solve the problems they create themselves—without making them look foolish or feel stupid while tired children or a spouse is looking on at the end of a long day in the park. The best organizations help these guests go home happy in spite of themselves.

Where Failures Happen

Though some moments of truth are especially susceptible to failure, an organizational failure to meet the customer's expectations can occur just about anywhere in the guest experience. This is why we spend so much time studying all aspects of the guest experience, identifying potential failure points, planning on how to prevent as many failures as possible, and preparing to fix the inevitable failures. The best failure is one that is discovered before it happened, but no service experience can be totally flawless for every guest no matter how much managers plan. An organization needs to develop a way to find and fix failures and problems at the time guests are having their experience.

The service product may be inadequate, inappropriate, or fail in some other way to meet the customer's expectations. For example, the ordered hamburger may not look like the one advertised on TV that attracted the customer to the burger stand, or it may be undercooked, spoiled, or just not as good as the customer expected. A service failure is the result. The intangible part of the delivery system can also fail. If the burger took an hour to get to the customer at the burger stand or if the line wasn't managed properly, the delivery system itself may have failed. The people part of the delivery system can certainly fail. If the burger-stand counter person is unfriendly, inept, poorly trained, or rude, then the experience is unlikely to meet the customer's expectations. Finally, there can be a failure in the environment or setting if the customer feels that the ambient temperature is too cold, a sudden rainstorm ruins the meal, or one customer collides into another making them drop their meals. These points of possible failure must all be planned for and managed to ensure that the service experience meets and, hopefully, exceeds the customer's expectations.

Severity of Failure and Recovery

zone of tolerance The range of service quality experienced that a customer will deem as satisfactory, even if aspects of the service are not fully up to expectations.

Service failure comes in degrees, ranging from insignificant mistakes that are barely noticed to catastrophic failures that make newspaper headlines. They also come in frequency from those that happen rarely to those that are often. Customers have what researchers call a **zone of tolerance**. Customers will tolerate most small and infrequent errors. They know that things don't work perfectly every time so they may brush off minor failures, especially if their prior experiences with that organization have been excellent and they expect to continue the relationship with it. But, once service drops below what the customer considers to be adequate service, the customer will become dissatisfied and frustrated with the company.[7] Some customer service experts

[7] Valerie Zeithaml, Mary Jo Bitner, and Dwayne Gremler, *Services Marketing: Integrating Customer Focus Across the Firm* (New York: McGraw Hill Education, 2018).

believe the organization should apologize even for these failures as they provide an opportunity to "wow."

Along the severity continuum is an infinite range of service errors. Since the customer defines the quality of the service experience, the customer also defines the nature and severity of the service failure. Different customers can be very unhappy or just mildly unhappy about the same failure just as different customers can be very happy or mildly happy about the same service. Some service recoveries fix the customer's problems, and other recovery efforts make things worse. Sometimes the best a manager can do is to neutralize the angry customer.

THE IMPORTANCE OF FIXING SERVICE FAILURES

When a guest has a problem, one of three outcomes usually occurs. The problem is fixed and the formerly unhappy guest leaves happy; the problem isn't fixed and the unhappy guest leaves unhappy; or the organization tries to fix the problem and fails or succeeds only in neutralizing the unhappy guest. Some researchers have categorized the types of service failures: monetary failures (e.g., being charged incorrectly), flawed service product (e.g., the room having a broken air conditioner), failed service delivery (e.g., the steak being overcooked), and lack of server attention (e.g., the waiter not coming back to check on the table).[8] According to the research the best way to recover depends on the type of failure. Monetary failures are best fixed by immediate monetary compensation; flawed service products are best fixed by an immediate exchange; and failed service deliveries are best fixed by redelivering the service. The best way to deal with a lack of attention, though, was less clear. Some monetary compensation either immediate or given later, an exchange or upgrade of a service product, a reperformed service delivery, or even just an apology may all help resolve this sort of service failure. This suggests that the best way to address a service failure may depend on the specific nature of the failure, its severity, and financial and non-financial cost to the customer. Hospitality organizations need to train their customer contact employees to be on the alert for failures and be ready, flexible, and quick in how they respond.[9]

Being successful in service-recovery efforts is critical, because a formerly unhappy guest who leaves happy may tell many others about a terrific experience. An unhappy guest may leave and tell as many others as possible about the terrible experience. A neutralized guest may leave and forget the whole experience and perhaps the organization as well. In instances of a total service catastrophe, neutralizing the unhappy customer may be the best the organization can hope for. If the surgeon removes the wrong leg, everyone on the cruise gets Legionnaires' disease, or the restaurant meal leads to food poisoning, recovery from the failure is nearly impossible. Even so, most modern hospitality organizations have developed disaster plans to prepare their employees for such situations.

Airlines have emergency teams for handling crashes, theme parks have quick-response teams for accidents, and hotels have fire teams for handling evacuations in emergencies. The team's primary responsibility is to handle the emergency situation, such as getting guests to safety. The best teams will also provide aid, some form of restitution, and comfort to the customers affected by the emergency, in order to restore, as much as possible, the customer's positive perception of the organization.

[8] Holger Roschk and Katja Gelbrich, "Identifying Appropriate Compensation Types for Service Failures: A Meta-Analytic and Experimental Analysis," *Journal of Service Research* 17, no. 2 (2014): 195–211.

[9] Detelina Marinova, Sunil K. Singh, and Jagdip Singh, "Frontline Problem-Solving Effectiveness: A Dynamic Analysis of Verbal and Nonverbal Cues," *Journal of Marketing Research* 55, no. 2 (2018): 178–192.

Courtesy of Ocean House

When The Ocean House in Rhode Island experienced a service failure caused by a fire alarm, after first ensuring customers' safety, the staff turned the potential service disaster into a party-like atmosphere by providing guests with champagne and creating a festive and fun mood.

A great example of how to do this was illustrated by The Ocean House, a luxury hotel and spa in Rhode Island. On a hot and sunny August day, with a packed house, a fire alarm went off. Hotel staff immediately evacuated guests. Although it was unclear whether there was an actual fire or not, the staff's first priority was to heed the alarm and safely evacuate guests from the building. While everyone appreciated the concern with safety, this action meant there were hundreds of guests standing around in the hot sun instead of enjoying the expected first-class luxury experience. Once the hotel staff had everyone safe, they sought to provide comfort by bringing the guests water and moving them to nearby local buildings to get them out of the hot sun.

While the staff had now resolved the guests' safety and comfort issues, there was a clear service failure that needed fixing. One staff member suggested that a way to improve the situation was to offer the now displaced guests champagne. This action turned an "ow" to a "wow" and turned the mood from concern and annoyance to festive and fun. The staff of The Ocean House clearly had been trained on how to prioritize guest safety and comfort, but had also been trained in the spa's cultural values to recognize the importance of doing what it could to turn potentially disastrous service failures into "wow" experiences.

The Price of Failure

Ultimately, retaining customers by providing excellent service and avoiding or fixing service failures is essential to organizational success. Frederick F. Reichheld and W. Earl Sasser Jr. showed that if a company can reduce its rate of customer defections (leaving the organization to go to a competitor) by only 5%, it can improve profits by 25 to 85%.[10] Since their now classic study, a lot of research effort has been dedicated to determining the lifetime value of a customer. Calculating and publicizing this value to employees gives everyone a strong sense of why it is so important to find and fix the service problems that cause customers to switch their support to other companies or use the service less frequently. It costs money to lose a customer.[11]

word of mouth Passing of information from person to person by means of oral communication.

When the lost revenue of unhappy customers who don't return is added to the lost revenue of customers who don't come because of the negative **word of mouth** from unhappy customers, service failures have created an expensive problem. Over a defecting customer's lifetime, how much potential revenue have you lost? Many companies have sought to make this estimate, and while results differ by the type of product being provided, they invariably show that the price of failure is highly significant for any business.

Consider the following examples. An analysis of Starbucks suggests the lifetime value of a customer is just over $14,000.[12] A study of a cruise line showed the lifetime value of customers ranged from $4,000 to $5,000.[13] Domino's Pizza estimated

[10] Frederick F. Reichheld and W. Earl Sasser, Jr., "Zero Defections: Quality Comes to Services," *Harvard Business Review* 68, no. 5 (1990): 105–111.

[11] For a review of literature on estimating customer lifetime value, see V. Kumar and Werner Reinartz, "Creating Enduring Customer Value," *Journal of Marketing* 80, no. 6 (2016): 36–68.

[12] Jeff Desjardins, "Calculating the Lifetime Value of a Customer," *Visual Capitalist*, January 27, 2016, http://www.visualcapitalist.com/calculating-lifetime-customer-value/.

[13] Paul D. Berger, Bruce Weinberg, and Richard C. Hanna, "Customer Lifetime Value Determination and Strategic Implications for a Cruise-Ship Company," *Journal of Database Marketing & Customer Strategy Management* 11, no. 1 (2003): 40–52.

that over a ten-year period a regular customer spends about $5,000.[14] Mazda Australia estimates the lifetime value of each customer is over $100,000,[15] while Carl Sewell of Sewell Cadillac in Dallas calculated that each of his customers was worth $332,000 in lifetime sales, service, and referrals.[16] The Ritz-Carlton estimates the lifetime value of its engaged guests at more than $1 million.[17] Thus, fixing service failures is clearly one of an organization's most essential activities. Of course, every business is different, and so every hospitality organization would benefit from taking the time to calculate the value of its long-term satisfied customers. Caesars Entertainment certainly takes this seriously. Their 200-person analytics team monitors every customer's trip in real time. This allows the company to step in and offer a complmentary meal or room, as long as the analytics, based on the customer's lifetime value, indicates the investment is worthwhile.[18]

George Rose/Getty Images

Caesars Entertainment used a 200-person analytics team to monitor customers in real time and allow them to provide rewards to loyal customers based on customer value.

The examples provided earlier reveal that, even for a small business, the lifetime value of a customer may be surprisingly large. To show how a restaurant might come up with numbers like these, assume the restaurant "wows" its patrons so much that some come back once a week and others once a month and spend an average of $20 each time they visit. The total value of each wowed customer's business for the next five years would be $5,200 for the weekly customer and $1,200 for the monthly customer. That's a lot of money to throw away by ignoring a complaint about one bad meal. These numbers get even bigger when the number of people that a positive word-of-mouth guest could bring to your hospitality organization is added in. If our "wowed" guest tells an average of five others who are also "wowed" and, in turn, tell five additional people, the multiplier effect is large. If our "wowed" guest spreads the word through social media, the multiplier effect can be enormous. Over the estimated life of a typical customer, this can add up to thousands of dollars in potential revenues.

Just as positive word of mouth has great value, negative word of mouth is extremely costly. Unhappy customers can be particularly harmful to a business, as they are approximately twice as likely to spread negative word of mouth as happy ones are to spread positive word of mouth. Research shows that customers who have bad experiences tell approximately eleven people; customers who have good experiences tell approximately six.[19] The internet is multiplying the influence of word of mouth even more. Word of mouth used to be one-to-one. Angry customers used to be limited to writing letters to corporate headquarters or the Better Business Bureau, putting up signs in their yard, or painting "lemon" on the car. Now, anyone with internet access can write a blog, tweet out their complaints or post comments on a social networking site; provide comments on a ratings site like TripAdvisor, Yelp, or

[14] Janelle Barlow and Claus Møller, *A Complaint Is a Gift: Recovering Customer Loyalty When Things Go Wrong* (San Francisco: Berrett-Koehler, 2008); Dominique Crie, "Consumers' Complaint Behaviour. Taxonomy, Typology and Determinants: Towards a Unified Ontology," *Journal of Database Marketing & Customer Strategy Management* 11, no. 1 (2003): 60–79.

[15] L. Hailey, "Lifetime Value Pays Small Business Dividends," *Dell.com*, accessed October 10, 2009.

[16] Carl Sewell and Paula Brown, *Customers for Life: How to Turn that One-Time Buyer into a Lifetime Customer* (New York: Pocket Books, 2002).

[17] Joseph A. Michelli, *The New Gold Standard: 5 Leadership Principles for Creating a Legendary Customer Experience Courtesy of the Ritz-Carlton Hotel Company* (New York: McGraw-Hill, 2008), 180.

[18] Bernard Marr, "Big Data at Caesars Entertainment—A One Billion Dollar Asset?," *Forbes*, May 18, 2015, https://www.forbes.com/sites/bernardmarr/2015/05/18/when-big-data-becomes-your-most-valuable-asset/#75066ed21eef.

[19] Christopher W. Hart, James L. Heskett, and W. Earl Sasser, Jr., "The Profitable Art of Service Recovery," *Harvard Business Review* 68, no. 4 (1990): 148–156.

some similar site; or create a dedicated website to tell the world about any offending company. If this person has a large following on the web and achieved "influencer" web status, the negative effect is greatly increased. In this day of instant worldwide communication, a customer can praise or complain and instantly reach millions of people. The benefits of avoiding negative word of mouth and turning it positive are obvious.

The Customer's Response to Service Failure

service recovery The organization's attempt to make right or compensate for a service failure.

The unhappy or dissatisfied customer is the focus of the **service recovery.** An unhappy customer can do any one or a combination of four actions.

Never Return

First, the customer can leave vowing never to return. Here, the company has lost a stream of potential future revenue. As already noted, lifetime customer values can be substantial, and when guests walk out vowing never to return, it all goes away. One main reason for empowering servers to provide on-the-spot service recovery is to keep dissatisfied customers from leaving unhappy. Fixing a service problem before the guest leaves your facility is the best thing you can do to diminish the impact of a failure and prevent the loss of that customer's future business.

Complain

The second action a customer can take is to complain to someone in the organization. A popular book on this subject is *Hug Your Haters.*[20] The best hospitality managers truly embrace complaints. They encourage guests to complain and thank them when they do. A complaint is a positive opportunity for the organization with several important benefits. For one thing, it gives the company the chance to make an unhappy guest happy; the organization can turn the lemon into lemonade.

Common wisdom in the hospitality field is that most disappointed customers simply go away unhappy. A classic and highly cited study suggested that only 1 disappointed customer in 20 actually complains to the company.[21] Yet, since the time of that study, organizations have increasingly embraced excellent customer service and their efforts to encourage unhappy customers to complain so problems can be resolved and customers retained. With more companies seeking customer feedback, with the ease of lodging complaints by a variety of methods (online, cell phone, in person), and with changing consumer expectations, customer complaining is a much more regular phenomenon. A recent Gallup poll of 13,000 customers showed that 59% of customers experienced problems with at least one company they bought products or services from in the past six months, but 79% of

AFP/AFP/Getty Images

Chinese customers mob a Kentucky Fried Chicken outlet in Beijing, angry over a coupon promotion gone awry.

[20] Jay Baer, *Hug Your Haters: How to Embrace Complaints and Keep Your Customers* (New York: Penguin Random House, 2016). See also Janelle Barlow and Claus Møller, *A Complaint Is A Gift: Using Customer Feedback as a Strategic Tool* (San Francisco: Berrett-Koehler publishers, 1996).

[21] Technical Assistance Research Programs Institute, *Consumer Complaint Handling in America: An Update Study*, TARP, 1985.

those customers indicated they had reported the problem to the company.[22] While this is good news for guestologists, it isn't all good news. Across industries, customers report they are dissatisfied nearly 75% of the time with how problems are resolved.[23] Failing a customer twice by not satisfactorily fixing a failure will have more impact on intent to return than merely failing to deliver the expected service.[24]

If guests can be encouraged to complain, the organization gets valuable information about where problems in the guest experience are located. The customers who return to the counter with undercooked hamburgers, complain to the front desk agent about their dirty room, tell the server about their unhappiness with the slow service, or write letters to the hotel manager describing their dissatisfaction, can all help identify problems in the service product, the service setting, and the delivery system including its personnel. At the same time, guests give the organization the opportunity to fix the problems before they tell others about their dissatisfaction and before other guests experience the same problem. With more guests willing to complain, companies have the potential to improve their services. But with most guests quietly leaving dissatisfied with how their problems are resolved, organizations are both missing an opportunity to improve and losing potential future business.

Organizations should encourage guests to complain, even teach them how to complain if necessary, and then measure and follow up on complaint resolution. Guests who suffer service failures and don't have their problem resolved to their satisfaction and quickly are more apt to leave without returning and to bad-mouth the organization. Examining individuals who complained about a brand or product by Twitter, one study showed that simply responding to the complaint, no matter how it was responded to (i.e., just an apology or some sort of resolution or compensation), increased the customer's willingness to pay more for the brand in the future. The study also showed that speed matters. Customers who received a response to their issue in five minutes or less were more willing to pay for the brand in the future than those who had more delayed responses.[25]

Some companies claim even stronger results from successful complaint resolution. They believe that, on average, 70% of their guests will stay with the organization if a complaint is resolved in the guest's favor, and a full 95% will do business again if the complaint is resolved favorably on the spot. This is why the benchmark hospitality organizations empower their frontline employees to handle many complaints quickly and in the best possible way they can, rather than seeking the manager's authorization first. As former Gaylord Hotels COO John Caparella said, "The only way to meet our mission of 'Flawless Service' is through the commitment and dedication of our front line employees. Our 'STARS' are the ones that are close enough to the customer to recognize and evaluate a problem and make it right for the customer and keep that customer."[26] This has been a point long championed by service scholars. Christopher Hart, James Heskett, and W. Earl Sasser wrote in their classic work, "The surest way to recover from service mishaps is for workers on the front line to identify and solve the customer's problem."[27] Just as handling a complaint well can be to the organization's benefit, handling it poorly or not at all can hurt badly. If a dissatisfied customer complains and then finds that the organization can't or won't fix the problem, the organization has now failed that customer twice, and everyone the customer knows

---

[22] John Timmerman and Daniela Yu, "Silver Lining of Customer Problems," *Gallup*, March 7, 2017, http://news.gallup.com/businessjournal/205445/silver-lining-customer-problems.aspx.

[23] Timmerman and Yu, "Silver Lining of Customer Problems."

[24] Yi-Fei Chuang and Yang-Fei Tai, "Research on Customer Switching Behavior in the Service Industry," *Management Research Review* 39, no. 8 (2016): 925–939.

[25] Wayne Huang, John Mitchell, Carmel Dibner, Andrea Ruttenberg, and Audrey Tripp, "How Customer Service Can Turn Angry Customers into Loyal Ones," *Harvard Business Review*, January 16, 2018, https://hbr.org/2018/01/how-customer-service-can-turn-angry-customers-into-loyal-ones. Accessed 2/2/2018.

[26] Robert C. Ford, Celeste Wilderom, and John Caparella, "Strategically Crafting a Customer-focused Culture: An Inductive Case Study," *Journal of Strategy and Management* 1, no. 2 (2008): 143–167.

[27] Hart, Heskett, and Sasser, "The Profitable Art."

will hear about it. A large sticker on the computer screens used by servers at T.G.I. Friday's reads "Every Guest Leaves Happy." Making sure no guest leaves unhappy is obviously to the organization's advantage. The excellent organizations want all of their dissatisfied customers to complain so they can fix whatever problems might have occurred.

Bad-Mouth the Organization

bad-mouth The spreading of negative comments and opinions about an organization by a dissatisfied customer.

The third action an unhappy customer can take is to **bad-mouth** the company, telling everyone who will listen about the terrible experience.[28] If the negative experience was very costly for the customer either financially or personally, the customer is even more likely to spread the bad word. The greater the costs to the customer, the greater the motivation to tell. If someone returns home after spending a lot of time and money flying to the Cayman Islands, staying in a hotel for a week, eating out, and paying admissions to various attractions, friends and neighbors will probably ask, "How was your vacation?" If it was a bad experience, the customer will make every effort to share that information with all who ask, tweet out their complaints, post their story to Facebook, and add the experience to TripAdvisor. The likelihood that anyone who listened to or read about that person's experience will also spend the time and money to go to the Cayman Islands will be substantially diminished. Obviously, the more important the experience is to the customer, the quicker the customer will become unhappy when the experience does not meet expectations. The unhappier a customer is, the more likely that person will complain, leave, and tell people about the experience.

Retaliate

Beyond bad-mouthing the organization, the fourth action an unhappy guest can take is to find a way to retaliate.[29] Getting back at the offending company can take several forms. Some customers get so angry that they conduct public bad-mouthing by taking their concerns to the press or their legislative representative. In rare cases, the retaliation can even be in the form of creating nongovernmental organizations (NGOs) to protest the organization and the practices that have led to the service failure. Airlines are a good example of an industry that has outraged so many people that angry customers have organized into groups to seek new legislation and redress for the airlines' passenger practices and apparent indifference to their guests' needs, wants, expectations and behaviors. As a result airlines face governmental mandates to make higher reimbursement payments for passengers bumped from flights and renewed calls for Passenger Bill of Rights legislation in the United States similar to that passed in Europe.[30]

Other retaliatory strategies are available to angry guests who believe the organization failed them in some way. They can picket organizational facilities, take out ads in newspapers publicizing whatever the organization did to anger them, post comments on websites, organize boycotts against the company, or file lawsuits that take company time and money to resolve. Retaliating guests may even take out their frustration on the company's employees. These actions by angry guests all have a cost for the organization. For example, when employees are abused by an angry guest, they themselves are likely to become angry with an employer that makes its customers so angry that employees get unfairly yelled at (or worse) by their customers.

[28] Na Young Jung and Yoo-Kyoung Seock, "Effect of Service Recovery on Customers' Perceived Justice, Satisfaction, and Word-of-Mouth Intentions on Online Shopping Websites," *Journal of Retailing and Consumer Services* 37 (2017): 23–30.
[29] Yany Grégoire and Robert J. Fisher, "Customer Betrayal and Retaliation: When Your Best Customers Become Your Worst Enemies," *Journal of the Academy of Marketing Science* 36, no. 2 (2008): 247–261.
[30] Scott McCartney, "Bumped Fliers May Get a Better Deal," *Wall Street Journal*, July 24, 2007.

Worst-Case Scenario

If the failure was severe enough, it turns the guest into the angry **avenger** that every organization fears. This is the company's worst-case scenario for a service failure, where the customer leaves vowing never to return, does not complain to the organization, switches to another service provider, bad-mouths the organization, and finds a way to retaliate. The company has not only lost any future business from the angry customer, but it has also lost the business of the many people who will hear and be influenced by the negative word of mouth. This dissatisfied customer has become a true avenger fighting against the organization. While a dissatisfied customer may tell eight or ten people about the problem, a true avenger is the person who creates a dedicated website or starts a blog in an effort to influence millions.

avenger A customer who has experienced a service failure and leaves vowing never to return, does not complain to the organization, switches to another service provider, bad-mouths the organization, and finds a way to retaliate.

The Value of Positive Publicity: Bad-Mouth versus Wow

On the other hand, the value of a "wowed" customer can be huge. Picture a family coming back home from a Caribbean island that caters to tourists. They have terrific tales to tell and tweet their friends and post on Facebook. Their experience exceeded their expectations. To have these enthusiastic promoters telling everyone they know about their great vacation is very much to the Caribbean island's advantage. This positive word of mouth has great value, not only for influencing others to go to the Caribbean paradise, but also for blunting negative word of mouth. If a potential customer hears strong testimonials or reads posts about a guest experience from three trusted friends, disregarding a complaining avenger's posts will be easier.

Credibility

Word of mouth is important for several reasons. People who tell other people tend to be more credible than impersonal or anonymous testimonials, especially if the source is seen as having greater expertise.[31] When your friend tells you a restaurant was bad, you no longer believe all the ads on television assuring you that the restaurant is a good place to eat. Not only is the information more credible, but it tends to be more vivid as well. For either good or bad word of mouth, the richness of the detailed personal experience of a friend is more compelling than any commercial advertisement.

Evangelists

Exceeding expectations creates the **evangelists** that every organization hopes to have. The best hospitality companies work hard to ensure that their guests have experiences so memorable they can't wait to get home and tell all their friends and relatives about what a terrific time they had, post to social media, or submit a glowing report on TripAdvisor. This positive word of mouth advertising reinforces the company's favorable public image.

evangelist Extremely satisfied, delighted guest who takes every available opportunity, and often creates opportunities, to praise the organization and recommend it to friends and acquaintances.

Like all companies that seek excellence, the best hospitality organizations work hard to identify and train their people to find and fix the inevitable problems quickly. These best companies plan for failures—by training, using simulations, telling stories to teach how employees have creatively fixed problems in the past, and celebrating employee efforts to find and fix service problems—with the intent of changing a problem into an opportunity to "wow" the guest and perhaps create an evangelist. In *The New Gold Standard: 5 Leadership Principles for Creating a Legendary Customer Experience Courtesy of the Ritz-Carlton Hotel Company,* Michelli reports a Ritz-Carlton example of a problem that was not even the hotel's fault but an employee fixed

[31] Jill Sweeney, Geoff Soutar, and Tim Mazzarol, "Factors Enhancing Word-of-Mouth Influence: Positive and Negative Service-related Messages," *European Journal of Marketing* 48, no. 1/2 (2014): 336–359.

it anyway. Some Ritz-Carlton hotels operate camps for kids. One guest reported, "My daughter spilled something on her pants soon after arriving there for a day. Our baggage was lost by the airline, and so she didn't have a change of clothes. Not only did the camp counselors have her clothes dry cleaned; they also went to Macy's and bought her a new outfit. I was floored. This is obviously above and beyond anything I would have expected."[32] Guests who get this kind of red-carpet treatment may become evangelists who not only become loyal repeaters but spread the company word far and wide.

DEALING WITH SERVICE FAILURES

The way in which an organization communicates its commitment to finding and fixing service failures to its employees will greatly impact its success in responding to failures. The organization trying to recover from failure can impress the customer positively or negatively. Research shows that for both positive and negative service recoveries, how the recovery is handled can be more important to the customer than the original failure.[33]

How the Recovery Is Handled

After a failure, the organization can either end up much better off or much worse off, depending on the customer's reaction to the recovery attempt. A small problem can become a big problem if the recovery effort is halfhearted or misguided. On the other hand, a big problem can be turned into an example of great service when handled quickly and effectively.

In one study of restaurants, the researchers discovered that the most important determinant of overall customer satisfaction after a service failure was customers' satisfaction with those responsible for dealing with failure: the personnel responsible for the service interaction. The organization's ability to recover from failure also had the largest impact on willingness to return and re-patronize the restaurant.[34] Lee, Singh, and Chan used a critical incident approach to conduct structured interviews with 75 hotel guests from 33 hotels in Hong Kong in which they asked the sample to describe negative experiences they had had with the hotel. They used text mining to identify patterns of service failures. As a result of their analysis, these researchers identified 50 keywords allowing them to organize service failures into eight clusters: guest arrival and departure (e.g., check-in, check-out, waiting lines); room amenities (e.g., internet, room size, bed); food services (e.g., buffet, cold, hot, slow); variety of choices (e.g., meals, menu); service personnel (e.g., staff, number); banquet services (e.g., large, choices); general food and beverage services (e.g., drinks, portions, restaurant); and communication (e.g., signage, entrance). For each of these failures a recovery strategy was identified as the best option for each type of failure. These ranged from compensation to a simple apology. The data analysis indicated that most failures occurred when hotels failed to deliver what had been promised and when there was a gap in external communication between hotel marketers making the promises and guests. In other words, when expectations set by marketing are not met by the actual experience provided, guests are dissatisfied.[35]

[32] Joseph A. Michelli, *The New Gold Standard*, 180.

[33] Yves Van Vaerenbergh, Chiara Orsingher, Iris Vermeir, and Bart Larivière, "A Meta-analysis of Relationships Linking Service Failure Attributions to Customer Outcomes," *Journal of Service Research* 17, no. 4 (2014): 381–398.

[34] Jerrold K. Leong and Woo Gon Kim, "Service Recovery Efforts in Fast Food Restaurants to Enhance Repeat Patronage," *Journal of Travel & Tourism Marketing* 12, no. 2–3 (2002): 65–93.; Ah-Keng Kau and Elizabeth Wan-Yiun Loh, "The Effects of Service Recovery on Consumer Satisfaction: a Comparison between Complainants and Non-complainants," *Journal of Services Marketing* 20, no. 2 (2006): 101–111.

[35] Myong Jae Lee, Neha Singh, and Eric SW Chan, "Service Failures and Recovery Actions in the Hotel Industry: A Text-Mining Approach, *Journal of Vacation Marketing* 17, no. 3 (2011): 197–207.

Service Recovery: A Message to Employees

Addressing service failure well has one more important outcome: It makes the organization a better place to work. It tells the employees how committed the organization is to customer satisfaction. Employees need to know that this commitment is more than a slogan. How the organization finds and fixes its service errors is a loud message to the employees about what the organization truly does believe in. Let us say that the management of Hotel A is defensive about customer complaints and keeps them secret (though employees will hear about them), resolves complaints as cheaply and quietly as possible, and blames employees for the complaints. The management of Hotel B, on the other hand, aggressively seeks out and fixes service failures. It disseminates findings about complaints and failures to employees, makes quick and generous adjustments for failure, and seeks solutions rather than scapegoats. Which organization's employees will give guests better service?

How the organization handles service recovery will also impact employee morale and satisfaction with the organization. After all, for whom would you rather work—a company that won't let you fix guest problems quickly and fairly, or one that empowers you to tell guests you will find a way to recover from service failures? Most will agree it is more fun and rewarding to work for a company that wants you to fix guest problems quickly and fairly than it is to work for one that doesn't. Research shows that when employees feel a company is committed to providing excellent service, and employees are supported in their efforts and rewarded for doing so, employee job satisfaction is significantly higher and turnover lower.[36]

The Yellow and Black Tags

Employees on the front line are often the first to notice or be informed of system faults or failures as they are the ones who observe or hear about customer problems. If they have been properly selected, trained, and motivated, they will report the need for system improvement. For example, a British Airways baggage handler at London's Heathrow Airport noticed that passengers waiting for their luggage at the carousel were asking him a strange question: How can I get a yellow and black tag for my bags? The passengers had noticed that bags with those tags arrived first, so they wanted the special tags. The baggage handler realized that because the passengers asking him the question were the first ones to arrive at the carousel, they had to be first-class passengers, who deplaned first. And, yet, they had to wait twenty minutes on average for their bags, while some other passengers were getting first-class luggage service. First-class passengers are highly profitable to airlines, and something was wrong with the service being provided to them.

The baggage handler's inquiries revealed that the passengers perhaps least deserving of "first-class" luggage service, those flying on stand-by, were getting it. Since they were the last to board, their luggage was loaded last and unloaded first. The baggage handler made a simple suggestion: load first-class luggage last. Although the idea was simple and had obvious merit, implementing it meant that BA had to change its luggage-handling procedures in airports all over the world, and that took time. But it was done, and the average time of getting first-class luggage from plane to carousel dropped from twenty minutes to less than ten worldwide, and under seven minutes on some routes.[37]

---

[36] Sean A.Way, Michael C. Sturman, and Carola Raab, "What Matters More? Contrasting the Effects of Job Satisfaction and Service Climate on Hotel Food and Beverage Managers' Job Performance," *Cornell Hospitality Quarterly* 51, no. 3 (2010): 379–397. See also Marshall Schminke et al., "Better than Ever? Employee Reactions to Ethical Failures in Organizations, and the Ethical Recovery Paradox," *Organizational Behavior and Human Decision Processes* 123, no. 2 (2014): 206–219.

[37] Alan G. Robinson and Sam Stern, *Corporate Creativity: How Innovation and Improvement Actually Happen* (San Francisco: Berrett-Koehler Publishers, 1997), 9–11.

A dedicated, motivated, observant employee saw a way to improve the system and got it done. He had no idea he would also end up receiving a service award, a cash award of $18,000, and two round-trip first-class tickets to the United States.

Looking for Service Failures

The most important key to finding service failures is to get all employees to look for and listen to guest complaints. Guests are generally willing to tell you when they think you've failed, but the hospitality organization that really wants to fix its failures makes sure everyone is looking and listening.

The Complaint as a Monitoring Device

Preventive strategies can reduce the number of problems, but some will inevitably occur, and the organization cannot fix problems it doesn't know about. The research shows clearly that the most important process strategy is to get unhappy guests to complain while they are still in the guest experience. This is a more difficult challenge than one might think. While some guests are all too happy to complain, most are not. They are unwilling to take the time, or they believe no one cares or will do anything even if they do complain, or they are too angry to say anything and they just leave. Hospitality organizations must let their guests know they and their employees are receptive to complaints and especially want to hear them before the guest leaves. Research on this issue has identified some important ways in which the organization can encourage and recognize customer complaints.

Encouraging Complaints

All service personnel should be trained and encouraged to solicit complaints. Because many service problems involve server errors, getting the servers to solicit complaints about their own performance may be a challenge. Management needs to make it very clear that employees will be better off reporting instead of hiding their mistakes, and also must show that it can be trusted to do what it says. If servers see that mistakes are punished more heavily than catching errors is rewarded, it will be difficult to find or fix the errors they make. Most people are less enthusiastic about admitting their mistakes than they are about sharing their successes, and the complaint strategy needs to accommodate this reality of human nature. Furthermore, it is difficult for guests to feel it is worthwhile to complain to the very person who just made them angry or offended them.

Body Language as a Complaint

Service personnel can be trained to read body language for clues to an unhappy guest. If a frowning guest walks by a Disney cast member, that person is supposed to inquire as to why "the unhappy face." Taking this initiative can elicit complaints that might otherwise go unmentioned. Food-service workers, hotel front desk agents, activity directors, and other people who interact directly with guests can also be trained to recognize the signs of unhappy people. Employees must also learn how to be receptive and sympathetic to the complaint once it is elicited and then act to fix the problem. Guests must perceive employees as interested and concerned. If guests do not think anyone cares, they generally won't say anything.

For example, a child visiting the Magic Kingdom at Disney world was excited to see that her favorite character, Captain Hook, was standing next to one of the rides posing for pictures and signing autographs. She too wanted her picture taken with the Captain and to get his autograph. As she got to the front of the line, the cast member in charge suddenly cut off the line and escorted the character off stage for a break. The child was heartbroken, and nothing her parents could say could cheer her up. That night at dinner an alert wait staff member noticed the sadness in the little girl's face and asked her, "How was your day?" After hearing her story and taking the order, the waitress told her shift supervisor the story of the sad little girl. The shift supervisor called the character supervisor to talk about this service failure. While a simple solution would have been to summon Captain Hook to the restaurant to greet the little girl, the two employees agreed that this would be out of character for the ill-mannered Captain. They then hit upon an in-character service-recovery strategy. A plush toy of Peter Pan was taken to the little girl's room and left along with the following note: "Dear Sally: I am sorry that Captain Hook was mean to you today, but he is sometimes mean like that. Next time I see him, I will tell him that he shouldn't be so mean to our guests. (signed) Peter Pan." The little girl was thrilled, and her parents told this story to anyone who would listen to them.[38] Server sensitivity to a little girl's nonverbal communication became a magical moment that turned an unfortunate situation around.

Don't Forget to Ask

Although already discussed in Chapter 12, this is a point worth reiterating. The most basic way to find out if there is a service problem is to simply ask the guest "Was everything OK?" Though there are a number of more sophisticated options—like comment cards, toll-free 800 numbers, surveys, focus groups, and reports from mystery shoppers, training employees to ask guests whenever the opportunity arises but especially at moments of truth in the service experience is the most basic way to find service failures. This training should also include how to respond if the guest says no. Employees should know how to follow-up, be taught ways they might resolve the service failure, and empowered to use them.

RECOVERING FROM SERVICE FAILURE

The organization failed. It got the guests in the door, and then it let them down. Now what? Hospitality organizations should train their employees to creatively resolve the problems when they find them. Scenarios, game playing, video recording, and role playing are good ways to train them on how to fix failures and respond to a disappointed or angry guest. Just as umpires can be trained to recognize balls and strikes through watching videos, hospitality personnel can be trained to recognize service errors and taught how to correct the failures they find.

Obviously, the more an organization depends on repeat business, the more critical it is for the organization to acknowledge and act on customer complaints. Some organizations report the results of their complaint investigations back to complaining customers in detail, including information on what people were affected and what systems were changed. In that way the organization shows it is responsive to the customer's complaint and gives that person a sense of participation in the organization that may positively enhance loyalty and increase repeat visits. If the complaint shows the organization a flaw that can be corrected, and if knowledge of the correction provides the customer with a sense of satisfaction for reporting the complaint, a true win-win situation can result. The key is, if there is a service failure, the company must take action.

Do Something Quickly

The basic recovery principle is to do something and do it quickly. While customers have a certain tolerance in terms of recovery speed, which depends on the nature of

[38] K. Taylor, "When Service Means Everything," *Association News*, November 2006.

the service and service failure, satisfaction with service-recovery efforts decreases as the amount of time taken to provide a resolution increases.[39] Strive for on-the-spot service recovery. Its many benefits are one major reason why benchmark organizations empower their frontline employees to such a great extent. The one answer a guest does not want to hear is, "I'll have to ask my manager." That's why a standing guideline for empowered employees of the best organizations is: Provide immediate service recovery.

The Ritz-Carlton is famous for empowering its employees to find and fix failures. Here are three of the "Ritz-Carlton Basics" that appear on the are taught to every employee:

- Any employee who receives a customer complaint "owns" the complaint.
- React quickly to correct the problem immediately. Follow up with a telephone call within twenty minutes to verify that the problem has been resolved to the customer's satisfaction. Do everything you possibly can to never lose a guest.
- Every employee is empowered to resolve the problem and to prevent a repeat occurrence.

How the problem came about or who caused it does not matter. Every employee is empowered to resolve it. The $2,000 each employee is authorized to use to recover from a service failure and achieve guest satisfaction backs up that philosophy.

Management must empower employees with the necessary authority, responsibility, and resources to act and act quickly following a failure. The higher the cost of the failure to the guest in terms of money, personal reputation, or safety, the more vital it is for the organization to train the server to recognize and deal with it promptly, sympathetically, and effectively. Of course, empowering employees to recover from failure will not be sufficient if recovery mechanisms are not in place. If the rest of the organizational systems are in chaos, empowering the front line won't do much good.

A necessary further step is that employees should inform their managers about system failures even if they have already initiated successful recovery procedures. If they don't, the problem may recur elsewhere. In part to help encourage employees to share how they handle service failures, Federal Express created the Golden Falcon Award to recognize employee initiatives in service recovery. Winners not only get a pin to commemorate their success, but they also have an article published in the company newsletter about what they did. In addition, they get a telephone call from a senior executive and receive ten shares of the company's stock.

All hospitality personnel should be trained to apologize, ask the guests about the problem, and listen in a way that gives guests the opportunity to blow off steam. Considerable research indicates that having the chance to tell someone in authority about the service failure and the problems it created is very important in retaining the guest's future patronage. This strategy is even more effective when the organization expresses its thanks for the complaint and offers a sincere apology with a tangible reward, even if it is small.[40] Many restaurants will apologize to guests who complain about a longer-than-expected wait and offer a free dessert as a small recognition of their sincere regret for disappointing the guest. Some restaurants do this even if the guest does not complain.

---

[39] Jens Hogreve, Nicola Bilstein, and Leonhard Mandl, "Unveiling the Recovery Time Zone of Tolerance: When Time Matters in Service Recovery," *Journal of the Academy of Marketing Science* 45, no. 6 (2017): 866–883.

[40] Xiaofei Li, Baolong Ma, and Chen Zhou, "Effects of Customer Loyalty on Customer Entitlement and Voiced Complaints," *The Service Industries Journal* 37, no. 13–14 (2017): 858–874; Miyoung Jeong and Seonjeong Ally Lee, "Do Customers Care About Types of Hotel Service Recovery Efforts? An Example of Consumer-Generated Review Sites," *Journal of Hospitality and Tourism Technology* 8, no. 1 (2017): 5–18.

Benefits of Quick Recovery

A quick reaction to service failure has numerous benefits. Solving a problem up front instead of over time reduces the overall expense of retaining guests. It is generally less expensive to fix a problem on the spot than it will be if the guest is further aggravated by the inability of the server to solve the problem without checking with the supervisor. This is where minor annoyance can become true anger and the reason the benchmark hospitality organizations empower their employees to fix the problem on the spot if at all possible. The sooner the guest is satisfied, the more likely the guest will remain with the hospitality organization and the sooner the organization will benefit from the guest's repeat business. Fix their problems and most guests will come back. Fix their problems on the spot and there is a very good chance that they will not only come back but will also likely recommend the organization to their friends. Reward programs and recognition for employees who have done an especially good job of recovering from a service failure offer strong incentives to other employees while providing role models of the organization's commitment to service quality.

How Do Customers Evaluate Recovery Efforts?

A service failure has occurred, and the organization has made an effort to recover from it. Does the guest feel fairly and justly treated? Three dimensions of justice—distributive, procedural, and interactive—need to be considered.[41] In fact, justice dimensions explain 85% of the variation in customer satisfaction with how complaints are handled.[42]

Distributive Justice

Distributive justice, or outcome fairness, is an assessment by the customers of the fairness associated with whatever compensation they received to rectify a service failure. What did the organization actually give or distribute to an unhappy customer as compensation for the problem? If the guest complains about a bad meal and gets only a sincere apology because that's all company policy calls for, some guests will feel unfairly treated; sometimes "We're sorry" isn't enough, in the guest's judgment, to compensate for the poor service. Once again, it all comes down to meeting the guest's expectations. The issue is difficult because each guest is different. For many guests, an apology is fair enough compensation for many service failures. For others, nothing is good enough to make up for the problem or difficulty that the service failure created for them. Finding satisfactory compensation may involve methodical trial and error on the organization's part, but the easiest way is to ask the guest. For example, a hotel could offer a disgruntled guest a choice of either a refund or an upgrade. Some hospitality service providers when confronted with an unhappy guest merely ask, "What would be a fair resolution to this problem?" as the best way to find out what the guest thinks is fair.

distributive justice The customer's feeling, after a complaint or service failure, that the outcome was fair.

Procedural Justice

Procedural justice refers to whether the customer believes company procedures for handling service failure are fair and not a procedural hassle full of red tape. Best Buy believes that not giving customers the best value possible is a kind of service failure, so it will pay customers a refund plus 10% if they show they were not given the lowest

procedural justice The customer's feeling that company procedures are fair and not a procedural hassle, especially after a complaint or service failure.

[41] Ronald L. Hess, Jr. and James Olver, "Failure and Complaint Handling in Marketing: An Organizational Justice Perspective," in *The Oxford Handbook of Justice in the Workplace*, eds. Russel S. Cropanzano and Maureen L. Ambrose (New York: Oxford University Press, 2015), 641–656.

[42] Ruiying Cai and Hailin Qu, "Customers' Perceived Justice, Emotions, Direct and Indirect Reactions to Service Recovery: Moderating Effects of Recovery Efforts," *Journal of Hospitality Marketing & Management* (2017): 1–23.

price in the area on a purchased product. Customers feel this is a fair policy. Customers also want an easy process for correcting failures. They feel that if the organization failed them, it is only fair that the organization makes it easy for them to receive a just settlement. In the earlier discussion of service guarantees, one of the most important features of good guarantees is that they are easy for a guest to invoke.

Interactional Justice

interactional justice The customer's feeling of being treated with respect and courtesy during interactions with the organization, especially after a service failure occurs; being given the opportunity to express complaints fully.

Interactional justice refers to the customer's feeling of being treated with respect and courtesy and being given the opportunity to express the complaint fully. It is the customer's perceptions of the sincerity the staff provides during the process of service recovery. If the customer has a complaint and staff hearing the complaint is rude, indifferent, or uncaring, the customer will feel unfairly treated.

Common sense suggests and research shows that a customer who is encouraged to complain and is then treated with respect, courtesy, and empathy is more likely to be satisfied with the experience, spread positive word of mouth, and repatronize the organization than one who was given a fair settlement but only with reluctance and discourtesy. One survey showed that only 13% of customers who were dissatisfied with the resolution to their problem said they would repurchase the product or service, whereas 73% of customers who were very satisfied with the problem resolution said they would repurchase.[43]

informational justice A type of interactional justice that refers to the customer's feeling of the fairness of the information and communication provided by the organization, especially after a service failure occurs.

Informational justice is a type of interactional justice that spotlights the importance of guests' satisfaction with the adequacy of the information and communication provided by the organization. Were employees of the organization candid with you, or did they not tell you what was going on, hide information, or simply did not communicate to you what the current situation was and what they knew? If a guest is unhappy about a flight delay, it is generally perceived as worse if the airline does not let the guest know the reason for the delay and how long it should realistically take to resolve. Recall from Chapter 11 on waits that an unexplained wait feels longer than an explained wait. Saying "We're sorry" shows the company is apologetic for the delay, but the guest still wants the service product she originally purchased: the flight from point A to point B. Feeling that the company was honest and forthright with information can go a long way with helping the guest to at least understand that there is a legitimate reason for the service failure.

How the Recovery Is Managed

Fairness can mean different things in different situations and with different people. A lot of research has been done to see which is more important and when. Studies have found that while all three justice dimensions influence customer satisfaction, there is no clear "most important" dimension.[44] Furthermore, the dimensions of justice are highly related to each other, so the most important dimension may depend on the context and the behaviors of the staff resolving the complaint.[45]

In fact, the research supports what common sense suggests should be the most effective service recovery. If something goes wrong, have a fair system in place to handle complaints, listen carefully and be empathetic to the guest. The complaint process should be easy-to-use and made available by an employee who seems genuinely apologetic for the failure, appreciative of the opportunity to fix it, and willing to provide fair and appropriate compensation for the pain and suffering caused by the failure.

[43] Daniela Yu and John Timmerman, "The Silver Lining of Customer Problems (Part 2)," *Gallup*, March 14, 2017, http://news.gallup.com/businessjournal/205913/silver-lining-customer-problems-part.aspx.

[44] See, for example, Steven J. Migacz, Suiwen Zou, and James F. Petrick, "The "Terminal" Effects of Service Failure on Airlines: Examining Service Recovery with Justice Theory," *Journal of Travel Research* 57, no. 1 (2018): 83–98; and Beomjoon Choi and Beom-Jin Choi, "The Effects of Perceived Service Recovery Justice on Customer Affection, Loyalty, and Word-of-Mouth," *European Journal of Marketing* 48, no. 1/2 (2014): 108–131.

[45] Jung and Seock, "Effect of Service Recovery," 23–30.

These effects of justice are well illustrated by the following example, where a customer emerged highly satisfied by what began as a horrendous service failure. Southwest reports a story of how a passenger wrote a letter thanking Southwest for a trip that took twenty-two hours. While most would think this is a cause for a major complaint, the customer saw it differently because of the actions taken by several customer service employees. It seems that weather had caused cancelled flights and closed airports for a traveler trying to get from Salt Lake City to Chicago. The customer service agent, working a seventeen-hour shift to help stranded customers, found a way to book the passenger on actual flights instead of sending him on his way to hope for the best on standby status. Booking a triple connection, the agent got him confirmed seats to his home. At the same time, another agent booked his bags directly to Chicago so they would be there when he finally arrived, and another agent met him at the end of the first leg of his trip and provided him with a snack. In the letter summarizing his experience, the passenger wrote, "Due to your amazing customer service, a flight plan that could have been a nightmare instead became a great story to tell. I received much more attention than expected because your organization truly under-promised and over-delivered."[46]

The important lesson that justice theory teaches is that different people will see failure and recovery through different perceptions of fairness. The different aspects of justice affect repurchase intentions, positive or negative word of mouth, and customer satisfaction.[47] The extent of dissatisfaction is affected by such factors as the customer involvement in co-production requirements; the length, frequency, closeness, and importance of the relationship to the customer; and the costs of switching to another provider.[48] The stronger guests feel about these factors, the angrier they will be when the organization fails them in some important way. One might then assume that satisfaction with service recovery would only be a function of how much the person gets (i.e., distributive justice) in compensation, but the prior research and the Southwest example shows this not to be the case. Instead, perceptions of service recovery are influenced by the fairness of the process used (procedural justice), the empathy of the employee (interpersonal justice), and the way in which the customer was kept informed (informational justice). The way in which the recovery is managed can thus either help or hinder the guest's future relationship with the organization.

There are a number of key lessons for service recovery that we can learn from the research on fairness: If there is a problem, fix it quickly. If the guest is a long-time loyal customer, fix it quickly and especially well. But solving it quickly and well does not mean just throwing money at a complaint, as that won't make it go away. Find out and care about the problem, be honest when solving the problem, and approach the solution fairly.

Service-Recovery Systems Analysis

Besides the individual tools and techniques discussed in the previous chapters, an overall strategy for failure analysis will serve the guestologist seeking to prevent any guest from being disappointed. Exhibit 13.1 presents a model that describes how managers should analyze their failures and their efforts at failure recovery. This exhibit shows that analyzing and correcting service failures has seven steps. The first three steps involve failure analysis, while the last four steps involve the recovery effort.

[46] T. Laraba, "Southwest Servant's Heart," *Spirit Magazine*, September 16, 2009.

[47] Cai and Qu, "Customers' Perceived Justice," 1–23.

[48] See David Cranage, "Plan to Do It Right: and Plan for Recovery," *International Journal of Contemporary Hospitality Management* 16, no. 4 (2004): 210–219.

EXHIBIT 13.1

The Steps of Failure Analysis and Recovery Efforts

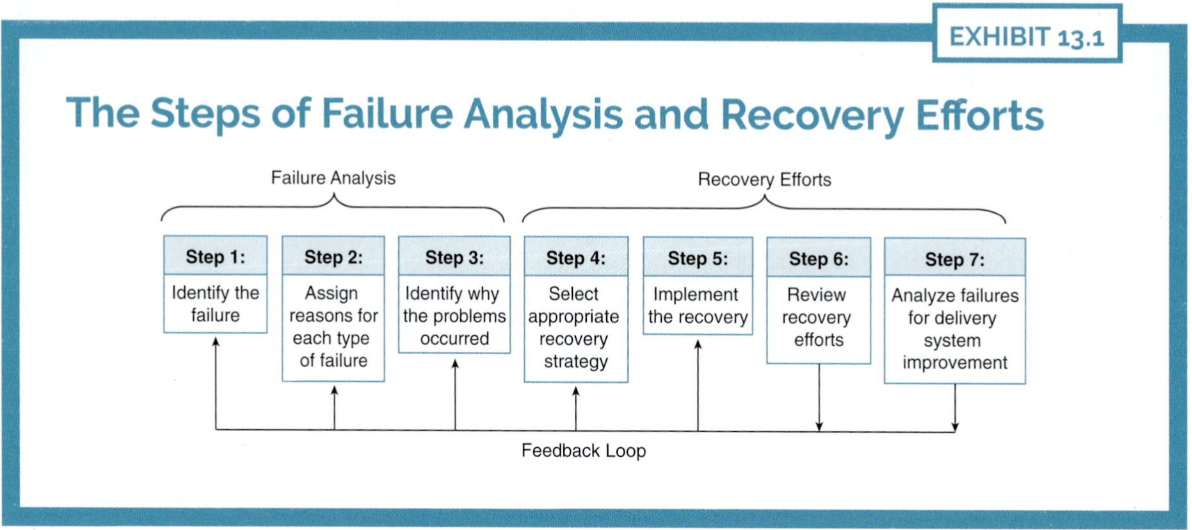

Specifically, the first step is to identify the failures. The second step is to put them into categories for further analysis. These steps require organizations to be on watch for service failures and to have a system in place to document and track any errors that occur. The third step is to assign reasons for each type of failure, attributing them to who was in charge, how often they happen, and whether those in charge could have controlled what happened. This step is not designed to focus on finding someone to blame or punish, but rather to identify why the problems occurred so the system can be changed, the employee involved can be trained, or the necessary changes can be made.

The recovery effort begins where the failure analysis ends. The fourth step of the model is to select the appropriate recovery strategy for each type of failure. Strategies can range from a simple apology to some level of compensation to no response at all. During the planning phase, companies must consider the types of failures that might occur and prepare appropriate responses for them. The fifth step is the implementation of the recovery. Its success is grounded in how fair customers perceive it to be, in terms of the justice types we have just discussed. The sixth step is to review the recovery efforts and follow up to see if they were successful. The organization should assess the extent to which the employees involved in attempting recovery performed appropriately and whether the details of the failure have been recorded and retained in the company database for future use and further study of failure causes.

Another critical component of a good failure analysis system is the feedback loop. Information obtained from each part of the process should be shared throughout the organization to help correct problems, prevent similar problems, and help teach other employees how to handle problems. While this feedback should occur throughout the process, in the seventh step the organization should look beyond the specific service failure incident and consider the implications of service failures for the entire service delivery system. For a system to "heal itself" it must be able to learn from its mistakes. The model seen here echoes the point of "the cycle going on" in the planning model presented in Chapter 10.

Characteristics of a Good Recovery Strategy

While the exact mechanisms of a good recovery system will depend on the specific nature of the business and its service product, in general a service-recovery strategy should satisfy several criteria.[49] First, the strategy should ensure the failure is addressed quickly and fixed in some positive way if possible. Second, recovery strategies must be communicated clearly to the employees charged with responding to customer dissatisfaction. The service people must know that the organization expects them to find and resolve customer problems as part of their jobs. Third, recovery strategies should be easy for the customer to find and use. Finally, they should be flexible enough to accommodate both the different types of failures and the different expectations that customers have of their guest experiences. The service-recovery strategy developed should be based on management understanding that because the customer defines the quality of the service experience, the customer also defines its failures and the adequacy of the recovery strategies.

No Better Makes It Worse

A strategy that does not improve the situation for the complaining customer is worse than useless because the organization makes plain that it can't or won't recover from failure even when informed of it. Most recovery strategies are in serious need of improvement. While the hotel industry does better than nearly all other industries, over 60% of customers who reported a problem reported that they were dissatisfied with the problem solution.[50] In trying to make things better, organizations may and often do make them worse.

Costs of Failure to Guests

One reason customers view many recovery strategies as inadequate is that they do not really consider all of the costs to the customer. Bad meal? Replace it. Theme park attraction broken? Give a complimentary one-day return pass. Busy signal on the telephone line for airport information? Interject a recorded apology. After such recovery efforts, the organization may think the relationship is back where it started but, for the customer, many other tangible and intangible costs may be associated with failures. The effective organization will try to identify these costs and include some recognition of them in selecting the appropriate service recovery. After all, the customer will think that the fact the service failed is "not my fault." Why should I have to wait on the side of the road for a long time because the rental car broke down? Why should I have to call back repeatedly to reservations because the airline messed up the original reservation? Why should I have to return ten miles to the restaurant because the drive-through people didn't get the order right?

Making It Right Is Not Enough

Customers clearly think that when a failure occurs, organizations need to do more than simply make it right by replacing it or doing it over again. Of course, organizations should do that, but they should do more. For example, if the failed meal causes the guest to be embarrassed in front of a client or boss, then the recovery strategy must not only include compensation for the meal but some consideration for the guest's other costs and emotional outlays as well. If a mom tells her kids about the terrific time they all will have at a famous resort, uses her only week of vacation to go there, and spends all the extra money she has so carefully saved, she has a lot at stake. If the experience fails somehow to meet the family's expectations, the mom loses her time, her money, and her credibility with the family. The outstanding hospitality organization systematically considers how to compensate guests for losses other than financial and makes extra effort to ensure that dissatisfied guests not only have their financial

49 Zeithaml, Bitner, and Gremler, *Services Marketing*.
50 Timmerman and Yu, "The Silver Lining."

Chip Somodevilla/Getty Images

After a horrendous customer service failure in which an overbooked customer was dragged off a United Airlines flight, despite an eventual apology and settlement, the CEO of United Airlines Oscar Munoz was required to testify in front of Congress about oversight of U.S. airline customer service.

losses addressed in a recovery effort, but the guests have their ego and esteem needs met as well. They want mom to go home a hero to her family.

Being Wrong with Dignity

Even when the guests themselves make mistakes, good hospitality organizations help to correct them with sensitivity. That way guests leave feeling good about their overall experience and appreciating how the organization's personnel helped them redeem themselves. Imagine how depressed you would feel if you came back to the parking lot after a long day at an amusement park to find that you have lost your car keys and are locked out of your car. Then you see the park's "Auto Patrol" coming to your rescue. They even make you a new set of keys for free! Even though such problems are not its fault, the guest-oriented organization believes that the guest needs to be wrong with dignity. It knows that guests who are angry at themselves may transfer some of that anger to the organization. To overcome this very human tendency, guest-centric organizations find ways to fix guests' mistakes so that angry, frustrated people leave feeling good because a bad experience has not been allowed to overshadow or cancel out all the good. By providing this high level of guest service, the hospitality organization earns the gratitude and future patronage of guests and enhances its reputation when such service successes are circulated to both external and internal customers.

Matching the Recovery Strategy to the Failure

The best recovery efforts match the nature and severity of failure. For example, if a restaurant is out of a certain menu item, compensating the guest with a "rain check" might be appropriate. If the failure is server inattentiveness, an apology by the manager would be a more appropriate response. Sometimes, customers demand more than is reasonable, and a company must respond while finding a way to stay within sensible limitations. For example, a customer claimed a Starbucks store had sold him two defective coffee makers with a total value of $500, neglected to include a promised free half-pound of coffee, and treated him rudely. The customer was not satisfied by company apologies, replacement and refund offers, and gifts. His suggested recovery strategy was that Starbucks take out a full-page ad of apology in the *Wall Street Journal,* give him a $2,500 coffee maker, and fund a shelter for runaway children.[51] Needless to say, the customer's demands were not met.

Categorizing the severity and causes of service failures is a useful way to show the type of recovery strategy that a hospitality organization might select. In Exhibit 13.2, the vertical axis represents the severity of the failure ranging from low to high. The horizontal axis divides service failures into those caused by the organization and by the guest. When severity is high and the failure is the organization's fault, the proper response is the red-carpet treatment, as in the case of a sold-out hotel "walking" a guest with reservations to a fully paid, upgraded room at another hotel. The organization needs to bend over backwards to fix this guest's problem and should consider trying to provide a "wow" level of recovery to overcome the negative feeling the

[51] Grégoire and Fisher, "Customer Betrayal."

EXHIBIT 13.2

Matching the Recovery Strategy to the Failure

Severity of failure	Organization	Guest
Relatively severe	Red-carpet treatment and apology	Provide help to the extent possible and apologize
Relatively mild	Apologize and replace	Apologize and extend sympathy

Cause of failure

guest will have after a severe failure. A less severe problem caused by the organization might be a server bringing a guest a cold food item that is supposed to be hot. A fitting solution here is to apologize and replace the item quickly. Providing a complimentary dessert might also be appropriate. McDonald's has a policy that anyone bringing a food item back to the counter with the complaint that it is cold is immediately given an apology and a replacement item with no questions asked.

The two general situations in which the guest caused the failure provide terrific opportunities for the organization to make guests feel positive about the experience even when they caused the failure. In a low-severity situation, a sincere apology is sufficient and will make the guest feel the organization is taking some of the responsibility for a situation that was clearly not its fault. Indeed, some organizations will do even more, if the cost to make a guest feel better is not too high. Many restaurants don't charge their guests for meals or items they don't like or want. Similarly, many different hotel brands offer service guarantees. The upper-right box represents situations where the problem is relatively severe and the guest or some external force created the problem. These are opportunities for the organization to be a hero and provide an unforgettable experience for the guest.

A Domino's delivery man showed up with pizzas at a house that was still smoldering from a devastating fire. The distraught couple, standing in the front yard of their ruined house looked up at the delivery man with some annoyance, said they hadn't ordered any pizza, and wondered if the delivery person couldn't see that they were overcome by the tragedy. The delivery man responded that he knew; he had passed the house earlier, saw it burning, and had told his manager. The two decided that it would be a kindness to cook up some pizzas and just give them to these people in their hour of sadness. The company became a hero to the couple—customers who didn't even know they were customers.

Learning From Failures

From a guestology view, a failure is an opportunity to improve. If the data collected show that older guests are having problems with reading the signs, then an organizational response would be to increase lettering size. If the data show that the source of customer dissatisfaction is other customers cutting in line, being too loud, or otherwise intruding on guest experiences, then policies and processes can be created to add rope lines, separate guests by a wider space, or institute cautioning measures. If the data show that the loyalty program is making promises on which the organization does not deliver, then the program must be revised to ensure that loyalty awards are easy to obtain, with accessible procedures, as valuable as promised, and actually available when desired. Finally, if the data show that the organization itself has policies, processes, and procedures that cause customer dissatisfaction or service failures, then it has valuable knowledge about what it needs to fix, improve, or change, what employee training to develop, and what innovations to make.

As is true of any data that report failures in any system, guest complaints are valuable data and should be collected and analyzed regularly. In an interview with Bruce Laval, retired vice president for planning and operations for the Walt Disney Company, he was asked how he found the things to fix. His response, as the inventor of the term *guestology,* should be a guide to all who wish to create a guest-focused organization: measure what you want to manage and, especially, everything that touches or impacts the guest. In a company like Walt Disney, that includes everything they do.

Service Recovery: Ow! to Wow!

Companies that have invested in the formation and operation of units designed to handle complaints can realize substantial returns on their investment. Putting money and effort into service recovery is good business. A Disney saying is, "Turn tragic moments into magic moments." The best hospitality organizations view a service failure as a great opportunity to create an unforgettable, outrageously positive response. If the guest is upset that the hotel is overbooked and her room is gone by the time she arrives tired and ready for bed, the hotel should not only drive her to a nearby hotel with the price of the room paid but should upgrade her room from whatever she had reserved. This guest who was denied her standard room but got a paid-for night in a VIP suite at another hotel might readily forgive the hotel that failed to save her a room. The organization extended its hospitality to a guest, then failed her. It should go the extra mile and then some to repair the damage. The right failure-recovery strategy can turn an irate guest, ready to head for the competition, into a raving fan who is happy to repay the organization with a lifetime of valuable support.

Consider the example of how a premium tour company, CruiseWest, once managed a problem that was clearly outside its control, and turned it into a memorable experience. Scott, driving a tour bus with twenty-five guests, was traveling from Fairbanks, Alaska, to Denali National Park for CruiseWest. Just outside Nenana, he was forced to stop at the end of a long line of busses from a number of other tour companies making the same journey. They were stopped because of a dangerous fire burning across the road in front of them, and there was no word on when it would be again safe to travel. Scott immediately called back to the supervisor in Fairbanks to report the situation. The supervisor told him to take the guests to a restaurant in Nenana while she sorted this out. While the group was dining, the supervisor called five bush pilots she knew of and arranged for them to fly to Denali. She then called Scott and told him to take the group to the Nenana airport where the bush pilots were now waiting, and who would fly the guests and Scott over the fire (and the fifteen waiting tour busses from the other tour companies). After the short flight, they landed near Denali at Healy where a bus picked them up and took them to their hotel to continue on with their scheduled tour activities. While this creative solution added nearly $10,000 to the operating cost of the tour, it was a far less expensive solution than what the other tour operators faced as they had to both reimburse their angry travelers for the unfulfilled trip experience and give them vouchers for another trip. This creative and quick solution to what might have otherwise been a complete disaster for CruiseWest guests turned an "ow" into a "wow." In fact, these guests indicated on their comment cards that the flight over the fire was the highlight of the trip and they could hardly wait to tell all their friends what a great cruise experience Cruise West provided. (As an aside, consider that the bus, and the unanticipated plane trip to Nenana, was really a "wait" for the real service product, the cruise. Because of the way the situation was handled, the guests actually ended up finding the wait for service to be a great moment on the trip!) A motivated and creative employee not only saved the trip and the costs of a major service failure but also created tremendous word of mouth for his company.

Even if you are not responsible for a failure, recovering is an important way to get the guest's attention with impressive service. When no one expects you to fix someone else's mistake and you do it anyway, people are wowed.

Successful Service Recovery

Although beginning a discussion with a definition is customary, we will end with one by service scholars Michel, Bowen, and Johnston who in defining effective service recovery state it is "the integrative actions a company takes to re-establish customer satisfaction and loyalty after a service failure (customer recovery), to ensure that failure incidents encourage learning and process improvement (process recovery) and to train and reward employees for this purpose (employee recovery)."[52] If the recovery actions the company takes are unsuccessful, then the company has added failure to failure. If the actions restore customer satisfaction and loyalty, then the recovery has succeeded from the customer's point of view, and that is the main thing. But from the company's perception, a truly successful service recovery will be a set of integrative actions that also improve the process and the employees involved. When the organization uses a successful service recovery, guests, employees, and the process are all better off.

LESSONS LEARNED

Lo 13.1 Explain how guests respond when the guest experience fails to meet their expectations.

- If the guest thinks you failed, you failed.

Lo 13.2 Describe how organizations should respond when the experience fails to meet guest expectations.

- Train your employees to listen with empathy.

Lo 13.3 Explain how organizations prepare their employees to find and fix failures.

- Find out and share with employees how much a dissatisfied guest costs; that will show your staff the importance of recovering from service failure.
- Train and empower your employees to find and fix failures.
- Don't punish employees for reporting failures they made, punish them for not reporting them.
- Even the best organizations fail a guest occasionally. Be prepared for failure; have a recovery strategy in place.

Lo 13.4 Explain why positive word of mouth is so valuable and bad word of mouth so harmful.

- Unhappy guests will tell twice as many people about bad experiences as happy guests will tell about good experiences.

Lo 13.5 Express why the recovery method for handling a service failure is so important.

- Encourage guests to tell you about problems and failures; a complaint is a gift.
- Service-failure recovery works only if the system works; even an empowered employee can't recover from service failure without support from the system.

---

[52] Stefan Michel, David Bowen, and Robert Johnston, "Why Service Recovery Fails: Tensions among Customer, Employee, and Process Perspectives," *Journal of Service Management* 20, no. 3 (2009): 253–273.

LO 13.6 State why fixing service failures quickly and fairly—on the spot, if possible—is so important.

- Fix their problems and most guests will come back; fix their problems on the spot and they will almost certainly come back.
- Don't cause a service-failure problem and then fail to fix it. Don't fail the guest twice.

LO 13.7 Recognize how to learn from service failures.

- When you work to solve the service failure, also work to improve the service delivery system.

LO 13.8 Describe how guests evaluate the hospitality organization's recovery efforts.

- Guests evaluate not just what they "get" to compensate for a service failure, but also the organization's procedures, how they were treated, and how information was shared with them during the service-recovery process.

LO 13.9 Match the recovery strategy to the failure.

- Find a fair solution, and know how guests determine what is fair.
- Find ways to help guests fix problems they caused.

KEY TERMS AND CONCEPTS

avenger 433
bad-mouth 432
distributive justice 439
evangelist 433
informational justice 440
interactional justice 440
procedural justice 439
service failure 421
service recovery 430
word of mouth 428
zone of tolerance 426

REVIEW QUESTIONS

1. Recall a service failure during a guest experience of your own.
   A. Describe the failure and your reaction to it.
   B. Describe the organization's response to the failure. Did your reaction to the failure seem to affect the organizational response?
   C. As a result of what happened, how do you feel about this organization now?
   D. If you were not completely satisfied, what could the organization have done to satisfy you and perhaps cause you to be even more loyal to the organization than before?
2. If you ran a hospitality organization, how would you plan to recover from failure?
   A. Would you give employees a list of common failures and their corresponding acceptable recovery strategies, or would you empower employees to use whatever recovery strategies they saw fit? Or both?
   B. Would you try to quick-fix problems immediately or look for longer-term solutions that might prevent future problems?
   C. What would be the characteristics of your service-recovery plan?
   D. One hospitality leader instructs employees to keep offering successively more significant remedies to failure until the guest smiles, then stop. Discuss this strategy.
3. Many service failures occurring during guest experiences at a hotel or at a restaurant can be predicted and fixed. Name two problems that a hotel and a restaurant probably cannot fix. What should the managers do if those failures occur?
4. A guest in your organization starts an argument with another guest who has tried to cut into a waiting line.
   A. Is this a service failure? If so, who or what failed? What should you as a manager do?
   B. If, rather than starting an argument, the first guest punches the second guest, what should you as a manager do?

5. Do you believe that a complaint is "a gift" from the complaining customer to the organization? If you have complained to organizations, has the reaction suggested that they believe you are presenting them with a gift?
6. According to this chapter, some experts suggest that apologizing for failures of which the guest may not even be aware might be a good idea. Do you agree?

ACTIVITIES

1. Have you recently experienced a service failure? If so, write a letter to the establishment's manager complaining about the dissatisfying or failed service experience you have had. (*Do not make up a false complaint!!!*) Describe how the organization responds to your complaint. How does the organization's recovery effort correspond to the suggestions for recovery offered in the chapter?
2. Have you recently experienced an exceptional service experience? If so, write a letter to organization complimenting the service. Send a copy to the company president. Report back on the results. It is okay to mention names in this letter.
3. Have you recently observed a service failure that someone else has experienced? If so, report how the organization recovered from the failure. Evaluate the recovery strategy based on the material presented in the chapter.
4. Divide into groups. For those who have been employees, describe service failures in which you have been involved. Have you been trained in how to recover from these failures? What recovery steps did you take? Pick the best service recovery and compare with the best of other groups. What lessons can be learned from these successful recoveries?
5. Have a classroom discussion on the topic "Who is more responsible for most service errors: servers or managers?" (Remember that managers plan and implement delivery systems.) Go out to some local restaurants or other hospitality organizations and ask some servers and some managers this question, "What service failures do guests most frequently experience in your place of business, and who is more responsible for most of them: servers or managers?" and report back your results.

ETHICS IN BUSINESS

A certain restaurant has no policy in place about service recovery, and servers have no specific authority to provide any free products to customers. A server in the restaurant sees that an error occurred at her table. In order to keep the customers happy (and to protect her tip), she gives them free drinks without getting permission to do so from her supervisor. A friend who tends bar gives her these drinks when he can do so unobserved. The server feels justified in doing this because her regular salary is low, and she depends on tips from satisfied customers for most of her income. Is her behavior unethical? Does the cost of the free item affect the appropriateness of her actions? Free soft drinks cost the restaurant only pennies. Complimentary drinks from the bar are much more expensive, and alcoholic beverages make up a considerable part of the restaurant's revenue. Does the server's motivation affect your answer—giving the free items because she wants to protect her tips, versus wanting to ensure that her customers have the best possible experience?

A second restaurant does have the policy of ensuring customer satisfaction, and servers have the authority to remove the cost of a meal if a customer is dissatisfied. A patron complains that she did not like her meal, although she did eat it in its entirety, said nothing during the meal, and the server saw no indication of a problem during the meal. The server is suspicious that the customer knows the company's policy and is simply trying to get a free meal, but he has no evidence to support this beyond his gut feeling. What is the right course of action?

CASE STUDY

Case 1: Pizza-to-Go

Bob Callahan led a very hectic business life consisting of hard work, long hours, and eating on the run. Bob also liked pizza. It is therefore no surprise that he did a lot of business with his neighborhood Pizza-to-Go outlet. About once a week, just before leaving work, Bob would call PTG; order a medium thin-crust pizza with olives, sausage, and double anchovies; and pick it up on his way home. The PTG people once forgot the sausage and once put pepperoni instead of olives, but Bob forgave them and never mentioned these small slipups. He could do with a little less sausage in his diet, and he liked pepperoni almost as well as olives anyway. Besides, they never got the anchovies wrong, and Bob's favorite part of the entire pizza experience was the overabundance of anchovies swimming in mozzarella cheese.

Last week Bob got home from work and kicked back, ready to enjoy a beer and some pizza fixed "his way." The pizza he took out of the box was fixed somebody else's way; it was covered with pineapple, broccoli, and what looked like a double order of onions. Bob couldn't imagine what kind of person would eat a combination like that. He called PTG immediately. The phone was answered by Vito Cifrese, who had been serving Bob regularly for about two years.

"Very sorry about that, Mr. Callahan. If you could just scrape those onions off this one time, next time you come in I'll comp you your regular order and I'll also throw in a small complimentary pizza with double anchovies for free!" Bob thought that was a pretty fair adjustment. He thanked Vito, scraped off the onions, and tried to eat the pizza. But the onion flavor remained. Bob couldn't finish the pizza; the combination of pineapple, broccoli, and onion flavor was too much for him.

That all happened on an early Monday evening. On Thursday of the same week, Bob called in and ordered the usual, plus a small pizza with double anchovies. When he got to Pizza-to-Go, Vito was nowhere to be seen. Bob identified himself to the counter server who handed over the two boxes. Bob explained that both items were to be "no charge" because of an error that had been made on a previous order.

The server laughed and said, "I don't think so. Check that sign out there. This is Pizza-to-Go. Pizza-for-Free is up the street."

Bob stayed calm and asked for Vito; he could straighten this out.

"Vito quit Monday night and said he never wanted to see another pizza."

"I've gotten one or two pizzas a week from you people for the past two years. My name's Bobby Callahan. Check under my name in your database and see if Vito left any special instructions."

"What database?" said the server.

Bobby gave up. He'd find another place to do business. "I'll just take the small pizza with double anchovies."

"You don't want the big one?"

"That's right."

"Even though you called in for it? Well, we can warm it up for somebody else, I guess, if anybody else wants a weird combo like olives, sausage, and anchovies."

Bob paid without tipping, left, got home, grabbed a beer, turned on TV, kicked back, opened the box, and took out a small pizza covered with onions.

1. Was service recovery called for in this situation?
2. If so, what recovery options would you have considered?
3. What should Bob Callahan do now?

Case 2: Recovery to the Max

Ben Sharpless, manager of the tackle store at Farney Spa and Fish Camp, had just finished explaining to new sales employee Max Gilley the importance of getting and retaining customers, recovering from service failure, and other basics of serving guests, whether they were fisher-folk who also had spa privileges or spa patrons who wanted to do a little fishing. About an hour later, Ben saw Max talking with regular customer Sally Higgins. He thought he would monitor Max's sales technique, so he moved to a spot where he could hear but not be seen.

Sally Higgins was saying,

"Max, I thought I'd fish down at the bend where you can see them feeding on the bottom."

"Ms. Higgins, you don't want to fish for those little minners. You want to put your bait about 30 feet out, where the big ones are. Here, what about this Orvis reel with the matching graphite rod and tackle box full of lures and other gadgets? I think that'll do the trick. But fishing's even better on the other side of the lake early in the morning. We've also got a fully equipped camping rig here that I can let you use, with the tent, the stove, all the supplies you could ever need. You can camp out, turn in early, and be up and at 'em with the dawn." Ms. Higgins agreed that it was a beautiful rig. Visions of huge trout leaped in her mind. Visions of a big sale leaped in the mind of store manager Ben Sharpless.

"What kind of car do you have, Ms. Higgins? A Mercedes E-300, isn't it? This stuff isn't going to fit in there. We just received a special-order Land Rover with matching trailer. You'll look good in that, and you can haul all this camping and fishing equipment in the trailer with room to spare. We could let you use that for a couple of days."

Manager Sharpless was really impressed with Max's results. Max and Sally finished the paperwork, Sally Higgins left, and Sharpless went to Max Gilley to congratulate him on a big sale.

"Gilley, you're quite a salesman. I don't know if I would have loaned her all that fancy camping equipment and the Land Rover, but that Orvis rod and reel plus a fully equipped tackle box is a big sale, maybe several hundred dollars, so I guess it's worth it."

Max looked puzzled. "No, Mr. Sharpless, you got it all wrong. Ms. Higgins was just out for a walk. We started to talk, and she told me the spa was busted. Uh-oh, I say to myself. "Service failure". I remembered what you told me: 'It costs several times as much to get a new guest as it does to keep a present guest, Max, so when you see any service failure, spa or fish camp, that service failure becomes yours to correct. You own that service failure until it's fixed, Max. And don't just fix it; go above and beyond. Anything we lose on that transaction will be made up in future business for the spa and fish camp. If we do lose money, what's the worst that can happen? We'll have a satisfied guest.' Wasn't that about it, Mr. Sharpless?"

Sharpless said, "Yes, Max, you learned well, but . . ."

"So I said to her, 'Since the spa is busted, why don't you go fishing?' Then I gave her the fishing tackle and the tackle box but I only loaned her the rest of the stuff. She seemed right happy, didn't she?"

Manager Sharpless sighed. "Max, if I hadn't been here, I guess you would have given her the whole darn tackle shop."

1. What do you think would have been an appropriate adjustment for this service failure? Or should a fish camp employee even be concerned about a spa service failure?
2. How can organizations encourage their employees to take ownership of service failures and try to fix them on the spot, without "giving away the store"?

Case 3: Letter of Complaint

Consider the following letter of complaint, an actual letter written by the lead author of this book, and tell how you would respond to it if you received it.

Mr. P.D. Bacon

Chief Executive Officer

Sun International Limited

27 Fredman Drive

Sandton 2031 Gauteng

Republic of South Africa

Dear Mr. Bacon:

I am writing to tell of an experience I had during my recent visit to one of your resorts, The Zambezi Sun. I want you to know that my experience had good and bad points to it. The good points are largely attributable to two of your employees, Mr. Craig Storkey and

Ms. Suzette Venter. The bad points are due to what seems to me to be policies and procedures that did not meet my expectations nor would I expect them to meet those of most American travelers. Thus, please consider this a letter of both compliment and complaint. Let me first detail the situation so you can see the reason for both my compliments and complaints.

In the late morning of June 24, my wife and I were standing in the porte-cochere of the Zambezi Sun in Victoria Falls, Zambia behind our transport to the airport. As I stepped back to avoid the downward closing tailgate of the transport van, a quickly moving jeep clipped my leg with its left side rear tire. Somehow, the tire grabbed my leg to make it stationary while it was wrenched and broken. While we do not know the vehicle number, we were later told it was a Zambian government vehicle. The result was two broken bones in my left leg. At the same time, apparently some hotel employees contacted both the hotel manager and the hotel clinic nurse.

The nurse did a competent job of calmly organizing my care. I was transported back to the hotel clinic (which had no working x-ray machine) and, while I was being interviewed by Zambian police about the accident, she called around to the local medical facilities to find a working x-ray so we could see the extent of damage to my leg. When she finally found one, she then contacted the local ambulance service to transport me. By this time the hotel manager had arrived and was talking to me in the clinic. He was reassuring and concerned. He told us that he would pay the ambulance fee cash requirement and put it on our bill so we could pay by credit card. We were concerned about how much cash we had to pay all that we had to in this cash-driven country. While we were surprised we would pay this fee, we appreciated his help.

The nurse was wonderful. After locating an x-ray and transport, she accompanied us to the Livingstone clinic where the doctor and x-ray were located. She was calm and reassuring throughout this ordeal. That was especially important to me and my wife as we contemplated the challenges of getting medical care in Zambia and then wondered how we would proceed from there to either home or our next medical treatment facility. After getting my leg x-rayed, the Zambian doctor put on a cast and told me I could travel onward. The nurse cautioned me that this might be a problem with a hard cast on an airplane so she persuaded the doctor to put on a cast that could be readily cut to relieve pressure while flying onward.

We then went back to the hotel where the manager had thoughtfully provided a room in the Royal Livingston for us at no charge. The nurse and he had agreed that I needed to stay on the ground that night in case any complications arose that would be harmful to my flying out. The nurse consulted with her supervisors in Johannesburg about what to do with me. They told her to Medivac me and would not approve any other means to transport me out of Zambia. Suzette then consulted with my travel insurance company which would not approve the fee for such transport. They told her that they would only pay for commercial transport and that if I wanted to go out by Medivac, it would be my financial responsibility. This is where the nurse really showed her medical expertise and decision-making skills. Since she was able to assess my physical condition and also knew the financial considerations of the options, she patiently and skillfully reviewed what I could do next. After some discussion, we agreed that flying commercially to Johannesburg the next day to seek further treatment was the best choice for me to make.

We found the nurse's handling of my situation remarkable and want to commend her for it. First, her response to my injury was quick, calm, and competent. She made a bad situation tolerable and reduced our level of panic by her calm demeanor and obvious professionalism. She exuded competence. Second, her management of the various steps involved in getting treatment was terrific. She handled it all and made sure we knew what was happening all the time. Third, she helped tremendously in going through the various options we had to carefully consider to decide what to do next. While she had to respect her own leadership's directions as to what to do, she also had to consider our needs and circumstances and we always felt she was considering her patient's needs first. In other words, we were tremendously impressed with her competence, calmness, and professionalism. You are fortunate to have such a terrific employee and you need to know that.

Now, however, I wish to make a complaint about your procedures for handling such situations. Perhaps we in the USA have a distorted picture of what the responsibility of a hotel is in such a situation because of the volume of personal injury litigation we have. I may even be more sensitive to this because I teach, conduct management development seminars, research, and write in the academic field of guest services management. Further, I live in Orlando where the Walt Disney Company has become the world benchmark for guest service excellence. From all these perspectives, I feel your company has much work to do before it matches the standards expected by today's upscale American traveler. For example, no American I know would ever expect to pay for an ambulance to be taken from an injury suffered in the hotel's own porte-cochere. No American would expect to be taken to an upscale hotel clinic that had no working x-ray machine. No American would expect to be asked to pay for emergency medical treatment resulting from an injury on hotel property, and no American would expect the hotel to ask him/her to pay for the meals or telephone calls made while trying to notify all the people that had to be notified to get on to the next destination. While I am certain the manager did all he was authorized to do, I would strongly encourage you to authorize him to do more. In the USA, a hotel manager would typically have picked up all these costs hoping that by doing so he/she could make the guest feel better (and less litigious) about being hit by a car on hotel property. Most of these costs are fairly minimal, especially food costs, and would have made a difference in the feelings that at least this guest had towards the hotel.

As we teach in our classes, this is the type of service failure that every hospitality organization fears. Once it happens, however, the organization should do everything it can to make the failure as tolerable as possible. We call this, in my own textbook on guest services management, the red-carpet treatment. While we greatly appreciated your manager's concern with our situation and his helpfulness in making arrangements to get us back to Johannesburg, we teach that a free room upgrade is only one part of the service-recovery effort available to recover from a major service failure like this.

While you may feel that I am overly influenced by what litigation has done to American hotel guest expectations, the point is that those are the expectations that your American guests now have and that you must meet if you wish to satisfy this market. I strongly urge you to revisit your procedures and consider revising them to meet the expectations of your guests no matter where they're from. In my opinion these are becoming the world class standards you must meet if you wish to be considered a world class hotel. There are many things that could have been done to mitigate the anguish I suffered, and world class hotels do the things that make a difference. I would encourage you to hold a simple brainstorming session with your general managers to consider failure scenarios and develop the best way to deal with various service failures like mine. This might help you think through the things that might have been done better here and which, for the most part, have nominal or little cost.

Thank you for the opportunity to share my thoughts with you. You have excellent people trying to do a terrific job in serving their guests, but based on my experience, your own procedures and service-recovery processes leave much to be desired. I hope you find this information useful and that you will publicly recognize the positive contributions that your employees made that made our bad situation less bad. My intent in sharing my complaint is to bring to your attention the need to think through the many other things that you might do to make this dissatisfied guest less dissatisfied. I think that a careful rethinking of some simple procedural changes would allow you to make this type of bad situation less bad for any future guests who suffer the misfortune I did. I urge you to take the time to consider them.

Sincerely,

Robert C. Ford, PhD

Professor of Management

1. What did the letter include or not include that a good complaint letter should contain?
2. What response should the hotel's CEO make to this letter?
3. How do you think the company actually responded?

4. Draft a response that you feel represents what the chapter teaches about how a complaint is a gift.

Case 4: The Hillsbrook Lodge

During the busy times of the year—ski season and the period when the leaves turned—a portion of visitors to New England bed and breakfast establishments sometimes made reservations at two or even three B&Bs. They knew that some B&Bs customarily overbooked, and these guests wanted to be sure they didn't end up after a long drive without a place to stay.

The Hillsbrook Lodge followed the practice of the other bed and breakfast places in its area. During those busy times of the year, the lodge customarily overbooked by 10 to 15%. At first, owners George and Audrey Spain didn't like to overbook; it seemed dishonest somehow. But the other owners were doing it, and the Hillsbrook Lodge couldn't afford to have anything less than 100% occupancy during the two periods of the year that enabled them to get sufficiently ahead financially to stay open during the leaner periods. Things usually balanced themselves out; the Hillsbrook Lodge overbooked by about 15%, and about 15% of the guests usually didn't show up.

The B&B owners in the area had a cooperative service-recovery plan. They networked and kept in touch, so that any owners finding themselves facing guests whose reservations could not be honored could usually make a few phone calls to find another acceptable accommodation for the guests nearby. But supply and demand did not always even out, so occasionally George and Audrey were in the uncomfortable position of telling guests with reservations that not only did they themselves have no room for the guests, but neither did anyone else in the area. Guests did not usually take that news very well. But under the pressures of the next day's activities, George and Audrey forgot these incidents quickly.

When the prime autumn weekend for viewing the turning of the leaves came, Audrey and George found they were grossly overbooked. In addition to the 15% overbooking they had reluctantly agreed to, they had each carelessly booked parties without the other's knowledge. So by the middle of Friday afternoon, all ten Hillsbrook rooms were taken, with several parties yet to come.

A fashionably dressed woman and a large man came into the lodge, announced that they were Bruno and Sophie Tattaglia from New York, and asked to check in.

"Hi, Mr. and Mrs. Tattaglia. Can I call you Sophie and Bruno? Welcome to Hillsbrook Lodge! We've got a little problem. More guests showed up than we thought we were going to get, so since we operate on a first-come, first-served basis, I'm sorry to say we're filled up. But I think I can find accommodations for you at one of the other B&Bs nearby. They're all quite fine."

Sophie Tattaglia protested, "But we had a reservation."

George said, "Well, unfortunately, a reservation doesn't always equal a room on one of the busiest weekends of the year. Let me make some phone calls and see what we can do for you."

George found accommodations for the Tattaglias about twenty miles away. "They don't have quite the view that we do, but it's a nice place," said Audrey. The Tattaglia couple was not smiling but they seemed to accept the situation. After they left, George said to Audrey, "Well, that wasn't so bad. We recovered pretty well, I thought. I hope these next people coming up the drive are as reasonable."

When Mr. and Mrs. Tattaglia got back to New York, they were still irritated about the Hillsbrook situation. George and Audrey Spain had thought about setting up a page on the web to make more people aware of the Hillsbrook Lodge, but they didn't really have the time or the expertise. Mrs. Tattaglia was self-employed as a creator of web pages. It was easy for her to set up a web page, available to anyone in the world, describing the Tattaglia experience at the Hillsbrook Lodge, soliciting other stories of negative experiences with the lodge, and urging potential visitors to New England not to patronize the Hillsbrook.

1. Overbooking is common in some parts of the hospitality and travel industry. Can you justify overbooking on ethical grounds?
2. Did the Hillsbrook Lodge have any alternatives to overbooking?
3. Once George and Audrey find out about the Hillsbrook page on the web, can you think of any service-recovery steps they might take?

Further readings on the topics in this chapter are listed in "Additional Readings" on pages 522–526.

Get the tools you need to sharpen your study skills. SAGE edge offers a robust online environment featuring an impressive array of free tools and resources.

Access practice quizzes, eFlashcards, video, and multimedia at **edge.sagepub.com/Ford2e**.

Visit **edge.sagepub.com/Ford2e** to help you accomplish your coursework goals in an easy-to-use learning environment.

SpaceX via Getty Images

14 Service Excellence: Leading the Way to Wow!

Hospitality Principle: Lead Others to Excel

If I tell you what to do, then the task is my responsibility, not yours. But if I inspire you to act on your own, the responsibility and results are yours. The difference in dedication is phenomenal.

—Norman Brinker,
Former CEO, Chili's
Restaurants

Learning Objectives

After reading this chapter, you should be able to:

14.1 Explain the overarching framework of the three *S*s—strategy, staffing, and systems.

14.2 Identify the challenges leaders of service firms will face in the future.

14.3 State the importance of innovation and managing change.

14.4 Differentiate between leading and managing.

14.5 Identify the key factors for service leadership.

14.6 Discuss the reasons why "it all ends with the guest."

INTRODUCTION

Ultimately, the logic behind guestology is simple. Study the guest, learn what that person really wants, expects, and does, and then provide it—plus a little bit more. A guestologist never stops studying the guest, using all the scientific tools available to know what the guest really wants, actually does, and truly values. Since guests change, and because service delivery is invariably a human process, the study is never complete. The service product, the environment, and the delivery system must also change to make sure each guest is satisfied enough to come back.

THE THREE *S*S: STRATEGY, STAFFING, AND SYSTEMS

Leaders of outstanding guest service organizations spend much time and effort studying the guest and using this information to shape their decisions on the three *S*s: strategy, staffing, and systems.

We have already covered a lot of ground in this book. We shall conclude by showing how the leader brings it all together and makes it happen both for today's guests and for all future guests.

Strategy

In this era when an amazing amount of information about guests and competition in providing services to those guests is available, only organizations that truly understand what guests want will survive and prosper. They first use this information to design a corporate strategy. They discover which of their competencies guests consider core and concentrate on making these core competencies better. They use the wants, needs, expectations, and capabilities of guests to sharpen their marketing strategies, budgeting decisions, organizational and production systems design, and human resource management plans and practices.

Southwest Airlines is an excellent example of a company that has used its understanding of the guest to discover and then provide what its passengers really want. Like most organizations, the airline originally used guest surveys to ask what guests wanted. Southwest learned that guests wanted cheap fares, on-time performance,

Courtesy of Southwest Airlines

Southwest provides what its customers want: low fares with reliable schedules and friendly service.

great meals, comfortable seats, free movies, and more. They quickly recognized that, human nature being what it is, if you ask people what they want—they want everything.

Southwest realized it couldn't give its customers everything because nobody could. Gourmet meals with wine in big comfortable seats and low fares—it can't be done. So Southwest did additional research to dig deeper into guest preferences and learned that customers really wanted low fares and reliable schedules with friendly service. The Southwest service product is exactly what its target market wanted and, more importantly, wanted enough to pay for and return to again and again. The point is the guestologist must dig deeper than the simple market survey of guest preferences to understand what preferences actually drive guest behavior. The organization can use the results from this deeper probing to match up the organization's core competencies and mission with what customers want. Even better for Southwest, giving guests what they want provided extra cost savings to Southwest; turning an airplane around between arrival and departure is considerably easier, faster, and cheaper without having to clean up all the mess and clutter caused by unwanted frills like food service.

The Key Drivers

The best guest service organizations have done what Southwest has done. They study their guests extensively to discover what the guests both want and value in the guest service experience and use this information to align all the elements of their corporate strategy with these expectations. On the basis of studying their targeted guest market, these organizations can identify the key drivers of the guest experience. These key drivers all contribute to the impression the guest takes away from the experience and play a large role in determining whether that guest will return. A trip to a theme park, or a visit to a restaurant or hotel, is a holistic experience to most people; excellent guest service organizations do the research necessary to identify all the separate components of this whole experience. Then, they manage those components.

basic guest expectations The fundamental components of the service experience that guests expect at a minimum

"wow" elements The characteristics and qualities that make a service experience memorable.

Drivers: The Basics.

In a sense, these key drivers can be divided into two categories. The first group includes those basic things guests expect the organization to provide if it is to operate in the particular market segment. A resort hotel must have attractively decorated, clean hotel rooms with the expected amenities like flat screen television, wi-fi, and good room service. A casual-dining restaurant must have good and reasonably priced food, fair waits, an appropriate number of adequately competent servers, clean rest rooms, and relatively prompt service. Guests expect these characteristics at a minimum. These are **basic guest expectations** the organization must meet; otherwise the guest will be dissatisfied. If the organization fails habitually to meet these basic expectations, it will fail altogether. The basic characteristics are the necessary *but not sufficient* guest experience aspects organizations must offer if they seek the reputation that attracts repeat business and leads to long-term success.

Drivers: The Wows.

The second group of drivers includes the characteristics and qualities that make the experience memorable. These are the **"wow" elements** that the excellent organizations find ways to provide in some or all parts of the guest experience. These organizations go beyond meeting the basic expectations with which guests arrive when they come in the door or onto the property to have a service need satisfied. They add the wow elements that make the experience memorable. It is the memorable experiences that compel guests to return again and again, and even motivate guests to become evangelists for the company who will tell all their friends about these exceptional organizations.

Disney, Olive Garden, The Ritz-Carlton, and most other guest service organizations continuously survey their guests to find out how well they can provide the basics that guests expect. However, these outstanding organizations go beyond the surveys to dig deeper to identify which key drivers provide guests with a "wow" experience.

For example, Disney knows its guests expect transportation to travel from one part of the Walt Disney World Resort complex to another. Disney surveys its guests to make sure they are satisfied with the transportation system. On the other hand, no one comes to the Walt Disney World Resort to ride a bus, and the transportation system seldom shows up in guest surveys as a source of satisfaction (except for the monorail), nor do guest opinions about the transportation system predict guest intent to revisit Disney. Even when the bus transportation isn't up to the guest's level of expectation, that minor service failure shows no relation to overall satisfaction or with intent to return. Unless the bus service is outrageously poor, dangerous, or grossly unsatisfactory in some other way, it has little or no impact on how guests react to the overall Disney experience. In contrast, the guest's perception of the quality of the rides and attractions, the dazzling nature of the fireworks displays, and the friendliness of cast member interactions with guests are highly correlated with guest satisfaction and intent to return, so they—and not bus service—become the focus of managerial concern: they are the key drivers.

Study, Study, Study

The point is that until you carefully study all the possible drivers, you don't know what factors in the service product, the environment, and the delivery system are the key drivers of guest satisfaction and intent to return. Many times, what management learns in such studies is a surprise because what management thought would be keys when it designed the components don't turn out to be so from the guest's point of view. This difference between what the organization delivers and what the guest expects is an important service gap that Len Berry identified, and it happens. No matter how much experience an organization has in surveying and studying guests, it will still be surprised occasionally by what guests say is really important to them or what they actually do regardless of what they say.

Accumulating Information

Excellent guest service organizations not only study their guests extensively, but also accumulate the information they have learned about guests, individually and collectively. Computerized databases and sophisticated techniques of data analysis allow the organization to know a great deal about its guests, either as a demographic or psychographic group or as individuals. The best organizations mine these databases using sophisticated data analytics to dig up as much as they can about what is important to their guests so they can ensure what is expected is delivered. More importantly, they can learn where their service is failing to meet expectations and what aspects of their service product, environment, or delivery system needs to improve.

A Key Driver: Personalize

The outstanding guest service organizations that attract repeat customers have an added advantage: they can accumulate information on their frequent guests and use this information to further customize the guest experience. In other words, they know that a key driver is to personalize the guest experience (everyone wants to be special and treated like an individual) in ways that make an emotional connection with the guest. Intelligent use of a customer database allows the best to get better at delivering this sort of personalized service. Guests like, feel good about, and want to return to organizations that give them personalized treatment. Customizing each guest's experience to match the guest's unique needs and expectations is becoming increasingly easy. Since the least expensive customer for a hospitality organization to get to come back is the one it already has satisfied, adding new and customized features that add a "wow" for those loyal guests is a cost-effective strategy for retaining their repeat business.

Technology

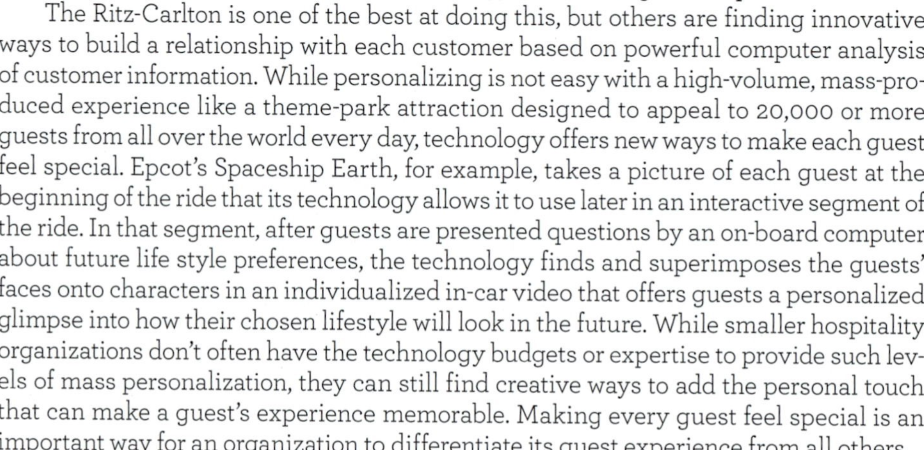

The Ritz-Carlton is one of the best at doing this, but others are finding innovative ways to build a relationship with each customer based on powerful computer analysis of customer information. While personalizing is not easy with a high-volume, mass-produced experience like a theme-park attraction designed to appeal to 20,000 or more guests from all over the world every day, technology offers new ways to make each guest feel special. Epcot's Spaceship Earth, for example, takes a picture of each guest at the beginning of the ride that its technology allows it to use later in an interactive segment of the ride. In that segment, after guests are presented questions by an on-board computer about future life style preferences, the technology finds and superimposes the guests' faces onto characters in an individualized in-car video that offers guests a personalized glimpse into how their chosen lifestyle will look in the future. While smaller hospitality organizations don't often have the technology budgets or expertise to provide such levels of mass personalization, they can still find creative ways to add the personal touch that can make a guest's experience memorable. Making every guest feel special is an important way for an organization to differentiate its guest experience from all others.

Finding out what makes that person feel special is one important role of guestologists and enables them to add the "wow" factor all guest service organizations want to provide to keep their guests coming back time and time again. The wow is the impact that providing the little bit more than the basic experience the guest expected can make; it can turn the satisfactory experience into a memorable one and keep the organization at the top of the customer's mind when thinking about where to go the next time that particular guest service is desired or when asked to make recommendations by others. "Wows" can be built into the service product, the environment, the service delivery system, or across all parts of the service experience. Based on the knowledge about how guests' likes and dislikes impact their emotions, the designers of the experience can build in those elements they expect will give the wow. They should, however, always follow up to find out if they were successful and, if not, should try to find out where and why they failed.

At Dorney Park. "Wows" don't have to be expensive, complicated, or elaborate, although they may be. Dorney Park and Wildwater Kingdom in Allentown, Pennsylvania, provides good examples of both a relatively inexpensive and a relatively expensive "wow" experience. The less expensive illustration is in their "Camp Snoopy" section of the park. While many rides are available for small children, Dorney also provides two simple, yet sizable, play areas. These areas are filled with small stones, so sand doesn't get into children's clothes and shoes. While these areas certainly aren't a major feature of the park, they provide a simple inexpensive experience that appeals to some children. If the children play there long enough, they'll likely have the chance to meet Snoopy, Charlie Brown, or another of the Peanuts characters. This creates a "wow" experience from a low-tech attraction.

At the other extreme, Dorney Park invests millions in its roller coasters. A recent addition, *Possessed,* hurtles the rider up (and then back down) two vertical spikes each with a 180-degree twist, with speeds reaching 70 mph. The purpose of the attraction is to provide an exhilarating ride, and the screams from the guests indicate that Possessed elicits a wow reaction.

Plan, Plan, Plan

Providing the guest with both the expected basic parts of the guest experience and the "wow" factors is the result of extensive planning. And as we know, planning starts with knowing the guest. Capacity and location decisions, the design of personnel policies, the selection of production equipment—all must be based on the organization's best estimates of what kind of experience the guests want, need, and expect from the organization as well as their capabilities. For example, if the organization's mission is to provide a cruise ship experience, then the first issue to resolve is where to locate the ship and how big to build it. If the organization's mission is to provide a casual-dining restaurant experience, then it must identify what food tastes, portion sizes, price points, locations, exterior appearances, and restaurant size it should have. These decisions can be correctly made only if based on solid and extensive market research, and guestologists use the best data they can find to make them. While many guest service operators still base these decisions on hunches and their own personal preferences, the outstanding ones always start with the guest and make sure that every decision is based on a thorough knowledge and understanding of the guest.

Get Constant Feedback to Drive Innovation

The best organizations also know that this discovery process is never ending; they constantly seek feedback from their guests about what works and what doesn't. Guest needs, wants, expectations, and capabilities change, and the best organizations respond to their guests' changes with changes of their own. Those organizations that constantly seek to exceed guest expectations build in their own future challenges. Today's "wow" is tomorrow's standard expectation for the guest who has been there and done that. The outstanding organizations are constantly seeking new ways to "wow" their guests, and they survey guests constantly to find out what these changing expectations are and then innovate their service product, environment, or delivery systems to meet them.

Technology

Emirates Air decided it needed to make an effort to get and use constant feedback in a way that could transform it and the air transport industry. Emirates Air learned from its customers' behaviors that its major competitors were increasingly the nimble technology companies who are becoming the primary sellers of flights in cyberspace. These technology companies were replacing Emirates in the minds of its loyal customers. Because Emirates Air didn't want to become a mere provider of a commodity (i.e., airline seats), it took the initiative to create its own information technology system that will be able to collect and analyze mountains of information with artificial intelligence to anticipate and fulfill each customer's travel needs before, during, and after a flight. By investing in the technology that is able to use guest feedback in a way that had never been done before, they hope to avoid being relegated to just a transportation company and instead become a lifestyle fulfillment company.[1] This innovative technology will give them a new ability to "wow" their guests, and give Emirates a competitive advantage in airline travel.

Culture Fills the Gaps

One last, but critically important issue in the strategy area is the organizational culture. Managers of outstanding hospitality organizations need to remember the

[1] Nicolas Parasie, "Emirates Air Flies into Uncharted Territory," *Wall Street Journal*, May 21, 2018, R8.

importance of the organizational culture in filling in the gaps between what the organization can anticipate and train its people to deal with and the challenges that arise in the daily encounters with a wide variety of guests. There is no way to anticipate the many things guests will do, ask for, and expect from the service provider. The power of the culture to guide and direct employees to do the "right thing" for the guest is critical. The best managers know the values, beliefs, and norms of behavior the culture teaches its employees ensure that the frontline employees do what the organization wants done in both planned and unanticipated situations.

The culture must be planned and carefully thought through to ensure the message sent to all employees is the one the organization really wants to send. An important part of any strategy is to ensure that everything the organization and its leadership writes, says, and does is consistent with the culture it wishes to define and support. The more intangible the service product, the stronger the cultural values, beliefs, and norms must be to ensure the guest service employee provides the quality and value of guest experience the guest expects and the organization wants to deliver.

Staffing

The second *S*, staffing, has become an increasingly important factor for all guest service organizations as they realize that the most effective way to differentiate themselves from their competitors is on the quality of the service encounters their customer contact personnel provide, especially at the moments of truth in the experience. In this day of widespread computerization and standardization, competitors can readily imitate the service product, the physical elements of the environment, and the technical aspects of the delivery system. It does not take long for one service organization to duplicate the successful differentiating factors of another. A chicken fajita wrapped in a soft tortilla that someone can hold while driving a car is an innovation for only as long as it takes competitors to offer one-handed fajitas in their drive-thrus as well. People, not fajitas, usually make the difference.

Getting the Right People for the Job

The challenge for a guestologist acting as a leader is to find, develop, and motivate the server to engage each guest on a personal, individual basis while still maintaining production efficiency and consistent quality in the service delivery process. Roller coasters at any major amusement park operate at a fast pace. The ride attendant greeting the arriving guests has just enough time to check the safety harnesses and tell each guest, "Keep your arms and hands inside the car, sit down, double check to make sure you have fastened your safety belt, and stay seated at all times." This encounter is highly mechanical and too short for the employee to do much more than repeat the scripted and important information before the next guest arrives and needs to be reminded of the same safety precautions. Repeating the same little speech feels to employees very much like working on the assembly-line job of Detroit automakers or Akron tire producers. About every six seconds a new guest, car, or tire arrives; the employee has to do or say something briefly, then the guest, car, or tire disappears down the assembly line to another worker's station. How can this job be made fun, fair, interesting, and important? While the ride attendants at least have the benefit of showing off their personality while interacting with a live human rather than just handling an inanimate tire or an auto, making such routine, repetitive jobs fun can be a challenge for both managers and employees.

Finding the right people and putting those people in these routinized jobs suited for them eliminates many of the problems in delivering high-quality guest experiences. People who are just good at and enjoy quickly establishing personal contact with guests can be identified through effective selection techniques. Nevertheless, even with the right types of people in these sorts of roles, these jobs can take an emotional toll on employees as well. Therefore, the best companies know they must find people with a great customer-oriented attitude who can be trained with the skills necessary for effective service delivery and motivated to perform exceptionally. While many management processes are involved in getting employees to deliver exceptional customer experiences, the best hospitality companies know that it begins with hiring the right people.

Future employees will expect more job challenges and increased opportunities to be responsible for the guest encounter. Future managers will have increasingly efficient mechanized production and delivery systems available to them with which to meet job challenges. Managers may have to choose between trusting these systems and trusting their employees to provide a high-quality and consistent service experience for their guests. The need to trust the employees will intensify as the competition for talented employees becomes greater. Good employees want to take the responsibility, and successful organizations will find ways to preserve the quality and value of the guest experience while empowering their employees to be responsible for guest satisfaction.

Training

The second part of the staffing issue is training. The right person in the right job must be trained to perform the job correctly and consistently. Many jobs in the guest service industry are repetitive, simple, or boring. They also require incredible attention to detail and concentration on task performance so that the employee provides the same service experience in the same flawless way for each guest. It is easy for employee Dave Johnson to zone out, daydream, or otherwise lose interest in saying "Thank you for visiting Six Flags" to the 20,000th guest. By that time his legs are tired, his attention span is short, and his interest in greeting one more person with a friendly smile and positive eye contact is about zero. Part of Dave's training should include how to cope with the emotional as well as the physical nature of the job. When the encounters are short—as at a fast-food drive-through window, convention check-in, or entry point for a theme-park attraction—the training challenge is particularly difficult.

Consider the role of restaurant servers. Recall that servers have three responsibilities in the guest experience: they deliver the service product (and co-create it on the spot), they manage the quality of the encounters or interactions between the co-producing guest and the organization, and they identify and fix the inevitable problems. Too many organizations train employees only for the first of these responsibilities and neglect the other two. In most instances, receiving the service product is just one element in the guest's determination of the quality and value of the guest experience. Servers must also be trained to deal effectively with the variety of knowledge, skills, abilities, personalities, and emotional states that different guests will bring to the guest experience. They must also be trained to look and listen for clues customers send when something has gone wrong and needs fixing.

Setting and Reinforcing the Standards

The third part of the staffing issue is the management responsibility to set performance standards, motivate employees to meet them, and maintain high levels of performance by rewarding employees who achieve those standards. Managers must master the skill of goal setting to define job responsibilities, the standards of performance, and management expectations to employees. SMART (*S*pecific, *M*easurable, *A*chievable, *R*esults-focused, and *T*ime-limited) goals must be clearly spelled out, reinforced, and rewarded by managers every day. Once a manager lets an employee provide service of less than outstanding quality, overlooks poor employee performance, or lets a "bad show" situation continue, the message goes out to everyone that managers

©iStockphoto.com/asiseeit

The best managers provide regular feedback in an appropriate setting, which reinforces the company's high standards.

don't always really mean what they say about providing high-quality guest service. Just as a guest has many moments of truth during the course of a single hospitality experience, employees have many moments of truth with managers every day. What happens during these moments of truth for the organization's internal customers—its employees—tells those employees a great deal about what management really believes in. The words and actions of all managers are where the organizational mission statement, corporate culture, and corporate policies about guest focus become real. Just as one employee at one moment of truth can destroy the guest's perception of the entire company, one supervisor who overlooks one violation of quality standards or poor job performance can destroy the way that employees look at the organization's mission. While most organizations have effective selection techniques and appropriate job training, many fall short in their commitment to training their leaders in the importance of continuous reinforcement. When managers let things slide, they miss the chance both to reinforce the positive cultural values and to coach away the negative aspects of employee performance.

Disney's policy of requiring its managers to spend time in the parks walking the walk and talking the talk is a vital part of how the message is sent to employees that everyone is responsible for guest service, including them. This policy also builds a sense of equality among the employees in that everyone is there to serve the guest.

Courtesy of Darden Restaurant

Darden's Olive Garden has a strong commitment to customer service, reinforced not just by words, but by the actions of their managers.

At Olive Garden. Ron Magruder, former president of Olive Garden, told the story about visiting some of his restaurants in Houston to see how they were doing. He arrived at one restaurant right at the peak of the lunchtime crowd and immediately learned the store manager was swamped. Two of her cooks had not shown up, and the restaurant was full of hungry and impatient customers. Ron, finding the manager in the kitchen trying to cook as fast as she could to keep up with orders, took off his coat, grabbed an apron, and joined her on the cook line. In the middle of this chaos, a phone call came in for the manager. It was another manager asking her if she had seen Ron yet. She tersely told the other manager not to bother her with such questions while the president of the company was working beside her at the next grill. The story got out rapidly, and there was no doubt in anyone's mind where Ron Magruder stood on customer service or the cultural values of Olive Garden. These kinds of stories do a powerful job of reinforcing the organization's commitment to its guest service mission, and they should be told.

Satisfaction from Satisfying

Similar jobs exist in the industrial sector, and job rotation, job enlargement, and job enrichment strategies have been tried with varying levels of success. The advantage guest service organizations offer to employees over most industrial settings is the presence of the guest and the positive feedback and stimulation that dealing with guests can bring. Once an employee learns how to derive satisfaction from doing something that makes a guest smile or finding ways to make a child happy, that employee gains an experience that can be as memorable for the employee as it is for the guest. These sorts of experiences give service employees a "something" to remember that increases their enjoyment of the job, as well as stories they can take home and talk about. Not only did they make "wow" memories for their guests, but in doing so, made "wow" memories for themselves. An important contribution to job satisfaction for most hospitality employees is the opportunity to create satisfaction for their guests. Regardless of how routine the task is, by showing off their personality, interaction skills, or problem-solving creativity to guests, employees can turn an "as expected" service into a memorable experience for both.

Many hospitality organizations have discovered that some of their best employees are older, retired people. They are often lonely, bored, and are looking for opportunities to develop positive contact with other people. Hospitality jobs are especially good at providing this particular opportunity to them. Some organizations that recruited older people because of labor shortages have found to their pleasant surprise that older people bring an enthusiasm for providing service that makes them great employees.

If you just *process* people, you get discouraged and bored in many hospitality jobs. If you *engage* people, the job becomes interesting. The challenge here is the short-cycle jobs where guest contact is so fleeting that the opportunity to engage guests is nearly nonexistent. As a contrasting example, consider the guides on a bus tour. With their longer time of contact, these employees can use various interpersonal skills to make the job personal, fun, and fulfilling for themselves and their guests. Because they have the time, they can interject their personalities to make the whole tour experience a function of their own ability to provide a memorable guest interaction. Many times, guides from extended tours stay in touch with guests for long after the tour has ended.

Loading a high-volume ride at Six Flags or serving a fast-food customer is a different matter and in many ways is a far greater challenge for both employees and management. Guests usually don't have time to notice employees and their individual contributions to the quality of the guest experience. The level of employee engagement and the subsequent satisfaction with providing exceptional customer service are considerably less, and these are the jobs that create the biggest challenges for managers seeking to provide their employees with jobs that are fun, fair, interesting, and important. Their challenge is to find ways to give each employee the opportunity to be unique, recognized, and noticed as an individual by the guest without compromising the speed and efficiency of the production process used to deliver the service product.

Employ the Guest

Just as organizations can benefit from thinking of their employees as internal customers or guests, they can also benefit from thinking of their customers as quasi-employees who must help co-produce their experiences in some way. Like employees, guests must be recruited, motivated, sometimes trained, and given the opportunity to "perform." Defining customers as co-producing employees gives the organization a different way of both looking at and thinking about their customers.

While the minimum customer performance—purchasing behavior—is what the most basic co-production requirement companies need from their customers, the guests can serve several other important functions. They can give helpful feedback to the organization regarding their level of satisfaction with the guest experience. In effect, they can be knowledgeable unpaid consultants. Guests are typically part of the service environment and help create the service experience for other guests. If being surrounded by other guests is an important part of each guest's experience, then how the guests are employed in helping to create each other's experience becomes an important part of the management process.

Most importantly for hospitality organizations, customers almost always have to co-produce hospitality experiences in some way. Knowing when we should or should not allow, encourage, or require the guest to co-produce part or all of the service experience is an important management decision. Guests can be required to create the salad they like at the salad bar, encouraged to clean up their own trash at the quick-serve restaurant, or allowed to check themselves out of the hotel. If the service delivery system is properly designed to ensure an excellent guest experience by accommodating varying guest skills and capabilities, these co-production strategies can benefit both the customer and the hospitality organization. The organization saves on labor costs, and knowledgeable, capable customers are likely to get a greater value from the hospitality experience served "their way" because they helped to produce it. In addition, they don't have to wait for service because they are producing it themselves.

Systems

The last *S* comprises all the organizational systems that support the guest experience. The best people in the world trained to perfection can't satisfy a guest if they deliver a bad product or deliver a good product late. In a huge, complex system like Walt Disney World Resort or a simple system like Ralph's Restaurant down on the corner, the whole system needs to be carefully managed so the right product is delivered to guests according to their expectations. Guests don't care that the organization forgot to rotate its stock so the eggs went bad, that the bed sheets are not clean yet because the laundry broke down, or that the person responsible for solving their problem is on break. They just want hot, fresh, properly cooked eggs, a clean room and a comfortable bed after a tough day on the road, and someone who will respond promptly to a legitimate concern. If these things don't happen, then the production system, the support system, the information system, or the organizational system has failed, and someone had better fix it fast.

Systems and Guestology

The most highly developed technical applications of guestology can be found in the systems area. Models of guest behavior in many situations can be built and used to understand and predict the ways in which the organization can satisfy the guest's expectations. Simulations are an important technique for achieving this, and with the increasingly user-friendly software packages, simulations will become more available and relevant to all types of hospitality organizations.

Once the planning process has gotten the design right and the measurement systems are in place to solicit guest feedback, the stage is set to use simulations of the entire guest experience to determine whether it all works as a system. By knowing what guests will do, theme parks can make sure the right capacity has been built into the attractions and all other features in the park, from rest rooms to merchandise outlets, to handle the number of guests expected on the design day. The design-day selection and the parameters used for the design day (such as the fifteen-minute average wait) drive the rest of the capacity decisions to ensure the "designed" experience can be provided to the guests. Since the design day is set at a high level of attendance by most theme parks, most guests on most days will experience a better-than-design-day experience because the lines will be shorter than designed capacity everywhere, from rest rooms to the best attractions.

The Wait

In many hospitality organizations, the most visible part of the guest experience is the wait for service. The wait system, therefore, requires extra organizational time and attention to ensure that the inevitable waits are tolerable and well within the limits guests will accept without becoming dissatisfied. Waiting periods are easily modeled and studied with simulation techniques and easy-to-use computer software. Everything—from the number of urinals at a convention center, to the number of front-desk agents at a hotel, to the number of seats on an airline route, to the time it takes to travel between points of interest on a bus tour, to the loading speed of a theme park attraction—can be simulated based on guest demand data. If you know how many guests are coming to your place of business and can estimate a predictable distribution to represent their arrival patterns and times for service, modeling how the waiting experience can be managed and balanced against capacity is relatively simple.

The management of waiting time is important both from the capacity standpoint and from the psychological standpoint. Since few organizations can build enough capacity to serve peak demand periods, and few hospitality organizations can stockpile their mostly perishable and intangible product, managing the wait is critical for all hospitality organizations. The greater the perceived value of the guest experience, the longer the guest will wait. Again, this area can benefit greatly from empirical research. How long guests will wait for anything before they give up and leave can be studied, measured, and understood. Some guests will wait hours to get into the hottest nightclubs or the trendiest restaurants. In contrast, they won't wait long at restaurants such as McDonald's, so that the organization knows it has to monitor service times constantly and follow strict procedural standards so food is delivered quickly. Wherever technology can be used to create virtual waits in place of an actual waits, both guests and organizations will benefit.

The management of strategy, staffing, and systems is the key to guest service excellence. They all count when creating a memorable guest experience, and they are all related. Making any strategic change will necessarily impact the service product, the environment, and the service delivery system. Ultimately, though, it all starts with the guest.

HOSPITALITY AND THE FUTURE

While no one knows what the future holds, every hospitality organization must make educated guesses in order to prepare for whatever happens. Such guesses will be needed for future strategy, staffing, and systems. And all will reflect the impact of changes in technology.

Service or Price

Technology

Service organizations will increasingly compete by differentiating its service or its price. A successful group of organizations in every service sector will seek to add value to each guest service experience (like at one of Four Seasons Hotels) or seek to define value on price alone (like a Red Roof Inn). By making sure they focus on a particular niche of the market, advertise to that niche, and then ensure they fulfill what they promise to do, these companies (like RyanAir, WestJet, or Southwest Airlines) will thrive. The effective use of new technology and process innovations in the service delivery system will allow those organizations that seek to focus on a price-conscious market niche to succeed in appealing to and satisfying this market segment. The efficient users of high technology will find ways to offer low prices, provide some unexpected technology-enhanced services to wow their customers, and still make money. The high end of the various service markets will succeed for the same reasons. They too will use technology, but for them technology is only a means to the end of providing the maximum amount of service their guests expect at a reasonable price for the service level. Both types of organizations will increasingly rely on technology to deliver the best value to their guests in the most efficient way. They can, consequently, make money through their efficiency where the less efficient competitors will fail. They will increasingly customize the product to each guest's expectations at the price point plus offer a little bit more as they can provide their employees with the necessary information to personalize the service in a prompt, friendly, and efficient way.

The hospitality businesses in the mass market between these two ends of the spectrum will have the most difficult challenge in the future as many are already having today. They will be challenged in offering guest services as personalized as the service-oriented firms in the marketplace have been able to offer and which guests now expect, while providing the low prices which the price-oriented firms in a competitive marketplace have also led guests to expect. This middle group of organizations seeking to serve the mass market may do neither very well, and may lose market share to companies that provide more specialized services at higher perceived value. These types of organizations may find themselves in the position of overpromising and under-delivering, which is not the way to have satisfied, loyal, or repeat guests.

People Making the Difference

The division between those hospitality organizations that figure out how to engage employees and those that use employees only from the neck down will widen, especially as technology, AI, and robots take on more of the routine tasks in delivering an experience. Value added to guest experiences through the use of the knowledge, skills, and abilities of employees will become a more important differentiating strategy as the decreasing costs and increasingly available technology make the hospitality product and service delivery system components (except for people) increasingly easy to duplicate and emulate by all competitors. If all burgers taste alike and cost the same, then the "feel-good" part of the burger service experience that the people create becomes an increasingly important part of the total. Advertising alone can't provide this difference and, in fact, may be counterproductive if guests don't get what the glowing ads lead them to expect.

Employees make the difference between simply providing a service product and co-creating one with the emotional connection that produces the memorable wow experience. The quality of employee encounters with guests will determine whether customer experiences are just a disappointment, satisfactory, or the type of exceptional experience that builds the positive word of mouth and repeat business on which everyone in the hospitality industry depends. If your guests are at least 70% repeat customers, as is true at the Walt Disney World Resort, you must be doing something right and, if their continued repeat business is vital to your organization's survival, you had better find a way to keep doing it.

Keeping Promises

The best guest service organizations of the future will use every tool and the most sophisticated data analysis at their command to figure out what the guest wants and then provide it in a way that is consistent with the guest expectations of value and quality. If they promise a high-quality experience and friendly service, they had better provide them or the customers will not come back. Most service organizations depend on repeat business, and to fail to meet their guests' expectations will cost them dearly in a competitive marketplace. Once you tell your customers what you will do for them, you've created an expectation for a hospitality experience that is a commitment and a promise. If the **guest promise** is broken or the commitment unrealized, guests will be

guest promise What you tell your customers that you will do for them (verbally, in writing, and/or through advertising).

unhappy and will tell everyone they know in person or anyone they are connected with on the internet about how unhappy they are. Few organizations can afford to break their promises, and the more a guest service organization depends upon the lifetime value of a guest's repeat business, the less chance it can take of violating that trust. Information and opinions about service quality and value are freely available and will become even more widespread as social media and customer review apps continue to grow. If a dissatisfied guest posts a negative comment about your service, that comment may be readily accessible on a computer somewhere forever. The internet has the capacity never to forget, and the more others' shared experiences are used to help customers make selections among guest service providers, the more critical it is to avoid failing the guest.

Technology

Many companies employ people or hire services to monitor social networking sites. If a customer posts a complaint on Facebook, TripAdvisor, or Instagram, an issue arises on a public discussion board or the company's own website or travel app, or someone tweets a criticism, the best companies have become proactive. They address the concerns or correct the errors before an issue or a service failure causes customers seeing negative reviews to go elsewhere or, even worse, escalates into a public relations nightmare. The job of social networking representative is part marketing and part public relations. A job classification that didn't even exist ten years ago will become an increasingly important part of the organization's communication strategy as it seeks to avoid the negative word of mouth that can now travel almost instantly across cyberspace to the entire world.

Tomorrow's "Wow"

The future will require managing information, managing people, understanding what each guest really wants more effectively (creating a **market niche of one** that allows the organization to build a relationship with each guest), and focusing on the organizational core competencies that satisfy these guest expectations. The future will also bring forth more knowledgeable customers with ever-rising expectations, and more competitors where they can spend their money. The more that competitors in the marketplace try to outdo one another in providing wow experiences, the more familiar these experiences will become. Yesterday's "wow" becomes today's expected basic level of service. Hospitality managers will need to engage the entire organization in constantly reviewing all aspects of the guest service product, the environment, and the service delivery system to find new and, hopefully, not easily duplicable features to create tomorrow's "wow" experiences.

market niche of one Identifying the specific needs of an individual customer, and attempting to fulfill those needs to deliver a personalized service experience.

Server-Customer Interactions

The easiest and most fruitful area in which to develop these features is in the interactions between servers and customers, where hospitality employees can make a "wow" experience happen. The challenge here is to give employees the ability, motivation, and opportunity to perform in novel ways without jeopardizing the quality and consistency of the service product. Human error is inevitable, and the need to blend technology and people to provide a high-tech and high-touch experience of consistently high quality will be the biggest and most interesting challenge for the future guestologist.

LEADING THE WAY INTO THE FUTURE

Regardless of the best predictions about the future, the successful hospitality organizations will all share one important capability: innovation. Embedded in the successful organizations is a recognition and willingness to adapt and change. They know the only constant is change, and they make sure their strategy is adaptable, their staff shares a willingness to innovate, and their systems are flexible.

Leading the Way Through Innovation

service innovations New services or service products that, when first offered, create a new service experience for guests.

Whatever the future holds, the leader's job will be to get everyone ready, willing, and able to embrace the inevitable changes the future will bring. Guestology can help managers prepare for and introduce **service innovations**. Like all benchmark hospitality organizations, Disney and Universal know repeat guests expect new experiences that will make their return visits worthwhile. While both theme parks already provide a richness and depth in the design of their attractions that offer layers of experience to returning guests, any organization that relies heavily on repeat visitors must find ways to keep the experiences enhanced and fresh. This is done by both continually updating existing attractions and adding new ones like Avatar at Disney and Harry Potter at Universal in order to encourage repeat guest visitations. A restaurant might offer new items on its menu, while retaining the old standbys. A cruise ship will add new destinations or add on-board amenities to balance the brand's promise of comfortable cruising with the need of guests for new and stimulating enhancements to the cruise ship experience. Yet, while the service product and the environment may change, the delivery of exceptional customer service must remain consistent.

Providing an innovative service experience relies on attracting and encouraging customers to experience something they have never seen or done before. To provide that experience, the company may have to produce something it has never done before either. For a radically new experience, this could mean risking a major investment in creating an experience that might turn out not to meet the needs of enough customers to be profitable. Creating a radically new cruise ship requires a lot of upfront investment; if customers don't like it after it is built, the company has made a very expensive mistake.

Types of Innovation

incremental innovation An innovation of an existing service product, process, marketing approach, resource supply, or organizational form.

radical innovation A totally new innovation that has a significant impact on a market and on the economic activity of firms in that market.

The classic research on innovation has evolved from the economist Schumpeter's definition and classification of innovation types. Schumpeter's definition suggests that innovation is an activity by which organizations or individuals bring inventions into the market for commercial purposes.[2] He identified five categories or types of innovations. These five are (1) the development and introduction of a new good (e.g., new service product); (2) the introduction of a new method of production (e.g., new delivery system); (3) the opening of a new market (e.g., targeting a new market niche); (4) new sources of production (e.g., new sources of raw material or semi-manufactured goods suppliers); and (5) new organizational forms or industries (e.g., sharing economy businesses).[3] In Exhibit 14.1, we illustrate each of these types of innovation in both an incremental form and a radical or disruptive form. **Incremental innovation** is where an invention is an improvement on or enhancement of an existing service product, process, marketing approach, resource supply or organizational form. **Radical innovation** is where there is something totally new in one of those categories that has a significant impact on a market and on the economic activity of firms in that market.[4]

As the exhibit shows, an incremental service product improvement might be exemplified by Walt Disney World's Epcot which was a new way of engaging guests in a service experience while a radical service product improvement would be

---

[2] Joseph A. Schumpeter, *The Theory of Economic Development: An Inquiry Into Profits, Capital, Credit, Interest, and the Business Cycle* (Cambridge, MA: Harvard University Press, 1934).

[3] Doris Omerzel Gomezelj, "A Systematic Review of Research on Innovation in Hospitality and Tourism," *International Journal of Contemporary Hospitality Management* 28, no. 3 (2016): 516–558.

[4] Clayton Christensen, *The Innovator's Dilemma: When New Technologies Cause Great Firms to Fail* (Cambridge, MA: Harvard Business Review Press, 2013).

EXHIBIT 14.1

Incremental and Radical Innovation in Service Product, Environment, and Delivery System

INNOVATION TYPE/ INNOVATION CATEGORY	PRODUCT INCREMENTAL EXAMPLES	PRODUCT RADICAL EXAMPLES	ENVIRONMENT INCREMENTAL EXAMPLES	ENVIRONMENT RADICAL EXAMPLES	DELIVERY SYSTEM INCREMENTAL EXAMPLES	DELIVERY SYSTEM RADICAL EXAMPLES
New Service Product	Epcot	Original Disneyland	Themed restaurants	Single admission theme parks	Bigger cruise ships	Fast food McDonald's
New Process	TripAdvisor	Netflix	Food trucks	Underwater hotels	Quick Serve	Uber, Lyft
New Marketing	Customer Relationship Management database providing information on guest preferences	Big data AI systems developing innovative bundlings of services based on patterns found across multiple databases	Guest-room redesign based on new demands for in-room technologies	Virtual visits with options for customization before arrival	Ads embedded in web pages	"Pushing" advertisements to guests cell phones based on purchasing behaviors
New Input Resources	Tofu, tempeh, and other meat substitutes	Lab-grown meat	Fast-fine dining	Vita Mojo (build your own dish, pay based on weight)	Farm-to-table restaurants	3D food printing
New Type Organization	Disneyland Paris	Space adventures	Segway instead of walking tours	Virtual reality tours	GrubHub	Airbnb

exemplified by the original Disneyland which is seen as a brand new way to provide the amusement park experience. Likewise, going across the top line in the table shows incremental and radical service product innovations in the other two aspects of the service experience—-service environment and service delivery systems. Included in this table are examples of each of Schumpeter's types of innovation categorized by service product, service environment, and service delivery systems. The point of this table is to show there are many ways to innovate, and Schumpeter's categories should spur innovative thinking by all hospitality organizations seeking to create future wows for their current guests.

The importance of innovation and the organization's support of innovative activity are especially important in a market where customer expectations can easily change. Not only do current customers want something novel in their service experiences, but your competitors are constantly innovating new ways to enjoy the experience that might be more attractive to your current customers. Once a customer experiences something new that is a value added to the existing service, it becomes part of the basic expectation for any future experiences. From that point on, the customer looks for something else to create the "wow" and only innovations can provide it.

Since so much of the service product, environment, and delivery systems are easily duplicated, it is challenging to innovate a service experience in ways that are not easily copied by competitors. As noted earlier, this puts an extra burden on leadership as the enthusiastic way in which employees embrace the service culture and deliver a memorable service product often becomes the only unique aspect of the service experience that can't be copied.

The services innovation literature tells us that for an innovation to succeed, both the company and the customer should find it in some way familiar.[5] For incremental innovations that make smaller changes in the service experience, creating a sense of familiarity is easier to achieve than it will be for a radical change, which may feel totally different from anything the company has done or the guest has experienced before. For any experience that is different from past experiences, both the company and the customer will have to learn new ways of performing their co-production roles in order to become successful in co-creating the new experience. The more radical the changes required, the more time and effort will be required to learn the new way of experiencing the service.

Leading innovation, then, requires leaders to use the principles and practices of guestology with both guests and employees. Guestology enables leaders to identify what and when guests need and want something new or different to satisfy their ever-changing expectations. Guestology also enables leaders to identify what and when employees need and want something new and different to successfully deliver the innovations that guests expect. Whether the innovation is a big deal or a minor change for the customer and employee, the skill of the leader to implement change successfully will make the difference between success and failure.

Management Innovation: William C. Coup, Innovative Champion

management innovation An innovation of a management practice, process, or technique that is new to the state of the art and is intended to further organizational goals.

The rational view of **management innovation** expands on Schumpeter's definition above and defines it as "the invention and implementation of a management practice, process or technique that is new to the state of the art and is intended to further organizational goals."[6] By that definition, William Cameron Coup provides a classic example of an innovator in one of the oldest hospitality and entertainment businesses: the circus.

Coup (1837–1895) literally ran away from home in Mt. Pleasant, Indiana, to join the circus. One summer day in 1853 at age 16, he quit his apprenticeship with a printer, packed his belongings, and walked to Terre Haute, Indiana, to find adventure. There he found a circus, P.T. Barnum's Grand Colossal Museum and Menagerie, and joined it as a roustabout.[7] This began a lifelong career in the circus where his many experiences allowed him to see how circuses were managed and what their challenges were. He gained his fame as an innovator by solving the very large challenge of mounting the "Greatest Show on Earth" on the railroad in 1872. Before Coup, circuses were hauled across their performance route by horses. This was a costly way to operate as the distance traveled each day decided where the circus would play that night. Some-

---

[5] For more on service innovation see Dominik Mahr, Annouk Lievens, and Vera Blazevic, "The Value of Customer Co-created Knowledge During the Innovation Process," *Journal of Product Innovation Management* 31, no. 3 (2014): 599–615; Carol Kelleher et al., "Value Proposal Co-Creation in Online Community-Based Idea Contests," in *Innovating in Practice*, eds. Tiziana Russo-Spena, Cristina Mele, and Maaria Nuutinen (Switzerland: Springer International Publishing, 2017), 291–316; Cathy A. En and Rohit Verma, "Introduction to the Cornell Hospitality Research Summit Special Issue: The New Science of Service Innovation in a Multipartner World," *Service Science* 8, no. 2 (June 2016): iv-ix.

[6] Julian Birkinshaw, Gary Hamel, and Michael J. Mol, "Management Innovation," *Academy of Management Review* 33, no. 4 (2008): 825–845, p. 825. See also Fariborz Damanpour, and William M. Evan, "Organizational Innovation and Performance: The Problem of 'Organizational Lag,'" *Administrative Science Quarterly* (1984): 392–409 for further support of key ideas contained in this definition.

[7] Fred Dahlinger and Stuart Thayer, *Badger State Showmen: A History of Wisconsin's Circus Heritage* (Baraboo, WI: Grote Publishing, 1998).

times this distance led to big towns with profitable large audiences, but sometimes this distance landed it in small towns where it couldn't break even. Coup figured that if he could put the circus on the railroad, it could play only in big, profitable locations. The 1872 profits of his railroad transported circus proved the value of his innovation.

To get an idea of how great this challenge was, imagine moving a city every day. One of his many innovations was the circus loading technique. By changing the traditional loading of wagons onto trains from side loading to end to end loading (see Photo 14-4), he could speed up the process of putting all the wagons and equipment on the train cars. This technique proved so successful that it was adopted by others, including the military, and is still used today as the roll-on roll-off technique for loading and unloading trucks and other vehicles on railcars.

Coup also developed other innovations that changed his industry. He is credited (by some) with creating the three-ring circus, developing the advance promotion strategy of posting advertising that remained in use as long as circuses were on the road, and creating a major aquarium. He also solved the problem of keeping the circus employees employed when the traveling season was over, by creating a permanent performing site, The Hippodrome in New York City. While his invention of the "circus loading" system was critical in putting the circus on a train, his other innovations reflect how he was able to "scale up" other innovations that he saw by solving the administrative and logistical challenges that scaling them up created.

Circus World Museum, Baraboo, Wisconsin

W. C. Coup is credited with innovations that radically changed the circus industry.

Coup was both a rational, incremental innovator and a radical one. The rational innovator is one who seeks ways to make an organization work more effectively. A rational innovator puts forward an innovative solution to address a specific problem the organization is facing and he or she then champions the implementation and adoption.[8] What Coup did shows how being a rational, incremental innovator can occur simultaneously with the radical approach of finding creative uses of available resources and opportunities. Coup was rational in seeing the value of using rail transport (the means) to achieve an end (making greater profits by avoiding small and unprofitable locations). But, at the same time, he had to experiment with different ways to use this new technological tool (means) in order to effect the result of transporting a circus on a train (end). The key characteristics of this type of innovators are that they know who they are (e.g., have traits and abilities to search out desired effects), know what they know (e.g., have knowledge of what they are doing), and know others (e.g., have social networks to access what they don't know and firm resources to allow them to try different means).[9] Coup had all of these.

Restaurant Incubators

An increasingly common technique to promote innovation is to provide entrepreneurs with access to incubators where they can get help with the organizational, legal, and financial challenges faced by startups. Although frequently used to help commercialize product and technology innovations, they are less common in hospitality.

[8] Birkinshaw, Hamel, and Mol, p. 828.

[9] Saras D. Sarasvathy, "Causation and Effectuation: Toward a Theoretical Shift from Economic Inevitability to Entrepreneurial Contingency," *Academy of Management Review* 26, no. 2 (2001): 243–263.

An example of a restaurant incubator is one established by Phil Romano, known for Romano's Macaroni Grill and Fuddruckers.[10] He developed an incubator at Trinity Groves, a 15-acre restaurant, retail, and entertainment center in West Dallas, to help new restaurants get off the ground with mentorship and funding from experienced restaurateurs. Another incubator is Washington, D.C.'s EatsPlace which operates as a neighborhood restaurant, food incubator, and restaurant accelerator by playing host to pop-up restaurants and guest-chef residencies. A third example is, Mi Kitchen es su Kitchen in Queens, New York, which allows new restaurant operators to use its space temporarily to train staff and develop a menu while their restaurants are under construction.[11]

Some innovative restaurateurs have found ways to create their own incubator to test new food offerings. When Tom Ferguson wanted to develop a burger food truck, he had a few advantages. By working out of his existing facility at Durham Catering Co. in Durham, North Carolina, he had ready access to a kitchen, staff, and equipment. The company offered doughnut and biscuit samples out the back door until it perfected the recipes. Ferguson says his in-house incubator gives him a fundamental advantage in developing new concepts: He can learn from trial and error with relatively low stakes. And it also makes it easy to kill ideas before he's in too deep. He abandoned a homemade pasta concept after realizing it wouldn't work with a quick-service model.[12]

Eco-Innovations

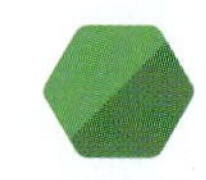

Sustainability

eco-innovations Innovations designed to reduce the environmental impact of people or businesses.

environmental impact The effect that the activities of people and businesses have on the ecological environment.

Innovations are being developed in hospitality as a response to customers' growing preference for eco-friendly products, and the cost of natural resources. These factors are causing organizations to find and adopt **eco-innovations** to reduce their **environmental impact** and reduce their use of natural resources. Eco-innovations have emerged in a wide variety of ways, from the very expensive to the simple and inexpensive. Eco-innovations include eco-friendly designs, implementing energy saving programs, focusing on purchasing locally produced foods, implementing a waste conservation program, installing green landscaping or even green roofs, and encouraging guests to use less electricity and water. Companies like Greenview help hotels benchmark their use of electricity, water, and greenhouse gas emissions so they can monitor how well they are performing on these metrics relative to both their own past performance and similar hotels.[13]

Eco-innovations can also help improve customer satisfaction, but only when companies educate customers as to the nature and beneficial impact of these practices.[14] Guests need to know that innovations like energy reducing practices and LEED green certifications don't just help the company save money, but provide benefits to guests and help the hospitality organization preserve the natural environment.[15] Eco-innovations can be salient, financially valuable, and viewed by stakeholders as an important ethical practice. Innovating in ways that benefit the environmental ecosystem requires leaders to understand and communicate the marketing, financial, and societal benefits that eco-innovations may provide. To gain the full benefit of such practices, they need to make sure that the guests understand both the practice and its implications.

---

[10] Kevin Hardy, "Test Run: Restaurant Incubators Let Operators Explore New Concepts Before Opening Their Doors to the Public," *QSR*, March, 2015, https://www.qsrmagazine.com/growth/test-run.

[11] Sumathi Reddy, "Stirring the Pot to Help Start-ups," *Wall Street Journal*, November 15, 2011, https://www.wsj.com/articles/SB10001424052970204323904577038501515209834.

[12] Hardy, "Test Run."

[13] Eric Ricaurte, "Hotel Sustainability Benchmarking Index 2017: Energy, Water, and Carbon," *Center for Hospitality Research Report* 17, no. 18 (2017), 3–17.

[14] Yixiu Yu, Xu Li, and Tun-Min Jai, "The Impact of Green Experience on Customer Satisfaction: Evidence from TripAdvisor," *International Journal of Contemporary Hospitality Management* 29, no. 5 (2017): 1340–1361.

[15] Melissa A. Baker, Eric A. Davis, and Pamela A. Weaver, "Eco-friendly Attitudes, Barriers to Participation, and Differences in Behavior at Green Hotels," *Cornell Hospitality Quarterly* 55, no. 1 (2014): 89–99.

LEADING AND MANAGING

We conclude by stressing an idea that has been implied throughout this book: if the goal of the best hospitality organizations is to provide excellence in service quality and value for its targeted customers through its employees, then managers must also be leaders. Managers are different than leaders although both are important. Managers manage inanimate things and processes. They order paper for the copier, get the payroll system working properly, organize tasks and schedules, and update the books. Leaders are different. They inspire people to perform their tasks with pride, with excellence, and on schedule because of a belief and commitment to the organization's mission. Leaders motivate employees to do the tasks they were hired, trained, and paid to do by managers. Leaders get employees to see their roles as something more important than just task performance. Instead, well led employees see their role as part of something greater than themselves and something that has value and importance to not only the organization, but to the larger society. While managers as **transactional leaders** are able to get people to do their assigned work (e.g., to take orders from guests) by trading pay for effort, effective leaders are able to go beyond this simple transactional relationship. Because of what they say, write, and do, these leaders inspire their employees to go beyond the routine and engage in their tasks with extraordinary care and commitment (e.g., to take orders from guests with authentic caring that guests remember). Leaders can convince their employees that what they do is an important part of contributing to an important mission by taking care to create jobs that are fun, fair, and interesting.

transactional leader A leader who focuses on supervision, policy, and performance; the transactional leader seeks to promote compliance with current policy and systems, using both punishments and rewards to meet specific goals, increase compliance, and enhance efficiency.

The best hospitality organizations realize they need their managers to be both: effective managers and effective leaders. Employees, like external customers must have their basic employment expectations met by a manager who carefully attends to the transactional parts of the employment relationship. Employees, also like external customers, find the "wow" in their employment when their managers are also **transformational leaders**, providing employees with opportunities to thrive and grow as individuals, to find a sense of accomplishment in jobs that are interesting, and to do work that is important as it has meaning and value.

transformational leader A leader who provides opportunities for employees to thrive and grow as individuals, to find a sense of accomplishment in jobs that are interesting to them, and to do work that is important as it has meaning and value.

The importance of the leader in hospitality organizations cannot be overemphasized. The leader is the teacher and role model of what the organization stands for, values, and believes. If the leader doesn't lead, all the efforts to discover the key drivers that cause the customer to seek out a particular hospitality experience, the expense of designing the service delivery system, and the effort to recruit and train the best people are wasted. Every day and in every way, the leader must set the example and show all employees what their value is to the organization and to the process of creating hospitality experience.

Everyone wants to feel that what they do has value and meaning to a purpose larger than enriching a company's top executives and stockholders. Leaders not only inspire their employees to realize their individual worth to the organization, they also help employees see what contributions they make to the greater good by doing their jobs with excellence. Telling people how important it is that they do their jobs well is not enough. All employees must understand and believe that their contributions make a difference and that doing well whatever they do is vital to an organizational mission.

Servant Leadership

One of the more effective leadership styles for doing these things that transform the organizational relationship with employees from a simple economic transaction to one that is enriching and inspiring is to become a **servant leader**. A servant leader is one who serves others by helping them to achieve their goals. There are six characteristics

servant leader A leader who serves others by helping them to achieve their goals; the servant leader shares power, puts others' needs first, and helps people develop so that they can perform as well as possible.

of a servant leader that help that leader become more than a transactional leader.[16] These leadership qualities include (1) valuing people—believing in them and listening to what they have to say; (2) developing people—providing them with learning, growth, encouragement, and efficacy; (3) building community—developing strong collaborative and personal relationships; (4) displaying authenticity—being open, accountable for one's own actions and open to learning from others; (5) providing leadership—foreseeing the future, setting goals, taking initiative; and (6) sharing leadership—facilitating and sharing power, empowering others.[17] This is not only a leadership style, but a way of living that encourages employees to find linkages between what they do, how they do it, and what the leader is asking of them. Reviewing these qualities employees can easily envision the positive nature of working for a manager that personifies them. A servant leader makes jobs fun, fair, interesting, and important.

All Jobs and People Have Value

Many organizations make efforts to show employees their jobs have value, but few do it as well as Disney. The Disney organization has inspired its employees to believe they are responsible for creating happiness for many who need it and many who would not otherwise have it. The tremendous publicity they provide to the "Give Kids the World" foundation and related ventures is not only a good thing to do, but it also inspires the people inside Disney that what they do is important and has value beyond the individual jobs they perform. The company reinforces this idea with the regular use of terms related to a theatrical production, such as *good show, bad show, on stage, off stage, and cast members*. These terms constantly remind all employees that their job has a greater purpose than merely sweeping up guest trash, working at a hamburger stand, or cleaning bathrooms. Each job has value and the person doing that job has value because of the contribution to the larger purpose. This is a vital part of inspiring people not only to do their jobs well, but to do them with enthusiasm, pride, and commitment. Obviously, not every employee or cast member will be deeply affected, but this idea is planted in so many employees' minds that it creates the strong cultural reinforcement that focuses everyone's attention on producing an "excellent show" for each guest. This is a powerful leadership technique and a valuable way to ensure that everyone stays focused on the guest.

Leaders, Employees, Guests, and the Larger Purpose

The lessons behind these leadership techniques are simple but worth recalling at this point. We expect each reader of this book has aspirations to lead, or why bother studying the management of hospitality organizations? The best companies know that if you want the frontline employees to deliver exceptional service to both internal and external customers, the message, vision, culture, and attitude must begin at the top. Leaders establish a culture of guest service excellence and reinforce it by word, deed, and celebration. Leaders are consistent in what they say and what they do. Leaders find ways to provide the incentives that motivate employees to exert effort, embrace the mission, and go above and beyond the job description by paying them fairly and making their jobs fun, fair, interesting, and important. Leaders give value to employees by showing them they are valued for both their contributions to the organization and their contributions to the larger purpose toward which the organization aspires. Leaders provide the guidance and feedback to help direct employee efforts and develop

---

[16] James Laub, "Defining Servant Leadership: A Recommended Typology for Servant Leadership Studies," in *Proceedings of the Servant Leadership Research Roundtable* (2004); Denise Linda Parris and Jon Welty Peachey, "A Systematic Literature Review of Servant Leadership Theory in Organizational Contexts," *Journal of Business Ethics* 113, no. 3 (2013): 377–393.

[17] Julia E. Hoch et al., "Do Ethical, Authentic, and Servant Leadership Explain Variance Above and Beyond Transformational Leadership? A Meta-analysis," *Journal of Management* 44, no. 2 (2018): 501–529.

employee skills. Leaders have the joy and the responsibility of making it all happen: motivated servers, a service-oriented culture, "wow" guest experiences, delighted and loyal repeat guests, and a firm foundation of organizational business success.

We have often used Disney as the benchmark, the standard, the reference point, so it is fitting that we conclude by showing what value Disney places on its leaders. From the beginning, Walt Disney intuitively felt a direct relationship must exist between leadership behaviors, the cast member experience, the guest experience, and customer loyalty. Eventually the organization was able to support the intuition statistically. According to Craig Taylor and Cindy Wheatley-Lovoy, based on their experience as executives with Disney,[18] "There is a direct link between leadership behaviors and a quality cast experience, a quality guest experience, and our business success. The correlation is strong and specific."[19] Taylor and Wheatley-Lovoy conclude, "In the business units in which cast members rate their leaders as outstanding in such behaviors as listening, coaching, recognition, and empowerment, the guest satisfaction ratings are the highest."[20]

The Leader's Challenge: Blending It All Together—Seamlessly

Finally, the leader blends together the strategy, staff, and systems so that everyone knows how and why to concentrate on the guest. The strategy must be right, the staffing right, and the systems right if the combined effort is to succeed in providing the outstanding guest experience the organization is in business to provide. If the leader sees that any element is not contributing to the employee's ability to provide outstanding experiences, the leader will fix it or have it fixed. Just as the organization wants to fix any guest problem that detracts from the guest experience, the outstanding leader wants to fix any employee problem that detracts from the employee's ability to provide an outstanding guest experience.

Exhibit 14.2 sums up all the elements leaders must manage if they are to meet this challenge effectively. They must:

- Define an organizational vision of what guest segment is to be served and what service concept will best meet their expectations.
- Select employees with service-oriented attitudes and train them in the necessary skills.
- Provide the incentives that will motivate empowered employees to deliver unsurpassed guest service.
- Ensure that employees have the proper resources to provide outstanding service.
- Design specific delivery systems that translate plans, employee skills, and resources into an experience that meets guest expectations and perhaps even wows the guest.
- Provide the measurement tools that allow employees (and co-producing guests) to see how well they are doing in providing the targeted or desired guest experience.

Measurement is critical for ensuring that all the other factors are correctly focused on achieving the best for the guest. If you don't know how you're doing, you don't know

[18] Craig R. Taylor and Cindy Wheatley-Lovoy, "Leadership: Lessons from the Magic Kingdom," *Training & Development* 52, no. 7 (1998): 22–26.

[19] Taylor and Wheatley-Lovoy, 24.

[20] Taylor and Wheatley-Lovoy.

EXHIBIT 14.2

Leadership Keys: Achieving the Best for the Guest

Skills + Incentives + Resources + Delivery System + Measurement – Vision = Unfocused Employees = Unfocused Service = **Confused Guests**

Vision + Incentives + Resources + Delivery System + Measurement – Skills = Untrained Employees = Probably Failed Service = **Disappointed Guests**

Vision + Skills + Resources + Delivery System + Measurement – Incentives = Unmotivated Employees = Lackluster Service = **Disappointed Guests**

Vision + Skills + Incentives + Delivery System + Measurement – Resources = Unsupported Employees = Inadequate Service = **Complaining Guests**

Vision + Skills + Incentives + Resources + Measurement – Delivery System = Unreliable Employees = Unreliable Service = **Unsatisfied Guests**

Vision + Skills + Incentives + Resources + Delivery System – Measurement = Uninformed Employees = Inconsistent Service = **Unfulfilled Guests**

Vision + Skills + Incentives + Resources + Delivery System + Measurement = **Unsurpassed Employees = Wow Service = Delighted Guests**

if you need to do better, so you don't know how to do better. If you try to improve guest service without any metrics, you will never know if you have succeeded.

Exhibit 14.2 shows how the guest and the guest's experience can be negatively affected when any one of these important leadership keys is missing or forgotten. Negative effects will not always occur. Just as service failures happen in the best-managed organizations, so can the frontline staff of poorly managed organizations sometimes provide successful guest experiences in spite of the organization and its faults. When one or more leadership keys are missing, however, the chances of consistent service success are reduced. The exact effect on the guest experience may not be predictable in precise terms, but it will not be a happy one.

Exhibit 14.2 only shows the effects that a missing leadership element can have on the guest experience. We do this to emphasize the role that leadership can play in affecting the guest experience. Although managers will do as good a job as they can of managing all of the parts of the service experience, they are going to have very little control over most of the nonhuman aspects of the system. Consequently, managers' capacity to change the service product, the service setting, and most components of the service delivery system will be limited. For example, if the dining room is already constructed, the menu set, and the kitchen equipped and set up, the manager may not be able to do much to manage the guest service product, environment, and the mechanical parts of the delivery system. In a way, this is good news. It enables managers to focus on the people part of the guest experience: the guests as part of the environment for each other, the guests as they participate in co-creating their own experiences, the servers as they try to contribute to outstanding experiences, and the back-of-the-house employees as they provide what their internal server-guests require. These many and ever-changing people elements of the guest service situation require and deserve each manager's attention. Using a theme restaurant as an example, perhaps it is fortunate that the elaborate fantasy setting and the frying system don't require the moment-to-moment attention that people often do.

If the organization's leaders lack an overall vision of a target market and its expectations, this lack will be evident from the top, disseminated throughout the culture, and may lead to unfocused service. Without good leadership, servers will not be sure of what exactly they should achieve, and guests will receive mixed messages and inconsistent experiences. If managers put untrained people in guest contact positions, service failures and disappointed guests are probable. If incentives are lacking or inappropriate, unmotivated employees will simply go through the motions of providing lackluster service experiences. Failure to provide resource support for people in both the front and the back of the house will prohibit even a motivated and guest-focused front line from providing adequate service. Similarly, flaws in the delivery system will keep the best of personnel from providing reliably satisfactory guest experiences, much less experiences that delight. As the saying goes, "a bad system will defeat a good person every time." Finally, if levels of service quality and guest satisfaction are not measured, employees will be frustrated by not knowing whether the guest experiences they are providing are achieving the organizational service vision, so in a hit-or-miss fashion, they will continue to provide inconsistent service.

Only when the elements are all in place can the leader be effective in enabling and empowering employees. Only then can empowered employees provide the "wow" experiences that fulfill the organizational vision of providing remarkable service to delighted guests.

The leaders of each hospitality organization have an awesome responsibility and challenge. These people must motivate and empower employees to do what must be done to create the guest experience with excellence. A poorly manufactured car can be recalled for a retrofit; a bad guest experience is a bad guest experience forever. A tire can be inspected many times by trained quality control engineers before it is sold; a guest experience cannot be inspected because it does not even exist for inspection before it is provided. The guest experience must be right the first time, or the server must be empowered to fix any problems on the spot.

Every manager from the chief executive officer to the frontline supervisor must ultimately make sure all this happens, that employees feel good about what they are doing, that they convey this feeling to guests, and that guests leave knowing the experience was worth every penny paid and maybe a little bit more. This is leadership that makes the difference between success and failure in today's hospitality organizations, and it will make the difference in the future. This is the leadership challenge.

Courtesy of Don Riddle Images

The essence of guest services in the hospitality industry is that it all begins and ends with the guest.

IT ALL BEGINS—AND ENDS—WITH THE GUEST

By now, you may be reciting the components of the guest experience in your sleep: service product plus service setting plus service delivery system. But isn't something or someone missing? If that is a model of the guest experience, where is the guest? Obviously you can't have a guest experience without a guest to experience it. That's the whole point: without the guest to initiate it, the components the organization has assembled—the carefully designed service product; the detailed and inviting setting; the highly trained, motivated servers; and the finest back-of-the-house people and facilities—are just an experience waiting to happen. Throughout this book, we have made the point that it all starts with the guest. We think it fitting that we conclude by saying: it all ends with the guest, too!

LESSONS LEARNED

LO 14.1 Explain the overarching framework of the three *S*s—strategy, staffing, and systems.

- Manage all three parts of the guest experience.
- Organize, staff, train, and reward around the guest's needs.
- Whatever is critical to organizational success should be measured and managed carefully.
- Train employees to think of the people they come in contact with as their guests.
- Prevent every service failure you can, find every failure you cannot prevent, and fix every failure you find—every time and, if possible, on the spot.

LO 14.2 Identify the challenges leaders of service firms will face in the future.

- Remember that the only thing that is constant is change. Lead innovation.

LO 14.3 State the importance of innovation and managing change.

- Exceeding guest expectations today may not even meet them tomorrow.

LO 14.4 Differentiate between leading and managing.

- Build a strong culture and sustain it with stories, rewards, and actions.
- Articulate a vision, transcending any single job, so that all employees have a sense of value and worth in what they do.
- Never stop teaching; inspire everyone to keep learning.

LO 14.5 Identify the key factors for service leadership.

- Create jobs that are fun, fair, interesting, and important.
- Lead by actions and words that consistently reinforce the service mission.

LO 14.6 Discuss the reasons why "it all ends with the guest."

- Guestologists start with the guests, both external and internal.
- It all ends with the guest!

KEY TERMS AND CONCEPTS

basic guest expectations 458
eco-innovations 474
environmental impact 474
guest promise 468
incremental innovation 470
management innovation 472
market niche of one 469
radical innovation 470
servant leader 475
service innovations 470
transactional leader 475
transformational leader 475
"wow" elements 458

REVIEW QUESTIONS

1. Assume that your hospitality instructor says, "Bringing together all the principles of strategy, staffing, and systems is the job of the hospitality leader."
   A. What leader or leaders do you think the instructor is talking about?
   B. Who has greater responsibility for "bringing it all together": the hospitality organization's CEO or the local unit manager?
   C. Steak and Bake International has a well-established corporate mission, vision, and strategy. Its delivery systems are all in place, and the individual units are fully staffed. You have just been hired to manage the local Steak and Bake. Do you have responsibilities with regard to strategy, staffing, and systems other than those of a caretaker?
   D. Based on any work observations you have made or organizational experiences you have had, how would you distinguish between a leader and a manager?
2. This book suggests that all people seek to be part of organizations or situations that give them a sense of being involved in and contributing to something greater than themselves. Reflect on organizations you have enjoyed being a part of or for which you have worked hard to help them succeed.

   A. Why did you enjoy them and work hard on their behalf?
   B. In your life, have you joined some organizations "to gain a sense of being involved and to contribute to something greater than yourself" and other organizations for entirely different (perhaps totally selfish or self-centered) reasons?
   C. How does all that relate to managing the guest experience in hospitality organizations?

3. Think back on hospitality organizations that you like and to which you feel loyal. What is it that they do to make you want to return and buy their services again and again? Is it that they provide the basic drivers of your satisfaction so well? Or is it that they provide some wow drivers in addition to the basics?

4. The book suggests that one key way to differentiate the guest experience and give it some wow is to personalize it, rather than simply "doing it by the numbers." Think about different hospitality organizations that you have patronized.
   A. Which aspects of service were "done by the numbers"?
   B. What did they do to personalize the experience for you?
   C. Could they have done more to personalize it, and if so, what?

5. Why is empowering the front line so important for hospitality organizations?
   A. Why is a strong organizational culture necessary for successful empowerment?
   B. Why is a strong organizational system necessary for successful empowerment?

6. Consider the probable growth and improvements in communications technology that will occur in the future. How will these changes affect several different types of hospitality organizations, including hotels, restaurants, and theme parks? How might a typical hotel and restaurant make use of the Internet?

ACTIVITIES

1. Be on the lookout for service failures. Try to locate the origins of the failures within Exhibit 14-2.

2. Divide into groups. Describe bosses or leaders that group members have had who made you feel good about your job or activity. What did the boss or leader do to make you feel that way? Have a similar discussion about bosses or leaders who had an opposite effect on you.

3. Interview four different employees in four different jobs. How do they feel about the jobs they do? What do their leaders do to make them feel either happy or otherwise in their work?

ETHICS IN BUSINESS

A number of critical stakeholders are affected by the process of delivering customer service.

There are, of course, the guests. But many other people and entities have a stake: employees, managers, the leaders of the business, the owners (or stockholders), suppliers, the government, and society. While it may seem difficult enough just to try to provide an exceptional customer service while making the company a fair profit, one inevitably is faced with a lack of resources (particularly financial), and compromises must be made.

You, the readers, are the emerging leaders, of both businesses and society. As a future business leader, to what extent do you feel you should compromise organizational profits to better satisfy the other stakeholders with whom you will interact? We are not talking about actions with an expected financial return—treating your customer better so that you will get repeat business, treating your employees better so that they will be more motivated, or donating funds to charities for good public relations—but rather making choices to benefit others when a financial profit is not likely to result, directly or indirectly.

- Do businesses have an obligation to provide good service?
- Do employers have a responsibility to provide for workers beyond what is needed to hire, retain, and motivate them?
- Do managers ultimately have responsibilities to those who are not the company's owners?
- Do businesses have an obligation to their communities beyond what helps with public relations or is required by law?

You may want to take some time to think about these issues as you conclude reading this book. Inevitably, you will need to consider these questions as you go forth in your career.

CASE STUDY

Case 1: The Penland Heights Resort

Nestled in the mountains of western North Carolina, the luxury-level Penland Heights Resort has been family owned for generations. The employees have also been members of families who have served the guests of the Penland Heights for all those generations. They and Tom and Laura Lunsford, the owner-operators, have taken a familial pride in providing the most outstanding guest service in the Blue Ridge Mountains.

For many years, the Penland Heights was the only employer in the mountain town of Penland. Then "progress" began to encroach on the town, in the form of fast-food outlets, a mall, tourists, and Florida families who picked off the prime mountain locations as sites for modernistic chalets. The Penland Heights maintained its dignity and its superiority, but the employees on whom the Heights had counted for so long were getting older, and the new generation just did not seem to have the same service values as their elders. Yet, what could the Penland Heights do? Most of the young people left the area as soon as they graduated from high school. Only the younger family members of the aging employees chose to stay in Penland to work at the Penland Heights.

Tom and Laura Lunsford dreaded the day when they and their guests would have to depend on "the new generation," and as had to happen, eventually the more youthful employees outnumbered the long-time loyal employees. The time also came that the service for which the Heights had long been famous began to slip. The senior Lunsfords felt the new generation just did not have the service values of their older family members. The Penland management had empowered the older folks to a high degree and was happy to do so. They thought they would have to exert much more control over their sons and daughters; otherwise the old resort would soon be on the auction block.

Their daughter Granada told them they were wrong. "These are great kids. They love this old barn of a place. Sure, their ideas . . . our ideas . . . are different from yours. But this world and this business are different from what they were when you were younger and took over the Heights. If you give us kids a chance, we will not only hold the line, we can bring the Penland Heights back to the level of the glory days."

1. What are the basic leadership issues in this case?
2. What leadership skills must Tom and Laura Lunsford either have or acquire to continue managing this hotel successfully under the changed social, cultural, and economic conditions of the times?
3. Do you think Tom and Laura, who are intelligent, well meaning, experienced, and highly motivated but somewhat old fashioned, are sufficiently adaptable to fit in with the "new breed" of employees? Can these old dogs learn new tricks? Or in all probability does the future of hotel leadership lie with their daughter Granada who, even though inexperienced, is more in tune with the times?

Case 2: The Hotel Kitchen

Jean Crine, a graduate of the Culinary Institute of America, works in a hotel kitchen as a sous chef. Unlike some hotel restaurants, which seem to exist only so that their hotels can refer to themselves as "full service," this restaurant is known to be one of the best in a fairly large city. Crine and a few other women hold responsible positions in the hotel, but most of the significant positions are held by men.

Crine shares a kitchen with the executive chef, three chefs, and two assistant chefs, all males. The atmosphere in the kitchen was very relaxed and was more social than professional until Crine was hired. When the executive chef isn't around, the other chefs tend to treat Crine like a little sister—teasing her about her clothing, her hair, her formal training (they all learned on the job), mistakes in her work, what she ate for lunch, and her lifestyle.

She has expressed her annoyance at this patronizing treatment, but her irritation has only prompted an increase in the teasing.

On one occasion, Jean noticed an assistant chef (subordinate in organizational level to her) tossing a large salad without wearing the required rubber gloves. She politely asked him not to do so. He responded by sticking a handful of garlic dressing into her mouth. She retaliated by dumping a jar of olives on him. Some of the olive juice splashed onto a chef working on the other side of the sink. He grabbed Crine and started shaking her. She told him to remove his hands, and he yelled that no woman would tell him what to do. The assistant chef was also yelling that no woman would tell him how to toss a salad. On another occasion, one of the chefs put a picture of a woman wearing only a chef's hat on the kitchen wall. Crine asked him to remove it, but he refused. Crine spoke to the executive chef, who made the chef take the picture down. He was furious.

The chefs complain that Crine is outspoken, easily offended, domineering, and rebellious. They claim she is the cause of all disharmony in the kitchen and detrimental to morale and production. The executive chef has spoken severely to her about her tendency to "overreact." Concerning the incident with the salad, Crine maintains that the assistant chef's sticking garlic dressing in her mouth was inexcusable and that her reaction was normal for any person with self-respect. She insists upon her right to be treated as a professional by her co-workers, despite their apparent feeling that women are not equal in ability to men. She feels that to tolerate treatment as an inferior in the world of high cuisine would put an end to her career.

Recently, Crine returned to the kitchen after a two-day absence. She remarked that it was good to see everyone again. One of the chefs replied, "Too bad the feeling isn't mutual. I wish you hadn't come back."

1. How could the organization have avoided this problem?
2. To what extent, if any, has Crine brought on her own difficulties? Or do you view her purely as the victim in the situation?
3. What should be done now?

Case 3: Millionaire Hotels

Wilbur Beck is manager of the Major Equipment Maintenance and Engineering Group for Millionaire Hotels, a southeastern chain. Reporting to Beck are four supervisors, each responsible for a district within the southeast. Assigned to each district are a work group leader and an engineer.

Millionaire Hotels uses the PERT/CPM technique to schedule all major maintenance on hotel equipment. The process includes estimating future requirements and then ordering parts and assigning teams to the different hotels to perform the scheduled maintenance. To meet this demand, the MEM&E Group is included in the PERT/ CPM chart's critical path. Therefore, all work must be done on time.

Beck has decentralized and delegated as much as he can. Within each district, the work group leader is responsible for ensuring that all schedules are met. Nelson Baldwin, supervisor of District I, has been on vacation for two weeks. A few days ago, engineer Frank Diasi came into Beck's office, stated that seven hotel engineering projects in his district were critically overdue, and said he could not possibly catch up without help. When Beck asked why the district was behind, Diasi said bluntly that work group leader Jim Clark devoted his time to "busy work" and did not do his job properly. Diasi said Clark had not performed satisfactorily at any time since his assignment to the district four months earlier.

Upon checking discreetly, Beck found that Diasi was apparently telling the truth. Everyone agreed that Clark was technically capable and personally likable, but for some reason he was not performing the duties required of his position. One employee commented that Clark did not seem to value his position very highly. Beck arranged to bail out District 1 by borrowing help from other districts, but something obviously had to be done about Clark.

When district supervisor Baldwin returned from his vacation, Beck questioned him. He said he had only recently become aware that Clark was performing poorly. He admitted that he had not kept close track of individual performance within his district because the group as a whole had been performing fairly well; he thought district results were what counted. He asked Beck for help in determining what to do about Clark. They reviewed Clark's background together.

Clark is fifty-four years old. He came to Millionaire five years ago from another major chain. When he arrived, he and top management both anticipated that he would soon become a group manager in a position similar to Beck's. However, although he appears to be quite good technically, he simply has not lived up to expectations. For the past couple of years, he has obviously resented taking orders from younger managers. A year ago, when Clark was in another district, Beck decided that he was adequate in his present job but was not then promotable. Clark became quite angry when he heard Beck's appraisal. Since that time, his attitude has been barely acceptable.

1. What do you suppose is wrong with Clark?
2. Who is at fault, if anyone?
3. What should be done now?

Case 4: The Management Seminar

"I'd like to sum up what we've been talking about during this four-week management seminar," said Professor Stilwell to Trina Morgan and nineteen other participating managers. "Research and practical experience both show that if you give your employees the opportunity, they will get together, discuss problems, analyze alternatives, and then come up with good decisions that they will implement with enthusiasm."

Morgan was persuaded that group discussion and group decision-making could work at Hoffman Restaurant, where she was manager. Once back at the restaurant, she called together the thirty servers and relayed this message.

"Our current service standards were established seven years ago. Last year we installed automated equipment in the delivery system to make your work easier, and raised your pay as a reward for work well done, but we have not changed the service standards. I am asking you to discuss the situation thoroughly and then to decide what the new standards should be in both the cocktail and food areas. I'll be back at 11 o'clock to hear what you have decided." Morgan thought surely that the employees would set high standards and, because they had made the decision themselves, would try extra hard to achieve them.

When Morgan returned, she listened to head server Rollie Morris, spokesman for the group: "Ms. Morgan, we appreciate your faith in us, and we are convinced that we have justified that faith by coming to the right decision. We talked it over and decided that, even with the automated equipment, which is now a part of the delivery system, the service standards are still too high. We have to just about kill ourselves to meet them, and we all go home dragging. Therefore, we unanimously agreed to abolish the standards. They make this place feel like a production line. We can deliver more wow if we are just left on our own."

The servers cheered and smiled. Morgan excused herself from the meeting, went to her office, and placed a call to Professor Stilwell.

1. Is there a leadership problem at Hoffman Restaurant?
2. What mistakes, if any, did Trina Morgan make?
3. What will Professor Stilwell say? How will he advise Trina Morgan?
4. Do you think his advice will work?

Further readings on the topics in this chapter are listed in "Additional Readings" on pages 526–528.

Get the tools you need to sharpen your study skills. SAGE edge offers a robust online environment featuring an impressive array of free tools and resources.

Access practice quizzes, eFlashcards, video, and multimedia at **edge.sagepub.com/Ford2e**.

Visit **edge.sagepub.com/Ford2e** to help you accomplish your coursework goals in an easy-to-use learning environment.

GLOSSARY

Achievement needs: (Chapter 7) The needs of individuals for significant accomplishments, setting and meeting high standards, and excelling in what they do.

Action plans: (Chapter 2) The specific plans that lay out the specifics of how the organization will operate, what everyone needs to do in the next time period, usually a year, what resources are available to implement them, and, through the assessment metrics, how valuable feedback will be elicited on progress in achieving the plan.

Advanced information system: A system that, rather than simply providing information, is able to respond to information and choose between alternatives.

Apprenticeship: (Chapter 6) A training program that combines on-the-job training with related one-on-one coaching-like instruction so that a worker learns how to perform a highly skilled craft or trade.

Arrival patterns: (Chapter 11) The patterns describing the number of customers arriving or entering a system in a given period of time.

Assessment center: (Chapter 5) A place where an array of tests are administered to measure the KSAs of individuals.

Authority-acceptance theory: (Chapter 7) Chester Barnard's theory of what authority is and why people do or do not accept it.

Avenger: (Chapter 13) A customer who has experienced a service failure and leaves vowing never to return, does not complain to the organization, switches to another service provider, bad-mouths the organization, and finds a way to retaliate.

Bad-mouth: (Chapter 13) The spreading of negative comments and opinions about an organization by a dissatisfied customer.

Basic guest expectations: (Chapter 14) The fundamental components of the service experience that guests expect at a minimum

Behavioral interview: (Chapter 5) A form of structured interview where applicants give specific examples of how they handled a specific problem or performance of a specific task in the past.

Beliefs: (Chapter 4) A body of ideas or tenets believed to be or accepted as true.

Benchmark organizations: Organizations that meet and often exceed customer expectations regarding service quality and value and that have a high degree of excellence in their services, processes, and business support systems; these organizations also frequently have a world-class reputation.

Big data: (Chapter 9) A massive volume of structured and unstructured data that is so large as to make traditional approaches to its analysis difficult or even impossible.

Blueprinting: (Chapter 10) A flowchart diagram of the events and contingencies in the service process, on paper or digitally, in blueprint format.

Brainstorming: (Chapter 2) As a qualitative forecasting tool, a method in which a group of people generate and share ideas in open discussion, often in a free-association way, about what the future may bring.

Brand image: (Chapter 2) The image or icon associated with a specific product, service, or organization, meant to help customers differentiate the organization's offerings from those of competitors.

Brand name: (Chapter 2) The name of a specific product, service, or organization, used to differentiate the organization's offerings from those of competitors.

Capacity day: (Chapter 11) The maximum number of guests allowed, by law or by the organization, in a service facility in a day or at one time, used like the design day to balance the costs to the organization of excess capacity and the costs to the guest (in terms of quality and value) of inadequate capacity.

Classroom training: (Chapter 6) Training provided to employees in a classroom setting, typically where an expert uses a lecture format to teach to employees.

Coaching: (Chapter 6) Training, where there is a relationship between an individual (teacher, supervisor, or trainer) and an individual or a team, and the coach teaches how to perform the job, provides feedback, and reinforces desired behaviors.

Co-creating: (Chapter 8) Guest involvement in creating the value and quality of the guest experience.

Comment card: (Chapter 12) A method for obtaining guest feedback, often in the form of a postcard, enabling guests to rate the quality of the guest experience by responding to a few simple questions.

Competitive advantage: (Chapter 1) Something an organization does or has that makes it somehow better than its competitors in the eyes of its targeted customers.

Co-production: (Chapter 8) The active producing or helping to produce and deliver the guest experience by guests themselves, ideally to the mutual benefit of guests and the organization.

Core competence: (Chapter 2) A specific factor or characteristic that a business sees as being a key strength for how it provides its service product.

Cost: (Chapter 1) The financial and non-financial burden incurred by a guest to obtain a service, including tangible quantifiable costs (like price) and intangible non-quantifiable costs like opportunity costs of foregoing alternative opportunities, annoyance at receiving unsatisfactory service, and so forth.

Critical incident: (Chapter 1) A memorable event that deviates significantly, either positively or negatively, from what the guests expects or considers normal in a service encounter.

Critical path: (Chapter 10) The sequence of activities from the start of a project to its completion having the greatest cumulative elapsed time, thereby determining how long the entire project will take.

Cross-functional structure: (Chapter 10) A method of organizing people and groups so as to enable them to work temporarily across the boundaries or functional units in which organizations are traditionally structured; also, an overlaying of a group or project team upon the traditional functional organizational structure to work on a task for a limited time, which creates multiple lines of authority.

Cross-functional training: (Chapter 6) A training program that teaches employees how to do other jobs, thus enlarging the workforce's capabilities.

Cross-sell: (chapter 9) Using an interaction with a guest who has come to the organization for one service as an opportunity to sell the guest another product or service.

Daily count: (chapter 9) A prediction arrived at by an information system after a relatively short period of time (e.g., an hour), and based on a combination of actual count, an attendance database, and knowledge of arrival-rate distributions, of how many guests will come into the service location during the whole day.

Data analytics: (chapter 9) A largely automated process that uses statistical analyses to search large datasets for useful information to support decision-making.

Decision support system (DSS): (chapter 9) An information system that, in addition to providing information, has the capability of responding to information, choosing between alternatives, and either making or helping to make a decision.

Deep acting: (Chapter 5) The process of changing inner feelings so that the expected emotion is also genuinely felt by the actor, thus allowing the emotion to be displayed with conviction and authenticity.

Delphi technique: (Chapter 2) As a qualitative forecasting tool, a rather formal process involving surveying experts to get their individual forecasts, then combining or averaging those forecasts, often followed by another round of estimates based on a sharing of the individual and combined forecasts, the goal being to arrive at a final combined forecast.

Design day: (Chapter 2) The day of the year the organization uses to calculate designed capacity. Capacity is built to meet or exceed demand at a percentage of the year where management believes the cost of turning guests away is less than the cost of building more capacity.

Differentiation: (Chapter 2) A strategy designed to create in the guest's mind desirable differences, either real or driven by marketing and advertising, between the service or product offered by the organization and other competing services and products.

Distributive justice: (Chapter 13) The customer's feeling, after a complaint or service failure, that the outcome was fair.

Eco-innovation: (Chapter 14) Innovations designed to reduce the environmental impact of people or businesses.

Econometric models: (Chapter 2) Elaborate mathematical descriptions of multiple and complex relationships, statistically assembled as systems of multiple regression equations; used in forecasting.

Economic needs: (Chapter 7) The needs of individuals for a steady and sufficient stream of income, necessary for purchasing the essentials in life (food, housing, and other necessities).

Economic ordering quantity (EOQ) model: (Chapter 9) A formula for calculating the optimum reorder size (number of units) of an item once the reorder point is reached; designed to minimize annual order and holding costs.

e-learning: (Chapter 6) Training that uses online resources and videos to deliver training content.

Emotional labor: (Chapter 5) The process of managing feelings and expressions to fulfill the interactional and emotional requirements of a job.

Employee development: (Chapter 6) A combination of work experience, education, and training, all of which combine to improve employee KSAs over time.

Empowerment: (Chapter 7) Giving employees authority and responsibility to make decisions and gain greater control over their work.

Environment: See *service environment*.

Environmental assessment: (Chapter 2) A careful examination of the present opportunities and threats in the external business environment, and forecast of the future environment, within which the organization operates to determine the impact of external factors on the organization and to discover the key drivers that will satisfy present and future guests; carried out as part of long-term strategic planning and sometimes called the long look around.

Environmental impact: (Chapter 14) The effect that the activities of people and businesses have on the ecological environment.

Equity theory: (Chapter 7) The theory that people consider what they get out of an endeavor (the outputs) and what they put into it (the inputs) and draw conclusions as to the fairness of the endeavor by comparing their ratio of outputs to inputs to the perceived ratio of others.

Ethical leadership: (Chapter 7) Leadership that is directed and driven by a respect for ethical beliefs and values, and respectful for the beliefs, dignity, and rights of others.

Evangelist: (Chapter 13) Extremely satisfied, delighted guest who takes every available opportunity, and often creates opportunities, to praise the organization and recommend it to friends and acquaintances.

Executive education: (Chapter 6) Training programs targeted at higher level leaders in organization.

Expectancy theory: (Chapter 7) The idea that organizations need to relate employee rewards directly to performance. If employees believe or expect that they can achieve a certain performance level by putting in a certain level of effort, that achieving this performance will lead to promised rewards, and if employees value these rewards sufficiently, then they will be motivated to put in the effort necessary to get the rewards.

Expectations: (Chapter 1) Characteristics that a guest hopes and assumes will be associated with a service experience.

External training: (Chapter 6) Training provided for organizational members by persons or institutions outside the organization.

Fire the guest: (Chapter 8) A relatively recent concept involving the refusal to serve certain guests who engage in unacceptable extreme behaviors; a philosophy contrary to "the guest is always right."

Fishbone analysis: (Chapter 10) An approach to problem solving that involves drawing a diagram, shaped like a fishbone, of the problem and its possible causes.

Fishbone diagram: (Chapter 10) A diagram, shaped like a fish skeleton, used in problem solving with the problem represented by the fish spine and the possible causes of the problem attached to the spine.

Focus group: (Chapter 2) As a qualitative forecasting tool, a group of people—frequently guests—discuss with a trained group discussion leader their future hopes and expectations of the organization; often used to sound out guests about planned organizational innovations.

Forecasting: (Chapter 2) Process of making predictions of future trends, or the impact of current trends on future business.

Formal group: (Chapter 7) A group of employees that exist because of the formal structure of an organization (a company, a shift, a team, etc.).

Goal setting: (Chapter 7) Setting goals for individual employees and units for the purpose of motivating higher performance. Setting specific and challenging goals can lead to higher performance levels than merely setting vague goals or telling people to do their best.

Green movement: (Chapter 2) A diverse set of political, scientific, and social movements advocating for sustainable management of resources and addressing issues of climate change.

Growth needs: (Chapter 7) The needs of individuals for learning and growing.

Guest experience: (Chapter 1) The sum total of the experiences (consisting of the service product, setting, and delivery system) that the guest has with the service provider on a given occasion or set of occasions; often referred to as service experience in other service industries.

Guest focus groups: (Chapter 12) A method of assessing service quality in which, typically, six to ten guests gather with a facilitator for several hours to discuss perceived problems and make suggestions. It provides in-depth information on how guests view the service they receive.

Guestologist: (Chapter 1) A specialist in identifying how hospitality organizations can best respond to the needs, wants, expectations, and behaviors of their targeted guest markets.

Guestology: (Chapter 1) The study of guests—their wants, needs, expectations, and behaviors—with the aim of aligning the organization's strategy, staff, and systems so as to provide outstanding service to guests.

Guest promise: (Chapter 14) What you tell your customers that you will do for them (verbally, in writing, and/or through advertising).

Hedonic treadmill: (Chapter 7) The tendency of people to return to a relatively stable level of happiness despite positive (or negative) events, purchases, or life changes.

Hiring from within: (Chapter 5) The practice of filling positions within an organization from employees already working for the organization.

Hospitality: (Chapter 1) An industry consisting basically of organizations that offer guests courteous, professional food, drink, and lodging services, alone or in combination, but in an expanded definition also includes theme park[s], gaming [centers], cruise ships, trade shows, fairs, meeting planning, and convention organizations.

Human resource management: (Chapter 5) The use of organizational systems to ensure that human talent is used efficiently and effectively to achieve organizational goals.

Human resource planning: (Chapter 5) The process of analyzing an organization's current human resource capabilities and the organization's human resources required to meet organizational objectives.

Incremental innovation: (Chapter 14) An innovation of an existing service product, process, marketing approach, resource supply, or organizational form.

Informal group: (Chapter 7) A social group that forms without guidance from the organization.

Informational justice: (Chapter 13) A type of interactional justice that refers to the customer's feeling of the fairness of the information and communication provided by the organization, especially after a service failure occurs.

Information-lean environment: (Chapter 3) An environment that does not require extensive information processing because there are few data to process.

Information overload: (Chapter 9) Literally, too much information; generally referring to a tendency of information systems and their users to generate and send too much information or non-useful information to guests and employees.

information-rich environment: (Chapter 3) An environment that requires considerable information processing because there are large amounts of data to process.

Information system: (Chapter 9) A system, often computerized, designed to get the right information to the right person in the right format at the right time so that it adds value to that person's decisions.

Integrated information system: (Chapter 9) A system designed to bring together diverse sources of organizational information to enable managerial decisions.

Interactional justice: (Chapter 13) The customer's feeling of being treated with respect and courtesy during interactions with the organization, especially after a service failure occurs; being given the opportunity to express complaints fully.

Internal assessment: (Chapter 2) A careful examination of the organization's present internal condition, its strengths—primarily its core competencies—and weaknesses; carried out as part of long-term strategic planning and sometimes called the searching look within.

Internal customers: (Chapter 1) Persons or units within the organization that depend on and serve each other.

Internal training: (Chapter 6) Training provided for organizational members by persons or groups within the organization itself.

Internship: (Chapter 6) A short-term work experience designed to familiarize employees with a particular role or career.

Job analysis: (Chapter 5) A systematic process through which information about the content of a job is gathered and analyzed to determine the exact job specifications and required competencies for the job.

Job performance standards: (Chapter 12) Standards that can help ensure success by providing employees with clear and specific performance expectations for each major duty associated with their jobs.

Juran Trilogy: (Chapter 10) Joseph Juran's model of quality: planning, control, and improvement.

Key driver: (Chapter 2) A primary factor within a guest experience valued highly by the guest and leading to guest satisfaction, determined by surveying and studying guests.

KSAs: (Chapter 1) An abbreviation for knowledge, skills, and abilities necessary to do a job.

Leadership: (Chapter 7) A process to influence others.

Lean environment: A service setting, environment, or servicescape requiring that guests process relatively little information; used when guests are generally unfamiliar with the environment; see also *information-rich environment*.

Low-price provider: (Chapter 2) An organization that tries to compete within its market primarily by maximizing operational or production efficiencies and minimizing organizational costs so as to offer the same service as competitors at a lower price.

Management by Objectives (MBO): (Chapter 7) A process of having each employee set specific and measurable goals, and then using the achievement of those goals as a key driver for that employee's performance assessment.

Management by walking around (MBWA): (Chapter 12) managers walk around observing the operation firsthand, looking for problems or inefficiencies, talking to guests and employees, and offering suggestions; sometimes referred to as walking the front.

Management innovation: (Chapter 14) An innovation of a management practice, process, or technique that is new to the state of the art and is intended to further organizational goals.

Managing information: (Chapter 9) Using information systems to get the right information to the right person in the right format at the right time.

Managing the wait: (Chapter 11) The organization's use of queuing theory and psychological techniques to minimize the negative impact on guests of inevitable waits.

Market niche: (Chapter 2) A gap in a market that an organization seeks out, focuses on, and attempts to fill to attract customers and compete successfully.

Market niche of one: (Chapter 14) Identifying the specific needs of an individual customer, and attempting to fulfill those needs to deliver a personalized service experience.

MBWA: (Chapter 12) See *management by walking around.*

Mentoring: (Chapter 6) A relationship in which an experienced manager is paired up with an individual early in the latter's career or when new to the organization.

Mission statement: (Chapter 2) An articulation of the organization's purpose, the reason for which it was founded and for which it continues to exist.

Moment of truth: (Chapter 1) Any key or crucial moment or period during a service encounter, a make-or-break moment; subsequently expanded by others to include any significant or memorable interaction point between organization and guest.

Motivation: (Chapter 7) The drive or compelling force that energizes people to do what they do in a given situation.

Multichannel, mutliphase queue: (Chapter 11) Two or more multichannel, single-phase queues in sequence. The guest waits to get to the front of one line, and then goes to the next available server. After receiving the first phase of service, the guest then gets into another line, wait to arrive at the front, then goes to the next available server/channel to receive the next phase of service.

Multichannel, single-phase queue: (Chapter 11) The customer begins in a single line that then feeds into multiple channels or stations for the service, each staffed by a server. The customer waits to get to the front of the single line, and then goes to the next available channel (server) for service.

Mystery shopper: (Chapter 12) Hired or in-house person who poses as a guest, methodically sample the service and its delivery, observe the overall guest service operation, and then submit a report to management.

Needs assessment: (Chapter 6) A process used to determine if perceived organizational problems or weaknesses should be addressed by training or by some other strategy.

Norms: (Chapter 4) Standards of behavior—spoken and unspoken, obvious and subtle—that define how members (and sometimes guests) are expected to act while part of the organization.

On-boarding: (Chapter 5) The process of integrating a new employee into an organization and its culture.

On-the-job training: (Chapter 6) Training where an experienced employee instructs a new employee on how to actually do the job while the trainee is actually performing the job.

Organizational culture: (Chapter 4) The shared philosophies, ideologies, values, assumptions, beliefs, attitudes, and norms that knit a community of different people together.

Organization as an information system: (Chapter 9) The idea that the organization itself should be considered as and structured as an integrated information network or system that connects all the departments and people that deliver the guest experience.

Pareto analysis: (Chapter 10) A problem-solving technique based on arranging the potential causes of an organizational problem in their order of frequency, from most to least.

PERT/CPM: (Chapter 10) PERT stands for Program Evaluation Review Technique, and CPM stand for Critical Path Method.

PERT/CPM Chart: (Chapter 10) A diagram, usually used in the planning of major projects, consisting of circles representing completed events, arrows representing the activities that must be done before an event can be considered completed, and includes a critical path indicating the sequence of events that must occur on time if the project is to be completed on time.

Poka-yoke: (Chapter 10) A device or procedure designed to prevent or immediately correct mistakes; "mistake-proofing" in Japanese.

Positive reinforcement: (Chapter 7) Providing rewards to employees for organizationally approved behaviors—namely, those associated with high levels of guest satisfaction—to encourage repetition of those behaviors.

Procedural justice: (Chapter 13) The customer's feeling that company procedures are fair and not a procedural hassle, especially after a complaint or service failure.

Process strategies: (Chapter 12) Means of comparing what is happening in the service experience against what is supposed to happen, usually but not always expressed as a measurable service standard.

Qualitative forecasting tools: (Chapter 2) Forecasting tools that use non-quantitative, subjective information to make projections.

Quantitative forecasting tools: (Chapter 2) Forecasting tools that use quantitative, objective information or data to make projections.

Quasi-employees: (Chapter 8) Term used to define the many different ways customers can help an organization be effective. Roles include not only co-producing their own experiences but also supervising, rewarding and motivating employees, training and supervising other guests, quality control consultants, part of other guest's experiences, and marketers.

Queue discipline: (Chapter 11) In hospitality settings, the organization's pattern or plan for how arriving guests are served; usually first-come, first-served.

Queuing theory: (Chapter 11) The theory of how waiting lines behave; same as waiting-line theory.

Queues: (Chapter 11) Waiting lines.

Radical innovation: (Chapter 14) A totally new innovation that has a significant impact on a market and on the economic activity of firms in that market.

Recognition needs: (Chapter 7) The needs of individuals for praise and attention from customers, colleagues, and/or superiors.

Recognition program: (Chapter 7) A program designed to provide a reward (financial and/or symbolic) to individuals who achieve a notable goal.

Recruitment: (Chapter 5) The process of finding candidates with the KSAs necessary to fill organizational positions.

Regression analysis: (Chapter 2) A statistical technique used to examine the relationship or degree of association between one or more variables to predict a dependent variable of interest; used in forecasting.

Retraining: (Chapter 6) Training designed to reinforce fundamental messages about the organization's mission while preparing employees for possible promotion and development

Revenue management: (Chapter 2) A technique for selling the right capacity to the right customer at the most advantageous price, to maximize both capacity use and revenue from all components of the service product.

Ritual: (Chapter 4) A symbolic act performed to gain and maintain membership or identity within an organization.

Role theory: The theory of how other people or groups influence us to behave or function in particular settings or situations.

Scenario building: (Chapter 2) As a qualitative forecasting tool, a group of people—frequently organizational employees—assume a certain future situation or set of circumstances, then try to assess its implications for the organization; sometimes called war gaming.

Selection: (Chapter 5) The process of selecting employees to fill organizational positions from the candidates with the necessary KSAs.

Self-efficacy: (Chapter 7) The beliefs of employees that their knowledge, skills, and abilities are sufficient to perform at the desired level.

Self-managed team: (Chapter 7) A team that is empowered to control its own task behaviors with relatively little external control.

Servant leader: (Chapter 14) A leader who serves others through them to achieve their goals; the servant-leader shares power, puts others' needs first, and helps people develop so that they can perform as well as possible.

Service: (Chapter 1) An action or performed task that takes place through contact between the customer or guest and representatives of the service organization.

Service delivery system: (Chapter 1) The human components and the physical production processes, plus the organizational and information systems, involved in delivering the service to the customer.

Service encounter: (Chapter 1) The person-to-person interactions or series of interactions between the customer and the persons delivering the service.

Service environment: (Chapter 1) The physical location and its characteristics within which the organization provides service to guests; same as service setting and servicescape.

Service experience: (Chapter 1) Same as guest experience but sometimes used in service industries that do not typically refer to their customers as guests.

Service failure: (Chapter 13) The organization's failure to deliver the promised service according to its own standards or the guest's expectations.

Service guarantee: (Chapter 12) An organization's written promise either to satisfy guests or to compensate them for any failure to satisfy them regarding the overall service or particular aspects of it.

Service innovations: (Chapter 14) New services or service products that, when first offered, create a new service experience for guests.

Service naturals: (Chapter 5) An individual who instinctively provides great service when presented with the opportunity

Service package, service product: (Chapter 1) The entire bundle of tangibles and intangibles provided by a hospitality organization to guests during a service experience.

Service-profit chain: (Chapter 7) The idea that organizational practices affect employee motivation, which affects customer satisfaction, which ultimately affects profitability.

Service quality: (Chapter 1) The difference between the service that the customer expects to get and the service that the customer actually receives.

Service recovery: (Chapter 13) The organization's attempt to make right or compensate for a service failure.

Servicescape: (Chapter 1) The physical location and its characteristics within which the organization provides service to guests; same as service environment and service setting.

Service setting: (Chapter 1) The physical location and its characteristics within which the organization provides service to guests; same as service environment and servicescape.

Service standards: (Chapter 10) The company's explicit expectations for how the different aspects of the service experience should be delivered every time to every guest.

Service strategy: (Chapter 2) The organization's plan for providing the experience guests expect.

Service value: (Chapter 1) The relationship of the quality of the service to its cost, or service quality divided by all costs incurred by the guest for service.

SERVQUAL: (Chapter 12) Standing for "service quality," SERVQUAL is the best-known survey instrument within the services field; measures customer perceptions of service quality along five dimensions: reliability, responsiveness, assurance, empathy, and tangibles.

Setting: See *service setting*.

Simulation: (Chapter 10) An imitation of a real or potential problem or organizational situation.

Simulation: (training) (Chapter 6) A training program that provides a realistic but controlled and safe environment for employees to learn or practice new skills.

Single-channel, multiphase queue: (Chapter 11) Two or more single-channel, single-phase queues in a sequence. The guest waits in one queue for service from a single server, and then moves on to wait in another queue for another phase of service from another single server.

Single-channel, single-phase queue: (Chapter 11) A type of queue where there is a single server and s single step.

Situational interview: (Chapter 5) A form of structured interview where applicants explain how they would handle a specific problem or task.

Skills training: (Chapter 6) Training designed to give employees the knowledge they need to do their jobs.

SMART goals: (Chapter 7) Goals that are Specific, Measureable, Attainable, Results oriented, and Time bound.

Social needs: (Chapter 7) The needs of individuals to be part of a group.

Strategic plan: (Chapter 2) The specific steps that detail how the organization intends to get from where it is to where it wishes to be in order to achieve its mission and vision.

Strategic premises: (Chapter 2) Assumptions about the future, based on the results of forecasting, on which the organization's strategic plan is based or premised.

Structured guest interview: (Chapter 12) An interview conducted according to a set pattern, usually involving a standard set of professionally developed, validated questions designed to gather guest perceptions of service quality.

Structured interview: (for job candidates) (Chapter 5) A job interview conducted according to a set plan, usually involving a standard set of questions designed to gather relevant personal and job-related data, providing a standardized method to evaluate candidates, and ensuring that all candidates are evaluated in a comparable way.

Succession plans: (Chapter 5) A long-term plan for the orderly progression of employees through key positions or key locations.

Surface acting: (Chapter 5) The process of modifying facial expressions and body language to display the expected emotions, but without the emotion being genuinely felt by the actor.

Sustainability: (Chapter 2) The use of resources in a way that protects the future environment and the ability of future generations to meet their own needs.

Symbol: (Chapter 4) A physical object that has organizational significance or communicates an unspoken message (for example, Mickey's ears for Disney).

Team: (Chapter 7) Two or more individuals, working together (either face-to-face or virtually) who are performing organizationally relevant tasks to achieve one or more common goals.

Text analytics: (Chapter 9) Linguistic, statistical, and machine learning techniques that can capture the information content of textual sources for use in business intelligence, exploratory data analysis, research, or investigation.

"The show": (Chapter 3) A Disney terms for everyone and everything that interfaces or interacts with guests on a Disney property.

Theming: (Chapter 3) The organization and presentation of the guest experience around a unifying idea or theme, often a fantasy theme, to give guests the illusion of being in a place and time other than "the here and now"; most often used in connection with theme parks and theme restaurants.

Time-series and trend analysis: (Chapter 2) Statistical methods for projecting past information or trends into the future; used in forecasting.

Training control group: (Chapter 6) A group of individuals that are similar to those being trained, except that they do not receive the training.

Transactional leader: (Chapter 14) A leader who focuses on supervision, policy, and performance; the transactional leader seeks to promote compliance with current policy and systems, using both punishments and rewards to meet specific goals, increase compliance, and enhance efficiency.

Transformational leader: (Chapter 14) A leader who provides opportunities for employees to thrive and grow as individuals, to find a sense of accomplishment in jobs that are interesting to them, and to do work that is important as it has meaning and value.

Universal service map: (Chapter 10) An elaborate and detailed blueprint that can be generally applied to a variety of service situations.

Unstructured interview: (Chapter 5) A selection technique in which interviewers make up questions as they go along, have no predetermined way to score applicants and relying on memory and intuition to evaluate candidates.

Values: (Chapter 4) Preferences for certain ideas, behaviors, and outcomes over others, used and promulgated within organizations to define for members (and sometimes guests) what is right and wrong, preferred and not preferred.

Virtual queue: (Chapter 11) A line that is not visible and allows consumers to be "in line" without actually having to stand in a line. Allows customers to engage in other activities while waiting for service.

Vision statement: (Chapter 2) An articulation of what the organization hopes to look like and be like in the future.

Waiting-line theory: (Chapter 11) The theory of how waiting lines behave; same as queuing theory.

Word of mouth: (Chapter 13) Passing of information from person to person by means of oral communication.

"Wow" elements: (Chapter 14) The characteristics and qualities that make a service experience memorable.

Yield management: (Chapter 2) A technique for managing the pricing of an organization's units of capacity, using forecasts based on past results, to maximize the profitability of that capacity; in other words, selling the right capacity to the right customer, at the right time, for the right price.

Zone of tolerance: (Chapter 13) The range of service quality experienced that a customer will deem as satisfactory, even if aspects of the service are not fully up to expectations.

ADDITIONAL READINGS

Chapter 1

Akaka, Melissa Archpru, and Stephen L. Vargo. "Extending the Context of Service: from Encounters to Ecosystems." *Journal of Services Marketing* 29, no. 6/7 (2015): 453–462.

Åkesson, Maria, Bo Edvardsson, and Bård Tronvoll. "Customer Experience from a Self-service System Perspective." *Journal of Service Management* 25, no. 5 (2014): 677–698.

Ali, Faizan, Muslim Amin, and Cihan Cobanoglu. "An Integrated Model of Service Experience, Emotions, Satisfaction, and Price Acceptance: An Empirical Analysis in the Chinese Hospitality Industry." *Journal of Hospitality Marketing & Management* 25, no. 4 (2016): 449–475.

Benoit, Sabine, Katrin Scherschel, Zelal Ates, Linda Nasr, and Jay Kandampully. "Showcasing the Diversity of Service Research: Theories, Methods, and Success of Service Articles." *Journal of Service Management* 28, no. 5 (2017): 810–836.

Berry, Leonard L. *Discovering the Soul of Service: The Nine Drivers of Sustainable Business Success.* New York, NY: The Free Press, 1999.

Bolton, Ruth, Anders Gustafsson, Janet McColl-Kennedy, Nancy J. Sirianni, and David K. Tse. "Small Details that Make Big Differences: A Radical Approach to Consumption Experience as a Firm's Differentiating Strategy." *Journal of Service Management* 25, no. 2 (2014): 253–274.

Bowen, David E., and Benjamin Schneider. "A Service Climate Synthesis and Future Research Agenda." *Journal of Service Research* 17, no. 1 (2014): 5–22.

Bowen, John, and Robert C. Ford. "Managing Service Organizations: Does Having a "Thing" Make a Difference?" *Journal of Management* 28: 3 (2002): 447–469.

Brinker, Norman, and Donald T. Phillips. *On the Brink: The Life and Leadership of Norman Brinker.* Arlington, TX: Summit Publishing Group, 1996.

Buswell, John, Christine Williams, Keith Donne, and Carley Sutton. *ServiceQuality in Leisure, Events, Tourism and Sport.* Oxfordshire, UK: Centre for Agriculture and Biosciences International, 2016.

Capodagli, B., and Lynn Jackson. *The Disney Way: Harnessing the Management Secrets of Disney in Your Company.* 3rd ed. New York, NY: McGraw Hill, 2016.

Carlzon, Jan, and Tom Peters. *Moments of Truth.* New York, NY: Harper Business, 1989.

Carù, Antonella, and Bernard Cova. "Co-creating the Collective Service Experience." *Journal of Service Management* 26, no. 2 (2015): 276–294.

Cathy, S. Truett. *Eat Mor Chikin: Inspire More People.* Looking Glass Books, 2002.

Chandler, Jennifer D., and Robert F. Lusch. "Service Systems: A Broadened Framework and Research Agenda on Value Propositions, Engagement, and Service Experience." *Journal of Service Research* 18, no. 1 (2015): 6–22.

Chase, Richard, and Sriram Dasu. "Psychology of the Experience: The Missing Link in Service Science." In *Service Science, Management and Engineering Education for the 21st Century,* edited by Bill Hafley and Wendy Murphy, 35–40. Denton, TX: Springer US, 2008.

Chathoth, Prakash K., Gerardo R. Ungson, Robert J. Harrington, and Eric SW Chan. "Co-creation and Higher Order Customer Engagement in Hospitality and Tourism Services: A Critical Review." *International Journal of Contemporary Hospitality Management* 28, no. 2 (2016): 222–245.

Cockerell, Lee. *The Customer Rules: 39 Essential Rules for Delivering Sensational Service.* Redfern, NSW, Australia: Currency Press, 2013.

Collier, Joel E., Donald C. Barnes, Alexandra K. Abney, and Mark J. Pelletier. "Idiosyncratic Service Experiences: When Customers Desire the Extraordinary in a Service Encounter." *Journal of Business Research* 84 (2018): 150–161.

Dickson, Duncan, Robert C. Ford, and Bruce Laval. "The Top Ten Excuses for Bad Service (and How to Avoid Needing Them)." *Organizational Dynamics* 34, no. 2 (2005): 168–184.

Dong, P., and Noel Yee-Man Siu. "Servicescape Elements, Customer Predispositions and Service Experiences: The Case of Theme Park Visitor." *Tourism Management* 55 (2013): 541–551.

Ford, Robert C., and David E. Bowen. "A Service-Dominant Logic for Management Education: It's Time." *Academy of Management Learning & Education* 7, No. 2 (2008): 224–243.

Ford, Robert C., and Duncan D. Dickson. "The Father of Guestology: An Interview with Bruce Laval." *Journal of Applied Management and Entrepreneurship* 13, no. 3 (2008): 80–90.

Ford, Robert C., Cherrill Heaton, and Stephen Brown. "Delivering Excellent Service: Lessons from the Best Firms." *California Management Review* 44, no. 1 (2001): 39–56.

Ford, Robert C. and Janet McColl-Kennedy. "Organizational Strategies for Filling the Customer Can-Do/Must-Do Gap." *Business Horizons* 58, no. 4 (2015): 459–468.

Gittell, Jody Hoffer. *The Southwest Airlines Way: Using the Power of Relationships to Achieve High Performance.* New York, NY: McGraw Hill, 2002.

Golubovskaya, M., Richard R. N. Robinson, and David Solnet. "The Meaning of Hospitality: Do the Employees Understand?" *International Journal of Contemporary Hospitality Management* 29, no. 5 (2017): 1282–1304.

Gremler, Dwayne D. "The Critical Incident Technique in Service Research." *Journal of Service Research* 7, no. 1 (2004): 65–89.

Heskett, James L., and W. Earl Sasser. *Service Breakthroughs: Changing the Rules of the Game.* New York, NY: Free Press, 1990.

Heskett, J., W. Earl Sasser, and Leonard A. Schlesinger. *The Service Profit Chain: How Leading Companies Link Profit and Growth to Loyalty, Service and Value.* New York, NY: Free Press, 1997.

Jaakkola, Elina, Anu Helkkula, and Leena Aarikka-Stenroos. "Service Experience Co-creation: Conceptualization, Implications, and Future Research Directions." *Journal of Service Management* 26, no. 2 (2015): 182–205.

Kandampully, Jay, Byron William Keating, BeomCheol Kim, Anna S. Mattila, and David Solnet. "Service Research in the Hospitality Literature: Insights from a Systematic Review." *Cornell Hospitality Quarterly* 55, no. 3 (2014): 287–299.

Kandampully, Jay, and David Solnet. *Service Management Principles: For Hospitality and Tourism.* Dubuque, IA: KendallHunt Publishing Company, 2015.

Kandampully, J., Byron William Keating, BeomCheol Kim, Anna S. Mattila, and David Solnet. "Service Research in the Hospitality Literature: Insights from a Systematic Review." *Cornell Hospitality Quarterly* 55, no. 3. (2014): 287–299.

Kandampully, Jay, Tingting Zhang, and Elina Jaakkola. "Customer Experience Management in Hospitality: A Literature Synthesis, New Understanding, and Research Agenda." *International Journal of Contemporary Hospitality Management* 30, no. 1 (2018): 21–56.

King, C. A., "What Is Hospitality?" *International Journal of Hospitality Management* 14, no. 3–4 (1995): 219–234.

Kinni, T., Michael D. Eisner, and Walt Disney Company. *Be Our Guest: Perfecting the Art of Customer Service.* New York, NY: Disney Editions, 2001.

Klaus, P. and Bo Edvardsson. "Striking the Right Balance: How to Design, Implement, and Operationalize Customer Experience Management Programs." In *Managing Consumer Services: Factory or Theater?* edited by Enzo Baglieri and Uday Karmarkar, 69–89. Switzerland: Springer, 2014.

Lemon, K. N., and Peter C. Verhoef. "Understanding Customer Experience Throughout the Customer Journey." *American Marketing Association* 80, no. 6 (2016): 69–96.

Levitt, T. "Marketing Intangible Products and Product Intangibles." *Harvard Business Review* 22, no. 2 (1981): 37–44.

Lipp, Doug. *Disney U: How Disney University Develops the World's Most Engaged, Loyal, and Customer-Centric Employees.* New York, NY: McGraw-Hill, 2013.

McColl-Kennedy, J. R., Anders Gustafsson, Elina Jaakkola, Phil Klaus, Zoe Radnor, Helen Perks, and Margareta Friman. "Fresh Perspectives on the Customer Experience." *Journal of Services Marketing* 29, no. 6–7 (2015): 430–435.

Michelli, J. *The New Gold Standard: 5 Leadership Principles for Creating a Legendary Customer Experience Courtesy of the Ritz-Carlton Hotel Company.* New York, NY: McGraw-Hill, 2008.

Ng, Sylvia C., Carolin Plewa, and Jillian C. Sweeney. "Professional Service Providers' Resource Integration Styles (PRO-RIS) Facilitating Customer Experiences." *Journal of Service Research* 19, no. 4 (2016): 380–395.

Ostrom, Amy L., Ananthanarayanan Parasuraman, David E. Bowen, Lia Patricio, and Christopher A. Voss. "Service Research Priorities in a Rapidly Changing Context." *Journal of Service Research* 18, no. 2 (2015): 127–159.

Parasuraman, A. P., Valerie A. Zeithaml, and Leonard L. Berry. "A Conceptual Model of Service Quality and its Implications for Future Research." *Journal of Marketing* 49, no. 4 (1985): 41–50.

Peng, Jianping, Xinyuan Zhao, and Anna S. Mattila. "Improving Service Management in Budget Hotels." *International Journal of Hospitality Management* 49 (2015): 139–148.

Pine, B. J., and James H. Gilmore. "The Experience Economy: Past, Present and Future." In *Handbook on the Experience Economy,* edited by Jon Sundbo and Flemming Sorensen, 21–44. Cheltenham, Glos: Edward Elgar Publishing Limited, 2013.

Pine, B. Joseph, and James H. Gilmore. "Welcome to the Experience Economy." *Harvard Business Review* 76, No. 4 (1998): 97–105.

Pizam, A., Valeriya Shapoval, and Taylor Ellis. "Customer Satisfaction and Its Measurement in Hospitality Enterprises: A Revisit and Update." *International Journal of Contemporary Hospitality Management* 28, no. 1 (2016): 2–35.

Radojevik, T., Nemanja Stanisic, Nenad Stanic. "Ensuring Positive Feedback: Factors that Influence Satisfaction in the Contemporary Hospitality Industry." *Tourism Management* 51 (2015): 13–21.

Rathmell, J. M. "What Is Meant by Service?" *Journal of Marketing* 30, no. 4 (1966): 32–36.

Rawson, A., Ewan Rawson, Conor Jones. "The Truth About Customer Experience." *Harvard Business Review* 91, no. 9 (2013): 90–98.

Sharp, Isadore. Four Seasons: *The Story of a Business Philosophy.* New York, NY: Penguin, 2009.

Sipe, Lori J., and Mark R. Testa. "From Satisfied to Memorable: An Empirical Study of Service and Experience Dimensions on Guest Outcomes in the Hospitality Industry." *Journal of Hospitality Marketing & Management* 26, no. 8 (2017): 1–18.

Solnet, David, and Jay Kandampully. "How Some Service Firms Have Become Part of 'Service Excellence' Folklore: An Exploratory Study." *Managing Service Quality: An International Journal* 18, no. 2 (2008): 179–193.

Subramony, Mahesh, Karen Ehrhart, Markus Groth, Brooks C. Holtom, Danielle D. van Jaarsveld, Dana Yagil, Tiffany Darabi et al. "Accelerating Employee-related Scholarship in Service Management: Research Streams, Propositions, and Commentaries." *Journal of Service Management* 28, no. 5 (2017): 837–865.

Susskind, Alex M., K. Michele Kacmar, and Carl P. Borchgrevink. "Guest–Server Exchange Model and Performance: The Connection Between Service Climate and Unit-Level Sales in Multiunit Restaurants." *Journal of Hospitality & Tourism Research* 42, No. 1 (2016): 122–141.

Tax, Stephen S., David McCutcheon, and Ian F. Wilkinson. "The Service Delivery Network (SDN) a Customer-centric Perspective of the Customer Journey." *Journal of Service Research* 16, no. 4 (2013): 454–470.

Tontini, Gérson, Graziela dos Santos Bento, Thaíse Caroline Milbratz, Barbara Kobuszewski Volles, and Daniela Ferrari. "Exploring the Nonlinear Impact of Critical Incidents on Customers' General Evaluation of Hospitality Services." *International Journal of Hospitality Management* 66 (2017): 106–116.

Treacy, Michael, and Fred Wiersema. *The Discipline of Market Leaders.* Reading, MA: Addison-Wesley, 1997.

Verhoef, Peter C., Katherine N. Lemon, Ananthanarayanan Parasuraman, Anne Roggeveen, Michael Tsiros, and Leonard A. Schlesinger. "Customer Experience Creation: Determinants, Dynamics and Management Strategies." *Journal of Retailing* 85: 1 (2009): 31–41.

Voorhees, Clay M., Paul W. Fombelle, Yany Gregoire, Sterling Bone, Anders Gustafsson, Rui Sousa, and Travis Walkowiak. "Service Encounters, Experiences and The Customer Journey: Defining The Field and A Call To Expand Our Lens." *Journal of Business Research* 79 (2017): 269–280.

Whitbread LC, "Good Night Guarantee." Premier Inn, Whitbread PLC, accessed February 2, 2018. https://www.premierinn.com/gb/en/why/sleep/good-night-guarantee.html

Wirtz, Jochen, and Christina Jerger. "Managing Service Employees: Literature Review, Expert Opinions, and Research Directions." *The Service Industries Journal* 36, no. 15–16 (2016): 757–788.

Wirtz, Jochen, and Christopher Lovelock. *Managing People for Service Advantage.* Hackensack, NJ: World Scientific, 2017.

Wood, Roy C., and Bob Brotherton, eds. *The SAGE Handbook of Hospitality Management.* Thousand Oaks, CA: Sage Publications, 2008.

Xiang, Zheng, Zvi Schwartz, John H. Gerdes, and Muzaffer Uysal. "What Can Big Data and Text Analytics Tell Us about Hotel Guest Experience and Satisfaction?" *International Journal of Hospitality Management* 44 (2015): 120–130.

Yelp, "Southwest Airlines," Yelp (blog), accessed February 2, 2018. http://www.yelp.com/biz/southwest-airlines-phoenix-3

Zeithaml, Valarie A., and Stephen W. Brown. *Profiting from Services and Solutions: What Product-centric Firms Need to Know.* New York, NY: Business Expert Press, 2014.

Chapter 2

Al-alak, Basheer Abbas, and Saeed A. Tarabieh. "Gaining Competitive Advantage and Organizational Performance through Customer Orientation, Innovation Differentiation and Market Differentiation." *International Journal of Economics and Management Sciences* 1, no. 5 (2011): 80–91.

Aldehayyat, Jehad S. "Organisational Characteristics and the Practice of Strategic Planning in Jordanian Hotels." *International Journal of Hospitality Management* 30, no. 1 (2011): 192–199.

Altinay, Levent, Alexandros Paraskevas, and SooCheong Shawn Jang. *Planning Research in Hospitality and Tourism.* New York, NY: Routledge, 2015.

Avci, Umut, Melih Madanoglu, and Fevzi Okumus. "Strategic Orientation and Performance of Tourism Firms: Evidence from a Developing Country." *Tourism Management* 32, no. 1 (2011): 147–157.

AZQuotes, "Tony Alessandra Quotes." AZQuotes, accessed February 3, 2018. http://www.azquotes.com/author/40353-Tony_Alessandra

Barth, Joe. "A Model for Wine List and Wine Inventory Yield Management." *International Journal of Hospitality Management* 30, no. 3 (2011): 701–707.

Bartlett, Kenneth R., Karen R. Johnson, and Ingrid E. Schneider. "Comparing Strategic Human Resource Development Approaches for Tourism and Hospitality Workforce Planning." *Journal of Human Resources in Hospitality & Tourism* 15, no. 4 (2016): 440–461.

Bassiouni, Dina H., and Chris Hackley. "Generation Z Children's Adaptation to Digital Consumer Culture: A Critical Literature Review." *Journal of Customer Behaviour* 13, no. 2 (2014): 113–133.

Berry, Leonard. "The Employee as a Customer." In *Services Marketing: Text, Cases & Readings*. Edited by Christopher H. Lovelock, 65–68. Englewood Cliffs, NJ: Prentice Hall.

Bhattari, Abha. "Applebee's Halts Millennial Chase." *Orlando Sentinel*, August 15, 2017, A8.

Black, Jane. "A Grown-up Guide to Fast-fine." *Wall Street Journal*, June 11, 2017. https://www.wsj.com/articles/a-grown-ups-guide-to-fast-fine-dining-1496923201.

Borges, Sérgio, and Nuno Gustavo. "Business Performance and Strategic Management Options in Hospitality: The Case of Lisbon City." *International Journal of Business and Management* 10, no. 9 (2015): 33.

Brotman, Stuart M. "The Real Digital Divide in Educational Technology," Brookings Foundation. January 28, 2016. https://www.brookings.edu/blog/techtank/2016/01/28/the-real-digital-divide-in-educational-technology/

Carpenter, Marian J., and Linda C. Charon. "Mitigating Multigenerational Conflict and Attracting, Motivating, and Retaining Millennial Employees by Changing the Organizational Culture: A Theoretical Model." *Journal of Psychological Issues in Organizational Culture* 5, no. 3 (2014): 68–84.

Carr, Nicholas. "How Smartphones Hijack Our Minds," *Wall Street Journal*, October 7–8. (2017): C1–2.

Cheng, David SY. "Analyze the Hotel Industry in Porter Five Competitive Forces." *Journal of Global Business Management* 9, no. 3 (2013): 52.

Choice Hotels International. "HOME." Choice Hotels International Inc. Accessed February 3, 2018. https://www.choicehotels.com.

Claveria, Oscar, Enric Monte, and Salvador Torra. "A New Forecasting Approach for the Hospitality Industry." *International Journal of Contemporary Hospitality Management* 27, no. 7 (2015): 1520–1538.

Collins, James Charles, and Jerry I. Porras. *Built to Last: Successful Habits of Visionary Companies*. New York, NY: Random House, 2005.

Custis, Christine. "The Role of Business Intelligence within the Hospitality Industry's Information Systems Strategy: Historical Concepts and Future Trends." *Journal of Management Policy and Practice* 13, no. 3 (2012): 82.

Darden Concepts Inc. "Frequently Asked Questions." Darden, Darden Corporation. Accessed February 3, 2018. https://www.darden.com/legal-notices.

Dawson, Mary, and Jeanna Abbott. "Hospitality Culture and Climate: A Proposed Model for Retaining Employees and Creating Competitive Advantage." *International Journal of Hospitality & Tourism Administration* 12, no. 4 (2011): 289–304.

Della Corte, Valentina, and Massimo Aria. "Coopetition and Sustainable Competitive Advantage. The Case of Tourist Destinations." *Tourism Management* 54 (2016): 524–540.

Denizci Guillet, Basak, and Ibrahim Mohammed. "Revenue Management Research in Hospitality and Tourism: A Critical Review of Current Literature and Suggestions for Future Research." *International Journal of Contemporary Hospitality Management* 27, no. 4 (2015): 526–560.

Dickson, Duncan, Robert C. Ford, and Bruce Laval. "Managing Real and Virtual Waits in Hospitality and Service Organizations." *Cornell Hotel and Restaurant Administration Quarterly* 46, no. 1 (2005): 52–68.

Eng, Dinah. "What Do Millennials Want? Hotels Have Some Ideas." *New York Times*, April 4, 2016, https://www.nytimes.com/2016/04/10/travel/millennials-hotels.html

Evans, Nigel. *Strategic Management for Tourism, Hospitality and Events*, 2nd Ed. Abingdon, Oxon: Routledge, 2015.

Evans, Nigel, George Stonehouse, and David Campbell. *Strategic Management for Travel and Tourism*. Burlington, MA: Butterworth-Heinemann, 2012.

Fenich, George G. *Planning and Management of Meetings, Expositions, Events and Conventions*. Upper Saddle River, NJ: Pearson Higher Ed, 2014.

Four Seasons Press Room. "Awards and Accolades for Four Seasons Hotels and Resorts." Accessed June 11, 2018. https://press.fourseasons.com/news-releases/awards-and-accolades-for-four-seasons-hotels-and-resorts/.

Granic, Isabela, Adam Lobel, and Rutger CME Engels. "The Benefits of Playing Video Games." *American Psychologist* 69: 1 (2014): 66–78.

Gretzel, Ulrike, Marianna Sigala, Zheng Xiang, and Chulmo Koo. "Smart Tourism: Foundations and Developments." *Electronic Markets* 25, no. 3 (2015): 179–188.

Hamel, Gary, and C. K. Prahalad. *Competing for the Future*. Boston, MA: Harvard Business School Press. 1994.

Hamm, Russell, Lauren Pinkus, Amanda Wilkins, and Maria Town. "The Impact of Web-Based Game Play on Soft Skills Education." Department of Labor, accessed February 3, 2018. https://www.dol.gov/odep/documents/Soft%20Skills%20Fact%20Sheet%20Fina17%2015_508%20compliant.pdf.

Harrington, J., Robert, Prakash K. Chathoth, Michael Ottenbacher, and Levent Altinay. "Strategic Management Research in Hospitality and Tourism: Past, Present and Future." *International Journal of Contemporary Hospitality Management* 26, no. 5 (2014): 778–808.

Harrison, Jeffrey S., and Caron H. St John. *Foundations in Strategic Management*. Mason, OH: Cengage Learning, 2013.

Hernandez, Daniela. "Seven Jobs Robots Will Create-or Expand." *Wall Street Journal*, April 30, 2018. https://www.wsj.com/articles/seven-jobs-robots-will-createor-expand-1525054021.

Hitt, Gabriel. "Gen Z Makes Its Labor Force Debut–Is Your Company Ready?" Universum Global Top 100. Universum Global, last revised 2017. http://universumglobaltop100.com/articles/gen-z-makes-its-labor-force-debut-is-your-company-ready.

Hitt, Michael A., R. Duane Ireland, and Robert E. Hoskisson. *Strategic Management Cases: Competitiveness and Globalization*. 12th ed. Boston, MA: Cengage Learning, 2017.

Huang, Chenchen, and Kathleen M. O'Brien. "The Impacts of Perceived Environmental Uncertainty, Outlook, and Size on Strategic Planning in Private Clubs." *Journal of Hospitality Marketing & Management* 24, no. 5 (2015): 554–571.

Huang, Leo, Chi-Yen Yung, and Evonne Yang. "How Do Travel Agencies Obtain a Competitive Advantage? Through a Travel Blog Marketing Channel." *Journal of Vacation Marketing* 17, no. 2 (2011): 139–149.

Huh, Chang, and Sean Chang Howook. "An Investigation of Generation Y Travelers' Beliefs and Attitudes towards Green Hotel Practices: a View from Active and Passive Green Generation Y travelers." *International Journal of Tourism Sciences* 17, no. 2 (2017): 26–139.

Jargon, Julie. "McDonald's Sales Show Improvement." *Wall Street Journal*, July 26, 2017. https://www.wsj.com/articles/mcdonalds-profit-rises-refranchising-drive-dents-revenue-1508851452.

Jiang, Yawei, and Brent W. Ritchie. "Disaster Collaboration in Tourism: Motives, Impediments and Success Factors." *Journal of Hospitality and Tourism Management* 31, (2017): 70–82.

Keller, Kevin L. *Strategic Brand Management: Building, Measuring, and Managing Brand Equity*. 4th ed. Boston, MA: Pearson, 2013.

Keupp, Marcus Matthias, Maximilian Palmié, and Oliver Gassmann. "The Strategic Management of Innovation: A Systematic Review and Paths for Future Research." *International Journal of Management Reviews* 14, no. 4 (2012): 367–390.

Khan, Natasha. "Robots Shift from Factories to New Jobs." *Wall Street Journal*, June 11, 2018, B4.

Kim, Heejun, Zheng Xiang, and Daniel R. Fesenmaier. "Use of the Internet for Trip Planning: A Generational Analysis." *Journal of Travel & Tourism Marketing* 32, no. 3 (2015): 276–289.

Kim, W. Chan, and Renée Mauborgne. *Blue Ocean Shift: Beyond Competing—Proven Steps to Inspire Confidence and Seize New Growth*. Boston, MA: Hachette Books, 2017.

Kimes, Sheryl E., and Jochen Wirtz. "Revenue Management: Advanced Strategies and Tools to Enhance Firm Profitability." *Foundations and Trends in Marketing* 8, no. 1 (2015): 1–68.

Köseoglu, Mehmet Ali, Cafer Topaloglu, John A. Parnell, and Donald L. Lester. "Linkages among Business Strategy, Uncertainty and Performance in the Hospitality Industry: Evidence from an Emerging Economy." *International Journal of Hospitality Management* 34 (2013): 81–91.

Koutroumanis, Dean A. "Technology's Effect on Hotels and Restaurants: Building a Strategic Competitive Advantage." *The Journal of Applied Business and Economics* 12, no. 1 (2011): 72.

McCartney, Scott S. "The Uber Airport Rules." *Wall Street Journal*, July 7, 2016, https://www.wsj.com/articles/you-cant-take-an-uber-home-from-these-airports-1467829592.

Mair, Judith, Brent W. Ritchie, and Gabby Walters. "Towards a Research Agenda for Post-disaster and Post-crisis Recovery Strategies for Tourist Destinations: a Narrative Review." Current Issues in *Tourism* 19, no. 1 (2016):

Michelli, Joseph. *The New Gold Standard: 5 Leadership Principles for Creating a Legendary Customer Experience Courtesy of the Ritz-Carlton Hotel* Company. New York, NY: McGraw Hill Professional, 2008.

Mok, Connie, Beverley Sparks, and Jay Kadampully. *Service Quality Management in Hospitality, Tourism, and Leisure*. Binghamton, NY: Routledge, 2013.

Morritt, Ron, and Art Weinstein. *Segmentation Strategies for Hospitality Managers: Target Marketing for Competitive Advantage*. Binghamton, NY: Routledge, 2012.

NetJets. "More Than 50 Years of Leadership: And Still Going Strong." NetJets, Berkshire Hathaway. Accessed February 3, 2018. https://www.netjets.com/AboutNetJets/

Okumus, Fevzi. "Facilitating Knowledge Management through Information Technology in Hospitality Organizations." *Journal of Hospitality and Tourism Technology* 4, no. 1 (2013): 64–80.

Okumus, Fevzi, Levent Altinay, and Prakash Chathoth K. *Strategic Management for Hospitality, and Tourism*. Abington, Oxon: Routledge, 2010.

Okumus, Fevzi, Mehmet Ali Köseoglu, Alfonso Morvillo, and Mehmet Altin. "Scientific Progress on Strategic Management in Hospitality and Tourism: A State-of-the-Art." *Tourism Review* 72, no. 3 (2017): 261–273.

Olive Garden Italian Kitchen. "Home." Olive Garden. Darden Concepts. Accessed February 3, 2018. www.olivegarden.com/home

Padhi, Sidhartha S., and Vijay Aggarwal. "Competitive Revenue Management for Fixing Quota and Price of Hotel Commodities under Uncertainty." *International Journal of Hospitality Management* 30, no. 3 (2011): 725–734.

Pechlaner, Harald, Monika Bachinger, Michael Volgger, and Elisabeth Anzengruber-Fischer. "Cooperative Core Competencies in Tourism: Combining Resource-based and Relational Approaches in Destination Governance." *European Journal of Tourism Research* 8 (2014): 5–19.

Peng, Bo, Haiyan Song, and Geoffrey I. Crouch. "A Meta-analysis of International Tourism Demand Forecasting and Implications for Practice." *Tourism Management* 45, (2014): 181–193. https://doi.org/10.1016/j.tourman.2014.04.005

Peters, Tom. *The Circle of Innovation: You Can't Shrink Your Way to Greatness.* New York, NY: Vintage Books 1997.

Peterson, Andrea. "Secrets of a Hotel Test Lab." *Wall Street Journal,* October 1, 2015. http://online.wsj.com/public/resources/documents/print/WSJ_-D001-20151001.pdf

Phillips, Paul, and Luiz Moutinho. "Critical Review of Strategic Planning Research in Hospitality and Tourism." *Annals of Tourism Research* 48 (2014): 96–120.

Playa Nicuesa Rainforest Lodge, "Sustainability: Eco-friendly Lodge Near Puerto Jimenez, Costa Rica." Nicuesa Lodge, accessed February 3, 2018. https://www.nicuesalodge.com/sustainability.aspx

Porter, Michael E. *Competitive Strategy: Techniques for Analyzing Industries and Competition.* New York, NY: The Free Press, 1980.

Prud'homme, Brigitte, and Louis Raymond. "Implementation of Sustainable Development Practices in the Hospitality Industry: A Case Study of Five Canadian Hotels." *International Journal of Contemporary Hospitality Management* 28, no. 3 (2016): 609–639.

Prud'homme, Brigitte, and Louis Raymond. "Sustainable Development Practices in the Hospitality Industry: An Empirical Study of Their Impact on Customer Satisfaction and Intentions." *International Journal of Hospitality Management* 34 (2013): 116–126.

Ritchie, Brent W., "Disaster Collaboration in Tourism: Motives, Impediments and Success Factors." *Journal of Hospitality and Tourism Management* 31 (2017): 70–82.

Ritchie, Brent W., John C. Crotts, Anita Zehrer, and George T. Volsky. "Understanding the Effects of a Tourism Crisis: The Impact of the BP Oil Spill on Regional Lodging Demand." *Journal of Travel Research* 53, no. 1 (2014): 12–25.

Robb, Brian J. *A Brief History of Disney.* London: Little, Brown Book Company, 2014.

Rosenbaum, Mark Scott, and Ipkin Anthony Wong. "Green Marketing Programs as Strategic Initiatives in Hospitality." *Journal of Services Marketing* 29, no. 2 (2015): 81–92.

Sakdiyakorn, Malinvisa, and Walanchalee Wattanacharoensil. "Generational Diversity in the Workplace: A Systematic Review in the Hospitality Context." *Cornell Hospitality Quarterly* (2017): 1–25.

Sandberg, Erik, and Mats Abrahamsson. "Logistics Capabilities for Sustainable Competitive Advantage." *International Journal of Logistics Research and Applications* 14, no. 1 (2011): 61–75.

Sloan, Julia. *Learning to Think Strategically.* 3rd ed. New York, NY: Taylor & Francis, 2016.

Smithson, Steve, Carlos Alberto Devece, and Rafael Lapiedra. "Online Visibility as a Source of Competitive Advantage for Small-and Medium-sized Tourism Accommodation Enterprises." *The Service Industries Journal* 31, no. 10 (2011): 1573–1587.

Society for Accessible Travel and Hospitality. "Home Page." Society for Accessible Travel and Hospitality (SATH). Accessed February 3, 2018. http://www.sath.org/.

Solnet, David, Australia Anna Hood, and Paul Barron. "Yet Another Challenge for Hospitality Managers–Generation Y: A Literature Review and Future Research Agenda." In *Proceedings of 2008 International CHRIE Conference,* p. 467–475. Atlanta, GA: 2008.

Solnet, David, Anna Kralj, and Jay Kandampully. "Generation Y Employees: An Examination of Work Attitude Differences." *Journal of Applied Management and Entrepreneurship* 17, no. 3 (2012): 36.

Sox, Carole B., Jeffrey M. Campbell, Sheryl F. Kline, Sandra K. Strick, and Tena B. Crews. "Technology Use within Meetings: A Generational Perspective." *Journal of Hospitality and Tourism Technology* 7, no. 2 (2016): 158–181.

Sox, Carole B., Sheryl F. Kline, and Tena B. Crews. "Identifying Best Practices, Opportunities and Barriers in Meeting Planning for Generation Y." *International Journal of Hospitality Management* 36 (2014): 244–254.

Southwest Airlines Co. "About Southwest." Southwest, Southwest Airlines Co. Accessed February 3, 2018. https://www.southwest.com/html/about-southwest/.

Starbucks, Inc. "Starbucks Mission Statement." Starbucks, access February 3, 2018, https://www.thebalance.com/starbucks-mission-statement-2891826.

Stewart, Jeanine S., Elizabeth Goad Oliver, Karen S. Cravens, and Shigehiro Oishi. "Managing Millennials: Embracing Generational Differences." *Business Horizons* 60, no. 1 (2017): 45–54.

Tavitiyaman, Pimtong, Hailin Qu, and Hanqin Qiu Zhang. "The Impact of Industry Force Factors on Resource Competitive Strategies and Hotel Performance." *International Journal of Hospitality Management* 30, no. 3 (2011): 648–657.

Tavitiyaman, Pimtong, Hanqin Qiu Zhang, and Hailin Qu. "The Effect of Competitive Strategies and Organizational Structure on Hotel Performance." *International Journal of Contemporary Hospitality Management* 24, no. 1 (2012): 140–159.

Testa, Mark R., and Lori Sipe. "Service-Leadership Competencies for Hospitality and Tourism Management." *International Journal of Hospitality Management* 31, no. 3 (2012): 648–658.

Thomas, R. David. *Dave's Way.* New York, NY: Berkley, 1992.

Thompson Jr., Arthur A., and Margaret A. Peteraf, *Crafting & Executing Strategy: The Quest for Competitive Advantage.* 21st ed. New York, NY: McGraw-Hill Education, 2017.

Toker, Sacip, and Meltem Huri Baturay. "Antecedents and Consequences of Game Addiction." *Computers in Human Behavior* 55 (Part B) (2016): 668–679.

Twenge, Jean M. "Have Smartphones Destroyed a Generation." *The Atlantic.* September 2017. https://www.theatlantic.com/magazine/archive/2017/09/has-the-smartphone-destroyed-a-generation/534198/.

Twenge, Jean M. *iGen: Why Today's Super-Connected Kids Are Growing Up Less Rebellious, More Tolerant, Less Happy—and Completely Unprepared for Adulthood—and What That Means for the Rest of Us.* New York, NY: Atria Books, 2017.

United States Census Bureau, "Population," Census.gov, U.S. Department of Commerce. Accessed September 15, 2017. https://www.census.gov/topics/population.html.

Van Deursen, Alexander JAM, and Jan AGM Van Dijk. "The Digital Divide Shifts to Differences in Usage." *New Media & Society* 16, no. 3 (2014): 507–526.

Wang, Xuan Lorna. "Relationship or Revenue: Potential Management Conflicts between Customer Relationship Management and Hotel Revenue Management." *International Journal of Hospitality Management* 31, no. 3 (2012): 864–874.

Wu, Doris, Chenguang, Haiyan Song, Haiyan Song, and Shujie Shen. "New Developments in Tourism and Hotel Demand Modeling and Forecasting." *International Journal of Contemporary Hospitality Management* 29, no. 1 (2017): 507–529. https://doi.org/10.1108/IJCHM-05-2015-0249.

Xiang, Zheng, Dan Wang, Joseph T. O'Leary, and Daniel R. Fesenmaier. "Adapting to the Internet: Trends in Travelers' Use of the Web for Trip Planning." *Journal of Travel Research* 54, no. 4 (2015): 511–527.

Xu, Xun, and Dogan Gursoy. "A Conceptual Framework of Sustainable Hospitality Supply Chain Management." *Journal of Hospitality Marketing & Management* 24, no. 3 (2015): 229–259.

Yang, Guo-liang, and Huan-ling Lu. "Analysis on Blue Ocean Strategy for Home Inns' Success." *Tourism Forum* vol. 2, (2011).

Yang, Jen-te. "Identifying the Attributes of Blue Ocean Strategies in Hospitality." *International Journal of Contemporary Hospitality Management* 24: 5 (2012): 701–720.

Yang, Yang, Wesley S. Roehl, and Jing-Huei Huang. "Understanding and Projecting the Restaurantscape: The Influence of Neighborhood Sociodemographic Characteristics on Restaurant Location." *International Journal of Hospitality Management* 67 (2017): 33–45.

Chapter 3

Abarbanel, Brett, Bo Bernhard, Ashok K. Singh, and Anthony Lucas. "Impact of Virtual Atmospherics and Functional Qualities on the Online Gambler's Experience." *Behaviour & Information Technology* 34, no. 10 (2015): 105–102.

Ali, Faizan, Muslim Amin, and Cihan Cobanoglu. "An Integrated Model of Service Experience, Emotions, Satisfaction, and Price Acceptance: an Empirical Analysis in the Chinese Hospitality Industry." *Journal of Hospitality Marketing & Management* 25, no. 4 (2016): 449–475.

Ali, Faizan, Woo Gon Kim, Jun Li, and Hyeon-Mo Jeon. "Make It Delightful: Customers' Experience, Satisfaction and Loyalty in Malaysian Theme Parks." *Journal of Destination Marketing & Management* 7 (2016) 1–11.

Areddy, James T. "In China, Disney Aims to Keep Security Behind the Scenes." *Wall Street Journal,* June 10, 2016. https://www.wsj.com/articles/in-china-disney-aims-to-keep-security-behind-the-scenes-1465464602.

Ariffin, Hashim Fadzil, Mohamad Fahmi Bibon, and Raja Puteri Saadiah Raja Abdullah. "Restaurant's Atmospheric Elements: What the Customer Wants." *Procedia-Social and Behavioral Sciences* 38 (2012): 380–387.

Augustin, Sally. *Place Advantage: Applied Psychology for Interior Architecture.* Hoboken, NJ: John Wiley & Sons, 2009.

Baek, Jooa, and Chihyung Michael Ok. "The Power of Design: How Does Design Affect Consumers' Online Hotel Booking?" *International Journal of Hospitality Management* 65 (2017): 1–10.

Ballantyne, David, Elin Nilsson, and Elin Nilsson. "All That Is Solid Melts into Air: the Servicescape in Digital Service Space." *Journal of Services Marketing* 31, no. 3 (2017): 226–235.

Bitner, Mary Jo. "Evaluating Service Encounters: The Effects of Physical Surroundings and Employee Responses." *Journal of Marketing* 54, no. 2 (1990): 69–82.

Bitner, Mary J. "Servicescapes: The Impact of Physical Surroundings on Customers and Employees." *The Journal of Marketing* 56, no. 2 (1992): 57–71.

Botha, Elricke. "Marketing Experiences for Visitor Attractions: The Contribution of Theming." In *The Handbook of Managing and Marketing Tourism Experiences,* edited by Marios Sotiriados and Dogan Gursoy, 343–362. Bingley, UK: Emerald Group Publishing Limited, 2016.

Caldwell, Clare, and Sally A. Hibbert. "The Influence of Music Tempo and Musical Preference on Restaurant Patrons' Behavior." *Psychology & Marketing* 19, no. 11 (2002): 895–917.

Cassidy, Tony. *Environmental Psychology: Behaviour and Experience in Context.* New York, NY: Psychology Press, 2013.

Chang, Kuo-Chien. "Effect of Servicescape on Customer Behavioral Intentions: Moderating Roles of Service Climate and Employee Engagement." *International Journal of Hospitality Management* 53 (2016): 116–128.

Cheng, Jen-Son, Ta-Wei Tang, Hsin-Yu Shih, and Tsai-Chiao Wang. "Designing Lifestyle Hotels." *International Journal of Hospitality Management* 58 (2016): 95–106.

Chiu, Yen-Ting Helena, Wan-I. Lee, and Tsung-Hsiung Chen. "Environmentally Responsible Behavior in Ecotourism: Antecedents and Implications." *Tourism Management* 40 (2014): 321–329.

Dedeoğlu, Bekir Bora, Kemal Gürkan Küçükergin, and Sevgi Balıkçıoğlu. "Understanding the Relationships of Servicescape, Value, Image, Pleasure, and Behavioral Intentions Among Hotel Customers." *Journal of Travel & Tourism Marketing* 32, no. sup1 (2015): S42-S61.

Disney, Walt. *Walt Disney Famous Quotes.* Disney's Kingdom Editions. Lake Buena Vista, FL: The Walt Disney Company, 1994.

Dong, Ping, and Noel Yee-Man Siu. "Servicescape Elements, Customer Predispositions and Service Experience: The Case of Theme Park Visitors." *Tourism Management* 36 (2013): 541–551.

Durna, Ufuk, Bekir Bora Dedeoglu, and Sevgi Balikçioglu. "The Role of Servicescape and Image Perceptions of Customers on Behavioral Intentions in the Hotel Industry." *International Journal of Contemporary Hospitality Management* 27, no. 7 (2015): 1728–1748.

Ellen, Tristan, and Ran Zhang. "Measuring the Effect of Company Restaurant Servicescape on Patrons' Emotional States and Behavioral Intentions." *Journal of Foodservice Business Research* 17, no. 2 (2014): 85–102.

Essawy, Mohamed. "The Impacts of E-atmospherics on Emotions and on the Booking Intentions of Hotel rooms." *Tourism and Hospitality Research* (2017). https://doi.org/10.1177/1467358417692393.

Fakharyan, Meysam, Sadaf Omidvar, Mohammad Reza Khodadadian, Mohammad Reza Jalilvand, and Leila Nasrolahi Vosta. "Examining the Effect of Customer-to-Customer Interactions on Satisfaction, Loyalty, and Word-of-Mouth Behaviors in the Hospitality Industry: The Mediating Role of Personal Interaction Quality and Service Atmospherics." *Journal of Travel & Tourism Marketing* 31, no. 5 (2014): 610–626.

Fjellman, Stephen M. *Vinyl Leaves: Walt Disney World and America.* Boulder, CO: Westview Press, 1992.

The Food Network, "Liquid Nitrogen Cocktails," Food Detectives, season 2, episode 9, directed by Bob Tuschman, aired July 16, 2009. New York, NY: Scripps Networks, 2018, Television.

Ford, Robert C. "Prime Time: The Strategic Use of Subconscious Priming to Enhance Customer Satisfaction." *Business Horizons* 57, no. 2 (2014): 269–277.

Gelderman, Cees J., Paul W. Th. Ghijsen, and Ronnie Van Diemen, "Choosing Self-service Technologies or Interpersonal Services—The Impact of Situational Factors and Technology-related Attitudes," *Journal of Retailing and Consumer Services* 18, 5 (2011): 414–421.

Gifford, Robert. "Environmental Psychology Matters." *Annual Review of Psychology* 65 (2014): 541–579.

Ha, Jooyeon, and SooCheong Jang. "Boredom and Moderating Variables for Customers' Novelty Seeking." *Journal of Foodservice Business Research* 18, no. 4 (2015): 404–422.

Hahn, Song-Ee, Beverley Sparks, Hugh Wilkins, and Xin Jin. "E-service Quality Management of a Hotel Website: A Scale and Implications for Management." *Journal of Hospitality Marketing & Management* 26, no. 7 (2017): 694–716.

Han, Heesup, and Sunghyup Sean Hyun. "Impact of Hotel-Restaurant Image and Quality of Physical-Environment, Service, and Food on Satisfaction and Intention." *International Journal of Hospitality Management* 63 (2017): 82–92.

Hanks, Lydia, Nathan Line, and Woo Gon Woody Kim. "The Impact of the Social Servicescape, Density, and Restaurant Type on Perceptions of Interpersonal Service Quality." *International Journal of Hospitality Management* 61 (2017): 35–44.

Hooper, Daire, Joseph Coughlan, and Michael R. Mullen. "The Servicescape as an Antecedent to Service Quality and Behavioral Intentions." *Journal of Services Marketing* 27, no. 4 (2013): 271–280.

Hyun, Sunghyup S., and Juhee Kang. "A Better Investment in Luxury Restaurants: Environmental or Non-environmental Cues?" *International Journal of Hospitality Management* 39 (2014): 57–70.

Jain, Rajinish, and Shilpa Bagdare, "Music and Consumption Experience: A Review," *International Journal of Retail & Distribution Management* 39, no. 4 (2011): 289–302.

Jang, Yeajin, Heejung Ro, and Tae-Hee Kim. "Social Servicescape: The Impact of Social Factors on Restaurant Image and Behavioral Intentions." *International Journal of Hospitality & Tourism Administration* 16, no. 3 (2015): 290–309.

Jani, Dev, and Heesup Han. "Testing the Moderation Effect of Hotel Ambience on the Relationships Among Social Comparison, Affect, Satisfaction, and Behavioral Intentions." *Journal of Travel & Tourism Marketing* 31, no. 6 (2014): 731–746.

Kim, Dohee, and Richard R. Perdue. "The Effects of Cognitive, Affective, and Sensory Attributes on Hotel Choice." *International Journal of Hospitality Management* 35 (2013): 246–257.

Kim, Hyeon-Cheol, Bee-Lia Chua, Sanghyeop Lee, Huey-Chern Boo, and Heesup Han. "Understanding Airline Travelers' Perceptions of Well-Being: The Role of Cognition, Emotion, and Sensory Experiences in Airline Lounges." *Journal of Travel & Tourism Marketing* 33, no. 9 (2016): 1213–1234.

Kim, Woo G., and Yun J. Moon. "Customers' Cognitive, Emotional, and Actionable Response to the Servicescape: A Test of the Moderating Effect of the Restaurant Type." *International Journal of Hospitality Management* 28, No. 1 (2009): 144–156.

Koenig, David. *Mouse Tales: A Behind-the-Ears Look at Disneyland.* Irvine, CA: Bonaventure Press, 1994.

Kotler, Philip. "Atmospherics as a Marketing Tool." *Journal of Retailing* 49, no. 4 (1973): 48–64.

Lee, Andy Hee, Basak Denizci Guillet, and Rob Law. "Tourists' Emotional Wellness and Hotel Room Colour." *Current Issues in Tourism* 21, no. 8 (2016): 1–7.

Lee, Seonjeong Ally, and Linda Shea. "Investigating the Key Routes to Customers' Delightful Moments in the Hotel Context." *Journal of Hospitality Marketing & Management* 24, no. 5 (2015): 532–553.

Li, Yaoqi, Hui Fu, and Songshan Sam Huang. "Does Conspicuous Decoration Style Influence Customer's Intention to Purchase? The Moderating Effect of CSR Practices." *International Journal of Hospitality Management* 51 (2015): 19–29.

Lin, Ingrid Y. "Effects of Visual Servicescape Aesthetics Comprehension and Appreciation on Consumer Experience." *Journal of Services Marketing* 30, no. 7 (2016): 692–712.

Line, Nathaniel D., Lydia Hanks, and Woo Gon Kim. "An Expanded Servicescape Framework as the Diver of Place Attachment and Word of Mouth." *Journal of Hospitality & Tourism Research* 42, no. 3 (2015): 476–499.

Loureiro, Sandra Maria Correia. "Medical Tourists' Emotional and Cognitive Response to Credibility and Servicescape." *Current Issues in Tourism* 20, no. 15 (2017): 1633–1652.

Loureiro, Sandra Maria Correia, Marta Almeida, and Paulo Rita. "The Effect of Atmospheric Cues and Involvement on Pleasure and Relaxation: The Spa Hotel Context." *International Journal of Hospitality Management* 35 (2013): 35–43.

Lyu, Jiaying, Liang Hu, Kam Hung, and Zhenxing Mao. "Assessing Servicescape of Cruise Tourism: The Perception of Chinese Tourists." *International Journal of Contemporary Hospitality Management* 29, no. 10 (2017): 2556–2572.

Magnini, Vince. "Designing Tourism Services in an Era of Information Overload." In *Design Science in Tourism*, edited by Daniel R. Fresenmaier and Zheng Xiang, 161–172. Switzerland: Springer, 2017.

Mari, Michela, and Sara Poggesi. "Servicescape Cues and Customer Behavior: A Systematic Literature Review and Research Agenda." *The Service Industries Journal* 33, no. 2 (2013): 171–199.

Meng, Bo, and Kyuhwan Choi. "Theme Restaurants' Servicescape in Developing Quality of Life: The Moderating Effect of Perceived Authenticity." *International Journal of Hospitality Management* 65 (2017): 89–99.

Min, Deedee Aram, Kyung Hoon Hyun, Sun-Joong Kim, and Ji-Hyun Lee. "A Rule-Based Servicescape Design Support system from the design patterns of theme parks." *Advanced Engineering Informatics* 32 (2017): 77–91.

Mossberg, Lena. "Extraordinary Experiences through Storytelling." *Scandinavian Journal of Hospitality and Tourism* 8, no. 3 (2008): 204.

Mullin, Molly H. "The Great Southwest of the Fred Harvey Company and the Santa Fe Railway." *Museum Anthropology* 20, 1 (1996): 79–80.

National Geographic. "Top 5 Parking Jobs: Crowd Control." YouTube video, 1:34, posted November 16, 2014. https://www.youtube.com/watch?v=PcKIsS1ShfI

Nilsson, Elin, and David Ballantyne. "Reexamining the Place of Servicescape in Marketing: a Service-dominant Logic Perspective." *Journal of Services Marketing* 28, no. 5 (2014): 374–379.

North, Adrian C., David J. Hargreaves, and Jennifer McKendrick. "In-store Music Affects Product Choice." *Nature* 390, no. 6656 (1997): 132.

Olmsted, Allison. "Travelers: Your Hotel Workout and Fitness Options Just Got Much Better," *Forbes*, April 26. Accessed February 7, 2018. https://www.forbes.com/sites/allisonolms/2017/04/26/travelers-your-hotel-workout-fitness-options-just-got-much-better/#69301d6d6c69.

Osman, Hanaa, Nick Johns, and Peter Lugosi. "Commercial Hospitality in Destination Experiences:

McDonald's and Tourists' Consumption of Space." *Tourism Management* 42 (2014): 238–247.

Peterson, A."It's Checkout Time, Kenny G: The New Hotel Music Strategy." *Wall Street Journal*, July 30, 2015: D1-D2.

Pine, B. Joseph, and James H. Gilmore. *The Experience Economy: Work Is Theatre and Every Business a Stage*. Boston, MA: Harvard Business School Press, 1999.

Pullman, Madeleine E., and Michael A. Gross. "Ability of Experience Design Elements to Elicit Emotions and Loyalty Behaviors." *Decision Sciences* 35, no. 3 (2004): 551–578.

Rafaeli, Anat, and Iris Vilnai-Yavetz. "Emotion as a Connection of Physical Artifacts and Organizations." *Organization Science* 15, no. 6 (2004): 671–686.

Rosenbaum, Mark S., and Carolyn Massiah, "An Expanded Servicescape Perspective," *Journal of Service Management* 22, no. 4 (2011): 471–490.

Sewell, Carl, and Paul B. Brown. *Customers for Life: How to Turn That One-Time Buyer into a Lifetime Customer.* New York, NY: Doubleday, 2002.

Sheng, Xiaojing, Xiaojing Sheng, Judy A. Siguaw, Judy A. Siguaw, Penny M. Simpson, and Penny M. Simpson. "Servicescape Attributes and Consumer Well-being." *Journal of Services Marketing* 30, no. 7 (2016): 676–685.

Silvis, Jennifer. "What's In A Theme?" *Health Care Design Magazine*. December 21, 2011. https://www.healthcaredesignmagazine.com/architecture/whats-theme/.

Spence, Charles, and Maya U. Shankar. "The Influence of Auditory Cues on the Perception of, and Responses to, Food and Drink." *Journal of Sensory Studies* 25, no. 3 (2010): 406–430.

Srivastava, Mala, and Dimple Kaul. "Social Interaction, Convenience and Customer Satisfaction: The Mediating Effect of Customer Experience." *Journal of Retailing and Consumer Services* 21, no. 6 (2014): 1028–1037.

Stacey, Rulon F., and Carolyn Wilson. "Benefits of a Co design Model in Healthcare Don't End with the New Building." *Frontiers of Health Services Management* 31, no. 1 (2014): 31–38.

Symonds, Paul. "Wayfinding Signage Considerations in International Airports." *Interdisciplinary Journal of Signage and Wayfinding* 1, no. 2 (2017): 60–80.

Tombs, Alastair, and Janet R. McColl-Kennedy. "Social-Servicescape Conceptual Model." *Marketing Theory* 3, no. 4 (2003): 447–475.

Tsai, Chang-Yen, Jeou-Shyan Horng, Chih-Hsing Liu, and Da-Chian Hu. "Work Environment and Atmosphere: The Role of Organizational Support in the Creativity Performance of Tourism and Hospitality Organizations." *International Journal of Hospitality Management* 46 (2015): 26–35.

Tuominen, Pasi P., and Mário P. Ascenção. "The Hotel of Tomorrow: A Service Design Approach." *Journal of Vacation Marketing* 22, 3 (2016): 279–292.

The Unusual Company Ltd., "Go Unusual Travel Ideas," *unusual hotels of the world*, The Unusual Company Ltd., access date February 6, 2018. http://www.unusualhotelsoftheworld.com/

Vilnai-Yavetz, Iris, and Anat Rafaeli. "Aesthetics and Professionalism of Virtual Servicescapes." *Journal of Service Research* 8, no. 3 (2006): 245–259.

Wakefield, Kirk L., and Jeffrey Blodgett. "Retrospective: The Importance of Servicescapes in Leisure Service Settings." *Journal of Services Marketing* 30, no. 7 (2016): 686–691.

Waldrep, Shelton S. "Monuments to Walt." In *Inside the Mouse: Work and Play at Disney World*, edited by Jane Kuenz, Shelton Waldrep, Susan Willis, and Karen Klugman, 212–213. Durham, NC: Duke University Press, 1995.

Wang, Chen-Ya, and Anna S. Mattila. "The Impact of Servicescape Cues on Consumer Prepurchase Authenticity Assessment and Patronage Intentions to Ethnic Restaurants." *Journal of Hospitality & Tourism Research* 39, no. 3 (2015): 346–372.

Chapter 4

"After Lawsuit, Denny's Restaurants Chain Buries Its Racist Image." *Lubbock Avalanche-Journal* (2002). http://lubbockonline.com/stories/040602/nat_0406020065.shtml#.WlUb4zOZNmB

Alvesson, Mats, and Stefan Sveningsson. *Changing Organizational Culture: Cultural Change Work in Progress*. 2nd ed. New York, NY: Routledge, 2015.

Brinker, Norman, and Donald Thomas Phillips. *On the Brink: The Life and Leadership of Norman Brinker.* Arlington, TX: Summit Publishing Group, 1999.

Büschgens, Thorsten, Andreas Bausch, and David B. Balkin. "Organizational Culture and Innovation: A Metaanalytic Review." *Journal of Product Innovation Management* 30, no. 4 (2013): 763–781.

Chen, Rose XY, Catherine Cheung, and Rob Law. "A Review of the Literature on Culture in Hotel Management Research: What Is the Future?" *International Journal of Hospitality Management* 31, no.1 (2012): 52–65.

Conţiu, Lia Codrina, Manuela Rozalia Gabor, and Flavia Dana Oltean. "Employee's Motivation from a Cultural Perspective—A Key Element of the Hospitality Industry Competitiveness." *Procedia Economics and Finance* 3 2012): 981–986.

Dawson, Mary, JeAnna Abbott, and Stowe Shoemaker. "The Hospitality Culture Scale: A Measure Organizational Culture and Personal Attributes." *International Journal of Hospitality Management* 30, no. 2 (2011): 290–300.

Deal, Terrence E., and M. K. Key. *Corporate Celebration: Play, Purpose, and Profit at Work*. San Francisco, CA: Berrett-Koehler, 1998.

Dickson, Duncan, and Robert Ford. "'We only need one rule.' Growing a Service Culture: An Interview with John Caparella, President and Chief Operating Officer the Venetian Las Vegas, the Palazzo Las Vegas, and Sands Expo and Convention Center." *Journal of Applied Management and Entrepreneurship* 17, no. 3 (2012): 98–114.

Ehrhart, Mark G., and Maribeth Kuenzi. "The Impact of Organizational Climate and Culture on Employee Turnover." In *The Wiley Blackwell Handbook of the Psychology of Recruitment, Selection and Employee Retention*, edited by Harold W. Goldstein, Elaine D. Pulakos, Jonathan Passmore, and Carla Semedo, 494–512. Malden, MA: Wiley-Blackwell, 2017.

Erhardt, Niclas, Carlos Martin-Rios, and Charles Heckscher. "Am I Doing the Right Thing? Unpacking Workplace Rituals as Mechanisms for Strong Organizational Culture." *International Journal of Hospitality Management* 59 (2016): 31–41.

Ford, Robert C., and Janet R. McColl-Kennedy. "Organizational Strategies for Filling the Customer Can-do/Must-do gap." *Business Horizons* 58, no. 4 (2015): 459–468.

Ford, Robert C., Celeste P. M. Wilderom, and John Caparella. "Strategically Crafting a Customer-focused Culture: An Inductive Case study." *Journal of Strategy and Management* 1, no. 2 (2008): 143–167.

Gregersen, Al B., and J. Stewart Black. "J. W. Marriott, Jr., on Growing the Legacy." *The Academy of Management Executive* 16, no. 2 (2002): 33–39.

Guchait, Priyanko, Ayşin Paşamehmetoğlu, and JeAnna Lanza-Abbott. "The Importance of Error Management Culture in Organizations: The Impact on Employee Helping Behaviors during Service Failures and Recoveries in Restaurants." *Journal of Human Resources in Hospitality & Tourism* 14, no. 1 (2015): 45–67.

Hallowell, Roger, David Bowen, and Carin-Isabel Knoop. "Four Seasons Goes to Paris." *The Academy of Management Executive* 16, no. 4 (2002): 7–24.

Han, Hyun Jeong. "The Relationship among Corporate Culture, Strategic Orientation, and Financial Performance." *Cornell Hospitality Quarterly* 53, no. 3 (2012): 207–219.

Hogan, Suellen J., and Leonard V. Coote. "Organizational Culture, Innovation, and Performance: A Test of Schein's Model." *Journal of Business Research* 67, no. 8 (2014): 1609–1621.

Howard, J., "Service with a Sneer." *New York Times*, November 6, 1994, http://www.nytimes.com/1994/12/04/magazine/1-service-with-a-sneer-990094.html

Hyatt. http://www.hyatt.jobs/explore-hyatt/mission-statement, accessed February 7, 2018.

Jet Blue. http://work-here.jetblue.com/category/get-to-know-us, accessed February 7, 2018.

Kao, Chiu-Ying, Sheng-Hshiung Tsaur, and Tsung-Chiung Emily Wu. "Organizational Culture on Customer Delight in the Hospitality Industry." *International Journal of Hospitality Management* 56 (2016): 98–108.

Kim, Min Gyung, Chung Hun Lee, and Anna S. Mattila. "Determinants of Customer Complaint Behavior in a Restaurant Context: The Role of Culture, Price Level, and Customer Loyalty." *Journal of Hospitality Marketing & Management* 23, no. 8 (2014): 885–906.

Kokt, Deseré, and Relebohile Ramarumo. "Impact of Organisational Culture on Job Stress and Burnout in Graded Accommodation Establishments in the Free State Province, South Africa." *International Journal of Contemporary Hospitality Management* 27, no. 6 (2015): 1198–1213.

Koutroumanis, Dean A., George Alexakis, and Barbara R. Dastoor. "The Influence Organizational Culture Has on Commitment in the Restaurant Industry." *Small Business Institute Journal* 11, no. 2 (2015): 27–40.

Kumar, Ramesh, Charles Ramendran, and Peter Yacob. "A Study on Turnover Intention in Fast Food Industry: Employees' Fit to the Organizational Culture and the Important of Their Commitment." *International Journal of Academic Research in Business and Social Sciences* 2, no. 5 (2012): 9–42.

LaBaton, Stephan. "Denny's Restaurants to Pay $54 Million in Race Bias Suits." *New York Times*, May 25, 1994, http://www.nytimes.com/1994/05/25/us/denny-s-restaurants-to-pay-54-million-in-race-bias-suits.html?pagewanted=all

Makovsky, K. "Behind the Southwest Airlines Culture." *Forbes* November 21, 2013. Accessed February 7, 2018. https://www.forbes.com/sites/kenmakovsky/2013/11/21/behind-the-southwest-airlines-culture/#39871af23798

McGee-Cooper, Ann, Duanne Trammell, and Gary Looper. "The Power of LUV: An Inside Peek at the Innovative Culture Committee of Southwest Airlines." *Reflections: The SoL Journal* 9, no. 1 (2008): 49–55.

Michelli, Joseph. *The New Gold Standard: 5 Leadership Principles for Creating a Legendary Customer Experience Courtesy of the Ritz-Carlton Hotel Company*. New York, NY: McGraw Hill Professional, 2008.

Rahimi, Roya. "Customer Relationship Management (People, Process and Technology) and Organisational Culture in Hotels: Which Traits Matter?" *International Journal of Contemporary Hospitality Management* 29, no. 5 (2017): 1380–1402.

Ricca, S. "Commitment to Culture." *Hotel and Motel Management* 244, no. 5 (2009): 28–29.

Rice, Faye, and A. Faircloth. "Denny's Changes Its Spots Not So Long Ago, The Restaurant Chain Was One of America's Most Racist Companies. Today it is a Model of Multicultural Sensitivity. Here is the Inside Story of Denny's About-Face." *Fortune,* May 13, 1996. http://archive.fortune.com/magazines/fortune/fortune_archive/1996/05/13/212386/index.htm.

Schein, Edgar H. *Organizational Culture and Leadership,* 5th ed. Hoboken, NJ: Wiley, 2016.

Schneider, Benjamin, Mark G. Ehrhart, and William H. Macey. "Organizational Climate and Culture." *Annual Review of Psychology* 64 (2013): 361–388.

Sharp, Isadore. Four Seasons: *The Story of a Business Philosophy.* New York, NY: Penguin, 2009.

Southwest Airlines Co. "Our History." Southwest Airlines Co. Accessed September 7, 2009. https://www.swamedia.com/pages/our-history-sort-by.

Tajeddini, Kayhan, and Myfanwy Trueman. "Managing Swiss Hospitality: How Cultural Antecedents of Innovation and Customer-Oriented Value Systems Can Influence Performance in the Hotel Industry." *International Journal of Hospitality Management* 31, no. 4 (2012): 1119–1129.

Trice, Harrison M. and Janice M. Beyer. *The Cultures of Work Organizations.* Englewood Cliffs, NJ: Prentice-Hall, 1993.

Tsang, Nelson KF. "Dimensions of Chinese Culture Values in Relation to Service Provision in Hospitality and Tourism Industry." *International Journal of Hospitality Management* 30, no. 3 (2011): 670–679.

Van Maanen, J. "The Smile Factory: Work at Disneyland." In *Refraining Organizational Culture,* edited by John P. Frost, P. L. Moore, C. Lundberg, M. Louis, and J. Martin, 66. Newbury, Park, CA: Sage, 1991.

Ueno, Akiko. "Which HRM Practices Contribute to Service Culture?" *Total Quality Management & Business Excellence* 23, no. 11–12 (2012): 1227–1239.

Waldrep, Shelton S. "Monuments to Walt." In *Inside the Mouse: Work and Play at Disney World.* Edited by Jane Kuenz, Shelton Waldrep, Susan Willis, and Karen Klugman, 212–213. Durham, NC: Duke University Press, 1995.

Wolff, C., "What Makes Kimpton Cool." *Lodging Hospitality* 11, no. 8 (2008): 42–43.

Zoghbi-Manrique-de-Lara, Pablo, and Jyh-Ming Ting-Ding. "The Influence of Corporate Culture and Workplace Relationship Quality on the Outsourcing Success in Hotel Firms." *International Journal of Hospitality Management* 56 (2016): 66–77.

Chapter 5

"50 HR and Recruiting Statistics for 2017." Glassdoor, Inc. Accessed January 3, 2018. http://resources.glassdoor.com/rs/899-LOT-464/images/50hr-recruiting-and-statistics-2017.pdf.

Arthur, Winfred Jr., Eric Anthony Day, Theresa L. McNelly, and Pamela S. Edens. "A Meta-analysis of the Criterion-Related Validity of Assessment Center Dimensions," *Personnel Psychology* 56, no. 1 (2003): 125–154.

Berry, Leonard L. *Discovering the Soul of Service: The Nine Drivers of Sustainable Business Success.* New York: The Free Press, 1999.

Bharwani, Sonia, and Parvaiz Talib. "Competencies of Hotel General Managers: A Conceptual Framework." *International Journal of Contemporary Hospitality Management* 29, no. 1 (2017): 393–418.

Bidwell, Matthew. "Managing Talent Flows through Internal and External Labor Markets." In *The Oxford Handbook of Talent Management,* edited by David G. Collings, Kamel Mellahi, and Wayne F. Cascio, 281–298. New York, New York: Oxford University Press, 2017.

Bowen, John, and Robert C. Ford. "Managing Service Organizations: Does Having a "Thing" Make a Difference?" *Journal of Management* 28, no. 3 (2002): 447–469.

Brinker, Norman and Donald Thomas Phillips. *On the Brink: The Life and Leadership of Norman Brinker.* Arlington, TX: The Summit Publishing Group, 1996.

Campion, Michael C., Michael A. Campion, Emily D. Campion, and Matthew H. Reider. "Initial Investigation into Computer Scoring of Candidate essays for Personnel Selection." *Journal of Applied Psychology* 101, no. 7 (2016): 958–975.

Casio, Wayne F., and John W. Boudreau. *Investing in People: Financial Impact of Human Resource Initiatives.* Upper Saddle River, New Jersey: FT Press, 2011.

Chen, Ziguang, Hongwei Sun, Wing Lam, Qing Hu, Yuanyuan Huo, and Jian An Zhong. "Chinese Hotel Employees in the Smiling Masks: Roles of Job Satisfaction, Burnout, and Supervisory Support in Relationships between Emotional Labor and Performance." *The International Journal of Human Resource Management* 23, no. 4 (2012): 826–845.

Clegg, Alicia. "Recruiters Turn to AI Algorithms to Spot High-Fliers." *Financial Times,* last modified July 13, 2017. Accessed January 3, 2018. https://www.ft.com/content/3045bbaa-6260-11e7-8814-0ac7eb84e5f1.

Colby, Sandra L., and Jennifer M. Ortman, "Projections of the Size and Composition of the U.S. Population: 2014 to 2060." Current Population Reports, P25-1143, U.S. Census Bureau. Washington, DC, 2014.

Crotts, John C., Robert C. Ford, Vincent C.S. Heung, and E. W. T. Ngai. "Organizational Alignment and Hospitality Firm Performance." *International Journal of Culture, Tourism and Hospitality Research* 3, no. 1 (2009): 3–12.

D'Innocenzio, Anne. "Getting in the Door Is Harder Now." *Orlando Sentinel*, June 5, 2018: A9.

Deery, Margaret. "Talent Management, Work-Life Balance and Retention Strategies." *International Journal of Contemporary Hospitality Management* 20, no. 7 (2008): 792–806.

Doyle, Alison. "Top 10 Nest Job Websites: Maximizing Your Online Job Search." The Balance. Last modified December 7, 2017. Accessed January 3, 2018. https://www.thebalance.com/top-best-job-websites-2064080.

Doyle, Alison. "Top 18 Niche Job Sites." The Balance. Last modified August 24, 2016. Accessed January 3, 2018. https://www.thebalance.com/top-niche-job-sites-2061866.

"Elite 100 Speaks to Eleven Madison Park's Daniel Humm." Elitetraveler. Accessed January 2, 2018. http://www.elitetraveler.com/features/elite-100-speaks-to-eleven-madison-parks-daniel-humm.

Farr, James L., and Nancy T. Tippins. eds. *Handbook of Employee Selection.* New York, New York: Taylor & Francis, 2017.

Ford, Robert C., Celeste P. M. Wilderom, and John Caparella. "Strategically Crafting a Customer-Focused Culture: An Inductive Case Study." *Journal of Strategy and Management* 1, no. 2 (2008): 143–167.

Gannon, Judie M., Angela Roper, and Liz Doherty. "Strategic Human Resource Management: Insights from the International Hotel Industry." *International Journal of Hospitality Management* 47, (2015): 65–75.

Gatewood, Robert, Hubert S. Feild, and Murray Barrick. *Human Resource Selection.* Boston, MA: Cengage Learning, 2016.

Gattis, Paul. "New Huntsville-based App Connects Jobs, Workers in Hospitality Industry." AL.com. Last modified October, 30, 2017. Accessed January 3, 2018.

Gibbs, Chris, Fraser MacDonald, and Kelly MacKay. "Social Media Usage in Hotel Human Resources: Recruitment, Hiring and Communication." *International Journal of Contemporary Hospitality Management* 27, no. 2 (2015): 170–184.

Gottfredson, Linda S. "Why G Matters: The Complexity of Everyday Life." *Intelligence* 24, no. 1 (1997): 79–132.

Gross, T. Scott, Andrew Szabo, and Michael Hoffman. *Positively Outrageous Service: How to Delight and Astound Your Customers and Win Them for Life.* 3rd Edition. New York: Allworth Press, 2016.

Hinkin, Timothy R., and J. Bruce Tracey. "The Cost of Turnover: Putting a Price on the Learning Curve." *Cornell Hotel and Restaurant Administration Quarterly* 41, no. 3 (2000): 14–21.

Hinkin, Timothy R., and J. Bruce Tracey. "What Makes It So Great? An Analysis of Human Resources Practices among Fortune's Best Companies to Work for." *Cornell Hospitality Quarterly* 51, no. 2 (2010): 158–170.

Holley, Peter. "A Robot That Functions 'Like Uber for Job Recruitment.'" *Orlando Sentinel*, May 2, 2018: A8.

Humphrey, Ronald H., Blake E. Ashforth, and James M. Diefendorff. "The Bright Side of Emotional Labor." *Journal of Organizational Behavior* 36, no. 6 (2015): 749–769.

Hunter, John E. "Cognitive Ability, Cognitive Aptitudes, Job Knowledge, and Job Performance." *Journal of Vocational Behavior* 29, no. 3 (1986): 340–362.

Hunter, John E., and Ronda F. Hunter. "Validity and Utility of Alternative Predictors of Job Performance." *Psychological Bulletin* 96, no. 1 (1984): 72–98.

Ineson, Elizabeth M. et al. "Seeking Excellent Recruits for Hotel Management Training: An Intercultural Comparative Study." *Journal of Hospitality & Tourism Education* 23, no. 2 (2011): 5–13.

Kim, Youngsang, and Robert Ployhart. "The Strategic Value of Selection Practices: Antecedents and Consequences of Firm-level Selection Practice usage." *Academy of Management Journal* (2017): 61, no. 1 (2018): 46–66.

Lian, Huiwen, Kai Chi Yam, D. Lance Ferris, and Douglas Brown. "Self-control at Work." *Academy of Management Annals* 11, no. 2 (2017): 703–732.

Lievens, Filip, and Paul R. Sackett. "The Effects of Predictor Method Factors on Selection Outcomes: A Modular Approach to Personnel Selection Procedures." *Journal of Applied Psychology* 102, no. 1 (2017): 43–66.

Lockyer, Cliff, and Dora Scholarios. "Selecting Hotel Staff: Why Best Practice Does Not Always Work." *International Journal of Contemporary Hospitality Management* 16, no. 2 (2004): 125–135.

Macan, Therese. "The Employment Interview: A Review of Current Studies and Directions for Future Research." *Human Resource Management Review* 19, no. 3 (2009): 203–218.

McCarthy, Julie M., Talya N. Bauer, Donald M. Truxillo, Neil R. Anderson, Ana Cristina Costa, and Sara M. Ahmed. "Applicant Perspectives during Selection: A Review Addressing 'So What?,' 'What's New?,' and 'Where to Next?'" *Journal of Management* 43, no. 6 (2017): 1693–1725.

McGinley, Sean P., Lydia Hanks, and Nathaniel D. Line. "Constraints to Attracting New Hotel Workers: A Study on Industrial Recruitment." *International Journal of Hospitality Management* 60 (2017): 114–122.

Merkulova, Natalia, Martin Kleinmann, Klaus Melchers, Tibor Szviresez Tresch. "A Test of the Generalizability of a Recently Suggested Conceptual Model for Assessment Center Ratings." *Human Performance* 29, no. 3 (2016): 226–250.

Moncarz, Elisa, Jinlin Zhao, and Christine Kay. "An Exploratory Study of US Lodging Properties' Organizational Practices on Employee Turnover and Retention." *International Journal of Contemporary Hospitality Management* 21, no. 4 (2009): 437–458.

Morgeson, Frederick P., Matthew H. Reider, and Michael A. Campion. "Selecting Individuals in Team Settings: The Importance of Social Skills, Personality Characteristics, and Teamwork Knowledge." *Personnel Psychology* 58, no. 3 (2005): 583–611.

Newman, Jerry. *My Secret Life on the McJob: Lessons from Behind the Counter Guaranteed to Supersize Any Management Style*. New York: McGraw-Hill, 2007.

"No.1 Eleven Madison Park." The World's 50 Best Restaurants. Accessed January 2, 2018. http://www.theworlds50best.com/The-List-2017/1-10/Eleven-Madison-Park.html.

"100 Best Companies to Work for 2017." *Fortune*. Accessed January 3, 2018. http://fortune.com/best-companies/.

Peters, Kim, and Tabitha Russell Wilhelmsen. "The Skills Challenge: How Four of the World's Best Workplaces Prepare Their Teams for the Future." *Fortune*. Last modified October 26, 2017. Accessed January 3, 2018. http://fortune.com/2017/10/26/best-companies-to-work-for-global/.

Pettersen, Normand, and Andre Durivage. *The Structured Interview: Enhancing Staff Selection*. Quebec, Canada: Presses De L'Universite Du Quebec, 2008.

Prafder, Erika. "Hilton Hotels Use Special Hiring Program to Recruit Veterans." *New York Post*. Last modified March 6, 2017. Accessed January 7, 2018. https://nypost.com/2017/03/06/hilton-hotels-use-special-hiring-program-to-recruit-veterans/.

Ree, Malcolm James, and James A. Earles. "Intelligence Is the Best Predictor of Job Performance." *Current Directions in Psychological Science* 1, no. 3 (1992): 86–89.

Rumbaugh, Andrea. "After 6 Weeks of Training, Freshly Minted Flight Attendants Soar." *Houston Chronicle*. Last modified March 4, 2017. Accessed January 2, 2018. http://www.houstonchronicle.com/business/article/After-6-weeks-of-training-freshly-minted-flight-10972075.php.

Ryan, Ann Marie, Lynn McFarland, Helen Baron, and Ron Page. "An International Look at Selection Practices: Nation and Culture as Explanations for Variability in Practice." *Personnel Psychology* 52, no. 2 (1999): 359–391.

Schmidt, Frank, L. "The Role of General Cognitive Ability and Job Performance: Why There Cannot Be a Debate." *Human Performance* 15, no. 1–2 (2002): 187–210.

Schmitt, Neal, ed. *The Oxford Handbook of Personnel Assessment and Selection*. New York, New York: Oxford University Press, 2012.

Schmitt, Neal, Richard Z. Gooding, Raymond A. Noe, and Michael Kirsch. "Meta-analyses of Validity Studies Published Between 1964 and 1982 and the Investigation of Study Characteristics." *Personnel Psychology* 37, no. 3 (1984): 407–422.

"SHRM Survey Findings: Using Social Media for Talent Acquisition—Recruitment and Screening." Society for Human Resource Management. Last modified January 7, 2016. https://www.shrm.org/hr-today/trends-and-forecasting/research-and-surveys/Documents/SHRM-Social-Media-Recruiting-Screening-2015.pdf.

Solnet, David, Robert Ford, and Char-Lee McLennan. "What Matters Most in the Service-Profit Chain? An Empirical Test in a Restaurant Company." *International Journal of Contemporary Hospitality Management* 30, no. 1 (2018): 260–285.

Sturman, Michael C. "The Compensation Conundrum: Does the Hospitality Industry Shortchange Its Employees—and Itself?" *Cornell Hotel and Restaurant Administration Quarterly* 42, no. 4 (2001): 70–76.

Southwest. "Charitable Giving." Accessed January 3, 2018. https://www.southwest.com/html/southwest-difference/southwest-citizenship/charitableGiving.html.

Sturman, Michael C., Robin A. Cheramie, and Luke H. Cashen, "How to Compare Apples to Oranges: Balancing Internal Candidates' Job-performance Data with External Candidates' Selection-test Results." *Cornell Hotel and Restaurant Administration Quarterly* 43, no. 4 (2002): 27–40.

Sturman, Michael C., and David Sherwyn. "The Utility of Integrity Testing for Controlling Workers' Compensation Costs." *Cornell Hospitality Quarterly* 50, no. 4 (2009): 432–445.

Swider, Brian W., Ryan D. Zimmerman, and Murray R. Barrick. "Searching for the Right Fit: Development of Applicant Person-Organization Fit Perceptions during the Recruitment Process." *Journal of Applied Psychology* 100, no. 3 (2015): 880–893.

Tracey, J. Bruce. "A Review of Human Resources Management Research: The Past 10 Years and Implications for Moving Forward." *International Journal of Contemporary Hospitality Management* 26, no. 5 (2014): 679–705.

Tracey, J. Bruce, Michael C. Sturman, and Michael J. Tews. "Ability Versus Personality: Factors That Predict Employee Job Performance." *Cornell Hotel and Restaurant Administration Quarterly* 48, no. 3 (2007): 313–322.

"The 25 Best Workplaces in the Bay Area." *Fortune*. Last modified April 26, 2017. Accessed January 3, 2018. http://fortune.com/2017/04/26/best-companies-bay-area-large/.

Van Iddekinge, Chad H., Stephen E. Lanivich, Philip L. Roth, and Elliott Junco. "Social Media for Selection? Validity and Adverse Impact Potential of a

Facebook-based Assessment." *Journal of Management* 42, no. 7 (2016): 1811–1835.

Viswesvaran, Chockalingam, and Deniz S. Ones. "Integrity Tests: Alternate Conceptualizations and Some Measurement and Practical Issues." In *The Wiley Handbook of Personality Assessment*, edited by Updesh Kumar, 50–73. Hoboken, NJ: Wiley-Blackwell, 2016.

Walsh, Kate, Song Chang, and Eliza Ching-Yick Tse. "Understanding Students' Intentions to Join the Hospitality Industry: The Role of Emotional Intelligence, Service Orientation, and Industry Satisfaction." *Cornell Hospitality Quarterly* 56, no. 4 (2015): 369–382.

Walsh, Kate, Michael C. Sturman, and Bill Carroll. "Preparing for a Successful Career in the Hospitality Industry." In *The Cornell School of Hotel Administration on Hospitality: Cutting Edge Thinking and Practice*, edited by Michael C. Sturman, Jack Corgel, and Rohit Verma, 21–36. New York: Wiley, 2011.

Wan, Yim King Penny, Ipkin Anthony Wong, and Weng Hang Kong. "Student Career Prospect and Industry Commitment: The Roles of Industry Attitude, Perceived Social Status, and Salary Expectations." *Tourism Management* 40 (2014): 1–14.

Wildes, Vivienne J. "Attracting and Retaining Food Servers: How Internal Service Quality Moderates Occupational Stigma." *International Journal of Hospitality Management* 26, no. 1 (2007): 4–19.

Xanthopoulou, Despoina, Arnold B. Bakker, Wido G.M. Oerlemans, and Maria Koszucka. "Need for Recovery after Emotional Labor: Differential Effects of Daily Deep and Surface Acting." *Journal of Organizational Behavior* 39, no. 4 (2018): 1–14.

Chapter 6

Albrecht, Karl. *At America's Service: How Your Company Can Join the Customer Service Revolution.* New York: Warner Books, 1988.

Barry, Sion. "Celtic Manor Resort Recruiting for New Hospitality Apprentices." WalesOnline. Last modified July 24, 2017. http://www.walesonline.co.uk/business/appointments/one-wales-leading-hotels-launches-13376752.

Berry, Leonard. *Discovering the Soul of Service–The Nine Drivers of Sustainable Business Success.* New York, New York: Free Press, 1999.

Bitner, Mary Jo. "Building Service Relationships: It's All About Promises." *Journal of the Academy of Marketing Science* 23, no. 4 (1995): 246–251.

Blanchard, P. Nick, and James W. Thacker. *Effective Training: Systems, Strategies, and Practices.* Upper Saddle River, New Jersey: Prentice Hall, 2010.

Brinker, Norman, and Donald Thomas Phillips. *On the Brink: The Life and Leadership of Norman Brinker.* Irving, Texas: Tapestry Press, 1999.

Chabris, Christopher, and Matthew Brown. "Review—A Big Anti-bias Experiment for Starbucks—After an Ugly Incident, the Coffee Chain Has a Chance to Test Whether Training Programs Produce Less Prejudiced Behavior." *Wall Street Journal*, April 28, 2018, C 3.

Chandler, Dawn E., Kathy E. Kram, and Jeffrey Yip. "An Ecological Systems Perspective on Mentoring at Work: A Review and Future Prospects." *Academy of Management Annals* 5, no. 1 (2011): 519–570.

Disney Institute "About Us." Accessed February 12, 2018. https://disneyinstitute.com/about/.

Disney, Walt. *Walt Disney Famous Quotes.* Disney's Kingdom Editions. Lake Buena Vista, FL: The Walt Disney Company, 1994.

Dolezalek, Holly. "We Train to Please." *Training* 45, no. 3 (2008): 34–35.

Forbes. "Forbes Travel Guide Global Star Rating Awards." *Forbes Travel Guide.* last modified January 31, 2014. https://www.youtube.com/watch?v=J-00u24Hlpw.

Forbes. https://www.forbes.com/sites/micahsolomon/2017/07/29/5-wow-customer-service-stories-from-5-star-hotels-examples-any-business-can-learn-from/#7e578cd633e6.

Ford, Robert C. "Combining Performance, Learning, and Behavioral Goals to Match Job with Person: Three Steps to Enhance Employee Performance with Goal Setting." *Business Horizons* 60, no. 3 (2017): 345–352

Ford, Robert C., Celeste P.M. Wilderom, and John Caparella. "Strategically Crafting a Customer-Focused Culture: An Inductive Case Study." *Journal of Strategy and Management* 1, no. 2 (2008): 143–167.

"Four Ways to Use Big Data in Employee Training." InsideBIGDATA. Last modified December 22, 2017. https://insidebigdata.com/2017/12/22/4-ways-use-big-data-employee-training/.

Fuhrmans, Vanessa."Hotels, Pearson Team for Tuition Program." *Wall Street Journal*, March 1, 2018, B6.

Garvey, Bob, Paul Stokes, and David Megginson. *Coaching and Mentoring.* Thousand Oaks, California: Sage Publishing, 2018. https://www.greatplacetowork.com/

Groth, Aimee, and Gus Lubin. "11 Things Starbucks Does Better than Almost Any Competitor." *Business* Insider, July 29, 2011. Accessed September 7, 2018. https://www.businessinsider.com/starbucks-does-better-2011-7.

"Hilton Worldwide University." Hilton Hotels. Accessed February 16, 2018. http://www.hwu-overview.com/introduction/university.html.

"Hotel Industry Partners with Peason to Offer Debt-free College Degrees to Employees." American Hotel & Lodging Association. Last modified February 28, 2018. https://www.ahla.com/press-release/hotel-industry-partners-pearson-offer-debt-free-college-degrees-employees.

"How Did U.S. Students Perform on the Most Recent Assessments?" The Nation's Report Card. Accessed January 4, 2018. https://www.nationsreportcard.gov/.

Kirkpatrick, Donald L. *Evaluating Training Programs: The Four Levels.* San Francisco, California: Berrett-Koehler Publishers, 1994.

Kline, Sheryl, and Kimberly Harris. "ROI Is MIA: Why Are Hoteliers Failing to Demand the ROI of Training?" *International Journal of Contemporary Hospitality Management* 20, no. 1 (2008): 45–59.

Kraiger, Kurt, Jonathan Passmore, Nuno Rebelo Dos Santos, and Sigmar Malvezzi, eds. *The Wiley Handbook of the Psychology of Training, Development, and Performance Improvement.* Malden, Massachusetts: John Wiley & Sons, Ltd., 2015.

Lacerenza, Christina N., Denise L. Reyes, Shannon L. Marlow, Dana L. Joseph, and Eduardo Salas. "Leadership Training Design, Delivery, and Implementation: A Meta-analysis." *Journal of Applied Psychology* 102, no. 12 (2017): 1686–1718.

Latham, Gary P., and Gerard H. Seijts. "Distinguished Scholar Invited Essay: Similarities and Differences Among Performance, Behavioral, and Learning Goals." *Journal of Leadership & Organizational Studies* 23, no. 3 (2016): 225–233.

Law, Rob, Daniel Leung, Norman Au, and Hee "Andy" Lee. "Progress and Development of Information Technology in the Hospitality Industry: Evidence from Cornell Hospitality Quarterly." *Cornell Hospitality Quarterly* 54, no. 1 (2013): 10–24.

Lee, Patrick C., and Martin R. Bugler. "Training Practices in the Hong Kong Hotel Industry: Managerial and Executive Perspectives." *Journal of Human Resources in Hospitality & Tourism* 16, no. 1 (2017): 88–107.

Li, Ning, Murray R. Barrick, Ryan D. Zimmerman, and Dan S. Chiaburu. "Retaining the Productive Employee: The Role of Personality." *The Academy of Management Annals* 8, no. 1 (2014): 347–395.

Magnini, Vincent P., and Earl D. Honeycutt Jr. "Face Recognition and Name Recall: Training Implications for the Hospitality Industry." *Cornell Hotel and Restaurant Administration Quarterly* 46, no. 1 (2005): 69–78.

Marriot, J. W. "Bill" Jr. "Good Training Leads to Service Excellence." Marriott. Last modified April 8, 2011. http://www.blogs.marriott.com/marriott-on-the-move/2011/04/good-training-leads-to-service-excellence.html.

Marriott, J. W. "Bill" Jr. "Hire Friendly, Train Technical." Marriott. Last modified January 27, 2014. http://www.blogs.marriott.com/marriott-on-the-move/2014/01/hire-friendly-train-technical.html.

Mest, Elliott. "Hilton Partners with Cengage to Offer Employees High School Diplomas, Training," Hotel Management. Last modified November 14, 2017. https://www.hotelmanagement.net/human-resources/hilton-partners-cengage-to-offer-employees-high-school-diplomas-training.

Newman, Jerry. *My Secret Life on the McJob: Lessons from Behind the Counter Guaranteed to Supersize Any Management Style.* New York, NY: McGraw-Hill, 2007.

Noe, Raymond A. *Employee Training and Development.* New York: McGraw-Hill, 2017.

Noe, Raymond A., Michael J. Tews, and Alison McConnell Dachner. "Learner Engagement: A New Perspective for Enhancing our Understanding of Learner Motivation and Workplace Learning." *Academy of Management Annals* 4, no. 1 (2010): 279–315.

"Novility Launches Hospitality Training." *Hotel Management.* Last modified May 14, 2015. https://www.hotelmanagement.net/tech/novility-launches-hospitality-training.

Parasuraman, Arun, Valarie A. Zeithaml, and Leonard L. Berry, "Servqual: A Multiple-Item Scale for Measuring Consumer Perc." *Journal of Retailing* 64, no. 1 (1988): 12–40.

Phillips, Jack J. *Handbook of Training Evaluation and Measurement Methods.* New York, New York: Routledge, 2016.

Ravichandran, Swathi, Kelly E. Cichy, Monica Powers, and Kara Kirby. "Exploring the Training Needs of Older Workers in the Foodservice Industry." *International Journal of Hospitality Management* 44 (2015): 157–164.

"The Ritz-Carlton Leadership Center." The Ritz-Carlton. Accessed January 4, 2018. http://ritzcarltonleadershipcenter.com/.

Roeder, Diame Fermin. "Mövenpick Hotels & Resorts Hosts 'Business Academy' Leadership Training in Dubai." HotelierMiddleEast.com, last modified July 1, 2017. http://www.hoteliermiddleeast.com/30746-movenpick-hotels-resorts-hosts-business-academy-leadership-training-in-dubai/.

Ruetzler, Tanya, William Baker, Dennis Reynolds, Jim Taylor, and Brian Allen. "Perceptions of Technical Skills Required for Successful Management in the Hospitality Industry—An Exploratory Study Using Conjoint Analysis." *International Journal of Hospitality Management* 39 (2014): 157–164.

Scott, Adriana. "Virtual Onboarding: A Close Look." *Society for Human Resource Management.* Last modified August 28, 2013. https://www.shrm.org/resourcesandtools/hr-topics/talent-acquisition/pages/virtual-onboarding.aspx.

Solomon, M. 2017. "5 Wow Customer Service Stories form 5-Star Hotels: Examples Any Business Can Learn From." *Fortune,* July 29, 2017. Accessed 1/2/2018.

Smith, Erica, and Ros Brennan Kemmis. "What Industry Wants: Employers' Preferences for Training." *Education+ Training* 52, no. 3 (2010): 214–225.

Tews, Michael J., and J. Bruce Tracey. "Helping Managers Help Themselves: The Use and Utility of On-the-Job

Interventions to Improve the Impact of Interpersonal Skills Training." *Cornell Hospitality Quarterly* 50, no. 2 (2009): 245–258.

Tracey, J. Bruce, Timothy R. Hinkin, Thao Li Bui Tran, Teresa Emigh, Michael Kingra, Jonathan Taylor, and David Thorek. "A Field Study of New Employee Training Programs: Industry Practices and Strategic Insights." *Cornell Hospitality Quarterly* 56, no. 4 (2015): 345–354.

"Training Top 125." *Training Magazine.* January/February 54, no. 1 (2017): 60–95.

"2017 Training Industry Report." *Training Magazine.* Accessed January 4, 2018. https://trainingmag.com/trgmag-article/2017-training-industry-report.

Waddoups, C. Jeffrey, "Did Employers in the United States Back Away from Skills Training during the Early 2000s?" *ILR Review* 69, no. 2 (2016): 405–434.

Wong, Simon C.K., and Patrick C. Lee. "Roles of the Hotel Training Professionals—Perspectives of Industry Practitioners." *International Journal of Hospitality & Tourism Administration* 18, no. 1 (2017): 61–83.

Chapter 7

Antonakis, John, and David V. Day, Eds. *The Nature of Leadership.* Thousand Oaks, CA: Sage Publications, 2018.

Avolio, Bruce J., John J. Sosik, Dong I. Jung, and Yair Berson. "Leadership Models, Methods, and Applications." In *Handbook of Psychology,* edited by Walter C. Borman, Daniel R. Ilgen, and Richard J. Klimoski, 277–307. New York: Wiley, 2003.

Babakus, Emin, Ugur Yavas, and Osman M. Karatepe. "Work Engagement and Turnover Intentions: Correlates and Customer Orientation as a Moderator." *International Journal of Contemporary Hospitality Management* 29, 6 (2017): 1580–1598.

Bailey, Dawn. "Is the Customer Really Always Right? A Hotel Company Invests in Its Employees First." NIST. Last modified July 27, 2017. https://www.nist.gov/blogs/blogrige/customer-really-always-right-hotel-company-invests-its-employees-first.

Barnard, Chester I. *The Functions of the Executive.* Cambridge, MA: Harvard University Press, 1968.

Bavik, Ali, Yuen Lam Bavik, and Pok Man Tang. "Servant Leadership, Employee Job Crafting, and Citizenship Behaviors: A Cross-Level Investigation." *Cornell Hospitality Quarterly* 58, 4 (2017): 364–373.

Berber, Nemania, Michael J. Morley, Agnes Slavić, and József Poór. "Management Compensation Systems in Central and Eastern Europe: A Comparative Analysis." *The International Journal of Human Resource Management* 28, no. 12 (2017): 1661–1689.

Berger, Lance A., and Dorothy R. Berger. *The Compensation Handbook.* 6th ed. New York, NY: McGraw-Hill, 2015.

Blader, Steven L., and Tom R. Tyler, "Testing and Extending the Group Engagement Model: Linkages between Social Identity, Procedural Justice, Economic Outcomes, and Extrarole behavior." *Journal of Applied Psychology* 94, no. 2 (2009): 445–464.

Blanchard, Ken. "Are You a Leader? Here's How to Tell." *Ken Blanchard Blog.* June 2014, https://www.kenblanchardbooks.com/2014/06/.

Blanchard, Ken, and Spencer Johnson. *The New One Minute Manager.* New York, NY: HarperCollins, 2015.

Brinker, Norman, and Donald Thomas Phillips. *On the Brink: The Life and Leadership of Norman Brinker.* Irving, TX: Tapestry Press, 2002.

Brown, Michael E., Linda K. Treviño, and David A. Harrison. "Ethical leadership: A Social Learning Perspective for Construct Development and Testing." *Organizational Behavior and Human Decision Processes* 97, no. 2 (2005): 120.

Chen, Mengyuan, Yijing Lyu, Yan Li, Xing Zhou, and Weiwen Li. "The Impact of High-Commitment HR Practices on Hotel Employees' Proactive Customer Service Performance." *Cornell Hospitality Quarterly* 58, no. 1 (2017): 94–107.

Cohen-Charash, Yochi and Paul E. Spector. "The Role of Justice in Organizations: A Meta-analysis." *Organizational Behavior and Human Decision Processes* 86, no. 2 (2001): 278–321.

Collins, Denis. *Essentials of Business Ethics: Creating an Organization of High Integrity and Superior Performance.* Hoboken, NJ: John Wiley & Sons, 2009.

Colquitt, Jason A., Donald E. Conlon, Michael J. Wesson, Christopher O. L. H. Porter, and K. Yee Ng. "Justice at the Millennium: A Meta-analytic Review of 25 Years of Organizational Justice Research." *Journal of Applied Psychology* 86, no. 3 (2001): 425–445.

Crotts, John C., Duncan R. Dickson, and Robert C. Ford. "Aligning Organizational Processes with Mission: The Case of Service Excellence." *The Academy of Management Executive* 19, no. 3 (2005): 54–68.

"Culture." Southwest Airlines. Accessed January 9, 2018. https://www.southwest.com/html/about-southwest/careers/culture.html.

Dahlin, Kristina, You-Ta Chuang, and Thomas Roulet. "Opportunity, Motivation and Ability to Learn from Failures and Errors: Review, Synthesis, and the Way Forward." *Academy of Management Annals* 12, no. 1 (2018): 252–277.

Dickson, Duncan, and Robert Ford. "'We only need one rule.' Growing a Service Culture: An Interview with John Caparella, President and Chief Operating Officer of The Venetian Las Vegas, The Palazzo Las Vegas, and Sands Expo and Convention Center." *Journal of Applied Management and Entrepreneurship* 17, no. 3 (2012): 98–114.

Drucker, Peter F. *The Practice of Management.* New York, NY: Harper, 1954.

"Fairmont Stands Out with Employee Recognition Programs." G02 Tourism HR Society. Accessed January 9, 2018. https://www.go2hr.ca/articles/fairmont-stands-out-employee-recognition-programs.

Ford, Robert C. "Combining Performance, Learning, and Behavioral Goals to Match Job with Person: Three Steps to Enhance Employee Performance with Goal Setting." *Business Horizons* 60, 3 (2017): 345–352.

Ford, Robert C., Frank S. McLaughlin, and John W. Newstrom. "Questions and Answers about Fun at Work." *People and Strategy* 26, no. 4 (2003): 18–33.

Freiberg, Kevin, and Jackie Freiberg. *Nuts! Southwest Airlines' Crazy Recipe for Business and Personal Success.* Austin, TX: Bard Press, 1996.

Gerhart, Barry. "Incentives and Pay for Performance in the Workplace." *Advances in Motivation Science,* 4 (2017): 91–140.

Gross, Scott T., Andrew Szabo, and Michael Hoffman, *Positively Outrageous Service: How to Delight and Astound Your Customers and Win Them for Life,* 3rd ed. (New York, NY: Allworth Press, 2016), 147.

Harding, C.B., dir. "Blue Collar Comedy Tour: The Movie." 2003; Burbank, CA: Warner Home video, 2007. DVD.

Herzberg, Frederick, Bernard Mausner, and Barbara Bloch Snyderman. *The Motivation to Work.* New York, NY: Wiley, 1959.

Heskett, James L., Thomas O. Jones, Gary W. Loveman, W. Earl Sasser, and Leonard A. Schlesinger. "Putting the Service-Profit Chain to Work." *Harvard Business Review* 72: 2 (1994): 164–174.

Hogreve, Jens, Anja Iseke, Klaus Derfuss, and Tönnjes Eller. "The Service–Profit Chain: A Meta-analytic Test of a Comprehensive Theoretical Framework." *Journal of Marketing* 81, no. 3 (2017): 41–61.

"Homepage." Great Place to Work. Great Place to Work Institute, 2017. Accessed 9/7/2018. https://www.greatplacetowork.com/.

Huang, Lei, and Ted A. Paterson. "Group Ethical Voice: Influence of Ethical Leadership and Impact on Ethical Performance." *Journal of Management* 43, no. 4 (2017): 1157–1184.

Huertas-Valdivia, Irene, Francisco Javier Llorens-Montes, and Antonia Ruiz-Moreno. "Achieving Engagement among Hospitality Employees: A Serial Mediation Model." *International Journal of Contemporary Hospitality Management* 30, no. 1 (2018): 217–241.

Johnson, Craig E. *Meeting the Ethical Challenges of Leadership: Casting Light or Shadow.* Thousand Oaks, CA: Sage Publications, 2012.

Johnson, Stefanie K., and Juan M. Madera. "Sexual Harassment Is Pervasive in the Restaurant Industry. Here's What Needs to Change." *Harvard Business Review Digital Articles* (January 18, 2018): 2–6.

Kanfer, Ruth, Michael Frese, and Russell E. Johnson. "Motivation Related to Work: A Century of Progress." *Journal of Applied Psychology* 102, no. 3 (2017): 338–355.

Kerr, Steven. "On the Folly of Rewarding A, While Hoping for B." *Academy of Management Journal* 18 no., 4 (1975): 769–783

Koenig, David. *Mouse Tales: A Behind-the-Ears Look at Disneyland.* Irvine, CA: Bonaventure Press, 2012.

Landry, Anaïs Thibault, Marylène Gagné, Jacques Forest, Sylvie Guerrero, Michel Séguin, and Konstantinos Papachristopoulos. "The Relation between Financial Incentives, Motivation, and Performance: An Integrative SDT-based Investigation." *Journal of Personnel Psychology* 16, no. 2 (2017): 61–76.

Latham, Gary P. *Work Motivation: History, Theory, Research, and Practice.* Thousand Oaks, California: Sage Publications, 2012.

Latham, Gary P., Franco Fraccaroli, and Magnus Sverke. "What Am I Supposed to Do in My Job? Set Goals and Appraise Your People." In *An Introduction to Work and Organizational Psychology: An International Perspective,* edited by Nik Chmiel, F. Franccaroli, and M. Sverke, 64–79. Hoboken, NJ: John Wiley & Sons (2017).

Lee, Allan, Sara Willis, and Amy Wei Tian. "Empowering Leadership: A Metaanalytic Examination of Incremental Contribution, Mediation, and Moderation." *Journal of Organizational Behavior* 39, no. 3 (2017): 306–325.

Lee, Michael Y., and Amy C. Edmondson, "Self-Managing Organizations: Exploring the Limits of Less-Hierarchical Organizing," *Research in Organizational Behavior* 37 (2017): 35–58.

Ling, Qian, Fang Liu, and Xiaoyi Wu. "Servant Versus Authentic Leadership: Assessing Effectiveness in China's Hospitality Industry." *Cornell Hospitality Quarterly* 58, no. 1 (2017): 53–68.

López-Cabarcos, M. Ángeles, Ana Isabel Machado-Lopes-Sampaio-de Pinho, and Paula Vázquez-Rodríguez. "The Influence of Organizational Justice and Job Satisfaction on Organizational Commitment in Portugal's Hotel Industry." *Cornell Hospitality Quarterly* 56, no. 3 (2015): 258–272.

Lynn, Michael. "Does Tipping Help to Attract and Retain Better Service Workers?" *Journal of Foodservice Business Research* 20, no. 1 (2017): 82–89.

Mathieu, John E., John R. Hollenbeck, Daan van Knippenberg, and Daniel R. Ilgen. "A Century of Work Teams in the *Journal of Applied Psychology.*" *Journal of Applied Psychology* 102, no. 3 (2017): 452.

Michelli, Joseph A. *The New Gold Standard: 5 Leadership Principles for Creating a Legendary Customer Experience Courtesy of the Ritz-Carlton Hotel Company.* New York, NY: McGraw-Hill, 2008.

Merrilees, Bill, Dale Miller, and Raisa Yakimova. "The Role of Staff Engagement in Facilitating Staff-led Value

Co-creation." *Journal of Service Management* 28, no. 2 (2017): 250–264.

Naim, Mohamma Faraz, and Usha Lenk. "Development and Retention of Generation Y Employees: A Conceptual Framework." *Employee Relations: The International Journal* 40, no. 2 (2018): 433–455.

Newman, Jerry M., Barry T. Gerhart, George T. Milkovich. *Compensation.* 12th ed. New York, NY: McGraw-Hill, 2017.

Ng, Thomas W. H., and Daniel C. Feldman, "Ethical Leadership: Meta-analytic Evidence of Criterion-Related and Incremental Validity." *Journal of Applied Psychology* 100, no. 3 (2015): 948–965.

Park, Sanghee, and Michael C. Sturman. "Evaluating Form and Functionality of PayforPerformance Plans: The Relative Incentive and Sorting Effects of Merit Pay, Bonuses, and LongTerm Incentives." *Human Resource Management* 55, no. 4 (2016): 697–719.

Park, Sanghee, and Michael C. Sturman. "How and What You Pay Matters: The Relative Effectiveness of Merit Pay, Bonuses and Long-Term Incentives on Future Job Performance." *Compensation & Benefits Review* 44, no. 2 (2012): 80–85.

Parker, Sharon K., Frederick P. Morgeson, and Gary Johns. "One Hundred Years of Work Design Research: Looking Back and Looking Forward." *Journal of Applied Psychology* 102, no. 3 (2017): 403–420.

Prince, Nicholas R., J. Bruce Prince, Bradley R. Skousen, and Rüediger Kabst. "Incentive Pay Configurations: Bundle Options and Country-Level Adoption." *Evidence-Based HRM: A Global Forum for Empirical Scholarship* 4, no. 1 (2016): 49–66.

"The Ritz-Carlton Legacy." Marriott. Accessed January 9, 2018. http://www.marriott.com/ritz-carlton-careers/history.mi.

Rosenfeld, Jake. "Don't Ask or Tell: Pay Secrecy Policies in US Workplaces." *Social Science Research* 65 (2017): 1–16.

Ruggless, Ron. "7 Best Practices for Sexual Harassment Training." *Nation's Restaurant News.* Last modified December 13, 2017. http://www.nrn.com/workforce/7-best-practices-sexual-harassment-training.

Seppala, Emma, and Marissa King. "Having Work Friends Can Be Tricky, but It's Worth It." *Harvard Business Review Digital Articles* (August 8, 2017): 2–4. https://hbr.org/2017/08/having-work-friends-can-be-tricky-but-its-worth-it.

Shen, Lucinda. "The 10 Biggest Business Scandals of 2017." *Fortune.* Last modified December 31, 2017. http://fortune.com/2017/12/31/biggest-corporate-scandals-misconduct-2017-pr/.

Simons, Tony. *The Integrity Dividend.* San Francisco, CA: Jossey-Bass, 2008.

Solnet, David, Robert Ford, and Char-Lee McLennan. "What Matters Most in the Service-Profit Chain? An Empirical Test in a Restaurant Company." *International Journal of Contemporary Hospitality Management* 30, no. 1 (2018): 260–285.

Sturman, Michael C. "The Compensation Conundrum: Does the Hospitality Industry Shortchange Its Employees—and Itself?" *Cornell Hotel and Restaurant Administration Quarterly* 42, no. 4 (2001): 70–76.

Tepper, Bennett J., Lauren Simon, and Hee Man Park. "Abusive Supervision." *Annual Review of Organizational Psychology and Organizational Behavior* 4 (2017): 123–152.

Topping, Alexandra. "Sexual Harassment Rampant in Hospitality Industry, Survey Finds." *The Guardian,* last modified January 24, 2018. https://www.theguardian.com/world/2018/jan/24/sexual-harassment-rampant-hospitality-industry-unite-survey-finds.

"Trends in Employee Recognition: A Report by World-at-Work," WorldatWork. Last modified May 2017. https://www.worldatwork.org/dA/d0815e4c41/trends-in-employee-recognition-2017.pdf.

Tuahene, Shekina. "Sexual Harassment: A Hospitality Problem," Hotel Owner, last modified January 10, 2018. https://www.hotelowner.co.uk/13209-sexual-harassment-and-the-hotel-industry/.

Turnage, Kim. "Self-Directed Teams: Beyond Empowerment to 51%." *Talent Plus,* 2015. http://talentplus.com/talent-plus-viewpoint-blog/35-leadership/745-self-directed-teams-beyond-empowerment-to-51.

Watson, Alastair W., Babak Taheri, Steven Glasgow, and Kevin D. O'Gorman. "Branded Restaurants Employees' Personal Motivation, Flow and Commitment: the Role of Age, Gender and Length of Service." *International Journal of Contemporary Hospitality Management* 30, no. 3 (2018): 1845–1862.

Weinstein, Bruce. "Business Leaders Get an 'F' in Ethics, Yet Again." *Fortune.* Last modified January 9, 2016. http://fortune.com/2016/01/09/ethics-business-leaders-gallup/.

Wolf, Clark. "Restaurant Business' 'Excruciatingly Slow' Reckoning on Sexual Harassment Just Won't Do." *Forbes.* Last modified January 4, 2018. https://www.forbes.com/sites/clarkwolf/2018/01/04/excruciatingly-slow-reckoning-in-restaurant-business-just-wont-do/#5f84ee14215a.

Wu, Xiaoyi, Michael C. Sturman, and Chunben Wang. "The Motivational Effects of Pay Fairness: A Longitudinal Study in Chinese Star-Level Hotels." *Cornell Hospitality Quarterly* 54, no. 2 (2013): 185–198.

"Yours is a Very Bad Hotel." SlideShare. Last modified March 30, 2007. https://www.slideshare.net/politicsjunkie/yours-is-a-very-bad-hotel/.

Chapter 8

Bateson, John. "Are Your Customers Good Enough for Your Service Business?" *The Academy of Management Executive* 16, no. 4 (2002): 110–120.

Bateson, John E. "Self-Service Consumer: An Exploratory Study." *Journal of Retailing* 61, no. 3 (1985): 49–76.

Bendapudi, Neeli, and Leonard L. Berry. "Customers' Motivations for Maintaining Relationships with Service Providers." *Journal of Retailing* 73, no. 1 (1997): 15–37.

Bettencourt, Lance A. "Customer Voluntary Performance: Customers as Partners in Service Delivery." *Journal of Retailing* 73, no. 3 (1997): 383–406.

Bitner, Mary J., William T. Faranda, Amy R. Hubbert, and Valarie A. Zeithaml. "Customer Contributions and Roles in Service Delivery." *International Journal of Service Industry Management* 8, no. 3 (1997): 193–205.

Bitner, Mary Jo, Amy L. Ostrom, and Matthew L. Meuter. "Implementing Successful Self-service Technologies." *The Academy of Management Executive* 16, no. 4 (2002): 96–108.

Bharwani, Sonia, and Vinnie Jauhari. "An Exploratory Study of Competencies Required to Co-create Memorable Customer Experiences in the Hospitality Industry." *International Journal of Contemporary Hospitality Management* 25, no. 6 (2013): 823–843.

Bolton, Ruth N., Anders Gustafsson, Janet McColl-Kennedy, Nancy J. Sirianni, and David K. Tse. "Small Details that Make Big Differences: A Radical Approach to Consumption Experience as a Firm's Differentiating Strategy." *Journal of Service Management* 25, no. 2 (2014): 253–274.

Bowen, David E. "Managing Customers as Human Resources in Service Organizations." *Human Resource Management* 25, no. 3 (1986): 371–383

Campos, Ana Cláudia, Júlio Mendes, Patrícia Oom do Valle, and Noel Scott. "Co-creation of Tourist Experiences: A Literature Review." *Current Issues in Tourism* 21, no. 4 (2018): 369–400.

Chase, Richard B. "Where Does the Customer Fit in a Service Operation?" *Harvard Business Review* 56, no. 6 (1978): 137–142.

Chathoth, Prakash, Levent Altinay, Robert James Harrington, Fevzi Okumus, and Eric SW Chan. "Co-production Versus Co-creation: A Process-Based Continuum in the Hotel Service Context." *International Journal of Hospitality Management* 32 (2013): 11–20.

Chathoth, Prakash K., Eric S.W. Chan, Robert J. Harrington, Fevzi Okumus, and Zibin Song. "Co-creating Customer Experience: The Role of Employees in Hospitality and Tourism Services." In *Co-Creation in Tourist Experiences, edited by* Nina Prebensen, Joseph Chen, and Muzaffer Uvsal, 109–125. NY, NY: Routledge, 2017.

Chathoth, Prakash K., Gerardo R. Ungson, Robert J. Harrington, and Eric S. W. Chan. "Co-creation and Higher Order Customer Engagement in Hospitality and Tourism Services: A Critical Review." *International Journal of Contemporary Hospitality Management* 28, no. 2 (2016): 222–245.

Chen, Sandy C., Carola Raab, and Sarah Tanford. "Antecedents of Mandatory Customer Participation in Service Encounters: An Empirical Study." *International Journal of Hospitality Management* 4 (2015): 65–75.

Chen, Sandy C., Carola Raab, and Sarah Tanford. "Segmenting Customers by Participation: An Innovative Path to Service Excellence." *International Journal of Contemporary Hospitality Management* 29, no. 5 (2017): 1468–1485.

Collier, Joel E., Michael Breazeale, and Allyn White. "Giving Back the "Self" in Self Service: Customer Preferences in Self-service Failure Recovery." *Journal of Services Marketing* 31, no. 6 (2017): 604–617.

Collier, Joel E., and Sheryl E. Kimes. "Only If It Is Convenient: Understanding How Convenience Influences Self-Service Technology Evaluation." *Journal of Service Research* 16, no. 1 (2013): 39–51.

DeCelles, Katherine A., and Michael I. Norton. "Physical and Situational Inequality on Airplanes Predicts Air Rage." *Proceedings of the National Academy of Sciences* 113, no. 20 (2016): 5588–5591.

Demirkan, Haluk, and Jim Spohrer. "Developing a Framework to Improve Virtual Shopping in Digital Malls with Intelligent Self-service Systems." *Journal of Retailing and Consumer Services* 21, no. 5 (2014): 860–868.

Dong, Beibei, and K. Sivakumar. "Customer Participation in Services: Domain, Scope, and Boundaries." *Journal of the Academy of Marketing Science* 45, no. 6 (2017): 944–965.

Etgar, Michael. "A Descriptive Model of the Consumer Co-production Process." *Journal of the Academy of Marketing Science* 36, no. 1 (2008): 97–108.

Ford, Robert C., and John T. Bowen. "Getting Guests to Work for You." *Journal of Foodservice Business Research* 6, no. 3 (2004): 37–53.

Ford, Robert C., and Duncan R. Dickson. "Enhancing Customer Self-Efficacy in Co-producing Service Experiences." *Business Horizons* 55, no. 2 (2012): 179–188.

Ford, Robert C., and Janet R. McColl-Kennedy. "Organizational Strategies for Filling the Customer Can-do/Must-do Gap." *Business Horizons* 58, no. 4 (2015): 459–468.

Ford, Robert C., Brendan Richard, and Michael P. Ciuchta, "Crowdsourcing: A New Way of Employing Non-employees?" *Business Horizons* 58, no. 4 (2015): 377–388.

Frow, Pennie, Janet R. McColl-Kennedy, Toni Hilton, Anthony Davidson, Adrian Payne, and Danilo Brozovic. "Value Propositions: A Service Ecosystems Perspective." *Marketing Theory* 14, no. 3 (2014): 327–351.

Godfrey, Kara. "Passenger Ban: Airlines to Create 'No Fly' List as Drunken Arrests SOAR." *Express*, September 8, 2017, https://www.express.co.uk/travel/articles/851781/airline-drunk-passengers-banned.

Grandey, Alicia A., David N. Dickter, and HockPeng Sin. "The Customer Is *Not* Always Right: Customer Aggression and Emotion Regulation of Service Employees." *Journal of Organizational Behavior* 25, no. 3 (2004): 397–418.

Greenbaum, Rebecca L., Matthew J. Quade, Mary B. Mawritz, Joongseo Kim, and Durand Crosby. "When the Customer Is Unethical: The Explanatory Role of Employee Emotional Exhaustion onto Work–Family Conflict, Relationship Conflict with Coworkers, and Job Neglect." *Journal of Applied Psychology* 99, no. 6 (2014): 1188–1203.

Halbesleben, Jonathon R. B., and Oliver K. Stoutner. "Developing Customers as Partial Employees: Predictors and Outcomes of Customer Performance in a Services Context." *Human Resource Development Quarterly* 24, no. 3 (2013): 313–335.

Harrison, Tina, and Kathryn Waite. "Impact of Co-production on Consumer Perception of Empowerment." *The Service Industries Journal* 35, no. 10 (2015): 502–520.

Haumann, Till, Pascal Güntürkün, Laura Marie Schons, and Jan Wieseke. "Engaging Customers in Coproduction Processes: How Value-Enhancing and Intensity-Reducing Communication Strategies Mitigate the Negative Effects of Coproduction Intensity." *Journal of Marketing* 79, no. 6 (2015): 17–33.

Heidenreich, Sven, Kristina Wittkowski, Matthias Handrich, and Tomas Falk. "The Dark Side of Customer Co-creation: Exploring the Consequences of Failed Co-created Services." *Journal of the Academy of Marketing Science* 43, no. 3 (2015): 279–296.

Heskett, James L., W. Earl Sasser, and Leonard A. Schlesinger. *The Service Profit Chain: How Leading Companies Link Profit and Growth to Loyalty, Satisfaction, and Value.* (New York, NY: Free Press, 1997.

Huang, Ming-Hui, and Roland T. Rust. "Technology-Driven Service Strategy." *Journal of the Academy of Marketing Science* 45, no. 6 (2017): 906–924.

Im, Jinyoung, and Hailin Qu. "Drivers and Resources of Customer Co-creation: A Scenario-based Case in the Restaurant Industry." *International Journal of Hospitality Management* 64 (2017): 31–40.

Jaakkola, Elina, and Matthew Alexander. "The Role of Customer Engagement Behavior in Value Co-creation: A Service System Perspective." *Journal of Service Research* 17, no. 3 (2014): 247–261.

Jaakkola, Elina, Anu Helkkula, and Leena Aarikka-Stenroos. "Service Experience Co-creation: Conceptualization, Implications, and Future Research Directions." *Journal of Service Management* 26, no. 2 (2015): 182–205.

Kostopoulos, Giannis, Spiros Gounaris, and Ioannis Rizomyliotis. "How to Reduce the Negative Impact of Customer Non-Compliance: an Empirical Study." *Journal of Strategic Marketing* 22, no. 6 (2014): 513–529.

Kyriazi, Gary. *The Great American Amusement Parks: A Pictorial History.* Secaucus, NJ: Citadel Press, 1976.

Lovelock, Christopher H., and Robert F. Young. "Look to Consumers to Increase Productivity." *Harvard Business Review* 57, no. 3 (1979): 168–178.

Lusch, Robert F., and Stephen L. Vargo. The Service-Dominant Logic of Marketing: Dialog, Debate, and Direction. New York, NY: Routledge, 2014.

Mathis, Elaine F., Hyelin Lina Kim, Muzaffer Uysal, Joseph M. Sirgy, and Nina K. Prebensen. "The Effect of Co-creation Experience on Outcome Variable." *Annals of Tourism Research* (2016): 62–75.

McColl-Kennedy, Janet R., Lilliemay Cheung, and Elizabeth Ferrier. "Co-creating Service Experience Practices." *Journal of Service Management* 26, no. 2 (2015): 249–275.

McColl-Kennedy, Janet R., Anders Gustafsson, Elina Jaakkola, Phil Klaus, Zoe Jane Radnor, Helen Perks, and Margareta Friman. "Fresh Perspectives on Customer Experience." *Journal of Services Marketing* 29, no. 6/7 (2015): 430–435.

McColl-Kennedy, Janet R., Paul G. Patterson, Amy K. Smith, and Michael K. Brady. "Customer Rage Episodes: Emotions, Expressions and Behaviors." *Journal of Retailing* 85, no. 2 (2009): 222–237.

McColl-Kennedy, Janet R., Stephen L. Vargo, Tracey S. Dagger, Jillian C. Sweeney, and Yasmin van Kasteren. "Health Care Customer Value Cocreation Practice Styles." *Journal of Service Research* 15, no. 4 (2012): 370–389.

Mims, Christopher. "The Customer-Service Quandary: Touchy Feely or Do It Yourself: Some Companies Want to Make You Their Friend; Others Make It Hard to Phone Them." *Wall Street Journal*, November 2, 2015. https://www.wsj.com/articles/the-customer-service-quandary-touchy-feely-or-do-it-yourself-1446440460

Morris, David Z. "Uber Says It Can and Will Ban Passengers for Hate." *Fortune*, August 18, 2017. http://fortune.com/2017/08/18/uber-ban-white-supremacists/

Mustak, Mekhail, Elina Jaakkola, Aino Halinen, and Valtteri Kaartemo. "Customer Participation Management: Developing a Comprehensive

Framework and a Research Agenda." *Journal of Service Management* 27, no. 3 (2016): 250–275.

Neuhofer, Barbara, Dimitrios Buhalis, and Adele Ladkin. "A Typology of TechnologyEnhanced Tourism Experiences." *International Journal of Tourism Research* 16, no. 4 (2014): 340–350.

Pinho, Nelson, Gabriela Beirão, Lia Patrício, and Raymond P. Fisk. "Understanding Value Co-creation in Complex Services with Many Actors." *Journal of Service Management* 25, no. 4 (2014): 470–493.

Planet Marriot Europe. "You Create, You Post, We Donate." planetmarrioteurope.tumbler, Tumblr, 2016. http://planetmarriotteurope.tumblr.com/post/115122877560/you-create-you-post-we-donate

Prahalad, Coimbatore K., and Venkat Ramaswamy. "Co-creating Unique Value with Customers." *Strategy & Leadership* 32, no. 3 (2004): 4–9.

Prahalad, Coimbatore K., and Venkat Ramaswamy. "Co creation Experiences: The Next Practice in Value Creation." *Journal of Interactive Marketing* 18, no. 3 (2004): 5–14.

Robertson, Nichola, Heath McDonald, Civilai Leckie, and Lisa McQuilken. "Examining Customer Evaluations across Different Self-service Technologies." *Journal of Services Marketing* 30, no. 1 (2016): 88–102.

Robson, Karen, Kirk Plangger, Jan H. Kietzmann, Ian McCarthy, and Leyland Pitt. "Game On: Engaging Customers and Employees through Gamification." *Business Horizons* 59, no. 1 (2016): 29–36.

Sampson, Scott E., and R. Bruce Money. "Modes of Customer Co-production for International Service Offerings." *Journal of Service Management* 26, no. 4 (2015): 625–647.

Schneider, Benjamin, and David Earl Bowen. *Winning The Service Game.* Boston, MA: Harvard Business Review Press, 88–89.

Smaliukiene, Rasa, Lai Chi-Shiun, and Indre Sizovaite. "Consumer Value Co-creation in Online Business: the Case of Global Travel Services." *Journal of Business Economics and Management* 16, no. 2 (2015): 325–339.

Smith, Oliver. "Air Rage Is on the Rise—and Sober Passengers Are Usually to Blame." *The Telegraph.* September 29, 2016. http://www.telegraph.co.uk/travel/news/air-rage-on-the-rise-sober-passengers-to-blame/

Vargo, Stephen L., and Robert F. Lusch. "Evolving to a New Dominant Logic for Marketing." *Journal of Marketing* 68, no. 1 (2004): 1–17.

Yoho, Keenan D., Robert Ford, Bo Edvardsson, and Fred Dahlinger. "Moving 'The Greatest Show on Earth': WC Coup as an Innovation Champion." *Journal of Management History* 24, no. 1 (2018): 76–98.

Chapter 9

Adomavicius, Gediminas, and Alexander Tuzhilin. "Toward the Next Generation of Recommender Systems: A Survey of the State-of-the-Art and Possible Extensions." *IEEE Transactions on Knowledge and Data Engineering* 17, no. 6 (2005): 734–749.

Baran, Roger J., and Robert J. Galka. *Customer Relationship Management: The Foundation of Contemporary Marketing Strategy.* Oxfordshire, England: Taylor & Francis, 2016.

Berry, Leonard L., and Neeli Bendapudi. "Clueing in Customers." *Harvard Business Review* 81, no. 2 (2003): 100–106.

Bindley, Katherine. "Domino's Tracking App Tells You Who Made Your Pizza–Or Does It?" *Wall Street Journal,* November 28, 2017. https://www.wsj.com/articles/dominos-tracking-app-tells-you-who-made-your-pizzaor-does-it-1511889445

Bitner, Mary J., Amy L. Ostrom, and Matthew L. Meuter. "Implementing Successful Self-service Technologies." *The Academy of Management Executive* 16, no. 4 (2002): 96–108.

Branscombe, Mary. "How Technology Is Transforming the Casino and Gaming Industry," *dinCloud* (blog), dinCloud. Accessed September 14, 2018. https://www.dincloud.com/blog/how-technology-transforming-the-casino-and-gaming-industry.

Buhalis, Dimitrios, and Rob Law. "Progress in Information Technology and Tourism Management: 20 Years on and 10 Years after the Internet—The State of eTourism Research." *Tourism Management* 29, no. 4 (2008): 609–623.

Bush, Michael. "Why Harra's Loyalty Effort Is Industry's Gold Standard." *Ad Age,* published October 5, 2009. http://adage.com/article/news/harrah-s-loyalty-program-industry-s-gold-standard/139424/

Carlin, Mary L. "High Touch V.S. Touch Screen." hospitalitytech, EnsembleIQ. February 19, 2008. https://hospitalitytech.com/high-touch-vs-touch-screen

De Mauro, A., Greco, M., & Grimaldi, M. "What Is Big Data? A Consensual Definition and a Review of Key Research Topics." In *AIP Conference Proceedings 97–104.,* Vol. 1644, no. 1. (February 2015).

"Fire the Worst Customers: Dorothy Lane Market Inc." *CIO Insight* 1, no. 34 (2006): 51.

Fowler, Geoffry A. "June Oven Review: Can Artificial Intelligence Beat Mom's Home Cooking?" *Wall Street Journal.* December 14, 2016. https://www.wsj.com/articles/june-oven-review-can-artificial-intelligence-beat-moms-home-cooking-1481729982

Jain, Jitendra. "Future Hotel Trends–8 Hotel Guest Demands that Will Shape Hospitality."

Hotelmarketer. September 18, 2008. https://hotelemarketer.com/2008/09/17/future-hotel-trends

Johnson, Lesley, Karl J. Mayer, and Elena Champaner. "Casino Atmospherics from a Customer's Perspective: A Re-Examination." *UNLV Gaming Research & Review Journal* 8, no. 2 (2004): 1–10.

Jones-Cooper, Brittany. "Starwood, Marriott, Hyatt Got Hacked: What You Need to Know." Yahoo Finance, Yahoo, published August 15, 2016. https://finance.yahoo.com/news/starwood-marriott-hyatt-got-hacked-what-you-need-to-know-163947160.html

Kim, DaeYoung. "The Moderating Effect of Individual and Organizational Factors on Information Technology Acceptance: The Case of US CVBs' Internet Marketing." *Journal of Travel & Tourism Marketing* 26, no. 3 (2009): 329- 343.

Kim, Henry M., Kelly Lyons, and Mary Ann Cunningham. "Towards a Theoretically-Grounded Framework for Evaluating Immersive Business Models and Applications: Analysis of Ventures in Second Life." *Journal for Virtual Worlds Research* 1, no. 1 (2008): 1–19.

Knutson, Ryan. "Call Centers May Know a Surprising Amount About You." *Wall Street Journal,* January 6, 2017. https://www.wsj.com/articles/that-anonymous-voice-at-the-call-center-they-may-know-a-lot-about-you-1483698608

Krontiris, Ioannis, Marc Langheinrich, and Katie Shilton. "Trust and Privacy in Mobile Experience Sharing: Future Challenges and Avenues for Research." *IEEE Communications Magazine* 52, no. 8 (2014): 50–55.

Levinsohn, B., and E. Gibson. "An Unwelcome Delivery." *Business Week,* May 4, 2009. http://www.mtpspin.ca/picture_library/Dominos_pizza.pdf

Levy, Steven. "Secret of Googlenomics: Data-Fueled Recipe Brews Profitability." *Wired Magazine.* May 22, 2009. https://www.wired.com/2009/05/nep-googlenomics/.

Loveman, Gary. "Diamonds in the Data Mine," *Harvard Business Review* 81, no. 5 (2003): 109–113.

Magnini, Vincent, Earl D. Honeycutt Jr. and Sharon K. Hodge. "Data Mining for Hotel Firms: Use and Limitations." *Cornell Hotel and Restaurant Administration Quarterly* 44, no. 2 (2003): 94–105.

Michelli, Joseph. *The New Gold Standard: 5 Leadership Principles for Creating a Legendary Customer Experience Courtesy of The Ritz-Carlton Hotel Company.* New York, NY: McGraw Hill, 2008.

Morrison, Scott. "So Many, Many Words." *Wall Street Journal,* January 28, 2008. https://www.wsj.com/articles/SB120129801401017897

Nambisan, Satish, and Priya Nambisan. "How to Profit From a Better 'Virtual Customer Environment.'" *MIT Sloan Management Review* 49, no. 3 (2008): 53–61.

Ngai, E. W. T., F. F. C. Suk, and S. Y. Y. Lo. "Development of an RFID-based Sushi Management System: The Case of a Conveyor-Belt Sushi Restaurant." *International Journal of Production Economics* 112, no. 2 (2008): 630–645.

Nickell, Joe A. "WELCOME TO Harrah's." *Business 2.0* 3, no.4 (2002): 48–54

Norton, Steven. "United's Strategy to Reduce Overbookings." *Wall Street Journal,* August 13, 2017. https://www.wsj.com/articles/uniteds-strategy-to-reduce-overbookings-1502676300

O'Donnell, Andy. "8 Virtual Reality Travel Experiences That Will Blow Your Mind: See the World Without Ever Leaving Your Couch." Lifewire, May 23, 2017. https://www.lifewire.com/virtual-reality-tourism-4129394

Perlroth, Nicole, and Mike Isaac. "Inside Uber's $100,000 Payment to a Hacker, and the Fallout." *New York Times,* January 12, 2018. https://www.nytimes.com/2018/01/12/technology/uber-hacker-payment-100000.html

Piccoli, Gabriele. "Information Technology in Hotel Management: A Framework for Evaluating the Sustainability of IT-Dependent Competitive Advantage." *Cornell Hospitality Quarterly* 49, no. 3 (2008): 282–296.

Piccoli, Gabriele, Luis D. Anglada, and Richard T. Watson. "Using Information Technology to Improve Customer Service: Evaluating the Impact of Strategic Opportunities." *Journal of Quality Assurance in Hospitality & Tourism* 5, no. 1 (2005): 3–26.

Pletz, John. "How Outmoded Technology Is Clipping United's Wings," *Crain's Chicago Business,* Crain Communication, published 10, 2016. http://www.chicagobusiness.com/article/20161210/ISSUE01/312109994/how-outmoded-technology-is-clipping-uniteds-wings.

Rosenbush Steven, and Michael Totty. "How Bid Data Is Changing the Whole Equation for Business." *Wall Street Journal,* March 10, 2013. https://www.wsj.com/articles/SB10001424127887324178904578340071261396666

Rubinstein, E., "Gaylord Hotels Extends Reservations. Table Seating Systems to Increase Customer Service Quotients with Solutions from NTN." *Nation's Restaurant News* 39, no. 26 (2005): 29–30.

Seibert, Warner. "How to Choose the Right Point of Sale System for Your Full-Service Restaurant." *Modern Restaurant Management.* January 12, 2018. https://www.modernrestaurantmanagement.com/how-to-choose-the-right-point-of-sale-system-for-your-full-service-restaurant/

SEO PowerSuite, "8 Major Google Ranking Signals in 2017." Search Engine Land, Third Door Media, published July 11, 2017. https://searchengineland.com/8-major-google-ranking-signals-2017-278450.

Solomon, Micah. "What in the World is Triple Five-Star Customer Service? Ocean House's Daniel Hostettler Spills the Beans." *Inc.* January 16, 2018. https://www.inc.com/micah-solomon/what-in-world-is-triple-five-star-customer-service-ocean-houses-daniel-hostettler-spills-beans.html.

Song, Haiyan, and Gang Li. "Tourism Demand Modelling and Forecasting—A Review of Recent Research." *Tourism Management* 29, no. 2 (2008): 203–220.

Stephens-Davidowitz, Seth, and Steven Pinker. *Everybody Lies: Big Data, New Data, And What The Internet Can Tell Us About Who We Really Are.* New York, NY: Harper Luxe, 2017.

Temin, D., B. Molloy, and J. Kolla. "For the Hype: What Every Business Leaders Needs To Know About Artificial Intelligence Now." *Forbes,* December 6, 2017, https://www.forbes.com/sites/daviatemin/2017/12/06/forget-the-hype-what-every-business-leader-needs-to-know-about-artificial-intelligence-now/

Vecant, Emily Flynn. "Window Seats: Virtual Tours Provide Exploration Without Jet Lag, Hassles, or Crowds." *Newsweek.* May 28, 2007. https://www.highbeam.com/doc/1G1-163800104.html

Yuan, Yu-Lan, Ulrike Gretzel, and Daniel R. Fesenmaier. "The Role of Information Technology Use in American Convention and Visitors Bureaus." *Tourism Management* 27: 2 (2006): 326–341.

Zeithaml, Valarie A., Roland T. Rust, and Katherine N. Lemon. "The Customer Pyramid: Creating and Serving Profitable Customers." *California Management Review* 43, no. 4 (2001): 118–142.

Chapter 10

Albrecht, Karl, and Ron Zemke. *Service America! Doing Business in the New Economy*. Homewood, IL: Dow Jones-Irwin, 1985.

Baines, Tim, and Howard W. Lightfoot. "Servitization of the Manufacturing Firm: Exploring the Operations Practices and Technologies that Deliver Advanced Services." *International Journal of Operations & Production Management* 34, no. 1 (2013): 2–35.

Barlow, Janelle, and Claus Møller, *A Complaint Is a Gift: Recovering Customer Loyalty When Things Go Wrong,* 2nd ed. San Francisco, CA: Berrett-Koehler Publishers, 2008.

Benavides-Chicón, Carlos Guillermo, and Bienvenido Ortega. "The Impact of Quality Management on Productivity in the Hospitality Sector." *International Journal of Hospitality Management* 42 (2014): 165–173.

Bitner, Mary Jo, Amy L. Ostrom, and Felicia N. Morgan. "Service Blueprinting: A Practical Technique for Service Innovation." *California Management Review* 50, no. 3 (2008): 66–94.

Bretthauer, Kurt M. "Service Management." *Decision Sciences* 35, No. 3 (2004): 325–332.

Calabrese, Armando, and Federico De Francesco. "A Pricing Approach for Service Companies: Service Blueprint As a Tool of Demand-based Pricing." *Business Process Management Journal* 20, no. 6 (2014): 906–921.

Chase, Richard B., and Douglas M. Stewart. "Make Your Service Fall-Safe." *Sloan Management Review* 35, no. 3 (1994): 35.

del Mar Alonso-Almeida, María, Frederic Marimon, and Merce Bernardo. "Diffusion of Quality Standards in the Hospitality Sector." *International Journal of Operations & Production Management* 33, no. 5 (2013): 504–527.

Demirkan, Haluk, and Dursun Delen. "Leveraging the Capabilities of Service-oriented Decision Support Systems: Putting Analytics and Big Data in Cloud." *Decision Support Systems* 55, no. 1 (2013): 412–421.

Dittman, David A., and James W. Hesford, "A Simulation-based Optimization Approach for Investment Decisions: A Case Study of Pure Allergy-Friendly Rooms." *Cornell Hotel and Restaurant Administration Quarterly* 48, no. 1 (2007): 48, 88–100.

Facella, Paul, and Adina Genn. *Everything I Know About Business I Learned at McDonalds: The 7 Leadership Principles that Drive Break Out Success.* New York, NY: McGraw Hill Professional, 2008.

Farrington, Thomas, Jiju Antony, and Kevin D. O'Gorman. "Continuous Improvement Methodologies and Practices in Hospitality and Tourism." *International Journal of Contemporary Hospitality Management* 30, no. 1 (2017): 581–600.

Fenich, George G. *Planning and Management of Meetings, Expositions, Events and Conventions.* New York, NY: Pearson Higher Ed, 2014.

Johnston, Robert. "Service Operations Management: Return to Roots." *International Journal of Operations & Production Management* 19, no. 2 (1999): 104–124.

Juran, Joseph M. "The Quality Trilogy." *Quality Progress* 19, no. 8 (1986): 19–24.

Kadry, Seifedine, Aremn Bagdasaryan, and Mohammad Kadhum. "Simulation and Analysis of Staff Scheduling in Hospitality Management." *7th International Conference on Modeling, Simulation, and Applied Optimization (ICMSAO)* (2017): 1–6.

Kandampully, Jay, Byron William Keating, BeomCheol Kim, Anna S. Mattila, and David Solnet. "Service Research in the Hospitality Literature: Insights from a Systematic Review." *Cornell Hospitality Quarterly* 55, no. 3 (2014): 287–299.

Kazemzadeh, Yahya, Simon K. Milton, and Lester W. Johnson. "Service Blueprinting and Process-Chain-Network: An Ontological Comparison." *International Journal of Qualitative Research in Services* 2, no. 1 (2015): 1–12.

Kingman-Brundage, J. "The ABCs of Service System Blueprinting." In *Designing A Winning Service Strategy: 7th Annual Services Marketing Conference Proceeding*, edited by M. J. Bitner and Lawrence A. Crosby, 30–33. Chicago, IL: American Marketing Association, 1989.

Kingman-Brundage, Jane. "Technology, Design, and Service Quality." *International Journal of Service Industry Management* 2, no. 3 (1991): 47–59.

Kingman-Brundage, Jane, and Lynn G. Shostack. "How to Design a Service." In *The AMA Handbook of Marketing for the Service Industries*, edited by C. A. Congram and M. L. Friedman, 243–261. New York, NY: American Marketing Association, 1991.

Kuo, Chen-Feng, and Douglas C. Nelson. "A Simulation study of Production Task Scheduling for a University Cafeteria." *Cornell Hospitality Quarterly* 50, no. 4 (2009): 540–552.

Lim, Chiehyeon, Min-Jun Kim, Ki-Hun Kim, Kwang-Jae Kim, and Paul P. Maglio. "Using Data to Advance Service: Managerial Issues and Theoretical Implications from Action Research." *Journal of Service Theory and Practice* 28, no. 1 (2018): 99–128.

Maglio, Paul P., and Jim Spohrer. "A Service Science Perspective on Business Model Innovation." *Industrial Marketing Management* 42, no. 5 (2013): 665–670.

Marriot International. "Learn to Love the Pickiest Customer." *Marriot: On the Move* (blog). May 31, 2016. http://www.blogs.marriott.com/marriott-on-the-move/2016/05/learn-to-love-the-pickiest-customer.html

McChesney, Chris, Sean Covey, and Jim Huling. *The 4 Disciplines of Execution: Achieving Your Wildly Important Goals.* New York, NY: Free Press, 2012.

McNeill, Richard G., and Ronald A. Evans,."So You Want to Build a Convention Center: The Case of Hope Versus Reality." *Journal of Convention & Event Tourism* 6, no. 1–2, (2005): 23–43.

Metters, Richard, and Ann Marucheck. "Service Management—Academic Issues and Scholarly Reflections from Operations Management Researchers." *Decision Sciences* 38, no. 2 (2007): 195–214.

Office of Secretary of Transportation. "Revised Departmental Guidance 2016: Treatment of the Value of Preventing Fatalities and Injuries in Preparing Economic Analyses." transportation.gov, U.S. Department of Transportation. Accessed January 2018. https://www.transportation.gov/sites/dot.gov/files/docs/2016%20Revised%20Value%20of%20a%20Statistical%20Life%20Guidance.pdf.

Radnor, Zoe, Stephen P. Osborne, Tony Kinder, and Jean Mutton. "Operationalizing Co-Production in Public Services Delivery: The Contribution of Service Blueprinting." *Public Management Review* 16, no. 3 (2014): 402–423.

Robinson, Peter, Paul Fallon, Harry Cameron, and John C. Crotts, eds. *Operations Management in the Travel Industry.* Wallingford, England: CABI, 2016.

Seymour, Tom, and Sara Hussein. "The History of Project Management." *International Journal of Management & Information Systems* 18, no. 4 (2014): 233–240.

Shingo, Shigeo. *Zero Quality Control: Source Inspection and the Poka-Yoke System.* Portland, OR: Productivity Press, 1986.

Shostack, G. Lynn. "Designing Services That Deliver." *Harvard Business Review* 62, no.1 (1984): 133–139.

Song, Haiyan, and Gang Li. "Tourism "Demand Modelling and Forecasting—A Review of Recent Research." *Tourism Management* 29, no. 2 (2008): 203–220.

Szende, Peter, and Alec Dalton. "Service Blueprinting: Shifting from a Storyboard to a Scorecard." *Journal of Foodservice Business Research* 18, no. 3 (2015): 207–225.

Talib, Faisal, Zillur Rahman, and M. N. Qureshi. "An Empirical Investigation of Relationship between Total Quality Management Practices and Quality Performance in Indian Service Companies." *International Journal of Quality & Reliability Management* 30, no. 3 (2013): 280–318.

Tang, Christopher S. "The Past, Present, and Future of Manufacturing & Service Operations Management." *Manufacturing & Service Operations Management* 17, no. 1 (2015): 1–3.

Tarí, Juan José, Iñaki Heras-Saizarbitoria, and Jorge Pereira. "Internalization of Quality Management in Service Organizations." *Managing Service Quality* 23, no. 6 (2013): 456–473.

Thompson, Gary M. "Deciding Whether to Offer 'Early-Bird' or 'Night-Owl' Specials in Restaurants: A Cross-Functional View." *Journal of Service Research* 18, no. 4 (2015): 498–512.

Tsang, Nelson KF, Louisa Yee-Sum Lee, and Hailin Qu. "Service Quality Research on China's Hospitality and Tourism Industry." *International Journal of Contemporary Hospitality Management* 27, no. 3 (2015): 473–497.

Verdouw, Cor N., J. Wolfert, A. J. M. Beulens, and A. Rialland. "Virtualization of Food Supply Chains with the Internet of Things." *Journal of Food Engineering* 176 (2016): 128–136.

Wang, Yulan, Stein W. Wallace, Bin Shen, and Tsan-Ming Choi. "Service Supply Chain Management: A Review of Operational Models." *European Journal of Operational Research* 247, no. 3 (2015): 685–698.

Wyckoff, Daryl D. "New Tools for Achieving Service Quality: A Cornell Quarterly Classic." *Cornell Hotel and Restaurant Administration Quarterly* 42, no. 4 (2001): 25–38.

Xiang, Zheng, Zvi Schwartz, John H. Gerdes Jr, and Muzaffer Uysal. "What Can Big Data and Text Analytics Tell Us about Hotel Guest Experience and Satisfaction?" *International Journal of Hospitality Management* 44 (2015): 120–130.

Chapter 11

Bae, Gumkwang, and Dae-Young Kim. "The Effects of Offering Menu Information on Perceived Waiting Time." *Journal of Hospitality Marketing & Management* 23, no. 7 (2014): 746–767.

Dickson, Duncan, Robert C. Ford, and Bruce Laval. "Managing Real and Virtual Waits in Hospitality and Service Organizations." *Cornell Hotel and Restaurant Administration Quarterly* 46, no. 1 (2005): 52–68.

Ford, Robert C. "Prime Time: The Strategic Use of Subconscious Priming to Enhance Customer Satisfaction." *Business Horizons* 57, no. 2 (2014): 269–277.

Gillam, Graham, Kyle Simmons, Donald Stevenson, and Elliott Weiss. "Line, Line, Everywhere a Line: Cultural Considerations for Waiting-Line Managers." *Business Horizons* 57, no. 4 (2014): 533–539.

Gumus, Seigha, Gordon Monday Bubou, and Mobolaji Humphrey Oladeinde. "Application of Queuing Theory to a Fast Food Outfit: A Study of Blue Meadows Restaurant." *Independent Journal of Management & Production* 8, no. 2 (2017): 441–458.

Heo, Cindy Yoonjoung, Seoki Lee, Anna Mattila, and Clark Hu. "Restaurant Revenue Management: Do Perceived Capacity Scarcity and Price Differences Matter?" *International Journal of Hospitality Management* 35 (2013): 316–326.

Hernandez-Maskivker, Gilda, and Gerard Ryan. "Priority Systems at Theme Parks from the Perspective of Managers and Customers." *Technology Innovation Management Review* 6, no. 11 (2016): 40–47.

Kaushik, Arun Kumar, and Vikas Kumar. "Investigating Consumers' Adoption of SSTs–A Case Study Representing India's Hospitality Industry." *Journal of Vacation Marketing* 24, no. 3 (2018): 275–290.

Kim, Seontaik, Li Miao, and Vincent P. Magnini. "Consumers' Emotional Responses and Emotion Regulation Strategies during Multistage Waiting in Restaurants." *Journal of Hospitality & Tourism Research* 40, no. 3 (2016): 291–318.

Kokkinou, Alinda, and David A. Cranage. "Using Self-Service Technology to Reduce Customer Waiting Times." *International Journal of Hospitality Management* 33 (2013): 435–445.

Laval, B. "Optimization of Walt Disney World Monorail System through Computer Simulation." In *Proceedings 8th Annual Simulation Symposium*, 1–10. Tampa, FL. March12–14, 1975.

Lee, Younghwa, Andrew NK Chen, and Traci Hess. "The Online Waiting Experience: Using Temporal Information and Distractors to Make Online Waits Feel Shorter." *Journal of the Association for Information Systems* 18, no. 3 (2017): 231–263.

Liang, Chih-Chin. "Queueing Management and Improving Customer Experience: Empirical Evidence Regarding Enjoyable Queues." *Journal of Consumer Marketing* 33, no. 4 (2016): 257–268.

Lin, YuTse, KangNing Xia, and LienTi Bei. "Customer's Perceived Value of Waiting Time for Service Events." *Journal of Consumer Behaviour* 14, no. 1 (2015): 28–40.

Maister, D. H. "The Psychology of Waiting Lines." In *The Service Encounter: Managing Employee/Customer Interaction in Service Businesses*, edited by J. Czepiel, M. R. Solomon, and C. F. Suprenant, 113–124. Lexington, MA: Lexington Books, 1985.

McGuire, Kelly A., and Sheryl E. Kimes. "The Perceived Fairness of Waitlist-Management Techniques for Restaurants." *Cornell Hotel and Restaurant Administration Quarterly* 4, no.: 2 (2006): 121–134.

Munichor, Nira, and Anat Rafaeli. "Numbers or Apologies? Customer Reactions to Telephone Waiting Time Fillers." *Journal of Applied Psychology* 92, no. 2 (2007): 511–518.

Mustapha, R. R., M. Z. F. Ibrahim, N. Ghazali, A. Salim, and Z. Ahmad. "Queuing Management: Installation of Distractions Towards Customer Satisfaction." In *Innovation and Best Practices in Hospitality and Tourism Research*, edited by Salamiah A. Jamal, Salleh Mohd Radzi, Norzuwana Sumarjan, Chemah Tamby Chik, and Mohd Faeez Saiful Bakhtiar, 15–18. Oxfordshire, England: Taylor and Francis, 2016.

Norman, Donald A. "Designing Waits that Work," *MIT Sloan Management Review* 50, no. 4 (2009): 23.

Oh, Haemoon, Miyoung Jeong, and Seyhmus Baloglu. "Tourists' Adoption of Self-Service Technologies at Resort Hotels." *Journal of Business Research* 66, no. 6 (2013): 692–699.

Pàmies, Maria del Mar, Gerard Ryan, and Mireia Valverde. "Uncovering the Silent Language of Waiting." *Journal of Services Marketing* 30, no. 4 (2016): 427–436.

Pàmies, Maria del Mar, Gerard Ryan, and Mireia Valverde. "What Is Going on When Nothing Is Going On? Exploring the Role of the Consumer in Shaping Waiting Situations." *International Journal of Consumer Studies* 40, no. 2 (2016): 211–219.

Pullman, Madeleine, and Svetlana Rodgers. "Capacity Management for Hospitality and Tourism: A Review of Current Approaches." *International Journal of Hospitality Management* 29, no. 1 (2010): 177–187.

Pullman, Madeleine, and Gary M. Thompson, "Evaluating Capacity-and Demand-Management Decisions at a Ski Resort." *Cornell Hotel and Restaurant Administration Quarterly* 43, no. 6 (2002): 25–36.

Rafaeli, Anat, Greg Barron, and Keren Haber. "The Effects of Queue Structure on Attitudes." *Journal of Service Research* 5, no. 2 (2002): 125–139.

Ramseook-Munhurrun, Prabha. "A Critical Incident Technique Investigation of Customers' Waiting Experiences in Service Encounters." *Journal of Service Theory and Practice* 26, no. 3 (2016): 246–272.

Reckard, E. S. "More Disneyland Rides to Get Shortcut System." *Los Angeles Times,* May 26, 2000. www.latimes.com.

Ryan, Gerard, Gilda-María Hernández-Maskivker, and Mireia Valverde. "Challenging Conventional Wisdom: Positive Waiting." *Tourism Management* 64 (2018): 64–72.

Sasikala, S., K. Indhira, and V. M. Chandrasekaran. "A Study on MX/GB/1 Retrial Queueing System with Bernoulli Vacation Schedule and Variable Server Capacity." *International Journal of Knowledge Management in Tourism and Hospitality* 1, no. 3 (2017): 263–277.

Shunko, Masha, Julie Niederhoff, and Yaroslav Rosokha. "Humans Are not Machines: The Behavioral Impact of Queueing Design on Service Time." *Management Science* 64, no. 1 (2017): 453–473.

Stefan, T. "R&D Comes to Services: Bank of America's Pathbreaking Experiments." *Harvard Business Review* 81, no. 4 (2003).

Sundari, S. Maragatha, and Miriam Cathy Joy. "Queueing Model of Optional Type of Services with Service Stoppage and Revamp Process in Web Hosting Queueing." *International Journal of Knowledge Management in Tourism and Hospitality* 1, no. 2 (2017): 241–262.

Torres, Edwin N., Ady Milman, and Soona Park. "Delighted or Outraged? Uncovering Key Drivers of Exceedingly Positive and Negative Theme Park Guest Experiences." *Journal of Hospitality and Tourism Insights* 1, no. 1 (2017): 65–85.

Weng, Shao Jen, Donald Gotcher, and Chen Feng Kuo. "Lining Up for Quick Service—The Business Impact of Express Lines on Fast-Food Restaurant Operations." *Journal of Foodservice Business Research* 20, no. 1 (2017): 65–81.

Wirtz, Jochen, and Christopher Lovelock. "Balancing Demand and Capacity." In *Services Marketing: People, Technology, Strategy,* (Chapter 9) 332–265. Singapore: World Scientific Publishing, 2016.

Wolfston, B. J. "Disney Chief Financial Officer Sees Changes Raising Customer Satisfaction." *Orange County Register,* April 11, 2000. www.ocregister.com.

Zhang, Yingsha, Xiang Robert Li, Qin Su, and Xingbao Hu. "Exploring a Theme Park's Tourism Carrying Capacity: A Demand-side Analysis." *Tourism Management* 59 (2017): 564–578.

Chapter 12

Assaf, A. George, Haemoon Oh, and Mike G. Tsionas. "Unobserved Heterogeneity in Hospitality and Tourism Research." *Journal of Travel Research* 5, no. 6 (2016): 774–788.

Ayres, Ian. *Super Crunchers: Why Thinking-by-Numbers Is the New Way to Be Smart.* New York, NY: Bantam Books, 2007.

Baker, Tim, and David A. Collier. "The Economic Payout Model for Service Guarantees." *Decision Sciences* 36, no. 2 (2005): 197–220.

Bartkus, Kenneth R., Roy D. Howell, Stacey Barlow Hills, and Jeanette Blackham. "The Quality of Guest Comment Cards: An Empirical Study of US Lodging Chains." *Journal of Travel Research* 48, no. 2 (2009): 162–176.

Bartkus, Kenneth R., Robert Mills, and David Olsen. "Clarifications on the Design of Customer Comment Cards: Question Type, Question Wording, and Writing Space." *Journal of Hospitality Marketing & Management* 24, no. 2 (2015): 216–228.

Bell, Chip R., and Ron Zemke. *Managing Knock Your Socks Off Service,* 2nd ed. Edited by Chip R. Bell and Dave Zielinski. New York, NY: AMOACOM, 2007.

Berezina, Katerina, Anil Bilgihan, Cihan Cobanoglu, and Fevzi Okumus. "Understanding Satisfied and Dissatisfied Hotel Customers: Text Mining of Online Hotel Reviews." *Journal of Hospitality Marketing & Management* 25, no. 1 (2016): 1–24.

Berry, Leonard L. "Competing with Quality Service in Good Times and Bad." *Business Horizons* 52, no. 4 (2009): 309–317.

Berry, Leonard L., and Anantharanthan Parasuraman. *Marketing Services: Competing Through Quality.* New York, NY: Free Press, 2004.

Berry, Leonard L., Eileen A. Wall, and Lewis P. Carbone. "Service Clues and Customer Assessment of the Service Experience: Lessons from Marketing." *The Academy of Management Perspectives* 20, no. 2 (2006): 43–57.

Blind, Knut. "A Taxonomy of Standards in the Service Sector: Theoretical Discussion and Empirical Test." *The Service Industries Journal* 26, no. 4 (2006): 397–420.

Blodgett, Jeffrey G., Donald H. Granbois, and Rockney G. Walters. "The Effects of Perceived Justice on Complainants' Negative Word-of-Mouth Behavior and Repatronage Intentions." *Journal of Retailing* 69, no. 4 (1993): 399–428.

Brito, Pedro Quelhas, and Meena Rambocas. "Assessing the Impact of Mystery Client Traits on Service Evaluation." *Journal of Services Marketing* 30, no. 4 (2016): 411–426.

Cantallops, Antoni Serra, and Fabiana Salvi. "New Consumer Behavior: A Review of Research on eWOM and Hotels." *International Journal of Hospitality Management* 36 (2014): 41–51.

Chen, Hanyu, Betty Weiler, Martin Young, and Yun Lok Lee. "Conceptualizing and Measuring Service Quality: Towards Consistency and Clarity in Its Application to Travel Agencies in China." *Journal of Quality Assurance in Hospitality & Tourism* 17, no. 4 (2016): 516–541.

CPP-LUXURY. "Ted Teng, CEO, Leading Hotels of the World to Create a New Business Model." CPPLUXURY: Business of Luxury, posted on July 29, 2015. Accessed January 21, 2018. https://cpp-luxury.com/ted-teng-ceo-leading-hotels-of-the-world-to-create-a-new-business-model/.

Crisafulli, Benedetta, and Jaywant Singh. "Service Guarantee as a Recovery Strategy: The Impact of Guarantee Terms on Perceived Justice and Firm Motives." *Journal of Service Management* 27, no. 2 (2016): 117–143.

Cronin Jr, J. Joseph, and Steven A. Taylor. "SERVPERF versus SERVQUAL: Reconciling Performance-based and Perceptions-Minus-Expectations Measurement of Service Quality." *The Journal of Marketing* 58, no. 1 (1994): 125–131.

Crosby, Philip B. *Quality Is Free: The Art of Making Quality Certain.* New York, NY: McGraw Hill, 1980.

Dedeoğlu, Bekir Bora, and Halil Demirer. "Differences in Service Quality Perceptions of Stakeholders in the Hotel Industry." *International Journal of Contemporary Hospitality Management* 27, no. 1 (2015): 130–146.

Devi, S. Suneetha, and A. Vidhyadhara Reddy. "A Conceptual Study of Mystery Shopping as an Ancillary Method for Customer Surveys." *Global Journal of Management and Business Research* 16 (2016): 2E.

Fabien, Louis. "Design and Implementation of a Service Guarantee." *Journal of Services Marketing* 19, no. 1 (2005): 33–38.

Ford, Robert C., Gary P. Latham, and Gwen Lennox. "Mystery Shoppers: A New Tool for Coaching Employee Performance Improvement." *Organizational Dynamics* 40, no. 3 (2011): 157–164.

Hahn, Song-Ee, Beverley Sparks, Hugh Wilkins, and Xin Jin. "E-service Quality Management of a Hotel Website: A Scale and Implications for Management." *Journal of Hospitality Marketing & Management* 26, no. 7 (2017): 694–716.

Hart, Christopher W. L. "The Power of Unconditional Service Guarantees." *Harvard Business Review* 66, no.4 (1988): 54–62.

Hays, Julie M., and Arthur V. Hill. "Service Guarantee Strength: The Key to Service Quality." *Journal of Operations Management* 24, no. 6 (2006): 753–764.

Hocutt, Mary Ann, and Michael R. Bowers. "The Impact of Service Guarantees on Consumer Responses in the Hotel Industry." *Journal of Hospitality & Leisure Marketing* 13, no. 1 (2005): 5–23.

Hogreve, Jens, and Dwayne D. Gremler. "Twenty Years of Service Guarantee Research: A Synthesis." *Journal of Service Research* 11, no. 4 (2009): 322–343.

Hospitality Net. "Hampton by Hilton's New 100% Hampton Guarantee." Hospitality Net, posted January 19, 2017. Accessed January 8, 2018, https://www.hospitalitynet.org/news/4080485.html.

Jin, Liyin, Yunhui Huang, and Yanqun He. "When Does a Service Guarantee Work? The Roles of the Popularity of Service Guarantees and Firm Reputation." *Tourism Management* 57 (2016): 272–285.

Köseoglu, Mehmet Ali, Gary Ross, and Fevzi Okumus. "Competitive Intelligence Practices in Hotels." *International Journal of Hospitality Management* 53 (2016): 161–172.

Ladhari, Riadh. "Alternative Measures of Service Quality: A Review." *Managing Service Quality: An International Journal* 18, no. 1 (2008): 65–86.

Lai, Ivan KW, Michael Hitchcock, Ying Yang, and Tun-Wei Lu. "Literature Review on Service Quality in Hospitality and Tourism (1984–2014): Future Directions and Trends." *International Journal of Contemporary Hospitality Management* 30, no.1 (2018): 1984–2014.

Latham, Gary P., Robert C. Ford, and Danny Tzabbar. "Enhancing Employee and Organizational Performance through Coaching Based on Mystery Shopper Feedback: A QuasiExperimental Study." *Human Resource Management* 51, no. 2 (2012): 213–229.

Lee, Ji-Eun, and Denver Severt. "The Role of Hospitality Service Quality in Third Places for the Elderly: An Exploratory Study." *Cornell Hospitality Quarterly* 58, no. 2 (2017): 214–221.

Levent, Altinay Alexandros Paraskevas, and SooCheong Jang. *Planning Research in Hospitality and Tourism* (2nd edition). New York, NY: Routledge, 2015.

Lin, Chin-Feng, and Chen-Su Fu. "Advancing Laddering and Critical Incident Technique to Reveal Restaurant Niches." *The Service Industries Journal* 37, no. 13–14 (2017): 801–818.

Liu, Chih-Hsing Sam, Ching-Shu Su, Bernard Gan, and Sheng-Fang Chou. "Effective Restaurant Rating Scale Development and a Mystery Shopper Evaluation Approach." *International Journal of Hospitality Management* 43 (2014): 53–64.

Lu, Carol, Celine Berchoux, Michael W. Marek, and Brendan Chen. "Service Quality and Customer Satisfaction: Qualitative Research Implications for Luxury Hotels." *International Journal of Culture, Tourism and Hospitality Research* 9, no. 2 (2015): 168–182.

Maguire, S., S.C. Lenny Koh, and C. Huang. "Identifying the Range of Customer Listening Tools: A Logical Precursor to CRM?" *Industrial management & Data Systems* 107, no. 4 (2007): 567–586.

McCaskey, David, and Stuart Symes. "Travel Inn: Everything You Want for a Good Night's Sleep–100 Per Cent Satisfaction Guarantee or Your Money Back." *International Journal of Contemporary Hospitality Management* 16, no. 3 (2004): 166–174.

McCollough, Michael A., and Dwayne D. Gremler. "A Conceptual Model and Empirical Examination of the Effect of Service Guarantees on Post-Purchase Consumption Evaluations." *Managing Service Quality: An International Journal* 14, no. 1 (2004): 58–74.

Migacz, Steven, Angela Durko, and James Petrick. "It Was the Best of Times, It Was the Worst of Times: The Effects of Critical Incidents on Cruise Passengers' Experiences." *Tourism in Marine Environments* 11, no. 2–3 (2016): 123–135.

Milner, Rebecca, and Adrian Furnham. "Measuring Customer Feedback, Response and Satisfaction." *Psychology* 8, no. 3 (2017): 350.

Minghetti, Valeria, and Emilio Celotto. "Measuring Quality of Information Services: Combining Mystery Shopping and Customer Satisfaction Research to Assess the Performance of Tourist Offices." *Journal of Travel Research* 53, no. 5 (2014): 565–580.

Mok, Connie, Beverley Sparks, and Jay Kadampully. *Service Quality Management in Hospitality, Tourism, and Leisure.* New York, NY: Routledge, 2013.

Moorthy, Krishna, Lim En Chee, Ooi Chuan Yi, Ooi Soo Ying, Ooi Yee Woen, and Tan Mun Wei. "Customer Loyalty to Newly Opened Cafés and Restaurants in Malaysia." *Journal of Foodservice Business Research* 20, no. 5 (2017): 525–541.

Morgan, Ivor, and Jay Rao. "Aligning Service Strategy through Super-Measure Management." *The Academy of Management Executive* 16, no. 4 (2002): 121–131.

Morgan, James. "5 Interactive Ways To Get Real-Time Feedback." Event Manager Blog, posted February 26, 2018. Accessed September 14, 2018. https://www.eventmanagerblog.com/interactive-real-time-event-feedback.

Mukherjee, Avinandan, and Prithwiraj Nath. "An Empirical Assessment of Comparative Approaches to Service Quality Measurement." *Journal of Services Marketing* 19, no. 3 (2005): 174–184.

Nikolaidis, Dimitrios, Sotiria Christina Chrysikou, and Kostas Alexandris. "Testing the Relationship between Hotel Service Quality and Hotel Brand Personality." *International Journal of Hospitality and Event Management* 1, no. 4 (2016): 355–369.

Nimri, Rawan, Anoop Patiar, and Sandra Kensbock. "A Green Step Forward: Eliciting Consumers' Purchasing Decisions Regarding Green Hotel Accommodation in Australia." *Journal of Hospitality and Tourism Management* 33 (2017): 43–50.

Oh, Haemoon, and Kawon Kim. "Customer Satisfaction, Service Quality, and Customer Value: Years 2000–2015." *International Journal of Contemporary Hospitality Management* 29, no. 1 (2017): 2–29.

Oh, Haemoon, and Sarah C. Parks. "Customer Satisfaction and Service Quality: A Critical Review of the Literature and Research Implications for the Hospitality Industry." *Hospitality Research Journal* 20 (1997): 35–64.

Ostrom, Amy L., and Dawn Iacobucci. "Retrospective: The Effect of Guarantees on Consumers' Evaluation of Services." *Journal of Services Marketing* 30, no. 4 (2016): 373–376.

Parasuraman, Arun, Leonard L. Berry, and Valarie A. Zeithaml. "Refinement and Reassessment of the SERVQUAL Scale." *Journal of Retailing* 67, no. 4 (1991): 420–450.

Peng, Hong, Wei Jiang, and Ruihuan Su. "The Effect of Service Guarantee Strength on Service Quality of Online Merchants." *International Journal of Services Technology and Management* 22, no. 1–2 (2016): 4–17.

Petrick, James F., Catherine Tonner, and Christina Quinn. "The Utilization of Critical Incident Technique to Examine Cruise Passengers' Repurchase Intentions." *Journal of Travel Research* 44, no. 3 (2006): 273–280.

Prasad, Kesh, Philip W. Wirtz, and Larry Yu. "Measuring Hotel Guest Satisfaction by Using an Online Quality Management System." *Journal of Hospitality Marketing & Management* 23, no. 4 (2014): 445–463.

Rauch, Dennis A., Michael Dwain Collins, Robert D. Nale, and Peter B. Barr. "Measuring Service Quality in Mid-Scale Hotels." *International Journal of Contemporary Hospitality Management* 27, no. 1 (2015): 87–106.

Rezaei, Jafar, Oshan Kothadiya, Lori Tavasszy, and Maarten Kroesen, "Quality Assessment of Airline Baggage Handling Systems Using SERVQUAL and BWM," *Tourism Management* 66 (2018): 85–93.

Richard, Brandon, Stevphen A. Sivo, Marissa Orlowski, Robert C. Ford, Jamie Murphy, David N. Boote, and Eleanor Witta. "Online Focus Groups: A Valuable Alternative for Hospitality Research?" *International Journal of Contemporary Hospitality Management* (2018).

Sainaghi, Ruggero, Paul Phillips, and Emma Zavarrone. "Performance Measurement in Tourism Firms: A Content Analytical Meta-Approach." *Tourism Management* 59 (2017): 36–56.

Santos, Jessica. "E-service Quality: A Model of Virtual Service Quality Dimensions." *Managing Service Quality: An International Journal* 13, no. 3 (2003): 233–246.

Sari, Ferika Ozer, Cagri Bulut, and Ige Pirnar. "Adaptation of Hospitality Service Quality Scales for Marina

Services." *International Journal of Hospitality Management* 54 (2016): 95–103.

Schweitzer, Fiona Maria, Walter Buchinger, Oliver Gassmann, and Marianna Obrist. "Crowdsourcing: Leveraging Innovation through Online Idea Competitions." *Research-Technology Management* 55, no. 3 (2012): 32–38.

Sipe, Lori J., and Mark R. Testa. "From Satisfied to Memorable: An Empirical Study of Service and Experience Dimensions on Guest Outcomes in the Hospitality Industry." *Journal of Hospitality Marketing & Management* 27, no. 2 (2018): 178–195.

Sowder, Jules. "The 100% Satisfaction Guarantee: Ensuring Quality at Hampton Inn." *Global Business and Organizational Excellence* 15, no. 2 (1996): 53–66.

Su, Ching-Shu, and Chen-Tsang Tsai. "The Implication of Mystery Shopping Program in Chain Restaurants: Supervisors' Perception." *Journal of Foodservice Business Research* 17, no. 4 (2014): 267–282.

Swanson, R., Scott, Yinghua Huang, and Baoheng Wang. "Hospitality-based Critical Incidents: A Cross-Cultural Comparison." *International Journal of Contemporary Hospitality Management* 26, no. 1 (2014): 50–68.

Tax, Stephen S., and Stephen W. Brown. "Recovering and Learning from Service Failure." *MIT Sloan Management Review* 40, no. 1 (1998): 75–88.

Tian, Jenny, and Sophia Wang. "Signaling Service Quality via Website e-CRM Features: More Gains for Smaller and Lesser Known Hotels." *Journal of Hospitality & Tourism Research* 41, no. 2 (2017): 211–245.

Tisch, Jonathan, and Karl Weber. *The Power of We: Succeeding Through Partnerships.* Hoboken, NY: Wiley & Sons, 2004.

Tontini, Gérson, Graziela dos Santos Bento, Thaíse Caroline Milbratz, Barbara Kobuszewski Volles, and Daniela Ferrari. "Exploring the Nonlinear Impact of Critical Incidents on Customers' General Evaluation of Hospitality Services." *International Journal of Hospitality Management* 66 (2017): 106–116.

Torres, Edwin N. "Deconstructing Service Quality and Customer Satisfaction: Challenges and Directions for Future Research." *Journal of Hospitality Marketing & Management* 23, no. 6 (2014): 652–677.

Torres, Edwin N., Howard Adler, and Carl Behnke. "Stars, Diamonds, and Other Shiny Things: The Use of Expert and Consumer Feedback in the Hotel Industry." *Journal of Hospitality and Tourism Management* 21 (2014): 34–43.

Tovmasyan, Gayane. "The Models of Assessing the Quality of Hotel Services and Its Application in the RA." *American Journal of Sociology* 22 No. 6(2) (2017): 2266–2271.

Tsang, Nelson K. F., Louisa Yee-Sum Lee, and Hailin Qu. "Service Quality Research on China's Hospitality and Tourism Industry." *International Journal of Contemporary Hospitality Management* 27, no. 3 (2015): 473–497.

Van der Wiele, Ton, Martin Hesselink, and Jos Van Iwaarden. "Mystery Shopping: A Tool to Develop Insight into Customer Service Provision." *Total Quality Management & Business Excellence* 16, no. 4 (2005): 529–541.

Van Vaerenbergh, Yves, Arne De Keyser, and Bart Larivière. "Customer Intentions to Invoke Service Guarantees: Do Excellence in Service Recovery, Type of Guarantee and Cultural Orientation Matter?" *Managing Service Quality: An International Journal* 24, no. 1 (2014): 45–62.

Wang, Ya Lan, Tainyi Luor, Pin Luarn, and Hsi Peng Lu. "Contribution and Trend to Quality Research-a Literature Review of SERVQUAL Model from 1998 to 2013." *Informatica Economica* 19, no. 1 (2015): 34–45.

Weed, Julie. "Checking in After Checkout." *New York Times*, May 27, 2013. https://www.nytimes.com/2013/05/28/business/hotels-work-harder-to-collect-customer-responses.html

West Inn & Suites. "Guest Comment Card for West Inn & Suites." Accessed January 21, 2018. http://www.westinnandsuites.com/guest-comments-en.html.

Worsfold, Kate, Ron Fisher, Ruth McPhail, Mark Francis, and Andrew Thomas. "Satisfaction, Value and Intention to Return in Hotels." *International Journal of Contemporary Hospitality Management* 28, no. 11 (2016): 2570–2588.

Wyckoff, D. Daryl. "New tools for achieving service quality." *Cornell Hotel and Restaurant Administration Quarterly* 24, no. 6 (1984): 78–91.

Xiang, Zheng, Qianzhou Du, Yufeng Ma, and Weiguo Fan. "A Comparative Analysis of Major Online Review Platforms: Implications for Social Media Analytics in Hospitality and Tourism." *Tourism Management* 58 (2017): 51–65.

Xiang, Zheng, Zvi Schwartz, John H. Gerdes Jr, and Muzaffer Uysal. "What Can Big Data and Text Analytics Tell Us about Hotel Guest Experience and Satisfaction?" *International Journal of Hospitality Management* 44 (2015): 120–130.

Yaoyuneyong, Gallayanee, Jeremy E. Whaley, Rochelle A. Butler, James A. Williams, Kenny L. Jordan Jr, and Laura Hunt. "Resort Mystery Shopping: A Case Study of Hotel Service." *Journal of Quality Assurance in Hospitality & Tourism* 19, no. 3 (2018): 358–386.

Chapter 13

Albrecht, Arne K., Gianfranco Walsh, and Sharon E. Beatty. "Perceptions of Group versus Individual Service Failures and Their Effects on Customer Outcomes: The Role of Attributions and Customer Entitlement." *Journal of Service Research* 20, no. 2 (2017): 188–203.

Albrecht, Karl. *At America's Service: How Your Company Can Join the Customer Service Revolution.* New York: Warner Books, 1988, 124–125.

Assaf, A. George, Alexander Josiassen, Ljubica Knežević Cvelbar, and Linda Woo. "The Effects of Customer Voice on Hotel Performance." *International Journal of Hospitality Management* 44 (2015): 77–83.

Ateke, Brown Walter, Asiegbu, Ikechukwu Francis, and Chinyere Stella, Nwulu. "Customer Complaint Handling and Relationship Quality: Any Correlation?" *Ilorin Journal of Marketing, 2,* no. 2 (2015): 16–34.

Baer, Jay. *Hug Your Haters: How to Embrace Complaints and Keep Your Customers.* New York: Penguin Random House, 2016.

Bambauer-Sachse, Silke, and Landisoa Eunorphie Rabeson. "Service Recovery for Moderate and High Involvement Services." *Journal of Services Marketing* 29, no. 5 (2015): 331–343.

Barlow, Janelle, and Claus Møller. *A Complaint Is a Gift: Recovering Customer Loyalty When Things Go Wrong.* San Francisco: Berrett-Koehler, 2008.

Bateson, John. "Are Your Customers Good Enough for Your Service Business?" *The Academy of Management Executive*16, no. 4 (2002): 110–120.

Berger, Paul D., Bruce Weinberg, and Richard C. Hanna. "Customer Lifetime Value Determination and Strategic Implications for a Cruise-Ship Company." *Journal of Database Marketing & Customer Strategy Management* 11, no. 1 (2003): 40–52.

Bhaskar, Shilpa. "Customer Complaint Behavior: An Examination of Cultural VS. Situational Factors." *Journal of Consumer Satisfaction, Dissatisfaction and Complaining Behavior* 28 (2015): 61–74.

Cai, Ruiying, and Christina Geng-Qing Chi. "The Impacts of Complaint Efforts on Customer Satisfaction and Loyalty." *The Service Industries Journal* (2018): 1–21. https: //doi: 10.1080/02642069.2018.1429415.

Cai, Ruiying, and Hailin Qu. "Customers' Perceived Justice, Emotions, Direct and Indirect Reactions to Service Recovery: Moderating Effects of Recovery Efforts." *Journal of Hospitality Marketing & Management* 7, no. 3 (2018): 323–345.

Cambra-Fierro, Jesus, Iguacel Melero, and F. Javier Sese. "Managing Complaints to Improve Customer Profitability." *Journal of Retailing* 91, no. 1 (2015): 109–124.

Casidy, Riza, and Hyunju Shin. "The Effects of Harm Directions and Service Recovery Strategies on Customer Forgiveness and Negative Word-of-Mouth Intentions." *Journal of Retailing and Consumer Services* 27 (2015): 103–112.

Cheung, F. Y. M., and W. M. To. "A Customer-Dominant Logic on Service Recovery and Customer Satisfaction." *Management Decision, 54,* no. 10 (2016): 2524–2543.

Cheung, M. F., and W. M. To. "The Effect of Organizational Responses to Service Failures on Customer Satisfaction Perception." *Service Business, 11,* no.4 (2017): 767–784.

Choi, Beomjoon, and Beom-Jin Choi. "The Effects of Perceived Service Recovery Justice on Customer Affection, Loyalty, and Word-of-Mouth." *European Journal of Marketing* 48, no. 1/2 (2014): 108–131.

Chuang, Yi-Fei, and Yang-Fei Tai. "Research on Customer Switching Behavior in the Service Industry." *Management Research Review* 39, no. 8 (2016): 925–939.

Cranage, David. "Plan to Do It Right: and Plan for Recovery." *International Journal of Contemporary Hospitality Management* 16, no. 4 (2004): 210–219.

Crie, Dominique. "Consumers' Complaint Behaviour. Taxonomy, Typology and Determinants: Towards a Unified Ontology." *Journal of Database Marketing & Customer Strategy Management* 11, no. 1 (2003): 60–79.

Crisafulli, Benedetta, and Jaywant Singh. "Service Guarantee As a Recovery Strategy: The Impact of Guarantee Terms on Perceived Justice and Firm Motives." *Journal of Service Management* 27, no. 2 (2016): 117–143.

Davidow, Moshe. "Organizational Responses to Customer Complaints: What Works and What Doesn't." *Journal of Service Research* 5, no. 3 (2003): 225–250.

De Matos, Celso Augusto, Jorge Luiz Henrique, and Carlos Alberto Vargas Rossi. "Service Recovery Paradox: A Meta-analysis." *Journal of Service Research* 10, no. 1 (2007): 60–77.

Desjardins, Jeff. "Calculating the Lifetime Value of a Customer." *Visual Capitalist,* January 27, 2016. http://www.visualcapitalist.com/calculating-lifetime-customer-value/.

Einwiller, Sabine A., and Sarah Steilen. "Handling Complaints on Social Network Sites–An Analysis of Complaints and Complaint Responses on Facebook and Twitter Pages of Large US Companies." *Public Relations Review* 41, no. 2 (2015): 195–204.

Ford, Robert C., Celeste Wilderom, and John Caparella. "Strategically Crafting a Customer-focused Culture: An Inductive Case Study." *Journal of Strategy and Management* 1, no. 2 (2008): 143–167.

Gelbrich, Katja, Jana Gäthke, and Yany Grégoire, "How a Firm's Best versus Normal Customers React to Compensation After a Service Failure." *Journal of Business Research* 69, no. 10 (2016): 4331–4339.

Giovanis, Apostolos, Pinelopi Athanasopoulou, and Evangelos Tsoukatos. "The Role of Service Fairness in the Service Quality–Relationship Quality–Customer Loyalty Chain: An Empirical Study." *Journal of Service Theory and Practice* 25, no. 6 (2015): 744–776.

Gong, Shuangping, Yonghui Dai, Jun Ji, Jinzhao Wang, and Hai Sun. "Emotion Analysis of Telephone Complaints from Customer Based on Affective

Computing." *Computational Intelligence and Neuroscience* 2015 (2015): 15–23.

Goodwin, Cathy, and Ivan Ross. "Consumer Evaluations of Responses to Complaints: What's Fair and Why." *Journal of Consumer Marketing* 7, no. 2 (1990): 39–47.

Grainer, Marc, Charles H. Noble, Mary Jo Bitner, and Scott M. Broetzmann. "What Unhappy Customers Want." *MIT Sloan Management Review* 55, no. 3 (2014): 31–35.

Grégoire, Yany, and Robert J. Fisher. "Customer Betrayal and Retaliation: When Your Best Customers Become Your Worst Enemies." *Journal of the Academy of Marketing Science* 36, no. 2 (2008): 247–261.

Groth, Markus, and Alicia Grandey. "From Bad to Worse: Negative Exchange Spirals in Employee–Customer Service Interactions." *Organizational Psychology Review* 2, no. 3 (2012): 208–233.

Hailey, L. "Lifetime Value Pays Small Business Dividends." Accessed October 10, 2009. Dell.com.

Hart, Christopher W.,James L. Heskett, and W. Earl Sasser, Jr. "The Profitable Art of Service Recovery." *Harvard Business Review* 68, no. 4 (1990): 148–156.

Hazée, Simon, Yves Van Vaerenbergh, and Vincent Armirotto. "Co-creating Service Recovery after Service Failure: The Role of Brand Equity." *Journal of Business Research* 74 (2017): 101–109.

Heidenreich, Sven, Kristina Wittkowski, Matthias Handrich, and Tomas Falk. "The Dark Side of Customer Co-creation: Exploring the Consequences of Failed Co-created Services." *Journal of the Academy of Marketing Science* 43, no. 3 (2015): 279–296.

Hess, Ronald L., Jr. and James Olver. "Failure and Complaint Handling in Marketing: An Organizational Justice Perspective." In *The Oxford Handbook of Justice in the Workplace*, edited by Russel S. Cropanzano and Maureen L. Ambrose. New York: Oxford University Press, 2015.

Hoffman, K. Douglas, Scott W. Kelley, and Holly M. Rotalsky. "Retrospective: Tracking Service Failures and Employee Recovery Efforts." *Journal of Services Marketing* 30, no. 1 (2016): 7–10.

Hogreve, Jens, Nicola Bilstein, and Leonhard Mandl. "Unveiling the Recovery Time Zone of Tolerance: When Time Matters in Service Recovery." *Journal of the Academy of Marketing Science* 45, no. 6 (2017): 866–883.

Hsiao, Yu-Hsiang, Li-Fei Chen, Yoon Leng Choy, and Chao-Ton Su. "A Novel Framework for Customer Complaint Management." *The Service Industries Journal* 36, no. 13–14 (2016): 675–698.

Hu, Mingyao, Elliot Rabinovich, and Hanping Hou. "Customers Complaints in Online Shopping: The Role of Signal Credibility." *Journal of Electronic Commerce Research* 16, no. 2 (2015): 95.

Huang, Wayne, John Mitchell, Carmel Dibner, Andrea Ruttenberg, and Audrey Tripp. "How Customer Service Can Turn Angry Customers into Loyal Ones." *Harvard Business Review*, January 16, 2018. Accessed 2/2/2018. https://hbr.org/2018/01/how-customer-service-can-turn-angry-customers-into-loyal-ones.

Hult, G. Tomas M., Forrest V. Morgeson, Neil A. Morgan, Sunil Mithas, and Claes Fornell. "Do Managers Know What Their Customers Think and Why?" *Journal of the Academy of Marketing Science* 45, no. 1 (2017): 37–54.

Hur, JungYun, and SooCheong Jang. "Toward Service Recovery Strategies: The Role of Consumer-Organization Relationship Norms." *Journal of Services Marketing* 30, no. 7 (2016): 724–735.

Jeong, Miyoung, and Seonjeong Ally Lee. "Do Customers Care About Types of Hotel Service Recovery Efforts? An Example of Consumer-Generated Review Sites." *Journal of Hospitality and Tourism Technology* 8, no. 1 (2017): 5–18.

Jishim, Jung, Heesup Han, and Mihae Oh. "Travelers' Switching Behavior in the Airline Industry from the Perspective of the Push-Pull-Mooring Framework." *Tourism Management* 59 (2017): 139–153.

Jung, Na Young, and Yoo-Kyoung Seock. "Effect of Service Recovery on Customers' Perceived Justice, Satisfaction, and Word-of-Mouth Intentions on Online Shopping Websites." *Journal of Retailing and Consumer Services* 37 (2017): 23–30.

Kau, Ah-Keng, and Elizabeth Wan-Yiun Loh. "The Effects of Service Recovery on Consumer Satisfaction: a Comparison between Complainants and Non-complainants." *Journal of Services Marketing* 20, no. 2 (2006): 101–111.

Kim, Min Gyung, Chung Hun Lee, and Anna S. Mattila. "Determinants of Customer Complaint Behavior in a Restaurant Context: The Role of Culture, Price Level, and Customer Loyalty." *Journal of Hospitality Marketing & Management* 23, no. 8 (2014): 885–906.

Kumar, V. "A Theory of Customer Valuation: Concepts, Metrics, Strategy, and Implementation." *Journal of Marketing* 82, no. 1 (2018): 1–19.

Kumar, V., and Werner Reinartz. "Creating Enduring Customer Value." *Journal of Marketing* 80, no. 6 (2016): 36–68.

Lee, Myong Jae, Neha Singh, and Eric SW Chan. "Service Failures and Recovery Actions in the Hotel Industry: A Text-Mining Approach." *Journal of Vacation Marketing* 17, no. 3 (2011): 197–207.

Leong, Jerrold K., and Woo Gon Kim. "Service Recovery Efforts in Fast Food Restaurants to Enhance Repeat Patronage." *Journal of Travel & Tourism Marketing* 12, no. 2–3 (2002): 65–93.

Lervik-Olsen, Line, Tor Wallin Andreassen, and Sandra Streukens. "What Drives the Intention to Complain?"

Journal of Service Theory and Practice 26, no. 4 (2016): 406–429.

Li, Xiaofei, Baolong Ma, and Chen Zhou. "Effects of Customer Loyalty on Customer Entitlement and Voiced Complaints." *The Service Industries Journal* 37, no. 13–14 (2017): 858–874.

Liu, Stephanie Qing, and Anna S. Mattila. "'I want to help'" versus 'I am just mad' How Affective Commitment Influences Customer Feedback Decisions." *Cornell Hospitality Quarterly* 56, no. 2 (2015): 213–222.

Marinova, Detelina, Sunil K. Singh, and Jagdip Singh. "Frontline Problem-Solving Effectiveness: A Dynamic Analysis of Verbal and Nonverbal Cues." *Journal of Marketing Research* 55, no. 2 (2018): 178–192.

Marr, Bernard. "Big Data at Caesars Entertainment—A One Billion Dollar Asset?" *Forbes*. May 18, 2015. https://www.forbes.com/sites/bernardmarr/2015/05/18/when-big-data-becomes-your-most-valuable-asset/#75066ed21eef.

Mattila, Anna S. "The Impact of Service Failures on Customer Loyalty: The Moderating Role of Affective Commitment." *International Journal of Service Industry Management* 15, no. 2 (2004): 134–149.

Michel, Stefan, David Bowen, and Robert Johnston. "Why Service Recovery Fails: Tensions among Customer, Employee, and Process Perspectives." *Journal of Service Management* 20, no. 3 (2009): 253–273.

Michel, Stefan, and Matthew L. Meuter. "The Service Recovery Paradox: True but Overrated?" *International Journal of Service Industry Management* 19, no. 4 (2008): 441–457.

Michelli, Joseph A. *The New Gold Standard: 5 Leadership Principles for Creating a Legendary Customer Experience Courtesy of the Ritz-Carlton Hotel Company*. New York: McGraw-Hill, 2008.

Migacz, Steven J., Suiwen Zou, and James F. Petrick. "The "Terminal" Effects of Service Failure on Airlines: Examining Service Recovery with Justice Theory." *Journal of Travel Research* 57, no. 1 (2018): 83–98.

Mikolon, Sven, Benjamin Quaiser, and Jan Wieseke. "Don't Try Harder: Using Customer Inoculation to Build Resistance Against Service Failures." *Journal of the Academy of Marketing Science* 43, no. 4 (2015): 512–527.

Min, Hyounae, Yumi Lim, and Vincent P. Magnini. "Factors Affecting Customer Satisfaction in Responses to Negative Online Hotel Reviews: The Impact of Empathy, Paraphrasing, and Speed." *Cornell Hospitality Quarterly* 56, no. 2 (2015): 223–231.

Murphy, Kevin, Anil Bilgihan, Marketa Kubickova, and Matt Boseo. "There Is No 'I' in Recovery: Managements' Perspective of Service Recovery." *Journal of Quality Assurance in Hospitality & Tourism* 16, no. 3 (2015): 303–322.

Nikbin, Davoud, Malliga Marimuthu, Sunghyup Sean Hyun, and Ishak Ismail. "Relationships of Perceived Justice to Service Recovery, Service Failure Attributions, Recovery Satisfaction, and Loyalty in the Context of Airline Travelers." *Asia Pacific Journal of Tourism Research* 20, no. 3 (2015): 239–262.

Ogbeide, Godwin-Charles A., Stefanie Böser, Robert J. Harrinton, and Michael C. Ottenbacher. "Complaint Management in Hospitality Organizations: The Role of Empowerment and Other Service Recovery Attributes Impacting Loyalty and Satisfaction." *Tourism and Hospitality Research* 17, no. 2 (2017): 204–216.

Ozuem, Wilson, Amisha Patel, Kerry E. Howell, and Geoff Lancaster. "An Exploration of Consumers' Response to Online Service Recovery Initiatives." *International Journal of Market Research* 59, no. 1 (2017): 97–115.

Pasamehmetoglu, Aysin, Priyanko Guchait, J. B. Tracey, Christopher JL Cunningham, and Puiwa Lei. "The Moderating Effect of Supervisor and Coworker Support for Error Management on Service Recovery Performance and Helping Behaviors." *Journal of Service Theory and Practice* 27, no. 1 (2017): 2–22.

Patterson, Paul G., Michael K. Brady, and Janet R. McColl-Kennedy. "Geysers or Bubbling Hot Springs? A Cross-Cultural Examination of Customer Rage from Eastern and Western Perspectives." *Journal of Service Research* 19, no. 3 (2016): 243–259.

Pollack, Birgit Leisen. "Effects of Exit Barriers on Word of Mouth Activities." *Journal of Services Marketing* 31, no. 6 (2017): 512–526.

Reichheld, Frederick F., and W. Earl Sasser, Jr. "Zero Defections: Quality Comes to Services. " *Harvard Business Review* 68, no. 5 (1990): 105–111.

Reynolds, Kate L., and Lloyd C. Harris. "When Service Failure Is Not Service Failure: An Exploration of the Forms and Motives of 'Illegitimate' Customer Complaining." *Journal of Services Marketing* 19, no. 5 (2005): 321–335.

Ro, Heejung. "Customer Dissatisfaction Responses to Restaurant Service Failures: Insights into Noncomplainers from a Relational Perspective." *Journal of Hospitality Marketing & Management* 24, no. 4 (2015): 435–456.

Ro, Heejung, and Anna S. Mattila. "Silent Voices: Nonbehavioral Reactions to Service Failures." *Services Marketing Quarterly* 36, no. 2 (2015): 95–111.

Robinson, Alan G., and Sam Stern. *Corporate Creativity: How Innovation and Improvement Actually Happen*. San Francisco: Berrett-Koehler Publishers, 1997.

Roschk, Holger, and Katja Gelbrich. "Identifying Appropriate Compensation Types for Service Failures: A Meta-analytic and Experimental Analysis." *Journal of Service Research* 17, no. 2 (2014): 195–211.

Schminke, Marshall, James Caldwell, Maureen L. Ambrose, and Sean R. McMahon. "Better than Ever? Employee Reactions to Ethical Failures in Organizations, and the Ethical Recovery Paradox." *Organizational Behavior and Human Decision Processes* 123, no. 2 (2014): 206–219.

Sengupta, Aditi Sarkar, M. S. Balaji, and Balaji C. Krishnan. "How Customers Cope with Service Failure? A Study of Brand Reputation and Customer Satisfaction." *Journal of Business Research* 68, no. 3 (2015): 665–674.

Sewell, Carl, and Paula Brown. *Customers for Life: How to Turn that One-Time Buyer into a Lifetime Customer.* New York: Pocket Books, 2002.

Sharma, Piyush, and Roger Marshall. "Investigating Individual Differences in Customer Complaint Behavior: Towards a Comprehensive Conceptual Framework." In *Marketing, Technology and Customer Commitment in the New Economy,* edited by Harlan E. Spotts, 97. New York: Springer Cham, 2015.

Shoot, Brittany. "This Woman-Led Startup Is Turning Flight Delays into Cash." *Fortune,* November 24, 2014, http://fortune.com/2014/11/24/airline-delays-cash/.

Soares, Raquel Reis, and João F. Proença. "Does Service Failure Context Matter? Customers' Response to Service Recovery." *Journal of Marketing Research and Case Studies* 2015 (2015): 1–11.

Stoller, Gary. "Tarmac Ordeal Renews Push for Fliers' Rights." *USA Today,* Aug. 11, 2009.

Sweeney, Jill, Geoff Soutar, and Tim Mazzarol. "Factors Enhancing Word-of-Mouth Influence: Positive and Negative Service-related Messages." *European Journal of Marketing* 48, no. 1/2 (2014): 336–359.

Taylor, K. "When Service Means Everything." *Association News,* November 2006.

Technical Assistance Research Programs Institute (TARP). *Consumer Complaint Handling in America: An Update Study.* Washington, DC: White House Office of Consumer Affairs (1985).

Timmerman, John, and Daniela Yu. "Silver Lining of Customer Problems." *Gallup.* March 7, 2017. http://news.gallup.com/businessjournal/205445/silver-lining-customer-problems.aspx.

Trianasari, Nana, Ken Butcher, and Beverley Sparks. "Understanding Guest Tolerance and the Role of Cultural Familiarity in Hotel Service Failures." *Journal of Hospitality Marketing & Management* 27, no. 1 (2018): 21–40.

Umashankar, Nita, Morgan K. Ward, and Darren W. Dahl. "The Benefit of Becoming Friends: Complaining After Service Failures Leads Customers with Strong Ties to Increase Loyalty." *Journal of Marketing* 81, no. 6 (2017): 79–98.

Van Vaerenbergh, Yves, and Chiara Orsingher. "Service Recovery: An Integrative Framework and Research Agenda." *The Academy of Management Perspectives* 30, no. 3 (2016): 328–346.

Van Vaerenbergh, Yves, Chiara Orsingher, Iris Vermeir, and Bart Larivière. "A Meta-analysis of Relationships Linking Service Failure Attributions to Customer Outcomes." *Journal of Service Research* 17, no. 4 (2014): 381–398.

Walsh, Gianfranco, William Magnus Northington, Patrick Hille, and David Dose. "Service Employees' Willingness to Report Complaints Scale: Cross-country Application and Replication." *Journal of Business Research* 68, no. 3 (2015): 500–506.

Way, Sean A., Michael C. Sturman, and Carola Raab. "What Matters More? Contrasting the Effects of Job Satisfaction and Service Climate on Hotel Food and Beverage Managers' Job Performance." *Cornell Hospitality Quarterly* 51, no. 3 (2010): 379–397.

Yang, Yefei, Peter KC Lee, and T. C. E. Cheng. "Operational Improvement Competence and Service Recovery Performance: The Moderating Effects of Role Stress and Job Resources." *International Journal of Production Economics* 164 (2015): 134–145.

Yilmaz, Cengiz, Kaan Varnali, and Berna Tari Kasnakoglu. "How Do Firms Benefit from Customer Complaints?" *Journal of Business Research* 69, no. 2 (2016): 944–955.

Yu, Daniela, and John Timmerman. "The Silver Lining of Customer Problems (Part 2)." *Gallup.* March 14, 2017. http://news.gallup.com/businessjournal/205913/silver-lining-customer-problems-part.aspx.

Zeithaml, Valerie, Mary Jo Bitner, and Dwayne Gremler. *Services Marketing: Integrating Customer Focus across the Firm.* New York: McGraw Hill Education, 2018.

Chapter 14

Antonakis, John, and Robert J. House. "Instrumental Leadership: Measurement and Extension of Transformational–Transactional Leadership Theory." *The Leadership Quarterly* 25, no. 4 (2014): 746–771.

Baker, Melissa A.,Eric A. Davis, and Pamela A. Weaver. "Eco-friendly Attitudes, Barriers to Participation, and Differences in Behavior at Green Hotels." *Cornell Hospitality Quarterly* 55, no. 1 (2014): 89–99.

Bass, Bernard M., and Ruth Bass. *The Bass Handbook of Leadership: Theory, Research, and Managerial Applications.* New York: Simon & Schuster, 2008.

Bilgihan, Anil, and Mohammad Nejad. "Innovation in Hospitality and Tourism Industries." *Journal of Hospitality and Tourism Technology* 6, no. 3 (2015).

Birkinshaw, Julian, Gary Hamel, and Michael J. Mol. "Management Innovation." *Academy of Management Review* 33, no. 4 (2008): 825–845.

Brooker, Ed, and Marion Joppe. "Developing a Tourism Innovation Typology: Leveraging Liminal Insights." *Journal of Travel Research* 53, no. 4 (2014): 500–508.

Camisón, César, and Vicente M. Monfort-Mir. "Measuring Innovation in Tourism from the Schumpeterian and the Dynamic-Capabilities Perspectives." *Tourism Management* 33, no. 4 (2012): 776–789.

Campo, Sara, Ana M. Diaz, and María J. Yagüe. "Hotel Innovation and Performance in Times of Crisis." *International Journal of Contemporary Hospitality Management* 26, no. 8 (2014): 1292–1311.

Chen, Ja-Shen, Don Kerr, Cindy Yunhsin Chou, and Chinhui Ang. "Business Co-creation for Service Innovation in the Hospitality and Tourism Industry." *International Journal of Contemporary Hospitality Management* 29, no. 6 (2017): 1522–1540.

Christensen, Clayton. *The Innovator's Dilemma.* New York: Collins Business Essentials, 2006.

Christensen, Clayton. *The Innovator's Dilemma: When New Technologies Cause Great Firms to Fail.* Cambridge, Massachusetts: Harvard Business Review Press, 2013.

Dahlinger, Fred, and Stuart Thayer. *Badger State Showmen: A History of Wisconsin's Circus Heritage.* Baraboo, WI: Grote Publishing, 1998.

Damanpour, Farivorz, and William M. Evan. "Organizational Innovation and Performance: The Problem of 'Organizational Lag.'" *Administrative Science Quarterly* (1984): 392–409

Dzhandzhugazova, Elena A., Ekaterina A. Blinova, Liubov N. Orlova, and Marianna M. Romanova. "Innovations in Hospitality Industry." *International Journal of Environmental and Science Education* 11, no. 17 (2016): 10387–10400.

Enz, Cathy A., and Rohit Verma "Introduction to the Cornell Hospitality Research Summit Special Issue: The New Science of Service Innovation in a Multipartner World," *Service Science* 8, no. 2 (2016): iv-ix.

García-Villaverde, Pedro M., Dioni Elche, Ángela Martínez-Pérez, and Mª José Ruiz-Ortega. "Determinants of Radical Innovation in Clustered Firms of the Hospitality and Tourism Industry." *International Journal of Hospitality Management* 61 (2017): 45–58.

Gomezelj, Doris Omerzel. "A Systematic Review of Research on Innovation in Hospitality and Tourism." *International Journal of Contemporary Hospitality Management* 28, no. 3 (2016): 516–558.

Grissemann, Ursula, Andreas Plank, and Alexandra Brunner-Sperdin. "Enhancing Business Performance of Hotels: The Role of Innovation and Customer Orientation." *International Journal of Hospitality Management* 33 (2013): 347–356.

Guttentag, Daniel. "Airbnb: Disruptive Innovation and the Rise of an Informal Tourism Accommodation Sector." *Current Issues in Tourism* 18, no. 12 (2015): 1192–1217.

Hardy, Kevin. "Test Run: Restaurant Incubators Let Operators Explore New Concepts Before Opening Their Doors to the Public." *QSR,* March, 2015, https://www.qsrmagazine.com/growth/test-run.

Hoch, Julia E., William H. Bommer, James H. Dulebohn, and Dongyuan Wu. "Do Ethical, Authentic, and Servant Leadership Explain Variance Above and Beyond Transformational Leadership? A Meta-analysis." *Journal of Management* 44, no. 2 (2018): 501–529.

Hon, Alice HY, and Steven S. Lui. "Employee Creativity and Innovation in Organizations: Review, Integration, and Future Directions for Hospitality Research." *International Journal of Contemporary Hospitality Management* 28, no. 5 (2016): 862–885.

Kandampully, Jay, Anil Bilgihan, and Tingting Christina Zhang. "Developing a People-Technology Hybrids Model to Unleash Innovation and Creativity: The New Hospitality Frontier." *Journal of Hospitality and Tourism Management* 29 (2016): 154–164.

Kelleher, Carol. A. O' Cheilleachair, A. Helkkula, and J. Peppard. "Value Proposal Co-Creation in Online Community-Based Idea Contests." In *Innovating in Practice,* edited by Tiziana Russo-Spena, Cristina Mele, and Maaria Nuutinen, 291–316. Switzerland: Springer International Publishing, 2017.

Koyuncu, Mustafa, Ronald J. Burke, Marina Astakhova, Duygu Eren, and Hayrullah Cetin. "Servant Leadership and Perceptions of Service Quality Provided by Front-Line Service Workers in Hotels in Turkey: Achieving Competitive Advantage." *International Journal of Contemporary Hospitality Management* 26, no. 7 (2014): 1083–1099.

Laub, James. "Defining Servant Leadership: A Recommended Typology for Servant Leadership Studies." In *Proceedings of the Servant Leadership Research Roundtable.* Virginia Beach, VA: Regent University, 2004.

Lee, Craig, Rob Hallak, and Shruti R. Sardeshmukh. "Innovation, Entrepreneurship, and Restaurant Performance: A Higher-Order Structural Model." *Tourism Management* 53 (2016): 215–228.

Ling, Qian, Fang Liu, and Xiaoyi Wu. "Servant Versus Authentic Leadership: Assessing Effectiveness in China's Hospitality Industry." *Cornell Hospitality Quarterly* 58, no. 1 (2017): 53–68.

Mahr, Dominik, Annouk Lievens, and Vera Blazevic. "The Value of Customer Co-created Knowledge During the Innovation Process." *Journal of Product Innovation Management* 31, no. 3 (2014): 599–615.

Megheirkouni, Majd. "Insights on Practicing of Servant Leadership in the Events Sector." *Sport Business and Management: An International Journal* 8, no. 2 (2018): 134–152.

Michel, Stefan, Stephen W. Brown, and Andrew S. Gallan. "An Expanded and Strategic View of Discontinuous Innovations: Deploying a Service-Dominant Logic." *Journal of the Academy of Marketing Science* 36, no. 1 (2008): 54–66.

Mohamed, Lamiaa Moustafa. "Assessing the Effects of Transformational Leadership: A Study on Egyptian Hotel Employees." *Journal of Hospitality and Tourism Management* 27 (2016): 49–59.

Nicolau, Juan Luis, and María Jesús Santa-María. "The Effect of Innovation on Hotel Market Value." *International Journal of Hospitality Management* 32 (2013): 71–79.

Nieves, Julia, Agustín Quintana, and Javier Osorio. "Knowledge-Based Resources and Innovation in the Hotel Industry." *International Journal of Hospitality Management* 38 (2014): 65–73.

Parasie, Nicolas. "Emirates Air Flies into Uncharted Territory," *Wall Street Journal*, May 21, 2018, p. R8.

Parris, Denise Linda, and Jon Welty Peachey. "A Systematic Literature Review of Servant Leadership Theory in Organizational Contexts." *Journal of Business Ethics* 113, no. 3 (2013): 377–393.

Patiar, Anoop, and Ying Wang. "The Effects of Transformational Leadership and Organizational Commitment on Hotel Departmental Performance." *International Journal of Contemporary Hospitality Management* 28, no. 3 (2016): 586–608.

Randhawa, Praneet, MiRan Kim, Clay M. Voorhees, Ronald F. Cichy, Jason P. Koenigsfeld, and Joe Perdue. "Hospitality Service Innovations in Private Clubs." *Cornell Hospitality Quarterly* 57, no. 1 (2016): 93–110.

Reddy, Sumathi. "Stirring the Pot to Help Start-ups." *Wall Street Journal*, November 15, 2011. https://www.wsj.com/articles/SB10001424052970204323904577038501515209834.

Ricaurte, Eric. "Hotel Sustainability Benchmarking Index 2017: Energy, Water, and Carbon." *Center for Hospitality Research Report* 17, no. 18 (2017), 3–17.

Salem, Islam El-Bayoumi. "Transformational Leadership: Relationship to Job Stress and Job Burnout in Five-Star Hotels." *Tourism and Hospitality Research* 15, no. 4 (2015): 240–253.

Sarasvathy, Saras D. "Causation and Effectuation: Toward a Theoretical Shift from Economic Inevitability to Entrepreneurial Contingency." *Academy of Management Review* 26, no. 2 (2001): 243–263.

Schumpeter, Joseph A. *The Theory of Economic Development: An Inquiry Into Profits, Capital, Credit, Interest, and the Business Cycle.* Cambridge, Massachusetts: Harvard University Press, 1934.

Slåtten, Terje, and Mehmet Mehmetoglu. "The Effects of Transformational Leadership and Perceived Creativity on Innovation Behavior in the Hospitality Industry." *Journal of Human Resources in Hospitality & Tourism* 14, no. 2 (2015): 195–219.

Tajeddini, Kayhan, and Myfanwy Trueman. "Managing Swiss Hospitality: How Cultural Antecedents of Innovation and Customer-Oriented Value Systems Can Influence Performance in the Hotel Industry." *International Journal of Hospitality Management* 31, no. 4 (2012): 1119–1129.

Tang, Ta-Wei, Michael Chih-Hung Wang, and Ya-Yun Tang. "Developing Service Innovation Capability in the Hotel Industry." *Service Business* 9, no. 1 (2015): 97–113.

Taylor, Craig R., and Cindy Wheatley-Lovoy. "Leadership: Lessons from the Magic Kingdom." *Training & Development* 52, no. 7 (1998): 22–26.

Tigu, Gabriela, Maria-Cristina Iorgulescu, and Anamaria Sidonia Ravar. "The Impact of Creativity and Innovation in the Hospitality Industry on Customers." *Journal of Tourism Challenges and Trends* 6, no. 1 (2013): 9–33.

Yu, Yixin, Xu Li, and Tun-Min Jai. "The Impact of Green Experience on Customer Satisfaction: Evidence from TripAdvisor." *International Journal of Contemporary Hospitality Management* 29, no. 5 (2017): 1340–1361.

Zach, Florian. "Collaboration for Innovation in Tourism Organizations: Leadership Support, Innovation Formality, and Communication." *Journal of Hospitality & Tourism Research* 40, no. 3 (2016): 271–290.

Zou, Wen-Chi, Qing Tian, and Jia Liu. "Servant Leadership, Social Exchange Relationships, and Follower's Helping Behavior: Positive Reciprocity Belief Matters." *International Journal of Hospitality Management* 51 (2015): 147–156.

INDEX